DATE DUE

JAN 26 1987			
DEC 0 9 1987			
JAN 25 1988			
GAYLORD			PRINTED IN U.S.A.

SYNTAX and SEMANTICS

VOLUME 18

A list of titles in this series appears at the end of this book.

SYNTAX and SEMANTICS

VOLUME 18

Diachronic Syntax: The Kartvelian Case

Alice C. Harris

Program in Linguistics
Vanderbilt University
Nashville, Tennessee

1985

ACADEMIC PRESS, INC.

(Harcourt Brace Jovanovich, Publishers)

Orlando San Diego New York London
Toronto Montreal Sydney Tokyo

ACADEMIC PRESS, INC.
Orlando, Florida 32887

United Kingdom Edition published by
ACADEMIC PRESS, INC. (LONDON) LTD.
24–28 Oval Road, London NW1 7DX

LIBRARY OF CONGRESS CATALOGING IN PUBLICATION DATA

Harris, Alice C.
Diachronic syntax.

(Syntax and semantics ; v. 18)
Includes index.
1. Kartvelian language—Case. I. Title. II. Series.
P1.S9 vol. 18 415 s 84-20448
[PK9052] [499'.96]
ISBN 0-12-613518-5 (alk. paper)

PRINTED IN THE UNITED STATES OF AMERICA

85 86 87 88 9 8 7 6 5 4 3 2 1

This work is dedicated
to the memory of my father

CONTENTS

PART II. RECONSTRUCTION

PART III. THE DEVELOPMENT OF SERIES I IN COMMON KARTVELIAN

PART IV. OTHER CHANGES RELATED TO CASE MARKING

PART V. KARTVELIAN AND LANGUAGE UNIVERSALS

PREFACE

The research reported here addresses several central questions in diachronic syntax, principally ones involving grammatical relations in historical perspective. It is shown how a general rule of Object Demotion may be added to a grammar, one of the mechanisms by which an ergative case marking system can become accusative, some other possible fates that may befall an ergative system, how a case may be extended to new functions, and how a productive inversion construction can arise—from the perspectives of morphology, syntax, and pragmatics.

This work demonstrates how a study of the history of a specific language family can contribute to the development of a theory of diachronic syntax, by providing concrete examples of some of the changes that are possible in natural language, and by providing evidence of intermediate stages of changes that have been completed in some dialects. It confirms the importance of the central grammatical relations 'subject', 'direct object', and 'indirect object', as well as the notion of 'chômeur', in the historical development of a language. The reinterpretation of clause structure provides evidence of the relevance of syntactic levels in a diachronic account of grammar.

At the same time, the research reported here demonstrates how linguistic theory can contribute to an understanding of a variety of phenomena in the Kartvelian languages, such as the otherwise unexplained distribution of *En*-Agreement in Old Georgian, distribution of ablaut grades previously reconstructed on phonological grounds, and marking of retired indirect objects.

One goal of this study is to establish the viability of internal reconstruction and the comparative method in syntax; it is shown here that these methods can be used effectively in the syntax of a language family in which the affinity between members is relatively close. This research illustrates several ways in which phonological, in addition to morphological, phenomena contribute to an understanding of syntactic changes. In this work I have attempted to marry the approach of theoretical syntax with the techniques of diachronic linguistics and a use of philological data.

In the initial phase of this research (1977–1979) I profited greatly from advice from Calvert Watkins. I am particularly grateful to him for convincing me of three things: the importance of reading as many texts as could be found, the value of learning everything possible about the historical phonology and morphology of these languages for its relevance to syntax, and the necessity of explaining the origin of every morpheme in Series I forms.

The help given to me by Maksime Kaldani and his associates in the Svan Department at the Linguistics Institute in Tbilisi was invaluable. I am grateful also to Levan Ghvinjilia, Guram Kartozia, and Omar Memishishi for data and discussion of issues in Laz and Mingrelian. This work was much improved by comments from scholars who read earlier drafts, to whom I am very grateful: Stephen R. Anderson, Lyle Campbell, B. G. Hewitt, and Dee Ann Holisky. I wish to express my thanks, too, to Jenifer Burckett-Evans, with whom I undertook a joint project on case marking and inversion in Svan. While the results are not published, they provided a preliminary study for my 1981 fieldwork in Svaneti.

I wish also to express my thanks to many consultants, among them Rusudan Babluani, Eteri Chkadua, Aneta Cindeliani, Tetnulda Japaridze, Davit Nizharadze, and Liana Xvitia. I am also grateful to those who helped me to reach remote villages and in other ways aided me in gathering data, and especially in this regard Guram Bedoshvili and Rusudan Babluani. My thanks also go to others who gave advice or helped in obtaining data: J. Neville Birdsall, John Greppin, Dee Ann Holisky, Brian Joseph, Guram Topuria, and Kevin Tuite.

In 1981 I was the guest of the Linguistics Institute of the Academy of Sciences of the Georgian SSR and am very grateful to the Director, Ketevan Lomtatidze, Co-director Guram Topuria, and all of the associates there for helping to make my visit both fruitful and enjoyable. I am indebted, too, to scholars at Tbilisi State University and at the Oriental Institute in Tbilisi for advice, stimulating discussions, and friendship. I wish also to thank the Central Scientific Library, the Library of the Linguistics Institute, and the Institute of Manuscripts—all of the Academy of Sciences of the Georgian SSR—the Library of Tbilisi State University, and the Library of the Kutaisi State Pedagogical Institute for helping me acquire or use needed materials.

This work was made possible by a National Science Foundation National Needs Postdoctoral Fellowship (1978–1979), the American Council of Learned Societies' exchange with the Academy of Sciences of the USSR (administered by the International Research and Exchanges Board, 1981), and National Science Foundation Grants BNS-7923452 and BNS-8217355 (1979–1985). Any opinions, findings, conclusions, or recommendations expressed in this publication are my own and do not necessarily reflect the views of the National Science Foundation. I thank the above organizations and their staffs for support and encouragement.

NOTES ON PRESENTATION

SOURCE CITATIONS

Examples from works with numbered texts and sentences are cited by text and sentence: e.g., "Asatiani 1974:**3** [18]" refers to sentence 18 in story 3 in Asatiani (1974). Examples from works in which numbering of this kind is not provided are cited by page and line; e.g., "Chikobava 1936: II, 2, 4" identifies line 4 on page 2 of part II of Chikobava (1936). In works with interlinear translation, such as Kluge (1916), only the lines of the original are counted. Biblical sources are cited by chapter and verse. Where more than one variant was available, and no indication is made as to the codex used, all manuscripts listed agree.

Genesis (Gen), **Exodus** (Ex), **Leviticus** (Lev). Examples from Genesis 3 are unpublished and were copied for me in the Institute of Manuscripts of the Academy of Sciences of the GSSR. Other examples from the Pentateuch are from the manuscript dating from 978 (Shanidze 1947, 1948).

Psalms. Manuscript A, in Shanidze (1960).

Prophets: **Jeremiah** (Jer), **Zechariah** (Zak), names of other prophets are given in full. Examples are from Blake and Brière (1961), with Blake and Brière (1963). The Jerusalem (I) manuscript dates from the middle of the eleventh century, and the Mt. Athos manuscript, termed O, was written in A.D. 978 at the convent of Oshki. A few examples from the book of Jeremiah come from the Vaxtangiseuli (W) manuscript, which is much later, and are from Danelia (1965).

Matthew (Mt), **Mark** (Mk), **Luke** (L), **John** (J). Matthew, from Blake (1976); Mark, from Blake (1974); Luke, from Brière (1955); John, from Blake and Brière (1950). The codices are indicated as "Ad," the Adysh or Adiši Gospels, A.D. 897; "A," the Opiza Gospels, A.D. 913; "B," the Tbeṭi Gospels, A.D. 995. Examples from the *xanmeṭi* (*khanmeti*) palimpsest fragments published in Birdsall (1971) are cited both by chapter and verse and by "Birdsall 1971."

Acts of the Apostles (Acts). From the Mt. Sinai manuscripts A, A.D. 977, and B, A.D. 974, in Garitte (1955).

1,2 Corinthians (1,2 Cor), **Ephesians** (Eph), **1 Thessalonians** (1 Thess), **1 Timothy.** Examples from the Epistles are from Dzotsenidze and Danelia (1974). The six manuscripts that constitute the A and B editions are dated to the tenth century or first half of the eleventh; the six that constitute the C and D editions are dated to the eleventh through fourteenth centuries.

Revelation (Rev). In Imnaishvili (1961); the A manuscript is dated A.D. 978, and B is also from late in the tenth century (Imnaishvili 1961: 127, 128). The Mt. Sinai manuscript (C) is considered by some scholars to be later (Birdsall 1980) and is not used here.

1 Esdras. In Birdsall (1972), dated to the seventh century (1972: 97).

EXAMPLES

Except for hyphens, examples from texts are cited as published, not according to an imposed norm. Quotations within a text in Svan are translated literally, that is, with the third person, although in context these may refer to the second person, as in example (6) of Chapter 11.

Examples not otherwise identified were elicited from native speakers. These record what was said, not normative forms; for example, the assimilated *k* is given in example (6) of Chapter 3, although 'fire' is usually cited as *lemesg*. There is a great deal of phonological variation, especially in Svan, even for a single speaker. For example, one language consultant used both *xäm* and *xän* for 'pig' and both *bwepš-* and *bopš-* for the plural stem of 'child'. All the variants given could not be included here; in no case are parallel forms not given by the consultants included.

GLOSSES

In general, glosses give only the material needed to interpret the examples in the context of the topic under discussion. In the gloss of verb forms, a pronoun preceding the English verb indicates person of the subject; that immediately following the verb indicates direct object; and the third, with 'to', signifies the indirect object. In each, the number of the English pronoun reflects whether number is recorded in the verb; singular indicates that no marking of plurality is present for the nominal bearing that grammatical relation. Although the Kartvelian languages do not distinguish gender in pronouns, the gloss marks gender of the referent. Hyphens separate elements of the gloss that correspond to elements of the Kartvelian original set off by hyphens; a slash sets apart elements of the gloss where no separation has been made in the original or where elements in the gloss do not correspond individually to the divisions made in the original. Variations of this general system are made according to the requirements of each chapter.

ABBREVIATIONS

ABL	ablative case
ABSL	absolutive case (used with reference to languages outside this family)
ACT	active
ADV	adverbial case
ALL	allative case
AOR	aorist
BEN	benefactive
CAUS	organic causative
CGZ	Common-Georgian-Zan
CK	Common Kartvelian
COL	collective
CONJ	conjunction
CZ	Common Zan
DAT	dative case
DES	designative case
DET	determiner (article)
DIM	diminutive (hypercoristic)
DO	direct object
ERG	ergative case (used with reference to languages outside this family)
EXCL	exclusive

GEN	genitive case
IMPERF	imperfect
INACT	inactive
INCEP	inceptive
INCL	inclusive
IO	indirect object
INF	infinitive
INST	instrumental case
LB	Lower Bal dialect of Svan
LENṬ	Lenṭex dialect of Svan
L-M	Laz and Mingrelian (= Zan)
MAS	masdar (deverbal noun)
MOD	modal particle
MP	mediopassive
NAR	narrative case
NEW III	New Series III
NOM	nominative case
OBJ	object
OLD III	Old Series III
P	predicate
PART	participle
PL	plural
PV	preverb
QUES	question particle
QUOT	quotative particle
REL	relative
S	subject
SBJ	subjunctive
ScM	screeve marker
SG	singular
SM	series marker
SUBJ	subject
TRANS, TR	transitive
I, II, III, IV	Series I, II, III, IV

TRANSLITERATION

Georgian *mxedruli* alphabet	Phonetic equivalent	Transliteration
ა	a	a
ბ	b	b
გ	g	g
დ	d	d
ე	e, ɛ	e
ვ	v, w	v
ზ	z	z
ჱ	ey	ey
თ	t	t
ი	i, ɪ	i
კ	ḳ	ḳ
ლ	l	l
მ	m	m
ნ	n	n
ჲ	y	y
ო	o	o
პ	p̣	p̣
ჟ	ž̇	ž̇

Georgian *mxedruli* alphabet	Phonetic equivalent	Transliteration
რ	r	r
ს	s	s
ტ	ṭ	ṭ
ჳ	vi, wi, *etc.*	vi
უ	w, u	u
ფ	p	p
ქ	k	k
ღ	γ	γ
ყ	q̣	q̣
შ	š	š
ჩ	č	č
ც	c	c
ძ	ʒ	ʒ
წ	ç̣	ç̣
ჭ	č̣	č̣
ხ	x	x
ჴ	q	q
ჯ	ǯ	ǯ
ჰ	h	h
ჵ	ho	ho

Additional symbols:

უ̂	w	w
ა̈, ა̈̄	ä, ǟ	ä, ǟ
ო̈, ო̈̄		ö, ȫ
უ̈, უ̈̄		ü, ǖ
ჷ	ə	ə
ჶ	f	f

Old Georgian ოჳ is transliterated as *u*. The symbols უ̂, ვ, and ჳ in Svan texts are all written here as *w*. The system described above for Old Georgian is used in the other languages. In reconstruction in Chapters 8 and 9, *w* is used to give a phonetic representation of an allomorph, elsewhere written as *v*.

In transliterating people's names, the following spellings are substituted for those listed above.

Georgian alphabet	Transliteration	Name transliteration
პ	p̣	p
ტ	ṭ	t
კ	ḳ	k
ყ	q̣	k
ჩ	č	ch
ჭ	č̣	ch
შ	š	sh
ჟ	ž	zh
ძ	ʒ	dz
ც	c	ts
წ	c̣	ts
ჯ	ǯ	j
ღ	γ	gh

I

Introduction

1

The Problem

1.1. BACKGROUND

Since the early 1970s, more and more attention has been focused on the problems surrounding ergativity. Linguists have struggled to understand how ergative systems work, how they fit into the general schema of a language, their implications for linguistic theory, and their place in the evolution of language. The purpose of this work is to study in depth several changes in case marking that have taken place in the Kartvelian language family and to relate those changes to what is known about changes of related types in other language families.

Many, perhaps all, types of syntactic rules can be classified on the basis of their alignment as ergative, accusative, and so on. The primary focus of this work, however, is case marking, and definitions are stated in terms of cases for the sake of simplicity. Although other approaches have been taken, most linguists in the West define a case marking system as ergative if it uses one case for direct objects and subjects of intransitive verbs and a different case for subjects of transitive verbs (Anderson 1976; Catford 1976; Comrie 1973, 1978; Dixon 1979; Plank 1979; Silverstein 1976). Ergative case marking contrasts with the type often referred to as accusative; in an accusative system, one case marks the surface subjects of all verbs and a different case marks surface direct objects. While these are the types most frequently discussed, several other types exist; one other is important in this work. A case system is said to be active if the subjects of transitives and of active intransitives are marked with one case, while a different case marks the subjects of inactive intransitives and direct objects. The three systems of case marking that are most important in this study are summarized in Table 1.1, after Sapir (1917). In Table 1.1, A and B represent distinct cases. The column headings refer primarily to surface grammatical relations.[1] By TRANSITIVE is meant a verb or a clause that has both a subject and a direct object; by INTRANSITIVE is meant a verb or a clause that is not transitive. Active verb forms are those that have surface subjects that are agentive, that control the action. Inactive verb forms are those with surface subjects which do not control the action; usually these subjects are semantic patients.

Studies of changes in case marking systems have described shifts from the accusative to the ergative type (Bynon 1980; Chung 1978; Hohepa 1969; Payne 1979; Pirejko 1979) and from the ergative to the accusative type (Anderson 1977; Comrie 1978; Payne 1980). However, none of these studies takes into account the distinct nature of the active case marking type. Yet the active type cannot be accurately described as an irregular variant of the ergative type, since it is both internally consistent and comparable across languages (Harris 1981b).

One linguist has taken the active type into account in proposing a theory of change in case marking systems. Klimov (1972, 1973, 1976, and elsewhere) has proposed that active patterns can evolve into ergative patterns and that ergative ones can develop into accusative types, but that the reverse changes cannot occur. He suggests that the intermediate stage, ergative, can be skipped over. The evolutionary changes sanctioned under this hypothesis are summarized in Figure 1.1.

Only in the Indo–Iranian branch of Indo–European can shifts in case marking types actually be documented with texts written before, during,

Table 1.1

Some Alignment Types[a]

	Direct object	Subject of intransitive		Subject of transitive
		Inactive	Active	
Ergative	A	A		B
Active	A	A	B	B
Accusative	A	B		B

[a]In this and subsequent tables, "Direct Object" includes just final direct objects of transitives.

Figure 1.1 Changes sanctioned by Klimov (1973).

and after the change. A number of these languages have shifted from the accusative to the ergative type (Anderson 1977; Payne 1979, 1980) and are thus counterexamples to Klimov's hypothesis.[2] Analysis suggests that changes of a parallel nature have taken place in Polynesian (Chung 1978), although this is not without dispute.

In order to understand the changes that take place in case marking systems, we must understand the mechanisms by which these shifts can take place. Among the mechanisms that have been discussed are (a) borrowing, (b) reinterpretation of a surface syntactic pattern that results from the application of a once-productive rule, (c) reinterpretation of nominalizations, and (d) the extension of a case from one function to another by a change in the existing case marking rules. As an example of the second, it has been suggested that in both Indo–Iranian (Anderson 1977; Payne 1979) and Polynesian (Chung 1978), passivization applied, producing a surface syntactic structure in which the initial direct object was identified with the intransitive subject, while the initial transitive subject was set apart by a different marking. Subsequent reinterpretation of this resulted in an ergative case system. Comrie (1978) suggests that an accusative system in some Mayan languages arose as a reanalysis of nominalizations, where the dependents of the nominalization were marked with an accusative pattern. As an example of the last, it has been suggested that in the Dyirbal pronominal system (Dixon 1977b) and in one set of verb forms in Mingrelian (Anderson 1977), the marking for transitive subjects was extended to intransitive subjects, thus creating accusative systems.

1.2. THE KARTVELIAN FAMILY

The Kartvelian language family is an important resource for studying changes in case marking systems for several reasons. First, all three of the case marking types defined in Table 1.1 are attested in the daughter languages. Second, these languages have undergone a number of distinct changes in the systems they employ for marking grammatical relations with cases. Third, one of the languages in the family, Georgian, has a long documented history, being continuously attested since the fifth century A.D. Finally, there is a broad base of research on these languages which can form the foundation for a diachronic study of their syntax. Although it is little known outside the Georgian Soviet Socialist Republic, there is a large collection of dictionaries, grammars, annotated texts, and other scholarly materials available for research on these languages.

The Kartvelian family consists of Georgian, Svan, Mingrelian, and Laz. The first three named are spoken in the Georgian SSR; the last is spoken in the Turkish province of Trabzon on the Black Sea coast and north of there, as well as in a few settlements inside Georgia. Except for Georgian, none are literary languages. Relationships among the languages of this family, established on the basis of phonological, morphological, and lexical correspondences, are represented in Figure 1.2.

The problems in Kartvelian that demand explanation involve accounting for the diversity of case marking types that are found among the languages of the family, as well as the diversity within the individual languages. Georgian is the best known of these; in it there are three series of tense–mood–aspect categories, each of which is said to use a different system of case marking. The system of Series I is accusative; in it all subjects are marked with the so-called nominative case, while all objects—both direct and indirect—are marked with the dative. In Series II, on the other hand, subjects of transitive and of active intransitive verbs are marked with one case, traditionally termed the narrative case (NAR);[3] direct objects and the subjects of inactive intransitives are marked with the nominative (NOM); and indirect objects are marked with the dative (Harris 1981b). This is summarized in Table 1.2.

The headings of the columns in Table 1.2 refer to surface grammatical relations. The active intransitives, which take a subject in the narrative case in Series II, include verbs such as *mušaobs* 'he is working', *tamašobs* 'he is playing', *ṭiris* 'he is crying', and other agentive intransitives (Harris

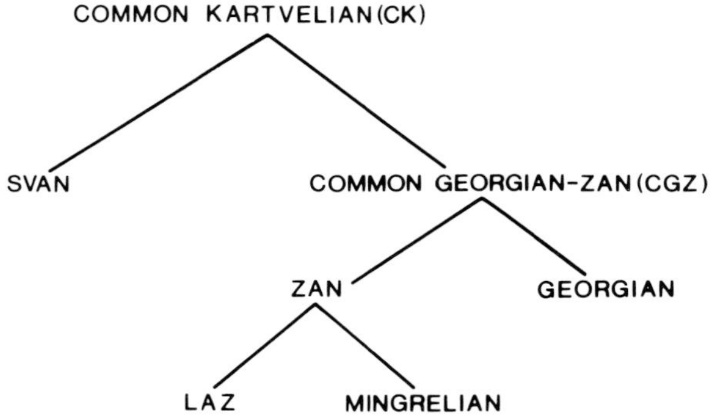

Figure 1.2 Relationships among the Kartvelian languages.

Table 1.2

Summary of Case Marking in Series I and II in Old Georgian

	Direct object	Subject of intransitive		Subject of transitive
		Inactive	Active	
Series I	Dative *-sa*	Nominative *-i/y*		Nominative *-i/y*
Series II	Nominative *-i/y*	Nominative *-i/y*	Narrative *-man*	Narrative *-man*

1981b; Holisky 1981a). Inactive intransitives include verbs of several derivational types, such as inceptives (*aṭirda* 'he burst out crying'), unaccusatives (*daixrčo* 'he drowned'), and passives (*damxrčvalia* 'he got drowned'). The distribution stated in Table 1.2 is supported by examples in §3.4.

The question of how Georgian and the other Kartvelian languages developed such complex systems has been addressed by several linguists. Anderson (1977), Aronson (1979), Boeder (1979), Deeters (1930), Pätsch (1967), Rogava (1975), and Zorrell (1930) have all suggested some version of a theory that Series I developed out of Series II by means of a process that made underlying direct objects surface obliques. According to this theory, underlyingly transitive clauses were made intransitive in Series I. This would explain why the subjects of all clauses in this series are in the nominative case and why the direct objects are in the dative case. At the same time it explains all the facts of agreement, with both the subject and the objects. In addition, it can account for the aspectual differences between the two series, as explained in Chapter 7.

The power of such a theory to explain so many facets of the syntax makes it a very attractive one. It is, however, based on a false premise, namely that case marking in Series II is of the ergative type. Only if it were ergative would we expect the subjects of all intransitives to be marked with the nominative case. But case marking in Series II of Old Georgian, the earliest attested of the Kartvelian languages, is of the active type, not the ergative (see Table 1.2 and Chapter 3). More specifically, when the direct object of a transitive verb is put into some other grammatical relation in Series II of Old Georgian, making the clause a surface intransitive, the subject remains in the NARRATIVE case; it is not put into the nominative case as the hypothesis outlined above assumes.

Examples of this from Old Georgian are of two sorts. In (2) we see examples of Direct Object Incorporation; (1) provides an example of an unincorporated object with the same verb.

(1) *ḳac-man vinme qo pur-i didi*
man-NAR someone he/make/it/II bread-NOM big
'A certain man made a big meal.' (L 14:16)

(2) a. *egreve saxed paṭiv-uqo ʒe-man*
same image/ADV respect-he/make/it/to.him/II son-NAR
mep-isa-man
king-GEN-NAR
'In like manner, the son of the king paid respect.'
(Abuladze 1957:30, 9)

b. *da man qma-qo da tkua*
and he/NAR noise-he/make/it/II and he/say/it/II
'And he cried out and said' (L 16:24)

In Chapter 14 an analysis of the construction in (2) is presented, and it is shown that clauses of this type are initially transitive and finally intransitive. The important point about these examples is that in the surface intransitives, as in (2), the subject is in the narrative case, not the nominative as would be required by the hypothesis outlined in the works cited above.

A second rule that puts underlying direct objects into another grammatical relation is Lexical Object Demotion, governed by only a few verbs in Old Georgian and occurring in Modern Georgian as well (Harris 1981:188–189). In example (3) from Old Georgian the initial direct object is the final indirect object.

(3) *ʒliersa qelmc̣ipe-sa . . . ʒlierta ḳac-ta*
strong ruler-DAT strong man-PL/NAR
sʒles
they/defeat/to.him/II
'Strong men defeated a strong ruler.' (Imnaishvili 1970d:224, 17)

The fact that it can undergo passivization shows that the dative nominal in such a construction is the initial direct object. Example (4) illustrates the analytic passive, and (5) the synthetic passive.

(4) *aramed ʒleul ikmna boroṭita mit codvita*
but defeated he/AUX/II evil/INST DET sin/INST
'But he was overcome by evil sin.' (Imnaishvili: 1970d:222, 43)

(5) *iʒlevis buneba-y, iʒlevian c̣es-ni*
it/defeat/MP/I nature-NOM they/defeat/MP/I law-PL/NOM

srbisani
course/GEN/PL/NOM
'Nature is defeated, the laws of the course are defeated.'
(Shanidze 1959:33, 6)

For each of these constructions, it is only initial direct objects that can become final subjects (on passives, see Appendix to Chap. 3). However, *ʒliersa qelmçipesa* 'a strong ruler' is not merely a direct object that has been idiosyncratically marked with the dative; it has undergone demotion to indirect-objecthood. That it is a final indirect object is shown not only by its case, but also by the fact that it triggers the indirect object agreement marker realized as *s-* in the verb form *s-ʒl-es*. A direct object would condition ∅ (see §12.1.1). In addition, the object does not condition number agreement, as shown by (6).

(6) *vervin* *sʒlo* *mat*
NEG/one/NAR he/defeat/to.him/II them/DAT
'No one could defeat them.' (Shanidze 1959:222, 6)

Under the conditions found in (6), plural direct objects trigger a suffix *-en/n*; plurality of indirect objects is not marked in the verb form (see Chap. 10). These facts lead to the conclusion that the objects in (3) and (6) are initial direct objects that are demoted to final indirect objects.[4]

It might be suggested that the construction in (3) and (6) is due to Armenian influence, since verbs meaning 'overcome, conquer, defeat' govern dative objects in Old Armenian (Jensen 1959:151). This possibility cannot be ruled out, but it is not relevant to the point here. The clause is intransitive on the surface in Georgian; it is Georgian grammar that determines the case of the subject. Even if Armenian influence were responsible for the construction, Armenian could not have determined the case of the subject in Georgian, because Armenian does not have a narrative–nominative alternation.

Lexical Object Demotion may also occur with a few verbs in other Kartvelian languages. Example (7) shows the operation of the rule in Laz, and (8) in Mingrelian.[5]

(7) *didnana-k . . .* *beropa-mušiš* *hiḳay-epe-s*
grandmother-NAR childhood-her/GEN story-PL-DAT
kogyoč̣ḳamṭu
she/begin/to.it/I
'Grandmother would begin stories of her childhood.'
(Dumézil 1937:119, 3)

(8) *orǰginə* *data-kə* *ndii-sə*
he/defeat/to.him/II Data-NAR ogre-DAT
'Data defeated the ogre.' (Bleichsteiner 1919:**VII** [12])

The significance of these examples is that in the Kartvelian languages, the subjects of detransitivized clauses are not necessarily in the nominative case. Sentences (3) and (6)–(8) show that the subjects of clauses to which Object Demotion in particular has applied are marked with the narrative case in Georgian and Laz, as well as in Mingrelian. Because Object Demotion is the sort of rule that has been thought to detransitivize clauses in Series I, these examples are especially important. They appear to disprove the assumption upon which the hypothesis sketched above is based, that the subject of detransitivized clauses will be in the nominative case. Thus, this hypothesis concerning the origin of Series I appears to be inconsistent with the facts of Georgian and Laz.

One of the results of the investigation reported here is to show that the hypothesis proposed by Anderson and others is correct in spite of this apparent anomaly. In Chapter 6 it is argued on the basis of case marking relics in Old Georgian, Laz, and Svan that CK must have had ergative, not active, case marking in Series II. The proposed hypothesis makes specific predictions with respect to additional phenomena of Kartvelian grammar, including ablaut and number agreement. In Part III of this work, an explicit statement of this hypothesis is made, and its implications with respect to these and other phenomena are explored. It is shown that ablaut, number agreement, and other phenomena support this hypothesis concerning the development of Series I; at the same time, this proposal provides an explanation for previously unexplained aspects of ablaut, series markers, number agreement, and so on. In Chapter 14, the CGZ change from the ergative to the active case marking system is traced in Old Georgian and its mechanisms described.

Laz and Mingrelian have each made additional, and different, changes. The case marking systems used today by these languages are described in Chapter 3. The changes that took place between CGZ and these daughters as well as additional changes in dialects of Georgian and of Laz, are explored in Chapter 15.

There is a third series in the Kartvelian languages, and its development is described in Chapter 13. It is argued here that while one part of Series III developed as a variant of Series I, the other parts developed as variants of Series II. It is shown that Series III also developed via a synchronic syntactic process, which is still productive today in Georgian. This rule is of the same general type as other rules that produce a surface syntactic configuration that has been reinterpreted in Indo–Iranian, Polynesian, Kartvelian, and other languages. It has been claimed that a reanalysis of

Series III in Georgian is in progress (Cole *et. al.*1980); the validity of this claim is also examined here.

It has been noted many times that there are two parts to historical analysis: The first is a reconstruction of an earlier stage, and the second is a study of the changes made from earlier stages to later ones. Part II of this study is a reconstruction of the case marking systems of Common Kartvelian. Reconstruction of some additional phenomena is included in Chapters 8–11. Most of Part III, as well as Part IV, is devoted to a study of the shifts in the case marking systems.

The diachronic shifts in case marking are studied from three points of view: the direction of change, the mechanism of change, and the concomitants of change. In terms of direction, the changes described here are of three types: ergative to accusative, ergative to active, and active to accusative. The second of these is a counterexample to one part of Klimov's theory, represented in Figure 1.1.

With respect to mechanism, examples of two types are investigated in this work. The development of Series I and its subsequent reanalysis as an accusative system is shown to have taken place via a once-productive rule of Object Demotion. The shift from ergative to active in Series II is shown to have proceeded in part by means of the rule of Object Incorporation, which made it possible for underlyingly transitive clauses to be reanalyzed as intransitive. The development of Series III took place via a still-productive rule of Inversion, which makes initial subjects indirect objects. The second type of mechanism exemplified here is the extension of a case to additional functions. It is shown that the changes that took place in Laz, Mingrelian, and Lower Ač̣arian involved the removal of one or more of the conditions on a rule.

I use the term 'concomitants of change' to describe morphological changes that occurred at about the same time as, or subsequent to, the syntactic ones. For example, in Laz, which generalized the active case marking throughout Series I and II, a number of morphological peculiarities developed in the verb, which now set those taking narrative case subjects apart from those taking nominative case subjects. In Chapter 16, morphological changes of this type are described for all of the Kartvelian languages. It is not suggested that the case marking shifts investigated here bear a directly causal relation to all or any of the concomitant changes described. However, study of the adaptations made by the different languages may lead to a better understanding of the major changes and the discovery of what, if any, real consequences such changes have in other parts of the grammar of a language. These concomitants are therefore described here as a contribution to future studies of the universal aspects of syntactic change.

NOTES

[1]A few languages with ergative case marking appear to assign cases on the basis of initial, rather than final, grammatical relations (see §6.6.1).

[2]Many linguists do not take Klimov's proposal seriously because of the overwhelming problem presented by the Indo–Iranian counterexample, because there seems to be little concrete foundation for the claims he makes (Figure 1.1), and because he seems to be claiming that the active is the more primitive type, in spite of his protestations to the contrary. His theory cannot, however, be dismissed out of hand in the present study because of his stature as a Kartvelologist (see Klimov 1962, 1964, and elsewhere).

[3]'Narrative' (*motxrobiti*) is used here because it is traditional in the work of Georgian linguists and because it does not prejudice the analysis. 'Active' is used here as the name of one system of distribution of cases (Table 1.1). 'Ergative' is used both as the name for a system of case distribution (Table 1.1) and as the name for a particular case, opposing absolutive, in some languages outside the Kartvelian family.

[4]Deeters (1930:97), citing Schuchardt, argues that *scxo* 'he anointed him' and *sca* 'he beat him' were true (surface) transitives, although they appear superficially to lack direct objects. With these verbs, the real direct objects were often omitted because they were understood. For example, with *sca*, which had the basic meaning 'give', the instrument could be the direct object, while the person receiving the blows was the indirect object. In addition to bearing direct object cases in some examples, the direct object nominal could become the subject of a passive, as in

(9) *isar-ni* *ecnes*
arrow-PL/NOM they/hit/to. him/MP/II
'The arrows hit him.' (Shanidze 1959:223, 33)

where the verb is formally a relative synthetic passive with the subject *isarni* and with the indirect object 'him' not appearing on the surface.

While Deeters was certainly correct in his analysis of *sca*, it does not apply to *ʒleva* 'defeat' in (3) and (6). The difference between the two verbs is shown both in the fact that *ʒleva* lacks a surface direct object and in the contrast between their passives. The syntax of *sca* 'beat' has changed, and in both the synthetic passive *icemeba* and the analytic passive *nacemi aris* the subject is the receiver of the blows, not the instrument. This reanalysis was underway even in Old Georgian, where "mixed" constructions occurred.

[5]The verb in (7) has cognates in Georgian and Mingrelian, but neither has this syntactic peculiarity. The verb in (8) has a cognate in Laz that is similar syntactically; the cognate in Georgian has quite different syntactic properties. Examples from all three languages may be found in Chikobava (1938:411, 435), in constructions that support the analysis provided here.

2

Theory and Method

2.1. SYNCHRONY

A diachronic study must be firmly based on consistent synchronic analyses. The foundation for the present investigation is presented in Harris (1981b) and in Chapter 3, supplemented in subsequent chapters. The principles upon which these analyses are based are set out in this section.

2.1.1. The Domain of Syntax

In the present work SYNTAX refers to the structure of sentences. It is assumed that we must understand the structure of clauses before we study the ways in which they may be combined to form more complex sentences. Limiting ourselves to simple clauses, we can trace the evolution of a clause type within a given language and compare types across languages. The structure of a clause may be reflected directly in case marking, agreement, word order, and, less overtly, in other phenomena amenable to study. The Kartvelian languages depend largely upon case marking and agreement to encode syntactic structure, occasionally making use of word order for this purpose; all three are used here as diagnostics by which to infer the structure of a clause.

Some linguists take the position that case marking and agreement fall into the domain of morphology, rather than that of syntax. Without a doubt, certain aspects of these phenomena do. The issues raised in Chapter 4 and part of Chapter 11, the actual FORMS of the case markers, certainly come under the study of morphology, because they relate to the SHAPES of the morphemes. In contrast, the functional distribution of cases is one direct reflection of syntactic structure. It is this alignment of cases and the changes that have taken place in this aspect of the Kartvelian languages that are at issue here. Morphological aspects of cases are studied for the contribution they may make to understanding the syntax of case marking.

2.1.2. Rule Alignment Typology

There has been a great deal of confusion in the literature concerning whether a given language is or is not ergative, or active, or accusative. The position taken here is that whole languages are not usefully categorized from this point of view. Alignment types are here understood as properties of rules, rather than of languages. This is consistent with the well-known fact that a given language may combine rules of differing alignment; for example, ergative case marking occurs with accusative agreement in Udi (Harris 1984), active case marking with accusative agreement in Laz (Chap. 3), and accusative case marking with active agreement in Choctaw (see Davies 1981). When one considers the variety of combinations that are attested, together with the fact that the issue of alignment is not limited to these two rules but relates also to word order (Derbyshire 1982), clause chaining (Dixon 1972), and other phenomena, it becomes clear that categorization of an entire language in terms of an alignment type is necessarily imprecise.

The alignment types defined in Table 1.1 cannot be taken either as exhaustive or as absolute. Other alignment types include the double-oblique (Payne 1980), neutral, and tripartite (see Comrie 1978); an additional minor type is described below in Chapter 16. Further, there is variation within each type; in §6.6.1, I distinguish two subtypes of ergative alignment, both attested. Beyond this, several studies have shown that ergative case marking is not the same in all languages (e.g., Austin 1982; Derbyshire 1982).

Active case marking is particularly poorly understood, perhaps because of the variety it may exhibit. In some languages, active case marking can be sensitive to controllability in context; that is, a given verb form may govern either the active or the inactive subject case according to context (Holisky 1983a; McLendon 1978). Alternatively, active case marking may be fully grammaticized, a given verb form governing a single subject case in all contexts (Harris 1981b). A further difficulty in understanding the active type, from the point of view of language universals, is that different verbs are interpreted as active or inactive by various languages; within a language there is typically not a perfect correlation between the controllability of an action and the syntax the verb governs. The fundamental difference between the active and inactive clause types is one of relational valence (see §2.1.4) rather than semantics. Thus, in a given language, the CLASS of inactive intransitives may contain certain verbs that are semantically active, and vice versa.

For the reasons stated above, alignment types in this work are applied only to individual rules, not to whole languages. The designations 'ergative,' 'active,' and 'accusative' are not treated as absolute. Thus, their chief value is as convenient labels for the various types. In addition, when Kartvelian material is interpreted from the point of view of general linguistics, these labels draw rough parallels between part of the structure of one language and that of another, though they are not here intended to indicate that structures are identical.

As early as 1942, Chikobava pointed out that the issue of alignment (in languages of the Caucasus) is independent of whether or not a particular language has the inversion construction, in which the underlying subject is marked with the dative case. The inversion construction may occur in languages with ergative case marking (e.g., Avar; Chikobava and Cercvadze 1962), in languages with active case marking (e.g., Georgian; Harris 1981b), and in ones with an accusative case system (e.g., Russian; Perlmutter 1978a, 1982:303–304). The presence or absence of this construction cannot be correlated with the alignment of any rule, though the dative-subject construction has sometimes been confused with active or with ergative case alignment.

While little credence is given to whole-language typologies by most Western linguists (see Voegelin, Ramanujan, and Voegelin 1960), some possible correlates of the various alignment types have been discussed; for example, it has been suggested that ergative case marking is typically accompanied by a lack of passivization. More extensive in this respect, however, is the work of Klimov (1972, 1973, 1977), who claims that there are typological correlates of ergative, active, and accusative languages. For example, he claims that the inclusion of animacy as a grammatical category is a property of "active languages" (1977). Klimov, however, does not first provide an objective way of typing languages in this sense and then make a rigorous study of correlations. If the secondary features do not fit his hypothesis, they are interpreted as relics of an earlier system (see Comrie 1976b). The correlations Klimov observes are thus impressionistic and at best represent tendencies.

2.1.3. Methodology

In working with Old Georgian, one must of course rely entirely upon manuscripts; in approaching the other Kartvelian languages, both textual material and language consultants are available. The problems involved in relying solely on one or the other of these approaches are well known. In order to circumvent—at least in part—both kinds of difficulties, sources of both types were used. In practice, hypotheses about the clause structure of each language were formulated on the basis of textual material and then checked against data elicted from consultants in the Soviet Union who were bilingual in Georgian and another Kartvelian language. Examples were elicted in three ways: (a) Consultants were asked to translate a Georgian sentence into their language. (b) Consultants were given a verb form known to be grammatical and were asked to make up a sentence illustrating its use. (c) Consultants were presented with a sentence and asked to make a grammaticality judgment; these examples were usually an altered version of a sentence from a text or of a sentence obtained earlier by (a) or (b).[1] In the chapters that follow, examples are given from texts and from consultants. Because parallel examples may be obtained from sister languages, elicited examples are particularly useful for illustrating similarities or differences among those languages.

A synchronic analysis is based primarily upon what is most general and productive in a language, not what is restricted or irregular. Synchronic analysis of productive case marking patterns in Chapter 3, as well as other analyses in other parts of this work, are based in the first instance on basic clauses. In practice, the following criteria were used to distinguish basic clauses from others: (a) Only clauses with simple syntactic structures were considered basic. (b) Clauses that were the least marked semantically and pragmatically were considered more basic. (c) Clause types governed by only a few verbs were not regarded as basic; for this reason, examples involving Lexical Object Demotion, such as (3) in Chapter 1, are not considered basic. Another criterion that is traditionally used to distinguish basic clauses, lack of morphological markedness, is not entirely appropriate for this group of languages, though it is applied with certain restrictions. As noted in Chapter 1, case marking in the Kartvelian languages differs by series; for comparative purposes, we need a separate description of the case system in each series in each language. The criterion of morphological simplicity would practically restrict us to Series II; this approach can be usefully applied in internal reconstruction (see Chap. 6) but does not allow for a synchronic description of series other than II. Even within Series II alone, unrestricted application of this criterion would give an unrealistic picture of the grammar, as it would nearly eliminate intransitive verbs. Almost all intransitives have a prefix *i-* or *e-* in Series II, serving one or another function. In order to include a fair sampling of verbs, it seems necessary to include intransitives bearing this prefix. Aside from the inclusion of forms with the *i-* or *e-* prefix and the use of morphologically marked forms in order to describe series other than II, the criterion of morphological simplicity is applied. The combined effect of the application of criteria (a)–(c) and the criterion of morphological simplicity in this limited form is the exclusion of the following marked or restricted constructions from consideration as basic clause types: synthetic causatives, inceptives, potentials, analytic passives, inversions, lexical object demotions, incorporated objects, and nonfinite verb forms. Each of these constructions is drawn secondarily into the analysis elsewhere in the work.

Since no assumption is made here that the alignment of any rule has broader implications (§2.1.2), the classification of a rule according to its alignment is not viewed as an end in itself. The purpose here is rather an accurate description of clause structure. In Chapter 3, alignment types are identified for each of Series I and II in each language for the purpose of comparison for reconstruction. In this work, the alignment of a given rule is determined solely on the basis of the distribution of its markers, as set out in the table of alignment types (Table 1.1), while allowing for the possibility of additional types not included there.

In some works on rule alignment, other criteria have been used in classifying a particular rule. Because some of these practices and assumptions are so widespread, it seems necessary to state why they have no place here.

1. Given that most languages mix rules of different alignment types, it is not logically possible to infer the alignment of one rule from that of another. This does not mean that there is not a tendency toward harmony of alignment types (see Chap. 16). It does mean that in the absence of a perfect correlation universally, arguing from the alignment of one rule to that of another is an invalid procedure.

2. Similarly, unless typological correlates of the sort proposed by Klimov are established as universal and absolute through the use of objective criteria and careful examination of a large base of data, they cannot be used to infer the alignment of any rule.

3. While it is true that the ergative case also serves as the instrumental or as the genitive in many languages having ergative case marking, this is not taken as the defining characteristic of that alignment type and therefore cannot form the basis for an argument that a case rule is or is not ergative.

4. The distribution of a case in one language is not evidence relevant to its distribution synchronically in a sister language. Since the functional distribution of cases may shift over time, the synchronic analysis must be made on the basis of language-internal facts only; and from comparison of these, the situation of the protolanguage may be inferred.

5. The alignment of case marking cannot be determined from the history of the morphemes themselves (see Chap. 4).

Although it may seem obvious to the reader that rule alignment cannot be identified through the use of these criteria, each of them has been applied to the Kartvelian family in the linguistic literature. If instead a single property—distribution—is taken as the defining characteristic of each alignment type synchronically, we have an objective basis for classification; we can then study additional phenomena to determine historical relationships and to look for possible correlates.

2.1.4. Theory of Clause Structure

The structure of a clause is understood here as the set of grammatical relations obtaining among the constituents of that clause. Because of the differential case marking in the various series in Kartvelian, syntax cannot, without a great many complications, be stated on cases. Because of the great freedom of word order, dominance and linear order are likewise an inappropriate basis for the statement of syntactic phenomena (Harris 1981b).

It has been shown that a description of Modern Georgian must make reference to three term grammatical relations: subject, direct object, and indirect object (Harris 1981b). The same relations are justified for each of the other Kartvelian languages by the fact that they are referred to by one or more syntactic rules: Causative Formation, Passivization, Version, Inversion, and others. The relations subject, direct object, and indirect object are accordingly assumed here.

It has been suggested that universally there are just two central grammatical relations, subject and object (e.g., Dik 1978:18; Faltz 1978). Indeed, there are some processes in the Kartvelian languages that refer to the notion 'object'; case marking in Series I in Georgian, Svan, and Mingrelian is one such rule, as is agreement in all series in Laz and Mingrelian. On the other hand, every Kartvelian language has more than one process that distinguishes between direct and indirect objects: agreement (Svan and many dialects of Georgian), case marking in Series II (all), Causative Formation (all), Inversion (all), and others. For this reason, direct object must be distinguished from indirect object in syntactic theory (see Dryer 1983).

A number of treatments of rule alignment are based upon a theory that recognizes the three relations intransitive subject (S), transitive subject (A), and transitive object (O), after Dixon (1972). Even if we add indirect objects as a fourth relation, this theory makes incorrect claims about the structure of the Kartvelian languages. In particular, the theory is not detailed enough to permit the description of an active case system (see Table 1.1), which is found in some Kartvelian languages. To remedy this situation, Dixon (1979:80) suggests the revised set, A, S_a, S_o, O. This still makes the claim that S_a and S_o are subtypes of S, or that they bear some special relationship; yet, it seems that there is no rule at any stage of any Kartvelian language that refers to S_a and S_o to the exclusion of other relations. There are, on the other hand, rules which relate A to S_a (e.g., case marking in Laz), A and S_a to S_o (e.g., case marking in Series I in Georgian, Svan, and Mingrelian), and S_o to O (e.g., *En*-Agreement; see Chap. 10). Thus, this shorthand is avoided here because it makes incorrect claims about the ways nominals may be grouped in this family.

A second assumption made here is that the structure of a clause may be different at various levels of derivation.[2] These differences may include variation in the grammatical relations borne by a particular nominal. Since subject and direct object relations may vary, and since transitivity is determined by the presence of nominals bearing these relations in a clause, it follows that transitivity may vary at different levels of derivation.

It is further assumed that a particular grammatical relation, or a particular role in the structure of a clause, may be borne by only one nominal at a given level of derivation. This principle, known as the Stratal Uniqueness Law (Perlmutter and Postal 1983b), particularly affects two analyses included here. In Chapter 11 it is assumed that the nominal that is the indirect object at initial levels of derivation does not bear that relation after Object Demotion has made the direct object an indirect object. As shown there, the evidence in the attested languages does not unambiguously support this view, though it is not inconsistent with it. Again, in §13.5, in evaluating a hypothesis involving reinterpretation of Series III, I assume that if the surface indirect object is being reinterpreted as subject, then the old surface subject must also be undergoing reinterpretation.

The importance of the notion 'retired term' in the syntax of Old and Modern Georgian has been firmly established (Harris 1979, 1981b). The Chômeur Law (Perlmutter and Postal 1983b:95–99, 109–122) may now be viewed as a language-particular condition on derivations. It makes correct predictions for the occurrence of chômeurs, one type of retired term, in a variety of constructions in Old and Modern Georgian; but alone it is not able to predict the occurrence of all retired terms in the language (Harris 1981b: Chap. 11). While universally valid generalizations predicting the occurrence of retired terms cannot yet be stated, the notion is motivated for Kartvelian languages and general linguistics. A retired term_i can be defined as a nominal which has as its last term relation term_i and which is finally a nonterm. For example, a retired indirect object is a nominal that is an indirect object and a final nonterm. In most dialects of the modern Kartvelian languages, retired indirect objects do not trigger indirect object agreement and are marked with a case other than that used for the surface indirect object (dative). The notion of retired indirect object is essential to an account of the behavior of the initial indirect object in the object demotion construction (see especially Chap. 12) and in inversion (Chap. 13). The same retirement relation in some other constructions is discussed in Chapter 11.

It is assumed here that cross-linguistic syntactic generalizations are best accounted for by positing a finite inventory of rules, as suggested within a transformational framework by Bach (1971) and Postal (1970) among others. It is further taken that such rules consist of a universal and one or more optional language-particular components (see Perlmutter and Postal 1983a).

A final assumption that requires some discussion concerns the relational valences governed by various finite verb forms. It is assumed here that, in addition to governing an indirect object, verb forms may govern an initial subject and/or direct object. These possibilities are illustrated from Laz in (1)–(3).

(1) *hemuk dido ḳai mç̌ums mç̌ḳudi*
he/NAR very well he/cook/it/I cornbread/NOM
'He cooks cornbread very well.' (Chikobava 1936, II:62, 5–6)

(2) *ḳinčik ç̌uṭa kelidušunu*
bird/NAR little it/think/II
'The bird thought a little.' (Dumézil 1937:101, 9–10)

(3) *eḳule ia mç̌ḳidi iç̌ven*
later that cornbread/NOM it/cook/I
'Then the cornbread cooks.' (Chikobava 1938:407)

In initial structure, (1) has a subject and a direct object, (2) a subject only, and (3) a direct object only. The initial direct object in (3) is obligatorily made a final subject by the rule of Unaccusative.

The principle that certain verb types govern initial intransitive direct objects was developed as the Unaccusative Hypothesis (Perlmutter 1978b; Perlmutter and Postal 1984); it has also been adopted in a version of the

Extended Standard Theory (see Chomsky 1982:256ff.). This analysis is implicit in traditional treatments of the grammar of Kartvelian languages, where clauses such as (3) are called PASSIVES and are said to be derived by CONVERSION of the direct object into subject, without expression of agent (e.g., Shanidze 1973:280–283, 355; see also Appendix to Chap. 3).

Support for the Unaccusative Hypothesis in Georgian comes from a variety of grammatical phenomena (Harris 1981b, 1982), and similar evidence is found in the sister languages. One value of recognizing that initial intransitive subjects, as in (2), differ from initial intransitive direct objects, as in (3), is that it permits a natural explanation of the fact that in the history of Kartvelian, the use of the narrative case spread from transitive subjects to the surface subjects of some, but not all, intransitives. In addition, it permits a natural treatment of the relationships between initial intransitive objects, as in (3), and final objects, as in (1).

In this work, the clause type illustrated in (1) is referred to as TRANSITIVE, that in (2) as ACTIVE INTRANSITIVE, and that in (3) as INACTIVE INTRANSITIVE. While these labels are appropriate for a majority of clauses, there exist examples of inactive intransitive clause structure that seem not to be semantically inactive, and so on. The clause type is determined by morphological and syntactic criteria—grammatical relations—not by the semantics of the verb (Harris 1982).

2.2. DIACHRONY

2.2.1. The Verb as the Locus of Syntax

In the Kartvelian languages the finite verb form encodes information concerning the structure of the clause it governs, indicating the transitivity of the clause, the syntactic construction type (e.g., causative or potential), and which nominals bear which term grammatical relations. Further, particular finite verb forms strictly govern the syntax of the clause and hence the case marking of the term nominals associated with them. This is true both of those verbs that govern regular, productive patterns and of those that govern an irregular marking. Consider as an example the root *cer-* 'write'. Forms of this root associated with the preverb *mi-* 'thither' or *mo-* 'hither' take an initial indirect object, while forms of the same root associated with other preverbs do not. (Forms of this root with other preverbs may have DERIVED, but not INITIAL, indirect objects; see Harris 1981b:93–95.) As another example, 'it is written' in the sense of 'spelled' or 'formed' is regularly expressed with the unaccusative (mediopassive) form, *icereba,* while 'it is/has been written' in the sense of 'composed' is most often expressed by means of the analytic passive, *dacerilia* (< *dacerili aris*). Use of these forms is related to the fact that the former cannot normally co-occur with an agent phrase, while the latter takes one freely (Harris 1981b:196–197). When we turn to lexical items for which the semantics does not agree with the relational valence, it is even more apparent that syntax may be lexically governed. For example, although intransitive verbs of controllable movement govern narrative case subjects in Series II (Holisky 1981a:109–119), the learner of the standard dialect of Modern Georgian must memorize the fact that the verb 'come, go' governs instead the nominative case, just as he must learn the irregular morphology of the verb. (This and other lexically governed exceptions to case marking in Georgian, Laz, and Svan are discussed in Chaps. 6 and 14.) The fact that in the Kartvelian languages syntax is partially lexically governed in this sense has important consequences for the historical study of this family.

First, the regularity of productive alternations, such as the Series I/Series II pattern illustrated by (4) and (5), gives us grounds for postulating that syntactic change is regular.

(4) *bavšv-i ṭiris*
child-NOM he/cry/I
'The child is crying.'

(5) *bavšv-ma iṭira*
child-NAR he/cry/II
'The child cried.'

This is parallel to the neogrammarians' hypothesizing that sound change is regular on the basis of the regularity of synchronic variation (Osthoff and Brugman 1878:ix; Weinreich, Labov, and Herzog 1968:115–116). In the present work, the concept 'regularity of syntactic change' is understood to refer, not to exceptionlessness of change, but rather to a RULE-GOVERNED ORDERLINESS OF CHANGE. With respect to case marking, this means that nominals bearing the same set of grammatical relations to the verbs that govern them will, under equivalent conditions, change case marking in the same way. We may take as an example the Laz extension of the Series II case marking system into Series I, as discussed in Chapter 15. The change is regular in the sense that nominals bearing the initial subject relation did, in the environment of Series I, cease to be marked with the nominative case, which is reconstructible in this function for CK, and begin to be marked with the narrative case. In this way, syntactic change is not random, but rule governed.

A second important consequence of the lexicalization of syntactic information is that lexical exceptions to change exist in syntax, just as they do in phonology and morphology. Exceptions and anomalies are one of the primary bases for internal reconstruction (Greenberg 1957:51; Kuryłowicz 1964:10; Meillet 1954:27; Watkins 1976). The lexicalization of exceptions provides a means of readily identifying and analyzing them, both within a language and among languages. Lexical relics are one basis for reconstruction in Chapter 6.[3] The regularization of such exceptions is one of the topics discussed in Chapter 14.

A further consequence of the lexicalization of syntax around a governing verb is that we can establish clausal equations as a basis of comparison, within a single language and among sister languages. Although phonological equations have long formed the basis for historical work in phonology, clausal correspondences have been conspicuously absent from historical syntax (see Watkins 1963:2). Jespersen's constructed examples representing a change in English case marking are one of the few instances of the use of this approach (see also Watkins 1964).

(6) *þam cynge licodon peran.*
the king likeden peares.
the king liked pears.
he liked pears. (Jespersen 1927:209)

Inasmuch as these sentences are not attested, they represent the syntax governed by 'like' as an abstraction from actually occurring examples, much as the correspondence

(7) Latin Gothic
t : þ

represents an abstraction from attested words.

It has been said that the notion of clausal correpondences is "incoherent" (Lightfoot 1979:8); yet in relatively closely related languages having a rich morphology, it is both possible and useful to compare clauses in this way. Attested correspondences for stages of Georgian, similar in approach to Jespersen's English ones, are used by Shanidze (1973:483–484) and are repeated in §6.2.2. Examples (8) and (9) illustrate a clausal correspondence between two languages, here Modern Georgian and Laz, respectively.

(8) *bič̣-eb-i a-xrč-ob-en nodar-s*
boy-PL-NOM they/drown/him/I Nodar-DAT
'The boys drown Nodar.'

(9) *bič̣-epe-k o-škvid-ap-en nodari*
boy-PL-NAR they/drown/him/I Nodar/NOM
'The boys drown Nodar.'

In these examples, the lexical items are cognates; and the verb tense (present), class (1), and series (I) are the same. In this sense they are directly comparable. One difference between (8) and (9) is that the former has its subject in the nominative case, while the latter has a narrative subject. The pair (8) and (9) is one example in support of the correspondence in (10), for this environment.

(10)	Georgian		Laz
	NOM-subject	:	NAR-subject.[4]

Other examples occurring under the same conditions of class and series support the same correspondence (see Chap 3). This is parallel to the fact that Latin *tres* 'three' and Gothic *þreis* 'three' are one example in support of correspondence (7); others occurring under the same conditions, in this instance those not meeting the conditions of Verner's Law as to the position of Indo–European accent, support the same correspondence.

In phonology certain facts safeguard against misidentifying a random similarity as a sound correspondence. As in the example above, it is essential that the meaning of the items compared be the same or nearly so. The correspondence must be supported in the same way by many examples (lexical items). Correspondences are most strongly supported by lexical items in which every sound corresponds, as in the example above, where we see also Latin *r* to Gothic *r*, *e* to *ei*, and *s* to *s*. Additional strength is provided by parallel correspondences—sharing point or manner of articulation—and by the fact that the multifaceted parallels all fit into a system.

In establishing clausal correspondences in this work, the following precautions are taken to insure that we are comparing structures that are descended form a common ancestor. First, the genetic relationships among the several languages has already been established through phonological and morphological correspondences, and these may be assumed here. Second, in order to guard against use of restricted patterns or of irregular verbs in establishing general patterns, many examples of each clause type are considered, and only basic clause types (see §2.1.3 above) are compared initially. Third, the regular syntactic systems compared are abstracted from clauses meeting the same conditions of class and series, which have been shown to be relevant to syntax in Kartvelian languages (see Harris 1981b); in this sense we can control for environment. Fourth, the morphological markers of class and series can be shown to be related in a regular way (Chapters 5 and 13), as can those of case (Chapter 4). This insures that the conditions relevant to the distribution of case markers are themselves genetically related. Fifth, just as phonetic correspondences are generally based on examples in which each segment in one language corresponds to each in the other, so our syntactic correspondences are founded upon clauses in which the various grammatical relations correspond. For example, in (8) and (9) we see not only the correspondence stated as (10), but also a Georgian direct object in the dative beside a Laz direct object in the nominative.

(11)	*Georgian*		*Laz*
	DAT-direct object	:	NOM-direct object

This correspondence, too, is supported by many examples; the regular relationship between the two correspondences lends support to each. Finally, each correspondence is part of a larger system, the alignment type of the rule. The individual correspondences, as well as the alignment type, can be related diachronically in plausible and clearly motivated ways.

2.2.2. Preliminaries to Syntactic Reconstruction

The principles established for the synchronic analysis of syntax apply mutatis mutandis to a diachronic investigation. Most important for present purposes are (a) that the analysis be founded on basic clauses and (b) that the reconstruction of case marking alignment be based solely upon the distribution of cases, not upon other properties of the language. These principles are set out in greater detail in §2.1.3 above.

It is the most ancient stage of a language that provides the basis for reconstruction. In internal reconstruction, the oldest attested stage is the input to the process of "undoing" the effects of change. In comparative reconstruction, it is the oldest stages derivable by internal reconstruction that are compared. For this reason I have relied most heavily upon the oldest available manuscripts (e.g., "Šušaniḳ" and the Adiši Gospels) for the purposes of reconstruction, while trying to provide a wider variety of attestation when the Old Georgian norm is described, as for example in Chapter 10.

In reconstruction and in the analysis of change, both the underlying form and surface realization must be taken into consideration. A contrast between underlying and surface representations is often the basis for reanalysis: It is important in the reinterpretation of Series I (Chap. 7) and the ergative-to-active shift (Chap. 14).

Timberlake (1977) has argued effectively that many syntactic changes have two parts—reanalysis and actualization. This principle is assumed here, and it is shown that the actualization of the ergative-to-active shift proceeded gradually (Chap. 6 and 14).

2.2.3. Methodology in Internal Reconstruction of Syntax

Whereas a synchronic analysis relies upon what is general and regular in a language, in internal reconstruction the exceptional and restricted has a special importance (Watkins 1976; see also references cited above, §2.2.1). It was observed in the preceding section that clausal relics exist in the Kartvelian languages and have an important role in internal reconstruction. In practice, however, it is not always easy to distinguish innovation from archaism. For this reason, it is useful for us to look at some of the properties of relics, with particular reference to syntax.

Exceptions tend to be regularized in the couse of time; a relic is likely to be replaced by a regular form. Examples of this are discussed in Chapters 6, 8, 10, 11, and elsewhere. The introduction of a literary norm may impede the natural processes of regularization. For this reason, relics may survive in a literary dialect and be leveled in nonliterary dialects and languages. An example of the dialectal leveling of irregularities is discussed in §6.2.1. A variety of instances of nonliterary languages or dialects simplifying the rather complex system retained by Standard Modern Georgian are discussed.

Relics are particularly likely to be retained in the most common words of a language (Meillet 1964:31–32). Those exceptions that are frequently repeated are more likely to be observed and acquired; those that are infrequently used are likely to go unnoticed and unlearned. In languages like those of the Kartvelian family, where the syntax of a clause is associated with a verb form, irregular syntax is also likely to be associated with commonly occurring words. It is this fact that explains the frequent association of irregular syntax with irregular morphology. That is, irregularities that are associated with frequently occurring forms are more likely to be retained, regardless of whether the irregularities are phonological, morphological, or syntactic. It cannot be assumed that there is any inherent relation between irregularity in morphology and in syntax, or that the one necessarily implies the other.

Since they are memorized and may be learned apart from the normal language acquisition, formulaic expressions of a language are likely to retain syntactic relics (Watkins 1976:317). An example of this is discussed in §6.2.2, and another in §11.2.1.

In actual reconstruction the language-internal search for evidence of earlier stages is combined with comparison of sister languages.

2.2.4. Methodology in Comparative Reconstruction of Syntax

The comparative method works hand in hand with internal reconstruction. The oldest form of each daughter language is compared with that of the others. If the evidence from the daughter languages agrees about some feature, that feature must be assumed to be reconstructible to the parent language, in the absence of evidence to the contrary. If all of the daughter languages exhibit two conjugational types, both must be reconstructed for the protolanguage; see §14.3.2. (Watkins, 1976:316, makes this point with respect to parallel marked and unmarked construction; see Hetzron 1976).

If, on the other hand, evidence from the daughters is conflicting, the comparative method consists in comparing hypotheses about the origin of the feature in question. (Of course, the comparison of hypotheses may be only implicit in the presentation.) If two values for a feature are attested, there are two obvious hypotheses as to which is original; if three values, three hypotheses, and so forth. Apart from this, one or more additional hypotheses may be suggested by the natural relations among the values attested or by internal evidence in one or more of the daughter languages.

For example, in Part II, it is shown that each of the systems of case marking shown in Table 2.1 is attested for Series II in at least one Kartvelian language or dialect. (An additional dialectal variant is discussed in Chapter 15).

In addition to the patterns attested, in Georgian, Laz, and Svan there is internal evidence to support postulation of a fourth pattern, shown in Table 2.2.

Table 2.1

Attested Case Patterns of Series II

Direct object	Subject of intransitive		Subject of transitive
	Inactive	Active	
NOM	NAR	NAR	NAR
NOM	NOM	NAR	NAR
NOM	NOM	NOM/NAR[a]	NAR

[a]NOM/NAR indicates that either may be used.

Table 2.2

Case Pattern of Series II, Indicated by Internal Evidence

Direct object	Subject of intransitive		Subject of transitive
	Inactive	Active	
NOM	NOM	NOM	NAR

Thus, we formulate four hypotheses: (a) that the protolanguage used the first pattern above, (b) that it used the second, (c) that it used the third, and (d) that it used the fourth. (For the sake of simplicity it is assumed here that the protolanguage used only one of these; other possibilities are discussed in Chapter 6.) As it is cumbersome to compare all four possibilities at once, the proposals outlined are compared in pairs in Chapters 5 and 6.

Having established reasonable hypotheses concerning the protolanguage, the accumulated body of knowledge of historical linguistics is brought to bear upon the evaluation of each hypothesis in comparison with the others. One element of this concerns indications that a feature is archaic or innovative, as described in the preceding section.

A second set of factors that must be considered involves relationships among the languages in the family, including the relative age of attested languages, sociocultural relations among the languages, and subgrouping. Each of these is discussed with particular reference to the Kartvelian family in §2.2.5.

One hypothesis will entail one or more changes in one language, while another will involve other changes in a different language. The relative plausibility of these changes must be evaluated. This may involve many different factors, such as the use of a known versus previously unknown mechanism, as well as change in a direction known to occur versus one believed not to occur. Or if, for example, borrowing is proposed as the mechanism of change, an evaluation of the plausibility of the change will question whether features of this particular type are believed to be susceptible to borrowing and whether there existed a pathway for borrowing, such as geographical proximity. In addition, the plausibility of a change concerns the presence or absence of a cause or motivation for the proposed change. Ultimately the evaluation of plausibility depends upon a notion of possible change (see Kiparsky 1974:257–258).

The plausibility of the reconstructed system must likewise be evaluated. One factor that must be taken into consideration from this point of view is the internal consistency of each reconstructed system. In addition, typology may provide a valuable tool for evaluating the plausibility of competing proposals (Campbell and Mithun 1980:32; Dressler 1971:9; Jakobson 1958; Watkins 1976:306). A hypothesis which has been developed on the basis of internal evidence, but which involves a type of system not attested, must be considered implausible.

Several studies in word order have made a different use of typology in reconstruction, based on the assumption that a language may be expected to develop in the direction of typological consistency, a proposal that might be referred to as "the typological consistency hypothesis." This approach has not gained wide acceptance (see criticism in Campbell and Mithun 1980:25–28; Jeffers 1976; Lightfoot 1979:162ff.; Watkins 1976). In the present work, alignment typology is not used as a method of reconstruction, just as the same approach, mutatis mutandi, is eschewed in synchronic analysis (see §2.1.3). The more general question of the validity of the typological consistency hypothesis with respect to rule alignment and alignment typology is the subject of Chapter 16.

In evaluating competing hypotheses, a final factor that should be taken into consideration is the explanatory value of the various proposals. Many changes will affect several parts of the grammar, and in some instances one hypothesis can be seen to account for and explain these additional aspects better than another.

2.2.5. Reconstruction in Kartvelian

In reconstruction it is important to keep in mind the relationships among the attested languages—subgrouping relations, relative age of attestation, and geographic and social relations. In the Kartvelian languages, the subgroupings stated in Figure 1.2 have been established by diachronic studies of phonetics, phonology, and morphology, and are widely, if not universally, accepted by Kartvelologists.[5] The relationships set out in Figure 1.2 determine in part how various correspondences are to be interpreted. Svan has a special importance in reconstructions because it split off earliest; the fact that a particular feature is attested in Svan and one other language suggests immediately that it is archaic.[6] Old Georgian has a different kind of importance in the reconstruction of CK. Because it is attested more than a millenium before any of its sisters, Old Georgian gives the most reliable kind of evidence concerning the age of various features.

Once we have ruled out chance resemblances and the effects of universals, a feature may be shared by two languages by virtue of (a) common inheritance, (b) parallel development, or (c) borrowing. By parallel development is meant an independent development of the same feature by two or more related languages (cf. Malkiel's 1981 'slant'). When a common innovation of this type is not independent, it may be termed 'borrowing'. The effects of both types of shared innovation must be factored out in order to determine which features are a shared inheritance and thus are to be reconstructed to the protolanguage. In the syntax of the Kartvelian languages, it is not always easy to distinguish common inheritance from common innovation.

Georgian exerts a strong influence on each of its sisters, and this has apparently been true for a very long time. Each of the sister languages is geographically contiguous with the Georgian-speaking area. Nearly all speakers of Svan, Laz, and Mingrelian in the USSR are bilingual with Georgian; community bilingualism provides an obvious vehicle for influence to flow from one language to another. Further, Georgian enjoys a special prestige in this region for many reasons. It has a far greater number of speakers than any other Kartvelian language. Through the course of history, Georgia has generally been associated with the politically strongest among Kartvelian elements.[7] Georgian has served, not only for Kartvelian speakers, but for certain other peoples of the Caucasus, as a lingua franca at various periods.

Perhaps most important, Georgian has a long literary history, which is rightly a source of pride to speakers of all Kartvelian languages. Further, Georgian is, with Russian, the language of schools, publications, and broadcasts and is included in the constitution as an official language in the Republic of Georgia.[8] In addition to adding to its prestige, the fact that Georgian is the language of these institutions insures that virtually all speakers of the smaller languages will have contact with Georgian, while far fewer Georgians have continued contact with another Kartvelian language. It may be noted that, as a mark of their identification with Georgian, most speakers of a Kartvelian language in the USSR, when asked their ethnic identity, reply not that they are Svan or Mingrelian, but that they are Georgian. This being so, it is not surprising that the literary language has long exerted a strong influence on its sisters, and this fact must be taken into account in reconstructing CK.[9]

As evidence of the extent of shared innovation within this family, consider the following (not exhaustive) list of features shared by Modern Georgian, Svan, and at least one of the Zan languages, but not found in Old Georgian (see also Topuria 1954):[10]

1. In Old Georgian, the preverb indicated direction or orientation; in the modern languages, it indicates perfective aspect in addition (see Chap. 5).
2. A future subseries (morphologically: present subseries + preverb) in Series I occurs in the modern languages, but not in Old Georgian (see Chap. 5).
3. Old Georgian has a habitual II or "permansive"; none of the modern languages has this (see Chap. 5).
4. In Inversion (see Chap. 13) in Old Georgian, the verb agreed in number with the nominative-nominal; in the modern languages it agrees with the dative-nominal.
5. In Old Georgian there was number agreement with direct objects in Series II (see Chap. 10); no modern language has this rule, though *Al*-Agreement in Svan is structurally similar (see §9.4).

6. In Old Georgian the dominant word order was NOUN MODIFIER and NOUN POSSESSOR; positionals preceded or followed head nouns. Each of the modern languages is characterized by a predominance of MODIFIER NOUN and POSSESSOR NOUN word orders and by exclusive use of NOUN POSITIONAL order.
7. Believed to be related to 6 above is the fact that Old Georgian used double case marking, the suffixation of an agreeing case on a genitive-marked possessor; none of the modern languages uses this productively.
8. In Old Georgian, formation of the plurals of substantives was principally fusional (see Chaps. 4 and 10); in the modern languages it is agglutinative, except as a conscious archaism in Georgian.

It is clear from the contrast between Old and Standard Modern Georgian in these respects that these features of the latter are recent developments; it is rightly inferred that the corresponding features of the other modern languages are likewise innovations, the result of either parallel development or borrowing from Georgian. These features demonstrate the powerful influence of Georgian on her sisters and show why we cannot make simple rules regarding reconstruction.[11] For example, if all of Old Georgian had been lost, we would be inclined to reconstruct MODIFIER NOUN, POSSESSOR NOUN, and NOUN POSITIONAL orders for CK (see 6 above), on the ground that it is attested in each daughter. In fact, Old Georgian evidence suggests that the reverse orders may be older. This does not mean that reconstruction is impossible in Kartvelian. It does mean that we must make the conservative assumption that borrowing and parallel development have always been important forces in these languages and that when there is substantial agreement among the daughter languages we look to all possible sources for additional types of evidence and proceed with caution.

Just as Georgian, especially the literary norm, may exert pressure to change, as in 1–8 above, it may likewise be a conservative influence. It is characteristic of recent innovations within Kartvelian, perhaps especially in Georgian dialects, that for a time the innovative form exists side by side with the corresponding conservative form from the literary dialect. For example, the Tušurian and Pšavian dialects of Georgian have generalized the use of the suffix *-av* (*-avis*) in the formation of the first evidential; beside this, the form dictated by the literary norm, *-ia* for many lexical items, continues to exist (Baramidze 1977:39). Syntactic examples of the same phenomenon are described in §6.2.1 and §15.3.4.

Areal influences from languages outside the Kartvelian family must also be taken into consideration. In the course of history, Georgia has been under the political influence of the Romans, Mongols, Turks, Persians, and Russians, among others. In such a situation, linguistic differences can be "marks of the solidarity of the group against all others" (Emeneau 1980b:41), and it is unlikely that the political dominance of these languages affected the syntax of the Kartvelian languages significantly.

Neighborly borrowing as a result of geographical contiguity and widespread bilingualism has unquestionably affected the lexicons of the Kartvelian languages. Svan development of two-base declensions has been attributed to close contact with other indigenous languages at an earlier period, while more recent loss of these declensions may be viewed as the result of renewed contact with other Kartvelian languages (Chantladze 1979:127).[12] It is likewise not unlikely that the presence of the evidential category, which occurs in many of the neighboring languages (see Friedman 1979), results, in part, from diffusion. However, the syntax and morphology of this category have clear internal sources (see Chap. 13). It has also been suggested that the case pattern reconstructible for Series I was borrowed from nearby Indo–European languages, but it is argued here that that hypothesis is untenable (Chap. 7). With respect to most of the other innovations that form the central issues discussed in the present work, borrowing from outside the family seems unlikely because the features do not exist in languages that are potential donors (but cf. §15.1).

An additional type of contact occurred through translation. Many of the oldest monuments of the Georgian language are translations from Greek or Armenian originals. It seems unlikely that either of these languages would have exerted much influence with respect to the case marking of subjects, direct objects, or indirect objects in finite clauses. At the time of translation, Georgian already had three distinct series, and the difficulties of making simple correlations between any one Georgian case and any Greek or Armenian case would tend to discourage this sort of influence. In one lexically governed pattern, as discussed in Chapter 1, it is possible that the case of the direct object was borrowed from Armenian; but, because of the lack of parallels, the influence of that language cannot be held responsible for the choice of the subject case even in this limited construction. In any event, the regular, productive patterns with finite verb forms clearly do not derive from these or other languages. With respect to other features, including the case marking of oblique nominals, the situation is different. Among the syntactic patterns discussed in the present work, it is the marking of retired indirect objects that presents the greatest difficulty in this respect (Chap. 11).

2.3. CONCLUSION

Several works have presented a pessimistic view of the possibilities of reconstruction in the field of syntax. I believe that the research reported here, together with parallel studies in other language families, provides grounds for cautious optimism as to what the comparative method and internal reconstruction can accomplish in the area of rule alignment. Again, some works have presented a nihilistic view of diachronic syntactic theory, suggesting in essence that there are no independent constraints on syntactic change. Although it is true that constraints cannot be formulated until a sufficiently large amount of data from a variety of language families is available, studies are accumulating. What is more promising, as observed especially in Chapter 17, is that there are enough parallels between developments studied in unrelated families to suggest that linguistically significant generalizations **are** there waiting to be captured.

NOTES

[1]The use of method (a), and to some extent (c), results in examples reflecting word order chosen by the investigator, rather than by the consultant. Although I frequently asked whether the word order were natural, the answer was nearly always affirmative. I infer from this that in Svan, Laz, and Mingrelian, as in Georgian, word order is essentially a pragmatically determined phenomenon, with the immediately preverbal position probably encoding focus. This question, however, requires further research.

[2]I depart from a relational grammar framework in taking a derivational approach; but see Perlmutter (1982) on syntactic levels.

[3]The importance of syntactic relics in reconstruction has already been demonstrated in Chung (1978), especially pp. 281ff. and 293ff.

[4]For at least one Laz dialect, this correspondence must be modified (see Chap. 15); this dialect is not considered further in the discussion here.

[5]Zan is sometimes referred to as Colxur or Kolxur, and Laz is also termed Chan or Č̣an. In the USSR, Laz and Mingrelian are usually treated as dialects of a single language, although they are not mutually intelligible. In the present work they are referred to as "languages" for convenience, since the resolution of this question seems to have no immediate linguistic consequences. As shown in Chapter 3, the two differ greatly in the features that are the central focus of this investigation.

[6]This principle has occasionally been erroneously interpreted to mean that every feature of Svan (or of an "archaic" dialect of Georgian) is necessarily ancient, ruling out the possibility of Svan (or the Georgian dialect) ever having changed independently (see Hetzron 1976:n. 6 on the same problem in Semitic).

[7]The kingdom of Colchis, comprising speakers of Mingrelian, Svan, and Georgian, is said to have enjoyed political power at one time.

[8]On the importance of such institutions in ethnic assimilation and language borrowing in the Caucasus, see Wixman (1980, esp. p. 112) with reference to the relation between Svan and Georgian.

[9]Emeneau (1980b:41ff.) has made the important observation that it is not always, as in the European situation, the prestige language/dialect that is imitated by speakers of other languages/dialects. Nevertheless, as shown by the facts enumerated above, the situation internal to the Kartvelian family is closer to the European case than to the Indian, discussed by Emeneau. It is on this basis that we may assume that influence generally flows from Georgian to its sisters. Machavariani (1980:216) concurs, citing "the strong influence of Georgian [on Svan]."

[10]Some dialects may be exceptions to some statements in the list.

[11]Schmidt (1978:248) suggests rules which are useful and generally valid, but which fail to take into consideration the possibility of changes such as 1–8 having occurred in prehistoric times. I suggest that Schmidt's rules be treated as conditions that are necessary but not sufficient for reconstruction.

[12]Some features of Svan declension have been interpreted as the result of contact with Adiγe, another Caucasian language (Sharadzenidze 1955:125–127; Topuria 1944:342–344).

II

Reconstruction

3

Synchronic Case Marking

3.1. INTRODUCTION

This chapter provides synchronic descriptions of the distribution of cases, in terms of function, for Old Georgian, Svan, Laz, and Mingrelian. These data provide the basis for the reconstruction of case marking patterns, undertaken in Chapters 5 and 6, and for the description of later changes, in Chapters 7–16. The present chapter is not, however, exhaustive. The data given here are derived only from the major dialects of each of the languages, but this is sufficient for immediate purposes and will limit the variety to a manageable amount. The variant case marking of the Naḳra-Laxamula subdialect of Svan is described in Chapter 6. The Artašen and Maxo subdialects of Laz and the Lower Aç̣arian dialect of Modern Georgian are discussed in Chapter 15.

The case patterns described in the present chapter are limited in other respects as well. Only Series I and II are described here for each language, Series III and IV being discussed in Chapter 13 and to some extent in 15–17. Further, the case marking patterns described here pertain to the common noun, not necessarily to proper nouns or to pronouns, and in no instance to the personal pronouns of the first and second persons. The latter use a single form for the narrative, nominative, and dative cases in all of the Kartvelian languages.[1] Both proper nouns and first and second person pronouns, as well as some other pronouns, are briefly treated in Chapter 4.

In this work I distinguish between the SYNTACTIC (grammatical) cases and the CONCRETE (or local) cases. In the Kartvelian languages, the concrete cases include the genitive, the instrumental, the vocative, and several locative cases.[2] Most of this monograph concerns the functions and distributions of the syntactic cases alone.[3] Each of the daughter languages has three cases, which, by various patterns, mark the subject, direct object, and indirect object. Naming these cases is difficult in the Kartvelian languages for several reasons. First, the functions of a single case change over time, yet it seems desirable to have a single name for it. Second, at a given time, a single case has such different functions in different case patterns that naming it is difficult. For example, in Modern Georgian the *-i/∅* case marks all subjects in Series I but only some subjects and all direct objects in Series II.

The usual names for cases are borrowed from languages where there is neither the change in function over time nor the variety of case marking patterns, so they are not really suitable for Georgian. For these reasons, I adhere to the traditional names for the cases; the reader must understand that the names are not accurate reflections of the functions. One case has two names: 'ergative' and 'narrative'. I have decided to use the latter to try to avoid prejudicing the analysis since *ergative* has a very particular meaning while *narrative* has no meaning outside this language family. The reader should note that this is the case that I referred to as ergative in Harris (1981b), though one of the results of that research was to show that case marking in Modern Georgian is of the active type, not ergative at all.

The description of case distribution for the daughter languages raises three problems. First, how are the case markers (morphemes), with such a variety of functions in the different languages, related historically? This question is morphological, rather than syntactic, and is dealt with in Chapter 4. Second, what is the relationship of the case marking pattern of Series I to that of Series II? Finally, what are the relationships of the patterns found in Series II of the various languages to one another? Of those in Series I? The second question is taken up in Chapter 5 and more extensively in Part III. The reconstruction of Series II on the basis of a comparison of the patterns of the daughter languages is the subject of Chapter 6, and the subsequent developments of those patterns are treated in Chapters 14, 15, and 16.

3.2. THE BASIS FOR THE DISTRIBUTION OF CASES

Three factors play a role in the determination of case assignment in at least some of the languages: the series to which the finite verb form belongs, the morphological class of the verb form, and the grammatical relations of the nominals. The notion of series was introduced in Chapter 1 and is discussed at greater length in Chapter 5. Grammatical relations and morphological class require some comment.

In order to discover the case marking patterns of each language, we must begin with the simplest syntactic constructions. In this chapter I give examples only of transitive sentences in which no rule has changed grammatical relations, together with examples of two types of intransitives. These are sufficient for determining the patterns of each language. Although analyses cannot be provided of the whole syntax of each language, the rules arrived at in this chapter also account for all of the constructions I am aware of in all of the languages, including unaccusatives and passives (described in the Appendix to this chapter), the inversion construction (described in detail in Chap. 13), the lexical object demotion construction (see Chap. 1), the incorporated object construction (§14.1.1), and causatives.

3.2.1. Grammatical Relations

We cannot determine grammatical relations on the basis of an arbitrarily chosen criterion such as case or agreement (see Johnson 1977). Nor is any single criterion adequate. Rather, it is necessary to consider a wide variety of both morphological and syntactic phenomena. In Harris (1981b), grammatical relations at various levels of derivation are established for Modern Georgian on the basis of the interaction of Person Agreement, Number Agreement, *Tav*-Reflexivization, Object Raising, Passivization, Causative Clause Union, Inversion, and a variety of other rules. The properties listed in Keenan (1976) are appropriate heuristics for identifying subjects and were also used here. Because the Kartvelian languages are widely divergent in case marking, but not in other aspects of syntax, it seems that it is justified to extrapolate from Modern Georgian to a certain extent.

It becomes clear from Harris (1981b) that there is a perfect correlation between Person Marking and final grammatical relations, as established on the basis of other rules. As I have no informants for Old Georgian, and as I cannot here provide complete analyses of the syntax of Svan, Laz, and Mingrelian, I use Person Agreement as an index of grammatical relations in each language.[4] There are a number of advantages to this choice:

1. The markers of Person Agreement correlate with final grammatical relations in every construction I know of in each language. For the most part, it is final grammatical relations that are relevant for case markings.

2. The markers of Person Agreement are relatively consistent from one language to the next. That is, there is morphological variation, caused chiefly by regular phonological change, but the relations are independently reconstructible. For example, the first person singular subject marker is *v-* in Georgian, *xw-* or *-w-* in Svan, and in Zan we find the allomorphs *w-*, *b-*, *p-*, *p̣- m-*, and ∅; Oniani 1978 reconstructs CK **xw-*.
3. The functional distribution of these morphemes is relatively stable.[5]
4. With one important exception (see Chap. 12), Person Agreement functions in the same way in Series I and II for each language.
5. Finally, Person Agreement is highly visible. Though ambiguities do exist, final grammatical relations are obvious to a great extent because they are advertised by Person Agreement markers.

3.2.2. Syntax, Semantics, and Morphological Class

The following definitions are assumed in this work. A clause or a verb is TRANSITIVE if it has both a subject and a direct object. A clause or verb is INTRANSITIVE if and only if it is not transitive. The transitivity of a clause must be specified with respect to a particular level of derivation; a clause may be transitive at one level and intransitive at another. (A more complete discussion of these issues appears in Harris 1981:179–190.) Except where it is stated to the contrary, transitive and intransitive in this work refer to the final level of derivation, as that is the level most relevant to case marking. In the examples used in this chapter, there is no conflict between the levels of derivation with respect to transitivity; each example is either transitive at all levels or intransitive at all levels.

It is not always obvious whether a clause is transitive or intransitive. Difficulties in identifying the transitivity of a particular clause arise out of the fact that all of the languages have a zero marker for agreement with a third person direct object and from the preference for dropping pronouns that are unemphatic. However, in this chapter only examples that are unambiguously transitive or intransitive are used.

Among intransitives, two types are found. In the simplest type, the final subject is also the initial subject. In others, the final subject is a direct object at a deeper level of derivation. Among clauses of the latter type, many subtypes are found; these are described briefly in the Appendix to this chapter.

On the basis of transitivity and grammatical relations three clause types are defined: (1) transitives, such as Old Georgian *ganiq̇vana* 'he took him'; (2) intransitives in which the surface subject is direct object at a more basic level, for example, Old Georgian *ganqma* 'it withered'; and (3) intransitives in which the surface subject is also the initial subject, for example, Old Georgian *mirbioda* 'he was running'.

The distinction between two syntactic types of intransitives in Kartvelian languages corresponds approximately to a dichotomy between active and inactive clauses. This distinction refers to controllability, agentivity, or volition on the part of the surface subject. A verb is said to be ACTIVE if it is controllable by the surface subject; it is said to be INACTIVE if is not controllable by the surface subject (see Harris 1982). Intransitives in which the surface subject is a direct object underlyingly are characteristically inactive, while intransitives in which the surface subject is the underlying subject are typically active.

The syntactic distinctions outlined above likewise correlate with a distinction between telic and atelic activities (see Holisky 1981a on Modern Georgian; also Holisky 1978). The difference is described in this way:

> Telic verbs describe action which is directed towards a goal or end point. The goal is understood as realized or attained in some grammatical forms and not realized in others. . . . Atelic verbs, on the other hand, denote activities which do not have to wait for a goal for their realization; they are realized as soon as they begin. (Holisky 1981a:138–139)

Intransitives with surface subjects that are also underlying subjects are characteristically atelic. Intransitives that have underlying direct objects that become their final subjects are typically either telic or stative.

The syntactic features and semantic categories defined above are notions of general linguistics; they are not limited to the Kartvelian languages. In this language family, these general categories and clause types are reflected in morphological classes—sets of finite verb forms that can be identified by a variety of criteria. In the various languages, the classes are recognized by different morphological diagnostics described in §3.3–3.6; yet Class 1 in Svan is cognate to Class 1 in each other language, and the same is true of the other classes. Transitive clauses contain Class 1 verb forms. Intransitives in which the surface subject is an underlying direct object contain Class 2 verb forms. Intransitive clauses in which the surface subject is an initial subject contain Class 3 verb forms.[6] The correlations described above among syntactic, semantic, and morphological properties are summarized in Table 3.1. In this table, as in subsequent tables in this chapter, 'transitive', 'intransitive', 'subject', and 'object' refer to the final level of derivation. 'Active (or inactive)' indicates that the majority of verbs of this class are active, though it is entirely regular for those transitives that are inactive to be members of this class.

The three complexes of properties set out in Table 3.1 are referred to here indifferently by their morphological (class) label or by the terms 'transitive', 'inactive intransitive', 'active intransitive'. Although it is clear that case marking is not determined directly by semantics (Harris 1982:299–304), the question of whether the morphological class or the syntax more closely corresponds to case marking is left open here because of changes that may have occurred in this respect historically and because neither can be said to correlate perfectly with case in transitional stages.

The syntactic properties correlate, albeit imperfectly, with semantics and morphology in the ways summarized in Table 3.1. The examples considered in the present chapter adhere to the characteristic correspondences described above. Exceptions to these correlations are here set aside in order to discover first the regularities of each language. Exceptions are discussed in Chapter 6 and in the Appendix to Chapter 14.

Table 3.1

Morphological–Syntactic–Semantic Correlations

Morphological	Syntactic	Semantic
Class 1	transitive	active (or inactive) telic
Class 2	intransitive initial direct object	inactive telic or stative
Class 3	intransitive initial subject	active atelic

3.3. SVAN

Unlike its sister languages, Svan possesses a complex variety of noun declensions. This chapter deals only with the most widespread of these, as distribution is most simply stated in this way; in Chapter 4 the variety of case endings are discussed.

There are three syntactic cases: the narrative, in *-d*, the dative, in *-s*, and the nominative, marked by umlaut (with or without breaking) or left unmarked (∅). The plural is formed with a suffix, usually *-ar*, *-al*, or a phonological variant of one of these, plus a case suffix.

The examples below illustrate the use of these cases in Series I; these examples are from the Upper Bal dialect; with respect to the distribution of cases, they are characteristic of Svan in general.

Series I Examples

(1) *dīna aṭwräli leṭwr-äl-s*
girl/NOM she/light/them/I candle-PL-DAT
'The girl lights candles.'

(2) *giorgi ḳatx-s äsqi*
Giorgi/NOM wooden/goblet-DAT he/make/it/I
'Giorgi makes a wooden goblet.'

(3) *tamara wisgw-s ixuriēle*
Tamara/NOM apple-DAT she/gather/them/I
'Tamara gathers apples.'

(4) *dede ičḳuārda*
mother/NOM she/think/I
'Mother was thinking.'

(5) *māre dīna-s xagərgälda*
man/NOM girl-DAT he/talk/to.her/I
'The man was talking to a girl.'

(6) *staman lemasksaxän ḳwešni*
pitcher/NOM fire/at it/break/I
'The pitcher breaks beside the fire.'

(7) *eǰa lädi amču sedni*
he/NOM today here he/stay/I
'He stays here today.'

(8) *xoča megm-är ləgx*
good tree-PL/NOM they/stand/I
'Good trees stand.' (Shanidze and Topuria 1939:369, 35–36)

In each of the examples above, it is the nominative-nominal that triggers subject agreement and is marked in this way as surface subject. The direct objects in (1), (2), and (3) and the indirect object in (5) are marked with the dative. We can make the generalization that in Series I, subjects are marked with the nominative and objects with the dative.

The examples below of Series II reveal a different distribution.

Series II Examples

(9) *dīna-d anṭwarāle leṭwr-äl*
girl-NAR she/light/them/II candle-PL/NOM
'The girl lit candles.'

(10) *sosruqw-d laxṭix šīra*
Sosrukw-NAR he/return/it/to.him/II millstone/NOM
nart-äl-s
Nart-PL-DAT
'Sosrukw returned the millstone to the Narts.'
(Shanidze and Topuria 1939:394, 8–9)

(11) *giorgi-d ḳatx-är änsqäle*
Giorgi-NAR wooden.goblet-PL/NOM he/make/them/II
'Giorgi made wooden goblets.'

(12) *dede-d adčḳūre*
mother-NAR she/think/II
'Mother thought.'

(13) *māre-d amaxw-s läxšiäle*
man-NAR enemy-DAT he/fight/to.him/II
'The man fought with his enemy.'

(14) *māre-d xočamd ädγirāle*
man-NAR well he/sing/II
'The man sang well.'

(15) *bepšw-d xwäi läišdirāle*
child-NAR much he/play/II
'The child played a lot.'

(16) *šed-är ädḳušuränx*
dish-PL/NOM they/break/II
'The dishes broke.'

(17) *gezal äntawän aprilisga*
child/NOM he/bear/II April/in
'The child was born in April.'

(18) *qän ädkarwän cxeḳisga*
pig/NOM it/lose/II woods/in
'A pig got lost in the woods.'

(19) *eǰ zurāl rokw čwädsōqän*
this woman/NOM QUOT she/crazy/II
' "The woman went crazy," he said.'
(Shanidze and Topuria 1939:373, 31)

In these examples we find a more complex situation: some subjects are marked with the narrative (*-d*) case (examples 9–15), while others are marked with the nominative (16–19). This distribution does not correspond to tne transitivity of the clause; examples (12)–(19) are all intransitive, but show different cases for the subjects. The marking is in no sense optional; examples (9)–(15) would be ungrammatical with a nominative case subject, those in (16)–(19) ungrammatical with a narrative case subject. The difference in the marking of the surface subject corresponds to distinctions among clause types, described in §3.2. In addition to the verbs in (12)–(15), other intransitives that govern narrative case subjects in Series II include *läigərgle* 'he talked', *ädkīzanāle* 'he laughed', *läičirxāle* 'he sledded', *läicuzāle* 'he swam', *läiç̣muriāle* 'he ran', *läiṭwīliēle* 'he yelled', together with these examples from the Lower Svan dialects: *lenbriāle* 'he sang', *lenbγə̄le* 'he howled, yelled', *entxēle* 'he hunted', *lenḳwarčxāle* 'he crawled', *lenḳrānkāle* 'he tumbled, somersaulted', *lenḳəldāle* 'he hurried', *lenḳupxiēle* 'he jumped, sprang', *lenrēç̣āle* 'he lamented', *esmāydāle* 'he ate the evening meal', *lenənəgzārwāle* 'he traveled', *lenžγə̄le* 'he cried out in fear', and many, many more. Other intransitives that govern nominative case subjects in Series II include the following from the Upper Bal dialect: *änṭebdä̆n* 'it warmed up', *ädḳilä̆n* 'it got locked', *ž'änpuḳwä̆n* 'it dried off', *ädkačä̆n* 'he got wounded', *änsq̇ä̆n* 'it was made'.

The verb forms in (9)–(11) are members of Class 1. The intransitives in (12)–(15) and others identified above as governing narrative case subjects in Series II are members of Class 3, while (16)–(19) and others listed above as taking subjects in the nominative are in Class 2. The three morphological classes are identified in Svan by the following criteria:

1. THE SUFFIX *-al* OR ITS PHONOLOGICAL VARIANTS. This occurs as a derivational suffix in all finite forms of many Class 3 verbs. (With these verbs it is also found in masdars (deverbal nouns) and participles.) An inflectional suffix of the same form is used optionally in some dialects with verbs of other classes to mark plurality of the direct object or repeated or habitual action (see examples (1) and (11) above and §9.4 and §13.4.4). Since Class 3 verbs may lack this suffix, its presence can be taken as a positive diagnostic, but its absence does not give a conclusive indication of class.

2. THE SUFFIX *-e* AS THE THIRD PERSON SINGULAR SUBJECT MARKER IN THE AORIST. In most dialects (but cf. Chap. 6), verbs of Class 1 and 3 take this suffix, contrasting with Class 2 verbs, which never have it.

3. THE SUFFIXES *-än* AND *-en*. Non-ablauting Class 2 verbs take a suffix of the form *-än*, *-ä̆n*, *-en*, *-an*, or *-ān* in the aorist. Although the form varies, this is found in all persons and numbers and in all dialects (Topuria 1967:194ff.). Ablauting Class 2 verbs lack this ending in the aorist, but characteristically have a suffix *-en/n* in the present tense. Class 1 and 3 verbs lack these suffixes.

These diagnostics are not absolute; nevertheless, taken together they provide a reliable way of distinguishing regular members of Classes 1–3:

Class 1. Do not have derivational *-al* etc.
Have *-e* in third person singular of aorist.
Lack *-än* etc., in aorist forms, and *-en* in the present.
Class 2. Do not have derivational *-al* etc.
Lack *-e* in third person singular of aorist.
Have *-än* etc., in aorist forms, or *-en* in the present.
Class 3. Have derivational *-al* etc.
Have *-e* in third person singular of aorist (except in parts of Lower Bal; see Ch. 6).
Lack *-än* etc., in aorist forms, and *-en* in the present.

We are now ready to characterize regular case marking in Series II of Svan. Class 1 and 3 verbs, as identified by the criteria stated above, govern narrative case subjects. Since Class 1 and 3 verbs are generally transitive and active intransitive, respectively, we can state that, in general, verbs of these types govern narrative case subjects in Series II, while inactive intransitives govern nominative subjects. This correlation is not, however, absolute, as there are some exceptions: a few intransitive verbs in Class 1, a few verbs that appear to be semantically active in Class 2, and so forth. The use of cases in both series is summarized in Table 3.2.

Table 3.2

Distribution of Cases in Svan

	Subject of Class 1	Subject of Class 3	Subject of Class 2	Direct Object	Indirect Object
Series I	NOM	NOM	NOM	DAT	DAT
Series II	NAR	NAR	NOM	NOM	DAT

By comparing this table with Table 1.1, we can see clearly that Series I has (nominative–)accusative type case marking. In this system, one case (the so-called nominative) marks all subjects, while another (the dative) marks direct objects. It is important to note, however, that this is not a typical example of accusative-type case marking, inasmuch as the case that marks direct objects also marks indirect objects; it nevertheless fits the *definition* of the accusative type perfectly. Series II, on the other hand, is an example of the active case marking type. In that system, one case, the narrative, marks subjects of transitive (Class 1) and active intransitive (Class 3) verbs, while another case, the nominative, marks subjects of inactive intransitives (Class 2) and direct objects.

3.4. OLD GEORGIAN

It is the oldest forms of Georgian that are relevant for the purpose of reconstruction, and only those are described here, except as later developments shed some light on the direction of evolution. Later developments in case marking in Georgian are discussed in Chapters 14 and 15.

Like its sisters, Old Georgian has three syntactic cases: the nominative (*-i*/*y*/*∅*), the narrative (*-man*), and the dative (*-s*(*a*)). (On the variants of each and the status of the nominative, see §4.4.)

The collective of a noun is composed of the root plus the collective marker *-eb* (discussed at greater length in §9.2.2) plus the appropriate case marker.

In the plural there are only three forms for all the cases. The suffix *-ni* marks the nominative, *-no* marks the vocative, and *-ta* marks all the other cases.

The examples below illustrate the distribution of cases in Series I in Old Georgian.

Series I Examples

(20) *romel-sa moscemda mas ḳact-moq̣uare*
which-DAT he/give/it/to.her/I her/DAT man-loving
ɣmert-i
God-NOM
'which philanthropic God gave to her'
(Imnaishvili 1970a:139, 25)

(21) *uḳuetu tvial-i šen-i marǯuene-y gactunebdes šen*
if eye-NOM your-NOM right-NOM it/offend/you/I you/DAT
'if your right eye should offend you' (Mt 5:29Ad)

(22) *mirbioda ert-i matgan-i*
he/run/I one-NOM them/from-NOM
'One of them was running thither.' (Mt 27:48)

(23) *rametu iglovda er-i misi mis zeda*
for he/mourn/I people(SG)-NOM his him over
'For his people mourned over him.' (Hosea 10:5)

(24) *mama-y tkuen-i ca-ta šina srul ars*
father-NOM your-NOM heaven-PL/DAT in perfect he/be/I
'Your Father in heaven is perfect.' (Mt 5:48Ad)

(25) *česmariṭeba-y upl-isa-y hgies uḳunisamde*
truth-NOM Lord-GEN-NOM it/endure/I forever
'The truth of the Lord endures forever.' (Psalm 116:2)

In each of the examples above, the nominative-nominal is the surface subject. The direct objects in (20) and (21) and the indirect object in (20) are marked with the dative case. We can make the generalization that in Series I, subjects are marked with the nominative while objects are marked with the dative.

The examples below show that in Series II the distribution is not the same as in Series I.

Series II Examples

(26) *xolo čuen γmert-man cecxl-i samsaxurebelad*
and us/DAT God-NAR fire-NOM to.use
moguca
he/give/it/to.us/II
'And God gave fire to us to use.' (Imnaishvili, 1970a: 154, 13)

(27) *da munkuesve sul-man ganiqvana igi*
and immediately spirit-NAR he/take/him/II him/NOM
udabno-d
desert-ADV
'And immediately the spirit took him to the desert.'
(Mk 1:12Ad)

(28) a. *uḳuetu niš da sasçaul aray ixilot*
if sign/NOM and wonder/NOM NEG you/see/it/II
(J 4:48Ad)

b. *uḳuetu ara ixilot sasçaul-eb-i da niš-eb-ı*
NEG wonder-COL-NOM sign-COL-NOM
'if you do not see sıgns and wonders' (J 4:48A,B)

(29) *aγimγerna qrma-man mucel-sa missa*
he/sing.out/II boy-NAR belly-DAT her
'And the boy in her belly sang out.' (L 1:41Ad)

(30) *ertsa zeda codvil-sa, romel-man šeinanos*
one over sinner-DAT which/REL-NAR he/repent/II
'over one sinner who would repent'[7] (L 15:7Ad)

(31) *da ganqma munkues ve leγv-i igi*
and it/wither/II immediately fig-NOM DET
'And immediately the fig withered.' (Mt 21:19Ad)

(32) *da aha iq̣o ḳac ert ierusaleym-s*
and behold it/be/II man/NOM one Jerusalem-DAT
'And behold there was a man in Jerusalem'. (L 2:25Ad)

These examples show that in Series II some subjects are marked with the narrative case (*-man*) while others are marked with the nominative (*-i/y/ Ø*).

There is a problem in the investigation of the system of case marking in Series II in Old Georgian, namely, that there are very few examples of active intransitives in the forms of Series II. In general, verbs of this type use Series I forms, even when the context requires Series II forms, as in (33) (see Kavtaradze 1954:23; Shanidze 1973:483–484).

(33) *da vitarca ixila iesu šorit, mirbioda*
and when he/see/it/II(AOR) Jesus far he/run/I(IMPERF)
da taq̣uanis-sca mas da
and worship-he/give/it/to.him/II(AOR) him/DAT and
γaγaṭ-q̣o qmita didita da
noise-he/make/it/II(AOR) voice/INST big/INST and
tkua
he/say/it/II(AOR)
'And when he saw Jesus afar, he ran (lit., WAS RUNNING) there and worshipped him, and cried with a loud voice and said'
(Mk 5:6–7Ad; example cited in Kavtaradze 1954:23)

The aorist (Series II) is the tense required in this context from the point of view of Georgian, and it is the tense used for the verbs *-sca* and *-q̣o* with which *mirbioda* is conjoined. For most active intransitives, no Series II forms are attested in Old Georgian, and Series I forms were used instead, as in this example. Shanidze (1973:483–484) also points out that, just for verbs of this type, the imperfect (Series I) was used to translate the Greek aorist; with verbs of other types, the Georgian aorist (Series II) translated the Greek aorist. A few active intransitives substituted Class I incorporated-object constructions just in Series II; *γaγaṭ-q̣o* in (33) is an example of this, corresponding to the active intransitive *γaγadebs,* which occurred only in Series I in Old Georgian (see §14.1.1).

In spite of the infrequency of examples of active intransitives in Series II, examples like (29)–(30) suggest that the narrative case was the regular marking for subjects of those Class 3 verbs that did occur in Series II. This is also consistent with subsequent developments. At later stages of the language, Series II forms of active intransitives become common, and they regularly govern narrative case subjects.

Examples (26)–(32) reveal that in Old Georgian, as in Svan, case marking in Series II varies by verb type, as outlined in Table 3.1.

In Modern Georgian the classes are distinguished on the basis of four morphological criteria (see Harris 1981b:259–267 for criteria and lists of verbs in each class). These classes are directly comparable to the same classes in Svan, though none of the morphological diagnostics are the same. While Classes 1–3 are clearly distinct in the grammar of Modern Georgian, they were not in Old Georgian; of the criteria used to distinguish classes in Harris (1981b), not one is entirely valid for Old Georgian.

In Old Georgian some verbs already possessed a conjugational trait that later became a more general mark of Class 3. These verbs oppose Series II forms with the prefix *i-* to Series I forms without a prefix; e.g., *ṭirs* 'he weeps-I' versus *iṭira* 'he wept-II'. Many verbs of all classes have a prefix *i-* in forms of both series, and it is only the opposition of *i-* to ∅ that identifies a verb as a member of Class 3. However, because many verbs of Class 3 lack this opposition, its absence does not give a conclusive indication of class (see §14.3.2 on *i-*).

Although Classes 1 and 3 were not thoroughly differentiated in conjugation in Old Georgian, Class 2 was distinct from both. Members of Class 2 generally had one or the other of the following distinctive present–stem formations: (a) Dynamic (nonstative) Class 2 verbs had present stems that usually included both a series marker (*-eb*, *-av*, *-am*, *-ev*, *-em*, *-ob*, or *-op*) and the suffix *-i*. Examples are *içu-eb-i-s* 'it burns' (Rev 19:20), *itk-um-i-s* (<**itkw-am-i-s*) 'it is said, told' (Shanidze 1959:38, 8); see Baramidze (1976) and note 5 of Chapter 8. (b) Many statives had present stems in *-ie*, e.g., *hg-ie-s* 'it lasts, endures' (J 6:27AB), *gipq̣r-ie-s* 'you have, hold it' (Imnaishvili 1970a:135, 27). Class 1 and 3 verbs never have stems with these structures in the present tense, and thus the presence of one of these characteristics positively identifies a verb form as belonging to Class 2. However, some Class 2 verb forms—mostly stative—have neither of these distinguishing characteristics, e.g., *ars* 'he is', *dgas* 'he stands'.

A second property is shared by many, but not all, Class 2 verbs. Forms of this class may have a suffix *-en/n* conditioned by plural final subjects (initial direct objects) in Series II. Since the same nominal also triggers plural subject agreement, the verb form shows double marking of plural agreement; e.g., *i-q̣v-n-es* 'they were', and *e-dg-n-es* 'they stood', where both *-n* and *-es* mark plurality. While verbs of Classes 1 and 3 may have the suffix *-en/n,* in these forms it is conditioned by the final direct object, rather than the final subject (see Chap. 10 on *En*-Agreement). Because some Class 2 forms lack *-en/n,* the absence of this marker provides no information concerning class.

The practical problem of classifying verbs in order to compare Old Georgian with its sister languages is solved here by applying the criteria above, together with comparing the classes of the same verbs in Modern Georgian. It is further assumed that intransitives will belong to Class 2 or 3. According to these diagnostics, the verbs in (26)–(28) are members of Class 1, those in (29)–(30) are in Class 3, and those in (31)–(32) in Class 2. The functional distribution of cases in both series is summarized for Old Georgian in Table 3.3.

A comparison of Tables 3.2 and 3.3 reveals that Svan and Georgian use the same two systems of case marking. An important difference involves the form of the marker of the narrative case; this is discussed further in Chapter 4. Like Svan, Georgian has an accusative system in Series I, where all subjects are marked alike, though this is not a canonical example of that type.

In the Series II system, subjects of transitive and intransitive active verbs are marked with one case (*-man*), while subjects of inactive intransitives and direct objects are marked with another (*-i/y/∅*). Series II case marking is usually called ergative, rather than active. I have argued at length that this is an inaccurate description of Modern Georgian (Harris 1981b:Chap. 16), and the same arguments apply to Old Georgian. I do not take this analysis of case marking to imply any claim about the alignment of any other rule in Georgian, about possible directions of change, about morphological categories or distinctions present or absent in the language, or about the psychology of Georgians. The label ‘active’ applied to this one case marking system is no more and no less than an objective statement of the functional distribution of cases.

Table 3.3

Distribution of Cases in Old Georgian

	Subject of Class 1	Subject of Class 3	Subject of Class 2	Direct object	Indirect object
Series I	NOM	NOM	NOM	DAT	DAT
Series II	NAR	NAR	NOM	NOM	DAT

3.5. LAZ

The syntactic cases in Laz are the nominative (∅), the narrative (*-k*), and the dative (*-s*). There is no collective. The plural is formed with the suffix *-epe* followed by a regular case ending (see Table 4.6 and §4.3.1.).

The examples below are from the village of Sarpi, part of the Xopian dialect; except as noted, they were elicited. Some dialectal variants are noted in Chap. 15. Although Series I is distinguished from Series II in the examples, they are grouped together since they have a single case marking system.

Series I Examples

(34) *baba-k* *mečaps* *skiri-s* *cxeni*
father-NAR he/give/it/to.him/I child-DAT horse/NOM
'The father gives a horse to his child.'

(35) *ḳoči-k* *q̣vilups* *γeǯi* [8]
man-NAR he/kill/it/I pig/NOM
'The man kills a pig.'

(36) *a'čkva* *ia* *ḳoči-k* *meele-ša* *čxu-epe*
again this man-NAR village-ALL sheep-PL/NOM
učumess
he/herd/it/I
'Again the man herds the sheep toward the village.'
(Asatiani 1974:**3**[86])

(37) *zaza-k* *oškvidaps* *nodari*
Zaza-NAR he/drown/him/I Nodar/NOM
'Zaza drowns Nodar.'

(38) *bere-k* *imgars*
child-NAR he/cry/I
'The child cries.'

(39) *oxorǯa-k* *mteli* *ndγa* *ičališeps*
woman-NAR whole day she/work/I
'The woman works all day.'

(40) *aya* *ḳoči-k* *ḳai* *ibirs*
this man-NAR well he/sing/I
'This man sings well.'

(41) *nodari* *iškviden*
Nodar/NOM he/drown/I
'Nodar drowns.'

(42) *ḳoči* *γurun*
man/NOM he/die/I
'The man dies.'

(43) *aya* *noškei* *yen*
this/NOM coal/NOM it/be/I
'This is coal.' (Asatiani 1974:**3**[27])

Series II Examples

(44) *baba-k* *cxeni* *meču* *skiri-s*
father-NAR horse/NOM he/give/it/to.him/II child-DAT
'The father gave a horse to his child.'

(45) *ḳoči-k* *doq̣vilu* *γeǯi*
man-NAR he/kill/it/I pig/NOM
'The man killed a pig.'

(46) *ḳoči-k-ti* *mu* *q̣vas* *ac̣i*
man-NAR-too what/NOM he/do/it/II now
'What should the man do now?' (Asatiani 1974:**3**[16])

(47) *bere-k* *isteru* *γoǯi-s*
child-NAR he/play/II yard-DAT
'The child played in the yard.'

(48) *ǯoγo-epe-k-ti* *lales*
dog-PL-NAR-too they/bark/II
'The dogs barked too.' (Asatiani 1974:**10**[15])

(49) *bere* *oxori-s* *doskidu*
child/NOM house-DAT he/stay/II
'The child stayed in the house.'

(50) *ḳoči* *doγuru*
man/NOM he/die/II
'The man died.'

(51) *oxoi* *domač̣u*
house/NOM it/burned/to.me/II
'My house burned down (on me)!' (Asatiani 1974:**3**[4])

It is clear from the examples that a single system operates in Series I and II in Laz. The case of the subject varies by class. Other intransitives that govern narrative case subjects include *imgars* 'he cries', *quaps* 'he yells', *xoronaps* 'he dances', *γaγalaps* 'he talks, speaks', and the following from Chikobava (1938): *dusṭvinu* 'he whistled' (314), *qiaps* 'it crows' (354), *çiaps* 'it peeps' (394), *xixinaps* 'it neighs' (428), *peṭelaps* 'it bleats' (306), and many more. Other intransitives that govern nominative case subjects include *iḳançuns* 'it shakes, is shaken', *dirdu* 'it grew' (Chikobava 1938:308), *diqven* 'it turns into' (Asatiani 1974: **50** [41]), and many similar examples.

The majority of verbs in Classes 1 and 3 take a series marker *-up*, *-ap*, and others (details in Chap. 9). Since all variants of the series marker end in a consonant, most verbs of these classes have consonant stems in Series I. However, even those that lack the series marker consistently end in a consonant; cited above we have *imgar-* 'cry', *ibir-* 'sing', *ister-* 'play', and others. Many Class 2 verbs are derived from the same roots as Class 1 verbs; these and other Class 2 verbs are formed with one of the following suffixes or circumfixes: *-u*, *i——e*, or *a——e* (Chikobava 1936:110–111). This leads to pairs of stems like those in Table 3.4. This contrast between the series markers of the form -VC (or a consonant-final root) and the formants (V)——V distinguishes Classes 1 and 3 from Class 2. The surprising fact is that, no matter how irregular or suppletive a verb is, if it is in Class 2 it generally has a stem form in -V; for example, ***r-e**-n* 'he is,' ***xe**-n* 'he sits', ***a-ǰer-e**-n* 'he believes' (see also examples in Chikobava 1936:170ff.).[9] Because the stem form (C- or V-final) determines three agreement phenomena (§16.1.4–16.1.6), the morphological contrast between Class 2 and Classes 1 and 3 is relatively prominent.

Table 3.4

Class 1 and 2 Examples in Laz[a]

Class 1	Class 2
*b-**o-ṭub-in-am*** 'I warm it' (Chikobava 1938:326)	*do-**ṭub-u**-n* 'it warms'
***n-çar-um**-s* 'he writes it' (Chikobava 1938:407)	***i-çar-e**-n* 'it is written' (Chikobava 1936:110)
*go-**ntx-ip**-s* 'he spreads it'	*gu-**i-ntx-e**-n* 'it spreads'
***o-škvid-ap**-s* 'he drowns him'	***i-škvid-e**-n* 'he drowns'

[a]The Series I stem of each example appears in boldface type.

There are no morphological criteria that distinguish clearly between Class 1 and 3. For practical purposes, those that are transitive are considered to belong to Class 1; and those that are intransitive, to Class 3.

Class 1 and 3 verbs govern narrative case subjects in Series I and II, while Class 2 verbs govern nominative subjects. Case marking in Laz is summarized in Table 3.5.

A comparison with Table 1.1, where case marking types are defined, shows that Laz has active-type case marking.[10] Subjects of transitives and of active intransitives are marked with one case (-*k*), while subjects of inactive intransitives and direct objects are marked with a second case (∅). All final indirect objects are in the dative (-*s*).

Table 3.5

Distribution of Cases in Laz

	Subject of Class 1	Subject of Class 3	Subject of Class 2	Direct object	Indirect object
Series I	NAR	NAR	NOM	NOM	DAT
Series II	NAR	NAR	NOM	NOM	DAT

3.6. MINGRELIAN

There are three syntactic cases in the noun in Mingrelian: the narrative (-*k*/*kə*/*ki*), the nominative (-*i*, realized as ∅ after a vowel), and the dative (-*s*). There is no collective; the plural is formed by the addition of the suffix -*ep*, followed by a case ending. Following a stem ending in *a* or *e*, either *l* is epenthesized between the stem vowel and the plural suffix or the final stem vowel deletes. The conditions governing this aspect of plural formation are stated in Kluge (1916:10). In some dialects, plural -*ep* becomes -*en* before a consonant-initial case marker (see Chikobava 1936:44ff.).

The language consultant for the examples below was from the village of Axali Xibula; this distribution characterizes all dialects of Mingrelian described in the literature.

Series I Examples

(52) *muma* *arʒens* *cxen-s* *skua-s*
father/NOM he/give/it/to.him/I horse-DAT child-DAT
'The father gives a horse to his child.'

(53) *ḳoč-i ʔviluns γe-s (γe-s<*γeǯ-s)*
man-NOM he/kill/it/I pig-DAT
'The man kills a pig.'

(54) *zaza oškviduans nodar-s*
Zaza/NOM he/drown/him/II Nodar-DAT
'Zaza drowns Nodar.'

(55) *baγana i(n)gars*
child/NOM he/cry/I
'The child cries.'

(56) *ʒγab-i teli dγas mušens*
girl-NOM whole day she/work/I
'The girl works all day.'

(57) *(a)te ḳoč-i ǯgiro ibirs*
this man-NOM well he/sing/I
'This man sings well.'

(58) *čkimi ǯimal-ep-i esxilcə va-mušena*
my brother-PL-NOM much not-they/work/I
'My brothers do not work this much.' (Kluge 1916: 86, 12)

(59) *ḳoč-i data re*
man-NOM Data/NOM he/be/I
'Data is a man.' (Bleichsteiner 1919:**VII** [8])

(60) *nodar-i iškvidu*
Nodar-NOM he/drown/I
'Nodar drowns.'

(61) *ḳoč-i γuru*
man-NOM he/die/I
'The man dies.'

The examples above show that in Mingrelian all subjects are in the nominative case in Series I, and all objects in the dative. Series II, on the other hand, differs somewhat from the patterns we have seen in the other languages.

Series II Examples

(62) *muma-k cxen-i (ki)meču skua-s* [11]
father-NAR horse-NOM he/give/it/to.him/II child-DAT
'The father gave a horse to his child.'

(63) *ḳoč-k(i) doˀvilu γeǰ-i*
man-NAR he/kill/it/II pig-NOM
'The man killed a pig.'

(64) *artišax muma-k aḳoḳatu skual-ep-i*
once father-NAR he/assemble/him/II child-PL-NOM
'Once the father assembled (his) sons.' (Kluge 1916:81, 17–18)

(65) *baγana-k ilaˀapu ezo-s*
child-NAR he/play/II yard-DAT
'The child played in the yard.'

(66) *baγana-k (k)ingaru*
child-NAR he/cry/II
'The child cried.'

(67) *ʒγabi-k (ko)sxap̣u*
girl-NAR she/dance/II
'The girl danced.'

(68) *sumar-kə ipirkə*
guest-NAR he/think/II
'The guest thought.' (Bleichsteiner 1919:**X**[3])

(69) *baγana-k ˀude-s kudoskidu*
child-NAR house-DAT he/stay/II
'The child stayed in the house.'

(70) *ḳoč-k doγuru*
man-NAR he/die/II
'The man died.'

(71) *c̣irua-kə geetuu*
church.service-NAR it/end/II
'The church service ended.' (Bleichsteiner 1919:**VIII**[3])

In Series II all surface subjects are marked with the narrative case, all surface direct objects with the nominative, and all surface indirect objects with the dative.

Although case marking does not distinguish between types of verbs in Mingrelian, some other rules do. The remarks made above concerning criteria for division into morphological classes in Laz apply also to Mingrelian; rules that distinguish classes are discussed in Chapters 15 and 16.

The functional distribution of cases in Mingrelian is summarized in Table 3.6. It is clear from the table that both series fit the definition of an accusative case system. However, the simplicity of this statement obscures

Table 3.6

Distribution of Cases in Mingrelian

	Subject of Class 1	Subject of Class 3	Subject of Class 2	Direct object	Indirect object
Series I	NOM	NOM	NOM	DAT	DAT
Series II	NAR	NAR	NAR	NOM	DAT

part of the situation, in that (a) different cass realize the accusative distribution in Series I and II and (b) only Series II has distinct cases for direct and indirect objects.

3.7. CONCLUDING STATEMENT

Accurate synchronic descriptions must be based upon regular productive patterns characteristic of a language or dialect as a whole. Exceptions and irregularities are very important for historical purposes but must be set aside in order to see the general picture first. The purpose of this chapter is synchronic description, so all of the examples given in it are regular and are representative of sentences of the same type. Irregular examples also occur, and they will play an important role in reconstruction; but consideration of these irregularities is deferred until Chapter 6.

In this chapter we surveyed case marking systems in the major dialects of each of the Kartvelian languages. We have found that (a) in Svan, Georgian, and Mingrelian, Series I and II have differing case marking systems and (b) both accusative and active systems are found in Kartvelian languages. We see in subsequent chapters that the analysis of case marking provided here accounts also for the other syntactic constructions in each language.

APPENDIX. CLASS 2 INTRANSITIVES

The purpose of this appendix is to acquaint the reader with the morphological and syntactic variety within Class 2. Several of the types discussed here are referred to later in this work. Although complete analyses and justifications of analyses cannot be provided here, for those constructions that occur in Georgian, they can be found in Harris (1981b) and (1982).

The diversity within Class 2 is unified by three characteristics:

1. The final subject of Class 2 verbs is an initial direct object.
2. The final subject of Class 2 verbs is in the nominative case in Series II (except in Mingrelian).
3. In Series III, Inversion does not apply to clauses containing Class 2 verbs.

Point 2 is discussed above in this chapter; point 3 is explained fully in Chapter 13. Point 1 is discussed more completely below. Each characteristic distinguishes Class 2 from both Class 1 and Class 3.

Class 2 includes both STATIVE and NONSTATIVE (DYNAMIC) verbs. Statives include both STATIVE PASSIVES, such as Georgian *sc̣eria* 'it is written,' and INVERSION VERBS, mostly affective verbs such as Georgian *uq̇vars*, Mingrelian *uʔors*, and Svan (Upper Bal) *xaläṭ* 'he loves him'. (Holisky 1978 provides diagnostics for statives in Georgian and discusses the relationship of this type to statives in other languages; I follow her definition here.) Statives in all four Kartvelian languages are quite irregular from a morphological point of view; some relevant aspects of the morphology of this type are discussed in Chapter 13.

As shown in Chapter 13, inversion verbs govern a rule, Inversion, which makes initial subjects final indirect objects.

Verbs that are not stative by Holisky's tests are nonstative, or dynamic. Dynamic intransitives of organic formation include markerless, prefixal, and suffixal varieties.

The MARKERLESS INTRANSITIVE is so called because it lacks a consistent (i.e., occurring in all forms of Series I and II) affixal exponent of class. Verbs in this group are the reflexes of one type of ABLAUTING INTRANSITIVES, and many of them retain ablaut still. The ablaut relation between these verbs and the corresponding transitives is explained by Gamkrelidze and Machavariani (1965) and is described in Chapter 8 below. The markerless intransitive occurs in all four languages, and this type includes several cognates. Examples are Georgian *tbeba* 'it warms up', *dneba* 'it melts', *šreba* 'it dries (off)'; Mingrelian *ṭibu(n)* 'it warms up', *γuru(n)* 'he dies', *skiru(n)* 'it dries, it goes out (of fire)', and the corresponding forms in Laz (Chikobava 1936:110–115; 1938:318–319); and Svan *degni* 'it goes out (of fire)', *kwerni* 'it rots', *ṭexni* 'he returns' (Topuria 1967:180–181). This type probably represents one of the oldest morphological types of intransitive in Kartvelian (Lomtatidze 1952; Machavariani 1959; Topuria 1942a) and therefore has a special importance for reconstruction.

PREFIXAL INTRANSITIVES are highly productive in all four languages. This group includes *i*-INTRANSITIVES and *e*-INTRANSITIVES; in Laz and Mingrelian, intransitives are also formed with *a*- and *o*-.

Both markerless and prefixal intransitives are of several types syntactically. Traditionally an ABSOLUTE and RELATIVE are distinguished, the latter having an indirect object and the former lacking one. Among prefixal intransitives, the distinction between absolute and relative forms is relatively consistently marked by the opposition of *i*- to other prefixes, *i*-marking absolute intransitives and the others marking relative forms. Examples are Mingrelian *i-ç̌aru(n)* 'it is written' versus *a-ç̌aru(n)* 'it is written to him, for him' (Chikobava 1936:113); Georgian *i-çereba* 'it is written' versus *e-çereba* 'it is written to him, for him', and Svan *i-č̣mi* 'it is mown' versus *x-e-č̣mi* 'it is mown for him' (Topuria 1967:179). (Zan *a*- is the regular reflex of CK **e*-.)

In all four languages, most of the markerless intransitives are UNACCUSATIVE clauses, structures with an initial direct object and no initial subject. These have been handled in traditional Georgian linguistics by including them as 'passives' (see handbooks), though it has also been observed that they are not truly passive (Blake 1932:234; Lomtatidze 1952; Machavariani 1959). The fact that these structures lack an initial subject is reflected in the fact that they cannot take an agent phrase, as shown by (72) from Georgian and (73) from Svan, and in the fact that their semantics exclude an agent or other initial subject; e.g., Georgian *ḷpeba* 'it rots'.

(72) *xač̣apuri* *cxveba* (**dedis mier*)
cheesebread/NOM it/bake/I mother by
'The cheesebread bakes (*by mother).'

(73) *lemesg* *degni* (**dīnoš*) [12]
fire/NOM it/go.out/I girl/INST
'The fire goes out (*by the girl).'

Comparison with examples (74) and (75) shows that the agent phrase is not ungrammatical in and of itself, but only when included in unaccusative clauses.

Prefixal intransitives include unaccusatives (Harris 1981b:Chap. 12; 1982), passives, potentials, and other syntactic types. PASSIVES, which differ from unaccusatives in having an initial subject, reflected as an agent phrase, are illustrated from Svan.

(74) *lāre* *ič̣mi* *māro-š/māre-šw*
hay/NOM it/mow/I man-INST
'The hay is mown by the man.'

(75) *lic* *xegwši* *bepšwš* *ečas*
water/NOM it/pour/to.him/I child/INST him/DAT
'Water was poured for him by the child.'

Example (74) is an absolute intransitive, bearing the prefix *i*-, while (75) is a relative intransitive, marked with *e*-. Markerless intransitives and prefixal intransitives are here regarded together as reflecting mediopassive voice.

Mingrelian and Laz recognize POTENTIALS as a morphological category, while in the other languages certain prefixal intransitives are open to a potential interpretation (see Chikobava 1936:110–115; Danelia 1976; Sherozia 1980). Mingrelian *i-č̣ar-e-(n)* 'it can be written' is an absolute potential contrasting with the relative potential *a-č̣ar-e-(n)* 'he can write it', as well as with the prefixal passive *i-č̣ar-u-(n)* 'it is written' (Chikobava 1936:113). In Mingrelian the potential consistently bears the suffix *-e* in the present, while other types bear the suffix *-u*. Absolute forms, marked by *i*-, consistently express the EPISTEMIC POTENTIAL; while relative forms, marked by *a*-, consistently express the ROOT POTENTIAL. Root potentials involve Inversion, and we may assume that potentials of both sorts have a complex structure.

SUFFIXAL INTRANSITIVES are formed with the suffix *-d* or, in Old Georgian, *-n* (Shanidze 1957b). The suffixal intransitive does not occur at all in Svan and is very infrequent in Mingrelian and especially in Laz (Chikobava 1936:114; Danelia 1976). This was earlier believed to be a structure borrowed from Georgian, but Danelia (1976:173–174) has argued that it is more probably an inherited type in Zan as well. In Georgian this type is productive in the formation of inceptives (see Holisky 1983b for a complete exposition); some examples of passives belong to this morphological type, e.g., *ḳet-d-eba* 'it gets done, made'.

ANALYTIC PASSIVES consist of a passive participle together with an auxiliary. With the auxiliary *qopna* 'be', this type is highly productive and frequent in Modern Georgian (see Harris 1981b:103–116, 203–204); e.g., *šeγebili iqo* 'it was painted', *dac̣erili-a* 'it is written'. While comparable structures are easily elicited in the other modern languages, they are infrequent in texts.

Although complete analyses cannot be included here, it is intended that this appendix serve only as a reference for terms used later in this work. While the types enumerated here are not identical in syntactic structure, they are unified by the characteristics listed at the beginning of this appendix.

NOTES

[1]Nebieridze (in press) makes the important point that an appositive to a first or second person pronoun must bear the case appropriate to its function, as describedin this chapter. The same is true of proper nouns. On this basis we are justified in saying that a particular instance of a first or second person pronoun represents a particular case.

[2]There is considerable contention over these points. The vocative is not always considered a case. Most, and perhaps all, locative cases, developed historically from prepositions or postpositions; some are regulary referred to as postpositions in the literature, though they cannot be distinguished from cases synchronically. None of these problems is relevant to the syntactic use of cases.

[3]At least some of the syntactic cases have concrete functions as well; for example, the dative typically indicates location, 'at, to'. Some syntactic uses of the concrete cases are discussed in Chapter 11. Thus, the distinction between syntactic and concrete cases is not absolute and is made here only for ease of reference.

[4]Number Agreement is a rule distinct from Person Agreement, with different distribution of markers and different conditions. It does not share with Person Agreement the features listed below. Some diachronic aspects of Number Agreement are discussed in Chapter 13.

[5]A change in the distribution of the third person object marker is described in Chapter 12, and some other changes in agreement are discussed in Chapter 16.

[6]There are actually four morphological classes (see Harris 1981:259–260). The fourth governs Inversion in all series, and a description of it is deferred to Chapter 13. Syntactically, semantically, and morphologically, Class 4 is a variant of Class 2; for the purposes of the present work the two are grouped together as Class 2.

[7]The intransitivity of this verb shows up more clearly in the example below, where the thing repented of is marked with a postposition.

(76) *sxua-ta* *mat* *ḳac-ta . . . .* *ara šeinanes*
other-PL/NAR DET/NAR man-PL/NAR not they/repent/II
mat *sakme-ta-gan*
DET/GEN deed-PL/GEN-from
'The rest of the men . . . did not repent of the deeds.' (Rev 9: 20)

It is usual for the thing repented of to be marked with a postposition (Blake 1932:259).

[8]This verb is used for 'kill' in hunting, not for 'slaughter'; this applies also to variants of this sentence cited below in this chapter, in Chapter 13, and in Chapter 15.

[9]I know of two exceptions to this generalization: verbs that appear to be inactive intransitives and which govern nominative case subjects but which have Series I stems ending in a consonant. These are *melams* 'it falls' (Chikobava 1936, Part II:45, line 18) and *ǰans* 'he sleeps' (Chikobava 1938:434). There are undoubtedly a few other exceptions as well.

[10]Klimov (1976) analyzes this as nominative–accusative case marking. He says that the nominative case has two allomorphs, *-k* and ∅, while the accusative has

∅. He concedes that the choice of which "allomorph" of the nominative is used is determined by whether the verb is active or inactive. This he interprets as a relic of an earlier "active" stage of the language; yet it is the productive way in which case marking is determined. Klimov's analysis is determined by his hypothesis (1973) that case change cannot proceed in certain directions (see Chap. 1).

[11]In (62) the optional affirmative particle, *ki*, is written as part of the verb; in verb forms beginning with *i*, such as (66), *ki* + *i* is realized as *ki*. In Mingrelian examples in this work, the particle is not glossed.

[12]Examples (73) and (74)–(75) are based on sentences given by Topuria (1967:180 and 179); the variants presented here were tested with informants in Mesṭia.

4

Reconstruction of Case Morphology

4.1. INTRODUCTION

This chapter is concerned with diachronic morphology, rather than syntax. The purposes of the chapter are

1. To distinguish clearly between the history of case markers (morphology) and the history of their functions and systems of distribution (syntax),
2. To show that in Kartvelian, the history of case endings contributes little to our understanding of case functions,
3. To show that the syntactic cases (narrative, nominative, and dative) were morphologically distinct from one another in CK, and
4. To establish the relationships between the case markers in the different languages and to show how they arose.

I begin by presenting, in §4.2, a summary of the major declensional types of nouns in each language. In §4.3 I sketch a theory of the origin of case endings, reconstruct the markers to CK, and present evidence to support the account. Section 4.4 is something of an aside, dealing with the special problem of nonarticulated forms in Old Georgian, which also support the general account presented in §4.3. Section 4.5 deals with the special problems of plurals, pronouns, and personal names.

Throughout, emphasis is placed on the three syntactic cases, since these are the ones relevant to the main issues of investigation reported here. Whole paradigms are presented, for the value that they may have in illuminating the history of the nominative, narrative, and dative. A number of suffixes are traditionally regarded as postpositions. Though there are reasons for considering some of them to be cases synchronically, they are not included here, as it is clear that they are positionals diachronically. Hence, just the traditional arrays of cases are included here.

4.2. SAMPLE DECLENSIONS

Except in Svan, nouns all belong to a single declensional type; differences result only from phonetic differences in the stem of the noun and are entirely straight-forward. A few details that contribute nothing to the general picture are omitted below.

4.2.1. Old Georgian

In Old Georgian we find eight cases: nominative (-*i*/y/∅), narrative (-*man*), dative (-*s*(*a*)), genitive (-*is*(*a*)), allative (-*isa*), instrumental (-*it*(*a*)), adverbial (-*ad*), and vocative (-*o*).[1] There is not complete agreement about the inventory of cases in Old Georgian. Some omit the vocative (but see Shanidze 1956), some collapse the allative with the genitive (but see Dzidzishvili 1956; Topuria 1956c). The functions of the cases that have not yet been introduced here are described in Topuria (1956a) and Imnaishvili (1957) and in the handbooks.

In monosyllabic stems ending in a consonant, the desinences are simply added, as for *ḳac*. Many polysyllabic stems undergo syncope, triggered by suffixes of the form -VC, as illustrated by *γrubel* in Table 4.1. When the

Table 4.1

Declension of Common Nouns in the Singular in Old Georgian

NOM	*ḳac*-(*i*) 'man'	*γrubel*-(*i*) 'cloud'
NAR	*ḳac-man*	*γrubel-man*
DAT	*ḳac-s*(*a*)	*γrubel-s*(*a*)
GEN	*ḳac-is*(*a*)	*γrubl-is*(*a*)
ALL	*ḳac-isa*	*γrubl-isa*
INST	*ḳac-it*(*a*)	*γrubl-it*(*a*)
ADV	*ḳac-ad*	*γrubl-ad*
VOC	*ḳac-o*	*γrubel-o*

Table 4.2

Singular Declension of Vowel-Stem Nouns in Old Georgian

NOM	*mepe-(y)* 'king'	*deda-(y)* 'mother'
NAR	*mepe-man*	*deda-man*
DAT	*mepe-s(a)*	*deda-s(a)*
GEN	*mep-is(a)*	*ded-is(a)*
ALL	*mep-isa*	*ded-isa*
INST	*mep-it(a)*	*ded-it(a)*
ADV	*mepe-d*	*deda-d*
VOC	*mepe-o*	*deda-o*

Table 4.3

Declension of Common Nouns in the Plural in Old Georgian

	'men'	'clouds'	'kings'	'mothers'
NOM	*ḳac-ni*	*γrubel-ni*	*mepe-ni*	*deda-ni*
NAR, DAT, GEN, ALL, INST, ADV	*ḳac-t(a)*	*γrubel-ta*	*mepe-ta*	*deda-ta*[a]
VOC	*ḳac-no*	*γrubel-no*	*mepe-no*	*deda-no*

[a]The form in *-ta* is infrequent as instrumental or adverbial; often postpositions are substituted for these cases in the plural (Imnaishvili 1957:271–272; Sharadzenidze 1956).

noun stem ends in a vowel and the desinence begins with a vowel, a variety of rules apply, depending on the quality of both vowels. While it is not necessary to give the details here, we can summarize the synchronic processes involved by saying that under these circumstances one or the other of the vowels either becomes nonsyllabic or is deleted. Two examples are given in Table 4.2. The occurrence of the formants in parentheses in Tables 4.1 and 4.2 is accounted for in §4.4.

The plural in Old Georgian is characterized by rather extreme syncretism; all cases except the nominative and vocative have a single form. Examples are given in Table 4.3. There was also, in Old Georgian, a collective, composed of the suffix *-eb* together with any (singular) case marker, as illustrated in Table 4.4. The collective was later reanalysed as plural; both are discussed in greater detail in Chapter 9.

Table 4.4

Partial Declension of Common Nouns in the Collective in Old Georgian

NOM	*ḳac-eb-(i)* 'men'	*γrubl-eb-(i)* 'clouds'	*mepe-eb-(i)* 'kings'	*ded-eb-(i)* 'mothers'
NAR	*ḳac-eb-man*	*γrubl-eb-man*	*mepe-eb-man*	*ded-eb-man*
DAT	*ḳac-eb-s(a)*	*γrubl-eb-s(a)*	*mepe-eb-s(a)*	*ded-eb-s(a)*

4.2.2. Laz

Declension in Laz is illustrated in Table 4.5. Data for Laz and Mingrelian are drawn mainly from Chikobava (1936), but his (synchronic) analysis differs from that presented here. Synchronically, we have the following desinences: nominative (∅), narrative (*-k*), dative (*-s*), genitive (*-š*(*i*)), allative (*-ša*), ablative (*-še*(*n*)), and instrumental (*-te*(*n*)).

The formation of the plural is illustrated in Table 4.6.

A comparison of Tables 4.5 and 4.6 shows an alternation between singular stems in final *-i* and plural stems lacking *-i*, as in *ḳoči*/*ḳoč-epe*; this occurs with inherited and borrowed consonant-final roots and is discussed further in §4.3.1.[2] With stems ending in vowels other than *-i*, the stem-final vowel conditions deletion of the first *e* in *-epe*.

Table 4.5

Declension of Common Nouns in the Singular in Laz

NOM	*ḳoči* 'man'	*ḳučxe* 'foot'	*orʒo* 'chair'
NAR	*ḳoči-k*	*ḳučxe-k*	*orʒo-k*
DAT	*ḳoči-s*	*ḳučxe-s*	*orʒo-s*
GEN	*ḳoči-š*(*i*)	*ḳučxe-š*(*i*)	*orʒo-š*(*i*)
ALL	*ḳoči-ša*	*ḳučxe-ša*	*orʒo-ša*
ABL	*ḳoči-še*(*n*)	*ḳučxe-še*(*n*)	*orʒo-še*(*n*)
INST	*ḳoči-te*(*n*)	*ḳučxe-te*(*n*)	*orʒo-te*(*n*)

Table 4.6

Partial Declension of Common Nouns in the Plural in Laz

NOM	*ḳoč-epe* 'men'	*ḳučxe-pe* 'feet'	*orʒo-pe* 'chairs'
NAR	*ḳoč-epe-k*	*ḳučxe-pe-k*	*orʒo-pe-k*
DAT	*ḳoč-epe-s*	*ḳučxe-pe-s*	*orʒo-pe-s*
GEN	*ḳoč-epe-š*(*i*)	*ḳučxe-pe-š*(*i*)	*orʒo-pe-š*(*i*)

4.2.3. Mingrelian

The set of forms traditionally included in the case inventory is listed and exemplified in Table 4.7. From a synchronic point of view, we find the case endings nominative (*-i*), narrative (*-k*),[3] dative (*-s*(*i*)), genitive (*-iš*(*i*)), instrumental (*-it*(*i*)), allative (*-iša*), ablative (*-iše*), designative

Table 4.7

Declension of Common Nouns in the Singular in Mingrelian

NOM	*ḳoč-i* 'man'	*ḳoṭo* 'pot'	*ḳaṭu* 'cat'
NAR	*ḳoč-k*	*ḳoṭo-k*	*ḳaṭu-k*
DAT	*ḳo-s*(< *ḳoč-s*)	*ḳoṭo-s*(*i*)	*ḳaṭu-s*(*i*)
GEN	*ḳoč-iš*(*i*)	*ḳoṭo-š*(*i*)	*ḳaṭu-š*(*i*)
ALL	*ḳoč-iša*	*ḳoṭo-ša*	*ḳaṭu-ša*
ABL	*ḳoč-iše*	*ḳoṭo-še*	*ḳaṭu-še*
INST	*ḳoč-it*(*i*)	*ḳoṭo-t*(*i*)	*ḳaṭu-t*(*i*)
DES	*ḳoč-išo*(*t*)	*ḳoṭo-šo*(*t*)	*ḳaṭu-šo*(*t*)
ADV	*ḳoč-o*	*ḳoṭo-t*	*ḳaṭu-o*

Table 4.8

Partial Declension of Common Nouns in the Plural in Mingrelian

NOM	*ḳoč-ep-i* 'men'	*ḳoṭu-ep-i* 'pots'	*ḳaṭu-ep-i* 'cats'
NAR	*ḳoč-en-k*	*ḳoṭu-en-k*	*ḳaṭu-en-k*
DAT	*ḳoč-en-s*	*ḳoṭu-en-s*(*i*)	*ḳaṭu-en-s*(*i*)
GEN	*ḳoč-ep-iš*(*i*)	*ḳoṭu-ep-iš*(*i*)	*ḳaṭu-ep-iš*(*i*)
ALL	*ḳoč-ep-iša*	*ḳoṭu-ep-iša*	*ḳaṭu-ep-iša*
INST	*ḳoč-ep-it*(*i*)	*ḳoṭu-ep-it*(*i*)	*ḳaṭu-ep-it*(*i*)

(*-išo*(*t*)), and adverbial (*-o/t*). This analysis assumes a productive synchronic rule,

(1) $i \rightarrow \emptyset$ / V + ____ ,

as well as deletion of final *-n* and *-t* under certain circumstances.

Plurals are exemplified in Table 4.8. This analysis includes the following additional rules among others:

(2) The noun pluralizer, *-ep*, is realized as *-en* before a case marker of the form -C(V).[4]

(3) Stem final *-o* is realized as *-u* before the noun pluralizer, *-ep/en*.

(4) Stem final *-e* and *-a* delete before the noun pluralizer, *-ep/en*.

The last is not illustrated here. Note that (4) also applies synchronically in Laz.

4.2.4. Svan

As indicated above, Svan is the only Kartvelian language with more than one declension. The analysis below is based on Sharadzenidze (1955).

I have here omitted some subtypes that exhibit variations due to phonological processes and reanalysis. I have also omitted dialectal variation, which is very complex.

The most common type is the first declension, shown in Table 4.9; it includes stems ending in consonants, *-a*, *-i*, *-o*, and *-u*. All plurals follow this type and they are not treated separately. An important subtype originally had a root-final vowel, which now shows up only in its umlauted variant in the genitive; for example, *kor* 'house/NOM' (< **kora*), *kor-äš* 'house-GEN' (< **kora-iš*).

In Svan *i* triggered umlaut; breaking of *ü* (to *wi*) and *ö* (to *we*) was common. In this declension, the umlauted variant has been generalized from the nominative to all other cases. For example, nominative *txwim* is from **txum-i*; the original form is preserved in the plural: *txum-är* (< **txum-ar-i*) 'head-PL-NOM', *txum-är-d* 'head-PL-NAR', and so on. Similarly, from CK **qan-*'ox', Topuria (1944:342) lists the following forms from Upper Bal and Lenṭex: nominative *qän*, narrative *qän-d*, dative *qän-s*, and so forth. In this Declension I, the desinences of the remaining cases are the following: narrative *-d*, dative *-s*, genitive *-iš* or *-eš*, instrumental *-šw* or *-wš*, and adverbial *-d*. (Dative *-s* is sometimes dropped in Svan; see note 2.)

The second declension is, according to Sharadzenidze, used mainly with those noun stems that end in a consonant and that are also declined according to the first declension. It is also used with some numbers. It is believed that in the past this declension was very widespread. This paradigm is an example of what is called in Caucasian studies a "two-base" declension. The nominative base, consisting of the root with an umlauted vowel, contrasts with the oblique base, in the present instance consisting of the nonumlauted root and the suffix *-w*. The dative is formed with *-w* alone, while the other cases add a second suffix: narrative *-em*, genitive *-(e)m-iš*, instrumental *-š*, and adverbial *-d* (see Table 4.10).

Sharadzenidze's third declension is used now only by a few pronouns; it is illustrated in Table 4.15 and discussed in §4.3.3., point 5.

Table 4.9

Declension I, Singular in Svan

NOM	*txwim*	'head, self'
NAR	*txwim-d*	
DAT	*txwim-s*	
GEN	*txwim-iš*	
INST	*txwim-šw*	
ADV	*txwim-d*	

Table 4.10

Declension II in Svan

NOM	*čäž* 'horse'	*žeγ* 'dog'
NAR	*čāž-w-em*	*žaγ-w-em*
DAT	*čāž-w*	*žaγ-w*
GEN	*čāž-w-(e)m-iš*	*žaγ-w-(e)*m-iš
INST	*čāž-w-š*	*žaγ-w-š(w)*
ADV	*čāž-w-d*	*žaγ-w-d*

Table 4.11

Declension IV in Svan

NOM	*māre* 'man'
NAR	*mār-a-d, mār-ēm*
DAT	*mār-a*
GEN	*mār-ēm-iš*
INST	*mār-oš*
ADV	*mār-a-d*

Table 4.12

Declension V in Svan

NOM	*ara* 'eight'
NAR	*arēm, arām-d, arāmnēm*
DAT	*arām*
GEN	*arēmiš*
INST	*arāmšw*
ADV	*arāmd*

The fourth declension is illustrated in Table 4.11.

Sharadzenidze suggests that this is not historically a two-base declension, as had been believed earlier. Instead, there is good internal evidence for reconstructing stems in final *-a* underlying all cases. The exponent of the nominative is then **-i*, which regularly triggers umlaut of *a* (*a* > *ä* > *e*, in many environments). The narrative *mārad* has simply the desinence *-d* added to the stem, as does the adverbial case form. She suggests that the instrumental *mārоš* is from *māra-šw*. Kaldani (1974:152) cites additional internal evidence for setting up stem-final *-a* historically. Sharadzenidze further suggests that the fourth and fifth declensions are related.

Table 4.12 illustrates the fifth declension. While the discussion above does not cover all the varieties that exist in Svan, it at least provides a starting point.

The plural in Svan is formed by adding a plural suffix, *-ar*, *-al*, *-är*, *-äl*, *ār*, and so on (see Sharadzenidze 1954), and declining the resulting stem by the first declension.

4.3. RECONSTRUCTION

In reconstructing cases, we are concerned with the inventory of the protolanguage, with the form of each desinence in the protolanguage, and with the function of each. The last of these is not considered in this chapter, and it should be remembered that the names used traditionally and in this work are somewhat arbitrary. With respect to inventory, an inspection of declension in the daughter languages tells us that some cases are probably not reconstructible to CK. In particular, the vocative is attested only in Old Georgian and is believed to come from the particle *o*, probably borrowed from Greek *ō* (Topuria 1956b). The allative, ablative, and designative seem to be secondary in the sense that they appear to be formed by the addition of suffixes, probably postpositions in origin, to the genitive (Gigineishvili and Sarjveladze 1978; Topuria 1937). Naturally, this is not to say that CK did not have an allative, an ablative, or a designative, but only that we cannot reconstruct them that far back (but cf. §11.2 on the allative). These subtractions leave us with an inventory consisting of nominative, narrative, dative, genitive, instrumental, and adverbial. Discussion of narrative is postponed to §4.3.2, while the others are discussed in §4.3.1.

4.3.1. Nominative, Dative, Genitive, Instrumental, and Adverbial of Singular Common Nouns

Table 4.13 gives the nominative, dative, genitive, instrumental, and adverbial case desinences. The nominative desinence **-i* can be traced in all

Table 4.13

Summary of Five Kartvelian Case Desinences

	CK	Old Georgian	Laz	Mingrelian	Svan
NOM	**i*	*i/y/Ø*	*Ø*	*i/Ø*	**i*
DAT	**s*	*s(a)*	*s*	*s(i)*	*s*
GEN	**is*$_1$	*is(a)*	*š(i)*	*(i)š(i)*	*iš/eš*
INST	**s*$_1$*i*	*it(a)*	*te(n)*	*(i)t(i)*	*wš/šw*
ADV	**d*	*d/a/ad*	—	*t/o*	*d*

four languages and is tentatively reconstructed on that basis. The *y* variant in Georgian and the ∅ alternant in Mingrelian are the result of productive synchronic rules that reduce *i* following a vowel (see n. 3 also). In Svan, **i* is reconstructible on the basis of internal evidence involving the stem vowel of other cases versus the stem vowel of the nominative (see Tables 4.10 and 4.11) or stem vowel of the singular versus that of the plural.

It is apparent that Laz has undergone reanalysis, such that the *i* that occurred in the nominative, genitive, and instrumental (as well as cases secondarily derived from them) was reinterpreted as part of the stem for roots that formerly terminated in a consonant. For example, *ḳoč* is a Kartvelian root, derived by regular sound changes from CK **ḳac*$_1$. As illustrated in Table 4.5, the present-day form of this stem is *ḳoči*. As part of this reinterpretation, the exponent of the nominative case, which probably already had the alternant ∅ after vowels (as in Mingrelian and Modern Georgian), was reinterpreted as ∅.

The nominative desinence was formerly reconstructed as **i*/**e* (see Machavariani 1970) on the basis of the Laz nominative plural, for example, *ḳoč-ep-e* 'men', and the Svan nominative plural ending *-are* in some forms. The suffix *-ar* occurs alone as a plural marker in Svan. Since *e* may trigger umlaut in Svan, it could have been responsible for the umlauted stem vowel in the nominative singular of the nouns in Tables 4.9–4.11; that is, **-e* could have been the Svan nominative case marker. However, Kaldani (1974) has shown that *-are* comes from **-ar-a-i*, where both **ar* and **a* are independently attested plural markers, and **i* is the nominative desinence. This explains a number of problems (see Kaldani 1969:65 and n. 7, p. 78), and shows that only **i*, not **e*, is to be reconstructed for Svan.

The plural in Laz has been reanalyzed. We can assume that Laz inherited the CGZ marker **eb*, with the Laz reflex *-ep*; this is suffixed directly to stems of all types, conditioning deletion of the stem-final *-i* discussed above. The suffix *-ep* was augmented with *-e*, inserted between *-ep* and the case endings probably for phonological reasons. Laz reanalyzed all case endings in such a way that they all begin with a consonant (see Table 4.5). In Mingrelian we see that just when the *p* of the plural would contact a consonant-initial case marker, *p* becomes *n* (see Table 4.8 and rule 2). Laz avoided the same *p* + C conflict by epenthesizing *e*.[5] This put *e* in all cases except the nominative, and it was natural for *e* to then be extended to the nominative and for the plural suffix to be reanalyzed as *-epe*. This account, together with Kaldani's (1974) analysis of Svan, makes it unlikely that the **i*/**e* alternation previously attributed to the nominative desinence ever existed.

An older form of the nominative case, the bare stem with ∅ marker, is discussed below; and a revision of the reconstruction is suggested in §4.6.

We must reconstruct at least *-*s* as an exponent of the dative, though it is not clear how this might account for the full variety found in Svan. In the first declension of Svan and in Laz, we find just -*s*. In Old Georgian we find -*s*, -*sa*, or -*as* (e.g., *adgilas*). One theory of the origin of this -*a* is discussed below. In Mingrelian we find -*s*, -*si*, or sometimes -*sə*, which may have originated in the same way as Georgian -*sa*. Analogous forms are also found in Georgian, e.g., *kalak-iti* 'city-INST'.

CK *s does not account for the dative found in the second, third, fourth, and fifth declensions of Svan; one of these is discussed in §4.3.3.

There is independent evidence from many CK roots that we must reconstruct three sets of spirants and affricates for CK; these are traditionally symbolized by s, s_1, and *š* (Gamkrelidze 1959; Machavariani 1963). The set symbolized by s_1 became s in Georgian and *š* elsewhere. The exponent of the genitive is set up as *is_1. The optional final -*a* in Georgian and -*i* in Laz and Mingrelian are probably related to those found also in the dative and referred to above. The initial *i* in Mingrelian is deleted productively by rule (1). The same rule probably operated at an earlier stage of Laz, but the desinence seems to have been reanalyzed, as suggested above. The *eš* variant in Svan is probably due to a secondary phonological process (see Kaldani 1974).

There are difficulties in the comparison of Georgian and Zan *t* with Svan *wš*/*šw*. The *w* of the Svan ending is believed to come from the *w*-base of the second declension, which in the instrumental must have been generalized to all declensional types. Metathesis of *w* is entirely regular in Svan, and it is this process that produces the variant *šw* from *w-š* (Sharadzenidze 1961: 222). There is a regular correspondence between Georgian and Zan *t* and Svan *šd*, which is reconstructed as CK *s_1t (Gamkrelidze and Machavariani 1965: 135ff.). Topuria (1977) suggests that the original form of the desinence of the instrumental case is one instance of this correspondence. The CK instrumental *s_1t developed regularly into Old Georgian, Laz, and Mingrelian -*t*. Topuria proposes that the Svan desinence -*wš* originated as Svan *-*w*-*šd*, where *šd* simplified to -*š* in this instance. He argues that *i* cannot be reconstructed as part of the desinence in CK. While the apparently isolated simplification of **šd* remains something of a problem, Topuria's account is convincing.

Even in the absence of an adverbial in Laz, this case is reconstructible in the inventory of CK. (The adverbial case is also known as the directional (*mimartulebiti*) or transformative (*gardakceviti*).) While Tables 4.1 and 4.2 represent the Old Georgian norm, Chikobava (1956b) has observed that in some instances we find -*a* in the function of the adverbial case (e.g., *ǰoǰoxet-a* 'to hell', *salocvel-a* 'to pray'), and that -*d* is not limited to the declension of vowel-stem nouns, but also occasionally occurs with consonant-stems (e.g., *betlem-d* 'to Bethlehem'). We may add that *-a* is found as a marker of the adverbial case in dialects of Georgian, both in the east (Imnaishvili 1966:90–91) and in the west (Dzotsenidze 1973:21, 47, 81, 119, 179, 210; Mikeladze 1980:94). In Mingrelian, too, *-o* and *-t* are separately attested as exponents of the adverbial (see Table 4.7). Devoicing of final stops is common in Mingrelian (i.e., the Mingrelian reflex of CK **d* is *t* in auslaut), and Mingrelian *o* is the regular reflex of CK **a*. Chikobava (1956b) argues that *-a* and *-d* are distinct exponents, combined in the Georgian desinence *-ad*. The same view may be taken of Mingrelian *-ot*, which occurs as the designative case (Topuria 1937), e.g., *ḳoč-iš-ot* < **ḳoč-iš-o-t* 'for the man,' and which is preserved, for example, in the adverbial plural of *bircx-ep-o(t)* 'fingernail/toenail' (Chikobava 1936:46). While the functions of *a/o* are not identical to those of *d/t*, the difference cannot yet be clearly determined; see also Chapter 11.

Of the two markers, only **d* can be reconstructed with confidence to CK; we must assume that the marker **a* is a CGZ development. I have assigned them both to a single case here, but in the future it may be possible to distinguish one set of functions for CK **d* and another for CGZ **a* and to clarify the development of *-ad* and *-ot*.

It is not obvious how the narrative fits in with the system discussed here, but its origin is dealt with in the next section. It is clear only that CGZ had *-k*. There is little agreement between Georgian and Svan and none with Zan.

4.3.2. An Outline of the Ancestral Article Hypothesis

Through the efforts of a number of scholars, a view has developed of the origin of some of the case markers via a definite article. Seminal papers on this hypothesis include Shanidze (1957d, esp. p. 365) and Chikobava (1939). Machavariani (1960) develops an important new aspect of the hypothesis. Other papers that have been influential include Chikobava (1956a), Dondua (1956a), and Vogt (1947b). The views of these scholars differ somewhat from each other; my own view, influenced by Greenberg's (1978) study of universals, is not the same as any one of these but has drawn from all.

In Old Georgian we find demonstrative pronouns, third person personal pronouns, and a definite article, all having the same form. They exist in a tripartite system consisting of a proximate (near the first person), a contingent (near the second person), and a remote member (far from both first and second persons) as shown in Table 4.14.[6]

The most important aspect of the declension of the pronoun–article is that for each pronoun there is one stem for the nominative case and an-

Table 4.14

Singular of Demonstrative, Third Person Pronoun, and Article in Oldest Georgian

	Proximate	Contingent	Remote
NOM	*ese*	*ege*	*igi*
NAR	*a-ma-n*	*maga-n*	*ma-n*
DAT	*a-ma-s*	*maga-s*	*ma-s*
GEN	*a-m -is*	*mag -is*	*m -is*
ALL	*a-m -is-a*	*mag -is-a*	*m -is-a*
INST	*a-m -it*	*mag -it*	*m -it*
ADV	*a-ma-d*	*maga-d*	*ma-d*

Table 4.15

Two-Base Declension of Pronouns in Laz and Svan[a]

	Laz	Svan
NOM	*a-ya* 'this (one)'	*a-la* 'this (one)'
NAR	*a-mu-k*	*a-m-n-ēm*
DAT	*a-mu-s*	*a-m-ən* / *a-m-i-s* / *a-ma-s* / *a-la-s*
GEN	*a-mu-ši*	*a-m-īš* / *amša*
ALL	*a-mu-ša*	—
ABL	*a-mu-še(n)*	—
INST	*a-mu-te(n)*	*a-m-n-oš*
ADV	—	*a-m-n-är-(d)*

[a]Svan after Sharadzenidze 1955:130 with Machavariani 1960:99.

other for all other cases. Each branch of Kartvelian preserves this in the declension of some demonstrative–third person pronouns, though some paradigms have been regularized. Two of those preserving the two-base declension are listed in Table 4.15.

Even though we cannot, with confidence, reconstruct the precise forms of the demonstrative–third person pronouns in CK, we are justified in assuming that (a) it had a two-base system for at least some pronouns, (b) the CK nominative was of the form V_iCV_j, where $V_i = V_j$, and (c) the oblique stem of some was **m*(V), certainly **ma* in CGZ.[7] Consideration of all the variants in all the languages would permit us also to conclude that (d) the remote member of the pair or triplet of forms contained the prefixal deictic *i-*,[8] while (e) the proximate member contained the prefixal deictic *a-*, perhaps also *e-*.

It is hypothesized here that the remote demonstrative pronoun (Stage 0), which could refer to something in discourse, developed into a definite article (Stage I), which marked a noun as “identified” or “known” previously in discourse. In this use it followed the noun and was unstressed; in its use as a demonstrative, on the other hand, it was stressed and usually preceded the noun (Imnaishvili 1957:563). Later, in addition to its definite uses, it developed some indefinite uses (Stage II). However, there continued to exist a contrast between those contexts in which the determiner occurred and those in which it did not. Finally, the unstressed article was absorbed into the noun form and the case distinctions of the article became those of the noun (Stage III).

This process in CK accounts for the origins of the nominative case marker **i* and of the forms of the narrative case that are found in Georgian and Svan. Chikobava (1956a) argues that the same process accounts for the optional final *-a* of the dative, genitive, and instrumental in Old Georgian.

It is theoretically possible that the absorption of the article is responsible for the renewal of older case markings, which had perhaps been eroded by phonological change. Alternatively it is possible that case had not previously been marked on the noun, but only on accompanying articles, and that this process is responsible for the creation of pristine case marking in the noun. There is good evidence that the nominative **i* is such a pristine case; this is discussed in §4.4. On the other hand, while there certainly was a narrative case in CK, it is not entirely clear whether it was marked only on the article, or on both the noun and article, as we see below.

4.3.3. How the Ancestral Article Hypothesis Accounts for Kartvelian Data

In this section I adduce arguments to support the ancestral article hypothesis and show in greater detail how the process worked and how it accounts for data in the daughter languages.

1. Old Georgian preserves an article in the sequence that would be required to produce a suffix; that is, the article follows the noun. This contrasts with the opposite order, where the pronoun–article has demonstrative function (Imnaishvili 1957:563): *ḳaci igi* ‘the man’ versus *igi ḳaci* ‘that man.’[9]

2. As shown above, some reflex of **i* is found in each of the daughter languages. A deictic prefix **i-* can likewise be reconstructed for the remote demonstrative in CK on the basis of Laz *ia* ‘that one/NOM’, Mingrelian

ina 'that one/NOM' (Chikobava 1936:79, 80), Georgian *igi* 'that one/NOM', and Svan *eǰa* < **iǰi* (Kaldani 1974).

3. Old Georgian preserves both the articulated (i.e., with the original article) and nonarticulated forms of the noun; e.g., *ḳac-i* versus *ḳac* 'man-NOM'. It is this fact that specifically supports the view that the nominative **i* is a pristine case marker. It is independently clear that the nonarticulated form of the nominative is older than the articulated; the distribution of the nonarticulated form was already highly restricted in the earliest Georgian, and eventually it died out completely. The exact distribution of the nonarticulated form also supports this hypothesis; it is discussed in detail in §4.4.

It is not suggested here that the desinence *-i* developed from the article that is actually found in Georgian. Rather, the demonstrative went through the entire sequence of events sketched in §4.3.2., then the process was repeated in Georgian alone through Stage I or II. In old Georgian the second round of the process was entering Stage II; the article was already found in indefinite specific uses (e.g., *navsa mas* boat/DAT ART 'into a (certain) boat' Mt 9:1Ad), though this is not frequent.[10] In this second round, the article did not get to Stage III, but died out before reaching it.[11]

4. The exponent of the narrative case in CK is reconstructed as **n/d* where the conditions that determine the alternants are not yet known.[12] In Georgian the entire narrative case of the article (remote demonstrative) became the new narrative case desinence of the noun; e.g., *ḳac-man* 'man-NAR'; compare *man* 'that one/NAR; he, she, it/NAR; the/NAR'. Here the *n* preserves the original exponent of the narrative case, while *ma* is the oblique stem (see Table 4.14). If we suppose that *-n* already served as the marker of the narrative case in the noun before the absorption of *man* in this function, it is not unreasonable that *n* deleted because of the following *m* of *man*. This would account for the lack of two layers of suffixes, which we would otherwise expect if the narrative case were already distinctly marked in the noun itself. The *n* alternant is also preserved in the narrative case form of the interrogative pronoun, *vin* 'who?', which, however, also serves as the nominative form (Chikobava 1939).

Svan preserves the *-d* variant of the narrative case in the first, fourth, and fifth declensions.

5. While Georgian preserves the full form of the oblique stem *ma-* and the case desinence in the narrative only, Svan preserves it in all oblique cases of the fifth declension, as pointed out by Machavariani (1960:99). He observes that in the paradigm of *ala* (Table 4.15), the dative *alas* must be the result of restructuring on the basis of the nominative *ala*; the oldest form must be *a-ma-s*. The following specific origins may be

posited for the forms in Table 4.12:

NAR *arāmnēm* < **ara-a-m(a)-n-ēm*

DAT *arām* < **ara-a-m* < **ara-a-m(a)-s*

GEN *arēmiš* < **arämiš* < **ara-a-m(a)-is*$_1$

The theory that the fifth declension derives from the articulated forms explains both why *-m-* is there at all and why it is not present in the nominative.[13]

6. The ancestral article hypothesis explains why we normally find neither *-i* (NOM) nor *-man* (NAR) with proper names in Old Georgian (but see example 17), though the other case forms do occur. Since proper nouns are meant to have unique reference, definite articles are not used with them. Since the article is not used with them, and since *-i* and *-man* have their origin in the article, *-i* and *-man* would not originally have occurred with proper nouns. Later, they were, of course, generalized to all nouns.

7. The same hypothesis explains why there are no proper nouns declined according to the fifth (*-m-*) declension in Svan (Machavariani 1960:98).

8. In Mingrelian the *i* of the remote demonstrative is preserved in the nominative, genitive, and instrumental, as well as in the dative of some nouns (see Table 4.7). In Laz, the *i* remains in the nominative, genitive, and possibly, as *e*, in the instrumental; see Table 4.5.

9. Finally, the hypothesized ancestral article is supported by Greenberg's (1978) study of the universals of this process. He shows that, in general, a postposed unstressed article, such as that which we see in Georgian, is a fruitful source of noun suffixes, which may take on gender or case marking functions, depending on the categories of the original article, or may become simply markers of nounness. Greenberg adduces a large number of examples to support universally the four stages of development. In addition, he states the contexts in which the nonarticulated form occurs and may be preserved as a relic (contrasting with the articulated form). As we see in the next section, these correspond exactly to the Old Georgian facts.

4.4. THE NONARTICULATED FORM IN OLD GEORGIAN

The hypothesis outlined in §4.3.2 entails that the articulated (derived from stem + article) form will eventually be generalized to all contexts. However, if we could "catch" a language in the midst of the process of change, before the articulated form is completely generalized, we should find that the nonarticulated form is retained systematically in some subset of the environments in which it was used in earlier stages. Old Georgian provides just this evidence. In the discussion below, I have drawn heavily from Imnaishvili's (1957) detailed study of the functions of the cases in Old Georgian, borrowing also some of his examples.

4.4.1. Universals

Greenberg (1978) has studied the universals of the development of a demonstrative to an article and finally to some noun marking which may indicate gender. He suggests that universally the nonarticulated form would be expected to be preserved in some of the following environments (1978:66ff.): (a) in negation, (b) in predicate nominals, (c) in locative and temporal expressions, (d) in incorporated object constructions, (e) in compounds, and (f) with numerals. Because we are dealing with the development of case suffixes, we must limit this list for each case to those functions in which it can be used. For example, the narrative case is never used as a predicate nominal, so we would not expect its nonarticulated form to be found in this function.

The list above consists of environments in which the article (definite; later: definite + indefinite specific) would not have appeared at earlier stages of its development. To Greenberg's list we can make two additions. In many languages that have definite articles, these articles generally do not occur with proper nouns or with personal pronouns (which may themselves be derived from demonstratives, as in Georgian). We can see that this is true by considering English. In English only a few proper nouns have the definite article: *the Hague*; personal pronouns never do: **the he*, **the she*. We have, therefore, (g) in proper nouns, and (h) in personal pronouns. In addition, Greenberg discusses the fact that subjects of existentials and objects are more likely to be indefinite, and therefore to preserve the nonarticulated form, than are subjects of other types of verbs (1978:66, 73–74; see Comrie 1976a)

With these universal considerations in mind, we are ready to consider the Old Georgian data.

4.4.2. The Nominative

The articulated form of the nominative case has *-i* (<*igi*), while the nonarticulated form is the bare stem (∅). The nominative case can occur in all of the contexts listed above, (a)–(h).

The nonarticulated form often occurs in negative expressions:

(5) *ara esvia mas švil*
not he/have/him/I him/DAT child
'He had no child.' (Mt 22:25Ad)

(6) *rametu sxua nav ara iq̣o mun*
for other boat/∅ not it/be/II there
'that no other boat was there' (J 6:22Ad)

When the very existence of the nominal is negated, as in these examples, the nominal cannot logically be definite and is therefore unlikely to have occurred with the article.

The nonarticulated form is frequently a predicate nominal. In the examples below, the predicate nominals *mšvid*, *mdabal*, and *ucxo* are in the zero form of the nominative.

(7) *rametu mšvid var da mdabal gulita*
for meek/∅ I/be/I and low/∅ heart/INST
'For I am meek and low of heart.' (Mt 11:29)

(8) *ucxo viq̣av*
foreign/∅ I/be/II
'I was a stranger.' (Mt 25:35)

This usage represents the Old Georgian norm for both Series I and II. The predicate nominal is generally indefinite nonspecific and would have lacked the article in Stage II of the development of the demonstrative into a case desinence.

The nominative case was used in time expressions, but not in the expression of location. The nonarticulated form is preserved in some of the former type, mostly in fixed expressions: *mraval žam* 'for much time', *mcired žam* 'for little time', N *c̣el* 'for N years', *c̣ut* N 'for N minutes', N *dγe* 'for N days', *dγe q̣ovel* 'every day', and so forth, where *žam, c̣el, c̣ut,* and *dγe* are nonarticulated forms.

The nonarticulated form occurs in the incorporated object construction, e.g., *γaγad-q̣o* 'noise-he/make/it', *lxineba-hq̣opdet* 'atonement-you/make/it' (Lev 10:17), *paṭiv-scemden* 'honor-they/give/it/to.him' (J 5:23AB). In each example, the initial incorporated noun is in nonarticulated form. This usage is explained by the fact that the incorporated object is most often, if not always, generic and nonspecific; it would therefore not have occurred with the definite article in Stage II.

The nonarticulated form occurs in compounds, e.g., *qma-maγali* 'voice-high', i.e., 'loud', *qel-mc̣ipebay* 'power', *perq-pačunieri* 'hairy-footed' (used as a classification of animals), *da-ʒmay* 'sister-brother', i.e., 'sibling', *col-kmari* 'husband-wife', i.e., 'couple', *deda-ḳaci* 'mother-man', i.e., 'woman'. In compounds, the individual elements are in nonarticulated form, though the whole NP may be marked with *-i/y* when it is in the nominative.

The nonarticulated form is common with numbers and other quantifiers, such as *mraval* 'many'.

(9) *movals dedaḳac ert*
she/come/I woman/∅ one
'A woman comes.' (J 4:7Ad)

(10) *romelsa akus xut queza krtilis da or tevz*
which he/have/it/I five loaf/∅ barley and two fish/∅
'who has five barley loaves and two fish' (J 6:9Ad)

(11) *da aha or ḳac gamočndes*
and behold two man/∅ they/appear/I
'And behold there appeared two men.' (L 24:4Ad)

(12) (*da hḳitxa mat: raodeni gakuns tkuen p̣uri?*)
('And he asked them: How many loves do you have?')

xolo mat hrkues: švid
and they/NAR they/say/it/to.him/II seven/∅
'And they said to him: seven.' (Mk 8:5Ad)

Counting in Old Georgian took the nonarticulated form: *ert*, *or*, *sam*, 'one, two, three' (Imnaishvili 1957:660).

Personal names in the nominative case occurred regularly in the nonarticulated form.

(13) *arkelaoz mepobs huriasṭans*
Archelaus he/reign/I Judea/DAT
'Archelaus rules in Judea.' (Mt 2:22B)

(14) *ixila simon da andria*
he/see/it/II simon/∅ and Andrew/∅
'He saw Simon and Andrew.' (Mk 1:16Ad)

Personal names do not take the definite article and therefore preserve the nonarticulated form in Old Georgian. Geographic names also lack the article; but many had already generalized the articulated form, though some examples preserve the nonarticulated form (see (23) below).

The pronoun has only nonarticulated forms; third person forms are listed in Table 4.14. In the first and second persons, too, we find only the nonarticulated form: *me*/**me-y* 'I-NOM', *tkuen*/**tkuen-i* 'you/PL-NOM' (see Imnaishvili 1957:489).[14]

With respect to grammatical relations, we find the following situation in Old Georgian. In Series II, the nonarticulated form occurs as the direct object of a fairly wide variety of verbs: *sca* 'gave', *iγo* 'took', *dasdva* 'put', *ipq̣ra* 'caught', *ixila* 'saw', *ḳla* 'killed', *igdo* 'threw', *uc̣oda* 'named', *q̇o* 'made', *hrkua* 'named', *kmna* 'made', *isxna* 'sit (TRANS, PL OBJ)', and others (Imnaishvili 1957:640). In both Series I and II the nonarticulated form functions frequently as the subject of various verbs meaning 'be' (Imnaishvili 1957:638) and occasionally as the subject of *abs* 'it hangs (STATIVE)', *eces* 'it will be given to him' (Imnaishvili 1957:639). Finally, the nonarticulated form may express the thing or person possessed with the various verbs of possession (Imnaishvili 1957:638); all of these undergo Inversion, and the possessed is the initial direct object and final subject (Harris 1981b: Chap. 8; Chap. 13 below).

Thus, we find the nonarticulated form of the nominative case in the full set of contexts where it might, on universal grounds, be expected to be preserved. Later, the articulated form was generalized, and in Modern Georgian it alone occurs in all of the contexts discussed above, with the following exceptions.[15] Compounds still preserve the ancient usage in the first element: *col-kmar-i* 'wife-husband-NOM', i.e. 'couple', *tav-ḳidur-i* 'head-hung-NOM', i.e., 'initial'. Pronouns, which have an irregular declension anyway, never developed articulated forms (examples above).

4.4.3. The Narrative Case

The narrative case is not used at all in some of the contexts listed in §4.4.1.; no form of it is found in predicate nominals (b), in locative or temporal expressions (c), in incorporated object constructions (d), or in compounds (e). The narrative functions only as the subject of Class 1 and 3 verbs in Series II. In this function, it can be in negation (a) or with numerals (f); however, in these contexts we find only the articulated form.

The nonarticulated form (∅) of the narrative case is found with personal names (g) and personal pronouns (h). The former is exemplified in (15)–(16).

(15) *iaḳob* *šva* *iuda*
Jacob/∅ he/beget/him/II Judas/∅
'Jacob begat Judas.' (Mt 1:2)

(16) *xolo mariam* *moiγo* *liṭra-y* *ert-i*
then Mariam/∅ she/take/it/II litre-NOM one-NOM
'Then Mariam took a litre.' (J 12:3)

The order used in otherwise ambiguous sentences like (15) is usually, but not invariably, SVO. The articulated form could alternatively occur:

(17) *isaḳ-man* *šva* *iaḳob-i*
Isaac-NAR he/beget/him/II Jacob-NOM
'Isaac begat Jacob.' (Mt 1:2Ad)

The articulated form of the narrative case eventually replaced the non-articulated in personal names, the pattern in (17) becoming general in Modern Georgian. In the personal pronoun, on the other hand, there has never been an articulated form: *man*, not **man-man* 'he-NAR'; *me*, not **me-man* 'I-NAR'; *šen*, not **šen-man* 'you-NAR' (see also §4.5).

4.4.4. The Dative Case

While there is excellent support for the ancestral article hypothesis for the nominative and narrative cases, the evidence relating to the dative, genitive, and instrumental is considerably weaker. The evidence presented here supports the ancestral article hypothesis by showing that in Old Georgian the nonarticulated forms of the dative case occurred in those contexts universally predicted by Greenberg's study. However, the articulated form of this case has not been generalized to the same extent as have those of the nominative and narrative. In some contexts in Modern Georgian, they exist side by side, with the articulated form being more "correct," more formal, *ḳac-is-tvis*/*ḳac-is-a-tvis* 'man-GEN-for'. But the articulated form of the dative sounds archaic as an ordinary object: *misca ḳacs* versus *misca ḳacsa* 'he gave it to a man'.

The articulated form of the dative is *-sa*, from *-s* plus the deictic prefix of the proximate demonstrative, *-a*. The nonarticulated form is *-s*, which we have shown to be the reflex of CK **-s*.

The nonarticulated form of the common noun normally does not occur as a surface direct object or indirect object (this includes the surface indirect object of the Inversion construction, which is an initial subject) or retired indirect object (Imnaishvili 1957:687, 688, 694), though the articulated form is used in all of these functions in Old Georgian.

Nonarticulated forms do occur as locatives and temporals, mainly in fixed expressions, both illustrated below.

(18) *da mašin gamočndes niš-i igi ʒ-isa*
and then it/appear/I sign-NOM DET/NOM son-GEN
ḳac-isa-y zeca-s
man-GEN-NOM heaven-DAT
'And then the sign of the son of man will appear in heaven.'
(Mt 24:30Ad)

(19) *mived dγe-s da ikmode saqurʒen-sa čem-sa*
you/go/II day-DAT and you/work/II vineyard-DAT my-DAT
'Go today and work in my vineyard.' (Mt 21:28Ad)

Example (19) also illustrates the most common use of the articulated form in a locative (*saqurʒensa*).

The nonarticulated form occurred in incorporated object constructions:

(20) *me* *natel-s-gcem* *tkuen* *c̣ql-ita*
I/NOM light-DAT-I/give/it/to.you/I you/DAT water-INST
'I baptize you with water.' (Mk 1:8Ad)

(21) *romel-sa* *gul-s-edva* *micema-y*
which/REL-DAT heart-DAT-it/placed/to.him/II giving-NOM
misi
him/GEN
'who planned to give him up (i.e., betray him)' (J 12:4A)

In the first of these examples, the incorporated noun is the initial direct object; in the second, it indicates a location, literally 'it was placed to him in the heart'.

The nonarticulated, rather than the articulated, form occurs in those compounds that make use of datives, e.g., *tav-s-mdebeli* 'he who is forbearing' (Abuladze 1973:174b), where *-s-* is the dative marker of the noun *tav-* 'head'.

The nonarticulated form is the norm for proper nouns in the dative:

(22) *aha* *angeloz-i* *upl-isa-y* *gamoučnda*
behold angel-NOM lord-GEN-NOM he/appear/to.him/I
čvieneb-it *iosep-s*
dream-INST Joseph-DAT
'Behold the angel of the Lord appeared to Joseph in a dream.'
(Mt 2:13Ad)

(23) *romel-ni* *iqvnes* *betlem-s*
which/REL-PL/NOM they/be/II Bethlehem-DAT
'who were in Bethlehem' (Mt 2:16Ad)

Finally, in personal pronouns the nonarticulated form is the norm; e.g., *me* 'I, me', *šen* 'you(SG)'. Some dialects have optional variants with *-a*: *mena* 'I, me,' *šena* 'you(SG)' (Martirosovi 1964:84–85); these may be interpreted as extensions of the articulated form to the pronoun.

4.4.5. The Genitive and Instrumental

The situations of the genitive and instrumental in Old Georgian are analogous to that of the dative. The nonarticulated form of the genitive is *-is*, the articulated is *-isa*. The nonarticulated form is preserved in certain time expressions (Imnaishvili 1957:718), in incorporated object constructions (e.g., *natl-is-cemay* 'light-GEN-giving' i.e. 'baptizing'), in compounds (e.g. *c-is-peri* 'sky-GEN-color', i.e., 'light blue', *er-is-tavi* 'people-GEN-head', i.e., 'prince'), in personal names (*mariam-is* 'Mary-GEN'), and as the only form of personal pronouns (e.g., *mis*, not **misa* 'his').[16] It is also found in expressions of measure (Imnaishvili 1957:719–720) and as the possessor of a noun that is itself in the nonarticulated form of the nominative (Imnaishvili 1957:719).

The nonarticulated form of the instrumental is *-it*, the articulated is *-ita*, and *-iti* is also found. The nonarticulated form is retained in Old Georgian in locative expressions (e.g., *kalak-it* 'out of the city'), with personal names (e.g., *moseis-it-gan* 'Moses-INST-from'; *ḳaiapays-it* 'Caiaphas-INST'),[17] and in personal pronouns (e.g., *mit*, not **mita*). The nonarticulated instrumental has many additional uses (see Imnaishvili 1957:723–730).

4.4.6. The "Absolutive Case"

In the handbooks on Old Georgian, the inventory of cases includes, in addition to the nominative, the 'absolutive case.' The absolutive case is what I have been referring to as the "nonarticulated form of the nominative case," that is, the bare stem. Most or all of the authors of the handbooks accept the ancestral article hypothesis (see Shanidze 1957d) and view the stem form as older than the nominative in *-i/y*, which took over its functions historically. Thus, there is no disagreement over the origin of *-i/y* or over the historical relationships between the bare stem and the suffixed form. I disagree with the writers of the handbooks only in that I cannot view the bare stem as a separate case. Being a distinct case entails having distinct functions. Yet the functions of the nonarticulated (stem) form are a proper subset of those of the articulated (suffixed) form.[18] If the stem form of the nominative is viewed as a distinct case, we have no explanation for the fact that it happens to occur in exactly those contexts in which we would, on universal grounds, expect to find the nonarticulated form preserved (see §4.4.1 above).

When the nonarticulated form of the nominative is viewed as a distinct case, it is given a status not accorded the nonarticulated forms of the narrative, dative, genitive, and instrumental, all of which are traditionally considered unemphatic forms of their respective cases or (in the instance of proper nouns and pronouns) parts of peculiar declensions. Giving the nonarticulated form of the nominative this status apart prevents our seeing the close relationship between the patterns of usage of all of the nonarticulated forms.

I conclude that the stem form is not a distinct case and should not be included in the inventory of cases. The stem form must be reconstructed as the oldest form of the NOMINATIVE case, preserved in environments that are predictable on universal grounds.

4.5. PLURALS, PRONOUNS, AND PROPER NOUNS

As shown in §4.2, all of the modern Kartvelian languages use agglutinative morphology in the formation of plurals; to the noun stem is suffixed a pluralizer, then a case marker, which is the same as in the singular. In Old Georgian, however, we had fusional morphology with syncretism, such that we found distinct desinences for the vocative (*-no* < *-n-o*) and nominative (*-ni* < *-n-i*), but a single exponent for the plural of all other cases (*-t*(*a*)). This suggests that formation of the plural of common nouns may have originally been radically different from what we find in the daughter languages and that it involved fusional morphology. But reconstruction of specific forms on the basis of a single language with so much syncretism would necessarily be little more than speculation.

While the third person pronouns, derived from demonstratives, have been discussed to some extent, little mention has been made of the first and second person pronouns. In all Kartvelian languages, a single form serves as nominative, narrative, and dative case, while there are distinct forms for the other cases. The first person singular is used as an example in Table 4.16 as its declension is characteristic also of the others in this group. On this basis, a single form is usually reconstructed for these three cases of each pronoun, e.g., first person singular **men*, reconstructed at least to CGZ (see discussion in Martirosovi:1964:84–103).

It is shown above that the nonarticulated form of personal names occurs frequently in Old Georgian; this was in fact the norm, though articulated

Table 4.16

Nominative, Narrative, and Dative Case Forms of the First Person Singular Pronoun in Kartvelian

	Old Georgian	Laz	Mingrelian	Svan
NOM	*me, men*	*ma, man*	*ma*	*mi*
NAR	*me, men*	*ma, man*	*ma*	*mi*
DAT	*me, men*	*ma, man*	*ma*	*mi*

forms are also found. On the basis of the fact that the nonarticulated forms of both nominative and narrative case were the bare stem, Machavariani (1970) reconstructs a distinct declensional pattern for personal names. While it coincides with that of common nouns in most respects, Machavariani's schema for personal names has a single form for the narrative and nominative cases: ∅. Notice, however, that the evidence to support this is rather scant, coming entirely from Old Georgian. A different possibility is that proper names originally had the same declension as common nouns, including ∅ for the nominative and **n* for the narrative. They did not develop articulated forms until quite late, since they had not originally taken articles. It is clear that the new narrative case marker, *-man*, was generalized at a more rapid rate than were the new exponents of the other cases, since we have few contexts in which the nonarticulated form is preserved. If we assume that the narrative case was always marked in the noun itself (not just on the article), then its ending, **n*, disappeared under the influence of *m* of *man*. (The opposite assumption, that case marking was only in the article leads necessarily to the conclusion that declension was the same for common and proper nouns.) This disappearance of **n* in common nouns could account also for its loss in the declension of proper names. Thus, proper names may well have had a narrative case in **n*, just as common nouns had; the **n* then disappeared in all noun declensions when it was lost in the common noun. This is consistent with the fact that narrative case **n* is retained in only a few forms. If this is the way the language developed, then we do not necessarily have to assume different declensional patterns for personal names and common nouns. Table 4.17 shows the declension of personal names in Old Georgian.

The existence of a single syncretic form for the three syntactic cases of the pronouns of the first and second persons and the use of the stem form of proper names as both nominative and narrative case in Old Georgian has been used to argue that there is, beside the accusative system of Series

Table 4.17

Declension of Personal Names in Old Georgian

NOM	*šušanik̥* 'Shushanik'	*abo* 'Abo'
NAR	*šušanik̥*	*abo*
DAT	*šušanik̥-s*	*abo-s*
GEN	*šušanik̥-is*	*abo-ys*
ALL	*šušanik̥-isa*	*abo-ysa*
INST	*šušanik̥-it*	*abo-yt*
ADV	*šušanik̥-ad*	*abo-d*
VOC	*šušanik̥*	*abo*

I and the active system of Series II, an "undifferentiated" system that spans all three series (Chikobava 1948:2–4). This hypothesis has two distinct aspects—synchronic (for Old Georgian) and diachronic. Must we set up a third system of case marking for proper names and pronouns in Old Georgian? No. To do so is an unnecessary complication in the grammar of an already complex language. The shared forms are most simply treated, as they are here, as syncretic forms of different cases. Chikobava further argues on the basis of these facts that CK originally had an undifferentiated case system; that is, that case was not originally used in the coding of grammatical relations. He views proper names and first and second personal pronouns as relics of this system. (A similar view is held by Boeder 1979:457 and Palmaiti 1978, 1979. See also Vogt 1947b:136.) This conclusion is not warranted on the basis of these facts. It is well known that pronouns often exhibit a case system that differs in type from the system for noun case marking in the same language (Silverstein 1976). Yet there is no independent evidence that either pronouns or proper nouns are necessarily conservers of case alignment systems. By itself, the fact that there is syncretism in the cases of pronouns and proper nouns in Kartvelian languages is not sufficient evidence for reconstructing a caseless protolanguage. Those who have used morphology to claim that there was a caseless system have not suggested how this might have developed into the syntactic systems actually attested in the daughter languages. Nor is there any reason to reject a priori the possibility that CK always used a single form for these pronouns and has always had maximal differentiation in the common noun. The fact that there is a firm basis for reconstruction of distinct functions for three grammatical cases in CK (Chaps. 6–12) makes it clear that the position taken by Chikobava (1948) is untenable.

4.6. RECONSTRUCTION OF CK CASES

Although the form of the narrative can be reconstructed as CK **n*, **d* on the basis of Georgian and Svan, no account has been proposed for Zan -*k*. Most Kartvelologists assume that although the exponent of the narrative case in Zan is apparently not derived from a CK protoform, the narrative case itself continues an earlier CK case, to which we may give the same name. This is consistent with the place of the narrative in the paradigms of the daughter languages (see §4.2), and with the history of the functions of the case (Parts II and III below). The origin of Zan -*k* is, however, not known. The most likely account is that Zan -*k* is from CGZ **ak* 'here' or **ik* 'there'. This is similar to the hypothesis described above concerning demonstrative pronouns, and such forms are a frequent source for nominal markers of many sorts (Greenberg 1978). Possible reasons for the replacement of the inherited form by *-k* in Zan are suggested in §15.2.

With respect to the inventory of cases, suggestions have been made that the genitive and instrumental originated as one, that the dative and adverbial were once one (Deeters 1927:20; Topuria 1944), that the instrumental and adverbial are related, and so forth. One such proposal, that the adverbial and narrative originated as a single case (Machavariani 1970; Schmidt 1976), finds support in the fact that both can be reconstructed to CK as **d* with some certainty. If this is correct, then the inventory of reconstructible CK cases is nominative, narrative–adverbial, dative, genitive, and instrumental. Though this hypothesis seems likely to be correct, the conservative course is taken here, treating the narrative and adverbial as separate cases.

It has been shown above that **i* is a shared marker for the nominative case and that *∅ is earlier in this function. Although **i* is shared by all four languages, it may not date to CK. First, the ∅ form is still found in Old Georgian, long after the dissolution of the protolanguage. Second, we might assume that the narrative and nominative were renewed at the same time. Yet the three main branches treat the renewal of the narrative so variously that we cannot assume a unified development for it. Thus, if we assume that the nominative and narrative were renewed at the same time, the diversity of development of the narrative leads us to suppose that **i* was a parallel, rather than a common, development. On the other hand, the renewal of the nominative may have preceded that of the narrative; that cannot be determined at this time.

In conclusion, the exponents of the cases in CK must have included at least those shown in Table 4.18. Also, I have argued that the syncretism that is found in the pronouns of the first and second persons is not sufficient cause for claiming that there was originally no differentiation of case in Kartvelian.

Table 4.18

Summary Reconstruction of CK Case Markers for Nouns in the Singular

NOM	*∅	GEN	**is*$_1$
NAR	**d*/**n*	INST	*(*i*)*s*$_1$*t*
DAT	**s*	ADV	**d*

NOTES

[1]I have followed Shanidze (1976:31ff.) in many respects and have borrowed examples from him. On the exclusion of the absolutive case, see § 4.4, especially §4.4.6.

[2]As part of a more general deletion of final vowels, *-i* may drop from the nominative (Zhghenti 1953:138–140). On the deletion of *-s* and *-k* in some dialects, see §15.5.

[3]While *-k* is always listed in the grammars, *-ku*, *-ki* and *-kə* are also found. In Mingrelian, nominative *-i* is dropped optionally by some speakers.

[4]Kluge (1916:10) records *-ep* also before cases beginning with consonants in the speech of Axali (Novo) Senaḳi: *nin-ep-s*, *nin-ep-k* (or *ninepəkə*) 'tongues'. In the dialect of my consultant from Axali Xibula, the plural morpheme has the form *-em* before cases with consonantal formants: *ḳoč-ep-i* 'man', but *ḳoč-em-s*, *ḳoč-em-k*.

[5]While epenthesis seems the probable origin of *-e* of *-ep-e* in Laz, *p* + C does occur, such as *p* + *t* in conjugation in the present tense (see paradigms in §16.1.4).

[6]Old Georgian had two remote pronouns, *igi* and *isi*, but the latter did not appear before the tenth century (Martirosovi 1964:168) and is therefore not included in Table 4.14. The members of the triplet had additional meanings beyond those stated here.

[7]On CK **a* > *u* in the environment of a bilabial in Zan, see §9.2.1.

[8]Kaldani (1974:151) reconstructs **iǰi* for the remote pronoun in Svan.

[9]Martirosovi (1979) observes that while this generalization is correct, there are exceptions to it. The use of the definite article in Old Georgian was less systematic than that in Greek or Armenian.

[10]The Opiza and Tbeṭi manuscripts omit *mas* in the above example.

[11]On the repetition of the process, drawing from the source demonstrative, see Greenberg (1978:76).

[12]While we cannot identify other clear Svan *d* to Georgian *n* correspondences to support this, there are *d*/*n* alternations within Georgian: (a) inchoative *d* < *n* (Shanidze 1957b), (b) third person plural subject marker of "present habitual," *-ed*, versus third person plural subject marker of "present," *-en*, and (c) third person singular subject markers, *-n* and *-d*, in certain screeves (see Arabuli 1980a; Rogava 1968).

[13]The second (*-w-*) declension may have a similar origin, though the details have not been worked out. On *w*/*v* > *m*, see §9.2 and Chapter 9, note 3.

[14]The form *tkuen-i* exists, but only as a possessive.

[15]Some nonliterary dialects, such as Xevsurian and Tušurian, retain the nonarticulated form (Shanidze 1957a).

[16]The form *misa* exists, but is the allative, not the genitive, case.

[17]Personal names may add *-is* before some case desinences; e.g., *davit-is-it-gan* 'from David' (Imnaishvili 1957:376; Shanidze 1976:42; etc.).

[18]One function of the bare stem is arguably distinct from those of the nominative case. In construction with verbs meaning 'name, call' or 'be named, be called', the epithet is often in stem form (e.g., Mt 1:21). Apparently, however, this construction is in flux, as the epithet could alternatively be marked with the nonarticulated form of the dative (Mt 23:8Ad), instrumental (Mt 23:8AB), or adverbial (J 15:15Ad), or be in apposition to an articulated form of the nominative (Mt 9:9Ad). See Schmidt (1980) on a similar use of the bare stem in Hittite.

5

Series II Predates Series I

Although the nominative, narrative, and dative desinences can be reconstructed for CK, neither the fact that they existed as cases distinct from one another nor the shape of their exponents gives us much help in reconstructing their syntax. The purpose of this chapter and the next is to reconstruct the syntax of case marking in CK on the basis of the systems shown in the daughter languages.

5.1. A PROPOSAL

Consider again the systems sketched in Chapter 3. We must, as a first step, assume that the systems of case marking used in Series I and II in CK were different from one another. Only Laz uses a single system for both series. According to the principle of archaic heterogeneity,[1] we must assume an early differentiation, followed by analogical restructuring in Laz. (The same conclusion is suggested by others, including Chikobava 1948, 1961:5; Deeters 1930; Schmidt 1966:52; and Shanidze 1942:291–292.)

When we compare Series I across the four languages, we find two patterns. Svan, Georgian, and Mingrelian all have in Series I a system of the accusative type, with all subjects marked by the nominative case (*∅, *-*i*) and all objects by the dative (*-*s*). Laz has active alignment in Series I, with active nominals marked with the narrative case (-*k*) and inactive with the nominative (∅). The alignment type found in Svan, Georgian, and Mingrelian must be reconstructed to CK for several reasons. First, given the subgroupings independently established for Kartvelian (Figure 1.2), a single pattern in all three subgroups is best explained as an inherited structure. Second, Laz has a single alignment type in Series I and II; Laz thus had an analogue for changing from the ancestral pattern to that found today. The other three languages do not have identical systems in Series I and II, and therefore had no immediate case analogue for changing Series I. Thus, while the Laz change from an original accusative system is easily accounted for, changes in the Series I systems of the other languages are not so simply explained. Third, the theory of the development of Series I as an accusative system is supported by facts considered in detail in Part III. On this basis I conclude that Series I in CK had accusative case marking, all subjects bearing the nominative case, and all objects the dative. Laz introduced an innovation to Series I, extending the system of Series II to both domains.[2]

When we compare Series II across all four languages, we find two systems. In Svan, Georgian, and Laz, case marking is active; subjects of transitives and of active intransitives are marked with the narrative case, while subjects of inactive intransitives and direct objects are marked with the nominative case. In Mingrelian, on the other hand, Series II case marking is accusative; all subjects are marked with the narrative, and direct objects with the nominative. The alignment type found in Svan, Georgian, and Laz must be considered the older for the following reasons. First, given the subgrouping within Kartvelian, and other things being equal, it must be assumed that a system found in all three subgroups is inherited. It is suggested in Chapter 6 that this active system was predated by a system with a somewhat different alignment; nevertheless, the active system of Series II in Svan, Georgian, and Laz must be older than the accusative system in the same series in Mingrelian. Second, Mingrelian has case marking with accusative alignment in both Series I and II. Although the systems are not identical (see Chap. 3), Series I provided an analogue for the restructuring of Series II case marking in Mingrelian. The development of Mingrelian Series II case marking out of an earlier active alignment is thus easily accounted for, while the reverse change in the sister languages would not be. Third, it is possible to provide a consistent acccount for the development of Series II case marking in the other languages (see below, especially Chapter 14).[3] On these grounds I conclude that active case marking, represented in Svan, Georgian, and Laz, is older in Series II than is the accusative type found in Mingrelian. Mingrelian introduced an innovation, expanding the functions of the narrative case in Series II. (The same conclusion is reached by others, including

Chikobava 1936:105; Deeters 1930:98; and Schmidt 1966:51.) Thus, comparision of the sister languages leads us to reconstruct distinct systems for Late CK, one accusative, the other (tentatively) active.

There is internal evidence that will permit us to go further back than this, to Early CK. An examination of the verbal categories and their expression in Old Georgian and in its sister languages leads to the conclusion that Series II is older than Series I. That this is so is shown by (a) the fact that the verbal forms of Series I are more complex than those of Series II, (b) the fact that Series I preserves a number of syntactic, morphological, and phonological traits of Series II as relics, and (c) the fact that we can see in the evolution of Georgian a development from Series I being marked relative to Series II towards the reversed relation. This is consistent with the principle that a newer formation tends to spread at the expense of the old.

Evidence to support the hypothesis that Series II is older than Series I is given below in §5.2, 5.3, and 5.4. It must be borne in mind, however, that some of the arguments adduced above, and expanded in §5.2 and in later chapters, in fact demonstrate only that Series II VERB FORMS are older than those of Series I. Because in the Kartvelian languages the verb form strictly governs the case pattern (see Chap. 3), for now we may assume as a working hypothesis that a case system correlated with Series II is also more ancient than that correlated with Series I. In §5.3 an argument is given to support DIRECTLY the age of a Series II case marking system relative to that of Series I. Further, the correctness of the hypothesis that a case system correlated with Series II is ancient is amply demonstrated by its explanatory power with respect to the origin of Series I (see Part III of this work).

5.2. TENSE, MOOD, AND ASPECT IN KARTVELIAN

It has already been explained that the series in the Kartvelian languages are sets of tense–mood–aspect paradigms. These paradigms are traditionally referred to as SCREEVES. In general, a screeve expresses one tense, one aspect, and one mood. For example, in Old Georgian the screeve that is called "aorist" expresses past time, indicative mood, and punctual aspect. Each screeve has a marker, which may be zero, a special ablaut grade, and/or one or more suffixes. Within a screeve, all other grammatical categories exist; every screeve has both active and mediopassive voice, has all versions, and so forth. With few exceptions, each person and number of each grammatical relation can be expressed in every screeve. In some instances the suffix of person and/or number interacts with the suffix that is the exponent of the screeve and in this way causes variation within a screeve.

5.2.1. The Series I and II Systems of Screeves in Old Georgian

There are significant differences between the inventory of screeves in Old Georgian after the ninth century and that of the oldest texts;[4] only the earliest system is described here. The description of screeves that follows is somewhat simplified, omitting details that are not relevant to reconstruction.

The inventory of screeves may be given as in Table 5.1. Series I opposes Series II aspectually, and this opposition is marked by the presence versus absence of a series marker, which for some verbs is zero. All of the forms of Series I are of durative aspect, while those of Series II are punctual, with the exception of the habitual II (Machavariani 1974; Schmidt 1963, 1966). The habitual II expresses durative, continuous (ongoing), or repeated action; Machavariani (1974:123) characterizes it as the only screeve that expresses only aspect, and not time or mood.

In each series, contrasting with the indicative screeves, there is a subjunctive; the same form also expresses the future indicative. In addition, there is an imperative in each series; this is incompletely distinguished from the past tense indicative of the corresponding series, differing from it only by minor markers (see Tables 5.2, 5.3, and 5.7).

In the indicative, past and present have distinct sets of forms. Future time is usually expressed by the subjunctive; it may also be depicted by the present (Natadze 1961) or through various analytic constructions (Kavtaradze 1960).

Thus, the habitual II corresponds to the present and the present habitual, the aorist to the imperfect and the imperfect habitual, the subjunctive II to the subjunctive I, and the imperative II to the imperative I.[5] The correspondence is imperfect, however, since the habitual II is not punctual

Table 5.1

Inventory of Screeves in Oldest Georgian

Series I	Series II
Present	Habitual II
Present habitual	—
Imperfect	Aorist
Imperfect habitual	—
Subjunctive I	Subjunctive II
Imperative I	Imperative II

Table 5.2

Paired Third Person Subject Markers in Old Georgian

	Singular	Plural
Set A	*-s*	*-en* (*-an*/ + *i* + ___; *-n*/ $\begin{bmatrix} V \\ -\text{high} \end{bmatrix}$ + ___)[a]
Set B	*-a* (*o*/*v* + ___)	*-es*
Set C	*-n*	*-ed*

[a]Apparently the observation that **en* > *an*/ + *i* + ___ was first made by Rogava (1968).

Table 5.3

Formation of Screeves in Old Georgian

	Series I: root + SM + ___		Series II: root + ___	
	Major marker	Minor marker	Major marker	Minor marker
Present indicative	*∅*/*i*[a] *∅*/*i*	A C	*i*	A
Past indicative	*d-*(*i*)/*od-e*[b] *d-i*/*od-e*	B A	*e*/*∅*/*i*	B
Future and subjunctive	*d-e*/*od-i*	A	*o*/*e*/*a*	A
Imperative	*d-*(*i*)/*od-e*	C	*e*/*∅*/*i*	C

[a]The present screeve marker *-i* is found in forms such as *ṭp-eb-i-s* 'it is getting warm', *i-ç̣er-eb-i-s* 'it is being written', and *ṭir-i-s* 'he is crying' (see §9.5).
[b]The distribution of *-i* versus *-e* with *-od* is discussed in Shanidze (1945).

like the rest of the screeves in its series, and since there are "extra" screeves in Series I.

Morphologically, the symmetry of the system is also imperfect. The various screeves are distinguished from one another by ablaut grade and by (a) the presence versus absence of a series marker (*-av*/*ev*, *-eb*, etc.), (b) the major screeve marker, which consists of one or more suffixes, and (c) the minor screeve marker, which is the specific exponent of the third person subject, chosen from those in Table 5.2.[6] The formation of the screeves of both series is schematized in Table 5.3. The Series I stem is formed by the addition of the series marker (SM). In both series, the screeve is formed by the addition of one of the indicated major screeve markers. The person and number markers for subject and object are added to this; the third person subject markers differ by screeve, as indicated by the specification of minor marker, referring by letter to sets specified in Table 5.2. An example conjugation is given in Table 5.7.

In Table 5.3, we see both symmetrical and asymmetrical elements. The symmetry is preserved in the partial use of the Series II major and minor screeve markers in the Series I screeve that corresponds in tense and mood (horizontally on the chart). For example, the subjunctive marker, *-e* (probably CK, see below), from Series II is repeated in the subjunctive of Series I. The destruction of the original symmetry, which has gone even further in Modern Georgian, is seen in the introduction of the present habitual and imperfect habitual and the introduction of additional major screeve markers; later the minor screeve markers were also altered in ways that helped to destroy the symmetry.

5.2.2. Origin of the System

The system described above was preceded by one consisting only of forms that are continued by Series II screeves. In this protosystem the primary opposition was aspectual (see e.g., Kavtaradze 1954:322; Schmidt 1966); the punctual (later, aorist) opposed the durative (later, habitual II).[7] A second opposition was that of indicative, including both durative and punctual, to subjunctive. The differentiation that is preserved as oppositions between different sets of third person subject markers (see Table 5.2) may be relic of an additional opposition, but is now not recoverable. This system, exemplified in Table 5.4, may be ascribed to Early CK.

The system represented in Table 5.4 was renewed by the creation of a new set of forms—all durative in aspect—to oppose the old set; at the same time the category of tense was introduced by reinterpreting old forms. At this stage there must have been a punctual past (aorist) of Series II opposing a durative past (imperfect) of Series I, a punctual imperative (imperative II) opposing a durative imperative (imperative I), and a punctual subjunctive future (subjunctive I). For each, the new was formed from the old by the addition of a series marker plus the suffix *d/od* plus the old

Table 5.4

Basic Oppositions in Early Common Kartvelian

Category	Form
Durative aspect	stem + **i*
Punctual aspect	stem + ?
Subjunctive	stem + **e*

major marker of past, imperative, or subjunctive future, respectively. The parallelism breaks down for the old durative. It could hardly be reinterpreted as the opposite of what it has once been. Instead, it continued to function as a durative, expressing no particular time. With it was paired a new durative that specifically expressed present time.

Table 5.5, which omits ablaut and the imperative, presents a simplified overview of the inherited and the innovative series. A number of details are debatable, but the table establishes the systematic correspondences—with respect to tense, aspect, mood, and their morphological expression—that most likely underlie the systems we find today in the several daughter languages.[8] As can be seen in Table 5.5, in Middle and Late Common Kartvelian, the series, each representing an aspect, were kept distinct by the series markers and the suffix **d*, as well as by ablaut (see Chap. 8), which does not appear in the table. The horizontally adjacent screeves, having a common tense and mood, were kept similar by the use of common major and minor makers.

Table 5.5

Basic Oppositions Reconstructed for Middle and Late Common Kartvelian

Innovative system (Series I)	Inherited system (Series II)
Present: root + SM + (**i*)	Habitual: root + **i*
(Minor markers A)	(Minor markers A)
present	—
indicative	—
durative	durative
Imperfect: root + SM + **d* + Ø/(**i*)	Aorist: root + Ø/(**i*)
(Minor markers B)	(Minor markers B)
past	past
indicative	indicative
durative	punctual
Subjunctive I: root + SM + **d* + **e*	Subjunctive II: root + **e*
(Minor markers A)	(Minor markers A)
irrealis	irrealis
durative	punctual

5.2.3. Development of the System in the Modern Languages

All of the modern languages have separately made changes in fundamental features of the system described above. We must attribute the similarity of the individual changes to a combination of (a) fulfilling the impetus of changes made during the period before division into distinct languages (i.e., slant; see Malkiel 1981:553) and (b) the influence of Georgian, as the only literary language, over its nonliterary sister languages.

All of the modern Kartvelian languages, with the exception of some conservative dialects, have made the following changes in the tense–mood–aspect system of CK:

1. The original durative versus punctual opposition has been reinterpreted as an imperfective versus perfective opposition (see Machavariani 1974).
2. This opposition is now expressed, at least in part, through the absence versus presence of a preverb (see Machavariani 1974:133, 136). In the original system the preverb did not have this function; the aspectual opposition was based on screeve differences, expressed by stem or suffix variation.
3. From Series II the habitual II screeve has been dropped.
4. To Series I has been added a new subseries, formed by the addition of a preverb to the older screeves. The preverb + present functions as a future, the preverb + imperfect as a conditional, and the preverb + subjunctive as a future perfective subjunctive. The old subjunctives have lost their function of expressing the future.

Each of these changes can be traced through Georgian in historical times.

This represents the general picture, but there are deviations from it. For example, Machavariani (1974:134) observes that Laz preserves the future meaning for the old subjunctive II, while also having the new future formed from preverb + present. Other variations of detail are described in Machavariani (1974:133–140).

Trends 3 and 4 as well as language-particular developments, destroyed the symmetry of the system represented in Table 5.5 (see Holisky 1981b on Modern Georgian). The various daughter languages, however, found ways to maintain certain facets of the system. Svan, for example, developed an opposition between a "two-theme" and a "five-theme," which exists only in the past tenses (aorist and imperfect). This refers to formal differences between first and second person singular subject forms on the one hand, and third person singular subjects and plural subjects of any person (inclusive or exclusive) on the other (see Topuria 1967). One result of this development in Svan is that the parallelism between the aorist and imperfect has been renewed.

An important point to be made here is that the decrease in the number of forms in Series II (loss of habitual II), the increase in the number of forms in Series I (creation of new future subseries), and the increase in the occurrence of Series I relative to Series II from Old Georgian into

Modern Georgian; see Shanidze 1957c, §46) are all consistent with the hypothesis that Series I is newer than Series II.

5.2.4. A Putative Problem

It has long been accepted by Kartvelologists of all persuasions that Series I is formed from Series II, the latter being the older (Boeder 1979:460–463; Chikobava 1942:233; 1943, 1948; Deeters 1930:115; Kavtaradze 1954:13; Nebieridze, in press; Pätsch 1952:5; Rogava 1975:275; Schmidt 1973:115). As above, this has been established on the grounds that the Series I forms are complex, relative to those of Series II. Machavariani (1974:129ff.) has, however, objected that for one type of verb this is not true. While he accepts that the Series I forms of 'kill' (e.g., *v-ḳl-av* 'I kill him') are derived historically from the Series II forms of this verb (e.g., *v-ḳal* 'I killed him') by the addition of a series marker (here *-av*), he objects that verbs like *-ç̣er-* and *-ṭex-* provide no evidence of such a diachronic relationship. Machavariani's objection is based upon the comparisons in Table 5.6 (1974:29–30). While accepting that for verbs like *ḳal*, Series I derives from Series II, Machavariani claims that for verbs like those in Table 5.6, Series II derives from Series I.

Machavariani's argument is, however, an artifact of the view of the individual series that is prevalent among Georgian scholars. They consider that the aorist is the base on which Series II is formed, and that the present is the base for the formation of Series I screeves. There is support for this view in Series I, since for many verbs the present screeve forms are actually part of the form of all other screeves, though there are some morphological changes involved.[9] For example, *v-ḳl-av* 'I kill him' (present) is contained in *v-ḳl-ev-d-(i)* 'I was killing him' (imperfect) and *v-ḳl-ev-d-e* 'I will kill him' (subjunctive I), with *av* > *ev*. In Series II, on the other hand, the notion of the aorist as stem is not workable. First, the aorist of a verb like *v-ç̣er-e* 'I wrote it' (aorist) is not contained in forms of the other screeves: *v-ç̣er-i* 'I write it' (habitual II) and *v-ç̣er-o* 'I will write it' (subjunctive II). Kiknadze (1947:320), arguing for the notion of the aorist as stem, suggests that the aorist marker *-e* is deleted under the influence

Table 5.6

Present and Aorist Forms of *ç̣er* and *ṭex*

	Series I		Series II	
ç̣er	*v-ç̣er*	'I write it'	*v-ç̣er-e*	'I wrote it'
ṭex	*v-ṭex*	'I break it'	*v-ṭex-e*	'I broke it'

of *-i* of the habitual II and *-o* of the subjunctive II in such instances. Note, however, that no such deletion occurs in other comparable situations; for example, the nominative (*-i*) and vocative (*-o*) case markers do not delete a preceding *-e*: *moçape-y* (<**moçape-i*) 'student, disciple (NOM)', *moçape-o* (VOC). In this example, *e* is part of a circumfix *mo—e*, which means that the environment is identical to that of the verb forms from a morphological as well as phonological point of view: (-)ROOT + *e* + *i*, (-)ROOT + *e* + *o*. The fact that *-i* and *-o* do not trigger deletion of a preceding *e* elsewhere makes it difficult to believe that the aorist form in *-e* is the stem for the other screeves of Series II. In addition, as long as we distinguish synchrony from diachrony, there is no reason to view one tense (screeve) of a series as derived synchronically from another in that series. While the habitual II and subjunctive II may or may not have been derived diachronically from the aorist, there is no advantage to viewing them this way synchronically. The alternative, which I support, is to derive a Series I stem and a Series II stem from the verb root; from the series stem, the individual screeves are then formed synchronically. From a diachronic point of view, Series I derived from Series II, not the present from the aorist.

In considering verbs of the type cited by Machavariani, it is necessary, for the reasons presented above, to consider each series as a whole, not just first person subject forms of the aorist and the present. A more complete paradigm is presented for comparison as Table 5.7, with all singular subject persons. It should be clear from Table 5.7 that selecting only the first person subject forms and comparing only the present (of a verb with a zero series maker) and aorist distorts the situation. When viewed as a whole, Series I is considerably more complex than Series II, even for verbs such as *çer* and *ṭex*. Even if we discount the Series I screeves that have no equivalent in Series II, and even if we do not consider the optional final *-i* of some forms, the number and complexity of formants in Series I are clearly greater than in Series II.

5.2.5. Conclusion

In this section I have argued that, because Series I is a morphologically complex version of Series II, it is reasonable to view the former as derived from the latter. Series I is formed from Series II by the addition of a series marker; individual screeves are formed from this stem by the addition of ∅ or the formant *d/od* and major and minor screeve markers, themselves from Series II.

The arguments presented above establish only that Series II verb forms are older than those of Series I. It is only by extension that we may infer

Table 5.7

Paradigm of *ç̣er* 'write' in Singular Subject Forms in Old Georgian

Series I		Series II	
Present	*v-ç̣er* *s-ç̣er* *ç̣er-s*	Habitual II	*v-ç̣er-i* *s-ç̣er-i* *ç̣er-i-s*
Present habitual	*ç̣er-n*		
Imperfect	*v-ç̣er-d-(i)* *s-ç̣er-d-(i)* *ç̣er-d-a*	Aorist	*v-ç̣er-e* *s-ç̣er-e* *ç̣er-a*
Imperfect habitual	*v-ç̣er-d-i* *s-ç̣er-d-i* *ç̣er-d-i-s*		
Subjunctive I	*v-ç̣er-d-e* *s-ç̣er-d-e* *ç̣er-d-e-s*	Subjunctive II	*v-ç̣er-o* *s-ç̣er-o* *ç̣er-o-s*
Imperative I	*ç̣er-d-(i)* *ç̣er-d-i-n*	Imperative II	*ç̣er-e* *ç̣er-e-n*

that the case marking associated with Series II is also older than that of Series I.[10] We are justified in making this inference as a working hypothesis because of the strong coherence in Kartvelian between the morphology of a verb form and the case pattern of the nominals it governs, because of the additional argument given in §5.3 below, and because of the explanatory value of this hypothesis as demonstrated in Part III of this work.

5.3. *ICIS* AND *UÇQ̇IS* 'KNOW'

The irregular verbs *icis* and *uçq̇is* 'know' provide a second argument that the use of narrative case subjects is older than the case system of Series I. In Old Georgian these verbs preserve the case marking system of Series II as a relic in Series I. Their status as relics is established on the basis of (a) their irregularity, described below, (b) the fact that *uçq̇is* died out in historical times, a step toward regularization, and (c) the fact that in some nonstandard dialects the case marking has been regularized (Imnaishvili 1959:185).

In Old Georgian, both verbs occur in Series I forms governing a narrative case subject and a nominative case direct object (see Chikobava 1948:65–69).

(1) *romel-man-igi* *ara* *icoda* *codva-y*
which/REL-NAR-DET NEG he/know/it/I sin-NOM
'he who did not know sin' (2 Cor 5:21)

(2) *rametu uçqoda* *γmert-man*
for he/know/it/I God-NAR
'For God knew it.' (Gen 3:5)

Could this case marking pattern be attributed to the verbs' being perfective presents as in Germanic? There is no doubt that the Series I forms of these verbs are derived from Series II forms, just as for all verbs. However, in Old Georgian the forms are not Series II forms. One sign of this is the use of the suffix *-od* in *i-c-od-a* in (1) and *ucq-od-a* in (2); this suffix characterizes Series I and is not found in Series II in the earliest texts (see note 4). Second, while the present screeve forms *u-çq-i-s* and *i-c-i-s* could be interpreted instead as forms of the habitual II, the forms of the present habitual, such as in (3), are unambiguously Series I forms (see Table 5.7).

(3) a. *romeli* *valn* *bnelsa* *ara* ***uçqin***
who/REL/NOM he/go/I dark/DAT neg he/know/it/I
vidre *valn* (J 12:35 Ad,B)
where he/go/I
b. *romeli valn bnelsa ara* ***icin*** *vidre valn* (J 12:35 A)
'He who goes in the dark does not know where he goes.'

Thus it is clear that these two verbs have forms that belong to Series I, yet govern the case marking pattern of Series II. This remains true of the verb *icis* even in Modern Georgian. The case marking governed by these verbs represents a relic of an earlier system (Series II) in a later one.[11]

5.4. CONCLUDING STATEMENT

There is a great deal of evidence to support the hypothesis that Series I developed out of Series II. However, much of this relates also to HOW that development took place; because it requires a lengthy exposition, this is deferred until Part III. The evidence referred to is therefore only summarized below.

As observed, the verbs *icis* and *uçqis* 'know' preserve the syntax of Series II as a relic in Series I. The general system of case marking in Series I, on the other hand, preserves the object demotion construction, which is associated with durative (later, imperfective) aspect of Series I (see Chaps. 7 and 11).

With respect to morphology, those categories that are not affected by the syntactic–aspectual development of Series I are retained there intact; these categories include the person and number agreement of subjects, version, inversion, synthetic passives, among others. The number agreement (*en*) associated with direct objects in Series II is retained in Series I only as a relic (see Chap. 10). The agreement of indirect objects is directly affected by the syntactic change that took place in Series I (see Chap. 12). The aspectual change is coded in the series markers of Series I, which directly indicate durative aspect, (see Chap. 9).

Finally, the phonological evidence that Series II is older than Series I is developed in Chapter 8. There it is shown that although the alternation between stem vowels *e* and *i* was originally phonological, they were reanalyzed as ablaut grades marking the surface transitivity of a clause. Only in this way can the distribution of the various ablaut grades in the daughter languages be explained.

On the basis of the arguments developed in this chapter and in Part III, I conclude that Series II predates Series I and that the case marking system of the former predates that of the latter. We now turn to a detailed examination of the case marking system of Series II, the most ancient in Kartvelian.

NOTES

[1]"If a number of cognate languages each have a system similar to its homologues in the other languages in some respects, but different in other respects—unless one can find a clear conditioning factor for differentiation—the relatively most heterogeneous system might be considered the most archaic, the closest to the ancestor, and the more homogeneous ones might be assumed to have arisen as a result of simplification" (Hetzron 1976:93).

Watkins (1976:315–316) also notes that where both a marked and an unmarked pattern are attested in several daughters, the comparative method requires that both be reconstructed in the protolanguage.

[2]Further support for this view is found in one Laz dialect that preserves a stage transitional between the reconstructed Series I system and the Series I system found in other Laz dialects. This dialect is described in §15.3.3. According to Chikobava (1936:181–182), in this dialect, orally transmitted poetry preserves instances of the reconstructed accusative system, although it is not acceptable in speech.

[3]Evidence that the Series II system in Mingrelian is transitional is that it violates otherwise valid linguistic universals, as discussed in §15.3.1.

[4]Beginning in the ninth century, the *šereuli ḳavširebiti* and the *šereuli xolmeobiti* are attested (Imnaishvili 1977, Kiknadze 1967, observation attributed to Sha-

nidze). The imperfect habitual, while it was originally thought to be a late innovation, did occur in the earliest texts (Kiknadze 1961).

[5]Many Kartvelologists consider, with good reason, that the present and present habitual are one screeve, permitting an alternation in the markers of third person subjects (Arabuli 1980a; Chikobava 1968a: 136, 163; Rogava 1968; Topuria 1953:521). The imperfect habitual is probably a secondary formation, Series I having already begun to expand in Old Georgian times.

[6]Third person subject markers are not traditionally analyzed in this way but are stated individually for each screeve. This obscures the fact that the minor markers of each Series II screeve were carried over to the corresponding primary screeves of Series I.

[7]This discussion is limited to organic formations; there is also a periphrastic subjunctive in Old Georgian (*mca*) and Svan (*u, w, ow, uw, oγ,* etc.) (Topuria 1967:61).

[8]The series markers are reconstructed in Chap. 9. The suffix **d* (?<**ed*) is reconstructed here on the basis of Georgian *d*, Laz *ṭ*, Mingrelian *d*, and Svan *d*, and is intended to stand also for other ancient markers of the imperfect (see Kaldani 1968; Machavariani 1980; Topuria 1967: 74, 81–84, 105–106). The suffix of the present–habitual II is reconstructed as **i* (?<**ey*; see Gamkrelidze and Machavariani 1965:227) on the basis of *i* in both screeves in Old Georgian (see Table 5.3, fn. *a*) and *i* in the present in Svan. The marker of the past tense is problematic, but Svan evidence supports both **i* and ∅ in the aorist (Kaldani 1978), and this is confirmed by all three of the other languages. Probably there were additional allomorphs of the past tense marker, one with the reflex *-e* in Old Georgian. The original distribution is not recoverable at this time. The exponent of the subjunctive can be reconstructed as **e* on the basis of Laz, Mingrelian *-a* (the regular reflex of CK **e*) in both subjunctives, Georgian *-e* in both, and Svan *-e* in both (see Chikobava 1929b:116ff.)

[9]Even so, for many verbs forms in Series I, including all synthetic passives, the whole present is not part of the other screeves; e.g., *v-ṭir-i* 'I cry', but *v-ṭir-od-e* 'I was crying'.

[10]This is emphasized here because the complexity argument has been used, notably in Chikobava (1948), with the implication that the relative age of the verb forms constituted proof of the relative age of the two case marking systems.

[11]The verbs 'know' may have developed this irregularity in the following way. When the syntactic construction that became Series I originated, these verbs did not govern Object Demotion (see Chap. 7), because this construction was associated with durative–imperfective aspect, and these verbs were atelic, not allowing the expression of aspectual opposition. Evidence that their direct objects remained direct objects is, in addition to the case marking itself, the occurrence of *-en* (see Chap. 10), as in

(4)	*iesu*	*icnoda*	*gulis*	***zraxva-ni***	*matni*
	Jesus/NAR	he/know/them/I	heart/GEN	thought-PL/NOM	their

'Jesus knew the thoughts of their heart(s).' (L 9:47)

6

Reconstruction of Series II Case Marking

In Chapter 5, I showed that a case marking system associated with Series II must be older than that of Series I. On the basis of the system of the active type found in Georgian, Laz, and Svan, I tentatively reconstructed CK Series II as belonging also to the active type. In this chapter I show that each of these languages has internal evidence of an earlier ergative system. On this basis, I reconstruct Series II case marking as originally ergative, having later developed into active.

It is useful here to consider again the difference between ergative and active types, as defined in Chapter 1 and repeated in Table 6.1. The sole difference between the two types we are concerned with in this chapter is

Table 6.1

Some Alignment Types[a]

	Direct object	Subject of intransitive		Subject of transitive
		Inactive	Active	
Ergative	A	A		B
Active	A	A	B	B
Accusative	A	B		B

[a]After Sapir (1917).

the marking assigned to the subjects of active intransitives, and it is on this that the discussion centers. In an ergative system, the subject of an active intransitive is marked like that of an inactive intransitive (case A); while in an active system, this nominal is marked like the subject of a transitive (case B). Thus, at issue is whether the subjects of active intransitives in CK were marked with the nominative or narrative case.

Section 6.1 takes up some methodological considerations in the use of internal reconstruction in syntax. In the sections that follow, examples of variation of subject case marking with basic and derived intransitives are presented. Variations with basic intransitives in Georgian are discussed in §6.2, examples from Laz in §6.3, and from Svan in §6.4. Mingrelian is omitted from the discussion in this chapter because it underwent further changes in Series II obscuring the original system, as described in Chapters and 15. In §6.5, variations in subject case governed by basic intransitives with cognates among the languages are presented. In §6.6, derived intransitives from all three languages are described. In §6.7 these data are interpreted using internal reconstruction, and it is argued that in CK an ergative system of case marking must have been used. Some additional characteristics of this CK system are discussed in §6.8. Section 6.9 presents an overview of the reconstruction made in Chapters 3 through 6 and of the changes that subsequently took place, which are discussed in more detail in Parts III and IV.

6.1. SYNTACTIC RELICS

On the basis of the discussion in previous chapters, it can be seen that in Kartvelian languages there is a strong cohesion between syntactic properties and morphological class membership. In general, semantic, syntactic, and morphological characteristics of intransitives fall together in the way summarized in Table 6.2. The morphological characteristics indicated here as "Class 2" and "Class 3" are different for each language and refer to the properties discussed in Chapter 3. The syntactic property stated as "initial subject" or "initial direct object" refers to the analysis described in §3.2.2 and in greater detail in Harris (1981b:Chap. 16) and in Harris (1982). The cases listed in Table 6.2 were established in Chapter 3 and refer to the subject case governed by these verbs in Series II in Georgian and Svan, and in both Series I and II in Laz; it is not applicable to Mingrelian (see Chap. 3). Although these characteristics generally coincide in the way indicated, there are exceptions in each language. The exceptions provide important evidence for internal reconstruction, and it is these that are the topics of §6.2, §6.3, and §6.4.

Table 6.2

Morphological–Syntactic–Semantic Correlations: Intransitives

Morphological	Syntactic	Semantic
Class 2	intransitive initial direct object nominative case	inactive telic or stative
Class 3	intransitive initial subject narrative case	active atelic

It was observed in Chapter 3 that active intransitives seldom occur in Series II in Old Georgian. Some verbs of this type substitute transitives in Series II (see Chap. 14), while others use a Series I form, even where Old Georgian needs Series II (see §3.4). In all of the modern languages this same class of verbs regularly uses Series II forms. Is the Old Georgian evidence to be taken as an indication that originally these verbs lacked Series II forms? We know that many of the verbs with basic reflexes in Class 3 date back to CK. For example, CK **ḳi* 'screech, cry out' (Klimov 1964:53) has reflexes in Georgian *ḳivis* (present), Svan (Lašx) *lenḳīle* (aorist), Laz *ḳiams*, Mingrelian *rḳians* (present). CK **br* (Klimov 1964:53) has reflexes in Svan (Lašx) *eǰnēm lenbriāle* 'he/NAR sang' and in Mingrelian and Laz *ḳočik ibiru* 'man/NAR sang'. Svan (Lašx) *lengwāne* 'he wept' is cognate with Mingrelian *ingaru*, Laz *imgaru*, and Georgian *iglova* in the same meaning (see Chikobava 1938:259; Topuria 1942b:495). CK **γar/γr* (Klimov 1964:201) has reflexes in Georgian, *man imγera* 'he/NAR sang', Svan *eǰnēm lenγarāle* (Lašx) in the same meaning. CK **bγa* 'howl, yell' has reflexes in Georgian *bγavis* (present), Laz *mγoraps,* Mingrelian *γorans* (present), and Svan (Lašx) *lenbγəle* (aorist). From this it is clear that basic active intransitives existed in CK. Since CK originally had only those verb screeves with direct reflexes in Series II, not Series I (see Chap. 5), we must assume that these CK verbs had forms in what became Series II. The restriction of most active intransitives to Series I in Old Georgian can only be a secondary development, undoubtedly reflecting the incompatibility between their atelic nature and the fact; that Series II expressed punctual–perfective aspect (see Holisky 1981a; Shanidze 1973:483–484). As we see below, a few active intransitives occur as relics in Series II, preserving the morphology that they had before Class 3 became distinct.

In the sections that follow, I present examples of verbs that show variation between narrative and nominative as the case governed for subjects in Series II. This sort of variation is not part of the productive patterns of the languages, except for Class 3 verbs in the Nak̹ra-Laxamula dialect (§6.4.1); it is highly restricted, and in all instances is lexically governed. In some instances the variation is between languages (§6.5, 6.6.2), in some between dialects (§6.2.1, 6.4.2) or between stages (§6.2.2) of a single language, in some it is synchronic in a single dialect (§6.3.1, 6.3.2, 6.4.1). Sections 6.2–6.5 deal with variations governed by basic intransitives; section 6.6.2 concerns variations with derived intransitives where the variants are not necessarily cognate but belong to the same narrowly defined subtypes.

The sorts of variation documented here clearly indicate change. In determining the direction of change and in reconstructing the original situation, we depend upon the method of internal reconstruction. This method is based upon the controlled use of exceptions as indications of the system of an earlier stage (Kuryłowicz 1964:10; Meillet 1954:27; 1964:46; Watkins 1976). With respect to the problem at hand, the regular system for Georgian, Laz, and Svan is for active intransitives to govern narrative case subjects in Series II, as described in Chapter 3 and summarized in Table 6.2. The few active intransitives that govern nominative case subjects are exceptions. Among basic intransitives, two types of exception are found, which can be characterized in terms of Table 6.2. (a) The first type has morphological and syntactic properties predominantly or entirely of Class 2; its semantics, however, are characteristic of Class 3. (b) The second type has inconsistent grammatical properties: They govern nominative case subjects in Series II but otherwise have syntactic and morphological characteristics of Class 3 verbs.

The status of an expression as a relic can be confirmed by certain established characteristics. Relics are likely to occur among the most common expressions of a language (Meillet 1964:31–32). They are likely to be regularized in the course of history. Relics are likely to be preserved in a literary language, particularly where prescriptive grammar is taught in schools.

In determining the direction of a change, it is important to take into consideration the relationships among the languages involved, as described in §2.2.5. In a language like Georgian with a long written history, we can sometimes trace changes through comparison of different stages. In languages like Svan and Laz that lack a written history, it may be more difficult to identify the direction of change. However, because we are dealing with closely related sister languages, if a direction of change can be clearly identified in Georgian, we are justified in assuming that the change took the same direction in the sister languages as long as there is no evidence to the contrary. Diffusion is always a possibility where related languages remain contiguous, and directions of influence need also to be taken into consideration in determining directions of change.

In §6.7, the method of internal reconstruction is applied, using the exceptions discussed in the sections that follow.

6.2. GEORGIAN

6.2.1. Active Intransitives in Class 2

The first set of exceptions discussed are of type (a) above, having a discrepancy between grammatical and semantic characteristics. Because there is little inconsistency among the grammatical properties of these verbs, they have not been thought of as irregularities or relics by other investigators.

In Old Georgian three verb roots are commonly used for ‘come, go’; the directional differences may be expressed by means of preverbs such as *mi-* ‘thither’, *mo-* ‘hither’, *aγ-* ‘up’, *aγmo-* ‘up here’, and so forth, which combine with any of these roots and have no effect on the syntax. In Old Georgian two of these three roots, *vid* and *qed*, occur in Series II. Two examples are cited below:

(1) *ese* *movida* *p̣ilaṭesa*
he/NOM he/come/II Pilate/DAT
‘He came to Pilate.’ (Mt 27:58B)

(2) *ese* *miuqda* *p̣ilaṭes*
he/NOM he/go/II Pilate/DAT
‘He went to Pilate.’ (Mt 27:58Ad)

Example (1) contains the verb *mo-vid* ‘come’, and (2) the verb *mi-qd* (√*qad*) ‘go’; a third verb, *val*, completes the set of roots that, with an appropriate directional preverb, indicated ‘come’, ‘go’.

The ‘come, go’ set could occur as active, controllable verbs, as in (1) and (2), or as inactive, noncontrollable ones, as in example (3).

(3) *da* *mqie-ni* *gamouqdes* *mas*
and grey-PL/NOM they/come.out/to.him/II him/DAT
‘And he got gray hairs.’ (Lit., ‘And gray hairs came to him.’)
(Hosea 7:9)

It is entirely characteristic of the Kartvelian languages that one verb form regularly governs only one case pattern as an active or inactive verb regardless of variation in activeness in a particular context. With few exceptions (see below), these verbs show consistent properties of Class 2 verbs, morphologically and syntactically.

During the course of Georgian, this set has been restricted in the following ways: (a) The verb *qad* has been lost in the meaning 'come/go'. (b) The remaining two roots combined to form a suppletive paradigm, which in Standard Modern Georgian retains its Class 2 morphological and syntactic properties. (c) Another root in the same meaning has the regular syntax of an active verb but remains highly restricted in use (see Shanidze 1973:510; Tschenkéli 1960–1974:1221, 1237).

(4) *gela-m gaiara saxlidan*
Gela-NAR he/go/II house/from
'Gela went out of the house.'

The verbs meaning 'sit' (*da-ǰdoma, da-sxdoma*), 'stand' (*a(γ)-dgoma, da-dgoma*), and 'lie' (*da-ç̣ola*) are a special class. They exist in paired active and inactive forms (e.g., 'stand up, move into a standing position' versus 'be standing'). The inactives fit the regular pattern of the language in being members of Class 2 with the syntactic characteristics typical of this class. Although we would expect the semantically active member of each pair to belong to Class 3, each belongs to Class 2 and governs the nominative case. This unexpected membership in Class 2 has been maintained in Standard Modern Georgian, e.g., *is daǰda* 'he/NOM sat down'.

In §2.1.2 it was observed that some languages classify a verb of a particular meaning as active, while other languages treat a verb of apparently the same meaning as inactive. For this reason, the verbs cited above might be dismissed as peculiarities of Georgian (or Kartvelian), were it not for certain facts. First, 'come, go' is attested with a narrative case subject, although this is extremely rare.

(5) *mama-man mat-man ksenepore ç̣arvida da ganq̣ida*
father-NAR their-NAR Ksenepore he/go/II and he/sell/it/II
q̣ovel-i-ve monag-eb-i tvis-i
all-NOM-even possession-COL-NOM self's-NOM
'Their father, Ksenepore, went and sold all his possessions.'
(Cxorebay Ksenaporesi da mokalakobay misi, Sin. 52:98; cited in Kiziria 1963:113, n. 4.)

Example (5) shows that although this verb is classified as a member of Class 2, speakers felt this classification to be inconsistent with its semantics in some contexts. The restrictions described above that were placed on the Class 2 verbs meaning 'come, go', and the fact that a new Class 3 verb in this meaning has been introduced, albeit in a limited way, add support to the view that speakers felt an inconsistency in the classification of these verbs.

Second, the distribution of the suffix *-en/n* in Old Georgian shows that speakers classified the active members of the 'sit', 'stand', and 'lie' pairs as grammatically active in spite of the fact that they governed nominative case subjects in Series II and had other syntactic characteristics of Class 2. In Chapter 10 it is shown that plural final subjects of Class 2 verbs condition the plural direct object marker *-en/n*, while those of Class 3 verbs do not. Final subjects of inactive members of the pairs 'sit', 'stand', and 'lie' may trigger this marker; final subjects of the active members do not; e.g., *e-dg-**n**-es* 'they stood to him', that is, 'he had them' (Kekelidze 1918:45, 19) versus *še-u-dg-es* 'they stood to him', that is, 'they followed him' (see §10.1.4 and §10.2.2). In general, plural nominative subjects trigger *En*-Agreement in Series II; the fact that subjects of these active verbs do not is evidence of inconsistency in the classification.

Third, irregularities in both of the sets discussed above, as well as some other irregularities, have been partially eliminated in several nonliterary dialects. The verbs most often cited by the various authorities on these dialects are the frequently occurring 'come, go' set and the 'sit up', 'stand up', and 'lie down' set. The dialects for which the use of narrative case subjects with these verbs has been recorded include Ḳaxian (Martirosovi and Imnaishvili 1956:131) and Kartlian (Imnaishvili 1974:238) in eastern Georgia; Mesxian (Dzidziguri 1941:251) in south Georgia; several dialects of west Georgia (Dzotsenidze 1973:69, 108, 167, 197–198, 226, etc.; Jajanidze 1970; Kiziria 1974); Fereidan (Chikobava 1927:217), spoken in Iran; and Ingilo (Imnaishvili 1966:140), spoken in Azerbaijan. The last two are not contiguous with other Georgian dialects. From available analyses of these dialects, it appears that in at least some, the literary standard coexists with the local standard; that is, *is c̣avida* 'he/NOM went' alternates with *man c̣avida* 'he/NAR went'. The importance of the latter construction in some dialects can be partially gauged by the fact that it is specifically cited by some authorities as one of the properties that distinguishes the regional from the literary dialect (e.g., Imnaishvili 1959:185).

The occurrence of constructions like *man c̣avida* is frequently attributed to Mingrelian influence. There are two problems with this account. First, several of the dialects in question are geographically distant from Mingrelian, and that small language exerts no cultural influence in eastern Georgia, Azerbaijan, and Iran. Second, Mingrelian has narrative case for all subjects in Series II, not only for subjects of active verbs. Yet in the dialects named, especially in those not contiguous with Mingrelian, it is principally verbs from the two sets discussed here that are cited as taking narrative case subjects; the verb 'be', for example, is prominently absent from examples of the use of the narrative case (references cited above).

The alternative explanation for these phenomena advanced to date in the literature is that they occur when an intransitive precedes a transitive (Dzidziguri 1941; Dzotsenidze 1973; Fähnrich 1967:37; Imnaishvili 1966:140; 1974:238; Kiziria 1974:76–77). Yet in each instance it is observed that narrative subjects also occur WITHOUT a following transitive. Further, the hypothesis that the occurrence of the narrative case is conditioned by the second verb does not account for the fact that examples cited are generally limited to active intransitives.[1] For example, Dzidziguri (1941:251) cites (6a,b), but nothing comparable to (6c).

(6) a. *mivida* ***ešmaḳ-ma*** *da xelit gaasuptava*
he/go/II devil-NAR and hand/INST he/clean/it/II
'The devil went and cleaned it by hand.'

b. *aman adga da c̣avida*
he/NAR he/stand.up/II and he/go/II
'He rose and went.'

c. **γonieri iq̇o ešmaḳ-ma da xelit gaasuptava*
strong he/be/II devil-NAR and hand/INST he/clean/it/II
('The devil was strong and cleaned it by hand.')

Thus the hypothesis proposed does not account for the grammaticality of (6b) or for the implied ungrammaticality of (6c).

The explanation proposed in the present work is that the occurrence of forms like *man c̣avida* 'he/NAR went' (where the literary dialect has only *is c̣avida*) represents a more complete actualization of the change than has taken place in the literary language (see Topuria 1923). Active intransitives are viewed here as a natural class in universal grammar, and the use of *man c̣avida* is considered a regularization of this verb with examples such as *man iṭira* 'he wept', *man imepa* 'he reigned', *man imarxula* 'he fasted', and so forth. This hypothesis explains why *man c̣avida* would occur in noncontinguous dialects and accounts for the nonoccurrence of **man iq̇o* 'he/NAR was'. At the same time, dialectal regularization is consistent with (a) the fact that a literary dialect with prescriptive norms is likely to preserve archaisms, (b) the fact that literary and dialectal norms may coexist in a single discourse (see §15.4), and (c) the possibility that context could determine which of the two coexistent norms was more likely to be followed in a given instance.

All of the verbs discussed in this section are exceptions of type (a), as defined in §6.1; that is, their grammar in the standard dialect is, on the whole, inconsistent with their semantics. This observation is not made from an external point of view but is based on the occurrence of properties of active verbs: the restricted narrative case subject in (5), the failure of *-en/n* to occur in Series II, and the partial regularization of narrative case subjects with these verbs in some dialects. These properties identify these verbs as active from the point of view of Georgian.

6.2.2. Basic Intransitives with Grammatical Inconsistencies

The second type of exception has inconsistent grammatical properties, governing nominative case subjects in Series II but otherwise having syntactic and morphological characteristics of Class 3 verbs. This type of relic has been studied by Shanidze (1973:483–484), and the examples below were first adduced by him.

(7) *katam-i q̣iva*
chicken-NOM he/crow/II
'The cock crowed.' (Mt 26:74; L 22:60; J 18:27)

All three versions consulted agree in this in each of the three locations cited. In Modern Georgian this is rendered

(8) *mamal-ma iq̣ivla*
cock-NAR he/crow/II
'The cock crowed.'

While several aspects of this sentence have changed, the most important for our purposes is the case of 'cock': nominative in Old Georgian, narrative in Modern Georgian. It is also probably not an accident that the morphology of the verb changed also (see §14.3.2): *q̣iva* to *iq̣ivla*.

As late as the eighteenth century, *mepa* 'reign' was used with nominative case subjects in *Kartlis Cxovreba*.

(9) *mepe ḳonsṭanṭine z c̣eli mepa*
monarch/NOM Constantine 7 year/NOM he/reign/II
'King Constantine reigned 7 years.' (Kauxchishvili 1973:277, 1)

In this volume of the history of Georgia, (9) is repeated dozens of times, with changes made for the name of the monarch and number of years. It seems that (9) was formulaic and that it is this fact that is responsible for its retaining archaic case marking (see §2.2.3). In Modern Georgian we find instead

(10) *tamar-ma imepa*
Tamar-NAR she/reign/II
'Tamar reigned.'

Given that different languages may classify verbs differently, on what basis are these identified as members of Class 3? Why can they not simply be viewed as regular members of Class 2? As explained in Chapter 3, in Old Georgian Class 3 verbs can only be identified as intransitives that lack Class 2 properties. Each of these verbs lacks the defining properties of Class 2 verbs (see §3.4). (a) They do not in Series I have a series marker and the suffix *-i*, which together characterize most dynamic verbs in Class 2. Instead they have, like most Class 1 and 3 verbs, only one of these two markers: *q̣iv-**i**-s* 'it crows,' *mep-**ob**-s* 'he reigns'. (b) They do not in Series I have the suffix *-ie*, which characterizes many statives in Class 2. (c) Their subjects, if plural, do not condition the *-en/n* pluralizer (see Chap. 10). In addition, these verbs do not have the *i/e-* prefix that characterizes prefixal intransitives, the suffix *-d* that is typical of suffixal intransitives, or the relics of ablaut that are found in many of the "markerless" intransitives. Thus, these verbs have none of the positive features that identify Class 2 verbs. Further, they are clearly members of Class 3 in Modern Georgian. Finally, this conjugational type can be reconstructed for Class 3 verbs in CK (see §14.3.2).

With the two verbs discussed in this section, the nominative case died out completely in this use and was replaced by the narrative. We can see, therefore, that this use of the nominative with active intransitives is a relic rather than an innovation.

6.3. LAZ

In Laz we find both of the types of relics defined above in §6.1: (a) verbs with predominantly Class 2 characteristics that appear to have the semantic properties of Class 3 and (b) intransitives having predominantly Class 3 characteristics but governing nominative case subjects in Series II. In Laz, since active case marking has spread from Series II to Series I, we find such exceptions in both series.

On the basis of the Laz data alone, it would be difficult or impossible to judge whether these irregularities are archaic or innovative; however, because they are of the same type as those in Georgian, where diachronic development shows them to be archaic features, we can see that these irregularities similarly represent relics in Laz.

6.3.1. Active Intransitives in Class 2

I begin by considering the three verb roots meaning 'come/go', which we saw to be irregular in Old Georgian. Corresponding to Georgian *val/*

vl is Laz *ul* (CGZ **vl*; Chikobava 1936:172; Klimov 1964:84), to Georgian *qad/qd* is Laz *xt/xṭ* and Svan *qad/qd/qed/qid* (CK **qad/qd*: Chikobava 1936:172; Klimov 1964:263), and to Georgian *ved/vid* is Laz *id* (CGZ **vid*: Klimov 1964:84). Each of these roots means 'come' or 'go' or some other variant with an appropriate preverb. In Laz the first and second roots are parts of a suppletive paradigm, just as the first and third are in Georgian. We saw that in Standard Georgian these verbs retain nominative case subjects as an archaism, though their case government has been regularized to narrative in Series II in a number of nonliterary dialects. In Laz both cases are used, as shown by the examples in (11), with nominative case subjects, and by those in (12), with narrative case subjects.

(11) a. *aç̣i bee-pe komu**lan** do dadalepeši visteat*
now child-PL/NOM they/come and "queen"/NOM we/play/it
. . . babaç̣oni
"doll"/NOM
'Now the children will come and we will play "queen" [and] "doll".' (Asatiani 1974:**15**[8])

b. *noγamisa žureneč dγaš-ḳule **ulun** baba-muši-š*
bride/NOM forty day-later she/go father-her-GEN
oxori-ša
house-ALL
'Forty days later the bride goes to her father's house.'
(Asatiani 1974:**17**[45])

c. *č̣inḳa mextu do kayezdu ia paa*
goblin/NOM he/go and he/take that money/NOM
'The goblin went and took that money.' (Asatiani 1974:**9**[11])

d. *aya dal-epe **ides**, **ides**, **ides** do mteli daγi*
this sister-PL/NOM they/go and whole forest/NOM
miḳiles
they/pass/it
'These sisters went and went and went, and passed by the whole forest.' (Asatiani 1974:**29**[8])

(12) a. *ia mamuni-k bee-ša **ulun** do bonups*
that midwife-NAR child-ALL she/come and she/bathe/him
'That midwife comes to the child and bathes him.'
(Asatiani 1974:**18**[4])

b. *ia ḳoč-epe-k komo**xtes**. ia ṭua yezdes*
that man-PL-NAR they/come that sack/NOM they/take
'Those men came. They took the sack.'
(Asatiani 1974:**3**[82])

It has been suggested that the use of narrative case subjects with intransitives in western dialects of Georgian is, in some instances, due to a neighboring transitive verb (see references, page 113). It is possible that this effect is responsible for the use of the narrative case in (12). Notice, however, that in (11a, c, d) the verb 'come,go' is likewise followed by a clause containing a verb that obligatorily governs a narrative case subject, yet the subject of the first clause is in the case required by its own clause. Thus, the "syntactic assimilation" of subject case is, at most, optional. Note too that in (12a) the direct object of the second verb, 'child', is not in the case that would be governed by that verb form, but in the form required for the clause in which it actually occurs, namely allative. That is, it is significant that it is just the subjects of intransitive verbs that exhibit this alternation. Further, the verbs with which this phenomenon is found are not a random group, but only active intransitives. The same verbs may undergo Inversion in Series III, as do verbs of Class 3 (see Chap. 13, n. 29). This, combined with the fact that narrative subjects are elicited in isolated sentences, shows that this phenomenon is not syntactic assimilation at all, but rule-governed variation. We may conclude from the data above that the use of the nominative case for subjects of these verbs represents an archaism, while the use of narrative case subjects is a step toward regularization, that is, conformity with the regular patterns of the language.

6.3.2. Basic Intransitives with Grammatical Inconsistencies

The verbs below can be shown to have the characteristics of Class 3, but, as these and other examples show, take nominative case subjects.

(13) *aɣne nisa mtii-ḳala . . . va* ***ɣaɣal****aps*
new daughter.in.law/NOM father.in.law-with not she/talk
'The new daughter-in-law does not talk with [her] father-in-law.'
(Asatiani 1974:**17**[41])

(14) *çiṭa čxomepe* ***isteṭ****eenan* [2]
little fish/PL/NOM they/play
'The little fish played.' (Asatiani 1974:**12**[149])

The verbs in (13)–(14) may optionally take a narrative case subject, as shown in (15) and (16).

(15) *entepe-k na* ***ɣaɣal****apan . . .*
they-NAR CONJ they/talk/I
'as they talk . . . .' (Asatiani 1974:**48**[23])

While my consultant volunteered only the narrative case with *γa(r)γal-* 'talk', he suggested both variants of *ste(r)-* 'play':

(16) a. *bere* **isters** *γoǰis*
child/NOM he/play/I yard/DAT
'The child plays in the yard.'
b. *bere-k* **isters** *γoǰis*
child-NAR
'The child plays in the yard.'

The (a) variant, with the nominative case, is preferred in (16), where the verb form is in Series I. With a verb form in Series II, the variant with the narrative case, (17b), was preferred.

(17) a. *bere* **isteru** *γoǰis*
'The child/NOM played in the yard.'
b. *berek* **isteru** *γoǰis*
'The child/NAR played in the yard.'

These examples seem to reflect (a) the archaic case marking dichotomy between Series I and II, (b) the accusative-type marking (all subjects in the nominative) reconstructed for Series I after it was reanalyzed (16a), (c) the analogical restructuring of Series I in Laz (16b), (d) the original ergative marking in Series II (17a), and (e) the development of active case marking in this series (17b).

6.4. SVAN

Up to now we have considered restricted variation between narrative and nominative case subjects for active intransitives in Series II. In §6.4.1, we see that the same sort of variation exists as a productive, regular pattern in one subdialect of Svan. In §6.4.2 we consider two examples of restricted variation between other dialects of Svan.

6.4.1. The Naḳra-Laxamula Subdialect

The subdialect described in this section is part of the Lower Bal dialect.[3] The features described here are not found in all parts of Lower Bal; in particular, the (a) examples in (18)–(26) were judged ungrammatical by all consultants in the Bečo Valley. This construction was also entirely unknown to my consultants from Upper Bal (Mesṭia and Leǰera) and to my consultant and research assistant, who had lived in both the Lašx and Lenṭex areas. I located these features in the village of Laxamula and in the Naḳra area. Beyond this, I did not determine the geographical boundaries of the features described here. I use the term 'Naḳra-Laxamula (sub)dialect' to refer to the Svan spoken in these areas with respect to the features described below, without a more precise geographic bounding.

In Chapter 3 it was shown that in Svan, Class 3 verbs govern narrative case subjects in Series II. While this is true generally, in the Naḳra-Laxamula dialect Class 3 verbs govern either narrative or nominative case subjects. All consultants reported that there is no meaning difference between the two variants; in particular, they do not differ according to controllable versus noncontrollable, purposeful versus nonpurposeful, or punctual versus durative. A large number of active intransitive verbs were tested with consultants; except as noted, the examples given below were confirmed with speakers from both villages.

(18) a. *čäž* *ädkinal* *däb-isga*
horse/NOM he/run/II field-in
b. *čäž-d* *ädkinale* *däb-isga*
horse-NAR he/run/II
'The horse ran in the field.'

(19) a. *bopš-är* *ädq̣aralx*
child-PL/NOM they/fight/II
b. *bopš-är-d* *ädq̣aralex*
child-PL-NAR they/fight/II
'The children fought/quarrelled.'

(20) a. *mare* *ädšwep̣inal*
man/NOM he/whistle/II
b. *mare-m* *ädšwep̣inale*
man-NAR he/whistle/II
'The man whistled.'

(21) a. *bepšw* *ädṭulal*
child/NOM he/yell/II
b. *bepš-d* *ädṭulale*
child-NAR he/yell/II
'The child yelled.'

(22) a. *mare* *megč̣ad* *ädšial*
man/NOM hard he/fight/II
b. *mare-m* *megč̣ad* *ädšiale*
man-NAR he/fight/II
'The man fought hard.'

(23) a. *mare* *xočamd* *ädγiral*
man/NOM well he/sing/II
b. *mare-m* *xočamd* *ädγirale*
man-NAR he/sing/II
'The man sang well.'

(24) a. *dina* *ädšdiral*
girl/NOM she/play/II
b. *dina-d* *ädšdirale*
girl-NAR she/play/II
'The girl played.'

(25) a. *lintw-isga* *bepšw* *ädčarxal* (*čarx-šw*)
winter-in child/NOM he/sled/II sled-INST
b. *lintw-isga* *bepšw-d* *ädčarxale* (*čarx-šw*)
child-NAR he/sled/II
'In the winter the child sledded.'

(26) a. *bepšw* *ädḳarčxal* *kor-s*
child/NOM he/crawl/II house-DAT
b. *bepšw-d* *ädḳarčxale* *kor-s*
child-NAR he/crawl/II
'The child crawled in the house.'

The (a) and (b) variants have, according to my consultants, exactly the same meaning; nor did they express a preference, giving first sometimes one variant, sometimes the other. Both variants are in the aorist, which is a Series II screeve.[4] There is, in my data, an absolute correlation between the use of the narrative case and the occurrence of the suffix *-e* in the verb form; that is, the nominative case with *-e* forms and the narrative case with forms lacking *-e* were judged absolutely ungrammatical for every verb by every consultant. The *-e* suffix occurs in third person subject forms of Class 1 (transitive) verbs in the aorist and does not occur with forms of Class 2 (inactive intransitive) verbs.

There is also, in my data, an absolute correlation between the *-al* (*-el*, etc.) suffix, which characterizes Class 3 verbs and the ability to occur in both of the patterns illustrated in (18–26).[5] That is, all Class 3 verbs that have the suffix *-al* may occur in both pattern (a) and pattern (b); verbs that lack *-al* or its variants occur only in one pattern or the other. Some Class 3 verbs lack *-al*, as in (27). Some that seem to be active intransitives are irregular members of Class 2, taking a nominative case subject without *-e*, as in (28). (The criteria used here for determination of class membership are as stated in §3.3.)

(27) *di-d* *ädsḳore*
mother-NAR she/think/II
'The mother thought.'

(28) *leti* *žeγ* *ädhaw* (Naḳra)
night dog/NOM he/bark/II
'Last night a dog barked, bayed.'

Both verbs lack the explicit marker of Class 3 (*-al*) and that of Class 2 (*-an*). Neither is flexible with respect to case and verb agreement (*-e*).

It is pointed out above that ergative and active alignment systems differ only in the marking assigned to the subjects of active intransitives. We see in (18)–(26) that this marking varies in the Naḳra-Laxamula dialect. The marking used with transitive and inactive intransitive verbs, illustrated below, is like that in other dialects (see Chap. 3 for additional examples from other dialects).

(29) Transitive
gela-d *diär* *kannaqe* (Naḳra)
Gela-NAR bread/NOM he/bake/it/CL.1/II
'Gela baked bread.'

(30) Inactive Intransitive
diär *kännaqan* (Naḳra)
bread/NOM it/bake/CL.2/II
'The bread baked.'

The transitive and inactive intransitive clauses illustrated in (29) and (30), as well as other clauses containing regular verbs of these classes, cannot occur in more than one pattern as those in (18)–(26) can.[6] The regular case marking systems of Series II in this dialect are summarized in Table 6.3. Comparison with Table 6.1 shows clearly that the first of these, representing the (a) examples, is the ergative type; the second, representing the (b) sentences, is active. We can see that the two types coexist in this series in Naḳra-Laxamula.

Table 6.3

Summary of Case Marking Systems in Series II in the Naḳra-Laxamula Dialect

Direct Object	Subject of Intransitive		Subject of Transitive
	Inactive	Active	
NOM	NOM		NAR
NOM	NOM	NAR	NAR

6.4.2. Variation among Svan Dialects

In the dialects described in this subsection, productive case marking in Series II is active, as illustrated in Chapter 3. In the Upper Bal and Lašx dialects,[7] the (a) constructions in (18)–(26) were judged ungrammatical and only the (b) variants were accepted. Variation between Upper Bal and Lašx on the one hand, and Naḳra-Laxamula on the other, are summarized more precisely in Table 6.4, which is limited to those elicited verbs that were cognate. The data labeled "Upper Bal" were obtained from speakers in Mesṭia. Dashes indicate that the verb was not tested in a dialect or that the verb is not used there.

Table 6.4

Some Verbs Governing Either Narrative or Nominative in Naḳra-Laxamula, Only Narrative in Upper Bal and Lašx

Naḳra-Laxamula	Lašx	Upper Bal	Meaning
ädγiral(e)	*lenγiräle*	*ädγiräle*	'he sang'
ädšial(e)	*lenšiäle*	*ädšiäle*	'he fought, made war'
ädšdiral(e)	*lenšdiräle*	*läišdiräle*	'he played'
ädṭulal(e)	*lenṭūle*	*läiṭwīliēle*	'he yelled'
ädšwepinal(e)	*lenšwepe*	*läišweṗ*	'he whistled'
ädcuṅal(e)	*laxūcuṅāle (REL)*	—	'he laughed'
ädqaral(e)	*lenqäriele*	—	'he fought'
ädḳarčxal(e)	*lenḳwarčxäle*	—	'he crawled'
eszelal(e)	*eszeläle*	—	'he passed by'
äntop(e)	*lentope*	—	'he shot a gun'
änḳonḳal(e)	*lenḳōnḳäle*	—	'he limped'
änḳəldal(e)	*lenḳəldäle*	—	'he hurried'
läiḳupxiel(e)	*lenḳupxiele*	—	'he jumped, sprang'

The verb 'he sledded', on the other hand, governs a narrative case subject in Upper Bal (*läičirxäle*), but nominative in Lašx (*edčīrxän*), and either in Naḳra-Laxamula (example 25).

6.5. BASIC INTRANSITIVES WITH VARIATION AMONG COGNATES

Consideration of cognates shows that for several, a nominative case subject occurs in Series II in one language and narrative in another. For example, CK **qad/qd* (Klimov 1964:263) 'come, go' may take nominative subjects in all three languages: Svan *eǯi anqad* 'he/NOM came', Old Georgian *igi ganqda* 'he/NOM went', Laz *ia moxtu* 'he/NOM came'; the reflex of this verb occurs alternatively with a narrative case subject in Laz and in a number of Georgian dialects (see §6.2.1 and §6.3.1). The root *gza* 'travel, go' is a basic intransitive in all three languages.[8] In Laz it takes a nominative subject.

(31) *ḳoči. . .* *meele-ša* *igzalu*
man/NOM village-ALL he/go/II
'The man went to the village.' (Asatiani 1974:**3**[50])

Its cognates in Georgian and Svan require a narrative subject: Georgian *man imgzavra* and *man imogzaura* both 'he/NAR traveled', Lašx *ejnēm lenənəgzārwāle* 'he/NAR traveled.'

The CK root **gor/gr* 'roll' (Klimov 1964:64) has basic intransitive reflexes in Georgian and Laz. In Laz, it requires a nominative subject, as in (32), while the Georgian reflex, in (33), requires narrative (see Holisky 1981a:116–119 on agentivity in Georgian).

(32) *ḳoči* *ingoru*
man/NOM he/roll/II
'The man rolled.'

(33) *ḳac-ma* *igora*
man-NAR he/roll/II
'The man rolled.'

The Laz Class 3 verb *γaγalaps* 'he talks' takes a nominative or narrative subject (see 13 and 15), while its Class 3 cognate requires a narrative subject in most Svan dialects (Lašx *ejnēm lengərgale* 'he/NAR talked'), but either in Naḳra-Laxamula (Laxamula *eǰi esgərgal* 'he/NOM talked'/ *eynem esgərgale* 'he/NAR talked'). Likewise Laz *isters* 'he plays' takes either nominative or narrative (see 16 and 17), as does its possible cognate in Naḳra-Laxamula (see 24); it takes only narrative in most Svan dialects (Upper Bal *bepšwd ädšdirāle* 'child/NAR played').[9]

In Georgian we find a Class 3 verb in *man ivaxšma* 'he/NAR supped'; the corresponding verb in Upper Bal and Lašx dialects of Svan, apparently borrowed, is in Class 2 and takes the nominative (Lašx *eǰi edwaxšmān* 'he/ NOM supped').[10] There are also CK roots of this type that govern only narrative subjects in each language in which they occur; see examples in §6.1.

6.6. TRANSITIVE–INTRANSITIVE PAIRS IN KARTVELIAN

We have seen that some basic intransitives are relics of an earlier stage when all intransitives must have governed nominative case subjects in Series II. Non-basic intransitives provide a different kind of evidence.

6.6.1. Generalized and Restricted Ergative

In this subsection, I distinguish briefly between two attested types of ergative case marking and compare them with active. In the following subsection, the implications of these facts for Kartvelian are explored.

In most of the languages with ergative case marking that have been described in the literature, the absolutive (nominative) case is used not only for the subject of basic intransitives, but also for the subjects of derived intransitives. Derived intransitives may include clauses in which the direct object of an otherwise transitive verb is (a) in an oblique case, (b) incorporated, or (c) unexpressed; they do not necessarily include derived reflexive intransitives (see below). An example of the first type from Yidiɲ is the transitive–intransitive pair in (34).

(34) a. *wagud̪a-ŋgu buɲa giba:l*
man-ERG woman/ABSL scratched
'The man scratched the woman.' (Dixon 1977a:274)

b. *wagu:d̪a giba:d̪iɲu buɲa:-nda*
man/ABSL scratched woman-DAT
'The man scratched [at] the woman.' (Dixon 1977a:274)

The property of interest here is that the subject in the intransitive, (34b), is in the absolutive (nominative) case, not in the ergative as in (34a). I will refer to ergative case marking comparable to (34) as GENERALIZED ERGATIVE.

A few languages have genuine ergative case marking yet use the ergative case, rather than the absolutive, in derived intransitives of the type discussed here. I will refer to this as RESTRICTED ERGATIVE marking. It is exemplified in (35) from Walbiri.

(35) a. *njuntulu-ḷu Ø-npa-tju pantu-ṇu ŋatju*
you-ERG Ø-2nd-1st spear-PAST me/ABSL
'You speared me.' (Hale 1973:336)

b. *njuntulu-ḷu Ø-npa-tju-ḷa pantu-ṇu ŋatju-ku*
-la me-DAT
'You speared at me.' 'You tried to spear me.' (Hale 1973:336)

This difference may be accounted for by permitting the rules that assign cases to refer to initial rather than final transitivity (Harris 1981c). Pairs comparable to (35) also occur in Udi (Panchvidze 1974), Rembarnga (McKay 1976), and Dargwa (Abdullaev 1971).

It is characteristic of an active case marking system, on the other hand, that the case of the subject of an intransitive is determined on the basis of the active–inactive dichotomy, rather than on the basis of intransitivity alone. Therefore, in transitive–intransitive pairs where the subject is the same, as in (34) and (35), a consistent active system would use the active (narrative) case for the subject of both transitive and intransitive. An example from Choctaw illustrates this principle.

(36) a. *Issoba shilli-li-tok*
horse comb-1.ACT-PAST
b. *Issoba ĩ-shilli-li-tok*
horse 3.DAT-comb-1.ACT-PAST
'I combed the horse.' (Davies 1981:242)

Here (a) is a canonical transitive, with the direct object 'horse'. When this object is put in the dative by a lexically governed rule, as in (36b), the subject is still marked with the form *-li*, which is cofunctional with the Kartvelian narrative case. That is, the subject of a clause in which Object Demotion has applied, such as (36b), is in the form also used for the subjects of transitives, such as (36a), not in the form used for the subjects of inactive intransitives, such as (37).

(37) *Sa-ka:passa*
1.INACT-cold
'I'm cold.' (Davies 1980:3)

This pattern of marking is characteristic of a language with active case distribution, as defined in Table 6.1.

6.6.2. Kartvelian

With respect to transitive–intransitive pairs, we must distinguish two major types.

In type I the subject of the intransitive is the direct object of the transitive; this type is represented by (29) and (30) above and by examples on pages 20, 52, and 56. In this type the intransitive member is semantically inactive and belongs regularly to Class 2, having the syntactic characteristics of this class, including a nominative case subject in Series II. This type is consistent with both ergative and active case marking and is therefore not relevant to determining whether CK had ergative or active case marking in Series II.

The second major type of transitive–intransitive pair, type II, involves an intransitive with a subject corresponding to the subject of the transitive. Here must distinguish among subtypes.

TYPE IIA. The first subtype involves an initial direct object in an oblique case. This occurs in each Kartvelian language as a lexically governed rule applying with only a few verbs and is illustrated by (38) below from Laz.

(38) *noγamisa-s ǰuma-muši-k gyaḳneps xe-s*
bride-DAT brother-her-NAR he/take/to.it hand-DAT
'Her$_i$ brother takes the bride$_i$ by the hand.'
(Asatiani 1974:**17**[33])

Additional examples from Georgian, Laz, and Mingrelian are cited as (3) and (6)–(8) in Chapter 1, and Modern Georgian examples are given in Harris (1981b:188–189). In the examples cited, the subject is in the narrative case, as would be expected with active case marking.

In Svan the same rule is lexically governed by 'see', illustrated in (39).[11]

(39) *eǰi xeçad bepš-s*
he/NOM he/see/to.him/II child-DAT
'He saw the child.' (Gagua 1976:102)

The object, *bepš-s* 'child', is shown to be a final indirect object by the fact that it bears the indirect object case and conditions the third person agreement marker, *x-*, which is limited to indirect objects. However, this nominal is not an initial indirect object, but an initial direct object, as shown by its behavior in inversion, illustrated in (40) and in example (21b) of Chapter 13.

(40) *mi eǰ mare ču miçwa*
I/DAT this man/NOM PV I/see/him/III
'I have seen this man.' (Gagua 1976:102)

In the inversion construction, the initial direct object is advanced to subject by Unaccusative; it is marked with the subject case and conditions subject person agreement (see Chap. 13). The initial indirect object, on the other hand, is retired and in Svan is marked with the adverbial case or with the genitive and adverbial together (see Chap. 11). These facts show that *mare* 'man' in (40) is the initial direct object. The verb *xeçad* takes an initial subject and direct object and lexically governs Object Demotion.[12]

TYPE IIB. A second subtype of type II intransitives, the incorporated object construction, is found only in Old Georgian. It is illustrated in (2a,b) of Chapter 1 and discussed in greater detail in §14.1.1. In this type, the subject of the intransitive clause is in the narrative case.

TYPE IIC. A third subtype involves unexpressed direct objects, such as 'he writes a letter' versus 'he writes'. Generally speaking, pairs of this kind do not occur in Georgian and Laz. Instead, the intransitive is regularly expressed by means of a form that is grammatically transitive, as illustrated by (41) from Laz.

(41) a. *nana-k* *palṭo* *muiçḳips*
mother-NAR coat/NOM she/take.off/it/II
'Mother took off [her] coat.'
b. *nana-k muiçḳips*
'Mother took it off.' 'Mother undressed.'

Georgian is like Laz in this respect, and a variety of syntactic evidence indicates that sentences like (41b) in Modern Georgian are transitive. Sentences of this sort may be derived by dropping unemphatic pronouns whose reference has been established in discourse. However, unlike sentences with ordinary Unemphatic Pronoun Drop, in examples like (41b) the understood direct object need not be established in discourse. In this sense, sentences like (41b), although transitive, function as intransitives.

Transitive–intransitive pairs with unexpressed objects do occur, though rarely, in Georgian—for example, *aginebs* 'he curses him'/*igineba* 'he curses'; however, verbs of the latter variety are limited to Series I. Therefore, although *igineba* is genuinely intransitive, the question of subject case in Series II does not arise. In Svan, on the other hand, pairs of this kind do occur as regular verbs, as illustrated with Series II forms in (42).

(42) a. *dede-d* *lerekw* *edīγāle*
mother-NAR clothes/NOM she/take.off/it/II
'Mother took off [her] clothes.'
b. *dede* *edīγalān*
mother/NOM she/take.off/II
'Mother undressed.'

(43) a. *dede-d* *anrekwe*
mother/NAR she/put.on/it/II
'Mother put it on.'
b. *dede* *enrekwān*
mother/NOM she/put.on/II
'Mother dressed.'

These examples are from Lašx; the same patterns were found in Naḳra, although the verb elicited was not the same as the one in (42): *kadšqužure* 'he took it off'–*kädšqužuran* 'he undressed'. Some verbs in Svan follow the pattern found more widely in Georgian and Laz, as illustrated by (44) from Naḳra.

(44) a. *pur-är-d* *ču* *lälemx* *çem*
cow-PL-NAR PV they/eat/it/II hay/NOM
'The cows ate hay.'

b. *pur-är-d* *lälemx* *mindor-isga*
cow-PL-NAR they/eat/it/II meadow-in
'The cows ate in the meadow.'

TYPE IID. A fourth subtype is reflexive, such as the Svan (b) examples below.

(45) a. *dede-d* *adbare* *gezal*
mother-NAR she/bathe/him/II child/NOM
'The mother bathed her child.'
b. *dede* *edbarān*
mother/NOM she/bathe/II
'The mother bathed [herself].'

(46) a. *māre-d* *adçabūre* *apxnik̹*
man-NAR he/shave/him/II friend/NOM
'The man shaved his friend.'
b. *māre* *edçabūrān*
man/NOM he/shave/II
'The man shaved [himself].'

(47) a. *dīna-d* *anmāre* *lezob*
girl/NAR she/prepare/it/II food/NOM
'The girl prepared food.'
b. *dīna* *enmārān*
girl/NOM she/prepare/II
'The girl prepared [herself].'

The examples above are from the Lašx dialect; similar facts were found in Nak̹ra, although the verbs were not necessarily the same; e.g., *kaakän* 'he bathed him', *kädkanan* 'he bathed [himself]'. These may usefully be compared with examples from Laz.

(48) a. *nana-k* *skiri* *bonups*
mother-NAR child/NOM she/bathe/him/I
'The mother bathes her child.'
b. *nana-k* *ibons*
mother-NAR she/bathe/I
'The mother bathes [herself].'

(49) a. *k̹ulani-k* *doxaziru* *gyari*
girl-NAR she/prepare/it/II food/NOM
'The girl prepared food.'
b. *k̹ulani* *dixaziru*
girl/NOM she/prepare/II
'The girl prepared [herself].'

With these and other verbs tested, the syntax in Georgian is essentially like that in Laz in this respect, although the verbs in a given meaning are not necessarily cognate; e.g., Georgian *moamzada* 'he prepared it'–*moemzada* 'he prepared'. Note that with the verb 'prepare', the construction in Laz and Georgian is like that in Svan, including case marking. With the verb 'bathe', on the other hand, Georgian and Laz substitute for the intransitive a transitive with an unexpressed direct object. Unlike ordinary Unemphatic Pronoun Drop, this construction makes it unnecessary to establish in context the referent of the direct object. In this sense, (48b) functions as an intransitive.

It is not clear a priori whether the final subject in (45b), (46b), and (47b) represents the initial subject or the initial direct object, advanced to subject by Unaccusative. At first glance, the evidence appears to support the second analysis since intransitives of this type have the morphology of verbs with which Unaccusative has applied. For example, the (b) examples in Svan have the suffix *-ān*, used in the aorist of verbs with which Unaccusative has applied. However, consideration of the facts discussed below in this section suggests that this analysis is incorrect. Nevertheless, the evidence offered by (46)–(49) may be considered less compelling than that offered by the other pairs discussed.

TYPE IIE. A fifth transitive–intransitive pattern can be seen in pairs in which the verb is one of the few Class 3 verbs that take an optional direct object, the vast majority taking no direct object at all (Harris 1981b:Chap. 12). In Georgian and Laz, both the intransitive and the transitive, both in Class 3, take narrative case subjects, as we would expect.

(50) Modern Georgian
a. *ḳac-ma imγera "suliḳo"*
man-NAR he/sing/II "Suliko"/NOM
'The man sang "Suliko."'
b. *ḳac-ma imγera*
'The man sang.'

(51) Laz
a. *aya ḳoči-k ḳai ibirs birapa-pe*
this man-NAR well he/sing song-PL/NOM
'This man sings the songs well.'
b. *aya ḳoči-k ḳai ibirs*
'This man sings well.'

These examples are unlike the ones considered above in that they involve an optional, rather than an unexpressed, direct object; syntactic evidence for this is found in Harris (1981b:181–187).

Now consider the following examples from Nak̦ra-Laxamula.

(52)	a.	*ej̆nēm*	*ädšdirale*	*pau*
		he/NAR	he/play/it/II	stick/NOM
	b.	*ej̆i*	*ätšdiral*	*paus*
		he/NOM	he/play/II	stick/DAT
		'He played with a stick.'		

Pau is a stick for playing a Svan game; the English translation fails to reveal that the structure of (52a) is comparable to English *he played ball/ croquet/baseball.*

(53)	a.	*mare-m*	*ädγirale*	*"lile"*
		man-NAR	he/sing/it/II	"Lile"/NOM
	b.	*mare*	*ätγiral*	*"lile-s"*
		man/NOM	he/sing/II	"Lile"-DAT
		'The man sang "Lile." '		

Consultants report that there is no meaning difference between the (a) and (b) variants. (53a) and (23b) form a pair parallel to Georgian (50) and Laz (51). But forms parallel to (53b), like (23a), fail to occur in Georgian or Laz. The Nak̦ra-Laxamula data are difficult to interpret, for we would not expect structures of the (b) type for transitive sentences in either an ergative or an active case marking system (see Table 6.1). It is possible that this case pattern was "analogically extended" on the models of (24a) and (23a) and Series I transitives. I believe that a more probable explanation is that in (52b) and (53b), *paus* and *liles* are not final direct objects, but obliques of some kind, probably the result of Lexical Object Demotion. That is, I suggest that these pairs are structurally parallel to (39). This is supported by the following facts.

1. The verb forms in (b) of (52)–(53) lack the suffix *-e*, which characterizes transitive verbs with third person singular subjects in the aorist. Instead, these forms are suffixless like the intransitives in (a) of (18)–(26) and like (39).
2. The initial direct object is in the dative, as in the Object Demotion construction.
3. In (b) of (52)–(53), the subject is in the nominative case as it is in the Object Demotion construction in Svan, (39).
4. The verbs (b) of (52)–(53) show agreement with the object, while those in the (a) examples do not. Third person indirect objects in Svan condition the prefix *x-*, while third person direct objects condition Ø. The agreement marker *x-* conditions *ad* > *at* (Topuria 1967:55). Thus, surface direct objects in the (a) examples contrast

with the surface indirect objects in the (b) examples, accounting for the *ad-* versus *at-* alternation. For these reasons, it is assumed in the discussion below that the (b) parts of (52)–(53) are examples of optional object demotion, type IIA above.

It is noteworthy that among intransitive verb forms of type II, the occurrence of nominative case subjects is significantly more limited in Georgian and Laz than in Svan. In object demotion (type IIA), Svan has a nominative subject, (39) and (b) of (52)–(53), while Georgian and Laz require narrative case subjects. The incorporated object construction requires narrative case subjects in Georgian and does not occur in the remaining languages. For unexpressed object constructions (type IIC), Georgian and Laz generally use a grammatically transitive construction. Those that are intransitive are restricted to Series I, where subject case is not an issue. Svan has nominative case for some unexpressed-object constructions, (42)–(43), and narrative for others, (44). Finally, in the five reflexive constructions tested, Svan used nominative case subject for four, while Georgian and Laz used this for only two expressions each. Because the languages differ from one another in this respect, we may assume that there has been change.

The data presented above include examples that are exceptions in various ways to the general correlations presented in Table 6.2. The Nak̩ra-Laxamula examples, (52b)–(53b), have Class 3 morphological characteristics but govern nominative case subjects in Series II.[13]

The (b) examples of (45)–(49) are also irregular in the following sense: In general, the subjects of Class 2 correspond to the direct objects of the correlated Class 1 forms (see Shanidze 1973:355; Topuria 1967:179).[14] In these Class 2 forms, the subjects correspond to the subjects, not to the direct objects, of the correlated Class 1 forms. Each of the transitive verbs illustrated selects an initial subject that is animate, while its direct object may be inanimate; the subject of each of the intransitive verbs in (b) of (45)–(49) must be animate. Thus, the fact that the verbs in these sentences are in Class 2 is an exception to the general pattern of the languages.

A third irregularity found in the data presented above concerns inconsistencies in the class-defining morphology of the verb forms in the intransitives in types IIC and D in Svan. At least some verbs of these types have the characteristics of Class 3 in Series I and properties of Class 2 or of both classes in Series II (Topuria 1967:237). Like the basic intransitive relics discussed in §6.2, §6.3, and §6.4, these intransitives are irregular in having inconsistent grammatical properties.

We see that in intransitive clauses there is variation that that indicates that change has occurred, and there is irregularity that requires explanation. However, without considering the language family as a whole, it is not clear which sort of intransitive is archaic and which is innovative. In the following section, that question is considered, and it is suggested that Svan is conservative in this respect.

Among the transitive–intransitive pairs discussed above, those where the intransitive governs a nominative case subject illustrate the kind of case distribution that is characteristic of generalized ergative case marking and which would not be expected in a case system of the active type. It is likewise this kind of transitive–intransitive pair that has been assumed to be the basis for the formation of Series I (see Chap. 1 and 7).

6.7. DISTINGUISHING INNOVATION FROM ARCHAISM

In §6.2 through §6.6, I present data that show variation in the subject case governed by basic (§6.2–6.5) and non-basic (§6.6) intransitives. The variation is between different dialects (§6.2.1 and §6.4.2), diachronic in a single language (§6.2.2), synchronic in a single dialect (§6.3.1, §6.3.2, and §6.4.1), between different languages (§6.5, and some instances in §6.6.2), or among various verbs of a single type (some instances in §6.6.2). In each instance, an intransitive verb with active semantics governs nominative case subjects under certain circumstances and narrative under others.

Variation of these sorts indicates change. Other things being equal, it is possible that either the nominative or the narrative variant is archaic, and these two possibilities are weighed against each other in this section.

If the examples with nominative case subjects in Series II, that is (1)–(3), (7), (9), (11), (13), (14), (a) of (16)–(26), (31), (32), (39), (42b), (43b), (b) of (45)–(47), (49b), (52b), (53b) and other examples in §6.5 are older, they are relics of a stage at which all intransitives governed nominative subjects in this series. The table of alignment types (Table 6.1) shows this to be an ergative case system. I refer to this possibility as the ANCESTRAL ERGATIVE HYPOTHESIS.

If, on the other hand, those examples are newer than the examples with narrative case subjects, they are innovations. This implies that the active case distribution which is productive today is ancient; and this view is termed the ANCESTRAL ACTIVE HYPOTHESIS.

According to the Ancestral Ergative Hypothesis, Series II had ergative case marking in Late CK[15]. This later shifted to the active type by (a) changing the marking assigned to the subjects of basic active intransitives, which became Class 3 verbs, and (b) replacing intransitive clauses like (39), (42b), and (43b) with ones like (38) or with transitives like (41b). This stage is preserved by Georgian, while in Laz the system of Series II spread also into Series I. Svan probably retained ergative case marking after it split off from CK (see pp. 136–137), but later, under the cultural influence of Georgian, followed the latter in replacing ergative with active case marking in Series II. Svan remains conservative in this change, retaining more nominative subjects with intransitive clauses (§6.6.2). The Naḳra-Laxamula dialect is most conservative in this respect, but even here the enormous cultural pressure of Georgian schools and other cultural institutions has resulted in the introduction of the innovative system, now coexisting with the archaic.

According to the Ancestral Active Hypothesis, on the other hand, the Kartvelian languages had active case marking at an earlier stage. The use of nominative case subjects with basic active intransitive verbs, such as (7), and with detransitivized verbs like (39) would be an innovation.[16] This development could be internally motivated or could represent a borrowing from a Caucasian language outside the Kartvelian family.[17] In this change, the Naḳra-Laxamula dialect must be interpreted as innovative, with the other Svan dialects and Georgian and Laz following its lead. This entails that examples such as (7) and (9) in Georgian and (11) and (13) in Laz are also innovations.

In the remainder of this section, I consider how each of these hypotheses accounts for the data available, and I argue that we must adopt the Ancestral Ergative Hypothesis.

Argument 1. First, there is evidence from the morphological structure of Class 3 verbs in the Naḳra-Laxamula dialect. As we saw in §6.4.1, there is an absolute correlation between the use of the narrative case in this dialect and the occurrence of the aorist suffix *-e* in the third person singular subject forms. The *-e* suffix is found in third person singular subject forms of the aorist with many transitives and never with inactive intransitives. Corresponding to this form of transitive aorists, first and second person singular subject forms have umlauted root vowels, as in Table 6.5. Thus the regular pattern is for the *-e* third person aorist to correspond to um-

Table 6.5

Singular Subject Forms in the Aorist of Transitive Verbs[a]

	'broiled it'	'destroyed it'	'darkened it'
1st person	*oxwṭqäb*	*oxwžöm*	*otbür*
2nd person	*axṭqäb*	*axžöm*	*atbür*
3rd person	*anṭqab-e*	*anžom-e*	*adbur-e*

[a]After Kaldani (1978:155).

lauted first and second person singulars. However, this is not what we find for the Class 3 verbs in *-al* in the Nak̩ra-Laxamula dialect; corresponding to third person in *-e* are first and second persons lacking umlaut, as in Table 6.6. Kaldani has shown that the pattern in Table 6.5 derives from the transitive verb root, the suffix **i*, which marked the aorist of transitive verbs, and the third person singular subject suffix **a* (Kaldani 1978). In the third person form, **i* plus **a* becomes *e*. In the first and second persons, **i* conditioned umlaut then dropped. If the *-e* suffix were original to Class 3 verbs, we would expect to find umlaut in the first and second person forms in Table 6.6.[18] Kaldani (1979; also Kaldani 1956:173) shows that one of the patterns for (inactive) intransitive verbs is derived from a Ø aorist marker plus a third person singular subject suffix **a*. This **a* conditions back umlaut in the root vowel; typically **e* becomes *ä* or *a* (see also Kaldani 1969), then drops. This gives the paradigm shown in Table 6.7.

If the verbs in Class 3 (active intransitives) had originally followed this pattern, having Ø suffixes in first and second persons in **-a* in third, we would find no change in the quality of the stem vowel in the first two and likewise none in the third person, since *a* did not affect a preceding *a* and these verbs have the suffix *-al*. When the third person **a* dropped, all three forms would be left with the same stem and suffix forms. This is

Table 6.6

Singular Subject Forms in the Aorist of Active Intransitives[a]

	'passed by'	'sang'
1st person	*otzelal*	*otγiral*
2nd person	*ätzelal*	*ätγiral*
3rd person	*ädzelal-e*	*ädγiral-e*

[a]After Kaldani (1978:150)

Table 6.7

Singular Subject Forms in the Aorist of Inactive Intransitives[a]

	'came'	'got lost'
1st person	*onqwed*	*otwep*
2nd person	*anqed*	*atwep*
3rd person	*anqad* < **an-qed-a*	*atwap* < **at-wep-a*

[a]After Kaldani (1979:219).

exactly what we find in the pattern type shown in Table 6.8 and illustrated in the (a) examples of (18)–(26). Thus the Class 3 paradigm lacking *-e* in this dialect could derive from the ∅, ∅, **-a* pattern of Table 6.7, which has been reconstructed for one kind of inactive intransitive (by Kaldani 1979). The Class 3 paradigm which has *-e* in this dialect (Table 6.6), on the other hand, could not derive from the **-i*, **-i*, **-i-a* pattern of Table 6.5, which has been reconstructed for transitives (by Kaldani 1978). This suggests that for Class 3 verbs, the ∅, ∅, **-a* pattern, with the reflexes shown in Table 6.8, is original and that the other pattern, with the reflexes shown in Table 6.6, is an innovation. Because of the absolute correlation between the verb morphology and the case marking shown in examples (18)–(26) and the general tendency toward such a correlation in the Kartvelian languages, we are justified in tentatively inferring that the use of the nominative case subject with Class 3 verbs, which is associated with the older verb morphology, is likewise older. If the use of the nominative case is older with Class 3 verbs, then intransitives of both classes used the nominative case, and thus ergative case marking is older than active. Other arguments below support this tentative inference.

Table 6.8

Singular Subject Forms in the Aorist of Active Intransitives[a]

	'played'	'sang'
1st person	*ot-šdir-al*	*ot-γir-al*
2nd person	*ät-šdir-al*	*ät-γir-al*
3rd person	*äd-šdir-al*	*äd-γir-al*

[a]After Kaldani (1978:152) and consultant work.

Argument 2. As observed above, the Ancestral Active Hypothesis entails that those intransitives with nominative case subjects discussed in §6.2–6.6 are innovative. Since there are only a few examples of this in each language, except the Naḳra-Laxamula dialect of Svan, this usage would be assumed to be a recent innovation. Given that the split of Svan from CK occurred before the seventh century B.C.,[19] the occurrence of this recent innovation in Laz, Georgian, and Svan must be due to diffusion. This implies the Naḳra-Laxamula dialect, where we find the greatest number of these forms, must be in the vanguard in this change, with other Svan dialects, Laz, and Georgian following its lead. This is a most unlikely hypothesis. The Laz and Georgians have virtually no contact with the communities where the Naḳra-Laxamula dialect is preserved, isolated high in the main chain of the Caucasus Mountains.

The Ancestral Ergative Hypothesis, in contrast, entails that those same clauses are archaic. Their small number is due to the fact that the actualization of the change from ergative to active system in Series II is nearly complete (see Chap. 14). According to this hypothesis, the change itself occurred much longer ago, probably in CGZ.

For the following reasons, it seems likely that Svan borrowed the innovative active case system from Georgian. (a) Unlike its sisters, Svan did not completely replace the inherited narrative (ergative) case marker when new functions developed. As suggested in §15.2, a change in the form of this case in the other languages may have accompanied the change in its function. (b) In the Naḳra-Laxamula subdialect, the change is incomplete and probably recent. More generally, Svan seems to retain more relics of the ergative system than do Georgian and Laz (see §6.6). (c) The data discussed in §14.2 seem to indicate that the reanalysis phase of the ergative-to-active shift had taken place a relatively short time before attested Old Georgian. If this is correct, the time frame proposed for the split of Svan from the rest of Kartvelian (see n. 19, this chapter) would indicate that the shift was after the CK period. (d) The fact that the reflexes of some CK active intransitives govern a narrative case subject in Series II of one language and nominative in a sister language (§6.5) suggests that the ergative-to-active shift did not occur in CK. Diffusion in this direction is consistent with the enormous cultural influence that Georgian exercises upon Svan (see Wixman 1980:112). For example, Svan speakers attend schools taught in Georgian, read Georgian newspapers and books, and, when asked about ethnic affiliation, reply that they are Georgian. This, together with the great respect for ancient Georgian literature, is consistent with Georgian influencing Svan.

In spite of the probability of this scenario, we cannot rule out the possibility that the ergative-to-active shift occurred *before* Svan split from its sisters, with the change simply being actualized more slowly there. In either case, the Ancestral Ergative Hypothesis implies that it is the Naḳra-Laxamula subdialect that has most effectively resisted Georgian influence in this respect. This may be compared with the fact that the Ecer-Laxamula subdialect, of which Naḳra-Laxamula is a part, alone among Svan dialects, has resisted Georgian influence to generalize the *-d* formant of the imperfect (Machavariani 1980, esp. p. 216).[20]

Argument 3. Meillet (1954:27, 1964:46) has emphasized the role of exceptions in linguistic reconstruction, and the importance of this approach for syntactic reconstruction has been reiterated by Watkins (1976).

The use of nominative subjects with active intransitives in Series II falls outside the general pattern of the attested Kartvelian languages, and these clauses are exceptions, as discussed in previous sections. As shown in §6.6, certain types of detransitivized clauses having nominative subjects also present syntactic irregularities. As exceptions, these provide the basis for reconstructing nominative case subjects for basic active intransitives and for detransitivized clauses of type II. That is, the principle of 'reconstructing on exceptions' supports the Ancestral Ergative Hypothesis.

ARGUMENT 4. Archaisms are particularly likely to occur in the most commonly used expressions of a language (Meillet 1964:31–32). As observed above, the nominative case subject is preserved with some of the most commonly used of the active intransitive predicates of the various languages, including those meaning 'come, go', 'sit down', 'stand up', and 'lie down'. These facts point to a system in which active, as well as inactive, intransitives took nominative case subjects; they are inconsistent with the Ancestral Active Hypothesis.

ARGUMENT 5. At least two active intransitive verbs occurred with nominative subjects in older Georgian and with narrative case subjects in the modern literary language (§6.2.2). (A few additional examples of a nominative-to-narrative shift are mentioned in Chapter 14 and its Appendix.) None of the sister languages provides the continuous attestation that would permit us to see the same change taking place. Because the shift can be seen to have been nominative-to-narrative in Georgian, we must infer that it took the same direction in the sister languages. This means that we must assume that the ergative distribution, rather than active, is archaic.

ARGUMENT 6. Some verbs that took nominative subjects in Old Georgian may take narrative subjects in some modern regional dialects (§6.2.1). If we make the assumption that the Old Georgian literary language represents in this respect an earlier stage of all the Georgian dialects, this difference constitutes a shift from nominative to narrative for these active intransitives. It is natural for irregularities to be eliminated, completely or in part, in dialects not governed by prescriptive norms. This development thus supports the Ancestral Ergative Hypothesis.

In evaluating a proposed reconstruction, one must also consider the linguistic change that it presupposes; in the present instance, it is the shift from ergative to active or from active to ergative that is at issue. To evaluate the putative reconstructions, we must consider whether the change involved is plausible, whether it is motivated, and whether it is internally consistent (see Chap. 2). The arguments below relate to these aspects of the evaluative process. I assume that either a shift from ergative to active or from active to ergative is plausible a priori.

ARGUMENT 7. There is an internal motivation for a shift from ergative to active; it is developed in greater detail in Part IV and is presented here only in summary form. Series III was developed fully only after the creation of Series I. This new Series consists of screeves in the evidential mood, all characterized by the application of a syntactic rule known as Inversion. Inversion applies to the subjects of transitive and active intransitive verbs and not to the subjects of inactive intransitives. This is probably a universal characteristic of the rule. In this way the new series introduced a grammatical feature that identified active intransitives with transitives. Ergative case marking, on the other hand, identifies active intransitives with inactive intransitives in the sense that their subjects are marked alike. However, a shift to active case marking in Series II would bring Series II into line with Series III in the sense that it would identify active intransitives with transitives in Series II by a shared subject case, just as they were identified with one another in Series III by a shared rule, Inversion. While we cannot assume a priori that a language will progress toward typological consistency, such changes are known to occur frequently (see Chap. 16). In this instance, a tendency to change in the direction of typological consistency provides a motivation for the change from ergative to active.

ARGUMENT 8. The positing of an ancestral ergative case system permits us to explain the development of Series I. The theory of how Series I developed is presented in detail in Part III and is only summarized here. Series I, representing durative aspect, originated as a construction that opposed Series II, which generally represented punctual aspect. Series I was characterized by a syntactic construction in which all clauses were surface intransitives. (Later, initial transitives were reanalyzed as transitive at the surface also.) As intransitives, they all governed nominative case subjects. This explains the origin of the use of this case for all subjects in Series I, but only if the case marking system were ergative with productive transitive–intransitive pairs like Svan (39) and unlike the Georgian and Laz construction exemplified by (38). This analysis of the origin of Series I, which is supported by a large number of independent arguments (see Chaps. 7–12), is consistent only with ergative case marking in Series II, not with an active system in that series. Thus, this constitutes a strong argument in favor of the Ancestral Ergative Hypothesis.

ARGUMENT 9. The Ancestral Ergative Hypothesis likewise permits an explanation of why Series I and II coexist. Other things being equal, we would expect that an innovative system, such as Series I, would replace, rather than coexist with, the ancient system (Series II), once the newer had been reanalyzed. Exactly this has taken place in some Pama Nyungan languages (Klokeid 1976, 1978). In other families, too, one type of case marking is known to have replaced another; but only occasionally has one come to coexist with another (see Chap. 17). The coexistence of two different types seems to require explanation. In Kartvelian the explanation is this: Series I developed when case marking in Series II was still ergative, and Series I existed as a productive syntactic variant of it. That is, ergative case marking existed throughout the language, though in Series I every verb was a surface intransitive and therefore had a nominative case subject. When the case marking system of Series II shifted from ergative to active, Series I could no longer function as a productive syntactic variant, though it continued to exist in the same surface form. The case marking and the morphology (see Chaps. 8–10, 12), however, became opaque, as they were no longer synchronically motivated. At this point the initially transitive clauses were reanalyzed as transitive also on the surface, and Series I came to be treated, as it is to this day, as a distinct case marking system apart from Series II and not synchronically relatable to it (see Harris 1981b:Chap. 9). This kind of explanation is possible only with the Ancestral Ergative Hypothesis.

On the basis of the arguments presented above, I conclude that Series II had ergative case marking at an earlier stage, and that this was eventually replaced by active case marking.

Two distinct questions arise in the analysis of the data presented above. First, what was the direction of change? Second, what was the mechanism of change? These two problems are logically distinct and must not be confused.

On the first question there has been substantial agreement among Kartvelologists. With the exception of Klimov (see n. 16), the view of those who have addressed the question has been that basic Class 3 verbs adopted narrative case subjects relatively recently. For example, Deeters has written: "The use of the active [narrative case] with intransitive verbs is contrary to its nature and must be interpreted as an extension that is not original" (1927:21). Others, notably Shanidze (1973:483–484), have also assumed that the use of the narrative with active intransitives in Georgian is secondary, that they originally had nominative case subjects. The present work differs from those named, not in reconstructing ergative case marking, but in using the label 'active' to characterize attested productive systems. Others have considered the productive systems in Series II of Georgian, Laz, and Svan to be ergative (see Harris 1981b:229–234 for a discussion of this from a synchronic point of view in Georgian). The present work also offers a different view of the mechanism by which this change took place; this distinct question is considered in Chapter 14.

6.8. FURTHER CHARACTERIZATION OF CK CASE MARKING

In the preceding section, it was shown that case marking in Series II in CK must have been ergative. There remain some additional details of the CK case system to be considered in this section.

6.8.1. Generalized or Restricted Ergative?

In §6.6.1, two types of ergative case distribution were defined and labeled 'generalized' and 'restricted'. In the generalized type, which seems to be more common, the subjects of derived intransitives are in the absolutive (nominative) case. In the restricted type, derived intransitives have subjects in the ergative (narrative) case.

Among the transitive–intransitive pairs presented in §6.6.2, we find derived intransitives with narrative case subjects and ones with nominative subjects. While the former sort is regular, the latter has irregular features, as shown. Because the use of the nominative in derived intransitives of these types is an exception to the general patterns of the language, we may assume that it is older than the narrative construction. This is confirmed by the fact that Svan is otherwise conservative with respect to the case changes considered here. Since the nominative construction with derived intransitives of the types illustrated in §6.6.2 is archaic, we may assume that Kartvelian had the generalized type of ergative case distribution.

The replacement of the nominative construction by the narrative in the reflexive subtype in Georgian is discussed in Chapter 14, especially §14.1.2.1. In Svan the nominative construction has been retained in many or most derived intransitives of type II. Derived intransitives, such as (b) of (42), (43), and (45)–(47), developed the morphological marking that would be consistent with this syntax, namely the suffix *-an*/*ān* of Class 2—but only in Series II, where the cases of subjects also differentiate the classes. In Series I, where classes do not differ syntactically, these verbs developed the Class 3 morphology (derivational *-al*/*āl*) that is consistent with their active semantics (see Table 6.2). For some, Series II forms have both the *-al*/*āl* of Class 3 and the *-an*/*ān* of Class 2 (Topuria 1967:237). The morphological inconsistencies of these forms may be assumed to have originated in this way.

There is additional evidence that ergative case marking in CK was of the generalized ergative type. As observed in argument 8 of §6.7 and in Chapter 1, this assumption is necessary in order to explain the origin of Series I case marking. That is, only if non-basic intransitives—specifically those which have undergone Object Demotion—have nominative case subjects, can we explain the origin of nominitive case subjects for the detransitivized sentences of Series I (see Table 6.9). There is a great deal of evidence to support this analysis of the origin of Series I presented in Chapters 7–12. Thus, an assumption of generalized ergative case marking is justified methodologically by its explanatory potential with respect to Series I in CK.

Table 6.9

Summary Reconstruction of Generalized Ergative Case Marking in CK

	Subject	Underlying direct object	Verb
Canonical transitive	narrative case	nominative case	transitive
Object demotion construction	nominative case	dative case	surface intransitive

The case rules reconstructed for CK may be stated as in (54).

(54) a. The final subject of a transitive is marked with the narrative case.

b. The final subject of an intransitive is marked with the nominative case.

c. A final direct object is marked with the nominative case.

d. A final indirect object is marked with the dative case.

These are not stated in the most compact form, but analytically for discussion of their separate parts in later chapters.

6.8.2. The Ancestral Mixed System Hypothesis

In §6.7 it was assumed that the protolanguage was either ergative or active, that is, that it had a consistent case system belonging to one of these two types. We must consider, in addition, the hypothesis that CK had a mixed system of some sort, perhaps the type attested in the Naḳra-Laxamula dialect. That is, this dialect could be viewed as preserving in Series II exactly the system that originally existed in that series. Is this a reasonable alternative to the Ancestral Ergative Hypothesis?

The combined force of arguments 2–6 in §6.7 is to establish that the direction of change is toward greater use of narrative case subjects with active intransitives verbs. This is entirely consistent with the Ancestral Mixed System Hypothesis since this could be interpreted as a loss of the ergative portion of the ergative–active system, rather than as a shift from ergative to active as suggested above. For example, we cannot rule out the possibility that both of the patterns illustrated in (18)–(26) existed at an earlier stage, with the (a) variant simply being lost with most verbs in other dialects.

Arguments 7–9 likewise do not necessarily contradict the Ancestral Mixed System Hypothesis. If we view (52b) and (53b) as Object Demotion constructions, then this pattern could have given rise to Series I just as proposed under the Ancestral Ergative Hypothesis.

Argument 1 in §6.7 does contradict the Ancestral Mixed System Hypothesis. It was shown there that the morphology of Class 3 verbs that have narrative case subjects in Naḳra-Laxamula is not original, and from this it was inferred that the case pattern is likewise not original. Yet this alone is not sufficient evidence for entirely rejecting the Ancestral Mixed System Hypothesis, since we cannot rule out restructuring the paradigm. In the remainder of this work, I will refer to the reconstruction of ergative case marking for Series II in CK, yet this must be understood as including the hereafter-unstated caveat that we cannot, with certainty, rule out the possibility that CK had, not consistent ergative case marking, but a mixed ergative–active system comparable perhaps to that found today in Naḳra-Laxamula. We can be certain of two aspects of the CK system: (a) The nominative case was used with active intransitives to a greater extent than in the daughter languages (excluding Naḳra-Laxamula) and (b) it was characterized by the transitive–intransitive pattern schematized in Table 6.9.

6.9. SUMMARY: THE GENERAL PICTURE

In this section I present a brief narrative summary of the results of the reconstruction in Chapters 3–6.

Early CK was characterized by an ergative case marking system, or possibly a mixed ergative–active system similar to that found today in the Naḳra-Laxamula dialect. At this stage only those verb forms existed that have as their reflexes in the daughter languages the forms of Series II. These forms expressed primarily aspectual and modal oppositions rather than temporal ones.

In Middle CK a new syntactic construction, Object Demotion, developed; this is schematized in Table 6.9. In this construction, all underlyingly transitive verbs were made intransitive by a rule that demoted direct objects to indirect-objecthood. Because the languages used generalized ergative case marking (defined above in §6.6.1), and because all clauses in the Object Demotion construction were surface intransitives, all had nominative case subjects. The reflex of this construction is Series I in all of the daughter languages. Series I, with the Object Demotion construction, opposed Series II aspectually, Series I representing durative aspect and Series II generally representing punctual aspect. This change also made possible the development of temporal oppositions as some screeves were partially reinterpreted.

In Late CK, Series III developed, characterized by a productive syntactic construction known as Inversion. It was probably at this stage that Svan split off from the rest of the family, and the Nak̩ra-Laxamula dialect retains ergative case marking in Series II as one productive system today.

During the CGZ period, the case marking system of Series II shifted from ergative to active. This may have been the indirect result of the development of Series III, in which the syntactic rule Inversion identifies active intransitives with transitives and distinguishes both from inactive intransitives. Because of the shift in case marking type in Series II, the forms of Series I could no longer be related to it by a productive synchronic rule; and as a result, the underlyingly transitive clauses in Series I were reanalyzed as transitive at the surface level as well. Throughout this reanalysis, the same case marking pattern was retained and was reinterpreted as an accusative system, with all subjects in the nominative case and all objects in the dative. This stage of development is preserved in Georgian.

In Laz, the new active case system of Series II spread into Series I, unifying the two series under one case marking type.

In Mingrelian, the narrative case, which had already been widened in scope from transitive subjects alone to subjects of active intransitives in CGZ, was now extended to include all subjects. Thus, both series in Mingrelian have accusative case marking, but the case markers are used differently in the two series.

Lastly, Svan has likewise shifted from ergative to active case marking in Series II. Probably this is the result of borrowing from Georgian, which is culturally dominant; however, we cannot rule out the possibility that the shift to active in Series II was begun in Late CK.

The summary above is based on the reconstruction made and justified in Chapters 3–6 and on changes described in greater detail in later parts of this work.

NOTES

[1]For example, the eleven examples cited in Dzidziguri contain only 'come, go' and 'stand up' verbs. Without independent tests of the type developed in Holisky (1981a), we cannot be certain of the view of the semantics of a particular verb in a given dialect (see §2.1.2). We are best informed by the remarks of those who have investigated these dialects at first hand and who report that those intransitives that take the narrative case in regional dialects are ones that "indicate the action of the subject" as opposed to ones that signify "its (the subject's) situation and being–existence" (Topuria 1923:115). Verbs that take narrative subjects in these dialects are "active, dynamic" (Topuria 1954:455); and they "express active action" (Jajanidze 1970:258).

[2]This example is actually in Series IV, but the same case system is used as in Series I and II in Laz; examples (16a) and (17a) show the same verb in Series I and II with nominative subjects.

[3]The syntax of this subdialect has apparently not been described before, except for the three examples given in Klimov (1973:239). Kaldani (1968:135), a native speaker of Laxamula, has commented on the productivity of the morphological type presented here. As shown below, the syntax is closely tied to the morphology.

[4]Except for (24), examples (18)–(26) were elicited by presenting the consultant with the equivalent Georgian sentence, each of which requires a narrative case subject: *cxenma irbina q̣anaši, bavšvebma ičxubes, ḳacma istẏina,* and so forth. In spite of this bias toward the narrative case subject, the nominative case was often the first offered.

With the proper intonation, the (a) verb forms can serve as imperatives, the nominative being used as vocative and the second person imperative (e.g., *ädš-diral*) being equivalent to the second person aorist without the subject person marker (e.g., < **ad-i-šdir-al* 'play!' contrasting with *ätšdiral* < **ad-x-i-šdir-al* 'you played', where the second person subject marker, **x*, conditions **d* > *t*); see Chap. 5 on the relation of imperative to aorist in Kartvelian.

[5]I am using the suffix *-al* and its variants here as in Chapter 3, to define a morphological class; I refer only to those verbs that have derivational *-al*. Note that Class 1 and 2 verbs may also, in some dialects, take inflectional *-al* to indicate plurality of the initial direct object or repeated action.

[6]It is reported that in some languages of Australia and New Guinea an ergative marker may be dropped when the meaning would be clear without it (e.g., Dixon 1979:72ff.). Such a process would not account for the data described here, for several reasons. First, the nominative case form (for some words) is not equivalent to the narrative form minus the case marker, e.g., *eǰnem/eynem* 'he/NAR' beside *eǰi* 'he/NOM'. Second, the nominative cannot be substituted for the narrative with Class I verbs, like (29), but only with Class 3 verbs.

[7]The consultant for the dialect identified here as Lašx had lived in both the Lašx and Lenṭex areas; her data generally represented the dialect of the former.

[8]The Svan form cited here has not been related to the Georgian and Laz forms

(see Gagua 1976:52ff.; Klimov 1964:62–63), but like them consists of the root *gza* and derivational affixes.

[9]On Laz *γa(r)γal* : Svan *gərgal*, see Schmidt (1962:69) and Zhghenti (1949:147). Laz *ster* probably corresponds to Svan *šdir* 'play'; on the regular derivation of Laz *t* (here *st*) and Svan *šd* from CK *$*s_1t$*, see Gamkrelidze and Machavariani (1965:135ff).

[10]On *vaxšm* in Georgian and Svan, see Gabliani (1925:177). Nozadze (1974:40) gives *ädwaxšmale* (Class 3) for this verb in Lower Bal.

[11]This syntactic property may be limited to the root *ç̣*, which is defective, occurring only in Series II and III (Gagua 1976:101). The root occurs also in Laz (Chikobava 1938:398; Gagua 1976:103), where it also governs Lexical Object Demotion:

(54) *siǰa-k bozo-s nuḳu-s komoçḳams*
groom-NAR girl-DAT face-DAT he/look/to.her/I
'The bridegroom looks the girl in the face.' 'The bridegroom looks at the girl's face.' (Dumézil 1937:117,6)

This especially brings out the difference between Svan and Laz with respect to Object Demotion: in this Laz example the subject is in the narrative, while in Svan (39) the cognate verb in the same construction has a nominative subject.

[12]There is also a noninversion construction for this verb in Series III (Gagua 1976:104-105); this in no way decreases the cogency of the evidence in (40).

[13]The form in (52b) has the *-al* suffix of Class 3 verbs and lacks the *-an* suffix of Class 2 verbs in Series II. This contrasts with a Class 2 form on the same root, such as Upper Bal *läxšdirän* 'he played with him'.

[14]Shanidze made this statement with respect to Georgian, but it is likewise valid for Laz and Svan; there are exceptions to this generalization in each of these three languages, as discussed here and in Harris (1981a).

[15]The periods here labeled 'Early CK', 'Middle CK', and 'Late CK' do not necessarily coincide with the periods so named in discussions of diachronic phonology. These terms are used here only to establish the relative chronology of changes in syntax and morphology.

[16]See Klimov (1973:64–65, 237, 239; 1976). Klimov supports his view that Kartvelian languages once had active case marking by the claim that active case marking is a more primitive type than ergative. See Comrie's review (1976b:259) on the internal inconsistency of Klimov's claims concerning Kartvelian.

[17]Kaldani (1955:137–139) has argued, on the basis of thirteenth century church rosters, that the present inhabitants of the village of Laxamula are not descended from ancient inhabitants of that place. He has suggested that the forebears of today's Laxamulians arrived sometime after the sixteenth century and, on the basis of Mingrelian surnames such as Č̣ḳadua and Kobalia, has proposed that they came there from Mingrelia. It is not clear how this proposal might apply to the Naḳra area, where my consultants bore the Svan surname Cindeliani. At any rate, we can definitely rule out Mingrelian as a source for the variant case marking found in Naḳra-Laxamula. In Series II in Mingrelian, all subjects bear the narrative case;

clearly this cannot explain case marking with Class 3 verbs in Naḳra-Laxamula, since it is the use of the nominative that is aberrant from the point of view of the other dialects.

[18]Kaldani (1978) shows that this pattern has indeed been extended to the forms of the verbs in Table 6.6 in the Upper Bal dialect.

[19]Vogt (1938) argues that Mingrelian and Georgian were already distinct at the time of Armenian settlement in the Caucasus (seventh century B.C.). Since it is agreed that Svan broke off from CK before Zan and Georgian split, the break between Svan and CGZ must have occurred before the seventh century B.C.

[20]The Laxamula dialect has been characterized as conservative in other respects as well, such as retension of *h* initially before *a* and *e* (Kaldani 1959b:96) and retension of the third person subject prefix (Kaldani 1979).

III

The Development of Series I in Common Kartvelian

7

An Account of the Development of Series I

In Part II it was shown that Common Kartvelian had ergative case marking in Series II screeves and that Series II is older than Series I. These facts have not escaped the attention of other linguists, and several hypotheses concerning the origin of Series I have been proposed. In §7.1, I describe the differences between Series II and Series I, in this way defining what it is that must be accounted for by an acceptable hypothesis of the diachronic relations between the series. In §7.2, I discuss existing hypotheses concerning the relations these series bear to each other. Finally in §7.3 I present an explicit proposal and some preliminary arguments to support it. More lengthy arguments are presented in the remaining chapters of this Part.

7.1. FACTS TO BE ACCOUNTED FOR

A theory of the mechanism of change from Series II to Series I should account for all of the differences between these two systems. If it restricts itself to case marking differences alone, a diachronic hypothesis will give an incomplete picture and will be inferior to a hypothesis that encompasses the language as a whole.

In Parts I and II we saw that aspect and the case marking systems used in Series I and II in Old Georgian differ. In addition, in Old Georgian there are two morphological features that distinguish Series I as a whole from Series II. In general, Series I verb forms have series markers and Series II forms lack them. For example, Table 7.1 lists forms of the verb *šeynebay* 'build', with third person singular subject and object. Here we see that the series marker *-eb-* occurs in all Series I forms and in no Series II forms. Other series markers in Old Georgian include *-av*, *-am*, *-i*, and *-ob*. Some verbs have a zero series marker; Table 7.2 lists forms for one such verb, *ç̣eray* 'write'; the forms are directly comparable to those in Table 7.1. This verb exhibits no series marker in Series I. Verbs that take series markers, like *šeynebay*, have the series marker in all Series I forms and in no Series II forms. In this sense, series markers distinguish Series I from Series II and must be accounted for by a hypothesis that would relate these series diachronically.

The second morphological marker that distinguishes Series I as a whole from Series II is ablaut grade. In Old Georgian ablaut had already been lost from many verbs, such as the one in Table 7.2. Gamkrelidze and Machavariani (1965) have studied ablaut in Kartvelian in detail and show that the pattern in Table 7.3 was characteristic of Kartvelian and was retained for some verbs in Old Georgian as well. Table 7.3 shows that, for some verbs, Series I was differentiated from Series II in part by ablaut

Table 7.1

Occurrence of Series Markers in Series I

Series I	Series II
a-šeyn-eb-s	*a-šeyn-i-s* 'he builds it'
a-šeyn-eb-d-a	*a-šeyn-a* 'he built it'
a-šeyn-eb-d-e-s	*a-šeyn-o-s* 'he will build it'
a-šeyn-eb-d-i-n	*a-šeyn-e-n* 'let him build it'

Table 7.2

Occurrence of Zero Series Marker in Series I

Series I	Series II
ç̣er-s	*ç̣er-i-s* 'he writes it'
ç̣er-d-a	*ç̣er-a* 'he wrote it'
ç̣er-d-e-s	*ç̣er-o-s* 'he will write it'
ç̣er-d-i-n	*ç̣er-e-n* 'let him write it

Table 7.3

Occurrence of *e*-Grade Ablaut in Series I

Series I	Series II	
dreḳ-s	*driḳ-i-s*	'he bends it'
dreḳ-d-a	*driḳ-a*	'he bent it'
dreḳ-d-e-s	*driḳ-o-s*	'he will bend it'
dreḳ-d-i-n	*driḳ-e-n*	'let him bend it'

grade. The forms in this table are representative, but ablaut may also involve other vowels; it is described more fully in Chapter 8.

We have now discussed four ways in which Series I differed from Series II: (a) aspect, (b) case marking system, (c) series markers, and (d) ablaut grade. Each of these must be explained.

With respect to agreement markers, there are two differences between Series I and II. In Old Georgian, a suffix *-en* was added to the form of transitive verbs having a plural direct object and to the form of inactive intransitives having a plural subject. There are additional restrictions on its occurrence, and it is described more fully in Chapter 10. The peculiarity of this morpheme that is of interest here is that it occurs in Series II, but not in Series I.

Series I also differed from II with respect to the distribution of the third person object agreement marker; this marker was realized as *h*/*x*/*s*/∅, depending on the following phonological environment. In describing the distribution of this morpheme in Classical Georgian, Shanidze (1957c) showed that in Series II it marks agreement with a third person indirect object. In Series I, on the other hand, it occurs with third person indirect objects, but also under certain circumstances with verb forms having a third person direct object and no indirect object. Example (1) illustrates respectively a Series I and a Series II form of the verb *ganḳurnebay* 'heal'.

(1) a. *rametu me gan-v-h-ḳurneb mat*
that I/NOM PV-1.SUBJ-3.OBJ-heal/I them/DAT
'that I heal them' (Hosea 11:3)

b. *ražams gan-v-ḳurno me israeyli*
when PV-1.SUBJ-heal/II I/NAR Israel/NOM
'when I would have healed Israel' (Hosea 7:1)

In the Series I form, (1a), the direct object, *mat* 'them', triggers third person object agreement, realized as *h-* before *ḳ*. In the Series II form,

(1b), the direct object *israeyli* 'Israel', does not trigger the marker *h*-. Additional examples cited in Shanidze (1957c:183–189) show that, in general, a third person direct object may trigger agreement in Series I, but not in Series II. This is discussed in greater detail in Chapter 12.

I have now enumerated six differences between Series I and II:

(2) a. aspect
b. case marking system
c. Series markers
d. ablaut grade
e. *-en/n-* plural marker
f. *h/x/s/∅* object marker

These features differentiate Series I as a whole from Series II, by virtue of their presence or absence in an entire series or their different realization in an entire series.

There are some additional differences, whose status is, however, not equivalent to those in (2), in that they do not characterize a series as a whole, but only some part of it. As Tables 7.1–7.3 show, some screeves of Series I have the formant *-d*, while this formant is not found in Series II.[1] On the other hand, the formant *-o* occurs in the Series II subjunctive (see third line of Tables 7.1–7.3), but is not found in Series I. In Series II aorist forms, certain verbs take the agreement marker *-o* for third person singular subject, such as *ako* 'he praised it'; this morpheme is not found in Series I. Similarly, the third person singular subject marker *-n* is limited to the present screeve in Zan (Chikobava 1936:89). While the reasons for these differences between Series I and II should be sought, they do not require explanation to the same extent that features (a)–(f) do. Any theory that would relate Series I to Series II must minimally account for these features.

Some of the Old Georgian characteristics (a)–(f) are not found in the sister languages. For example, in Svan there is neither *En*-Agreement with direct objects, (e), nor use of *x/∅* (cognate to Georgian *h/x/s/∅*) to mark direct objects in Series I, (f). Nor does Svan have additional features that distinguish Series I as a whole from Series II. Details concerning case marking and aspect in Svan are in Chapters 3 and 5, while ablaut and series markers are discussed in Chapters 8 and 9 respectively.

Each of the Zan languages has a morphological feature not found in the related languages, one characteristic of which is that it occurs only in Series I. In Mingrelian, a suffix *-k* occurs just in the present screeve, with first or second person singular subjects (Chikobava 1936:96–97, 135; Lomtatidze 1946:131). The examples in Table 7.4 illustrate the occurrence of this morpheme; examples are from Chikobava (1936:137). However, while the suffix *-k* is limited to Series I, it does not characterize Series I as a whole, as it does not occur in the imperfect, conditional, or subjunctive I.

It is believed that the suffix *-r* of Laz is related to Mingrelian *-k* (Asatiani 1973; Lomtatidze 1946). In Laz, *-r* occurs in the first and second persons singular and plural, and may be found in all screeves of Series I (Lomtatidze 1946:133; Marr 1910:65, 58). Marr cites examples *viq̇vert* 'we are', *iq̇vert* 'you-PL are' as evidence for the former, and the imperfects, *bxerṭi* 'I was 'sitting', *xerṭi* 'you were sitting' as evidence of its occurrence throughout Series I.

Both the *-k* of Mingrelian and the *-r* of Laz are believed to be secondary developments and not part of CK (Deeters 1930:55; Lomtatidze 1946). Since Series I seems to have developed in CK, these suffixes would not appear to be relevant to the establishment of this series. In any case, neither characterizes the series as a whole, having originally been limited to the present screeve (Lomtatidze 1946:133). Both morphemes are discussed in Chapter 16. Laz and Mingrelian do not offer other characteristics that would add to the list in (2).[2]

It is useful to consider also which categories of Series II are preserved in Series I. The root of the verb is essentially the same, except for the effects of ablaut; there are a few suppletive verbs that have one root in Series I and an unrelated root in Series II.

The occurrence and form of the preverbs are the same in Series I and II in Old Georgian. Preverbs indicate direction, orientation, and other spacial nuances of the action described by the verb. In the modern languages, preverbs indicate perfective aspect, but this is considered a later development (Machavariani 1974).

Other morphology is shared in Series I and II. The screeve formants *-i* and *-e* (Zan *-a*) occur in both series: The former is found in Series I in the present of some verbs (Old Georgian *iç̣erebis* 'it is written'), and in Series II in the habitual II (*cadis* 'he tries it'); see also §9.5. The formant *-e* occurs in Series I in the subjunctive I (*aṭpobdes* 'he will heat it'), and

Table 7.4

Occurrence of *-k* in Mingrelian

Present (Series I)		Aorist (Series II)	
b-zim-un-k	'I measure it'	*b-zim-i*	'I measured it'
zim-un-k	'you measure it'	*zim-i*	'you measured it'
zim-un-s	'he measures it'	*zim-u*	'he measured it'

in Series II in the subjunctive II (*gantpes* 'it will heat up') and elsewhere (see Chap. 5).

Except for the third person singular object discussed above, person markers are shared between Series I and II. For example, we find Old Georgian *vc̣er* 'I write, am writing it' in Series I and *vc̣ere* 'I wrote it' in Series II, where *v-* indicates first person in both forms. Similarly, the second person object marker *g-* occurs in Series I *mo-g-ḳlavs* 'he kills you' and in Series II *mo-g-ḳla* 'he killed you'. Additional examples may be found in the handbooks, which show that other person markers occur in both Series I and II in all four languages. While the plural marker *-en/n* (see above) is limited to Series II, the plural markers Georgian and Zan *-t* and Svan *-d* and *-x* are not limited, but mark plurality in Series I or II. For example we find Old Georgian *vc̣ert* 'we write it' in Series I and *vc̣eret* 'we wrote it' in II. The third person markers fuse person and number agreement, such that in Old Georgian *-s*, *-n*, *-a*, and *-o* mark third person singular subjects, and *-en*, *-an*, *-n*, *-ed*, and *-es* mark third person plural subjects. Which of these forms occurs is determined by the screeve and by the preceding phonological environment. With the exceptions noted above, each form is found in both series.

Finally, the syntactic constructions involving version (creation of an indirect object), inversion, causatives, and voice differences, as well as the morphological exponents of these constructions, are the same in Series I and II.

We can summarize this section by observing that there are six features that distinguish Series I as a whole from Series II as a whole in at least one Kartvelian language. As we saw in Part II, aspect can be reconstructed for CK as a system that opposes imperfective, durative (Series I) to perfective, punctual (Series II); reflexes of this system exist in all of the daughter languages. In all of the Kartvelian languages except Laz, different case marking patterns characterize Series I and II. In every Kartvelian language, Series I is characterized by the occurrence of series markers for at least some verbs. The ablaut system reconstructed for CK distinguishes Series I from II (Gamkrelidze and Machavariani 1965), and this is partially preserved in all the languages. The object pluralizer *-en* occurred only in Series II; it is found only in Georgian. The third person singular person agreement marker distinguishes Series I from II by its different distribution; this characteristic of its occurrence is limited to Georgian. These facts must be accounted for by any theory that would relate Series I to Series II.

In addition, several morphemes occur only in one series or the other but do not characterize all screeves of the series. These include Georgian, Svan, Mingrelian *-d* and Laz *-ṭ-*, as well as Mingrelian *-k* and Laz *-r*.

7.2. EXISTING HYPOTHESES

The complexity of the relationship between Series I and II in the Kartvelian languages requires an explanation in historical terms, and the observation that Series II is older than Series I has spawned a variety of hypotheses to relate the two systems historically. In this section, these hypotheses are briefly reviewed.

7.2.1. Borrowing

There are remarkable similarities between CK and Proto–Indo-European in the areas of vowel inventories, ablaut and sonant systems, and canonical form of morphemes (Gamkrelidze 1967; Gamkrelidze and Machavariani 1965; Machavariani 1966; cf. Schmidt 1971), while in some other respects the Kartvelian languages are typologically similar to the languages of the north Caucasus—the occurrence of ejective consonants, polypersonalism of the verb, and certain aspects of the system of nominal declension. Viewing the syntactic organization of the simple clause in this light, Machavariani (1966) suggests that while the system in Series II is original to Kartvelian, the system of Series I was borrowed in the course of long contact between Kartvelian and Indo–European languages.

One important problem with such a hypothesis is that it is untestable: there is no type of data that could disprove it. The most that can be done is to establish that some other explanation is plausible.

A further problem is that this theory fails to explain any of the features listed in section 7.1 as distinguishing Series I from II. In particular, Machavariani's claim that the accusative-type case marking system of Series I was borrowed from Indo–European fails to explain the way in which this system is realized in Kartvelian. Taking the ergative-type system of Series II in CK as the historical starting point, Machavariani's hypothesis does not explain why the *-i* (nominative) case should be chosen, rather than the narrative, to mark all subjects. (The case name, "nominative," is rather deceptive in this sense, labeling as it does both the subject case of accusative systems and the absolutive case of ergative systems.) There can be no universal proscription against the use of an ergative (narrative) as the general subject case in such a situation, since exactly such a distribution is found in certain Mayan languages. For example, in Yucatec the so-called ergative marks the subjects of transitives in the past tense (comparable to Kartvelian Series II) and of all verbs in the present (comparable to Kartvelian Series I); see Blair (1964). This system can be represented as Table 7.5 and can be contrasted with Kartvelian as represented in Table 7.6. The system found in Yucatec and represented in Table 7.5 is not to

Table 7.5

Distribution of Markers in Yucatec[a]

	Direct object	Subject of intransitive	Subject of transitive
Present system	A	B	B
Past system	A	A	B

[a]"A" and "B" in Table 7.5 are used as in the table of alignment types (Table 1.1), not in the way Mayanists use these labels. In Yucatec these markers are part of the verb complex.

Table 7.6

Distribution of Cases in Georgian and Svan

	Direct object	Subject of intransitive	Subject of transitive
Series I	C	A	A
Series II	A	A	B

be expected a priori, but neither does Machavariani's theory of borrowing provide any explanation of why it was the *-i* case (A) that Kartvelian put in the function of representing the subject in Series I. Nor does this theory offer any basis for the use of the dative case to mark the direct object, a function not found for it in any other series.

In addition, the theory of borrowing fails to relate the newly developed case marking systems to the other features that distinguish Series I from II, including aspect, series markers, ablaut, *-en* pluralizer, and the distribution of *h/s/x/Ø*, as set out in §7.1.

7.2.2. Reanalysis of Nominalizations

Braithwaite (1973) has suggested that Series I forms originated as masdars with the auxiliary *qopna* 'be', and that the case marking they govern results from this. Since the verb *qopna* governs a nominative case subject in Series II, if Series I forms originated as periphrastics using this auxiliary, it is entirely reasonable that their subject should also be marked with the nominative. The cases of the direct and indirect object must also be accounted for. In Old Georgian, we find the initial direct object of nominalizations marked with the genitive case or with the dative case; the initial indirect object is marked with the dative, allative, or with the postposition *-tvis* (Harris 1979). It is therefore not implausible that the dative marking of both objects derives historically from their role as retired objects of nominalizations.[3] Braithwaite's hypothesis also has the virtue of accounting for the occurrence of series markers in Series I, since these morphemes are found in nominalizations (e.g., Old Georgian *ašeynebs* 'he builds it', *aγšeyneba* 'building'). Braithwaite also relates this to aspectual differences between the series.[4]

There are several problems with this hypothesis. First, it does not explain why we find *e*-grade ablaut in Series I and the masdar. As described more fully in Chapter 8, both *e*-grade and *i*-grade are found in Series II. It is not clear on this hypothesis why *e*-grade should have been generalized for the masdar and for the Series I forms said to be derived from it.

Second, the facts of Person Agreement are not consistent with nominalization analysis. In periphrastic structures in Georgian, the agreement markers normally occur on the finite auxiliary, not on the nonfinite verb form; examples of periphrasis are the passive in (3) and a future in (4); see Kavtaradze (1960:199).

(3) *gardagorvebul iq̣o lodi igi*
rolled/away it/be/II stone/NOM DET
'The stone was rolled away.' (Mk 16:4)

(4) *arcaγa q̣opad ars*
NEG/too to.be it/be/I
'And it will never be; and it is never to be.' (Mt 24:21AB)

Examples (3) and (4) are from Old Georgian; the fact that the auxiliary bears agreement is typical of such constructions in Kartvelian languages. However, Braithwaite's analysis might still be correct if the originally periphrastic construction had been reinterpreted as a simple finite verb form. This reanalysis would explain why the initial subject triggers Subject Person Agreement, and why the initial indirect object triggers Indirect Object Person Agreement. It does not, however, explain why direct objects trigger *h/x/s/∅* in Series I but not in Series II (see example (1) above).

Third, this hypothesis does not explain the fact that *-en* plural marker is triggered by direct objects in Series II, but not in Series I.

In sum, the nominalization hypothesis explains aspectual differences, (a), case marking differences, (b), and the occurrence of series markers, (c). However, it fails to account for ablaut, (d), the distribution of the *h/x/s/∅* marker, (e), or that of the *-en* pluralizer, (f).

7.2.3. Intransitive with Oblique Object

Zorrell (1930:93) suggests an explanation for Series I case marking, which has been echoed in several forms by other linguists. Zorrell proposes that the direct object in Series I is marked with the dative case as a sort of locative expression. He explicitly compares the Series I construction with the German expressions *er malt an einem Bild* (versus *er malt ein Bild*) and *er schreibt an einem Brief* (versus *er schreibt einen Brief*) where the object, *Bild, Brief,* is treated as an oblique, marked with a preposition *an*. Comparable examples in English are *he knits on a scarf* versus *he knits a scarf* and *he read in the book* versus *he read the book.* Zorrell apparently felt it unnecessary to explain the use of the nominative case as a subject case in Series I, since subject marking is the normal function of a case named "nominative."

Deeters (1930:115; 1963:59) likewise suggests that the notional direct object is to be understood as a locative, associating this with a participle—*er bau-end-ist am-Hause.* He sees this as an explanation of both the case and the occurrence of *h/x/s/∅* agreement. He goes further than Zorrell in proposing explicitly that historically Series I was intransitive.

Pätsch (1967) also sees Series I forms as originally nontransitive, that is, not distinguishing transitive from intransitive in an overt way. If (Series II) case marking were ergative, and if clauses in Series I were not transitive, then their subjects would be expected to bear the nominative (unmarked) case. Like Zorrell and Deeters, Pätsch considers the direct object to be an oblique object in Series I. She further suggests a correlation between this hypothesis and the aspectual differences between the two series.

Rogava (1975) agrees that Series I was originally intransitive, while the logical direct object was grammatically an oblique *(ubralo damateba).* Rogava compares the original Series I forms with the so-called labile construction, which is found in languages of the North West and North East Caucasian families, as well as other languages of the world. Western linguists call this construction the 'antipassive'. Both terms refer to clauses in which the direct object of a transitive verb is either left unexpressed or is put into an oblique case, often the dative. Rogava suggests that at first Kartvelian had the (Series II) construction,

(5) *man* *mḳis* *igi*
he/ERG he/mows/it/II it/NOM
'He mows it.'

out of which developed the labile intransitive construction of Series I:

(6) **igi* *mḳis*
he/NOM he/mows/I
'He mows.'

He suggests that later a direct object was added "by analogy," but in the dative case, as a general object case:[5]

(7) *igi mḳis mas*
it/DAT
'He mows it.'

Anderson (1977:349–352), like Zorrell and Rogava, notes the similarity of Kartvelian's Series I to sentences like *John shot at Bill* (versus *John shot Bill*) and *John chewed on his steak* (versus *John chewed his steak*), where the direct object occurs as an oblique object. Anderson suggests that objects are demoted, making the clauses intransitive, and thus accounting for the case marking in an ergative-type system. He goes on to observe that in other, unrelated languages, the demotion of an object is correlated with imperfective or durative aspect, which contrasts with a construction not involving demotion, which is correlated with perfective or punctual aspect.

Aronson (1979:300–303) suggests that the opposition between the direct and indirect objects is neutralized in Series I (p. 300) or that the dative-marked patients of transitive verbs in Series I "were indeed indirect objects, or, better, non-direct objects" (p. 301). He suggests that the series markers were intransitivizing suffixes and relates the formation of Series I to the aspectual differences observed (pp. 301–302). Aronson explicitly argues for the non-direct objecthood of the patient in Series I on the grounds that in Series I, but not in Series II, it triggers the indirect object marker *h/x/s/∅*.

Boeder (1979:462–463) gives a similar analysis, also drawing the parallel with the labile or antipassive of the North West Caucasian languages and other languages of the world. He too notes that the antipassive is normally associated with imperfective or durative aspect and contrasts with a perfective or punctual, as in Kartvelian.

Thus, a number of linguists have observed this parallelism of the Kartvelian Series I to the antipassive, which involves a direct object marked with an oblique case; they have observed the same correlation with aspectual differences; and they have noted that this is related to the fact that the third person direct object in Series I often shows INDIRECT-object-like agreement (*h/x/s/∅*). In Chapter 1 I showed that this hypothesis is inconsistent with the active-type case marking found in Old Georgian and reconstructible for CGZ. In Part II, however, I showed that, we must reconstruct a case marking system with ergative alignment for Series II in CK. Therefore, although the intransitive hypothesis is inconsistent with the system attested in Old Georgian, it is not inconsistent with the system reconstructed in Part II.

7.3. AN EXPLICIT PROPOSAL

In the next three chapters I present new evidence for an analysis similar to the "intransitive with oblique object" hypothesis, but here made explicit. New arguments are based on ablaut (Chapter 8), series markers (Chapter 9), and the *-en* pluralizer (Chapter 10).

I propose that the grammar of Proto-CK contained a rule of Object Demotion:

Object Demotion: Direct objects become indirect objects.

Such a rule would have no effect on the subject-hood of the underlying subject. Applying to a transitive initial structure, it would produce an output that lacked a direct object. Without a direct object, the clause would be intransitive at superficial syntactic levels (Harris 1981b:186). This analysis therefore predicts that such clauses would have all of the properties of final intransitive clauses and that the initial direct object would have all of the properties of a surface indirect object.

The Chômeur Law states that a consequence of Object Demotion in Kartvelian is that the initial indirect object becomes an indirect object chômeur. Therefore, my proposal claims that the initial indirect object once had all of the properties of indirect object chômeurs. As discussed in Harris (1981b), in the Kartvelian languages indirect object chômeurs also occur in inversion forms (pp. 119ff.). Retired indirect objects, of which indirect object chômeurs are a subtype, also occur in organic causatives (pp. 81–85), analytic passives (pp. 110–112), as well as with nonfinite verb forms (Chap. 10). In all of these constructions, the properties of retired indirect objects can be studied, and it can be determined whether or not the predictions made by Object Demotion are borne out by the data.

This analysis for initial transitives with an indirect object can be represented as the network shown in Figure 7.1, which corresponds to (8) and examples in other Series I forms.

(8)	*vano*	*deda-s*	*ceril-s*	*cers*
	vano/NOM	mother-DAT	letter-DAT	he/write/it/I
	'Vano writes a letter to [his] mother.'			

With respect to initial intransitive clauses, we must distinguish two types. An active intransitive has an initial subject and no initial direct object (see Chap. 3). Lacking a direct object, it does not meet the input conditions for Object Demotion, and the rule cannot apply. The subject

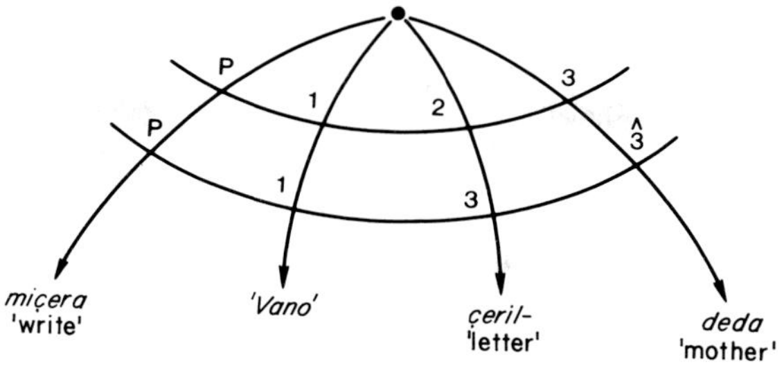

Figure 7.1 Initial transitives with an indirect object: 1, subject; 2, direct object; 3, indirect object; 3̂, indirect object chômeur (see §2.1.4); P, predicate.

and the optional indirect object are unaffected; this is given in Figure 7.2, which corresponds to (9) and other forms in Series I.

(9) *vano* *ṭiris*
vano/NOM he/cry/I
'Vano cries.'

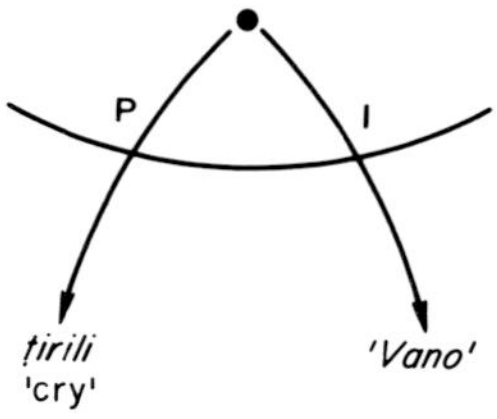

Figure 7.2 Initial active intransitives: 1, subject; P, predicate.

A second type of initial intransitive is the inactive intransitive, which has an initial direct object (and optional indirect object), but has no initial subject (Chapter 3, this volume; Harris 1981b:191–203, 239–241; Harris 1982; Shanidze 1973:§346; Tschenkéli 1958:253). In Series II, a rule of Unaccusative applies obligatorily in all such structures to make the direct object the subject. Under the present proposal, clauses of this type in Series I would meet the input conditions of both Unaccusative and Object Demotion; the proposal makes no prediction as to which rule would apply. What we find is that Unaccusative, not Object Demotion, applies to inactive intransitives in Series I; this is given in Figure 7.3, which corresponds to (10) and similar examples in Series I.[6]

(10) *isini* *arian*
they/NOM they/be/I
'They are.'

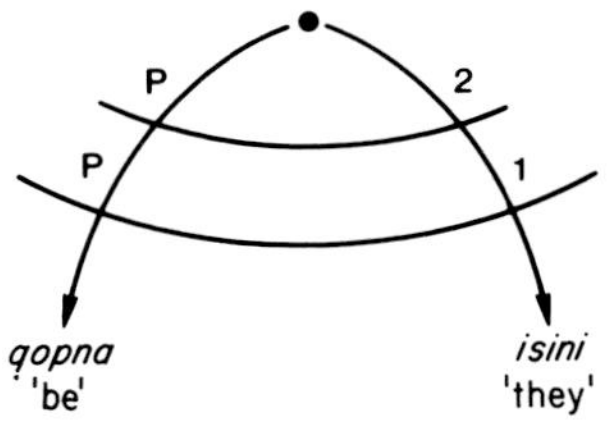

Figure 7.3 Initial inactive intransitives: 1, subject; 2, direct object; P, predicate.

It is proposed that during the period of CGZ, structures like (8) were reinterpreted, such that the initial direct object was reanalyzed as final direct object, and initial indirect object as final indirect object. The effects of this reanalysis are described in §15.1.

NOTES

[1]The formant *-d* does occur in the so-called mixed subjunctive and mixed habitual screeves of Old Georgian Series II (Imnaishvili 1977; Kiknadze 1967); however, these screeves are not attested until the ninth century (Imnaishvili 1977:13) and are considered secondary developments (Shandize 1945:843). Svan secondarily extended this suffix, *-da*, to aorist forms of some verbs (Topuria 1967:158–159, 166).

[2]The suffixal formants of inactive intransitives (unaccusatives, passives, and potentials) in Zan occur only in Series I (Chikobava 1936:111). It is most likely that these formants, *-e* and *-u*, derived from series markers *-ep/em/en* and *-up/um/un* (see Chap. 9). Series markers *-eb* and *-en* of Georgian and Svan, respectively, are used in the same function.

[3]Braithwaite suggests that the objects were marked with the dative in Series I, not for the reason given here, but because this is the marking used for objects of verbs having nominative subjects in Series II. Indirect objects were indeed marked with the dative in Series II, but verbs having nominative case subjects in this series had no final direct objects in Old Georgian, and therefore there existed no such precedent for their marking (see Chaps. 1 and 3).

[4]Braithwaite proposes that Series I in Modern Georgian derives SYNCHRONICALLY from Series II. However, the two case marking systems in Modern Georgian cannot be related by synchronic rules (Harris 1981b:Chap. 9). Although this analysis is an impossible one synchronically for Modern Georgian, it presents an interesting possibility diachronically, and it is in this way that I have considered it here.

[5]This suggestion is rather problematic. The dative became a "general object case" only after the inception of Series I; in Series II, which Rogava, too, recognizes as representing the original situation, the surface DIRECT object is only in

the nominative, not in the dative. If the direct object was added subsequently "by analogy," it would seem that it should be in the nominative. If, on the other hand, the dative object is part of the labile construction, as in some other languages, then it is not clear why it should not have been present from the beginning.

[6]The correct prediction is made by the Final 1 Law (Perlmutter and Postal 1983b:100–101) in conjunction with the analysis proposed here.

8

Ablaut

The proposal made in §7.3 entails that when Object Demotion was a productive rule of grammar, all Series I verb forms were surface intransitives and therefore had all of the grammatical properties of surface intransitives. In this chapter it is shown that (a) in Early CK before the introduction of Series I, transitive verb forms, for at least some verb types, were distinguished from intransitive forms of the same root by ablaut and (b) in Series I these verbs had the ablaut grade of the intransitive stem after the introduction of that series. Later, when Object Demotion ceased to be a productive rule and Series I was reanalyzed, the dialects made different adaptive changes in the original ablaut system.

8.1. ABLAUT IN MONOMORPHEMIC VERB STEMS IN CK

Old Georgian verbs present a bewildering array of stem forms, apparently determined by the series, screeve, subject person, transitivity, and conjugational type of the verb. While the various ablaut classes were described and classified long ago and the problems surrounding them stated, many of those problems were solved only in 1965, when Gamkrelidze and Machavariani presented a complete study of the problems of the ablaut system of CK (Gamkrelidze and Machavariani 1965).[1] The facts presented in this section and in §8.3 below, as well as many of the examples cited, are drawn from Gamkrelidze and Machavariani (1965).

The so-called markerless intransitive represents one of the oldest conjugational types in Kartvelian (Machavariani 1959; Topuria 1942a). Verbs of this type, in the original system, make use of a contrast in ablaut grades to distinguish Series I from II and transitive from intransitive, as summarized for one class of verbs in Old Georgian in Table 8.1 (Gamkrelidze and Machavariani 1965:205).[2]

Table 8.1

The System of Ablaut in Monomorphemic Verb Stems in Old Georgian

	Transitive	Intransitive
Present (Series I)	*v-cwet* 'I wear it out'	*v-cwt-eb-i* 'I wear out, am worn out'
Aorist (Series II)	*v-cwit-e* 'I wore it out'	**v-cwet* 'I wore out, was worn out'

As noted in Table 8.1, the intransitive aorist for this verb is unattested; it is reconstructed on the basis of oppositions in intransitives, such as those in Table 8.2. Verbs like those in Table 8.2, however, either lack corresponding transitives or have restructured their transitives using causative morphology (e.g., present *v-a-ṭp-ob* 'I heat it', with the circumfix *a—ob*); see Gamdrelidze and Machavariani (1965:205, n. 1) and Table 8.17, this volume.

As shown in Tables 8.1 and 8.2, the intransitive aorist and transitive present have the *e*-grade (normal grade) of the root, the transitive aorist has the *i*-grade (reduced grade), and the intransitive present has ∅-grade (zero grade). The forms in Tables 8.1 and 8.2 are all first person subject forms (marked by *v*); in the intransitive aorist, third person subject forms have ∅-grade roots, not the *e*-grade used for first and second persons: *cwt-a* 'it wore out, was worn out', where *-a* marks the third person singular subject.

One morphological class in Svan preserves the ablaut system as shown in Table 8.3 (examples from Topuria 1967).[3]

Table 8.2

Ablaut in Monomorphemic Intransitives in Old Georgian

	Verb *ṭep*	Verb *deg*
Present (Series I)	*v-ṭp-eb-i* 'I get warm'	*aγ-v-dg-eb-i* 'I stand up'
Aorist (Series II)	*gan-v̇-ṭep* 'I got warm'	*aγ-v-deg* 'I stood up

Table 8.3

The System of Ablaut in Monomorphic Verb Stems in Svan

	Transitive	Intransitive
Present (I)	*ṭix-e* 'you return it'	*ṭex-n-i* 'you return'
Aorist (II)	*a-ṭəx*< **a-ṭix*[a] 'you returned it' *a-ṭix* 'he returned it'	*a-ṭex* 'you returned'

[a]On the origin of the regular *ə/i* alternation in the transitive aorist, see Gamkrelidze and Machavariani (1965:208) and Topuria (1979b:31).

While the verb stem in Table 8.3 preserves the original *i* versus *e* opposition representing transitive versus intransitive in Series II, it has restructured the present. Like most verbs in Svan, *ṭix* added a thematic marker in the present and so did not preserve the original ablaut grade associated with an athematic present.[4] For this and similar verbs, *e*-grade of the transitive present can be reconstructed on the basis of the masdar, *li-ṭex*, the masdar being a form constructed on the transitive Series I stem (Gamkrelidze and Machavariani 1965:208–209). A few verbs, however, preserved the original athematic transitive present with *e*-grade, as illustrated in Table 8.4.

Table 8.4

The System of Ablaut in Monomorphemic Verb Roots in Svan

	Transitive	Intransitive
Present (I)	*x-i-ḳed* 'you destroy it'	*ḳed-n-i* 'you are destroyed
Aorist (II)	*e-x-i-ḳ* (< * *-ḳd*) 'you destroyed it' *an-ḳid* 'he destroyed it'	*an-ḳed* 'you were destroyed'

Although a large number of morphological changes and productive phonological processes camouflage the basic oppositions, Gamkrelidze and Machavariani are able to reconstruct, on internal evidence alone, an original system that included athematic intransitive aorist in *e*-grade, athematic transitive present in *e*-grade, and thematic transitive aorist in *i*-grade. The system they propose for an earlier stage of Svan is represented here as Table 8.5. (Gamkrelidze and Machavariani 1965:214). An exactly analogous system is internally reconstructible in Georgian. Although Laz and Mingrelian do not preserve ablaut in monomorphemic roots (Gamkrelidze and Machavariani 1965:214–225; Gudava 1974), we may reconstruct such a system for some stage of CK.

Table 8.5

Reconstruction of Ablaut System in Monomorphemic Verb Roots in Svan

	Transitive	Intransitive
Present (I)	**w-qed* 'I take it'	**w-qd-en-i* 'I go'
Aorist (II)	**w-qid-e* 'I took it'	**w-qed* 'I went' **qd-a* 'he went'

8.2. BEYOND MONOVOCALICITY: A PROPOSAL

Gamkrelidze and Machavariani (1965:243; Gamkrelidze 1966:76) propose to account for the alternations in Tables 8.1–8.5, as well as other types described by them, by means of the Principle of Monovocalicity:

In a polymorphemic form, only one morpheme may occur in the normal grade.

This accurately describes the forms presented, including the fact that we have *e*-grade (normal grade) in the athematic transitive present and athematic intransitive aorist, and other grades in the thematic transitive aorist and intransitive present. As they note (p. 372; Gamkrelidze 1966:82), the Principle of Monovocalicity cannot, however, explain why we get *i*-grade roots in some forms with normal grade suffixes, but ∅-grade roots in other forms, also with normal grade suffixes. The hypothesis I propose below explains the distribution of the various ablaut grades; it in no sense disproves the Principle of Monovocalicity, but rather supplements it.

It is hypothesized here that when only Series II existed, thematic transitives with the vowel *i* opposed athematic intransitives with the stem vowel *e*. The alternation must have arisen as a productive phonological process, including at least the Vowel Reduction process, (1).

(1) Vowel Reduction
$e \rightarrow i / C\_\_C + V(C)$

While there still existed only the forms of Series II, this alternation was reinterpreted as a morphological marker serving to distinguish transitive from intransitive forms. As proposed in Chapter 7, the creation of Series I involved the rule of Object Demotion, which made direct objects indirect objects. All Series I forms were thus surface intransitives, and, therefore, it was the intransitive stem form, with *e*-grade, that formed the basis for all Series I forms. The forms labeled 'transitive' in the tables of examples in this chapter were originally underlying transitives that were surface intransitives in Series I. When Series I was reinterpreted, these forms were reanalyzed as surface transitives.

At some time after the reanalysis of the *i*-grade versus *e*-grade opposition as a marker of transitive versus intransitive, a new rule of vowel reduction was introduced:

(2) Syncope

$$\begin{bmatrix} \text{V} \\ -\text{high} \end{bmatrix} \rightarrow \emptyset / \text{C} \_\_\_ \text{C} + \text{V(C)}$$

Rule (2) applies in the same environment that (1) did. While in Svan it may apply to vowels of all timbres, in Old Georgian it applied just to *a, e, o,* deleting *a* or *e*, but reducing *o* to *w* (Topuria 1979c). Thus, the original scope of syncope in (2) is not clear. When this rule was introduced into the grammar, it applied to the output of vowel reduction, rule (1). Hence, we find Old Georgian intransitive aorists in *e*-grade, except where (2) applied: **cwet-a* became *cwt-a*, where **cwet-a* is reconstructed as the basic underlying form synchronically for Proto-Georgian. In the transitive aorist, on the other hand, the basic underlying form was already *cwit-e*. Syncope never affects *i* in Georgian (Topuria 1979c), and hence no change occurred. In the athematic transitive present the input conditions of syncope are met only in third person subject forms, since there are no other suffixes of the form -V(C); this accounts for *v-cwet*. In the intransitive present, the suffix *-eb(i)* triggers syncope, and we get **cwet-eb-i* becoming *cwt-eb-i* synchronically.[5]

The proposal can be summarized as in Table 8.6, which represents the Old Georgian underlying forms corresponding to the surface forms represented in Table 8.1. The situation is Svan is made clearer in §8.3 below.

The proposal advanced here is based on the assumption of a theoretical model that permits various levels of derivation, an assumption not made by Gamkrelidze and Machavariani. In addition, this proposal makes certain claims that must be justified: (a) that *e*-grade can be reconstructed as

Table 8.6

Summary Reconstruction of the Underlying Forms of Monomorphemic Roots in Old Georgian

	Transitive	Intransitive
Present (I)	*v-cwet* 'I wear it out'	**v-cwet-eb-i* 'I wear out, am worn out'
Aorist (II)	*v-cwit-e* 'I wore it out'	**v-cwet* 'I wore out, was worn out'
		**cwet-a* 'it wore out, was worn out'

the underlying form for intransitives in Series I, (b) that rule (2) applied as a productive synchronic rule more recently than did rule (1), and (c) that it is plausible that the *i/e* alternation marked transitive versus intransitive forms in Series II. Evidence to support each of these claims is presented in §8.4.

8.3. ABLAUT IN BIMORPHEMIC VERB STEMS IN CK

Bimorphemic verb stems in CK present a considerably more complex picture.[6] Gamkrelidze and Machavariani (1965:180) establish for Old Georgian the sort of system shown in Table 8.7. Vogt (1947a:44) shows that such stems originated as a root and suffix; we reconstruct this as **der-eḳ*. The forms in Table 8.7 are like those in Table 8.1 in that the *i*-grade shows up only in the transitive aorist.

Table 8.7

The System of Ablaut in Bimorphemic Verb Stems in Old Georgian

	Transitive	Intransitive
Present (I)	*v-dreḳ* 'I bend it'	*v-drḳ-eb-i* 'I bend, am bent'
Aorist (II)	*v-driḳ-e* 'I bent it'	*v-derḳ* 'I bent, was bent'

Gamkrelidze and Machavariani (1965:179–194) describe the forms in Table 8.7 in the following way: The transitive aorist represents the ∅-grade of the root and the *i*-grade of the suffix. The intransitive aorist shows *e*-grade of the root and ∅ of the suffix, while the transitive present shows ∅-grade of the root and *e* of the suffix. The intransitive present shows ∅-grade of the root and of the suffix, with *e*-grade of the secondary suffix (*-eb*).

I suggest that the surface forms represented in Table 8.7 correspond to the underlying forms in Table 8.8. The *i* vocalism of the transitive aorist

Table 8.8

Summary Reconstruction of the Underlying Forms of Bimorphemic Stems in Old Georgian

	Transitive	Intransitive
Present (I)	**v-der-eḳ* 'I bend it'	**v-der-eḳ-eb-i* 'I bend, am bent'
Aorist (II)	**v-der-iḳ-e* 'I bent it'	**v-der-eḳ* 'I bent, was bent'

was diachronically derived by rule (1) but had been reanalyzed as part of the morphology of transitives in Series II.

In the transitive present and transitive aorist, the rule of syncope applies just as stated in rule (2). In the intransitive present, the rule applies as expected, except that *-eb* does not undergo syncope. The suffix *-eb*, in all of its functions, is always an exception to syncope; see §8.4.2. The synchronic derivation of the surface form, *vderḳ*, of the intransitive aorist, is discussed below.

In Zan the system of ablaut in Series I and II has been restructured on the basis of the transitivity of the verb form after reanlaysis; Gamkrelidze and Machavariani (1965:187ff.) give the forms in Table 8.9. A series of phonological changes have affected the forms shown here. In every instance, Zan *dir* must come from **dr̥*, which has the reflex *dr* in Georgian. Every instance of a bimorphemic stem involves a sonant in this position, originally a part of a complex sonant system. Thus, Zan *dirk* comes from **dr̥k*. The suffixal *-iḳ* found in the transitive forms is the regular reflex of CK **iḳ*, and represents the *i*-grade. Thus, the transitive forms in Table 8.9 correspond to the Old Georgian *i*-grade of the suffix (transitive aorist of Table 8.7), while the intransitive forms correspond to the Old Georgian ∅-grade (intransitive present in Table 8.7).[7] Zan also preserves a reflex of the *e*-grade in the form *dir-aḳ*, found in the masdar, the past participle, and the intransitive forms of Series III; the latter are discussed in Chapter 13. CK **e* is realized as Georgian *e* and Zan *a* in most phonetic environments. Gamkrelidze and Machavariani observe that Mingrelian *dir-aḳ* could not have come from **der-eḳ*, since that would have the reflex **dar-aḳ*, which is not found. Thus, there is no Zan form that corresponds to Old Georgian *der-ḳ* (intransitive aorist) or to the hypothetical underlying form **der-eḳ*. On the other hand, *dir-aḳ* preserves the Proto-Zan form corresponding to Old Georgian *dr-eḳ* (transitive present). (See Gamkrelidze and Machavariani 1965:78ff., 188ff. for discussion of the above.)

On the basis of these facts, Gamkrelidze and Machavariani reconstruct for Zan a system analogous to that in Old Georgian, represented in Table 8.7. I would suggest in addition that the surface forms they reconstruct

Table 8.9

The System of Ablaut in Bimorphemic Verb Stems in Zan

	Transitive		Intransitive	
Present (I)	*dir-iḳ-un-s*	'he bends it'	*dir-ḳ-u(n)*	'he bends, is bent'
Aorist (II)	*dir-iḳ-u*	'he bent it'	*do-dir-ḳ-u*	'he bent, was bent'

correspond in Proto-Zan to underlying forms analogous to those reconstructed for Georgian in Table 8.8. In the course of time the Zan system was changed in three important respects. When the underlying transitives of Series I were reanalyzed as surface transitives (see Chap. 7), the transitive forms of Series I were restructured using the stem that represented the transitive in Series II, namely stem form **der-iḳ-*. Second, the rules governing sonants required that *r̥* became *ir* in these contexts in Zan, but *r* in Georgian. Third, the fact that the transitive Series I had been restructured, together with the fact that the intransitive in Series II is mostly thematic, and therefore ∅-grade, meant that the root **der* would surface only in the first and second person subject forms of the intransitive aorist. Therefore the basic underlying form of the intransitive of Series II was reinterpreted as that form that occurred in all other screeves and in the third person subject forms of the aorist, namely, *dir-ḳ* coming from **dr̥-ḳ*. In this way, a Proto-Zan system analogous to the Georgian one in Table 8.8 was restructured as shown in Table 8.10.

Table 8.10

Summary Reconstruction of Underlying Forms of Bimorphemic Verb Stems in Zan

	Transitive	Intransitive
Present (I)	*dr-iḳ-	*dr-ḳ-
Aorist (II)	*dr-iḳ-	*dr-ḳ-

In Svan, bimorphemic verb stems were not preserved; verbs originally of this form were simplified into monomorphemic stems by the loss of the sonant **r* or **l* (Gamkrelidze and Machavariani 1965:194ff.).

There is no attestation of the postulated basic form **der-eḳ*, and only Georgian preserves the form *der-ḳ* in the intransitive aorist. Notice that rule (2) would lead us to expect only *dr-eḳ* from **der-eḳ*. There are a few other instances that may involve syncope as a progressive, rather than regressive rule in Old Georgian (Gamkrelidze and Machavariani; 1965:273ff.). Some examples are listed in (3); forms from Imnaishvili (1971:211).

(3) *mo-v-s-dreḳ-d* < **mo-v-s-der-eḳ-ed*
gan-v-a-bnev-d < **gan-v-a-bnev-ed*

In Svan, syncope is progressive in many instances, though regressive syncope as in (2) also applies (Topuria 1979c:149ff.). We find *e* deleting in the mirror image of the environment of (2), but only in some dialects and in some forms. We can describe the process in Svan as (4), though it is less general than this would suggest.

(4) $e \rightarrow \emptyset/(C)V + C \_\_\_ C$

One example of this is the contrast between the so-called relative (having an indirect object) and absolute (lacking an indirect object) forms of the intransitive. In the Lašx dialect we find the forms *e-m-e-qd* 'you came to me' (Topuria 1967:199), contrasting with *an-qed* 'you came' (Topuria 1967:196). Topuria observed the generality of this opposition, proposing that Upper Bal *ot-e-q̣č* 'I left it' comes from Lenṭex *ätw-e-q̣č*, which comes from **atw-e-q̣eč* (Topuria 1967:199).

A more complex set of oppositions involves *e*-grade of the first syllable and ∅ of the second, alternating with *e* or *o* of the first, ∅-grade of the second and *e*-grade of the third; the examples in Table 8.11 are from Topuria (1967:41). The forms in Table 8.11 are from the present screeve; the suffix *-en* occurs with ablauting verbs only in Series I (Topuria 1967:179), and this opposition therefore could not exist in Series II. The verbs in Table 8.11 have corresponding transitives in *i*-grade, if they have corresponding transitives at all (Topuria 1967:41). The Lenṭex dialect of Svan lacks syncope in general, and it preserves the postulated underlying forms in both the absolute and relative intransitives: *ṭex-en-i, x-e-ṭex-en-i* (Topuria 1967:181). Syncope is a productive phonological rule in other Svan dialects today (Kaldani 1955:174; 1959a:223–224; 1962:201–203).

Almost all linguists who have considered the problem of ablaut in Kartvelian have associated it in part with dynamic or moveable stress in the protolanguage; Schmidt (1962:21ff.) gives a useful summary of different positions on this question. Gamkrelidze and Machavariani (1965:370) also adopt this position, suggesting that Old Georgian *der-ḳ* is the reflex of an

Table 8.11

Ablaut Grades in Intransitives in Svan

Absolute	Relative
ṭex-n-i 'he returns'	*x-e-ṭx-en-i* 'he returns to him'
peš-n-i 'he gets tired'	*x-e-pš-en-i*
pxež-n-i 'it spreads'	*x-e-pxž-en-i*
geb-n-i 'it gets dirty'	*x-o-gb-en-i*
kwec-n-i 'it cuts'	*x-e-kwc-en-i*
kwer-n-i 'it rots'	*x-e-kwr-en-i*
twep-n-i 'it gets lost'	*x-o-twp-en-i*
sed-n-i 'he remains'	*x-e-sd-en-i*
p̣er-n-i 'it flies'	*x-e-p̣r-en-i*

earlier CV́C-VC stress pattern, while Old Georgian *dr-eḳ* results from an earlier CVC-V́C pattern. The pattern of CK stress and its interrelationship with syncope has not been worked out; it is not yet known how to explain in which environments rule (2) applied and in which (4) applied. However, we can assume that rule (4), governed by stress, explains the occurrence of the surface form *v-der-ḳ* in Old Georgian from the underlying form **v-der-eḳ* proposed in Table 8.8. The same rule explains the surface form *ṭex-n-i* in Svan from underlying *ṭex-en-i*, attested in the Lenṭex dialect; this is the analysis proposed by Topuria (1967:181) and Machavariani (1980:208). Finally, rule (4), together with dynamic stress, explains the alternation illustrated in Table 8.11.

8.4. EVIDENCE TO SUPPORT THE PROPOSAL

It has been shown that the surface forms listed for Old Georgian in Tables 8.1 and 8.7 and for Svan in Table 8.4 can be synchronically derived in a straightforward way from underlying forms like those proposed in Tables 8.6 and 8.8, respectively. The Svan forms in Table 8.3 and the Zan forms in Table 8.9 are derived in a similar way, except that they underwent a restructuring of the paradigm on the basis of the transitivity of the verb form at the time when Series I was reanalyzed, as proposed in Chapter 7.

The reconstruction proposed here can be represented as in Table 8.12, which shows underlying forms, generalized for the whole series, not limited to present and aorist screeves. With respect to monomorphemic stems, Table 8.12 represents the ablaut grade of the verb root. With respect to bimorphemic stems, Table 8.12 represents the ablaut grade of the suffixal element of the stem, the root element being always in *e*-grade in the underlying form.[8]

The analysis summarized in Table 8.12 differs from the analysis proposed by Gamkrelidze and Machavariani in that it represents underlying forms and in that it posits a normal grade (*e*-grade) in the intransitive

Table 8.12

Summary Reconstruction of the System of Ablaut in CK

	Transitive	Intransitive
Series I	*e*-grade	*e*-grade
Series II	*i*-grade	*e*-grade

Series I forms. Because of the latter difference, evidence to support my hypothesis is presented in this section.

8.4.1. Reconstruction of *e*-Grade in Series I Intransitives

I have proposed the reconstruction of an original underlying *e*-grade in part on the basis of the fact that this form is preserved in Svan in verbs of the type illustrated in Table 8.3 and in those of the type illustrated in Table 8.4. In addition, *e*-grade intransitive presents are preserved in a few verbs in Old Georgian, as shown in Table 8.13. The optional loss of *v* is a regular phonological process after a vowel and before a nonhigh vowel (Shanidze 1976:88). As Table 8.13 shows, the paradigm of this verb has been restructured on the basis of series, such that *e*-grade has been generalized for Series I and *i*-grade for Series II. The complementarity of this restructuring with that of Svan (Table 8.3) and Zan (Table 8.9) makes the system reconstructed in Table 8.12 all the more plausible. In like manner, the preservation of *e*-grade in the initial intransitive present of this verb supports the specific reconstruction of normal grade as the underlying form for the Series I intransitives.

Table 8.13

Ablaut in *bnev*-type in Old Georgian

	Transitive		Intransitive	
Present (I)	*gan-a-bnev-s*	'he strews it'	*gan-i-bnev-i-s*	'it is strewed'
Aorist (II)	*gan-a-bni(v)-a*	'he strewed it'	*gan-i-bni(v)-a*	'it was strewed'

The reconstruction ın question is also supported by the fact that the rule needed to derive the surface forms, rule (2), is independently necessary. It is needed to account for phemomena discussed in §8.3, §8.4.2, and §8.4.3.

The Ø-grade attested in surface forms such as *v-cwt-eb-i, v-ṭp-eb-i,* and *v-dr-ḳ-eb-i* could not be derived from an underlying *i*-grade, since syncope never applies to *i* in Georgian (Topuria 1979c:153).

Consider the alternative analysis proposed by Gamkrelidze and Machavariani (1965). For Svan they reconstruct the form **w-qd-en-i* 'I come' (p. 214). They suggest that the attested form *qed-n-i* 'he comes' derives via a form attested in Lenṭex, *qed-en-i,* from **qd-en-i* (p. 212). They go on to point out that this is part of a Svan tendency to avoid initial consonant clusters. It is proposed that originally the epenthetic vowel "must have been a short neutral vowel, which later took on the timbre of the vowel *e* under the influence of the vowel of the suffix *-en*" (p. 212). There is no possible way to disprove such an account.

8.4.2. The Relative Chronology of Rules (1) and (2)

According to the proposal outlined in §8.2, rule (1) ceased to apply as a synchronic phonological alternation at a stage of CK before (2) was introduced. It is proposed here that the *i* versus *e* alternation had been reinterpreted as a grammatical marker, that is, as ablaut, long before the *e* versus ∅ alternation was reanalyzed as ablaut. To support this claim, it is important to note that the *i*-grade is found only in the thematic transitive of Series II, as outlined in §8.1 and §8.3 above. In contrast, ∅-grade, derivable from an underlying *e*-grade, is found in a very wide range of environments in both series. The remainder of this subsection is devoted to observing the generality of rule (2) in this sense. It must be noted from the outset, however, that rule (2) had partially died out as a productive process before the earliest attested manuscripts.

Rule (2) is needed to account for alternations in noun and adjective declension, such as *mezobel* 'neighbor/NOM' versus *mezobl-is* 'neighbor-GEN', on the one hand, or *mezobl-eb-i* 'neighbor-COL-NOM', on the other; here the stem form *mezobel* becomes *mezobl* when followed by *-is* 'GEN' (or *-it* 'INST', *-ad* 'ADV') or by *-eb-* 'COL'.

In the verb system, this rule accounts for a variety of alternations, both in Series I and II. In Series II we find the opposition *gan-v-ṭep* 'I warmed up' versus *gan-ṭp-a* 'it warmed up', as discussed above in §8.1. The same rule accounts for the opposition between intransitive aorist forms (first and second person subjects) and intransitive habitual II and subjunctive II forms of the same person; all of these screeves are in Series II. This opposition is summarized in Table 8.14 (examples from Imnaishvili 1971:242). Here the aorist is athematic, while the habitual II is marked with *-i* and the subjunctive II with *-e*; both suffixes trigger syncope.

Still within Series II, the application of the same rule can be seen in the forms of intransitives formed with the suffix *-en*, (examples from Imnaish-

Table 8.14

Syncope in Habitual II and Subjunctive II of Markerless Intransitive in Old Georgian (√ *ṭep* 'warm up')

	Aorist	Habitual II	Subjunctive II
1st singular subject	*gan-v-ṭep*	*gan-v-ṭp-i*	*gan-v-ṭp-e*
2nd singular subject	*gan-s-ṭep*	*gan-s-ṭp-i*	*gan-s-ṭp-e*

vili 1971:240).[9] Table 8.15 shows that the intransitive formant *en* becomes *n* if followed by the third person singular subject marker, *-a*, the formant of the habitual II, *-i*, or the formant of the subjunctive II, *-e*; it has its full form only in the athematic aorist, first and second person subjects.

Table 8.15

Syncope in Conjugation of Intransitive in Series II in Old Georgian (√ *c̣ux* 'grieve, be sad, displeased')

	Aorist	Habitual II	Subjunctive II
1st singular subject	*še-v-c̣ux-en*	*še-v-c̣ux-n-i*	*še-v-c̣ux-n-e*
2nd singular subject	*še-s-c̣ux-en*	*še-s-c̣ux-n-i*	*še-s-c̣ux-n-e*
3rd singular subject	*še-c̣ux-n-a*	*še-c̣ux-n-i-s*	*še-c̣ux-n-e-s*

The operation of the same rule can be seen in the contrast between the forms of a given verb with a singular direct object versus forms of the same verb with a plural direct object. Table 8.16 (examples from Imnaishvili 1971:226, 237, 238) illustrates the plural marker, *-en*, in full form in the first and second person subject forms of the aorist; when followed by the third person aorist subject marker, *-a*, or by the habitual II formant, *-i*, *-en* syncopates to *-n*. In addition, Table 8.16 illustrates the application of syncope in the verb root, in all forms except the athematic first and second person subject forms with singular direct object in the aorist.

Table 8.16

Syncope in Plural Object Marker in Old Georgian (√ *ḳal* 'kill')

	Aorist		Habitual II
	3. singular object	3. plural object	3. plural object
1st singular subject	*mo-v-ḳal*	*mo-v-ḳl-en*	*mo-v-ḳl-n-i*
2nd singular subject	*mo-h-ḳal*	*mo-h-ḳl-en*	*mo-h-ḳl-n-i*
3rd singular subject	*mo-ḳl-a*	*mo-ḳl-n-a*	*mo-ḳl-n-i-s*

In Series I forms, the operation of syncope can be seen in the form of the verb stem occurring with a series marker, illustrated in Table 8.17 (examples from Imnaishvili 1971:206, 207); the full forms of these verb roots are illustrated in Tables 8.14 and 8.16. The series markers themselves undergo syncope when followed by the third person plural subject marker of the present, *-en*, or present habitual, *-ed*, as shown in Table 8.18 (examples from Shanidze 1976:94). The series marker also syncopates when followed by the formant of the imperfect habitual, *-idi*, or that of the subjunctive I, *-ide*, as shown in Table 8.19 (examples from Shanidze 1976:94, 95). (The formants *-idi* and *-ide* are further analyzable.) The same

Table 8.17

Syncope in Verb Root in Thematic Present in Old Georgian

Series marker *-ob*		Series marker *-av*	
v-a-ṭp-ob	'I warm it up'	*v-ḳl-av*	'I kill him'
a-ṭp-ob		*h-ḳl-av*	
a-ṭp-ob-s		*ḳl-av-s*	

Table 8.18

Syncope in Series Marker *-av* with Plural Subject Markers (√ ḳal 'kill')

	3rd singular subject	3rd plural subject
Present	*ḳl-av-s* 'he kills him'	*ḳl-v-en* 'they kill him'
Present habitual	*ḳl-av-n*	*ḳl-v-ed*

Table 8.19

Syncope in Thematic Marker *-av* with Screeve Formants (√ *ḳal* 'kill')

	Present	Imperfect habitual	Subjunctive I
1st singular subject	*v-ḳl-av* 'I kill him'	*v-ḳl-v-idi* 'I was killing him'	*v-ḳl-v-ide* 'let me kill him'
2nd singular subject	*h-ḳl-av*	*h-ḳl-v-idi*	*h-ḳl-v-ide*
3rd singular subject	*ḳl-av-s*	*ḳl-v-idi-s*	*ḳl-v-ide-s*

series marker syncopates when followed by the screeve marker of intransitives, *-i*, as shown in Table 8.20 (examples after Shanidze 1976:110).

Syncope also applied in forms of Series III and in nonfinite forms. The former are discussed, together with ablaut in Series III, in Chapter 13. The masdars (nominalizations) in *-ay* show syncope of the series marker or of the verb root in verbs having an athematic Series I, as shown in

Table 8.20

Syncope in Series Marker *-av* with Intransitive Formant *-i*. (√ *xaṭ* 'paint')

Transitive		Intransitive	
da-v-xaṭ-av	'I paint it'	*da-v-i-xaṭ-v-i*	'I get painted'
da-xaṭ-av		*da-i-xaṭ-v-i*	
da-xaṭ-av-s		*da-i-xaṭ-v-i-s*	

Table 8.21 (examples from Shanidze 1976:86, 136). The older masdar formant *-omay* also triggers syncope, shown in Table 8.22 (examples from Shanidze 1976:119, 136), as does the present participle in *m__el* and *m__ar*, shown in Table 8.23 (examples after Shanidze 1976:136, 137), where the thematic markers *-av* and *-am* syncopate to *-v* and *-m*, respectively, and the verb root *zard* syncopates to *zrd*.

Table 8.21

Syncope in *-ay* Masdar in Old Georgian

Finite form	Masdar
v-h-par-av 'I cover it'	*par-v-a-y* 'covering'
aγ-u-tku-am 'I promise it to him'	*aγ-tku-m-a-y* 'promising'
aγ-v-zard-e 'I raised him'	*aγ-zrd-a-y* 'raising'
gan-v-qad-e 'I took it out'	*gan-qd-a-y* 'taking out'

In spite of the great generality of the application of this rule, there are environments in which it did not apply in Old Georgian. The endings *-in*, which marks third person singular subject imperative II, and *-it*, which marks plurality of the first or second person subject in the aorist for a few verbs, do not trigger syncope; for example, *gan-ṭep-i-n* 'may it warm up!' (not the expected **gan-ṭp-i-n*) and *gan-v-ṭep-i-t* 'we warmed up' (not the expected **gan-v-ṭp-i-t*). The sequence *-i-t* seems to have been lately formed from simple *-t*, which is still frequent: *gan-v-ṭep-t* 'we warmed up'. Some morphemes fail to trigger syncope only sometimes, under conditions that

Table 8.22

Syncope in *-omay* Masdar in Old Georgian

Finite form	Masdar
da-v-a-dger 'I stood firm'	*da-dgr-om-a-y* 'standing firm'
aγ-v-deg 'I stood up'	*aγ-dg-om-a-y* 'standing up'

Table 8.23

Syncope in Present Participle in Old Georgian

Finite form	Participle
v-h-par-av 'I cover it'	*m-par-v-el-i* 'protector'
aγ-u-tku-am 'I promise it to him'	*aγ-m-tku-m-el-i* 'one who makes a promise'
aγ-v-zard-e 'I raised him'	*m-zrd-el-i* 'educator'
v-xaṭ-av 'I paint it'	*m-xaṭ-v-ar-i* 'painter'

cannot yet be specified; for example, compare *dreḳ-ed* 'they bend it' (not **drḳ-ed*) with *ḳl-v-ed* 'they kill him' from **ḳal-av-ed* (Table 8.18). Another type of exception is the target that meets the input conditions for the rule but fails to undergo it. Such exceptions are the series markers *-eb*, *-ob*, *-ev*, and *-em*, which never undergo syncope in the environments illustrated for *-av* and *-am* in Tables 8.18—8.23 (for examples, see handbooks). Roots like *xaṭ* in Table 8.20 appear to be exceptions to syncope, but Gamkrelidze and Machavariani (1965:240ff.) have shown that this is due to the fact that they derive from original long vowels, which were not syncope targets.

Because of the exceptions mentioned above, we cannot formulate syncope as a simple phonological rule of Old Georgian. However, because of the great generality of its application, we can conclude that a rule like (2) was fully productive in a stage of the language not long before attested Old Georgian.

Topuria (1979c) shows that syncope—rules (2) and (4)—is also widespread in Svan, but less so in Zan. He concludes that it is a late rule (page 169).

The fact that the rule of vowel reduction, or the alternation *e* versus *i*, is so restricted in comparison with the very general rule of syncope, or *e* versus ∅ alternation, is evidence that the latter was productive much later than the former. In this sense, it supports the hypothesis proposed in §8.2.

8.4.3. The *i* versus *e* Alternation as a Marker of Transitivity

The proposal made in §8.2 makes the claim that transitive forms were distinguished from intransitive forms of the same verb in part by means of the quality of the stem vowel. In this section, I consider whether or not that is a plausible claim.

The most obvious support for the claim that *i* versus *e* distinguished transitive from intransitive in Series II in the protolanguage is the fact that this alternation still serves this purpose in Svan. Examples of this are given in Tables 8.3 and 8.4. Although the domain of *i* was extended to include transitives in Series I after reanalysis of that series, verbs of the *ṭex* type in Svan clearly show the plausibility of such a syntactic function of the morphological alternation.

Although the Zan languages replaced *e*-grade with ∅-grade as the underlying form, it maintains a similar alternation as one of the markers of transitive versus intransitive (see Table 8.9).

Such a marker is not only plausible in general, however, but it is well founded specifically for Georgian. In Series II forms of verbs of the *cwet* or **der-eḳ* types (Tables 8.1 and 8.7), we find that the *i* versus *e* alternation is maintained throughout the paradigm. That is, we find *i*-grade in all transitive forms in Series II. Table 8.24 (examples after Imnaishvili 1971:225, 228, 230) illustrates forms of the transitive varying for the person and number of the subject; all forms in the table have a third person singular direct object and no indirect object. Transitive forms with plural direct objects also consistently use the *i*-grade of the stem; for example, *mo-dr-iḳ-n-a* 'he bent them' from **mo-der-iḳ-en-a; mo-dr-iḳ-n-es* 'they bent them' from **mo-der-iḳ-en-es*. These forms have the suffix *-en*, marking object plurality; this is discussed in greater detail in Chapter 10. Forms of the transitive with non–third person objects also maintain the consistent *i*-grade of the stem; for example, *mo-m-i-dr-iḳ-e* '(you) bend it to me', where the oblique 'to me' has been advanced to indirect object, as shown by *m-i-*.

Table 8.24

i-grade in Transitive Series II Paradigm (**der-eḳ* 'bend')

	Aorist	Habitual II	Subjunctive II
1st singular	*mo-v-dr-iḳ-e*	*mo-v-dr-iḳ-i*	*mo-v-dr-iḳ-o*
2nd singular	*mo-s-dr-iḳ-e*	*mo-s-dr-iḳ-i*	*mo-s-dr-iḳ-o*
3rd singular	*mo-dr-iḳ-a*	*mo-dr-iḳ-i-s*	*mo-dr-iḳ-o-s*
1st plural	*mo-v-dr-iḳ-e-t*	*mo-v-dr-iḳ-i-t*	*mo-v-dr-iḳ-o-t*
2nd plural	*mo-s-dr-iḳ-e-t*	*mo-s-dr-iḳ-i-t*	*mo-s-dr-iḳ-o-t*
3rd plural	*mo-dr-iḳ-es*	*mo-dr-iḳ-i-an*	*mo-dr-iḳ-o-n*

In contrast, all forms of the intransitive in Series II have *e*-grade of the stem, or ∅-grade, which is derived from underlying *e*-grade by rule (2). This is shown in Table 8.25 (examples after Imnaishvili 1971:242).

A comparison of Tables 8.24 and 8.25 shows that in the third person subject forms of the aorist and in all persons of the habitual II, the phonological environment is identical for the transitive and intransitive. In other screeves the phonological environment is structurally similar, except

Table 8.25

e-grade in Intransitive Series II Paradigm (**der-eḳ* 'bend')

	Aorist	Habitual II	Subjunctive II
1st singular	*še-v-der-ḳ*	*še-v-dr-ḳ-i*	*še-v-dr-ḳe*
2nd singular	*še-s-der-ḳ*	*še-s-dr-ḳ-i*	*še-s-dr-ḳ-e*
3rd singular	*še-dr-ḳ-a*	*še-dr-ḳ-i-s*	*še-dr-ḳ-e-s*
1st plural	*še-v-der-ḳ-it*	*še-v-dr-ḳ-i-t*	*še-v-dr-ḳ-e-t*
2nd plural	*še-s-der-ḳ-it*	*še-s-dr-ḳ-i-t*	*še-s-dr-ḳ-e-t*
3rd plural	*še-dr-ḳ-es*	*še-dr-ḳ-i-an*	*še-dr-ḳ-e-n*

for the first and second person subject forms of the aorist. The fact that the transitive consistently shows the *i*-grade and the intransitive the *e*-grade or Ø-grade is evidence that the *i*-grade of the stem had been reinterpreted as the underlying form of the transitive and the *e*-grade as that of the intransitive. This supports the analysis proposed in §8.2 above.

8.5. RESTRUCTURING THE PARADIGMS

When Series I underlying transitives were reanalyzed in the way suggested in Chapter 7, the original ablaut system reconstructed in Table 8.12 no longer made any sense. It was intolerable that the Series I transitives should be like the intransitives of both series, but unlike the corresponding transitives of Series II. The different languages restructured their paradigms in a variety of ways.

The ablauting verbs of Zan and the *ṭex*-type verbs of Svan were restructured according to the transitivity of the verb forms, or along the vertical axis of the example tables (see Tables 8.3 and 8.9). In Zan there is a simple opposition of *i*-grade to Ø-grade, which had been reanalyzed as the underlying form of the intransitive. In Svan we find *i*-grade opposing the underlying form with *e*-grade, while Ø-grade could be derived from the latter, as in Georgian.

In Georgian, vertical restructuring occurred by a quite different means. For a number of verb stems, the old transitive was replaced with a new one that was formally a causative, bearing causative morphology; for example, the root *ṭep* (Gamkrelidze and Machavariani 1965:205). In Series I, all causative circumfixes included the prefixal element *a-* and a suffix of the form -VC or -VCVC; thus all triggered syncope. For this reason, in Georgian, verbs restructured in this way have forms like *gan-v-a-ṭp-ob* 'I warm it' derived from **gan-v-a-ṭep-ob* by the then-productive rule (2). Hence we find forms like *gan-v-a-ṭp-e* from **gan-v-a-ṭep-e*. For this verb and others like it, the underlying form is *e*-grade for all forms. Transitive opposes intransitive by affixal markers, not by ablaut.

In Georgian, verbs in *-ev* were restructured according to series, that is, along the horizontal axis. Examples of this type are shown in Table 8.13. For these verbs, the *i*/*e* alternation was reinterpreted as a marker of series, where *i* occurs in the underlying form of Series II, and *e* in those of Series I.

A third type of restructuring in Old Georgian also involved the replacement of the old markerless intransitive with the prefixal intransitive. However, in this type the transitive aorist stem form was taken as basic and is repeated in the intransitives of both series. This type is illustrated in Table

8.26 (examples after Shanidze 1976:109). This type of restructuring is based on taking the transitive Series II form to be basic, and extending it to the intransitive as a whole (see Table 8.27). This is analogous to the restructuring of the whole transitive paradigm with causative morphology as discussed above. In the type represented in Table 8.26, the whole intransitive paradigm has been based on mediopassive morphology.

Table 8.26

Ablaut in *pen*-type in Old Georgian

	Transitive	Intransitive
Present (I)	*mi-h-pen-s* 'he spreads it out on something'	*mi-e-pin-eb-i-s* 'it spreads out on something'
Aorist (II)	*mi-h-pin-a*	*mi-e-pin-a*

In Georgian, the *e*-grade of the Series I forms of the underlyingly transitive verbs are preserved only for those verbs with an athematic present. It can happen that a given verb root has both an athematic present with the old *e*-grade and a thematic present restructured on the basis of the old aorist stem (*i*-grade). Such a verb is *č̣er* 'catch' shown in Table 8.27 (examples from Modern Georgian: Tschenkéli 1960–1974:2241–2244). A similar example is the root *kreč̣/krič̣* 'shave'. For these verbs, the intransitive has been restructured as in Table 8.26. Thus, the vocalism originally restricted to the transitive of Series II has extended throughout the paradigm.

Table 8.27

Ablaut and Restructured Transitive Forms of *č̣er* in Georgian

	Original opposition	Restructured forms
Series I	*v-i-č̣er* 'I catch it'	*v-i-č̣ir-av* 'I catch it' *v-i-č̣ir-eb* 'I catch it'
Series II	*da-v-i-č̣ir-e*	*da-v-i-č̣ir-e*

8.6. SUMMARY

Gamkrelidze and Machavariani (1965) solve several long-standing problems of the phonological and morphological structure of the Kartvelian languages by reconstructing the Old Georgian, Svan, and Zan systems of ablaut presented in Tables 8.1, 8.7, 8.3, and 8.9, respectively. They do not explain why the Ø- and *i*-grades may be found in identical phonological environments (see Tables 8.24 and 8.25). Nor do they explain why the *i*-grade should be limited to the transitive aorist.

In this chapter it has been shown that the forms underlying the CK ablaut systems reconstructed by Gamkrelidze and Machavariani can all be represented by the schema in Table 8.12. It is not necessary to give different schemas for monomorphemic and bimorphemic stems. We can make the generalization that *i*-grade is found in the final stem morpheme of transitive forms of Series II, while all other stem morphemes have basic underlying forms with *e*-grade, reduced to Ø-grade in the environment C ____ C + V(C). It has been shown that the stem alternation *i* versus *e* served as a marker of transitive versus intransitive in Early CK.

Finally, it has been shown that there is a syntactic motivation for the distribution of underlying forms with *e*-grade versus *i*-grade. Series I forms were originally all surface intransitives and, therefore, made use of the stem form that had already been generalized as the intransitive. This both explains the fact that all Series I forms had underlying *e*-grade in common with Series II intransitives and supports the hypothesized intransitivization in Series I.

APPENDIX. OTHER ABLAUT PATTERNS

An analysis similar to that described above accounts for additional verb types which are found in Georgian but which seem to have no parallels in the sister languages. For the class represented by the root *ḳal* (see Gamkrelidze and Machavariani 1965:225), it is necessary only to note that the underlying form is *ḳal* and that it does not oppose transitive to intransitive by means of ablaut grades (see Tables 8.16–8.19). The occurrence of Ø-grade follows automatically from rule (2). In Modern Georgian, however, the paradigm has been restructured on the horizontal axis, and the occurrence of *a* stem vowel is no longer predictable on the basis of phonological environment; for example, Modern Georgian *mo-v-i-ḳal-i* 'I killed him for myself', not **mo-v-i-ḳl-i*.

The class represented by *č̣er* 'cut' in Old Georgian can be described in the same way. There is no evidence that it made use of vowel alternation to mark transitive versus intransitive. The occurrence of Ø-grade is predictable in Old Georgian but has been restructured in Modern Georgian along the horizontal axis.

A third class is exemplified by the root *qed* 'come/go, bring/take' (additional examples in Topuria 1942a:968). In Old Georgian we find a transitive aorist with root vowel *a* opposing an intransitive aorist with root vowel *e* or the Ø-grade derived from it; Series I forms share the *e*/Ø of the intransitive aorist, as predicted. In Svan, on the other hand, the verb has been restructured, in a way analogous to that in Table 8.3. That is, one root form is generalized for the transitives of both series while another is generalized for the intransitive. In the intransitive we find *e* root vowel; for example, Lenṭex *qed-en-i* 'he comes' (Topuria 1967:242), Lašx *lāy-qed* 'you went' (Topuria 1967:197). But in Svan the transitive has, not the *a* we find in Georgian, but *i*, as the verb in Table 8.3 has; for example, Lenṭex *qid-e* 'he brings it', *an-qid* 'he brought it' (Topuria 1967:242). We may assume that for this verb, too, Georgian preserves the original distribution and perhaps the original vocalism. By Old Georgian this system had already been partially restructured; for other verbs of the same type we find a system restructured either along the horizontal axis or in a way analogous to Table 8.26. For example, we find the forms in Table 8.28; beside *izrdebis*, we find also *izardebis*. Like the oppositions *i* versus *e* versus Ø, the opposition *a* versus **e* versus Ø cannot be accounted for on a phonological basis alone, since we find habitual II *zardis* 'he raises him' beside present *zrdis* 'he raises him', where the phonological environment is apparently identical. We may suppose therefore that *zard*, like *qad*, was originally limited to the transitive of Series II, while *zrd*, from **zerd*, was found in surface intransitives, including all Series I forms. Thus *a* versus **e* was another marker of transitivity.

Table 8.28

Ablaut in the Root *zard* in Old Georgian

	Transitive		Intransitive	
Present (I)	*zrd-i-s*	'he raises him'	*i-zrd-eb-i-s*	'he grows'
Aorist (II)	*zard-a*		*i-zard-a*	

NOTES

[1]Gamkrelidze and Machavariani (1965) is summarized in Gamkrelidze (1966) and discussed in Tsereteli (1966). It is reviewed in Lehmann (1968) and Schmidt (1968). A German translation has recently appeared; see References. Previous discussions in Western European languages of the problem of ablaut in Kartvelian include Deeters (1963), Schmidt (1962), and Vogt (1939).

[2]I do not accept the notion of a 'present stem' and 'aorist stem', but prefer the concept of Series I and Series II stems for the reasons stated in §5.2.4. However, in the present chapter I follow the tradition of citing present and aorist, since in ablaut they are characteristic of their whole series.

[3]The forms vary slightly from one dialect to another. See Topuria (1979b:30–32) for details. In the Upper Bal dialect, the third person singular subject form of intransitive *a-täx* is reconstructible as *an-tex-a*, with *e*-grade. The *ä* is due to a general back umlaut, $e \rightarrow ä / \_\_\_ C \begin{bmatrix} V \\ +\text{back} \end{bmatrix}$ in Upper Bal (see Kaldani 1979:219; Topuria 1927:310(§5), 1967:196).

[4]As used traditionally, 'thematic marker' is a cover term for series markers, such as Georgian *-eb*, Zan *-up*, *-un* (see Chap. 9), and screeve markers, such as *-e* of the subjunctive (see Chap. 5). A verb is said to have a thematic aorist if the aorist is formed with an affixal marker, such as *-i* or *-e*, and to have an athematic aorist if it has no reconstructible affixal formant in the aorist. A verb is said to have a thematic present if it has a nonzero series marker, such as those listed above, or a present screeve marker, such as *-i*.

[5]It has been suggested that earlier forms of the present markerless intransitive lacked the series marker, *-eb* and so forth (Baramidze 1976:93; Machavariani 1959:101; Osidze 1963:16; Rogava 1954:83). This is supported by Laz facts and by some Old Georgian forms, such as those found in Table 8.13, containing a verb of another ablauting type. I find this evidence convincing and support the reconstruction of the present intransitive **v-cwet-i* (Table 8.6) and **v-der-eḳ-i* (Table 8.7). This analysis, however, is independent of the proposals made in this chapter, and I have followed the more conservative course of including the attested *-eb* in the tables named.

[6]As used here, 'stem' refers to a verb root, together with those suffixes that may occur in all screeves, including the causative marker (see Vogt 1947a).

[7]Zan languages preserve the output of (2), as in *dirḳ-* < **dr̥ḳ-* < **dereḳ-*, but the rule is not productive (see Topuria 1979c:167ff.).

[8]This generalization may be extended to the (transitive) aorist of the causative, where we find forms such as *v-a-dr-eḳ-i-e* 'I caused him to bend it' from **v-a-der-ek-i(v)-e*, where the causative marker *-e(v)* occurs in *i*-grade. It is not clear why the second stem syllable does not undergo rule (2).

[9]These forms are usually referred to as passives. In Modern Georgian they are, with a few exceptions, inchoative (see Appendix to Chap. 3). Shanidze (1957b:37) characterizes them as denominals having a middle or intransitive meaning in Modern Georgian.

9

The Origin of Series Markers

If we are to account completely for the development of Series I out of a system that formerly contained only Series II, we must account for those properties that distinguish the series formally. One of these is the series marker.[1] As used in this work, SERIES MARKER refers to all those affixes that, for a particular verb, occur in ALL Series I forms and in NO Series II forms. Series markers occur with verbs of all types, though some verbs have the series marker Ø.

9.1. A PROPOSAL

It is suggested here that the original function of series markers was to mark the aspectual character of Series I. It is proposed that the series marker indicated durative aspect and that it originated as the collective marker. Series markers may have developed the secondary functions of marking surface intransitivity and Object Demotion.

A word must be said about the notion 'collective'. Chafe (1970:191) calls this the "aggregate" and characterizes it by saying that in a sentence containing an aggregate, "the class . . . is regarded as an undifferentiated whole, not as composed of separate individuals."

It is hypothesized here that the marker that originally indicated that a class of objects was to be viewed as an undifferentiated whole in CGZ was adopted to indicate that a series of separate actions or a continuing action was likewise to be regarded as an undifferentiated whole, grammatically opposing a view of the same actions as individual instances. In this way durative aspect of Series I was expressed through the affixation of a collective marker, while the punctual aspect of most of Series II was indicated by the lack of such a marker. This is analogous to the absence of a marker to indicate singular.

In the sections below, series markers and the collective marker are discussed in turn.

9.2. COMMON GEORGIAN-ZAN

9.2.1. Series Markers

In Old Georgian we find the series markers listed in Table 9.1. The series markers *-em* and *-op* each occur in only one highly irregular verb (Shanidze 1976:89); the series marker *-ev* occurs in only two verbs (Shanidze 1976:88). The remaining series markers listed in Table 9.1 each occur in a large number of verbs.

The series marker *-i* is discussed separately in §9.5. The other series markers in Table 9.1 are of the form *-VC*, where the vowel is nonhigh and where the consonant is labial. Several linguists have proposed that the vocalism in the various series markers is related. Specifically, it has been proposed that *-ob* is derived from **w-eb* or **v-eb* and that *-ov* comes from **w-ev* or **v-ev* (Deeters 1930:126, 210; Gamkrelidze and Machavariani

Table 9.1

Series Markers Attested in Old Georgian[a]

—	—	—	—	*-i*
-em	*-ev*	*-eb*	—	—
-am	*-av*	—	—	—
—	—	*-ob*	*-op*	—

[a]There is some internal evidence for reconstructing *-ov* (Kavtaradze 1954:142ff.; Shanidze 1976:89; Vogt 1947a:57), *-om* and *-ol* (Deeters 1930:218) as former series markers in Georgian. They would pose no problem for the analysis presented here. The suffixes *-an*, *-al*, and *-el* (Kavtaradze 1954:152ff.) and the 'primary suffixes' (Vogt 1947a) are not series markers in the sense defined here.

1965:274ff.; Osidze 1963:16). A wide variety of evidence has been cited in the works named, to support such a derivation, including the parallelism of certain noun roots and their related verbs, such as noun root *šv-* (*švili* 'child') and verb *šŏb-s* 'she bears' from **šv-eb-s*, and the alternation of the verb form *mepob* 'reign' with *meupeb* 'reign'.

It has been noted that *e* and *a* are often functionally parallel in Old Georgian suffixes (Vogt 1947a:75ff.). In addition, the series markers *-av* and *-am* are realized as *-ev* and *-em*, respectively, in certain screeves of Series I; for example, *v-ḳl-av* 'I kill him', but *v-ḳl-ev-d* 'I was killing him'. Chikobava (1964) gives additional arguments to relate these suffixes historically.

The similarity of the consonantal element has also not escaped notice. It seems probable that *v* of the series markers became *b* in many instances (see Gamkrelidze and Machavariani 1965:263, n. 1). Thus, it is likely that **ew* becomes Georgian *-ev*, which becomes *-eb*, and **w-ew* becomes Georgian *-ov*, which becomes *-ob*.

In the Javax dialect of Georgian, *-eb* is substituted for *-av* in certain screeves of Series I (Topuria 1963:182). In the same dialect and Mesxian, *-an* and *-en* are substituted for *-av* and *-ev*: *-ev* > *-em* > *-en; -av* > *-am* > *-an*. A verb that takes one series marker in Standard Modern Georgian is likely to take another in a regional dialect (Topuria 1963:182). For example, in Kartlian, *-am* is more productive than in the literary dialect; and instead of literary *movxarš-av-t* 'we will cook it by boiling', we find Kartlian *mofxarš-am-t* (Imnaishvili 1974:204). Such alternations between dialects are very common and suggest that the change that accounts for the variation is somewhat haphazard.

In Laz and Mingrelian we find the series markers listed in Table 9.2. The variants with *u* vocalism are most common; they vary freely with *i* and *ə* vocalism in Mingrelian. The series markers with *a* vocalism are also fairly widespread, while the variants with *e* and *o* vocalism are infrequently attested (Natadze 1959). The Mingrelian *-uan* is believed to have developed from a fusing of two morphemes, *-u-an*, reinterpreted as a single series marker; this *u* is the same element that accounts for the development of *-ob* from **w-eb* in Georgian, and it occurs in many of the same verbs (Gamkrelidze and Machavariani:1965:61, 277). The suffix *-mer/mel* and its Atinian variant *-lem* are believed to represent a Laz development (Chikobava 1936:173–174).

It is believed that the consonants we find in the series markers of Zan developed from **w/v*, becoming Zan *m*, which we find in the Viç–Arkab and Atinian dialects, then becoming *n* in Mingrelian (Gudava 1974:137); Laz *m* became *p* in the Xopian dialect.

Table 9.2

Series Markers in Zan[a]

Laz		Mingrelian
Xopian	Viç–Arkab and Atinian	
-ip	*-im*	*-in*
-ep	*-em*	*-en*
-ap	*-am*	*-an*
-op	*-om*	
-up	*-um*	*-un*
		-ən
		-uan
-mer/mel	*-mer/mel/lem*	

[a]After Chikobava (1936:131ff., 173–174).

Table 9.3

Vowel Correspondences in Phonologically Neutral Environment

CK	Georgian	Svan	Zan
**e*	*e*	*e*	*a*
**a*	*a*	*a*	*o*
**o*	*o*	*o*	*u/i*

Table 9.4

Correspondence of Georgian *a* to Zan *u* in Labial Environment[a]

Georgian *a*	Zan *u*
sami 'three'	*sumi* 'three'
mama 'father'	*muma* (Mingrelian) 'father'
mamali 'rooster'	*mumuli* 'rooster'
γame 'night'	*γuma* (Mingrelian) 'last night'

[a]From Gudava (personal communication).

Zan underwent a Great Vowel Shift, which accounts for the correspondences listed in Table 9.3. While Table 9.3 shows the general correspondences, in certain labial environments CK **a* became Zan *u* (Gudava 1979:82); compare with examples in Table 9.4. We can state the conditions of this change as in rule (1).

(1) $a \rightarrow u/ \_\_\_ m$

The change *a* becomes *u* in Zan also occurred in other labial environments, including #*m*C ___ and ___ C*v*, the labial element being lost in the latter environments; for example, the correspondences Georgian *msxali* 'pear' to Zan *(m)sxuli*; Georgian *idaq̣vi* 'elbow' to Zan *duʔi* (Gudava, personal communication); Georgian *mxari* 'shoulder' to Zan (*m*)*xuǯi* (Chikobava 1938:57).[2]

In considering the reconstruction of CGZ series markers, it is important to note that it is not possible to set up a one-to-one correspondence between any Georgian series marker and any Zan series marker. For example, verbs that have Zan *-up/um/un*, or their free variants with *i* or *ə* vocalism, may correspond to Georgian verbs that take no series marker (∅), to Georgian verbs that take *-av*, or to Georgian verbs which take *-i*. Zan *-ap/am/an* may correspond to *-eb*, *-av*, *-am*, *-em*, *-ob*, or *-i* in the cognate Georgian verbs (Natadze 1959). Although there is a partial functional differentiation between the various series markers in each language, we cannot make functional equations that correspond to phonetic ones. Reconstructed correspondences must therefore be made on a phonetic basis, with the assumption that the functional differentiations are at least partially secondary.

On the basis of the vowel correspondences shown in Tables 9.3 and 9.4, and in rule (1) and the consonant development proposed by Gudava (1974:137) and Gamkrelidze and Machavariani (1965:263, 274), we can set up the series marker correspondences in Table 9.5. Gudava sets up an intermediate stage **om*, which assumes that the Great Zan Vowel Shift applied before the assimilation of this vowel to the labial consonant (rule 1). If this is correct, Laz *-om/op*, which occurs only infrequently (Natadze 1959:138), may be a relic of this stage. The sporadically attested *-em*, *-ep*, *-en* may similarly be a relic of CK **e*, which failed to undergo the Great Vowel Shift.

Table 9.5

Series Marker Correspondences: Georgian, Laz, and Mingrelian

Georgian			Laz		Mingrelian
			Viç–Arkab and Atinian	Xopian	
-av	*-am*		*-um* (*-im*)	*-up* (*-ip*)	*-un* (*-in/ən*)
-ev	*-em*	*-eb*	*-am*	*-ap*	*-an*

We may assume that *v* developed into *m* and *b* in different dialects, just as Zan *m* developed into *p* in Xopian, and into *n* in Mingrelian.[3]

Gamkrelidze and Machavariani have suggested that CK was originally characterized by a monovocalic system having only an undifferentiated *ə, which could take different timbres. During CK times, this evolved to phonemic **a*, **e*, **o*, **ā*, **ē*, and **ō*. They view the **a* and **e* qualities as primary, with **o* derived chiefly from **we* or **wa* (Gamkrelidze and Machavariani 1965:366ff). This early lack of differentiation between **e* and **a* leads them to reconstruct a single suffix **aw*/*ew* with the Old Georgian reflexes *-av*, *-ev*, *-eb*, and when preceded by **w*, the reflexes *-ov*, *-ob* (Gamkrelidze and Machavariani 1965:274). If we combine this with the fact that in the series marker -V*m* is from -V*v* (Gudava 1974:137), we may conclude that a single CK suffix **aw*/*ew* developed under a variety of conditions into the series markers listed in Table 9.5. Under this hypothesis, the **a* variant has the reflexes *-av*, *-am* in Georgian, *-um* in Viç–Arkab and Atinian by rule (1), *-up* in Xopian and *-un* in Mingrelian by further consonantal change, and *-im*, *-ip*, *-in*, *-ən* by productive alternation. The **e* variant, on the other hand, has the reflexes *-ev*, *-em*, *-eb* in Georgian, *-am* and *-ap* in Laz, and *-an* in Mingrelian; **w-ew* has the reflex *-ov* and *-ob* in Georgian and *-uan* in Mingrelian.

9.2.2. Collective Markers

In Old Georgian we find a three-way opposition between (a) the singular, which bears no special marker, (b) the plural, which bears an inflectional marker indicating at once plurality and case, and (c) the collective, which bears an agglutinative suffix *-eb*, together with a case marker (see Dondua 1956b). For example, we find the forms listed in Table 9.6 for the root *saxl-* 'house' in the dative case.

The syntax of the *-eb* form in Old Georgian and its evolution throughout the history of the language have been studied by Chikobava (1968a, 1968b) and by Kiziria (1955); the discussion in this section is based in part on their observations, but in many respects does not represent their opinions.

Table 9.6

Dative Case Forms of Singular, Collective, and Plural in Old Georgian

Singular	Collective	Plural
saxl-sa	*saxl-eb-sa*	*saxl-ta*

The collective is formally a singular, triggering singular number in the verb, both as a subject and as an object, as shown in the examples below.

(2) a. *arγara moiqsenos merme saxel-eb-i mati*
NEG he/remember/it/II/ then name-COL-NOM their
'Then he will no longer remember their names.' (Hosea 2:17)
b. *q̣ovel-ni uḳetureba-ni matni moviqsenne*
all-PL/NOM evil-PL/NOM their I/remember/*them*/II
'I remember all their iniquities.' (Hosea 7:2)

(3) *sir-eb-i aγprinda*
bird-COL-NOM he/flew.up/I
'The birds flew up.' (Kekelidze 1918:115, 16)

(4) *rayta ara višeynot saxl-eb*
for NEG we/build/it/II house-COL/NOM
'that we will not build houses' (Jer 35:9 O)

In (2a) the collective direct object, *saxelebi mati*, does not condition direct object number agreement; in contrast, the plural direct object in (2b), *q̣ovelni uḳeturebani matni*, does trigger the agreement marker *n* (< *en*), described in greater detail in Chapter 10. If *sir-ni*, a formal plural, were substituted for the subject in (3), it would require the verb form *aγprindes* 'they flew up', with the third person plural subject marker *-es* instead of the singular *-a*. Thus, these examples show that collectives condition singular agreement, both as objects and as subjects.

Within the structure of the noun phrase, the collective has other grammatical characteristics of the singular, though not exclusively. Articles, possessors, and adjectival modifiers are often in the singular, as set out in Table 9.7. As Table 9.7 shows, there is a singular and a plural form for the pronominal possessor; the collective usually takes the same form as the singular. Similarly, Table 9.7 shows a singular and a plural for the

Table 9.7

Concord with Singular, Collective, and Plural in Old Georgian

	Singular	Collective	Plural	
Article	*saxl-sa mas*	*saxl-eb-sa-mas*	*saxl-ta mat*	'the house(s)'
Pronominal possessor	*saxl-sa čem-sa*	*saxl-eb-sa čem-sa* *saxl-eb-sa čem-ta*	*saxl-ta čem-ta*	'my house(s)'
Adjective	*saxl-sa did-sa*	*saxl-eb-sa did-sa* *saxl-eb-sa did-eb-sa*	*saxl-ta did-ta*	'big house(s)'

article; the collective uses the singular. With respect to modifying adjectives, the collective may take the singular form or a collective.

The Old Georgian inflectional plural was lost, and the collective in *-eb* took on the function of marking plurality. In Modern Georgian there is only a two-way contrast between the singular and the plural: *saxl-s* 'house-DAT' versus *saxl-eb-s* 'house-PL-DAT.'[4] In the course of this change, the *-eb* form acquired the characteristics of triggering plural number agreement in the verb and plural concord in modifying adjectives, possessors, and coreferential pronouns, the old article having been lost.

It must be observed that not all Kartvelologists have considered *-eb* a collective. Notably, Shanidze (1976:31), Kiziria (1955), and Chikobava (1968b) consider *-eb* simply a newer marker of the plural. I am inclined to agree with Vogt, who suggests that although *-eb* was a collective marker, Old Georgian texts do not always maintain a strict differentiation between the plural *-ni/ta* and the collective *-eb* (1947b:132–133). Note that a plural marker could also fill the function in the verb as hypothesized here; but in that case we would expect an emphasis on repetition rather than duration, on many individual instantiations of an action rather than on a collection or aggregate of an action.

In Standard Modern Georgian the pluralizer *-eb* is used with all nouns and predicate adjectives in all cases, though the Old Georgian *-ni/ta* is occasionally used in literary contexts. While the standard dialect has only *-eb*, some regional dialects have variants of this, usually coexisting with the literary norm. A part of the Ingilo dialect retains the form *-ev* (G. Imnaishvili 1966:100, n.1). "The *-ev* suffixal plural is also retained as a relic" in some Georgian geographical names (Shanidze 1973:137). Ḳaxian retains the occasional variant *-em* (Martirosovi and Imnaishvili 1956:75). (Kartlian has the variant *-ep*, but this seems to be secondarily derived by assimilation (Imnaishvili 1974:181).) Xevsurian retains a partial contrast between a collective and plural, with the collective markers *-ob*, *-ov* (Chincharauli 1960:59). Thus, for the consonantal element of the noun suffix, we find most of the variants listed for the verb suffix in Table 9.1: *m, v,* and *b*, with the vocalisms *e* and *o*.

In the sister languages no reflex of the old noun pluralizers (*-ni*, *-ta*) remains in that function. The morphemes that mark plurality in substantives in Laz and Mingrelian are listed in Table 9.8 beside the one used in Modern Georgian. Laz uses *-epe* with all nouns, except that *e* is elided when used with stems ending in a vowel (Chikobava 1936:44–50). The development of *-epe* from *-ep* with an epenthetic *e* is discussed in §4.3.1. In some dialects of Mingrelian, *-ep* occurs in all noun cases (Kluge 1916:10 on the dialect of Axali Senaḳi). In the speech of my consultant from Axali Xibula, *-em* is found before case markers with an initial consonant (nar-

Table 9.8

Pluralizers in Substantives

Modern Georgian	*-eb (-em/ev/ob/ov)*
Laz	*-ep-e*
Mingrelian	*-ep (-em/en)*

rative *-k* and dative *-s*), and *-ep* before those case markers that have an initial vowel. Chikobava (1936:44–50) records *-en* before consonants and *-ep* before vowels.

Georgian *-eb*, Laz *-ep-e*, and Mingrelian *-ep* are regarded as cognates. However, Table 9.3 would lead us to expect Zan **a* corresponding to Georgian *e*. Gamkrelidze and Machavariani have pointed out that there are a number of instances where we systematically find Georgian *e* corresponding to Zan *e*; these occur just in substantives. They propose to account for this through a secondary process of umlaut. Umlaut was triggered by *-i*, which occurs in six case endings, then was generalized throughout the paradigm. In addition to the correspondence of the plural marker, this process accounts for correspondences like Georgian *cxeli* 'hot' to Laz–Mingrelian *čxe*, Georgian *çveti* 'droplet' to Laz–Mingrelian *ç̌veti*; and Georgian *xeli* 'hand' to Laz–Mingrelian *xe* (Gamkrelidze and Machavariani 1965:160ff).

9.2.3. Comparison and Reconstruction

Consider the comparison between the noun pluralizers and the series markers used in the daughter languages, listed in Table 9.9. Table 9.9 lists only the major variants discussed here. The vocalism of the reconstructed

Table 9.9

Comparison and Reconstruction of Series Markers and Collectivizer–Pluralizers[a]

	CGZ	Georgian	Laz	Mingrelian
Series Markers	**ev*	*-ev, -em, -eb*	*-am, -ap*	*-an*
	**av*	*-av, -am*	*-um, -up*	*-un*
	**v-ev*	*-ob*		*-uan*
Collectivizer–pluralizer	**ev*	*-ev, -em, -eb*	*-ep-e*	*-ep, -em, -en*

[a]Here **v* denotes the sonorant that has the reflexes *u, w,* and *v* in Kartvelian languages.

collective marker is without problems, given the secondary umlaut in Zan discussed above. Because of the contexts in which it is found, Mingrelian *-en* must be considered secondary; it is thus clear that a labial consonant must be reconstructed for the collective marker. The status of Georgian *-ev* as a relic form (Shanidze 1973:137) requires us to consider this the protoform. Thus, **ev* must be reconstructed independently for the collective–pluralizer and for the series marker. On the basis of the Old Georgian collective versus plural opposition, preserved in the Xevsurian dialect, I assume that CGZ **ev* was originally a collective marker and that it was later generalized as the plural marker in Georgian, Laz, and Mingrelian.

The varying developments of the two suffixes are due to the differing phonological environments in which they occurred. In the substantive, **ev* was often followed by a case marker with the initial segment *i*, since the nominative, genitive, and instrumental cases contain this phoneme (see Chap. 4). In Zan, the **a* (< CK **e*) would have undergone umlaut, conditioned by this *i*, resulting in *e*, as in the stems of substantives discussed above. This vocalism was then generalized throughout the paradigm. The shift *v* to *m* to *b*, then in Zan to *p*, is nonconditioned and haphazard (see n. 3).

In the verb, **ev* would not have been followed by *i* in Zan to the same extent as in the substantive. In Zan, *i* does occur as a screeve marker in Series I, but only in those screeves that have the stem augment *ṭ/d* (based on Chikobava 1936:130–141). We find, for example, *b-zum-um-ṭ-i* 'I was measuring it', where *um* is the reflex of **ev*. In this environment umlaut did not apply to the output of the Great Vowel Shift, and we find *a* < CK **e*. In both Georgian and Zan, **ev* occurred after **v* in some verb forms; in Mingrelian this became *-uan* (< **uam*), and in Georgian *-ob*. The consonant of **ev* underwent the same haphazard changes in the verb as in the substantive, with different reflexes being generalized in various dialects. In addition, the reflexes of **ev* in the verb differ from those in the substantive in that the latter was made general for all substantives without exception, while in the verb the exact form of the series marker is still governed by the particular verb. For these reasons, the series markers retain various reflexes of the vocalic element in Laz and Mingrelian and various stages of the consonantal changes in Georgian.

Notice that positing Georgian *-eb* as the latest stage in the development of this suffix is consistent with several observed facts. It is expected that the newest form will be the one generalized. The series marker *-eb* (together with its variant *-ob*) is the most frequently encountered and the most productive in Georgian (Shanidze 1973:397). It is this suffix that has been generalized as the plural marker at the expense of the old inflectional plural, *-ni/ta*. Finally, the newness of this series marker in contrast with

-am, *-av*, and so forth is consistent with the fact that *-eb* never undergoes syncope, while *-am* and *-av* do (see Chap. 8).

The assumption that the series marker comes from the collective marker provides an explanation of the occurrence of the series marker just in Series I: this series expressed durative aspect, and it was the collective suffix that marked this.

9.3. SVAN

In Svan the formants listed in Table 9.10 occur in Series I forms and do not occur in Series II forms (Topuria 1931:162ff.). The suffixes *-esg* and *-ešg* take the form *-ēsg*, *-isg*, *-es(ḳ)*, *-ēšg* or *-ešḳ*. These do not bear any apparent relation to any series marker in any of the sister languages, and we shall assume that they are a Svan development. Of the remaining suffixes, Topuria reports that *-er* and *-el* (or *-ēl*) are each found in only one verb (Topuria 1931:162).

It has been suggested that Svan *-em* is equivalent to the Georgian series marker *-am*. We find *-em* with some of the same roots that Georgian *-am* occurs with, as in Table 9.11 (Topuria 1967:162). In other instances the Georgian series marker seems to have changed; for example, Svan *a-nqw-em* beside Georgian *a-mx-ob-s* 'he overthrows him', where Georgian *-ob* seems to have come from **v-ev* (cf. *da-a-mxv-e* 'you overthrew him').

Topuria (1967:241–242; 1979b:33ff.) has also suggested that Svan *-en* is equivalent to Georgian *-eb*. As evidence for this, he cites the parallel functions of the suffixes, including its function as the series marker with

Table 9.10

Series Markers in Svan

-em	*-en*	*-er*	*-el*	*-esg*	*-ešg*	—
—	*-in*	—	—	—	—	*-i*

Table 9.11

Svan *-em* to Georgian *-am* Correspondence

Svan	Georgian	
x-a-b-em (Upper Svan)/*x-a-b-en* (Lašx)	*a-b-am-s*	'it ties it (to something)'
i-kw-em	*i-cv-am-s*	'he puts it on (himself)'

transitive verbs, with inactive intransitive verbs, in deverbal nouns, and as a formant in some screeves of Series III.[5]

The pluralizers in Svan occur in many forms. They vary by dialect, and the use of a particular marker or markers is governed by the lexical item, or sometimes by the semantic class to which it belongs. Some of the pluralizers are listed by dialect in Table 9.12. The lists are not meant to be exhaustive.

In the Upper Bal dialect alone, there are more than twenty-five markers of plurality in substantives (Sharadzenidze 1954). Most of these are predictable or partially predictable positional variants of *-ar*. The form of the suffix is affected by *r* and *l* alternations, mostly as a result of dissimilation, by lengthening of the suffixal vowel after a root vowel, and by umlaut (regressive vowel harmony). It is probable that *-ar* and its variants are the newest of the morphemes listed, being by far the most widespread (see Sharadzenidze 1954:197). Kaldani (1974) has established that the *-ar* suffix is derived from **-er-a*. Elsewhere he has shown that **e* becomes *ä* (> *a*) in the environment of a following back vowel, which subsequently drops (Kaldani 1968, 1969). He presents cogent arguments for the existence of *-a* in the plural. He suggests that *-a* is an ancient pluralizer and the sequence **-er-a* originally functioned as a marker of the collective-plural

Table 9.12

Some Pluralizers in Svan Dialects[a]

Dialects	Pluralizer
Upper Svaneti	
Upper Bal	*-är*
	-äl
	-u
	-a
	la——a
Lower Bal	
Laxamula	*-u*
	-ow
Čubexe	*-u*
	-ol
Lower Svaneti	
Lašx	*-ēl*
	-ar
Lenṭex	*-ar*
	-ra

[a]From Kaldani 1955:153; 1959a: 218; 1974:159, 161; Sharadzenidze 1954.

(Kaldani 1974:161–162). Kaldani shows that the variants of *-ar* and *-al* evolved from a common form with the vocalic element **e*; in this way he accounts for the suffixes listed for Upper Bal and the Lower Svan dialects in Table 9.12.[6]

One of the pieces of evidence cited by Kaldani is the occurrence of either *-a* or *-er* in the ancient forms of family names. In Svaneti, a family was named for the senior male member; to his name were added the genitive marker *-š* or *-iš* and the pluralizer *-a* or *-er*. For example, from the forename *Seṭel*, are derived *Seṭel-š-ēr* or *Seṭel-š-a*, literally 'those of Seṭel' (Kaldani 1974:155). It is also important to observe what has replaced those forms. Where the ancient narrative poetry has *Gabi-š-a*, contemporary Svan has *Gabiāni*; where once there was *Urzäyša*, we find *Urzaiāni* (Gabliani 1925:195; Kaldani 1974:155). That is, *-an* (? < *en* + *a*) has replaced the ancient Svan pluralizer in the formation of names. These also function as plurals, as can be seen from the plural verb agreement in sentences such as Georgian *Gabiani ambobdnen* 'Gabiani were talking' (Kaldani 1974:155), where *-nen* is a marker of plural subjects. The suffix *-an*, therefore, must function as a pluralizer in a way similar to *-a* or *-er*.

Turning to the suffix *-u* of Upper Bal, we find that it occurs (a) alone with certain adjectives, (b) following *-er* or a variant with certain nouns, and (c) as *w* preceding *-ar* or *-al* with certain nouns. (Here *w* and *u* may have been positional variants; see Gamkrelidze and Machavariani 1965:25–38.) Redundant indication of plurality is not uncommon. It is not clear at this time whether Upper Svan *-u/w* is related to Lower Bal *-ow*, nor from what these may ultimately derive.[7]

From the discussion above, we can see that there are some suggestive parallels between some of the Svan pluralizers and some of the series markers. However, at this time the origins of all the various series markers cannot be accounted for, nor can a single pluralizer be reconstructed. While some of the Svan series markers may be related to ones in Georgian, as Topuria has suggested, it is not possible at this time to relate the two sets in a systematic way.

There is some evidence that series markers were not part of the original Series I forms: (a) A number of scholars support the position that the Series I intransitive originally lacked the series marker (see Chap. 8, n. 5). (b) The transitives of ablauting verbs generally lack series markers; for example, Old Georgian *vcwet* 'I wear it out', *vdreḳ* 'I bend it', Svan *ṭixe* 'you return it', *xiḳed* 'you destroy it' (see Chap. 8). Ablauting verbs are generally considered to preserve an archaic situation morphologically. (c) In Mingrelian, those masdars (nominalizations) that preserve *a*-grade (the reflex of CK **e*-grade) lack series markers (Gudava 1974:136). These forms, retaining the ancient ablaut grade that characterized Series I, may also retain the archaic morpheme structure and reflect a stage where series markers were not used. Together, this evidence and the lack of clear parallels between Svan and its sisters suggest that series markers may have developed in CGZ, with diffusion of the structure but not of the specific morphemes, accounting for the occurrence of some series markers in Svan. Series markers may have developed as a functional replacement for ablaut as part of the morphology that distinguishes Series I from II.

9.4. A FUNCTIONAL PARALLEL

In the preceding sections I have proposed that the collective marker of substantives was used in Georgian, Laz, and Mingrelian as a formant of Series I, originally as a marker of durative aspect. It has been observed that the reconstructions of the historical linguist must necessarily be constrained by known language universals (Jakobson 1958:23). We must avoid reconstructing a system of a type not known to occur among the languages of the world. It is the purpose of this section to briefly describe a productive system structurally similar to the one reconstructed here.

The productive substantive pluralizers in contemporary Svan are used also in some dialects to indicate iterative, or repeated, action—in finite verb forms, in masdars, and in participles (Sharadzenidze 1954:192–193; Topuria 1967:231–232, 234). Some examples of this use of *-āl*, *-iēl*, and *-ər* are given below.

(5) a. *ǰ-i-ç̣wīl-a*
you/married/III
'You have married (once).' (Sharadzenidze 1954:192)

b. *ǰ-i-ç̣wīl-**āl**-a*
you/married/PL/III
'You have married many times.' (Sharadzenidze 1954:192)

(6) a. *x-o-γ-ēšg-i*
he/takes/him/from.him/I
'He carries her off from him.' (Topuria 1967:82)

b. *i-γ-ešg-**āl**-w-n-i-x ecriš bušw-ār*
they/take/her/I Eceri/GEN bastard-PL/NOM
'The Eceri bastards will be carrying her off (repeatedly).' (Gabliani 1925:197, 4)

Closely related to this is the use of these same suffixes to mark plurality of the direct object. Examples (7) and (8) are from Topuria (1967:233, see also p. 234).

(7) a. *a-ṭwr-en-i* (Lašx)
he/lights/it/I
'He lights a candle.'
b. a-ṭwr-en-***āl***-*i*
'He lights candles' or 'He lights a candle many times.'

(8) a. *a-mār-e* (Upper Bal)
he/prepares/it
'He is preparing one thing.'
b. *a-mār-**äl**-i*
'He is preparing many things' or 'He is preparing repeatedly.'

The use of the substantive pluralizers *-ar*, *-al*, and so forth to mark repeated action, as in (5)—(8), is similar to the reconstructed use of the collective marker to indicate durative action. The existence of this productive system in contemporary Svan makes the CGZ reconstruction all the more plausible.

9.5. THE PROBLEM OF SERIES MARKER -*i*

The suffix *-i* is usually listed with the series markers *-av*, *-am*, *-eb*, and so forth in Georgian, but it is not clear that it has always had the same status. Chikobava (1940:23; 1943; 1948:73ff.) has suggested that this *-i* is from the screeve formant *-i* of the habitual II. There has been much discussion of this question in the literature, but many of the objections raised are really to peripheral claims of this theory (see Kavtaradze 1954:12–15; 1961; Kiknadze 1947; 1961:267ff.). Only two portions of this hypothesis are relevant here, namely, whether this is indeed the origin of *-i* and whether or not *-i* is a series marker.

When a language introduces a new series of verb forms that maintain the categories of the old series of verb forms, as Kartvelian introduced Series I maintaining the old categories of person, number, tense, voice, and mood, we would naturally expect that the morphology for representing these categories in the old system would find its way into the new. In Kartvelian, the Series II markers of subject person and object person and of subject number and object number are carried into Series I. The markers of transitivity (ablaut grade of the stem) and voice are found in Series I and in II. The same markers of version are found in Series I and II. And the screeve markers of the subjunctive II, *-e*, and of the imperative II, *-e*, are likewise found in Series I (see Chap. 5). It should therefore not be at all surprising that the exponent of the habitual II would be found also in Series I.

The suffix *-i* is found in the present, both with and without some other series marker. For example, we have ***šl-i-s*** 'he spreads it,' ***dg-eb-i-s*** 'he stands', and ***v-h-ḳitx-v-i*** (< **v-h-ḳitx-av-i** by regular syncope; see §8.4.2). Even in Old Georgian, the occurrence of *-i* in the present was limited mostly to verbs that had no other series marker, such as *šlis*, and to intransitives like *dgebis*.

The suffix *-i* differs from other series markers in the following respects: (a) Unlike all other series markers, *-i* does not occur in the masdar or participial forms of the verb. Thus we find *ḳitxvay* from **ḳitx-av-ay, mḳitxveli* from **m-ḳitx-av-eli*, but corresponding to *šl-i-s* we have *šlay*, not **sliay*, and *mšleli*, not **mšlieli.* (b) Unlike all other series markers, *-i* does not occur in first evidential forms. We find *-eb* retained in *u-γ-**eb**-i-e-s*, but *-i* dropped in *u-šl-i-e-s*. (c) Unlike all other series markers, *-i* does not occur in causatives. Beside *a-b-am-s* 'he ties it', we find *a-b-m-evin-eb-s* 'he causes him to tie it', where the series marker *-am* is reduced to *-m*; but beside *šl-i-s* we find *a-šl-evin-eb-s* 'he causes him to spread it'. It is possible to explain all of these facts in either of two ways. The series marker *-i* may be seen as the victim of a vowel deletion process. The alternative view is that *-i* was originally a screeve marker, not a series marker; this hypothesis also explains its failure to occur in all of the environments named above.

The question of whether or not *-i* is a series marker should center on the definition given at the beginning of this chapter. We may say that *-i* does not occur in Series II, since the *-i* of the habitual II is clearly a screeve marker and therefore may be a different morpheme. It is not obvious whether or not *-i* occurs in all forms of Series I, since the forms lend themselves to more than one interpretation. The two analyses are summarized in Table 9.13. According to the analysis given in the left-hand column, the series marker *-i* is carried throughout the Series I conjugation of this verb. It is followed in the imperfect, imperfect habitual, subjunctive I, and imperative I by the formant *-d* and formants of the individual

Table 9.13

Two Analyses of Series I Forms of *cday* 'try' in Old Georgian (Third Person Singular Subject Forms)

Present	*cd-i-s*	*cd-i-s*
Present habitual	*cd-i-n*	*cd-i-n*
Imperfect	*cd-i-d-a*	*cd-id-a*
Imperfect habitual	*cd-i-d-i-s*	*cd-id-i-s*
Subjunctive I	*cd-i-d-e*	*cd-id-e*
Imperative I	*cd-i-d-e-n*	*cd-id-e-n*

screeves. According to the analysis in the right-hand column, the common formant for the last four screeves is *-id*, not *-d*; the suffix *-i* is not found in every screeve of Series I. With other verbs, this formant can be found both in the form *-d*, for example, *c̣er-d-a* 'he was writing it', and as *-id*, for example, *xed-v-id-a* 'he was seeing it'. In order to be able to settle this question, it would be necessary to give a complete account of the occurrence of *-ed*, *-id*, and *-d*; but it is not yet possible to explain all of the occurrences of these forms, and the question must here remain unresolved.[8]

The remaining evidence concerning the origin of *-i* is equally uncertain and contradictory. There is no series marker in Laz or Mingrelian corresponding to *-i*, but there is in Svan. In Svan we must distinguish two types of *-i*. The first I describe is found in examples like Upper Bal *yə-rm-i* 'he catches it' and *i-rd-i* 'he raises him'. It seems to be carried through Series I in forms such as *yə-rm-e-y-da* 'he was catching it' and *i-rd-e-y-da* 'he was raising him'. Gamkrelidze and Machavariani have hypothesized that Georgian and Svan *-i* come from **ey* and that the *-ey* element following the root in these imperfect forms is a direct continuation of that **ey*. The second *-i* in Svan is parallel to *-e*, *-a*, and Ø, the choice of these being lexically determined. These elements function as markers of the present screeve, not of the entire series. Further, in the present they may follow a series marker; for example, *x-o-γ-ēšg-i* 'he takes it from him'. In the rest of the series there is no sign of this *-i*: *x-o-γ-äšg-da* 'he was taking it from him' from **x-o-γ-ēšg-da* (see Kaldani 1969).

It is useful to distinguish two *-i* suffixes in Georgian also. In addition to the one shown in Table 9.13, we find an *-i* that may occur after series markers and is restricted to the present. After the series marker *-eb*, we find *i* in forms like *dg-eb-i-s* 'he stands', but in the imperfect form *dg-eb-od-a* 'he was standing' there is no *-i*. We find *-i* without a series marker in *e-l-i-s* 'he waits' beside *e-l-od-a* 'he was waiting' with no *-i*. This *-i* occurs mostly with verbs that represent relics of ancient types, such as the markerless intransitive (see Chap. 8, n. 5); this suggests that this *-i* itself is ancient.

On the basis of both Svan and Georgian, we must posit two CK suffixes that have the reflex *-i*. We may safely conclude that the *-i* that occurs in forms such as Georgian *dgebis, elis* and Svan *xoγēšgi*, and that is clearly not characteristic of all Series I forms, is a continuation of the habitual II formant, *-i*, just as the *-e* of the subjunctive I is a continuation of the formant *-e* of the subjunctive II. This *-i* is found in the Old Georgian present and present habitual; this may also be the *-i* that follows the *-ed/id/od/d* in the imperfect habitual. It thus characterizes the present and habitual screeves in Old Georgian.

The *-i* in Svan *yərmi* and *irdi* and Georgian *cdis*, on the other hand, may be a true series marker. If Gamkrelidze and Machavariani are right, it came from **ey*, and its functional origin cannot be further traced at this time.

9.6. ALTERNATIVE ANALYSES

In the published literature, few alternative proposals have been made concerning the origin of series markers. I know of only two.

Chikobava (1942) argues that the ergative construction, specifically in Caucasian languages, is neither active nor passive in the sense of European languages, but rather neutral with respect to voice. He maintains that Series I contrasts with Series II in that while the latter has the neutral ergative construction, Series I is activized and involves something more like the European accusative. It is in the context of of this discussion that he remarks that specific morphological means—namely, thematic markers (series markers)—make possible the activized situation in Series I. In Georgian, he continues, these morphemes are the formants of the active voice, and the activization of the verb is inherently related to the causative. The relation between the present stem and the aorist stem is essentially the same as that between a causative and its corresponding base (Chikobava 1942:233).

The proposal is not elaborated in terms of specific morphology. One possible interpretation is that the claim is being made that the present stem is formed from the aorist stem by means of a causative affix. In Old Georgian a causative was formed from a noncausative base with the prefix *a-* and a suffix Ø, *-in*, or *-ev/iv*, where *-ev* represents the Series I form corresponding to *-iv* in Series II, usually reduced to *-i*; for example, *mo-a-ḳl-v-i-a* from *mo-a-ḳl-av-iv-a* (based on Takaishvili 1974). The Series I form of the causative suffix *-ev* is the same as the reconstucted protoform of the series marker. Thus, the passing remark by Chikobava referred to above finds support in specific affixes.

The problems with the proposal made in Chikobava (1942) involve not the morphology, but the relations referred to among verbal categories. The notion that in a language a given verb may have an active form as well as a form that is neutral with respect to voice is puzzling. The statement that Series I represents an activized situation is difficult to reconcile with the fact that Series I forms include mediopassives (unaccusatives) and passives, as well as actives; for example, *aṭpobs* 'he warms it', *ṭpeba* 'it warms up', *gamṭpari ars* 'it is warmed', *içereba* 'it is written'. Further, a relationship between Series I and the causative is difficult to reconcile with the fact that causatives are invariably transitive (Harris 1981b:Chap.

5), while Series I is believed to have originally been exclusively intransitive in surface structure (Aronson 1979:300–303; Pätsch 1967; Rogava 1975; etc.). On these grounds, the proposal that a causative or active marker is the source of series markers must be rejected.

Aronson (1979:301) suggests "that the present stem formants (e.g., Geo. *-av*, *-am*, *-eb*, etc.) [i.e., series markers] were in function a type of intransitivizing (and hence imperfectivizing) derivational suffix." As observed above, there is little doubt that Series I originally represented imperfective aspect and was limited to surface intransitives. To this extent, the proposal at hand is entirely plausible. However, in the passage cited, Aronson does not go on to relate the series markers to specific morphological origins that might be expected to have or develop an intransitivizing function. That is, no evidence is adduced to support the claim that the primary function of these markers was to intransitivize clauses. In general, intransitivizing affixes in Georgian, Laz, and Mingrelian are limited to the prefixes *i-*, *e-*, *a-*, and *o-*, and the suffix *-d*, not one of which appears to be homologous to series markers.

As we have seen, little work has been done on the origin of series markers. Extant hypotheses are either inconsistent with what is known of the syntax and verb categories expressed by Series I or are unsupported by specific morphological evidence. In contrast, there is good phonological, morphological, and syntactic support for the hypothesis developed here.

9.7. CONCLUSION

In each Kartvelian language there occur formants which characterize Series I verb forms as a whole and which do not occur in Series II. In Georgian, Laz, and Mingrelian, these formants all developed from a single form, *-*ev*. The collective marker of Old Georgian, *-eb*, and the plural markers of Laz and Mingrelian, *-epe*, *-ep*, *-em*, and *-en*, developed from a common form, *-*ev*, which originally functioned as an exponent of the collective. The collectivizer, *-*ev*, was used in Series I forms to mark durative aspect; it indicated that a set of actions was viewed as a whole, just as it indicated that a set of substantives was viewed as a whole. This hypothesis is consistent with the nature of Series I as a set of screeves expressing durative aspect.

NOTES

[1]These morphemes are usually called THEMATIC MARKERS. However, screeve markers, such as the aorist formant *-e*, are also often referred to as thematic

markers. As used in the present work, a SERIES MARKER characterizes every form of a particular type of a given verb in Series I. SCREEVE MARKERS, on the other hand, characterize only particular screeves, not whole series. In the present work, THEMATIC MARKER is a cover term for series markers and screeve markers.

[2]In CK the masdar was formed from the Series I transitive stem (Gamkrelidze and Machavariani 1965:208–209). In Zan, the labial consonant that conditions *a* > *u* drops in the masdar, leaving *-u*; for example, Laz *o-č̣ar-u* 'writing' beside *č̣ar-um-s* 'he writes it', and Mingrelian *č̣ar-u-a* 'writing' beside *č̣ar-un-s* 'he writes it' (forms from Chikobava 1936:174, 177). The labial consonant is also lost from the Zan Class 2 series marker *-u* < **om* < **am* < **av* (see also Danelia 1976; Gudava 1974; Nadareishvili 1970).

[3]The consonant correspondences are haphazard, not systematic. While labial consonants are the same in many cognate pairs, in the following they are not: Georgian *vin* : Laz *min* 'who?', Georgian *vlṭ* : Laz *mṭ* 'flee' (Chikobava 1938:319), Georgian *tiva* 'hay': Laz–Mingrelian *tipi* 'grass' (Chikobava 1938:132), Georgian *vs* : Laz–Mingrelian *pš, š* 'fill, full' (Chikobava 1938:240, 333), Georgian *mxari* : Laz *pxuǯi* 'shoulder' (Chikobava 1938:57), Georgian *mxali* : some western dialects *pxali* 'puree' (Chikobava 1950:VII:227), and Georgian *bγav* : Laz *mγor* 'howl, cry out'. Within Georgian we find alternations of *v* with *m* in the first person marker (Melikishvili 1977), of *v* with *p* in *moc̣ape, mosc̣avle* 'pupil, student'. See also Kaldani (1964:232), Kavtaradze (1964a:210–211), and Schmidt (1962:53) on haphazard changes and correspondences involving labial consonants.

[4]Collectives can now be formed lexically with *-eb-a* and *-ob-a*; for example, *ḳac-eb-a* 'mankind' beside *ḳac-eb-i* 'men' and *sṭudenṭ-ob-a* 'student body' beside *sṭudenṭ-eb-i* 'students'. See also Martirosovi (1958).

[5]Topuria also suggests that **en* (*n*) replaces the series marker *-eb* in certain forms in Georgian. For example, beside *ṭrial-eb-s* 'he turns-I' we find *u-ṭrial-n-i-a* 'apparently he turned-III'. If the *n* in the latter is actually related to the series marker *-eb* in the former, it would be partially parallel to the behavior of the series markers *-am* and *-av* in Georgian: *xaṭ-av-s* 'he paints it-I' and *da-u-xaṭ-av-s* 'apparently he painted it-III'; *a-b-am-s* 'he ties it-I' and *da-u-b-am-s* 'apparently he tied it-III'. In spite of this parallelism, it is by no means clear that is the correct analysis of *n* in *uṭrialnia*.

[6]Kaldani has also suggested that Svan collective **er-a* is parallel to a Georgian collective marker *-el* (1974:161–162).

[7]Kaldani (1969:68–69) has shown that the Svan suffixes *-ar*, *-aw*, and *-am* are functionally equivalent; we find Lower Bal *c̣ad-aw*, a name given to red cattle, where the first morpheme is 'red' and the second is a collective; *č̣er-am*, a name given to variegated cattle, where the first element is 'variegated' and the second is a collective; and *ḳvam-ar*, a name given to smoke-colored cattle, where the first element is from *ḳväm* (smoke) and the second is a collective.

[8]For example, it is not clear why we should find *ḳl-v-id-a* 'he was killing it', *ḳl-v-id-i-s*, and so on with no normal grade syllable. Nor is it clear why we find *dr-eḳ-d* rather than *dr-ḳ-ed*. See Gamkrelidze and Machavariani (1965:273–275).

10

The Plural Agreement Marker *-en*

In Chapter 7 it was shown that one of the features that distinguishes Series II from I is the occurrence of the plural direct object agreement marker *-en*. The purpose of the present chapter is to account for that difference. First, the distribution of this suffix in Series II of Old Georgian is described, and it is established that even in Old Georgian the use of this suffix in Series II was dying out.[1] In §10.2, I explore where *-en* would be expected to occur in Series I, if the rule assigning it were extended to that set of forms. It is shown that there are relics of the use of this suffix—and of the redundant marking of number—in just those verb types where our analysis would lead us to expect them.

10.1. THE DISTRIBUTION OF *-EN* IN OLD GEORGIAN

In this section it is shown that *-en* is triggered by final direct objects, by initial direct objects that are the final subjects of *i*- and *e*-intransitives, by initial direct objects that are the final subjects of analytic passives, by initial direct objects that are the final subjects of stative passives, and by direct objects that are the final subjects of inversion constructions. This would suggest that all nominals that are direct objects at any level trigger *-en*. However, some kinds of direct objects regularly fail to trigger *-en*. It is shown that one sort of failure of the direct object marker *-en* to occur is to be explained on phonological grounds. The other must be a grammaticized exception, perhaps the first stage in the eventual total loss of *-en* in Georgian.

The underlying form of the suffix discussed here is *-en* (Chikobava 1929b). However, in most forms in Old Georgian it appears as *-n*, reduced by syncope (rule 2 discussed in Chap. 8).

10.1.1. Final Direct Objects that Trigger *-en*

In Old Georgian, the suffix *-en* is triggered by plural direct objects. This is shown by the contrast between examples (1) and (2). The potential trigger and the *-en* suffix appear in boldface type in these examples and throughout this chapter.

(1) a. *da daviviçq**ne*** *me-ca* ***švil-ni*** ***šenni***
and I/forget/them/II I/NAR-too child-PL/NOM your
'And I, too, have forgotten your children.' (Hosea 4:6)
b. *vixil**en*** ***otx-ni*** ***angeloz-ni***
I/see/them/II four-PL/NOM angel-PL/NOM
'I saw four angels.' (Rev 7:1)

(2) a. *daiviçqa* *israeyl-man* ***šemokmed-i*** ***tvisi***
she/forget/him/II Israel-NAR maker-NOM self-GEN
'Israel has forgotten her maker.' (Hosea 8:14)
b. *vixile* ***sxua-y*** ***angeloz-i***
I/see/him/II other-NOM angel-NOM
'I saw another angel' (Rev 7:2)

The examples in (1) have plural direct objects (marked with the nominative plural, *-ni*); they trigger *-en* in the governing finite verb form. The examples in (2) have singular direct objects (marked with the nominative singular, *-i* or *-y*); there is no *-en* in the verb forms that govern them.

The contrast between (1b), which is in Series II, and (3), which is in Series I, demonstrates that *-en* was generally restricted to Series II.

(3) *romel-ni* *hxedvides* *mat*
which-PL/NOM they/see/it/I them/PL/DAT
'which saw them' (Rev 11:11B)

In (3), as in (1b), the direct object is plural. In (1b), the plural direct object triggers *-en*, but in (3) it fails to do so. In fact, *-en* never occurs in

Series I in this function. All tense–aspect categories of Series II, including the habitual II, aorist, subjunctive II, and imperative II, may bear *-en*.

The *-en* suffix is triggered by plural direct objects of all persons. This is established by the following examples, where (4) and (5) illustrate first person plural direct objects and (6) illustrates second person plural direct objects.

(4) *xolo sačmel-man* ***čuen*** *ara çargvidginnes ɣmert-sa*
but food-NAR us/NOM NEG it/commend/us/II God-DAT
'But food (meat) will not commend us to God.' (1 Cor 8:8AB)

(5) *damparenit* ***čuen***
you.PL/cover/us/II us/NOM
'Cover us!' (Hosea 10:8)

(6) *rametu otx-ta gan kar-ta*
for four-PL/GEN from wind-PL/GEN
c-isa-ta šegḳribne ***tkuen***
heaven-GEN-PL/GEN I/gather/you.PL/II you/PL/NOM
'For I have gathered you from the four winds of heaven.'
(Zak 2:6)

In (4)–(5) the direct object is *čuen* 'us', and in (6), *tkuen* 'you(PL)'. Both trigger *-en*, as shown. Example (1) shows that third person plurals also trigger *-en*.

In (5), the prefix *m-* (*damparenit*) is a first person object agreement marker, also used in the singular. In (4), a different prefix, *gv*, (*car-**gv**-idginnes*), occurs. This is a fusional affix indicating both first person (inclusive) object and plurality of that object; it is never used with a singular object. Thus, in (4) direct object plurality is marked redundantly—both by the first person plural object marker *gv-* and by the general plural direct object marker *-en*.

In the examples cited thus far, the direct object whose plurality triggers *-en* is present in the surface structure. This marker is also used when the unemphatic plural direct object is dropped, as in (7).

(7) *vis šeguvedren*
who/DAT you.SG/commend/us/II
'To whom did you commend us?' (Abuladze 1960:35,30)

As we know, in Series II, direct objects are marked with the nominative case. As discussed in §9.2.2, this case may take different forms. The old form *-ni*, a fusional marker that indicates both plurality and the nominative case, occurs frequently. The collective *-ebi* is infrequent in Old Georgian. Under certain circumstances, the bare stem of a noun may be used where a plural is intended, as in the examples in (10) below. It is often said that only the *-ni* plural triggers *-en* in the verb form; Shanidze (1976:159) cites the following examples in support of this (glosses and translations added):

(8) ***šen šehmusren tav-ni***
you/NAR you/break/them/II head-PL/NOM
vešap-ta-ni
dragon-PL/GEN-PL/NOM
'You broke the heads of dragons.' (Psalm 73:13)

(9) ***šen šehmusre tav-eb-i vešap-isa-y***
you/break/it/II head-PL-NOM dragon-GEN-NOM
mis
DET/GEN
'You broke the heads of the dragon.' (Psalm 73:14)

In (8), the direct object in *-ni* triggers *-en* in the verb form. In (9), the direct object in *-ebi* fails to trigger *-en*. Note, however, that there are nominative plural nominals that do not bear the *-ni* ending but do trigger *-en* in the verb. The first and second person plural pronouns in (4)–(6) do not bear the *-ni* suffix, but they do trigger *-en* in the verb form.[2] In (7), the trigger nominal is not even present in the surface structure, yet it triggers *-en*. In (10) bare stem (absolutive form) plurals trigger *-en*.[3]

(10) a. *romel-ta esxnen* ***col***
which-PL/DAT sit/them/to.them/MP/II wife
'those who had wives' (1 Cor 7:29)

b. *ixilna* ***simon da andrea***
he/see/them/II Simon and Andrew
'He saw Simon and Andrew.' (Mk 1:16B)

From these examples we must conclude that it is not only nominals in *-ni* that trigger *-en*; the rule that assigns *-en* is sensitive to the grammatical relations of the nominals and to plurality, not to the specific morpheme *-ni*.[4] The correct generalization, then, is that plural direct objects trigger *-en*, while singulars and collectives do not.

Derived direct objects trigger *-en* as do nominals that are direct objects at all levels of derivation. The occurrence of *-en* with derived direct objects is illustrated in (11)–(12).

(11) *rametu ganamravlna* ***eprem sakurtxevel-ni***
for he/CAUSE/increase/them/II Ephrem altar-PL/NOM
'For Ephrem increased the altars.' (Hosea 8:11)

(12) *da ganrcxnes mat* ***samosel-ni***
and they/wash/them/II they/PL/NAR clothes-PL/NOM
mat-ni *da ganaspeṭaḳnes*
their-PL/NOM and they/CAUSE/white/them/II
'And they have washed their robes and made them white.'
(Rev 7:14B)

The verb in (11) and the second one in (12) are organic causatives. Their final direct objects are plural and trigger *-en*.

10.1.2. Initial Direct Objects that Trigger *-en*

Subjects of inactive intransitive verbs also trigger *-en* in the verbs that govern them. This is one of the bases on which these nominals can be identified as initial direct objects (see Appendix to Chap. 3). Initial direct objects that advance to subject may occur with a verb form in any one of a number of morphological categories. It is shown here that plural initial direct objects trigger *-en* whether they are the final subjects of *i*-intransitives, *e*-intransitives, analytic passives, stative passives, or inversion constructions.

The examples in (13) illustrate the occurrence of *-en* with *i*-intransitives.

(13) a. *da* ***ušǰulo*** *xikmnnes*
and iniquity do/them/MP/II
'And iniquities were committed.' (1 Esdras 1:46–48)
b. *rayta ara ganiḳitxnet*
that NEG question/you.PL/MP/II
'in order that you not be questioned' (L 6:37)
c. *ganivtnes* ***gul-ni*** ***mat-ni***
divide/them/MP/II heart-PL/NOM their-PL/NOM
'Their hearts are divided.' (Hosea 10:2)

The verb 'be' is also in the morphological category of *i*-intransitives. It is illustrated in (14).

(14) a. *šišuel iq̇vnes*
naked be/them/MP/II
'They were naked.' (Gen 3:7)
b. *da iq̇o* ***siq̇mil-i*** *kueq̇anasa zeda*
and be/it/MP/II famine-NOM earth/DAT on
'And there was a famine on earth.' (Gen 12:10)

In (14b) the final subject is singular and does not trigger *-en*; it contrasts with (14a), which has a plural final subject and the *-en* marker.

In Old Georgian, plural final subjects trigger plural agreement, marked as *-(i)t* in the first and second persons and variously (*-es*, *-en*, etc.) in the third. As shown here, plural direct objects trigger *-en*. If a given plural nominal is a direct object initially and subject finally, it triggers both types of markers. In (13c) the plural nominal *gulni matni* 'their hearts' triggers *-en* (> *-n*), the marker of plural direct objects, and *-es*, the marker of third person plural subjects in the aorist: *gan-i-vt-**n**-es*. In inactive intransitive verb forms, all subjects originate as direct objects. Therefore, all plural subjects trigger two plural markers. It is for this reason that traditional grammars of Old Georgian list conjugations like those in Table 10.1 for *i*-intransitives. As Table 10.1 shows, in Series I the plural paradigm contrasts with the singular of the same person by just one morpheme, the final suffix *-(i)t* or *-an*. But in Series II, each plural contrasts with the singular of the same person by two morphemes: *-en* and *-(i)t* or *-es*.

Table 10.1

Partial Conjugation of *i*-Intransitive in Old Georgian[a]

	Present (Series I)	Aorist (Series II)
Singular		
1	*davic̣erebi*	*davic̣ere*
2	*daic̣erebi*	*daic̣ere*
3	*daic̣erebis* 'it is written'	*daic̣era* 'it was written'
Plural		
1	*davic̣erebit*	*davic̣ere**n**it*
2	*daic̣erebit*	*daic̣ere**n**it*
3	*daic̣erebian*	*daic̣er**n**es*

[a]Shanidze (1976:110–111).

In Old Georgian, the derivation of the *e*-intransitive is essentially like that of the *i*-intransitive, though most *e*-intransitives have a final indirect object. Example (15) shows that initial direct objects (final subjects) of *e*-intransitives trigger *-en* in the finite verb form that governs them.

(15) a. *tu ganepinnian* ***ṭred-ni*** ***igi*** *xe-sa* *mas*
if spread/them/MP/II dove-PL/NOM DET tree-DAT DET
'if the doves leave (from) the tree' (Imnaishvili 1970c:241,22)

b. ***q̇ovel-ni*** ***ḳerp-ni*** *daexnian* *da*
all-PL/NOM idol-PL/NOM cut/them/MP/II and
šeimusrnian
break/them/MP/II
'All the idols were cut and broken.' (Shanidze 1935:46, 9–10)

In (15a) the initial direct object, *ṭredni igi* 'the doves', is the *en*-trigger.

In Old Georgian, like Modern Georgian, there exists an analytic passive, morphologically a past passive participle plus a finite form of an auxiliary verb. In this construction, too, the initial direct object that is a final subject triggers *-en* if it is plural, as shown by (16).

(16) a. *vidre* ***mta-ni*** *arγa dabadebul iqv**nes***
until mountain-PL-NOM NEG created be/them/MP/II
'before the mountains were created' (Psalm 89:2)

b. ***igini*** *nugešiniscemul iqv**nen***
they/PL/NOM comforted be/them/MP/II
'They shall be comforted.' (Mt 5:4)

In (16a) the initial direct object *mtani* 'mountains' triggers *-en*, realized in the finite auxiliary.

The stative passive also has a direct object that advances to subject. If it is plural, this nominal, too, triggers *-en* in Series II.

(17) ***sxua-ni*** *eḳid**n**ian cer-ita perq-ta*
other-PL/NOM hang/them/MP/II big.toe-INST foot-PL/GEN
mat-ta-γta
they-PL/GEN-INST
'Others hang by the big toes of their feet.'
(Kekelidze 1946:107, 36)

In (17), the initial direct object *sxuani* 'others' triggers *-en* as a final subject, it also triggers the third person plural subject marker for the habitual II, *-an*.

The fifth category that is characterized by a direct object that advances to subject is the inversion construction; it is morphologically, syntactically, and semantically related to the stative passive. Inversion involves, as well, an initial subject that is demoted to indirect object (see Chap. 13). The initial direct object, if plural, triggers *-en* in Series II. Examples are in (18).

(18) a. *šeeçqal**nes*** ***igini*** *iesu-s*
he/pity/them/INV/II they/PL/NOM Jesus-DAT
'Jesus pities them.' (Mt 20:34AB)

b. *da mun gesm**nen***[5] ***siṭqua-ni*** ***čemni.***
and there you/hear/them/INV/II word-PL/NOM my
'And there you will hear my words.' (Jer 18:2 I)

In §10.1.1, it was demonstrated that plural final direct objects in Series II trigger *-en* in the finite verb forms that govern them. In this section it has been shown that this marker is also triggered by direct objects that are final subjects in five morphological categories.

10.1.3. Subjects and Objects that Do Not Trigger *-en*

The purpose of this section is to show that *-en* is not triggered by indirect objects, subjects of final transitive verbs, subjects of active intransitives, or direct objects that are demoted to indirect object.

The examples in (19) have plural indirect objects and are in Series II, but the plural nominals do not trigger *-en*.

(19) a. *da egvipṭ-it mouc̣ode* ***švil-ta*** ***mista***
and Egypt-INST I/call/to.him/II child-PL/DAT his
'And I have called (to) his children out of Egypt.' (Hosea 11:1)

b. *da* ***tkuen-****ca gesma siṭqua-y igi*
and you/PL/DAT-also you/hear/it/INV/II word-NOM DET
c̣ešmariṭeb-isa-y
truth-GEN-NOM
'And you too heard the word of truth.' (Ephes 1:13CD)

c. *miage* ***mat*** *sakmita matita*
you.SG/give/it/to.him/II them/PL/DAT deed/INST their
'Reward them (IO) according to their deeds.'
(Psalm 27:4)

Example (19) contains instances of indirect objects in all three persons. Example (19a) is a surface intransitive with an indirect object; (19b) is an inversion construction, showing that the initial subject that is demoted to indirect object does not trigger *-en* [cf. example (18) above]; (19c) is a surface transitive, though its direct object is unexpressed. These examples show that under no circumstances do indirect objects trigger *-en*.

The examples in (20) have plural transitive subjects. The failure of *-en* to occur in these clauses shows that subjects of transitives are not *en*-triggers.

(20) a. *tus ra-y sc̣amot anu ra-y*
if what-NOM you.PL/eat/it/II or what-NOM
suat
you.PL/drink/it/II
'[Do not worry] what you will eat or what you will drink.'
(Mt 6:25Ad)

b. *ganiqves samosel-i čemi*
they/divide/it/II clothing-NOM my
'They divided my clothing.' (Mt 27:35)

The examples in (21) show that subjects of active intransitives do not trigger *-en*.

(21) a. *romlisa tana isiʒves* ***q̣ovel-ta*** ***mepe-ta***
which with they/fornicate/II all-PL/NAR king-PL/NAR
kueq̣an-isa-ta
earth-GEN-PL/NAR
'with whom all the kings of the earth have committed fornication' (Rev 17:2)

b. ***čuen . . .*** *visc̣rapet* *p̣irisa* *tkuen-isa* *xilvad*
we/PL/NAR we/hurry/II face/GEN you/PL-GEN to.see
'We hurried to see your face.' (1 Thess 2:17)

The verb forms in (21) differ from those in §10.1.2 in that the latter are inactive intransitives, while these are active intransitives. In addition, those in §10.1.2 have nominative case subjects and may have the *-en* pluralizer, while those in (21) have subjects in the narrative case and do not have the *-en* marker.

Finally, a few verbs in Old and Modern Georgian govern Lexical Object Demotion, which demotes direct objects to indirect objects, both in Series I and in Series II. Evidence that the nominals are indeed underlying direct objects in Modern Georgian is given in Harris (1981b:188–189). Evidence that they are surface indirect objects is found in the fact that they trigger Indirect Object Agreement, occur in the dative case in Series II, and do not trigger *-en*, as shown in the examples in (22).

(22) a. *sʒlo* ***or-ta-ve*** ***mat*** *da*
he/overcome/him/II two-PL/DAT-even DET/PL/DAT and
ereoda
he/defeat/him/I
'He overcame them both and was defeating them.' (Acts 19:16)

b. ***perq-ta*** *gaḳoco*
foot-PL/DAT I/kiss/it/to.you/II
'I will kiss your feet.' (Kekelidze 1918:46, 8)

These examples show that a plural direct object that is demoted to indirect object does not trigger *-en*.

It has been shown that in Series II, *-en* is triggered by final direct objects and by initial direct objects that are final subjects in five morphological categories and that it is NOT triggered by subjects of transitive or of active intransitive verbs or by indirect objects, including direct objects demoted to final indirect-objecthood. On this basis we can state the following generalization:

(23) In Series II, a plural direct object that is a final subject or direct object triggers *-en* in the verb that governs it.

This is the equivalent of saying that plural subjects of inactive intransitive verbs and final direct objects trigger *-en* in Series II or that *En*-Agreement is a rule of active alignment as defined in Chapter 1.

The rule *En*-Agreement, then, has active alignment and occurs in Series II but not in Series I. Case marking in Old Georgian is also a rule of active alignment in Series II but not in Series I (see Chap. 3). Thus, *En*-Agreement and case marking should coincide in Series II. In all of the examples above, nominative plurals in Series II are *en*-triggers, and nominals of other cases never trigger *-en*.

In §10.1.4. we shall see that rule (23) does not account for the failure of *-en* to occur in two morphological verb types.

10.1.4 Failure of *-en* to Occur

In some instances, *-en* fails to occur when it is expected. For example, parallel to (10b), the Adiši and Opiza manuscripts have the verb form *ixila*, without *n* (< *en*), though the manuscripts are alike here in other relevant respects. Similarly, parallel to (18b), the Athos manuscript has the verb form *gesmen*, without *En*-Agreement, though the verse is otherwise essentially the same in the two versions. Such omissions may be harbingers of the later loss of this rule.

A few isolated verbs are always exceptions to *En*-Agreement. For example, the *i*- and *e*-intransitives of the verbs *darγueva* 'destroy, raze' and *kceva* '(re)turn' do not take *n* (Imnaishvili 1975:80). The latter verb has other syntactic peculiarities; see examples (21) in Chapter 14. The verbs 'come, go' are exceptions in that they govern nominative case subjects in Series II (see §6.2.1); they are like (narrative case) subjects of other active intransitives in not taking plural *-en* marking. For example, we find *mouqdes* and *movides* 'they came' (Mt 4:11Ad A and B, respectively), not **mouqdnes* or **movidnes*.

The verbs 'sit', 'stand', and 'lie' are in pairs, each with an active and an inactive member. The active member of each pair is an exception in taking a nominative case subject (see §6.2.1); they are like (narrative case) subjects of other active intransitives in not taking plural *-en* marking, for example, *gare-moadges* 'they took a stand outside [the camp]' (Rev 20:9). The inactive member of each pair regularly takes a nominative case subject. If plural, this subject may condition *En*-Agreement; this occurs most often when the verb is used in the meaning 'have', illustrated in (24), as well as (10a).[6]

(24) *romelsa edgnes tav-ni švidni*
which/DAT stand/them/to.it/MP/II head-PL/NOM seven
'on which stood seven heads' i.e., 'which had seven heads'
(Rev 12:3)

In addition, there are two morphological types in which *-en* is expected on the basis of the rule formulated above but in which it regularly fails to occur. One such type is the so-called markerless intransitive, a nonproductive dynamic intransitive that in productive derivations is replaced by other intransitives (see Appendix to Chap. 3). The examples in (25) show that a plural initial direct object (final subject) with a verb of this subclass does not trigger *-en*.

(25) a. *raymetu* ***igini*** *ganʒγen*
because they/PL/NOM satisfy/them/MP/II
'For they shall be satisfied.' (Mt 5:6)

b. ***tual-ni mat-ni*** *ċarmoscviven*
eye-PL/NOM their-PL/NOM consume/them/MP/II
'And their eyes shall consume away.' (Zak 14:12I)

The nominals expected to trigger *-en* in (25) appear in boldface type. It is clear from case marking, from the behavior of these verbs in Series III, and from the relations between the intransitive verbs in (25) and the corresponding transitives, that the nominative nominals in (25) are initial direct objects that are final subjects (see Appendix to Chap. 3). Yet unlike the initial direct objects that are final subjects illustrated in (13)–(18), those in (25) regularly fail to trigger *-en*. [The suffix *-en* in (25) is the plural *subject* marker for the subjunctive II of these verbs.] This fact is noted in the handbooks. The failure of *-en* to occur in the markerless intransitive must be treated synchronically as an exception; this verbal type is nonproductive and contains few members.

The second morphological category where plural direct objects in Series II fail to trigger *-en* is the inceptive. The examples in (26) show the failure of *-en* to occur in this category.

(26) a. *da* ***q̇ovel-ni mta-ni*** *da* ***borcu-ni***
and all-PL/NOM mountain-PL/NOM and hill-PL/NOM
damdablden
low/them/INCEP/II
'And every mountain and hill will become low.' (Lk 3:5)

b. *aramed ganmartldit*
but justified/you.PL/INCEP/II
'But you are justified.' (1 Cor 6:11AB)

Case marking and behavior in Series III show the nominative-nominals in (26) to be initial direct objects that are final subjects. The failure of these nominals to trigger *-en* is noted in the handbooks.

In the remainder of this section I establish the existence of a rule of *N*-Deletion and show that this, together with other regular rules of Old Georgian phonology, accounts for the fact that *-en* plural marker never shows up in inceptives.

The plural suffix *-en*, reduced by syncope to *-n*, is often omitted after a verb root ending in *n*. Examples (27a) and (28a) illustrate the omission of *-n* even where it is triggered by a plural direct object.

(27) a. *da ikmnes* ***kuxil-ni*** ***da qma-ni***
and make/them/MP/II thunder-PL/NOM and voice-PL/NOM
'And there were voices and thunderings.' (Rev 8:5A)
b. *da ikmnes* ***kuxilni da qmani*** (Rev 8:5B)

(28) a. *ikorc̣ined*
marry/them/MP/II
'Let them be married.' (1 Cor 7:9AB)
b. *ikorc̣in**n**ed* (1 Cor 7:9CD)

The verb forms in both (27) and (28) are *i*-intransitives. The suffix *-n* is omitted in the (a) examples because it would be juxtaposed with a stem in *n* (*kmn, korc̣in*).

According to Takaishvili (1974: n. 78), plural *n* is sometimes omitted from the causative form *vacemin**n**e*, where it would be juxtaposed with *n* of the causative circumfix *a——in*, as illustrated in (29).[7]

(29) *taq̇uanis-vacemine* *mas* ***q̇ovel-ni***
worship-I/CAUS/give/it/to.him/II he/DAT all-PL/NOM
ḳac-ni
man-PL/NOM
'I shall cause all men to worship him.'
(Ioani Okrop̣. Cxor. 255v, 18–19; Takaishvili 1974: n. 78.)

The verb root *cem* is made causative by the addition of the circumfix *a——in*; in this environment *-en* may not occur.

Another *-n* is used in the formation of the evidential (Series III) of one class of verbs, as in (30) from Modern Georgian.

(30) *u-tamaš-**n**-i-a* 'he apparently played'
*u-čxub-**n**-i-a* 'he apparently quarrelled'
*u-brʒol-**n**-i-a* 'he apparently fought'
*u-ṭir-**n**-i-a* 'he apparently cried'
*u-cigur-av-**n**-i-a* 'he apparently skated'

But if the formant *-n* would be juxtaposed with *n* in the stem, the former deletes, as (31) shows.

(31)	*u-sṭven-i-a*	'he apparently whistled'
	u-cin-i-a	'he apparently laughed'
	u-xvrin-i-a	'he apparently snored'
	u-rben-i-a	'he apparently ran'

(Forms in (30) and (31) from Tschenkéli 1960–1974)

There are no geminate consonants in Georgian, except where they are separated by a morpheme boundary. The examples in (27)–(31) show that even when they would be separated by a morpheme boundary, geminate *n*'s are generally simplified in Georgian. We can state this as (32).

(32) *N*-Deletion
$n \rightarrow \emptyset / n$ ____

There are many instances where *N*-Deletion fails to apply, such as (15a), (27b), and (28b). Nevertheless, the rule often applies in Old Georgian.

In Old Georgian the inceptive is formed with yet another *-n* suffix (also from **en*), which dissimilates to *d* after *l, r,* or *n* (Shanidze 1957b). If the *-n* plural were used in the inceptive, such as that in (26a), the plural *-n* would be juxtaposed with the inceptive *-n*: **damdabl-n-n-en* from **damdabl-en-en-en*, where the first suffix is the inceptive formant, the second is the marker of the plural initial object, and the last is the marker of the plural subject in the subjunctive II. After syncope (rule 2 of Chap. 8) has applied, producing **damdabl-n-n-en*, the input conditions are met for either *N*-Deletion or *N*-Dissimilation. If deletion precedes dissimilation, we get **damdabl-n-n-en* to **damdabl-n-en* to *damdabl-d-en*, the form that is attested in (26a). From this I conclude that the phonological rules applied in this order and that this accounts for the failure of *en-* plurals to occur in the inceptive in Old Georgian. Later in Georgian the inceptive *-n* was replaced by *-d* in all phonetic environments, leaving the omission of *-n* in the inceptive category a synchronically unmotivated phenomenon.

We must conclude that the productive rule of *En*-Agreement is correctly stated for Old Georgian as (23). We must add that the nonproductive morphological category of markerless intransitives is an exception to the rule, as are the isolated verbs named in this section. The productive morpho–syntactic category of inceptives is not an exception to (23). The failure of the marker *-n* (< **en*) to occur in the inceptive is phonologically motivated from a synchronic point of view in Old Georgian.

The complete loss of *En*-Agreement was facilitated by the fact that regular phonological rules blocked the occurrence of -n (< **en*) in the surface structures of all inceptives and often in verb forms with a stem ending in *n*. The reanalysis of the inceptive formant left the omission of -*n* from this category synchronically unmotivated and further eased the loss. It subsequently disappeared from the language altogether.

10.2. THE SUFFIX -*EN* IN SERIES I

10.2.1. The Role of -*en* in the Formation of Series I

If Series I was indeed formed as an aspectual variant of Series II, we would expect that all morphological categories of Series II would be carried over to Series I. In Series I verb forms, we do find the same categories of tense, mood, version, voice, causation, and most importantly, of person and number as in Series II, with the exception of -*en* and the prefix -*h*/*s*/*x*/∅, which is discussed in Chapter 12. We must explain why -*en* was not carried over to Series I.

If -*en* had been carried over to Series I, in what sorts of clauses would we expect to find it? According to rule (23), -*en* is triggered only by those plural direct objects that are final subjects or direct objects. If the hypothesis proposed in Chapter 7 is correct, at the inception of Series I there were no final direct objects in this series. Direct objects of transitive verbs were demoted to indirect object by the Object Demotion rule. The examples in (22) show that in Old Georgian, objects demoted by an analogous, but lexically governed, rule do not trigger -*en*. Similarly, -*en* would not have been triggered by initial direct objects of transitive verbs, if the *En*-Agreement rule had been extended to Series I.

Direct objects of initial intransitive verbs did not undergo Object Demotion in Series I but were prompted to subject by Unaccusative just as in Series II. That this is so is shown by the fact that they are marked with the nominative case and trigger subject agreement in both series (see Figure 7.3). If the *En*-Agreement rule were extended to Series I, as all other agreement rules were, we would expect it to be triggered just by plural subjects of inactive intransitive verbs. In this section it is shown that there are relics of the use of this marker with verbs of this type in Old Georgian and in Laz–Mingrelian.[8]

10.2.2. Old Georgian

The marker of direct object plurality is preserved as a relic with Series I forms of a few verbs in Old Georgian. In these forms, the plural marker usually takes the form -*an* instead of -*en*. The reasons for this discrepancy in the quality of the vowel cannot be fully explained here, but it has been noted above that *a* in verb suffixes of the present screeve correspond to *e* in other screeves (*-av* to *-ev*, *-am* to *-em* in Chap. 9). Some verbs discussed below occur in clauses to which only Unaccusative applies, while others occur in clauses to which Inversion and Unaccusative apply. The first examples are therefore analogous to examples (13)–(17), while the last are analogous to the examples in (18) above.

The verbs 'sit', 'stand', and 'lie' may be either active or inactive. In Series II only the latter type occurs with *-en*, as we would expect (see §10.1.4). In Series I it is just the inactives that preserve the marker of direct object plurality. In (33a) the subject (initial direct object) is singular and triggers *-s*, the third person singular subject marker for the present screeve. In (33b) it is plural and triggers both *-n* (< **-en*) as a direct object and *-an* as a subject; analogous redundant plural marking in Series II was observed in §10.1.2.[9] Example (33c) is in the present habitual, where the third person subject marker is *-ed*.[10]

(33) a. *da mesatxevle-y igi . . .dga-s*
and fisherman-NOM DET/NOM stand/him/MP/I
'And the fisherman stands.' (Shanidze 1959:223, 37–38)
b. *da* ***xe-ni*** ***igi*** *dga-**n**-an*
and tree-PL/NOM DET/NOM stand/them/MP/I
'And the trees are standing.' (Kekelidze 1918:27, 2)
c. *romelsa* ***qar-ni*** *ara u-dga-**n**-ed*
which/DAT ox-PL/NOM NEG stand/them/to.him/MP/I
'to whom no oxen stand' i.e., 'who has no oxen'
(Abuladze 1960:8, 29)

For the verb root *sx* in (34), we find singular subject forms with *-s* and plural subjects redundantly marked with *-en-ed* or *-en-an*.

(34) a. *purcel-i a-sx-s maradis*
leaf-NOM set/it/MP/I always
'The leaf is ever on it.' (Shanidze 1959:232, 25)
b. *rametu* ***qorc-ni*** *a-sx-**en**-ed ʒesa mas*
for flesh-PL/NOM set/them/MP/I son/DAT DET/DAT
adam-is-sa
Adam-GEN-DAT
'For there was flesh on the son of Adam.'
(Shanidze 1959:113, 20)
c. ***romel-ni*** *bnelsa . . .sx-**en**-an*
which/REL-PL/NOMdark/DAT sit/them/MP/I
'who sit in the dark' (L 1:79Ad)

Similar forms occur with *ç̣ev* 'lie'.

(35) a. *c̣arved adgil-sa mas, sada lom-i c̣ev-s*
I/go/II place-DAT DET/DAT where lion-NOM lie/him/MP/I
'I went to the place where the lion lies.'
(Kekelidze 1918:305, 23)

b. *c̣v-**an**-an **mraval-ni***
lie/them/MP/I many-PL/NOM
'Many lie' 'many sleep.' (1 Cor 11:30)

In the examples below, the root *gav* syncopates to *gv* when followed by the plural marker.

(36) a. *da h-gav-n igi ganmrq̣unelsa*
and resemble/him/to.him/MP/I he/NOM spoiler/DAT
mas devsa
DET/DAT devil/DAT
'And he resembles the spoiler, the devil.'
(Shanidze 1959:113, 10)

b. *vitar h-gv-**an**-an **marṭvil-ni** upal-sa*
how resemble/them/to.him/MP/I martyr-PL/NOM lord-DAT
čuen-sa
our-DAT
'[And see] how the martyrs resemble our lord.'
(Shanidze 1959:256, 8)

In (36a), *-n* is a third person singular subject marker used in the present habitual; see Table 5.2.

The verb root *ku* means both 'have' and, when used with a directional preverb, 'bring, take'. The forms *kun, kon* derive from **ku-an* or **ku-en*.

(37) a. *xolo ʒe-sa ḳac-isa-sa ara a-ku-s*
but son-DAT man-GEN-DAT NEG he/have/it/INV/I
sada-mca tav-i miidriḳa
where-REL head-nom he/bend/it/II
'But the son of man does not have a place to lay his head.'
(Mt 8:20Ad)

b. *rametu **siṭq̣ua-ni saɣmrto-ni** g-ko-**n**-an*
for word-PL/NOM godly-PL/NOM you/have/them/INV/I
šen
you/DAT
'For you have the words of God.' (Ingorokva 1913: R, 40–41)

An example with *rc̣mena* 'believe' is given as (18) in Chapter 13.[11] In all of the examples in (33)–(37), the nominative nominal is a direct object that advances to subject by Unaccusative, with or without the application of Inversion. It is these nominatives alone which when plural, trigger the object plural marker *-en/-an* as well as the subject plural marker *-en*, *-ed*, or *-an*.

From the examples above we can see that *En*-Agreement once applied in Series I. However, even in Old Georgian the rule was not productive in Series I, but was preserved only as a relic. This is supported by several facts. First, it does not occur in the newer *i*- and *e*-intransitives, but only with the most commonly occurring of the ancient verbs. Second, although the pattern described above is the regular one for the verbs that do take this redundant agreement (Kavtaradze 1954:172; Imnaishvili 1971:209, 211; Shanidze 1973:416; Suxishvili 1976:21ff.), these same verbs have some anamolous forms. That is, *-an* or *-n* may occur sporadically in the third person singular (e.g., *a-ku-n-s* 'he has it'). For those verbs that reanalyzed *-n/-an/-en* as part of the verb root (see below), this reanalysis was already underway. Finally, it is characteristic of a nonproductive rule that it would be restricted to a few forms, in this instance to the third person and to the present and present habitual screeves. If it were productive in Series I, as in II, we would expect it in all plural persons and in all screeves of the series.

When Series I was reanalyzed, the redundant plural marking no longer made sense, and several steps were taken. Productive derivational types restricted *-en* to Series II, where the rule was transparent. Among the ancient verb types that preserved it in Old Georgian, some retain it in Modern Georgian. Thus, in the present screeve, *gav-s* 'he resembles him' still opposes *gv-an-an* 'they resemble him' (< **gav-en-en*), and *ç̣ev-s* 'he is lying' still opposes *ç̣v-an-an* (< * *ç̣ev-en-en*) 'they are lying'. Number agreement in all series has changed since Old Georgian, such that in inversion, the unaccusative nominal (initial direct object) is not a number agreement trigger; therefore, some of the singulars no longer oppose plurals of the same type as in Old Georgian. The verb 'have, bring, take' has specialized the old root *ku*, with the *a*-prefix, to the present screeve: *a-kv-s* 'he has it/them'. The form *kon* (< **ku-an*) is reserved for the other screeves of Series I. This specialization was in progress in Old Georgian, so that even then the original *ku* could be found only in the present singular (see Kavtaradze 1954:158ff.). An analogous suppletive relation exists in Modern Georgian between the original *q̣av* 'bring, take', now restricted to the present, and *q̣van* (< **q̣av-en*), now used as the stem for all other screeves. Neither of these verbs reserves the form derived from *en* for plurals or the one that originally lacked *en* for singulars.

The analysis usually given for this *-an* in Old Georgian is that it represents the relic of a series marker or other stem formant. The linguists who have made this analysis, however, have noted that it leaves unexplained the fact that it occurs only in the third person plural forms (references cited above). In addition, it fails to explain why this suffix is restricted to inactive intransitive verbs.

10.2.3. Laz–Mingrelian

Verbs of the same type, though not necessarily cognate with the Old Georgian verbs discussed above, preserve the *-n* (< **en*) in both Laz and Mingrelian. The forms in Table 10.2 are from Laz and are drawn from Chikobava (1936:87, 89, 90–91).

Table 10.2

Conjugation of 'Be' in Present Screeve in Laz

	Singular	Plural
1	v-o-re 'I am'	v-o-re-t (/boret) 'we are'
2	(o)re 'you are'	(o)re-t 'you-PL are'
3	re-n 'he is'	re-***n***-an 'they are'

I propose the following analysis of these forms. The third person singular subject marker *-n* in *ren* is cognate to the third person singular subject marker *-n* in the present habitual in Old Georgian (Set C in Table 5.2); for example, *c̣er-n* 'he writes it'. The Laz suffix *-an* in *renan* is the same as the Old Georgian third person plural subject marker *-en*, with the variant *-an*, in the present screeve (Set A in Table 5.2). The Laz suffix *-n* in ***renan*** is the same as Old Georgian *n, en, an,* the exponent of *En*-Agreement. As in Georgian, the old plural object marker, *-n* (< **en*) is retained only in the third person plural subject forms in the present screeve. As in Georgian, this *-n* occurs only with unaccusatives in Series I. Chikobava (1936:91) lists the examples in Table 10.3, and additional examples are discussed in §16.1.4–16.1.6. While in Georgian *En*-Agreement in Series I is retained only in a few relics (§10.2.2), in Zan its reflex,

Table 10.3

Singular and Plural Third Person Forms of Inactive Intransitives in Laz

Singular	Plural
xe-n 'he sits'	*xe-n-an* 'they sit'
γuru-n 'he dies'	*γuru-n-an* 'they die'
irde-n 'he grows'	*irde-n-an* 'they grow'

-n-, became part of the productive agreement marking for unaccusatives in the present screeve.

In forms like *re-n-an* 'they are', Chikobava analyzes the first suffix, *-n*, as the third person subject marker, analogous to the prefix *v-* for the first person; the *-an* is the plural marker. This analysis may be correct synchronically, but from a historical point of view, it fails to explain two facts.

First, Chikobava's analysis does not explain why the ending *-n-an* is restricted to inactive intransitive verbs. Table 10.4 shows that the third person plural subject of transitive and active intransitive verbs is marked with *-an* alone, not with *-n-an* (examples from Chikobava 1936:91).[12] If Chikobava's account were diachronically correct, we would expect the third person singular subject marker governed by active verbs, *-s*, to be followed by an agglutinative pluralizer: **-s-an*. The hypothesis advanced in the present work, on the other hand, explains why *-n-an* would be limited to inactive intransitives; originally *-n* (< **en*) was triggered by plural initial direct objects, while *-an* was triggered by plural final subjects, resulting in the same kind of redundant plural agreement found in Old Georgian (see §10.1.2 and 10.2.1).

The second problem with Chikobava's analysis is that if *-n* in *re-n-an* is serving as the person marker, parallel to *v-* and ∅ of the first and second persons, we would expect to find the agglutinative pluralizer *-t*, just as in the first and second persons (see Table 10.2). That is, if the third person is structurally comparable to the other two persons, as suggested by Chikobava, we would expect **re-n-t*, which cannot be ruled out on phonological grounds. The hypothesis advanced here, on the other hand, explains *-an* as the same inflectional marker of third person plural surface subjects that is found in other paradigms (see Table 10.4).

Finally, both Shanidze's hypothesis that *-an*/*-n* discussed in §10.2.2 is a screeve marker and Chikobava's hypothesis that *-n* in Laz and Mingrelian

Table 10.4

Third Person Subject Agreement in Present of Transitive and Active Intransitives in Laz

Singular	Plural
hemuk imxor-s he/NAR he/eats/it/I	hemtepek imxor-an they/NAR they/eat/it/I
hemuk idušun-s he/NAR he/thinks/I	hemtepek idušun-an they/NAR they/think/I
hemuk xorxum-s he/NAR he/saws/it/I	hemtepek xorxum-an they/NAR they/saw/it/I

is an agglutinative person marker fail to account for the fact that it is in exactly the same type of verb that the three languages preserve this relic in the present screeve.[13]

On the basis of these facts from Georgian and Laz–Mingrelian, I conclude that at an earlier stage the rule was as in (23), except that it was not then restricted to Series II; it had the form given in (38).

(38) A plural direct object that is a final subject or direct object triggers -*en* in the verb that governs it.[14]

10.3. SUMMARY

In this chapter it has been shown that the object pluralizer -*en* was triggered in Series II by initial direct objects that were final subjects or direct objects. Although this is the same set of nominals that could be marked with the nominative case, the plural marker cannot be considered to be triggered by the case marker itself, for reasons cited in §10.1.1. It has been shown that nominals bearing other grammatical relations, including initial direct objects that are final indirect objects, do not trigger this marker (§10.1.3). Even in Old Georgian this rule had begun to die out (§10.1.4).

If -*en* had been extended to Series I, as all other agreement markers were, it would have been triggered only by initial direct objects that were final subjects, not by all direct objects (§10.2.1). There are relics of this morpheme in the third person plural forms of the present screeve in Old Georgian, Laz, and Mingrelian. Other explanations that have been offered for this morphology are inadequate. I conclude that *En*-Agreement, like other morphology, was originally extended to Series I and that the rule was triggered only by those plural initial direct objects that were final subjects. At the inception of Series I, this meant that in that series the rule was triggered only by the subjects of inactive intransitives. But when Series I was reanalyzed without Object Demotion, the old system for assigning -*en* became opaque. It was then lost as a productive rule from Series I and probably soon thereafter began to drop from Series II.[15] The morpheme itself was retained as a relic only in a few commonly occurring verbs of the type in which it had originally appeared productively. Since -*en* was not productive in Series I in Old Georgian, Laz, and Mingrelian, it is not surprising that it is restricted to a few verbs (in Old Georgian), to the third person, and to the present screeve.

NOTES

[1]The rule *En*-Agreement is preserved in some nonstandard modern dialects, either in its original form or in a restricted form; for example, Xevsurian (Chincharauli 1960:101ff.) and Ač̣arian (Nizharadze 1957:45; 1975:144).

[2]The nominative case of the third person plural pronoun, like that of nouns, is in *-ni*, for example, *igini*.

[3]In (10a) the *en*-trigger is not a final direct object, but an initial direct object, like those in §10.1.2. In this chapter, initial grammatical relations are represented in the verb glosses.

[4]The *-ni* (< **n* + *i*) nominative plural seems similar to the *-en* plural marker of the verb. The relationship between them is explored in Chikobava (1929b), Pochxua (1961), and elsewhere.

[5]In certain forms, this particular verb occurs with *n* in its stem (*smin*). However, from the minimal contrast between *gesma* in (19b) and the form in (18b), both aorists, it is clear that the *n* in the latter is triggered by the plural final subject (initial direct object).

[6]Blake (Lake *et al.* 1928:295) attributes the use of *dgomay* 'stand' to mean 'be' or 'have' to Armenian influence; see also (33c). In Old Georgian *sxomay* 'sit, set', see (10a) and (34b), *konebay, q̣olebay* 'take' and other verbs are also used to mean 'have' (see Deeters 1954).

[7]However, it seems that the *n* of causative *in* is sometimes omitted; see example (12a) of Chapter 14. This makes it uncertain that the *n* omitted from (29) is the plural *n*.

[8]In the two verbs 'know', *En*-Agreement is retained in Series I; e.g., *ic-n-oda* 'he knew them' (L 9:47); see §5.3.

[9]Attempts have been made to relate the third person plural subject markers *-en* and *-an* (set A of Chap. 5) diachronically to the plural direct object marker *-(e)n*, but no systematic account has been given of the development. Whether or not these suffixes are diachronically related, they are synchronically distinct in Old Georgian.

[10]Suxishvili (1976) has collected many examples of stative verb forms in Old Georgian, and a number of the examples in this section were first cited by him.

[11]Imnaishvili (1975:84–85) lists the following additional roots as having Series I forms with this *-an*: *tnv* 'desire', *ḳum* 'smoke [of things]', *qv* 'have, take', *č* 'be visible', *qm* 'need', and *brʒ* 'fight'. All of these are apparently inactive except the last; however, this too has Class 2 characteristics, including a masdar in *-ola*, use of *-od* in Series I, use of *e-* prefix, and sometime government of nominative case subject (see Abuladze 1973:36, Imnaishvili 1961:142–147).

[12]In the present screeve, *-n* is the third person singular marker with inactive intransitives, while *-s* fills this function with verbs of other types (see §16.1.5).

[13]In Laz and Mingrelian, just as in Georgian, the unaccusative nominal in the inversion construction ceased to be a trigger of number agreement; therefore, none of the languages preserve *-n* (< * e-*n*) in that construction.

[14]Boeder (1979:450) has suggested that the original distribution of the *-en* marker can be determined on the basis of case marking. This is methodologically unsound;

the distribution of *-en* must be determined on comparative and internal evidence from *En*-Agreement only (see Chap. 16). While (38) is likely the correct formulation for an earlier stage of these languages, the fact that initial direct objects in the incorporated object construction trigger *En*-Agreement (§14.1.1.1) makes it necessary to reformulate (23) for Old Georgian.

[15]As a result of this reanalysis, *En*-Agreement in Old Georgian does not apply in the first evidential screeve (Series III), which is derived diachronically from Series I, though the rule does apply in the other screeves of Series III, which are based on Series II (Chap. 13).

11

Case Marking in the Object Demotion Construction

In Chapter 6, I showed that the original case marking in CK must have been ergative. In this chapter, I show how an ergative case system, together with the Object Demotion analysis proposed in Chapter 7 accounts for the system of cases in Series I. In addition, I reconstruct the marking assigned to retired indirect objects and show that this correctly accounts for the marking of objects in Series I.

11.1. ERGATIVE CASE ALIGNMENT AND OBJECT DEMOTION

In Part II, it was shown that for Early CK we must reconstruct a single case system with ergative alignment, which has as its reflex the Series II systems of the daughter languages. The specific case assignment rules reconstructed in Chapter 6 are repeated in (1).

(1) Case Assignment in Early CK

a. The final subject of a transitive is marked with the narrative case.

b. The final subject of an intransitive is marked with the nominative case.

c. A final direct object is marked with the nominative case.
d. A final indirect object is marked with the dative case.

Rule (1a) could alternatively be stated in terms of an 'ergative nominal', where this is defined as the subject of a transitive. Rules (1b) and (1c) could be collapsed by referring to an 'absolutive nominal', defined in general linguistics as a subject of an intransitive or a direct object. The rule is divided into two parts here for ease of reference below. Recall that the labels 'narrative case' and 'nominative case' are traditional in the Kartvelian languages and refer to a specific marker in each language (see Chaps. 3 and 4).

In Chapter 7, I proposed that a rule of Object Demotion applied to derive Series I; the rule is repeated here as (2).

(2) Object Demotion: Direct objects become indirect objects.

I have proposed that the rules in (1), the only term case marking rules in Early CK, account for the origin of the case patterns we find in Series I. In the paragraphs below, I show how (1) and (2) together correctly account for each clause type. The discussion is limited to Old Georgian, Svan, and Mingrelian; as shown in Chapter 5, Laz has reanalyzed the syntax of Series I.

When rule (2) applies to an initially transitive clause, it makes the initial direct object a final indirect object. All of the case assignment rules of (1) refer to the final level of derivation alone. Rule (1d) marks the initial direct object (= final indirect object) with the dative case. As the result of the application of (2), the clause is detransitivized, but the subject remains subject. Rule (1b) will mark the subject of the detransitivized clause with the nominative case. This is the pattern we find for Series I forms in Old (and Modern) Georgian, Svan, and Mingrelian, as shown in (3)–(5) below and in examples (20)–(21), (1)–(3), and (52)–(54) in Chapter 3.

(3) Svan
dīna *iqāne* *miča ši-är-s*
girl/NOM she/smell/it/I her hand-PL-DAT
'The girl smells (sniffs) her hands.'
(Shanidze and Topuria 1939:368, 28)

(4) Old Georgian
adidebs *sul-i* *čem-i* *upal-sa*
it/magnify/it/I soul-NOM my-NOM lord-DAT
'My soul magnifies the Lord.' (L 1:46)

(5) Mingrelian
ʒγab(i) var-ia-s ragadanc-o
girl-NOM negative-QUOT-DAT she/say/it/I-QUES
'[And] if the girl says "no"?' (Samushia 1979:26, 25)

These and other examples show that (1) and (2) together account for simple transitive clauses in Series I.

Both types of intransitive have a final subject and no final direct object; they are unaffected by rule (2). Rule (1b) assigns them nominative case. The examples below, as well as (4)–(8), (22)–(24), and (55)–(61) in Chapter 3, show that intransitives of both types have nominative case subjects in Series I.

(6) Svan
a. *miča la-cl' ēser čigar abano-isga*
her PL-age.mate/NOM QUOT always bath.house-in
isṭγunälx.
they/bathe/I
' "Those her age always bathe in the bath house," she said.'
(Shanidze and Topuria 1939:368, 29)
b. *al mindor-isga xag xoša ǰihra*
this field-in it/stand/I big oak/NOM
'In this field stands a big oak.'
(Davitiania, Topuria, and Kaldani 1957:37, 27)

(7) Old Georgian
a. *da meupebdes upal-i mat zeda*
and he/reign/I lord-NOM them on
'And the Lord will reign over them.' (Micah 4:7 I)
b. *romel-i-igi iċuebis ċumċub-ita*
which/REL-NOM-DET it/burn/I brimstone-INST
'which burns with brimstone' (Rev 19:20)

(8) Mingrelian
a. *ḳvinča čviṭanc*
mountain.finch/NOM he/whistle/I
'The mountain-finch whistles.' (Samushia 1979:17, 18)
b. *isə kvara-ša almas-i aluʒən-ia*
him/DAT stomach/ALL diamond-NOM it/lie/to.him/I-QUOT
' "A diamond lies in his stomach," he said.' (Kluge 1916:88, 9)

These examples show that in all three languages the subjects of both types of intransitive are in the nominative; this is correctly accounted for by (1b).

When rule (2) applies to a clause that has an initial subject, direct object, and indirect object, the initial direct object becomes indirect object, just as in examples (3)–(5). The Chômeur Law predicts that the initial indirect object in this situation will become a retired indirect object.[1] In §11.2 we take a closer look at the case marking assigned to this nominal, and in Chapter 12 the agreement it triggers is discussed. The examples below show that the initial subject and direct object in such a sentence are correctly case marked by rules (1b) and (1d), respectively. (All elicited Svan examples in this chapter are from the Upper Bal dialect.)

(9) Svan
giorgi *al* *ambäw-s* *xaṭūli* *tamara-s*
Giorgi/NOM this news-DAT he/tells/it/to.her/I Tamara-DAT
'Georgi tells this news to Tamara.'

(10) Old Georgian
romel-sa *moscemda* *mas* *ḳact-moq̇uare*
which/REL-DAT he/give/it/to.her/I her/DAT man-loving
γmert-i
God-NOM
'which philanthropic God gave to her'
(Imnaishvili 1970a:139, 25)

(11) Mingrelian
muma *arʒens* *cxen-s* *skua-s*
father/NOM he/give/it/to.him/I horse-DAT child-DAT
'The father gives a horse to (his) child.'

Thus, rules (1b) and (1d) make the correct statement of case marking for at least the initial subject and direct object of these sentences.

Finally, we have intransitives with an indirect object. They are unaffected by rule (2), and (1b) and (1d) correctly assign the nominative to the subject and the dative to the indirect object, as the examples below show.

(12) Svan
māre *xemšeräl* *xexw-s*
man/NOM he/complain/to.her/I wife-DAT
'The man complains to his wife.'

(13) Old Georgian
igi *geṭq̇oda* *tkuen*
he/NOM he/speak/to.you/I you/PL/DAT
'He spoke to you.' (L 24:6)

(14) Mingrelian
dida *uragad* *ʒγabi-s*
mother/NOM she/talk/to.her/I girl-DAT
'The mother talks to the girl.'

Thus, while (1) alone states the case marking system reconstructible for CK Series II, the interaction of (1) and (2) makes the correct statements about the case marking of subjects, direct objects, and indirect objects in Series I and in this way accounts for the origin of the case distribution found with those verb forms.[2] The only case assignment that has not yet been accounted for is that of initial indirect objects occurring in initially transitive clauses in Series I. In §11.2 I reconstruct the marking assigned to retired indirect objects in other constructions in CK. In §11.3 I show that this is consistent wih the Object Demotion analysis and the marking assigned to initial indirect objects in that construction.

11.2. RECONSTRUCTION OF MARKING ASSIGNED TO RETIRED INDIRECT OBJECTS

A retired indirect object is a nominal which bears a final nonterm relation (i.e., is not a final subject, direct object, or indirect object) and which bore the indirect object relation as its last term relation.

Retired indirect objects lack some or all of the properties of final indirect objects. In the Kartvelian languages they do not trigger Person Agreement or Number Agreement—the latter relevant only in certain constructions—and have case marking that is wholly or partially different from that of final indirect objects. In addition, they have other syntactic traits that distinguish them from indirect objects. At the same time, retired indirect objects correspond to the final indirect objects of the same verbs in other constructions (Harris 1981b).

Retired indirect objects occur in a variety of constructions. They may occur with all types of nonfinite forms, including participles, masdars, and infinitives (so-called masdars in the adverbial or masdars in the genitive.)[3] Participles are used not only as adnominal modifiers, but also in periphrastic constructions, notably an analytic passive. In causatives, if there is an initial indirect object in the embedded clause, it is realized as a retired indirect object. Finally, in inversion in Series III, if there is an initial indirect object, it is realized as a retired indirect object.

The status of these nominals as retired indirect objects in inversion follows from the Chômeur Law (Harris 1981b:Chap. 8). The Chômeur Law was originally proposed as a universal, but has been shown not to apply in some languages (Perlmutter and Postal 1983b:95–99, 109–122). Nevertheless, viewed as a condition on derivations, it is valid in every Kartvelian language. This condition is essential to understanding the behavior of initial indirect objects in the inversion construction; together with the analysis presented in Chapter 13, it predicts the chômeurhood of this nominal. Its status as a retired indirect object in each language can be seen from case marking in the examples presented below in this section. Because the Chômeur Law applies generally in this language family, it makes a specific prediction for the object demotion construction, namely that the initial indirect object in an initially transitive clause would have been a retired indirect object.

The status of retired indirect objects in some other constructions is poorly understood (see Harris 1981b:Chaps. 11 and 12). However, it is clear from the treatment of these nominals under various grammatical rules that they form a unified class in each of the Kartvelian languages.

For each of the languages, examples presented below include the inversion construction, as that is both the best understood of the constructions involving retired indirect objects and the one syntactically most similiar to Object Demotion in Series I, at least with respect to the treatment of initial indirect objects. For each language, examples are given from other constructions according to availability.

11.2.1. Svan

Retired indirect objects are most often marked with the so-called genitive–adverbial, that is, the genitive case marker (*-iš/eš*, with the form *-äš* in some nouns, Kaldani 1974:152), followed by the marker of the adverbial case (*-d*). The examples in (15b)–(18) are inversion in Series III, those in (19)–(20) are in construction with a masdar, and those in (21)–(22) in construction with an infinitive. In each, the retired indirect object appears in boldface type.

(15) a. *segz-d miča apxneg-är-s xäkwe*
Segz-NAR his friend-PL-DAT he/say/it/to.him/II
'Segz said to his friends'
(Davitiani, Topuria, and Kaldani 1957:10, 37)

b. *ašxw ladeγ segz-s xokwa* ***natelad-äš-d***
one day Segz-DAT he/say/it/III Natelad-GEN-ADV
'One day Segz (apparently) said to Natelad'
(Davitiani, Topuria, and Kaldani 1957:11, 23)

(16) *di-s lōxγiräla* ***gezl-äš-d*** [4]
mother-DAT she/sing/to.him/III child-GEN-ADV
'The mother (apparently) sang to (her) child.'

(17) *merab-d läkw, ere läir lok loxoda*
Merab-NAR he/say/it/II that book/NOM QUOT he/give/it/III
meri-š-d
Meri-GEN-ADV
'Merab said that he had given the book to Meri.'

(18) *di-s čäž loxoda* ***gezl-äš-d***
mother-DAT horse/NOM she/give/it/III child-GEN-ADV
'The mother (apparently) gave a horse to (her) child.'

Examples (15b)–(18) are inversion constructions, while (15a) represents a noninversion clause similar to (15b).

(19) *gela-s xaḳu al ambwi*[5] *kalīmwi*
Gela-DAT he/want/it/I this news/GEN tell/MAS
di-eš-d
mother-GEN-ADV
'Gela wants to tell this news to (his) mother.'

(20) *gelas xaḳu läir-i līzzi*
Gela/DAT he/want/it/I letter-GEN send/MAS
dīnä-š-d
girl-GEN-ADV
'Gela wants to send a letter to the girl.'

(21) *gela ačäd läir-i lazizd* ***dīnä-š-d*** [6]
Gela/NOM he/go/II letter-GEN send/INF
'Gela went to send a letter to the girl.'

(22) *gela ačäd korte* ***di-eš-d***
Gela/NOM he/go/II house/to mother-GEN-ADV
ward-l-e lahwed
rose-PL-GEN give/INF
'Gela went home to give roses to (his) mother.'

While genitive–adverbial marking seems to be the most widespread in prose texts and in elicited examples, the adverbial case alone may be used in speech and is found in traditional narrative poetry, as shown by the examples below. In (24) the retired indirect object in inversion is in the adverbial; (23) illustrates the use of the dative for the corresponding final indirect object in Series II.

(23) *amī zisx sga läyç̌wēn plaṭok-s*
its blood/NOM in he/smear/it/II handkerchief-DAT
'He smeared its blood in the handkerchief.'
(Shanidze and Topuria 1939:369, 25)

(24) *zisx* *eser* *sga* *loxč̣ōna* ***plaṭok-d***
blood/NOM QUOT in he/smear/it/III handkerchief-ADV
' "He (apparently) smeared the blood in the handkerchief,"
(s)he said.' (Shanidze and Topuria 1939:372, 34)

Parallel to (16) is (25), with the retired indirect object in the simple adverbial instead of the genitive–adverbial (M. Kaldani, personal communication, 1981).

(25) *di-s* *lōxγirǟla* ***gez̧al-d***
mother-DAT she/sing/III child-ADV
'The mother (apparently) sang to (her) child.'

(26) *gigo-s* *xōkwa* ***glex-är-d*** ***miča***
Gigo-DAT he/say/it/III peasant-PL-ADV his
'Gigo has said to his peasants'
(Shanidze, Topuria, and Gujejiani 1939:46, 8)

Example (26) may be compared with (15a, b), which contain the same verb.

11.2.2. Mingrelian

In Mingrelian, retired indirect objects are marked with the allative case, *-(i)ša*, or the dative, *-s*. The (b) examples in (27)–(29) illustrate the use of the allative in inversion in Series III, while the (a) examples show the corresponding nominal in the dative in Series I or II.

(27) a. *rezo* *ačukens* *vard-em-s* *dida-s*
Rezo/NOM he/give/it/to.her/I flower-PL-DAT mother-DAT
'Rezo gives flowers to (his) mother.'
b. *rezo-s* *vard-ep-(i)* *(k)učukebu* ***dida-ša***
Rezo-DAT flower-PL-NOM he/give/it/III mother-ALL
'Rezo (apparently) gave flowers to (his) mother.'

(28) a. *dida* *ubirs* *skua-s*
mother/NOM she/sing/to.him/I child-DAT
'The mother sings to (her) child.'
b. *dida-s* *ubiru* ***skua-ša***
mother-DAT she/sing/III child-ALL
'The mother (apparently) sang to (her) child.'

(29) a. *tik* *ǰima-s* *para* *komeču*
he/NAR brother-DAT money/NOM he/give/it/to.him/II
'He gave money to (his) brother.' (Chikobava 1936:104)

b. *tis* ***ǰima-ša*** *para* *komeučamu(n)*
he/DAT brother-ALL money/NOM he/give/it/III
'He (apparently) gave money to (his) brother.'
(Chikobava 1936:104)

The retired indirect object of a masdar is marked with the allative in (30b), while the final indirect object of a comparable finite clause is in the dative in (30a).

(30) a. *rusudan-k* *durtinu* *çigni* *lamara-s*
Rusudan-NAR she/return/it/to.her/II book/NOM Lamara-DAT
'Rusudan returned the book to Lamara.'
b. *rusudan-s* *oḳo* *çigniš* *dortinapa* ***lamara-ša***
Rusudan-DAT she/want/it book/GEN return/MAS Lamara-ALL
'Rusudan wants to return the book to Lamara.'

In (31a) the recipient is in the dative, while in the causative (31b) it is in the allative; both sentences are in Series II.

(31) a. *muma-k* *cxeni* *(ki)meču* *skua-s*
father-NAR horse/NOM he/give/it/to.him/II child-DAT
'The father gave a horse to (his) child.'
b. *babu-k* *cxeni* *(ki)miočamapu* *tengiz-is*
grandfather-NAR he/CAUSE/give/it/to.him/II Tengiz-DAT
mota-ša
grandchild-ALL
'The grandfather made Tengiz give a horse to (his) grandchild.'

Example (32), which may be compared with (27a) above, also illustrates the allative case for the initial indirect object of the embedded clause.

(32) *muma-k* *rezo-s* *očukebapu*
father-NAR Rezo-DAT he/CAUSE/give/it/to.him/II
vard-ep-i ***dida-ša***
flower-PL-NOM mother-ALL
'Father made Rezo give flowers to (his) mother.'

Finally, (33)–(35) exemplify the use of the allative for the retired indirect object of various analytic constructions formed with a past participle. Example (33) is a periphrastic perfect, (34) is an analytic passive.

(33) *ates* *dənačina* *apun-ia* ***čkin-da***
he/DAT ordered/PART he/has-QUOT us-ALL
' "He has ordered it for us," he said.' (Xubua 1937:72, 26)

(34) *atena* ***čkim-da*** *re* *moc̣arili*
this/NOM me-ALL it/be/I written/PART
'This is written to me.' 'This is attributed to me/blamed on me.'

Example (34) is ambiguous because of the double meaning of the verb.

The allative case has two distinct uses in Mingrelian: (a) It indicates direction toward or to a destination; this concrete use is illustrated in (35).

(35) *diaḳon-k* *midaraʔ* *xoǯ-ep-i* *γal-ša*
deacon-NAR he/drive/it/II ox-PL-NOM creek-ALL
'The deacon drove the oxen to(ward) the creek.'
(Kluge 1916:83, 18)

(b) It has a use that is syntactic in the sense of Chapter 4. This use, the marking of retired indirect objects, is illustrated above.

The allative marker -(*i*)*ša* derives historically from the genitive -(*i*)*š* plus the adverbial -*a* (or -*d-a*); see §11.2.5, Chikobava (1956b), and Topuria (1937). It is, nevertheless, a single simple case synchronically. Note that in pronouns, illustrated in (33) and (34), we find the possessive stem (*čkin-* 'our', *čkim-* 'my') plus -*da*.

Although only the allative was elicited as marking for retired indirect objects, in texts the dative can also be found, as in (36).

(36) ***mešare-s*** *kaγard-iši* *gurapa*
traveller-DAT reading.writing-GEN teaching/MAS
'[The priest began] teaching reading-and-writing to the traveller.' (Kluge 1916:82, 10)

Thus, in Mingrelian, retired indirect objects are marked with the allative or the dative.

11.2.3. Laz

In Laz, retired indirect objects are marked with the allative case, -*ša*. The (b) examples in (37)–(38) illustrate the use of this case in inversion in Series III, while the (a) examples show the corresponding nominal in the dative case in Series I.

(37) a. *rezo-k* *mečaps* *nana-s* *pukir-epe*
Rezo-NAR he/give/it/to.her/I mother-DAT flower-PL/NOM
'Rezo gives flowers to (his) mother.'

b. *rezo-s* *pukir-epe* *nučamun* ***nana-ša***
Rezo-DAT flower-PL/NOM he/give/it/III mother-ALL
'Rezo (apparently) gave flowers to (his) mother.'

(38) a. *nana-k* *ubirs* *skiri-s*
mother-NAR she/sing/to.him/I child-DAT
'The mother sings to (her) child.'
b. *nana-s* *ubirun* ***skiri-ša***
mother-DAT she/sing/III child-ALL
'The mother (apparently) sang to (her) child.'

The use of the allative for a retired indirect object with a masdar is illustrated in (39b); this may be compared with (39a), which shows dative marking with a corresponding final indirect object.

(39) a. *rusudani-k* *lamara-s* *ketabi*
Rusudan-NAR Lamara-DAT book/NOM
kaguktinu
she/return/it/to.her/II
'Rusudan returned the book to Lamara.'
b. *rusudani-s* ***lamara-ša*** *ketabi-š* *goktinu*
Rusudan-DAT Lamara-ALL book-GEN return/MAS
unon
she/want/it/I
'Rusudan wants to return the book to Lamara.'

The allative may also be used to mark the retired indirect object in causatives and in analytic passives, as shown in (40) and (41), respectively.

(40) *baba-k* *rezo-s* *nočapaps* *pukir-epe*
father-NAR Rezo-DAT she/CAUS/give/it/to.him/I flower-PL/NOM
nana-ša //***nana-šeni***
mother-ALL mother-for
'Father made Rezo give flowers to (his) mother.'

(41) *cxeni* *mečameri* *ren* ***skiri-šeni***// ***skiri-ša***
horse/NOM given/PART it/be/I child-for child-ALL
'A horse is given to (someone's) child.'

Examples (40) and (41) suggest that in at least some constructions *-šeni* may be used in place of the allative to mark retired indirect objects. The postposition *-šeni* means 'for'. In Modern Georgian, the postposition *-tvis* both means 'for' (benefactive, delegative, etc.) and marks retired indirect objects (Harris 1981b:171–173). It is entirely possible that Laz, or this dialect of Laz, has been influenced in this respect by Georgian, since children may attend Georgian schools in the village that this consultant comes from. Alternatively, it is possible that the consultant was responding to the ambiguity inherent in the Georgian sentences with which (40) and (41) were elicited. While *-šeni* in (40) and (41) may be due to contamination of one sort or another, we can be sure that the allative marker (-*ša*) is not, since there is no parallel use of a similar case in Modern Georgian.

The allative in Laz, like that in Mingrelian, derives diachronically from the genitive **iš* plus **a* or **d-a* (see §11.2.5).

11.2.4. Old Georgian

11.2.4.1. Description

In Old Georgian, three distinct markings are used for retired indirect objects; they may be marked with the articulated form of the dative (-*sa*), with the allative (-*isa*//-*isad*(*a*)), or with the postposition -*tvis*, which governs the genitive case.

The marking of the retired indirect object in inversion in Series III has been studied by Getsadze (1957), and many of the examples below are drawn from his work. The use of the dative is illustrated in (42), the allative in (45), and -*tvis* in (46).

(42) a. ***romel-ta*** *mieca* *vecxl-i* *igi*
which/REL-PL/DAT he/give/it/III silver-NOM DET
'to whom he had given the silver' (L 19:15A)
b. ***çmidasa ɣmrtis mšobel-sa*** *šemivedrebiet.*
holy God/GEN parent-DAT I/commend/you/III
'I have commended you to the holy parent of God.'
(Abuladze 1960:35, 31–32)

Example (42a) may be compared with the same passage in the Adiši and Tbeṭi manuscripts, where the whole clause is in Series II instead of III, as in (43).

(43) *romelta misca* *vecxli igi*
he/give/it/to.him/II
'to whom he gave the silver' (L 19:15AdB)

Example (42b) may be compared with the line that precedes it in the same text, which is in Series II rather than Series III.

(44) *vis* *šeguvedren*
whom/DAT you/commend/us/II
'To whom did you commend us?' (Abuladze 1960:35, 30)

Thus, (43) and (44) show that the dative retired indirect objects of (42a, b) correspond to dative final indirect objects of Series II.

The retired indirect objects marked with the allative in (45) and with *-tvis* in (46) correspond to final indirect objects marked with the dative in other series, as shown by examples (47)–(49).

(45) a. *aha esera miuṭevebies* ***šenda*** *ɣmert-sa codva-y igi*
behold he/leave/it/III you/ALL God-DAT sin-NOM DET
'Behold God has forgiven you the sin.'
(Kekelidze 1918:311, 24)

b. *aç̣ me aɣmitkuams* ***upl-isada***
now I/DAT I/vow/it/III lord-ALL
'Now I have vowed to the Lord' (Marr 1911:T, 88)

(46) *ganbč̣obay ubrʒanebies* ***urč-ta*** ***da***
judging he/order/it/III rebel-PL/GEN and
gandgomil-ta-tvis
backslider-PL/GEN-for

'He has ordered to (for) the rebels and backsliders a judgement.' (Kekelidze 1946:10, 8–9)

(47) *uḳuetu ara miuṭevnet ḳac-ta*
if NEG you/leave/them/to.him/II man-PL/DAT
šecodebani matni
sin/PL/NOM their
'if you will not forgive men their sins' (Mt 6:15)

In (45a) and (47), 'sin' is the initial direct object, and the person forgiven (*šenda, kacta*) is the underlying indirect object.

(48) *aɣutkuan aɣtkumay upal-sa*
they/vow/it/to.him/II vow/NOM Lord-DAT
'They will vow a vow to the Lord.' (Isaiah 19:21)

(49) *ara ç̣midata mat sul-ta ubrʒanis*
NEG clean DET spirit-PL/DAT he/order/it/to.him/II
'He orders (to) the unclean spirits. (Mk 1:27Ad)

In (46), where there are conjoined nominals as the retired indirect object, only the second bears the postposition, while both bear the case (genitive) governed by the postposition. This is the regular pattern for conjoined nominals governed by a postposition. Examples (47)–(49) show that the allative and *tvis*-marked retired indirect objects of (45)–(46) correspond to dative final indirect objects of Series II.

With participles, the retired indirect object may be in the dative, as illustrated in (50), or in the allative, illustrated in (51).

(50) *moivlina gabriel angeloz-i. . . kalçul-isa*
he/sent/MP/II Gabriel angel-NOM virgin-ALL
txovil-isa ***kmar-sa***
engaged/PART-ALL husband-DAT
'The angel Gabriel was sent to a virgin, engaged to a husband.'
(L 1:26–27B)

(51) a. *tu micemul iqos* ***misa*** *mamisa mier čemisa*
if given it/be/II him/ALL father by my
'if it were given to him by my father' (J 6:65AdA)
b. *rayta vicodit γmrt-isa mier moničebul-i* ***čuen-da***
that we/know/it/I God-GEN thru given/PART-NOM us/ALL
'in order that we might know that which is given to us through God' (1 Cor. 2:12AB)
c. *romel mocemul ars* ***tkuen-da***
which/REL/NOM given/PART/NOM it/be/I you/PL/ALL
kriste iesu-ys mier
Christ Jesus-GEN through
'which is given to you through Jesus Christ' (1 Cor. 1:4AB)

The use of the dative or allative in (50)–(51), respectively, is not determined by the case of the governing participle; the participles are not themselves in the dative in (50) or in the allative in (51). The use of these two cases is determined by the grammatical relation of the nominals they mark, here, retired indirect object.

Now we turn to the infinitive, which has been studied in detail by Chxubianishvili (1972), from which some of the examples below are drawn (pp. 74–77). The Old Georgian infinitive involves some problems, since it permits a wider variety of marking for its terms than does any other construction. This is discussed in greater detail below. Example (52) illustrates retired indirect objects in the dative, and (53) in the allative.

(52) a. *ǰer ars-a micemad xarḳ-i* ***ḳeisar-sa***
right it/be/I-QUES give/INF tribute-NOM Caesar-DAT
'Is it right to give tribute to Caesar?' (Mk 12:14AB)
b. *mašin ubrʒana dadebad ǰačv-i* ***ked-sa***
then he/order/it/to.him/II put/INF chain-NOM neck-DAT
missa
her
'Then he ordered them to put a chain on her neck.'
(Imnaishvili 1970a:138, 8)
c. *rametu γirda. . . micemad* ***glaxaḳ-ta***
for it/worth/I give/INF poor-PL/DAT
'For it would have been good . . . to give it to the poor.'
(Mt 26:9Ad)

(53) a. *ǰer-ars-a* ***ḳeisr-isa*** *xarḳ-isa* *micemad*
right-it/be/I-QUES Caesar-ALL tribute-ALL give/INF
'Is it right to give tribute to Caesar?' (L 20:22Ad)

b. *iç̣qo* *peṭre* *siṭquad* ***misa*** *da* *hrkua*
he/begin/it/II Peter say/INF him/ALL and he/say/it/II
'Peter began to speak to him and he said' (Mk 10:28AB)

For the sake of completeness it must be added that other constructions in Old Georgian also have retired indirect objects, notably the causative and the masdar. Unfortunately, no special study has been made of the marking of retired terms with these constructions as has been done for the infinitive and for inversion in Series III. Example (54) illustrates the retired indirect object of a masdar in the dative, and (55) in the allative.

(54) *ǰer* *ars* *xarḳ-isa* *micema-y* ***ḳeisar-sa***
right it/be/I tribute-GEN give/MAS-NOM Caesar-DAT
'Is giving tribute to Caesar right?' (Mt 22:17AB)

(55) *ç̣es ars xarḳ-isa micema-y* ***ḳeisr-isa***
law Caesar-ALL
'Is giving tribute to Caesar lawful?' (Mt 22:17Ad)

In view of the fact that the importance of lexical government of case patterns has been emphasized in this work, it is necessary to point out that in this instance the choice of one or another case for retired indirect objects is apparently not lexically governed. For example, *brʒaneba* 'order' takes an indirect object; in Series III the retired indirect object may be marked with *-tvis,* as in (46), or with the dative (*mibrʒanebies šemasmenelta* 'I have ordered the accusers', Acts 23:30A). Similarly, *micema* 'give' in Series III may have its retired indirect object marked with the allative (*mimicemies matda* 'I have given it to them' Imnaishvili 1970b:194, 12) or with the dative, as in (42a). In the other constructions, too, a single verb may govern the dative (*miç̣utomad sazomsa* 'to attain (their) measure' Abuladze 1957:33, 26) or the allative (*miç̣utomad γmrteebisa* 'to attain/reach (his) gods', Abuladze 1957:144, 29). In some instances one manuscript has the dative (*ganmzadebad upalsa* 'to prepare [them] for the Lord', L 1:17AB), while another has the allative in the same context (*ganmzadebad uplisa* 'to prepare [them] for the Lord', L 1:17Ad).

Aside from its function of marking retired indirect objects, the dative is used syntactically to mark final indirect objects in all series (see Chap. 3; §11.1; Chap. 13). It also has concrete uses, including the marking of location, time expressions, and comparison (see Chap. 4; Imnaishvili 1957:685–703; Kiziria 1959). The allative in its concrete uses indicates goal, place toward which, person toward whom, benefactive, designative, and the 'ethical dative' or person affected (see Gigineishivli and Sarjveladze 1978; Imnaishvili 1957:491–495, 710–712; Martirosovi 1959). The postposition *-tvis*, in its concrete functions, is a marker of benefactive, designative, or delegative.

11.2.4.2. Internal Reconstruction

Form. In the Old Georgian examples above and below, a number of distinct forms are glossed as ALL (allative); one example of each type is entered for comparison in Table 11.1. With common nouns there exist both forms like *upl-isada* and *upl-isa;* in common nouns, the latter forms are syncretic with the genitive case forms (see Tables 4.1 and 4.2). In proper nouns, the allative in *-isa* is distinct from the genitive, which for proper nouns has the desinence *-is* (see Table 4.17). In first and second person pronouns, only forms in *-da* are found, while in the third person, both *-da* and *-a* are found, the latter being more frequent.

The genitive case in Old Georgian nouns has the form *-is(a),* which can be identified in the forms in Table 11.1. In pronouns, the genitive (possessive) stem is used, though the genitive stem contrasts with the dative only in the first and third persons singular: *čem-* 'my' versus *me* 'I/NOM/NAR/DAT,' and *mis-* 'his' versus *mas* 'him/DAT'. Once we factor out the root and genitive of each nominal, we find that they can be divided into two types—those with the additional suffix *-d(a)* and those with the additional suffix *-a,* as in Table 11.2. Thus, from the point of view of mor-

Table 11.1

Summary of Allative Case Forms

upl-isada	'to the Lord'	Example (45b)
ḳeisr-isa	'to Caesar'	Example (53a)
čuen-da	'to us'	Example (51b)
mat-da	'to them'	John 18:29Ad
mat-a	'to them'	John 18:29AB

Table 11.2

Allative Forms in *-da* and in *-a* in Old Georgian

-da	*-a*	
upl-isa-da	*upl-is-a*	'to the Lord'
—	*davit-is-a*	'to David'
mis-da	*mis-a*	'to him'
čem-da	—	'to me'

phology, it appears that in Proto-Georgian there were two distinct cases, which, however, had fallen together by attested Old Georgian.[7] It will be recalled from Chapter 4 that there is reason to reconstruct both **d* (to CK) and **a* (to CGZ) as markers of the adverbial case, though this may have once been two distinct cases. We may say that the two types that function as allatives in Old Georgian are derived historically from the genitive plus one or both of the two adverbial desinences. This is confirmed by comparison with Mingrelian (see below).

It should be noted that the picture presented above differs slightly from the view of many Kartvelologists, who consider the *-isa* forms to have been derived by deletion of *d* from *-isad(a)* (e.g., Martirosovi 1959). There is no independent support for deletion of *d* in such an environment. Nevertheless, for our purposes it is necessary only to note that there is good reason to believe that the allative case in Old Georgian derives historically from the genitive plus the adverbial case endings.[8]

The form of the dative case is reconstructed in Chapter 4.

FUNCTION. In order to reconstruct the CK situation, we must consider in detail the relationships among the three ways of marking retired indirect objects in Old Georgian. The postposition *-tvis* does not really belong in a reconstruction of this function, as it is clearly new in Georgian. In (46), as in other Old Georgian examples of the use of *-tvis* that have been adduced in the literature (Getsadze 1957), as well as examples I have found in reading Old Georgian texts, it is always possible to interpret *-tvis* as a concrete postposition in one of the meanings named above. In Standard Modern Georgian, on the other hand, it is the only productive way of marking retired indirect objects in the inversion construction of Series III, in infinitives, with masdars, in causatives, and so forth (Harris 1981b, Chap. 11). While examples of a syntactic use of *-tvis* in Old Georgian may exist,[9] it is clear from the course of its development in Georgian and from the lack of parallels in its sister languages (but see above on Laz) that the use of *-tvis* in this function is a relatively recent development in Georgian and should be disregarded in reconstructing CK.

With respect to the dative and the allative, we must consider the various constructions separately. It has been observed a number of times that the Old Georgian norm for the marking of the retired indirect object in Inversion in Series III is the allative (*-isa-da*), and that the use of the dative in this function is an exception (Danelia 1965:76; Getsadze 1957:465, 469; Imnaishvili 1957:687; and references cited by these authors). In this construction the dative has been entirely lost as a marker of the retired indirect object (Getsadze 1957:469): in some of the mountain dialects we find the allative (Martirosovi 1959:119), in some of the western dialects a form derived from this (e.g., *miza;* Martirosovi 1959:109), while in Standard Modern Georgian we find only *-tvis* (Harris 1981b:Chaps. 8 and 11). These facts suggest that in this construction, the use of the dative is original, replaced by the allative (genitive–adverbial) and then by *-tvis* in the standard literary language.

When we turn to the infinitive construction, we encounter special problems in the interpretation of the marking of retired indirect objects. First, it has been argued that the allative (genitive–adverbial) case occurs because the construction governs the genitive, and concord with the infinitive (itself historically derived from a masdar in the adverbial case) requires the addition of the adverbial (e.g., Imnaishvili 1957:710). It is indeed true that a genitive following its head noun agrees with it in case, as in (56).

(56) *ʒe-y* *ḳac-isa-y*
son-NOM man-GEN-NOM
'the son of man' (L 22:69, etc.)

Nevertheless, the fact that retired indirect objects are also marked with the allative in inversion, as in (45), with participles, as in (51), and with masdars, as in (55), suggests that in the infinitive construction the allative is assigned for the same reason, not because of concord.

A second problem is that this construction governs a greater variety of marking for its retired terms than any other nonfinite construction. In particular, its direct object may be marked with the nominative, dative, genitive, or allative case (Chxubianishvili 1972:75–78), while retired direct objects of other constructions in Old Georgian are not, in general, marked with the nominative (Harris 1979). Because the infinitive governs the same cases for direct objects that are governed by finite verbs (i.e., nominative and dative), as well as those that are governed by deverbal nominals (i.e., genitive and genitive–adverbial), the infinitive is traditionally considered to have, in some instances, 'verbal rection', and in others, 'nominal rection' (e.g., Chxubianishvili 1972; Martirosovi 1955). If this view of the infinitive is correct, then we might expect the use of the dative case to mark retired indirect objects to last longer in this construction than in others. That is, if the use of the dative to mark retired indirect objects was nearly dead even in Old Georgian, as suggested above, we might nevertheless find it with the infinitive, as part of verbal rection. The evidence from this construction must therefore be viewed somewhat differently from that from other constructions.

It appears that the dative was indeed used more frequently to mark retired indirect objects of infinitives than to mark those of the inversion construction. I interpret this as an artifact of the dual rection of infinitives.

That is, on the one hand, infinitives could have nominal rection with the retired direct object in the genitive or allative and with the retired indirect object in the case elsewhere used productively for this relation—the allative. This possibility is illustrated in (53). In (53a) *xarḳisa* 'tribute' is ambiguously genitive or allative (see Table 4.1 on the declension of common nouns), while *ḳeis(a)risa* 'to Caesar' is unambiguously allative (see Table 4.17 on the declension of personal names). On the other hand, infinitives could have verbal rection with the direct object in the nominative or dative and the indirect object in the dative, as in (52). It is this additional possibility, then, that accounts for the more frequent occurrence of dative indirect objects with the infinitive in Old Georgian. For completeness it must be noted that mixed rection can also occur, where the initial direct object bears the case of a final direct object but where the initial indirect object bears the marking of a retired term.

Chxubianishvili states the following restriction on the marking of (retired) objects with infinitives: first and second person (retired) objects with infinitives are always marked with the allative (= genitive–adverbial), never with the dative (1972:78; see also Imnaishvili 1957:710). That is, while we find, for example, *čemda* 'me/GEN/ADV' with the infinitive, we never find *me* 'me/DAT', even though there is no such restriction on the use of *me* as a dative to mark a final indirect object. Thus, the use of the dative to mark retired indirect objects with the infinitive is limited to third person nominals. In the two collections available to me of examples of the use of the dative to mark retired indirect objects in Inversion (Danelia 1965:76; Getsadze 1957), there is, similarly, no instance of the use of the dative for a retired first or second person indirect object. Thus, the use of the dative to mark retired indirect objects with both the infinitive and the inversion construction appears to be limited to third person nominals. A restriction of this type supports the hypothesis formulated above that the dative originally marked retired indirect objects and was later replaced in this function by the genitive–adverbial.

Unlike the two constructions discussed above, the participle, including its use in periphrastic constructions, has not been studied in detail from the point of view of the marking assigned to retired indirect objects. Examples above show that both the dative and the allative occur in this function in Old Georgian. In Modern Georgian the nominal is productively marked with *-tvis,* like other retired indirect objects (Harris 1981b:110–112, 171–173). Under certain circumstances it may be marked with a dative, even in Modern Georgian (examples in Imnaishvili 1957:689ff.). The use of the dative as a marker of retired indirect objects of analytic passives is restricted both dialectically and lexically in the modern language (details in Harris 1981b: 111–112). Even though the dative is retained in this function in Modern Georgian, the fact that it is restricted in these ways supports the hypothesis formulated above that the dative is original in this function.

As noted above, there are other constructions in Georgian in which a retired indirect object occurs. None of these constructions in Old Georgian has been studied from the point of view of the marking of the retired indirect object. In at least one—the synthetic causative—the dative still occurs as a marker of the retired indirect object (see Shanidze 1973:§431; Vogt 1971:§2.75). This use, however, is restricted by dialect, by lexical item, and by person of the nominals involved (Harris 1981b: 83–85). This construction may likewise be interpreted as evidence that the dative was once general in this function and later was restricted.

Since in the Kartvelian languages the use of the dative to mark retired indirect objects is not widespread, we should consider the possibility that this usage was introduced as a syntactic calque through translation from another language. In Matthew 22:17 the Adiši manuscript has the allative, while the Tbeṭi and Opiza texts have the dative; see examples (54) and (55). Knowing that the latter two represent revisions from a Greek original (Blake 1974:446; Lake, Blake, and New 1928:291), we might hypothesize that the allative of the inherited Kartvelian construction was replaced by the dative, under the influence of the Greek version, where the dative is found. The dative is found in this function in other places in the Adiši text (for example, Mark 12:14), as well as in "Šušaniḳ" (example 52b), "Limonari" (example 42b), the "Balavariani" (33, 26), "Ḳimeni I" (231, 37), and other works; but none of these rules out the possibility that this use of the dative entered the language through borrowing in a broader sense. In fact, it is impossible, in principle, to show that this usage was not borrowed.

On the other hand, since all of the Kartvelian languages use the dative to mark final indirect objects, there is no reason to suppose that the use of the dative in marking retired indirect objects is borrowed. Many languages, including neighbors of Georgian (Panchvidze 1960), use the same cases and patterns in nonfinite as in finite constructions. This being so, I hypothesize that the use of the dative in this function is inherited. This is supported by the fact that in Georgian, retired direct objects may be marked with the dative (see Imnaishvili 1957:689–693), just as the final direct object is in Series I. It is unlikely that this usage could have been borrowed, since the marking of final direct objects with the dative is not widespread among any of Georgia's neighbors. If there are more instances of the dative as a marker in the Tbeṭi and Opiza manuscripts than in the Adiši, I suggest that it is because the Greek original influenced the choice between two parallel inherited expressions. We may consider the dative in this function to be an additional example of an inherited expression found in Old Georgian but lost in all of the modern Kartvelian languages (see §2.2.5). Since there is good reason to relate the marking of retired indirect objects to that of final indirect objects (see Imnaishvili 1957:693), I tentatively assume that the use of the dative in this function is an inherited expression.

In conclusion, while there is some variation by construction, retired indirect objects in Georgian are in general marked by the dative or the allative (genitive–adverbial). Because of its restricted distribution—according to different parameters in various constructions—the dative may be considered the oldest in this function. The use of the allative was the productive pattern in Old Georgian, at least for the two constructions that have been studied in detail; it is completely absent from Standard Modern Georgian but is retained in some dialects.[10] The postposition *-tvis* was used very rarely, if at all, in this function in Old Georgian but is completely productive in Standard Modern Georgian. In all likelihood, the use of the dative in this function has persisted for so long because its use as the marker of all final indirect objects provides an analogue for its use as a marker of retired indirect objects. On the basis of these facts, I conclude that the dative was original in this function in Old Georgian and that it was mostly replaced by the allative (< genitive–adverbial), which was in turn replaced by *-tvis* (in the literary dialect).

11.2.5. Comparative Reconstruction

The facts presented above are summarized in Table 11.3. In the chart, a dash indicates only that examples are not available, not that the expression is ungrammatical. The absence of the various types of examples is explained in the relevant subsections above. Although this is not indicated in Table 11.3, the use of the dative for retired indirect objects was rejected by consultants for each construction tested in Svan, Mingrelian, and Laz. For example, (16) with a dative *gezals* 'to the child' instead of the genitive–adverbial was judged ungrammatical.

In evaluating the data summarized in Table 11.3, it should be kept in mind that the allative case of Mingrelian, Laz, and Old Georgian derives historically from the genitive case plus the adverbial case (Gigineishvili and Sarjveladze 1978; Martirosovi 1959; Topuria 1937; etc.). In Mingrelian, Laz, and Old Georgian, the allative is used also to indicate direction; in Svan a postposition usually performs this function.[11] The markers of the genitive and those of the adverbial, from which the allative derives, are cognate, as discussed above and in Chapter 4.

Table 11.3

Summary of Marking Assigned to Retired Indirect Objects

	Inversion in Series III	Analytic passive	Masdar	Infinitive	Causative
Svan	GEN–ADV ADV	—	GEN–ADV	GEN–ADV	—
Mingrelian	ALL	ALL	ALL DAT	—	ALL
Laz	ALL	ALL (*-šeni*)	ALL	—	ALL (*-šeni*)
Old Georgian	DAT ALL	DAT ALL	DAT	DAT ALL	DAT

It is clear that the allative (< genitive–adverbial) is to be reconstructed at least to CGZ. The fact that 'direction towards which' is expressed by postpositions in Svan, rather than by the genitive–adverbial, may suggest that the use of this case sequence to mark retired indirect objects in Svan is borrowed later from its sisters and not inherited from CK. Because of the age of Old Georgian relative to its sister languages and because of the relationships within the Kartvelian family, discussed in Chapter 2, we must also tentatively reconstruct the dative case as a marker of retired indirect objects. Since the dative was restricted from the earliest times, as observed in §11.2.4.2, it appears to be older in this function than the genitive–adverbial, though we cannot rule out the possibility that the two always coexisted.[12] On the whole then, the data suggest that the dative is older in this function and that the allative developed in CGZ and was borrowed by Svan (as genitive–adverbial) for this syntactic function only.

Because there is some variation by construction, we cannot absolutely rule out the possibility that originally there was greater divergence in this respect. Nevertheless, there is a high degree of internal consistency in each language, as well as correspondence between the languages in the marking assigned to retired indirect objects.

On the basis of the comparative data presented above, I suggest that for CGZ, and possibly CK, we reconstruct rule (57).

(57) A retired indirect object is marked with the dative or genitive–adverbial case.

Earlier it probably had the form in (58).

(58) A retired indirect object is marked with the dative case.

This could be combined with (1d) to give the simpler rule (59).

(59) An indirect object is marked with the dative case.

11.3. THE RETIRED INDIRECT OBJECT IN SERIES I

According to the analysis proposed in Chapter 7, Series I originated as a productive construction involving Object Demotion, later reanalyzed. Since Object Demotion is the demoting of the initial direct object to indirect-objecthood, if we assume that there can be only one indirect object at any level of derivation, then we would expect that the initial indirect object is not a final indirect object (until the construction was reanalyzed). The Chômeur Law predicts that the initial indirect object would be an indirect object chômeur, a type of retired indirect object. If rule (57) was in effect at this time, then we might expect to find initial indirect objects marked with either the dative or the genitive–adverbial in Series I. On the other hand, if the reasoning of §11.2.5 is correct, and the dative is actually older in this function, then we would expect to find only that case assigned to initial indirect objects of Series I.

Both possibilities do occur in Old Georgian, as shown in (60); the initial indirect object appears in boldface type.

(60) a. *momitxrobda* *igi* ***čemda-mo*** *qovelta*
he/pronounce/it/to.me/I he/NOM me/ALL-hither all/DAT
amat siṭquata
DET word/PL/DAT
(Jer 36:18W, cited in Danelia 1965:80)

b. *mitxrobda* ***me*** *igi qovelta amat siṭquata.*
he/pronounce/it/to.me/I me/DAT
'He pronounced all these words to me.' (Jer 36:18 IO)

However, similar examples occur in Series II, where the initial indirect object has always been final indirect object, as in (61).

(61) a. *me* *migigo* *šenda-mi*
I/NAR I/answer/it/to.you/II you/ALL-thither
(Jer 12:1W, cited in Danelia 1965:80)

b. *me migigo šen*
you/DAT
'I will reply to you.' (Jer 12:1 IO)

While examples like (60a) and (61a) are very infrequent, they are interesting because the nominal marked with the allative case triggers Person Agreement, which, as a rule, is conditioned only by nominals in the nominative, narrative, and dative cases.[13]

I suggest that the facts considered in this chapter are best accounted for by the following scenario. In Early CK, rules (1a–c) and (59) applied; it was natural for retired indirect objects to be marked in the same way as final indirect objects, and they did not at that time play an important role in the grammar. When, in Middle CK, Object Demotion began to apply generally, the same rules were employed, accounting for the marking assigned to nominals in Series I. When Series III was added, the same rules still applied (see Chap. 13). Since both Object Demotion and Inversion may create retired indirect objects, this grammatical relation now played a much larger part in the grammar, contributing to a need for marking retired objects differently from final indirect objects. In CGZ, Series I forms were reinterpreted, such that the initial direct object that had been made a surface indirect object by Object Demotion was now reinterpreted as (initial and) final direct object. At the same time, the initial indirect object that had been retired as a consequence of Object Demotion was reinterpreted as (initial and) final indirect object. As a result of this reinterpretation, the rules of case assignment were reanalysed. While the rules of (1) were retained in Series II, the rules of (62) were introduced for Series I.

(62) a. A final subject is marked with the nominative case.
b. A final object is marked with the dative case.

The rules of (62) retained exactly the case distribution that had always existed with Series I forms but now assigned them on the basis of reinterpreted final grammatical relations. A dual case marking system is retained even today, and the marking of Series I cannot be derived synchronically from that of Series II in Georgian (Harris 1981b:Chap. 9), Svan, or Mingrelian.

The reinterpretation of retired indirect objects as final indirect objects in Series I must have renewed pressure on the grammar to distinguish overtly between final and retired indirect objects. We may infer that it was at this point that the genitive–adverbial, which later still became the allative, was introduced to this function. The fact that the genitive–adverbial functioned as an allative in Old Georgian, Laz, and Mingrelian suggests that this form first developed in that concrete function after Svan had split from CK. Then, because of the semantic closeness of the notions of 'direction toward which' and 'indirect object', the allative marker could easily be extended to the syntactic function of marking retired indirect objects, fulfilling a need that had arisen because of the creation of Series I and III and the reinterpretations of Series I. Because of the continued geographical proximity and cultural interinfluences, the syntactic function of the genitive–adverbial could be borrowed into Svan without that language ever developing to any extent the concrete function of the allative case.

The occasional use of the allative for final indirect objects, as in (60a)–(61a), is a Georgian development, which never really took hold. Although this use of the allative is not unknown in the third person, it is chiefly limited to the first and second persons. This phenomenon might be viewed as an unsuccessful attempt to differentiate the dative from the nominative and narrative case forms of the first and second person personal pronouns, these three cases having a single syncretic form (see Table 4.16). In the literary language, the postposition *-tvis* was already beginning to be used to mark retired indirect objects, and the allative would thus have been free to mark final indirect objects. However, this change did not take hold, and constructions like those illustrated in (60a)–(61a) dropped out of the language. The first and second person pronouns remain syncretic for the nominative, narrative, and dative.

The hypothesis presented in Chapter 7 and elaborated here gives an internally consistent account of the distribution of cases in Series I and II for final terms as well as for final retired indirect objects. It is, at the same time, consistent with language universals as we know them at this time (see Chap. 17).

NOTES

[1]The Chômeur Law actually predicts that the indirect object will become an indirect object chômeur. However, indirect object chômeurs are not distinguished from other retired indirect objects in Modern Georgian (Harris 1981b:Chap. 12), Old Georgian (Harris 1979), or the other Kartvelian languages (§11.2, this volume).

[2]Inversion and other clause types are also correctly marked by the rules in (1), as discussed in Chapter 13.

[3]Chxubianishvili (1972) has argued that the masdar in the adverbial is synchronically an infinitive in Old Georgian. I have assumed the same analysis for cognate constructions in the sister languages, but the reconstruction of retired indirect object marking is in no way dependent on this assumption.

[4]While Object Demotion leaves the indirect objects of intransitives unaffected, as explained in §11.1, in active intransitives Inversion does not, as described in Chapter 13.

[5]One consultant gave the form *ambäwi*.

[6]A postposition can be used instead of the genitive–adverbial in (20) and (21), and for some speakers is preferred; *dīnäš-te* was suggested as a variant in (21) and *dīna-te* in (20). The postposition *-te* appears to be a lexically governed variant; see Harris (1981b:295, n.1) on a lexically governed variant to retired term marking in Modern Georgian. The adverbial for the retired term marking in Modern Georgian. The adverbial for the retired indirect object with this verb must, however, be quite old, as it appears in narrative poetry:

tatriš	*lašg-är-d*	*meckwil*	*xozzax*
Tatri-GEN	troop-PL-ADV	emissary/NOM	they/send/them/III

'They have sent an emissary to Tatri's troops.'

(Shanidze, Topuria, and Gujejiani 1939:46, 44)

[7]While there is no functional distinction between the two types in the third person pronoun, it appears that there is some difference between the two types in common nouns. Further study is necessary to determine this.

[8]Imnaishvili (1957:491–495) has argued that *da* is instead a postposition that governs the genitive case. For arguments that it is cognate with the adverbial case marker **d*, see Chikobava (1956b) and Martirosovi (1959).

[9]It is stated in the linguistic literature that *-tvis* is used in this function in Old Georgian (Getsadze 1957; Imnaishvili 1957:687, 710; Shanidze, quoted in Getsadze 1957:465).

[10]The allative case is no longer used in Georgian except as the case governed by a few postpositions, for example *čemda mimart* 'toward me', *šenda miuxedavad* 'regardless of you'.

[11]I cannot say with certainty that in Svan the genitive–adverbial case cannot be used with allative function. It was not used by my consultants, nor have I found textual examples or discussion of it in the linguistic literature.

[12]In Harris (1979) I tentatively reconstructed the dative case or *da,* that is, the allative, in this function for Proto-Georgian, on the basis of a comparison of Old with Modern Georgian.

[13]Danelia (1975) attributes agreement of this kind to the influence of other languages, especially Greek. There are other examples similar to (60a) and (61a), but where the nominal does not trigger agreement, for example, 1 Cor 7:1.

12

The Picture That Emerges

In this chapter, the final argument in favor of the Object Demotion analysis is adduced (§12.1), and all of the evidence for this hypothesis is summarized (§12.2).

12.1. PERSON AGREEMENT IN OLD GEORGIAN

12.1.1. Third Person Objects

In Old Georgian, direct objects of all persons in Series II, if they are plural, trigger the plural marker *-en/n* discussed in Chapter 10. Both singular and plural third person direct objects in this series trigger a ∅ for Person Agreement. The occurrence of a ∅ with third person direct objects in Series II is illustrated in the examples below.

(1)	*siṭquani,*	*romel*	*da-ç̣er-n-a*	*baruk*
	words/PL/NOM	which/REL/NOM	PV-write-PL-3S	Baruch/NAR

'the words, which Baruch wrote' (Jer 36:27O)

(2) *da ara p̣o-es*
and NEG find-3S/PL
'And they did not find it.' (Mt 26:60Ad)

(3) *ḳacman vinme q̣-o p̣uri didi*
man/NAR someone make-3S bread/NOM big
'A certain man made a big meal.' (L 14:16)

The verb forms *daçerna, p̣oes,* and *q̣o* contain no overt marker of Direct Object Person Agreement.

Third person indirect objects in the same series, on the other hand, trigger a non-null marker of Person Agreement. The form of the marker varies in the following ways:

1. In some texts, called *xanmeṭi*, the marker always takes the form *x*.
2. In other texts, called *haemeṭi*, it always has the form *h*.
3. Still others, for which the term *sannarevi* has been coined (Imnaishvili 1971), have *x*, *h*, *s*, ∅, or sometimes other variants in different phonetic environments (see Shanidze 1957c).[1]

The use of these markers to indicate a third person (singular or plural) indirect object is illustrated below. Example (4a) is from a *xanmeṭi* text, (4b) and (5) from *sannarevi* texts.

(4) a. *mašin movida moçapeta tana da* ***x****-rku-a*
then he/come/II disciple/PL/NOM to and 3IO-say-3S
mat
them/DAT (Mt 26:45, Birdsall 1971:65)
b. *mašin movida moçapeta da* ***h****-rku-a mat*
3IO-say-3S
'Then he came to the disciples and said to them'
(Mt 26:45AdAB)

(5) *ganṭexa da mi-s-c-a mat*
he/break/it/II and PV-3IO-give-3S them/DAT
'He broke it, and he gave it to them.' (L 24:30Ad)

In (4a) the third person indirect object marker has the form *x*, in (4b), *h*, and in (5), *s*.

The examples above illustrate that in Series II, third person direct objects trigger a ∅ person marker, while indirect objects trigger a person marker that may be realized as *x, h, s,* ∅, and so forth, depending upon the type of text and the phonetic environment.[2] In the first and second persons, direct and indirect objects have identical marking, as summarized in Table 12.1. Here and below, the discussion is based on the singular for simplicity; the plural follows the same principles (see handbooks).

It has been observed that while the direct object in Series II triggers ∅, in comparable examples in Series I the same object triggers *x*/*h*/*s*/∅ (Shanidze 1957c). The examples below, directly comparable to (1)–(3), are in

Table 12.1

Object Agreement Markers in Series II of Old Georgian

	Direct object	Indirect object
1st person	*m-*	*m-*
2nd person	*g-*	*g-*
3rd person	∅	*x*/*h*/*s*/∅-

Series I and show that there is a significant difference in this respect between Series I and II.

(6) *da me da-v-**s**-çer-d çignsa zeda melnita*
and I/NOM PV-1S-3IO-write-ScM book on ink/INST
'[He pronounced all these words to me] and I wrote them in the book with ink.' (Jer 36:18 O)

(7) *da ara **h**-pov-eb-d-es*
and NEG 3IO-find-SM-ScM-3S/PL
'[And the chief priests and all those of the council searched for false witness . . .] and did not find it.' (Mt 26:60AB)

(8) *da **h**-q̇-op-d-en sasçaulebsa da nišebsa*
and 3IO-make-SM-ScM-3S/PL wonder/COL/DAT and sign
'And they will make wonders and signs.' (Mk 13:22A)

In (6), the direct object triggers Indirect Object Agreement; in (1), a Series II example with the same verb, it does not. The same is true of (7) and (2), and (8) and (3).

For verbs like those in (1)–(3) and (6)–(8), it is generally true that the direct object in Series II triggers ∅, while the same object in Series I usually triggers *x*/*h*/*s*/∅ (Shanidze 1957c:§42). There are, however, exceptions of all types to this generalization (Shanidze 1957c:§42). The marker *x*/*h*/*s*/∅ for the direct object in Series I is more likely to occur with some verbs than with others; that is, there is lexical variation. The earliest texts were more consistent in their use of *x* or *h* to mark direct objects in Series I (Shanidze 1926:314).

Because there is a great deal about this morpheme that is not yet understood or accounted for, we must be very cautious in our interpretation of the Old Georgian facts.[3] Nevertheless, the generalization stated by Shanidze retains its validity and accounts for a large number of attested verb forms, especially in the oldest texts.

The following hypothesis accounts for the series discrepancy in the distribution of the third person indirect object marker *x*/*h*/*s*/∅ discussed above. Before the creation of Series I, third person indirect objects triggered *x*, while third person direct objects triggered Ø. These rules, like the other rules of Person Agreement, were based entirely on final grammatical relations. When Series I was created through the application of Object Demotion, in underlyingly transitive sentences the direct object became the surface indirect object, and thus a *x*-trigger if third person. Well before attested Old Georgian, Series I was reinterpreted; since the initial direct object was no longer a surface indirect object, the occurrence of *x* in Series I was, in many verb forms, unmotivated. Eventually *x* was made regular (see Chap. 15). The relatively unsystematic nature of this rule in Old Georgian is due to the restructuring that was then going on. This hypothesis, then, supports the analysis of the origin of Series I advanced here and partially explains the distribution of the third person indirect object marker and the discrepancy in this respect between Series I and II.[4]

A different explanation for the distribution of the third person *x*/*h*/*s* marker is implicit in Shanidze (1957c) and other works, namely that this marker is triggered by those final objects that stand in the dative case. This is without doubt a correct generalization synchronically, and a synchronic description was precisely his aim. From a diachronic point of view, this account only removes the burden of explanation by one step; that is, it remains to be explained why direct objects stand in the indirect object case (dative) just in Series I. Put another way, to say that *x*/*h*/*s* is triggered by those final objects that are in the dative case does not in any sense account for the origin of Series I or for the other specific phenomena that have been considered in Chapters 7–11. However, while a correlation between the dative case and the third person *x*/*h*/*s* marker does not explain the origin of the distribution described above, it probably was responsible for the fact that this distribution remained for a time after the reinterpretation of the syntax of Series I. After the reanalysis of Series I (see Chap. 15), the strong correlation between the verbal affix and the case of its trigger probably made it possible for the discrepancy between Series I and II to be retained.

12.1.2. Other Agreement Markers

The discussion above is limited to the third person object marker *x*/*h*/*x*/Ø because this is the only Person Agreement marker whose distribution in Series I differs from that in Series II. It seems worth considering briefly why this is the only marker of Person Agreement that differs in this way. (The term *Person Agreement* here specifically excludes *En*-Agreement.)

In Old Georgian, as in the sister languages, the rules of Person Agreement have accusative alignment. One set of forms, listed in Table 12.2, marks all subjects, another, represented in Table 12.1, marks direct objects. A third, also listed in Table 12.1, marks indirect objects, except as discussed in §12.1.1. In Table 12.2, the variant of the second person subject marker is determined phonetically; that of the third person singular is determined phonetically and by screeve (see Table 5.2).

In Series II, one of the affixes listed in Table 12.2 is triggered by every singular surface subject in Old Georgian, regardless of the type of construction in which it occurs. In the sister languages, affixes cognate to these are similarly assigned to all final subjects (see Oniani 1978). On this basis I assume that a similar distribution existed in CK.[5] We would expect that the same system would be extended to Series I, and indeed we find the same set of subject markers assigned on the same basis in Series I and II in Old Georgian and the sister languages (Oniani 1978).

Initial direct objects that are demoted to indirect-objecthood in Series I would be expected to trigger the indirect object markers listed in Table 12.1. Since in the first and second persons these are identical to the direct object markers, we would not be able to differentiate between them. The third person marker in Old Georgian is discussed above. In the sister languages, there is no difference between the distribution of the object markers in Series I and II (Chikobava 1936:92, 97–98; Topuria 1967:15ff). I assume that they, like Georgian later, restructured the distribution of the indirect object morpheme to reflect the reanalyzed surface structure (see Chap. 15).

In Series I, retired indirect objects would have occurred only in clauses having an initial subject, direct object, and indirect object. In Old Georgian, because of the morpheme structure rules of the language, there is no way of telling whether the retired indirect objects in clauses of this type trigger agreement or not.[6] These rules have been studied in detail by Imnaishvili (1971:318ff.), and the discussion below is based on his work. In Old Georgian there was a morpheme structure rule, given in (9).

Table 12.2

Subject Agreement Markers (Singular) in Old Georgian

1st person	*v-*	
2nd person	*h/x/s/∅-*	
3rd person		*-s, -a/o, -n*

(9) If in a clause two objects trigger agreement, the morpheme representing the person lower on the hierarchy deletes, where the hierarchy is
first person > second person > third person.

There are seven ways in which object markers could potentially co-occur, and this rule accounts for six of them. The possibilities are listed in Table 12.3. That is, if the direct object is first person, the indirect object could be second person or third person, and so on. Coreferentiality between direct and indirect object did not occur. Rule (9) correctly states that a first person object, regardless of whether it was direct or indirect, is favored morphologically at the expense of either second or third person objects. Similarly, second person objects are favored at the expense of third. Two examples are given below; additional ones are cited by Imnaishvili.

(10) *mo-m-ṭac-es* *me* *šen-gan*
PV-1DO-carry.off/3S/PL me/NOM you-from
'They carried me off from you.' (Imnaishvili 1966:61, 11)

(11) *aç̣ vin mi-m-ṭac-a šen čem-gan*
now who/NAR PV-1IO-carry.off-3S you/NOM me-from
'Now who carried you off from me?' (Kekelidze 1918:142, 17)

Both examples are in Series II. In (11) the direct object is second person, the indirect object first person; in (10) the grammatical relations of the persons are reversed. In both, it is the first person object that is actually marked, illustrating the correctness of generalization (9). Example (11) illustrates incidentally that a final indirect object is occasionally not marked with the dative case, yet triggers Indirect Object Agreement. (Additional examples of a similar type, from both Series I and II, are cited in Danelia 1965:80 and 1975.)

Because of the existence of rule (9), examples of the indirect object triggering agreement would actually show up only if the indirect object were on a level with or higher on the hierarchy than the direct object. Since Series I occurs less frequently in Old Georgian texts than Series II,

Table 12.3
Potential Co-occurrences of Object Markers

Direct object	Indirect object
first person	second person, third person
second person	first person, third person
third person	first person, second person, third person

and since examples with first and second person indirect objects do not occur frequently in either series, it is altogether difficult to find relevant examples; one is given as (12). (See also 1 Cor 16:15. These examples, however, are not from very early texts.)

(12) *amas mcnebasa* *še-g-vedreb* *šen*
this commandment/DAT PV-2IO-commit/I you/DAT
'I commit this commandment to you.' (1 Tim 1:18)

(The first person subject marker is regularly deleted when there is a second person object marker, as in (12); see Imnaishvili 1971:316ff.) Examples like (12) suggest that retired indirect objects in Series I might have triggered agreement. We can by no means be sure of this, however, since the surface syntax of Series I had been reinterpreted well before the earliest extant texts and since a rule with such infrequent application would probably have been among the first to be restructured.

In theory, we should also be able to determine whether a third person indirect object in Series I, the reflex of a retired indirect object, triggered agreement in Old Georgian when a third person direct object was present. It is likely, however, that another morpheme structure rule would have deleted one of the two *h/x/s* markers in such a case (see Shanidze 1957c: §27). Examples of two such morphemes do occur, for example, *x-x-iṭqoda* 'he said it to him', a Series I form. It is possible that one *x-* represents the direct object (which earlier was a surface indirect object), while the other represents the indirect object (which was a retired indirect object before reinterpretation of Series I). On the other hand, it appears more likely that this is a scribal error, especially in view of the fact that the first *x-* is erased (see Birdsall 1971:65, 11 and note); such double marking can also be found in Series II.

In sum, we have no very clear evidence as to whether the retired indirect object in Series I originally triggered agreement. What evidence there is in Old Georgian seems to suggest that it did, but of this we can by no means be certain.

Except for the distribution of the third person object marker, there appears to be no difference between the assignment of Person Agreement affixes in Series I and II in any of the languages. Nor would we expect any difference on the basis of the facts outlined above.[7]

12.2. SUMMARY OF EVIDENCE SUPPORTING THE OBJECT DEMOTION HYPOTHESIS

I began this study by asking how we can account for the variety of case marking patterns that exists among the Kartvelian languages. It was suggested that the explanation is diachronic. The following proposals have been made (1–3 in Part II and 4 in Chap. 7):

1. Series II predates Series I.
2. Case marking in Series II was originally a rule of ergative alignment.
3. Ergative case marking was of the generalized type (see §6.6.1); that is, it was final, not initial, transitivity that was relevant to assignment of cases.
4. Series I was derived from Series II diachronically by (reinterpretation of) a once-productive rule of Object Demotion, which made initial direct objects into final indirect objects.

The Object Demotion Hypothesis (4) is entirely dependent on hypotheses 1–3; that is, if 1, 2, or 3 were untrue, 4 would make no sense. Evidence to support 1–3 is presented in Chapters 5 and 6, respectively, and will not be reviewed here.

According to the Object Demotion Hypothesis, Series I originated as durative aspect, contrasting with the predominantly (see Chap. 5) punctual aspect of Series II. Associated with durative aspect (Series I) was a wholly productive rule that demoted the initial direct object of a transitive clause to indirect-objecthood. Indeed, Series I is to be reconstructed as representing durative aspect in CK (Machavariani 1974).

The aspectual opposition of Series I to Series II is indicated morphologically by a contrast between the presence or absence of a series marker (having the form Ø for some verbs). These verbal suffixes, formants of Series I, are derived from the marker of the collective (later plural) in nominals; in this way they represent durative aspect as an "undifferentiated whole" (see Chap. 9).

At the time that the syntactic rule was productive, the case marking system of the language was ergative (see Chap. 6). Since Object Demotion made direct objects into indirect objects, there were no sentences in Series I that were surface transitives; all underlying transitives were surface intransitives.[8] As case marking was based on surface grammatical relations, all subjects, being subjects of surface intransitives, were assigned the nominative (i.e., absolutive) case. Since direct objects of transitives were made surface indirect objects, they bore the indirect object case, dative, as did indirect objects of initial intransitives. In clauses having an initial subject, direct object, and indirect object, the last of these was retired as a result of the application of Object Demotion. It was marked, as were other retired indirect objects, with the dative case (see Chap. 11). Thus, the single rule of Object Demotion, together with general principles established elsewhere (Harris 1981b and references cited there), accounts for the origin of the Series I case marking pattern attested in Svan, Mingrelian, and Georgian and reconstructible for Late CK.

In CK there existed a rule of ablaut which, for a number of verbs, distinguished transitive from intransitive by means of a contrast between *i*-grade and *e*-grade (Gamkrelidze and Machavariani 1965, 1982). When Series I was introduced, the forms in it, being exclusively intransitive in surface structure, were all in *e*-grade. This accounts for the previously unexplained fact that *i*-grade was limited to Series II, while *e*-grade and the Ø-grade later derived from it, occur both in Series I and in Series II (see Chap. 8).

In Old Georgian there was a rule *En*-Agreement, which was limited to Series II for the most part. When the distribution of this morpheme is studied in a large number of constructions, we find that in Series II it is, with some exceptions, triggered by plural direct objects that are final subjects or direct objects. If the rule applied in the same way in Series I, where the application of Object Demotion leaves no final direct objects, its occurrence would be limited to those inactive intransitive verb forms that have a plural final subject. In fact, we find relics of the occurrence of this morpheme in plural forms of inactive intransitives in Series I in Georgian, Laz, and Mingrelian (see Chap. 10). We may assume that when the syntax of Series I was reanalyzed, the original distribution of *-en* was no longer synchronically motivated in Series I and it became nonproductive in that series and later in Series II as well.

Finally, it is shown in §12.1 that the third person indirect object marker, *x*/*h*/*s*/Ø, is triggered by indirect objects in both series and also by final direct objects in Series I only. This is further evidence that direct objects of transitive verbs were, at an earlier stage, surface indirect objects in Series I.

I have proposed that a once-productive syntactic rule, Object Demotion, created surface structures that were later reinterpreted. Positing a rule of this kind enables us to account in a unified way for all of the features that distinguish Series I as a whole from Series II, as first discussed in Chapter 7:

(13) a. Aspect
b. Case marking system
c. Series markers
d. Ablaut grade
e. *-en*/*n* plural marker
f. *x*/*h*/*s*/Ø object marker

A different way of viewing the diachronic analysis is in terms of individual facts to be accounted for. Looking at the problem in this way, we can summarize the arguments in favor of Object Demotion as (14).

(14) In Series I:
  a. The direct object has the indirect object case.
  b. The subject has the case of intransitive subjects.
  c. The indirect object has one of the cases of retired indirect objects.
  d. The direct object of a transitive clause triggers indirect object agreement.
  e. The direct object of a transitive clause does not trigger direct object plural agreement (*-en/n*).
  f. All verbs have one of the ablaut grades that characterize intransitives.

In (14), 'the indirect object case' and other general characterizations refer to the situation in Series II and throughout the language in CK.

Note that because of the complexity of the facts listed under (14), it is not enough to say that the change in CK consisted of the direct object being case-marked as an indirect object. In order to account for all of the facts listed here, we must say that the initial direct object *becomes* the (grammatical) indirect object; it does not merely acquire one property of indirect objects. These facts thus support the hypothesis that Object Demotion was once productive in Series I.

Either way of viewing the facts, (13) or (14), establishes that Object Demotion must have applied in CK. A construction of this kind is attested in a variety of other languages, many of them, like CK, having ergative case marking (Abdullaev 1971:132–133; Anderson 1976:21–22; Chung 1978:54, 56; Dixon 1972, 1977a; Jacobsen 1969; Klokeid 1976, 1978; Reed, Miyaoka, and Jacobson 1977:184, 230–231; Woodbury 1977:323). The Object Demotion analysis arises in a natural way out of the case marking system reconstructed for CK in Chapter 6—an ergative system. At the same time, the Object Demotion Hypothesis provides a basis for explaining the later reanalyses made by the various daughter languages (see Chap. 5; discussed in greater detail in Chap. 15).

NOTES

[1]*Xanmeṭi* means 'more *x*'s', and *haemeṭi*, 'more *h*'s'. The names reflect the fact that these texts, older than the *sannarevi*, were discovered later, and had, from

the point of view of *sannarevi*, more *x*'s or *h*'s. *Sannarevi* means 'with *s*'s mixed in'.

[2]Briefly, in *sannarevi* texts $h \rightarrow \emptyset$ / ___ V and $h \rightarrow s$ before alveolar and post-alveolar stops and affricates. (For additional variants, see Shanidze 1956c:§27–32.) Though *h* is the basic underlying form in *sannarevi* texts, relative dates of manuscripts and comparative evidence suggest that *x* was original.

[3]The unexplained problems include the following: (a) *x*/*h*/*s* for a direct object in Series I is usual with a preverb and not with forms lacking a preverb (Imnaishvili 1971:163–205). (b) A morpheme of the same form and phonological distribution marks second person subjects in Old Georgian, while in Svan *x*- marks the second person subject and is part of the first person subject marker (*xw*-) (Topuria 1931). (c) In *xanmeṭi* and *haemeṭi* texts the third person indirect object marker occurs with nearly all mediopassives.

[4]Gamkrelidze (1979:47) suggests that originally the prefix *x*/*h*/*s*/∅ marked direct objects as well as indirect. His argument, based on the fact that in *xanmeṭi* texts *x* almost invariably occurs with *i*-intransitives, is a compelling one. If this is correct, we must nevertheless assume that at a later stage this morpheme was restricted to indirect objects, including those surface indirect objects in Series I that are underlying direct objects. That is, while the original distribution of *x*- may have included all direct objects, it is clear that later it had a different distribution, triggered only by surface indirect objects.

[5]Chikobava 1950:054 suggests that in Georgian the verbs originally agreed with the direct objects of transitives and with the subjects of intransitives, not with the subjects of transitives. This proposal is based on the rules that determine the co-occurrence of agreement markers in Old Georgian, which favor the object marker at the expense of the subject. If this suggestion is correct, this type of agreement must have disappeared very early, as no more direct evidence of it is attested in Kartvelian.

[6]Other examples of retired terms triggering agreement are discussed in Lawler (1977) and Allen and Frantz (1978).

[7]This is not meant to be a complete study of agreement in Old Georgian, as it is limited to the few aspects of this process that are relevant to the creation of Series I. For a complete discussion of agreement in Kartvelian, see Oniani (1978).

[8]A few initial transitives were made intransitive by Inversion, a rule that applied to some clauses in all series. This construction is discussed in Chapter 13.

IV

Other Changes Related to Case Marking

13

Inversion and the Origins of Series III and IV

In each of the Kartvelian languages there is a construction traditionally known as 'inversion', it is illustrated by (1) from Old Georgian.[1]

(1) *da dγesasçaul-ni tkuenni sʒulan sul-sa*
and holiday-PL/NOM your it/hate/them/INV/I sour-DAT
čemsa
my
'And my soul hates your holidays.' (Isaiah 1:14 O)

Georgian grammarians describe this construction as one in which the logical subject is a grammatical object and the logical direct object is a grammatical subject (e.g., Chikobava 1968a).

One purpose of this chapter is to show that, from the point of view of case marking, the construction illustrated in (1) is just a special instance of an inactive intransitive and requires no special case marking rules or pattern. The remainder of the chapter is an investigation into various aspects of the history of Series III, which triggers Inversion for subjects of Class 1 and 3 verbs. In §13.2 I develop in broad outline a hypothesis of the origin of Series III. Section 13.3 deals with the place of Series III in the verb system in terms of both pragmatics and morphology. In §13.4 I discuss the variegated history of Number Agreement in the inversion construction. Section 13.5 addresses the question of whether Series III has undergone or is undergoing reinterpretation, while §13.6 discusses the relative chronology of the origin of Series III and other changes, as well as the alignment of the Inversion rule.

Although Inversion and Series III are tied closely together, it is important to maintain the distinction between the two. Series III forms of Class 1 and 3 verbs govern Inversion; Series III forms of Class 2 verbs do not. While the inversion construction occurs obligatorily in Series III forms of Class 1 and 3 verbs, it may also occur in other series, as discussed below. Thus, inversion is not limited to Series III, and not all Series III forms are characterized by inversion.

The inversion construction is used in a variety of different situations, varying to some extent from language to language: (a) In each Kartvelian language at least some affective verbs govern Inversion, as in (1). For some verbs Inversion appears to be obligatory, for a few optional. (b) In each language, Series III (in Laz, Old Series III) forms of Class 1 and 3 verbs govern Inversion. (c) In at least some Kartvelian languages, the unintentionality of actions may be marked by using inversion, in contrast to using the direct construction, which is unmarked in this respect. Examples are (9b) and (10). (d) In Laz and Mingrelian, root potentials govern Inversion; examples are (6b) and (8b). (e) Inversion is also used in some other contexts, which are not discussed here, such as the desiderative in Modern Georgian (Harris 1981b:242).

13.1. THE SYNTAX OF THE INVERSION CONSTRUCTION

In this section I present an analysis of the syntax of inversion from a synchronic point of view. This will be the basis for the discussion of diachronic problems treated in subsequent sections. In addition, this section will show that inversion in Series I and II is a subtype of inactive intransitives, in support of the claim made in Chapter 3 to the effect that this construction requires no special treatment with respect to case marking.

The rule of Inversion makes an initial subject the surface indirect object. In (1) and the examples discussed in this section, the initial subject is semantically an experiencer. If there is an initial direct object, it is a final subject in the inversion construction. The grammatical relations are schematized in Table 13.1, using (1) as an example.

In §13.1.1, arguments in support of the initial grammatical relations of Table 13.1 are adduced; in §13.1.2, evidence in support of the final relations is presented. Some of the arguments are made for all four languages. Others are not relevant to all, such as *En*-Agreement, which is found productively only in Old Georgian. For others, certain data are not available. Each argument is discussed only very briefly for it seems unnecessary

Table 13.1

Grammatical Relations in Inversion

	suli čemi 'my soul (DAT)'	*dγesascaulni tkuenni* 'your holidays (NOM)'
Initial	Subject	Direct object
Final	Indirect object	Subject

to present in detail arguments that have been previously made available (Harris 1981b: Chap. 8).

13.1.1. Evidence for Initial Grammatical Relations

The data introduced below show a variety of reasons for analyzing the dative-nominal as the initial subject, and the nominative-nominal, if there is one, as the initial direct object.

13.1.1.1. Relation to Noninverted Constructions

First, the inversion construction, where the experiencer of a particular verb is in the dative, alternates with the direct (unmarked) construction, where the same nominal is in the case appropriate to a final subject. In the Old Georgian examples below, the parallel constructions are used in different manuscripts of a single text.

(2) Old Georgian
a. *hq̣uarobdit mṭerta tkuenta*
you/love/him/I enemy/PL/DAT your (Mt 5:44Ad)

b. *giq̣uarded mṭerni tkuenni*
you/love/them/INV/I enemy/PL/NOM your
'Love your enemies.' (Mt 5:44AB)

With this particular verb, Laz continues the direct construction, and Mingrelian continues inversion.

(3) Laz
nugzari-k q̣orops manana-s [2]
Nugzar-NAR he/love/her/I Manana-DAT
'Nugzar loves Manana.'

(4) Mingrelian
nugzar-s uˀors manana
Nugzar-DAT he/love/her/INV/I Manana/NOM
'Nugzar loves Manana.'

The root 'love' in Georgian, *qvar-*, is cognate to Laz *q̣or-* and to Mingrelian *ʔor-*, with regular correspondences. Although Laz lacks inversion with *q̣or-*, it has the construction with some predicates, as illustrated in (5) in the Maxo dialect.

(5) Laz
čarči-s sum neḳna uγuṭu
bazaar-DAT three door/NOM it/has/it/INV/I
'The bazaar had three doors.' (Chikobava 1936, II:53, 4–5)

In Laz and Mingrelian, there is a potential form of the verb, and the root potential (see Appendix to Chap. 3) governs Inversion. Example (6b) illustrates inversion with the root potential, contrasting with the direct construction, (6a). Georgian lacks the potential as a productive category, but for this lexical item, maintains the same contrast between inversion and direct constructions, (7).

(6) a. Mingrelian
iprčkilek musiḳa-s
I/hear/it/I music-DAT
'I am listening to music.'
b. *marčkile musiḳa*
I/hear/it/INV/I music/NOM
'I (can) hear music.'

(7) Georgian
a. *vismen musiḳa-s*
I/hear/it/I music-DAT
'I am listening to music.'
b. *mesmis musiḳa*
I/hear/it/INV/I music/NOM
'I hear music.'

Example (8b) and the second clause of (8c) are Laz examples of the root potential form.

(8) Laz
a. *oxorǯa-k sankis kodiǯeru*
wife-NAR as tho she/believe/it/II
'The wife behaved as though she believed it.'
(Chikobava 1929a:38, 37)

b. *gurami-s var aǯeren skani ambai*
Guram-DAT NEG he/believe/it/INV/I your news/NOM
'Guram cannot believe your news.'

c. *cxeni-k-na* *turums . . . xoǰi-s* *va* *atoren-ki*
horse-NAR-CONJ he/draw/I ox-DAT NEG he/draw/INV/I
'A horse draws, but an ox cannot draw.'
(Chikobava 1936, II:4, 29)

Although these examples might suggest otherwise, the noninverted construction can also be used with negation (e.g., *mušeni va iǰer?* 'why don't you believe it?' Chikobava 1929a:12, 30), and the potential may be used in the affirmative. In Modern Georgian there exists an alternation comparable to that in (8a, b), but without the potential category: *viǰereb* 'I believe it' without inversion, *mǰera* 'I believe it' with inversion.

Inversion may express unintentional action, as in (9b) and (10).

(9) Svan
a. *bepšw-d* *čuadkarwe* *xäm*
child-NAR he/lose/it/II pig/NOM

b. *bepšw-s* *čuätkarwän* *xäm*
child-DAT he/lose/it/INV/II
'The child lost a pig.'

(10) Mingrelian
čkimi osuriskua-s *oskveburi* *komoǰ-kə*
my daughter-DAT appropriate husband-NAR
kaašu
she/acquire/him/INV/II
'My daughter got an appropriate husband.'
(Kipshidze 1914:64, 16)

If in each language the inversion construction is related to the direct (a) examples by a systematic rule or set of correspondences, we can account for the fact that each of the pairs above has similar selection restrictions; for example, the Laz verb in (8c) requires that its initial subject be animate. Similarly, a rule of Inversion will account for the systematic relationship of the inventories of initial terms; both verb forms in (9) require two arguments. Finally, without a rule of Inversion, the rules that relate syntactic structures to semantic representations would have to be complicated to account, for example, for the fact that in (6a) it is the nominative-nominal that hears, in (6b) the dative-nominal.

13.1.1.2. Reflexivization

Reflexivization has been studied in Modern Georgian, and it has been shown that nonsubjects do not condition occurrence of the full pronoun, *tav-* (Harris 1981b: 23–27, 205–210, and *passim*). While this cannot be tested in Old Georgian, observation of its use in texts and perusal of collected examples of reflexives (e.g., Martirosovi 1964:105–108) suggest that in simple constructions it is only subjects that can be *tav-* triggers.[3] It is reasonable to assume that the rule is approximately the same in Old as in Modern Georgian. Example (11) shows that in Old Georgian subjects trigger *Tav*-Reflexivization.

(11) *nuvin* *tav-sa* *tvissa* *actunebn*
no.one/NOM self-DAT self's he/deceive/him/I
'Let no one deceive himself.' (1 Cor 3:18)

Example (12) shows that the dative-nominal is a trigger of *Tav*-Reflexivization in inversion.

(12) *uḳuetu visme* *brʒen egonos* *tavi* *tvisi*
if someone/DAT wise he/seem/him/INV/II self/NOM self's
'if someone believes himself wise' (1 Cor 3:18AB)

Only on an analysis where the dative-nominal, *visme* 'someone', in (12), is a subject at some level of derivation, can (12) be reconciled with the general constraint that triggers of *Tav*-Reflexivization must be subjects.

Svan appears to share this constraint on Reflexivization in approximately the same form. In Series I and II, subjects may trigger the reflexive pronoun, *txwim*, as shown in (13a) and (13b).

(13) a. *č̣q̇inṭ* *miča txwim-s* *apšwdi* [4]
boy/NOM his self-DAT he/praise/him/I
'The boy praises himself.'
b. *č̣q̇inṭ-d* *miča txwim* *apäšwd*
boy-NAR his self/NOM he/praise/him/II
'The boy praised himself.'

In inversion constructions, the nominative-nominal was not accepted as a trigger of Reflexivization, as shown in (14a).

(14) a. **miča txwim-s* *č̣q̇inṭ* *xopšdwa*
his self-DAT boy/NOM he/praise/him/INV/III
('The boy has praised himself.')
b. *č̣q̇ inṭ-s* *miča txwim* *xopšdwa*
boy-DAT his self/NOM
'The boy has praised himself.'

Examples (14b) and (15)–(17) show that in inversion, the dative-nominal does trigger Reflexivization.

(15) *çqinṭ-s xaläṭ miča txwim*
boy-DAT he/love/him/INV/I his self/NOM
'The boy loves himself.'

(16) *txwim xam mašen eser xaläṭ*
self/NOM pig/DAT QUOT he/love/him/INV/I
' "A pig loves himself most of all," they say.'
(Davitiani 1973:42, 9)

(17) *dīna-s eser txwim čubow xočwmina*
girl-DAT QUOT self/NOM down she/pull/her/INV/III
' "The girl apparently pulled herself down from the tree," she said.' (Shanidze and Topuria 1939:373, 13–14)

Laz and Mingrelian seem to lack Reflexivization, at least with a reflexive pronoun, though there are attested sporadic occurrences that seem to be a calque on the Georgian *tav-*, from 'head' (Martirosovi 1964:108–109). Although a complete investigation of Reflexivization cannot be conducted for Old Georgian and has not been for Svan, on the basis of the similarity of the languages, we are justified in assuming that the constraints established on the basis of Modern Georgian existed in a similar, if perhaps not identical, form in the languages exemplified. It follows that the dative-nominal of the inversion construction must be a subject at some level of derivation.

13.1.1.3. *EN*-AGREEMENT

A third argument for the initial relations claimed in Table 13.1 is based on the rule of *En*-Agreement, described in Chapter 10. It is shown there that this plural agreement marker is triggered by final direct objects and by nominals that are initial direct objects and final subjects, drawing examples from five different constructions of the latter type. Further, it is shown that a nominal that is a subject at all levels of derivation cannot trigger *-en*. The plural nominals in the inversion examples of (18) in Chapter 10 and in (18) below trigger the *-en/n* plural direct object marker (here *-an*; see §10.2.2); a further example is (42) below.

(18) *upalo, mrçm**anan** me **siṭqua-ni šenni***
Lord/VOC I/believe/it/INV/I I/DAT word-PL/NOM your
'Lord, I believe your words.' (Abuladze 1955:75, 29)

If the nominative-nominals in inversion are analyzed as initial direct objects, the occurrence of the *-en/n* marker is predicted by the general rule discussed in Chapter 10. If, on the other hand, these nominals were analyzed as subjects at all levels of derivation, the grammar would require a rule to the effect that in inversion, subjects trigger *En*-Agreement AND DIRECT OBJECTS DO NOT, while in other constructions it is just direct objects that control this rule.

13.1.2. Evidence for Final Grammatical Relations

In this section I adduce three arguments for analyzing the dative-nominal as final subject.

13.1.2.1. PERSON AGREEMENT

As pointed out in Chapter 3, Person Agreement is relatively consistent throughout each language and across the Kartvelian languages. Since each language may have agreement with subjects, direct objects, and indirect objects, this rule provides important evidence concerning grammatical relations when considered together with other phenomena. Agreement markers are given in tabular form in Table 13.2 for reference in connection with the discussion that follows. Examples that illustrate their use can be found in the handbooks and elsewhere in this book.

Table 13.2

Productive Singular Agreement Markers in Kartvelian

	Old Georgian	Svan[a]	Laz	Mingrelian
Subject				
1	*v*—	*xw*—	*v/b/p/ṗ*—(*r*)	*v/b/p/ṗ*—(*k*)
2	*x/h/s/∅*—	*x/∅*—	—(*r*)	—(*k*)
3	—*s,a/o,n*	—*s,e,a,∅*	—*s,u,n*	—*s,u,n*
Direct object				
1	*m*—	*m*—	*m/b/p/ṗ*—	*m/b/p/ṗ*—
2	*g*—	*ǰ*—	*g/k̇*—	*g/r*—
3	∅	∅	∅	∅
Indirect object				
1	*m*—	*m*—	*m/b/p/ṗ*—	*m/b/p/ṗ*—
2	*g*—	*ǰ*—	*g/k̇*—	*g/r*—
3	*x/h/s/∅*—	*x/∅*—	∅	∅

[a]Third person prefix with the forms *l*-, *n*-, and *y*- may be productive in some dialects of Svan (see Kaldani 1979; Oniani 1978:93–94). The Svan suffix *-e*, while it originated as a screeve marker **i* plus the third person singular subject marker *-a* (Kaldani 1978), has been extended to all plural subject persons and is therefore not truly a third person singular subject marker. The same may be said of *-a*.

In each Kartvelian language, the affixes labeled 'subject markers' are conditioned by every final (grammatical) subject, regardless of construction. Similarly, the indirect object and direct object markers are conditioned by all final objects, as indicated. A dash represents the position of the verb stem. Slashes separate phonological variants (see Chikobava 1936:87–89, 97), while commas separate variants that are determined by verb type and/or by screeve. The suffixes placed in parentheses occur with certain verb types in certain screeves and are discussed in detail in Chapter 15; in screeves in which they do not occur, the second person subject marker in Laz and Mingrelian is Ø. In Svan and Old Georgian direct object and indirect object marking are distinct for the third person; this is discussed in detail in Chapter 12. In Georgian, Laz, and Mingrelian, *x* + *i* is realized as *u*, but *x* never shows up as such in Zan. In some forms of Georgian, *x*/*h*/*s* deletes before vowels, while in Svan the corresponding *x* deletes before consonants. Table 13.2 is limited to singular markers; plurals are marked in part by agglutinative morphology and in part by inflectional. The table gives only the most frequent variants and is intended only as an aid to the interpretation of examples.

The examples below show that in the inversion construction the dative-nominal is not only the initial subject, but also the final indirect object, as specified in Table 13.1. While this nominal has the properties of initial subjects described in §13.1.1, it conditions indirect object agreement. Examples with first person singular dative-nominals have been selected because they condition a non-null marker, which is the same in all four languages. The dative-nominal itself, however, is dropped when it is unemphatic; it is, therefore, absent from some of the examples.

(19) Old Georgian
da me, iovane, romel-sa m-esmoda da
and I John which-DAT 1/IND/OBJ-hear/it/INV/I and
v-xedevdi amas qovelsa
1/SUBJ-see/it/I this/DAT all
'and I, John, who heard and saw all this' (Rev 22:8)

The first person object (*m*-) and subject (*v*-) markers are separated from the rest of the verb form and are separately glossed in this section. Example (19) includes a verb that governs the inversion construction, *mesmoda*, and one that does not, *vxedevdi*. Though the two verbs have the same initial subject—*me* 'I'—and they are conjoined, the initial subject in the inversion form is marked with the object marker *m*-, and the initial subject in the direct form is marked with the subject marker *v*-. (The case of the initial direct object *amas qovelsa* 'all this' is determined by its relation to the verb closest to it.)

The same contrast between *v-* and *m-* can be seen also in the Mingrelian examples in (6) above. The (a) example illustrates the direct construction, where the agreement marker *v-* undergoes metathesis with *-i-* and assimilation: *i-p-rčkile-k* from **v-i-rčkile-k* (see Chikobava 1936:96 on this process in Laz). Inversion is illustrated by (6b), where *m-* indicates first person singular indirect object: *m-a-rčkile.*

We can see the same first person object marker in the Laz example,

(20) *ar eššeγi m-iq̇oun*
one donkey/NOM 1/OBJ-have/it/INV/I
'I have one donkey.' (Asatiani 1974:**1**[12])

In each of the examples discussed above, we see that the experiencer conditions object, not subject, agreement in the inversion construction.

The Svan examples below have first person plurals, distinguishing inclusive from exclusive. The basic forms of subject markers are inclusive *l—d*, exclusive *xw—d*; of the object markers, inclusive *gw—*, exclusive *n—*. Example (21a) illustrates the direct construction, where the experiencer is final subject and triggers *l—d*; (21b) illustrates inversion, where the same nominal is final indirect object and conditions the marker *gw—*.

(21) a. *ç̣ərni zisx-ild-s ečaw l-eç̣äd* (< **l-eç̣äd-d*)[5]
red blood-DIM-DAT there 1/INCL/SUBJ-see/it/II
'We saw red blood there.' (Gabliani 1925:198, 27)

b. *xexw i gezal dēsa gw-iç̣wa*
wife/NOM and child/NOM NEG 1/INCL/OBJ-see/it/INV/III
'We have not seen (our) wives and children.'
(Gabliani 1925:198,4)

Thus, the initial subject conditions indirect object markers in inversion in all four languages.

In Table 13.1 it is proposed that the initial direct object is the final subject in inversion; the sentences below show that this nominal has one property of final subjects: conditioning subject agreement. In the Old Georgian example, (22), the third person nominal triggers the subject marker *-s*.

(22) *ra-y g-ineb-s*
what-NOM 2IO-want/INV-3S
'What do you want?' (Imnaishvili 1970a:137, 19)

The Svan example, (23), illustrates the use of the first person singular subject marker agreeing with the final subject (= initial direct object).

(23) *dede-s mišgwa mam xw-alṭäna*
mother-DAT me-GEN NEG 1/SUBJ-she/love/INV/III
'My mother apparently does not love me.' (Gagua 1976:160)

The Mingrelian example, (24), shows the second person final subject marker *-k*.

(24) *uˀor-k*
he/love/INV/I-2/SUBJ
'He loves you.'

In Laz, we see the second person final subject marker, *-r*:

(25) *var miʒiru-r*
NEG I/see/INV/III-2/SUBJ
'[How long it is that] I have not seen you.'
(Dumézil 1937:122, 3)

In the Inversion construction, the initial subject (= final indirect object) always triggers indirect object person agreement, the initial direct object (= final subject) conditions subject person. Of course, in some examples the markers are obscured by morphophonological processes, by syntactic processes, or by the occurrence of Ø. Number agreement is differently determined and is treated in §13.4.

13.1.2.2. Class 2 Verb Morphology

Inversion forms constitute a proper subset of Class 2 verbs. In this subsection it is shown that inversion forms have the properties that were used to define Class 2 in Chapter 3. In addition, they show certain characteristics, not discussed here, which distinguish them from other Class 2 verbs and which could be used to justify a fourth class, which then would share many properties with Class 2.[6] In the discussion below, it should be borne in mind that affective verbs that condition Inversion are morphologically irregular. The statements made below apply to only some of them; the generalizations are based rather on other, more regular, types of inversion.

In Chapter 3 it was observed that in Svan the following characteristics of Class 2 verbs distinguish them from verbs of Class 1 and 3:

(26) a. They do not have derivational *-al* etc.
b. They lack *-e* in third person singular of aorist.
c. They have *-än* etc., in aorist forms, or *-en* in the present.[7]

The examples cited above in this chapter show that all of these features also characterize inversion forms. For example, *čuätkarwän* 'he lost it' in (9b) illustrates the use of the formant *-än*; this suffix does not show up in the noninversion form, (9a), *čuadkarwe* 'he lost it'. Similarly, the inversion form lacks the *-e* third person singular agreement marker of the aorist, which, however, is found in the noninverted form. The form in (9b) (as well as its (a) counterpart) likewise lacks the suffix *-al* that characterizes Class 3 verbs, as illustrated in examples (5) and (13)–(15) of Chapter 3. In Svan, then, verb forms in the inversion construction have all of the defining properties of Class 2 verbs and none of those of Class 1 and 3 verbs.

In Laz, Class 2 is differentiated from Classes 1 and 3 by the fact that the former has present tense stems ending in a vowel, while the latter have present tense stems ending in a consonant. The final segment of the present stem, in turn, conditions three other properties. For Class 1 and 3 verb stems, which end in a consonant, the third person singular subject marker in the present tense is *-s*, the third person plural in the same screeve is *-an*, and the first and second persons singular have Ø suffixes. On the other hand, for Class 2 verbs, with present stems ending in a vowel, the corresponding suffixes are *-n*, *-nan*, and *-r*.

Inversion forms in Laz share these properties with other Class 2 verbs, supporting their inclusion in that class. In (8c) we see corresponding inversion (*ator-e-n* 'it can draw') and noninversion (*tur-um-s* 'it draws') forms of a single verb root. In the former, the present stem is *a-tor-e*; that is, it is vowel-final. The corresponding noninversion form, on the other hand has the present stem *tur-um*.

Mingrelian is similar to Laz in these respects. In addition, Class 2 verbs in Mingrelian, and to a lesser extent in Laz, use a series marker *-u* (< **um*) (see Chap. 9, note 2, and Danelia 1976). We find, for example, Mingrelian *ič̣ḳiru-**u**-(n)* 'it is cut', *očkar-**u**-(n)* 'he is in a hurry' (Danelia 1976:165), *γur-**u**-(n)* 'he dies'. The same formant is used in Series III forms of Class 1 and 3 verbs; for example, *duˀvil-**u**-(n)* 'he has killed it', *m(e)učam-**u**-(n)* 'he has given it', *ungar-**u**-(n)* 'he has cried.'

In Old Georgian, most Class 2 verbs differ from those of Classes 1 and 3 in having present stems formed either with a series marker plus *-i* or with the suffix *-ie*. In addition, most Class 2 verbs have *En*-Agreement with plural final subjects. Some, but not all, inversion verbs have present stems formed with the suffix *-ie,* for example, *gipq̇ries* 'you have, hold it' (Imnaishvili 1970a: 135, 27). It is shown in §13.1.1.3 that plural final subjects condition *En*-Agreement in inversion forms.

Thus, in Svan, Laz, Mingrelian, and Georgian, there are clear morphological reasons for including inversion forms as a subtype of Class 2.

13.1.2.3. Case Marking

In this section it is shown that in each series, for each language, the initial subject of inversion is case marked as a final indirect object, while the initial direct object of the construction bears the subject case. This varies by language, as the case assignment rules vary. At the same time it is established that, with respect to case patterns governed, inversion forms are like other Class 2 forms and that there is no need to make special mention of inversion in any case assignment rules.

Old Georgian and Svan. In Old Georgian in Series I, all final subjects are in the nominative and all final indirect objects in the dative (see Chap. 3). This generalization applies to (1), as summarized in Table 13.1. The final subject is *dγesasçaulni tkuenni* 'your holidays', which is in the nominative. The final indirect object is *sulsa čemsa* 'my soul', in the dative.[8]

In Series II, final indirect objects are likewise marked with the dative; final subjects of Class 2 verbs bear the nominative case. Both are illustrated in the Series II example, (12). The nominal *visme* 'someone' is dative, as the final indirect object; while *tavi tvisi* 'himself' is nominative, as the final subject of an inactive intransitive (Class 2) verb form.

Svan has the same general case marking patterns in Series I and II as Georgian; in both series, the subjects of Class 2 verbs are in the nominative, while final indirect objects are in the dative. The general case marking applies also in inversion, as (27) shows.

(27) a. *lic* *xapənda* *māra*
water/NOM he/thirst/it/INV/I man/DAT
'The man was thirsty for water.' (Topuria 1967:159)

b. *lic* *axpənda* *māra*
water/NOM he/thirst/it/INV/II man/DAT
'The man became thirsty for water.' (Topuria 1967:159)

Case marking in both languages supports the analysis proposed in Table 13.1, namely the final subjecthood of the initial direct object and the final indirect-objecthood of the initial subject.

Laz. Case marking in Laz is consistent over Series I and II. In both, final indirect objects are marked with the dative, and final subjects of Class 2 verbs with the nominative. These are illustrated in (5), (8b), (8c), (20), and (28).

(28) *tinatini-s* *var* *unon* *γvini*
Tinatin-DAT NEG she/want/it/INV/I whiskey/NOM
'Tinatin doesn't want whiskey.'

In (28), for example, *γvini* 'whiskey' is case marked as the final subject of a Class 2 verb always is; *tinatinis* is in the dative, as are other final indirect objects.

MINGRELIAN. In Series I, Mingrelian uses the nominative for all final subjects and the dative for all final objects. Both relations are illustrated in (4), (6b), (29) and (30).

(29) *guram-s vaǰers skani ambe*
Guram-DAT NEG/he/believe/it/INV/I your news/NOM
'Guram can't believe your news.'

(30) *tinatin-s γvin(i) vaḳo*
Tinatin-DAT whiskey/NOM NEG/she/want/it/INV/I
'Tinatin doesn't want whiskey.'

In this respect, then, Mingrelian is like its sister languages. At first glance, however, it would appear to differ from its sisters in Series II because final subjects in inversion are marked with a different case. For other verb forms, all final subjects in Series II govern the narrative (*-k*) case; examples of this can be found in Chapter 3. In the inversion construction, too, the final subject (= initial direct object) is marked with the narrative case, as the examples below show.

(31) *mara čxom-k vaač̣ʔopu*
but fish-NAR NEG/he/catch/it/INV/II
'But he could not catch a fish.' (Kluge 1916:79, 3)

(32) *osur-s meç̣onu te boši-k*
woman-DAT she/like/him/INV/II this boy-NAR
'The woman liked this boy.' (Xubua 1937: 1, 6)

(33) *cira-sə keeʔoropu ǰimušier-kə*
maiden-DAT she/love/him/INV/II Jimsher-NAR
'The maiden fell in love with Jimsher.' (Kipshidze 1914: 75, 25)

Examples (32) and (33) are quoted by Uridia (1960:167), who also provides parallel examples from both series:

(34) a. *is kaγard-i va daguredəni*
he/DAT reading. writing-NOM NEG he/learn/it/INV/I
'[that] he could not learn reading and writing'
(Kipshidze 1914:7,23)

b. *is kaγardi-k va dagurin*
he/DAT reading. writing-NAR NEG he/learn/it/INV/II
'He could not learn reading and writing.' (Uridia 1960:168)

Both examples in (34) have inversion; and in both the final subject (*ka-γardi-* 'reading and writing') is marked like other final subjects in its series, and the final indirect object (*is* 'he/DAT') is marked like other final indirect objects. Thus, inversion in Series I and II is the same as the inversion construction in Series I and II of the other Kartvelian languages. The actual cases used to mark the nominals in this construction in Series II differ, but only because general case marking in Series II of Mingrelian differs. This fact confirms both the analysis of inversion proposed above and the general statement of case marking in Mingrelian made in Chapter 3.

13.1.3. Conclusion and Reconstruction

On the basis of the facts presented above, we must conclude that in inversion the dative-nominal is the underlying subject and surface indirect object, while the nominative-nominal is the underlying direct object and final subject. The initial grammatical relations are supported by the necessity of relating the surface subject of noninverted constructions to the dative-nominal of inversion (§13.1.1.1) and by data concerning Reflexivization (§13.1.1.2) and *En*-Agreement (§13.1.1.3). The final grammatical relations are supported by the facts of Person Agreement (§13.1.2.1), by the verbal morphology that indicates class membership (§13.1.2.2), and by case assignment (§13.1.2.3).

Additional support for the proposed initial grammatical relations comes from the facts of number agreement in some of the dialects (see §13.4.2, 13.4.3, 13.4.4), while other aspects of number agreement confirm the final relations stated in Table 13.1 (see §13.4.1, 13.4.3, 13.4.5, 13.4.6).

I conclude further that inversion forms are to be included as a subtype of Class 2, with no change in the case rules stated for each language in Chapter 3.

As a construction, inversion is shared by all of the Kartvelian languages, though the environments in which it applies are not identical. Inversion applies with at least some of the affective verbs in each language, and we can identify some cognates that trigger it. For example, CK **sm-* 'hear' governs inversion in each branch of Kartvelian, as shown by the examples below.

(35) Svan
ali *segz-s* *ka xesmi*
this/NOM Segz-DAT PV he/hear/it/INV/I
'Segz hears this.' (Davitiani, Topuria, and Kaldani 1957:10, 37)

(36) Mingrelian
ragadi *masime(n)*
talk/NOM I/hear/it/INV/I
'I hear (the) talk(ing).' (Chikobava 1938:314)

Laz has apparently lost this construction with this verb (Chikobava 1938:314). Georgian has *mesmis* 'I hear it'. In many instances, however, inversion verbs in the various languages appear not to be related to forms in the sister languages. In other instances, inversion has apparently been lost with an inherited verb; Laz seems to have lost inversion with many affective verbs, such as **sm* 'hear' and CGZ **q̇war* 'love'.

Sherozia (1980) has argued that the potential construction, which involves inversion in the types illustrated in (6b), (8b), (8c), (31), and (34), also goes back to CK. On the basis of the facts presented above, we can conclude that inversion existed in Common Kartvelian and that it occurred at least with some affective verbs and possibly in other environments as well. As a syntactic construction, inversion must be reconstructed to CK.

13.2. THE ORIGIN OF SERIES III

Intersecting the categories of tense, mood, and aspect is a fourth opposition, which Aronson (1977:13) has referred to as 'status'. In Kartvelian the status of a verb is evidential (unseen) or nonevidential (seen); the evidential or unseen is the marked member of the opposition.

Series III is a set of screeves that express the evidential. In the present work, the traditional name 'evidential' is used for this status of the verb as a whole, while 'first evidential' and 'second evidential' are the names of particular screeves. Among the functions of Series III are the following:[9]

1. The various screeves express the perfect, pluperfect, future perfect, and so on. There is also a periphrastic perfect and a periphrastic pluperfect in some of the languages, consisting of past participle and the auxiliary 'have'; for example, Georgian *nanaxi makvs* 'I have seen it' and *nanaxi mkonda* 'I had seen it'.
2. Series III forms provide an unmarked statement of a negation of a past tense action. This contrasts with a negation in the aorist, which marks the intentionality of failure to perform the act.
3. Series III forms may state that an action took place that was not directly witnessed or was not participated in by the speaker; this function is here referred to as the 'unseen' after the Georgian terminology. There are other means of expressing the unseen, which are discussed in §13.3.

For uniformity of translation, the English perfect, pluperfect, and future perfect have been used for most Series III examples cited here; 'apparently' is used to translate the unseen where this is required.

In Series III, Class 1 and 3 verbs govern inversion obligatorily in all four languages; for Laz this statement applies to Old Series III. The examples below illustrate inversion in Series III in Laz with a Class 1 and a Class 3 verb; the corresponding Series I and II forms of these sentences appear as examples (35), (45), and (38) in Chapter 3.

(37) *ḳoči-s* *uq̇vilun* *γeǰi*
man-DAT he/kill/it/INV/III pig/NOM
'The man has killed a pig.'

(38) *bere-s* *umgarinun*
child-DAT he/cry/INV/III
'The child has cried.'

Here the syntactic construction is the same as that involved in the Series I and II examples discussed in §13.1. The initial subjects, here *ḳoči* 'man' and *bere* 'child', are in the dative case; and the initial direct object, *γeǰi* 'pig' in (37), is in the nominative. Similarly, the dative nominals trigger Indirect Object Agreement, realized as *u-* (< **x + i*) in (37) and (38) (see §13.1.2.1), as *m-* in (39), and as *g-* in (40).

(39) *man* *m-i-q̇vilun* *γeǰi*
I/DAT 1/OBJ-CV-kill/it/INV/III pig/NOM
'I have killed a pig.'

(40) *sin* *g-i-q̇vilun* *γeǰi*
you/DAT 2/OBJ-CV-kill/it/INV/III pig/NOM
'You have killed a pig.'

Inversion in Series III is in other respects comparable to inversion discussed above.

Class 2 verbs do not govern inversion in Series III, as illustrated by (42) (see also (42) and (50) of Chap. 3).

(41) *ḳoči* *doγureleren*
man/NOM he/die/III
'Apparently the man (has) died.'

A number of languages neighboring the Kartvelian family have status as a verb category with distinct morphological expression. Friedman (1979:339) names the following in this regard: Macedonian, Bulgarian, Turkish, Albanian, Avar, Tadjik, and Azerbaijani. The category could, therefore, be considered an areal feature. Is Series III then borrowed from one of its neighbor languages? While the development of the evidential may have been influenced by surrounding languages, it is clear that there are internal sources both for the verb morphology and for the clause syntax. The sources of the verb morphology are identified below; it was shown in §13.1.3 that the Kartvelian languages make use of inversion in other series as well and that it is reconstructible to CK.

In the remainder of this section, I discuss in broad outline a theory of the internal development of Series III in CK. Additional details and related problems are discussed in subsequent sections. The part of the hypothesis that is presented in this section owes much to a number of works by Chikobava (especially 1948 and 1962) and to Kavtardze (1956) and Natadze (1955). In the belief that most readers will not be interested in the full variety of morphology in Series III, I have omitted many details; a very complete treatment is provided in Natadze (1955).

13.2.1. Second Evidential and Related Forms of Classes 1 and 3

Inversion is a device for removing the subject or the speaker from the action expressed by the verb in one of the following senses: (a) It may indicate that the action was unintentional. For some lexical items, the unintentionality is grammaticized and inversion is used generally; for example, Modern Georgian *uq̣vars* 'he loves him'. For other lexical items it is optional, the inverted structure being marked for unintentionality; for example, Georgian inverted *mičịravs* 'I have it, I hold it' contrasting with noninverted *vičẹr* 'I catch it'. (b) In Zan inversion marks an event as a root potential, in contrast to an actual occurrence; for example, (8c) *turums* 'it draws, does draw' versus *atorens* 'it can draw'. These expressions mark an event as not actually realized, as involuntary or unintentional on the part of the initial (logical) subject.

One component of the meaning of the evidential is likewise unintentionality or nonvolitionality. This component is present in negatives, such as (21b) and (25), and in some affirmative examples as well. The use of inversion in removing the subject or speaker from the action in a general way is also related to the unseen function of Series III. Because inversion already served as a distancing device in CK (§13.1.3), it was natural that it should occur also in the emerging evidential—Series III.

The morphology of Series III exists independently in other series. We begin by looking at the aorist of so-called relative intransitives (or *e*-intransitives), that is, surface intransitives that have an indirect object. Relative intransitives include inversion constructions and certain other Class 2 verbs. In the aorist, relative intransitives consist formally of an optional preverb (PV), the prefix *e*-, the verb root, and the suffixes that mark the screeve and agreement with subject and direct object (*-n-es* and *-a* below). Example (42) shows an inversion form in the aorist, and (43), another kind of relative intransitive.

(42) *še-e-cqal-n-es* *igini* *iesu-s*
PV-REL-pity/INV-OBJ/PL-SUBJ/PL them/NOM Jesus-DAT
'Jesus pitied them.' (Mt 20:34AB)

(43) *da e-šeyn-a* *kalak-sa mas*
and REL-settle-3/SUBJ/SG city-DAT DET
'And he settled in the city.' (Mt 2:23AdA)

This morphology, together with the inversion construction, came to be associated with the second evidential screeve in forms of Class 1 and 3 verbs. A hypothetical example using Modern Georgian morphemes may make this clearer. A form *e-č̣ir-a* 'he had it, held it, kept it' functioned as the aorist of the inversion example cited above in this section; it contrasted with *i-č̣ir-a* 'he caught it'. The beginnings of Series III most probably lay in using forms like *eč̣ira* more and more in the expression of the pluperfect, the negative past, and the unseen, as 'he had caught it (and hence had it)' or 'apparently he caught it'. This we can identify as the first step towards the development of the second evidential as an independent screeve.

All of the morphology of Series II forms of relative intransitives was taken over to the screeves of Series III, except that relating only to the imperative, since there was no imperative in Series III. Old Georgian presents the most complete inventory of screeves and probably best represents the original morphology. For the time being, one screeve of Series III, the first evidential, is left out of our discussion. The other screeves of Series III can be paired with those of Series II as shown in Table 13.3. In each series, the habitual expresses an action without a specific time reference (see Chikobava 1948:78–80; Machavariani 1974:123). The habitual III is infrequent (see Sarjveladze 1972, citing Shanidze); both habituals

Table 13.3

Partial List of Screeves in Old Georgian

Series II	Series III
Habitual II	Habitual III
Aorist	Second evidential
Subjunctive II	Subjunctive III
Imperative II	

died out in Georgian. (Sarjveladze suggests that the habitual III originated as late as the tenth century A.D.) The aorist is a simple past, and the second evidential is a pluperfect or past.

The major screeve marker of the habitual, *-i*, is used also in the habitual of Series III. Of the aorist screeve markers used in Old Georgian, *-e* has been generalized in the Series III past (the second evidential), though Ø occurs in certain environments. All three screeve markers of the subjunctive II are used also in the subjunctive III and occur under the same conditions. In addition, the third person singular and plural markers of final subjects are transferred from the Series II screeves to the corresponding ones in Series III. That is, in the aorist and second evidential we find singular *-a* and plural *-es* (set B), while in the other screeves we find singular *-s* beside plural *-en/an/n* (set A); these serve as minor screeve markers (see Table 5.2). A partial comparison of the morphology of these screeves is summarized in Table 13.4 (see Table 5.3, which summarizes Series I and II.). The person and number markers of Series I and II were likewise maintained in Series III, the subject markers referring to the surface subjects and the object markers to surface objects, as in other inversion constructions.

Table 13.4

Some Parallels of Screeve Formation in Old Georgian

	Series II		Series III	
	Major marker	Minor marker	Major marker	Minor marker
Present	*i*	A	*i*	A
Past	*e/Ø/i*	B	*e/Ø*	B
Future and subjunctive	*o/e/a*	A	*o/e/a*	A

The morphology in Svan differs from that in Georgian, but preserves the same parallels. In Svan, Series II has two screeves, and Series III three; again we omit the first evidential from the discussion that follows. Table 13.5 compares the morphology of relative intransitives (e.g., 9b) in Series II with that of Class 1 and 3 verbs in Series III. The major markers in Table 13.5 are not screeve markers as such, but are used only with surface intransitives and only in the screeves noted here. The minor markers are the third person singular final subject markers. In Series III, the Georgian markers of Table 13.4 are suffixed to a stem consisting of *e* plus root, while those of Table 13.5 are attached to a stem with the form *i* plus root. Georgian *e* does not regularly correspond to Svan *i*, but to Svan *e*. It is probable that Svan has restructured this prefix on the model of the

Table 13.5

Some Parallels of Screeve Formation in Svan

	Series II		Series III	
	Major marker	Minor marker	Major marker	Minor marker
Past	*-än* (etc.)	∅	*-än* (etc.)	∅
Subjunctive	*-ēn* (etc.)	*-s*	*-ēn* (etc.)	*-s*

first evidential since certain second evidential forms exceptionally retain *e-* rather than *i-* (Topuria 1967:176). Laz and Mingrelian have restructured Series III morphology in a more thoroughgoing way; see §13.3.

In this way, already-extant Series II inversion forms came to be used in a predominantly evidential function. These forms became part of an independent Series III, however, only when three other changes took place: (a) The first evidential, omitted from the preceding discussion, was developed. (b) The general patterns of all Series III screeves were extended to verbs that, for one reason or another, lacked relative intransitive forms in Series I and II. (c) Paradigms developed for Class 2 verbs. The order in which these changes are listed here and discussed below does not necessarily reflect the order in which they occurred.

13.2.2. First Evidential of Classes 1 and 3

In Old Georgian there are, in the present screeve, two patterns for the formation of underlyingly transitive inversion forms, as in (44).

(44) *m-gon-ie-s* 'I believe it'
g-gon-ie-s 'you believe it'
h-gon-ie-s 'he believes it'

(45) *m-i-pqr-ie-s* 'I hold it'
g-i-pqr-ie-s 'you hold it'
u-pqr-ie-s 'he holds it'

While the paradigm in (44) is quite likely very old, only the pattern in (45) has been taken over into the first evidential; that is, all Class 1 and 3 verbs use the vowel prefix (*i* > *u*/*x* + ___ +, in the third person, with deletion of *x* in many dialects). The various affixes used in the present tense forms of the verb in (45) appear also in the first evidential forms in the paradigm in (46).

(46) *mi-ç̣er-ie-s* 'I have written it'
g-i-ç̣er-ie-s 'you have written it'
u-ç̣er-ie-s 'he has written it'

The suffix *-ie* is not a screeve marker as such, but is used only with certain relative intransitive forms. In (44)–(46), as in other inversion forms, the affixes *m-*, *g-*, **x-* mark agreement with the surface indirect object (see Table 13.2), while *-s* indicates third person final subject. This *-s* is part of the set A third person subject markers and is used in the present and first evidential alike.

Again, the morphology of the first evidential in Svan is not the exact phonological correspondent of that in Georgian, but the Svan first evidential[10] shows the same relationship to the forms of inversion in the present tense, namely, both use the prefix *a-* or *i-* (in the third person, *i* > *o*/*x* + ___+) together with the invariant suffix *-a*. Compare, in this respect, the paradigm of an inversion verb in the present (Series I) in (47) with that of a Class 1 verb in the first evidential (Series III) in (48).

(47) *m-i-tr-a* 'I know him'
ǰ-i-tr-a 'you know him'
x-o-tr-a 'he knows him' (Topuria 1967:85)

(48) *m-i-mar-a* 'I have prepared it'
ǰ-i-mar-a 'you have prepared it'
x-o-mar-a 'he has prepared it' (Topuria 1967:169)

13.2.3. Generalization of the Forms

A second development that must have taken place in making Series III an independent set of paradigms was the generalization of the productive forms to those verbs which because of irregularities, lacked regular intransitive forms in *e-* in Series II. For example, the verb 'kill' has an irregularly derived intransitive in Series II, but its Series III forms are entirely regular. Table 13.6 lists first an example of the regular relationship, *ç̣er*, then several verbs with regularized Series III forms. The Series II form listed is the aorist, the Series III form is the second evidential; all terms are third person singular.[11] As shown in Table 13.6, those verbs that had irregular Series II intransitives (*mo-ḳud-a*) or which had Series II intransitives derived by a pattern that was no longer productive (*še-ḳrb-a*) made use of the Series II transitive stem in forming a second evidential as part of an independent Series III.

Table 13.6

Comparison of Forms in Old Georgian

Series II			
Transitive	Intransitive	Series III	
(da)-ç̣er-a	*(da)-e-ç̣er-a*	*(da)-e-ç̣er-a*	'write'
(mo)-ḳl-a	*(mo)-ḳud-a*	*(mo)-e-ḳl-a*	'kill'
(gan)-ṭex-a	*(gan)-ṭq̇d-a*	*(gan)-e-ṭex-a*	'break'
(še)-ḳrib-a	*(še)-ḳrḃ-a*	*(še)-e-ḳrib-a*	'gather'
(gan)-a-ṭp-o	*(gan)-ṭp-a*	*(gan)-e-ṭp-o*	'warm up'

13.2.4. Class 2 Forms

A further change necessary to the development of an independent Series III was linking the forms discussed above with a paradigm having comparable functions for Class 2 verbs. Whereas the paradigm used for Series III forms of Class 1 and 3 verbs was associated with the expression of unintentional action, those used for Series III forms of Class 2 verbs were associated with the perfect. The past passive participle plus the copula provided a source for the morphology of Class 2 verbs in Series III.[12] In Table 13.7 some examples of past participles are compared with first evidential forms; the Svan examples (Lenṭex dialect) are from Topuria (1967:204, 220–221), and the Georgian from Imnaishvili (1971:240, 242). Table 13.7 shows the formal relationships between past passive participles and the Series III forms of Class 2 verbs in Svan and in Old Georgian. In

Table 13.7

Comparison of Past Participle and Periphrastic First Evidential in Svan and Old Georgian

	Past participle	Periphrastic first evidential
Svan	*me-ṭex-e* 'returned'	*ä-me-ṭex-e xwi* 'I returned'
		ä-me-ṭex-e xi 'you returned'
		ä-me-ṭex-e li 'he returned'
	lə-šix, lə-šx-e 'burned'	*čwa-l-šix-e xwi* 'I (am) burned'
		a-l-šix-e xi 'you (are) burned'
		a-l-šix-e li 'he (is) burned'
Old Georgian	*da-mal-ul* 'lost'	*da-mal-ul var* 'I am lost'
		da-mal-ul xar 'you are lost'
		da-mal-ul ars 'he is lost'
	gan-m-ṭp-ar 'warmed'	*gan-m-ṭp-ar var* 'I am warmed'
		gan-m-ṭp-ar xar 'you are warmed'
		gan-m-ṭp-ar ars 'he is warmed'

Svan two formants of the past passive particple are *me—e* and *lə—e* (*lə—∅*), and these circumfixes occur also in the Series III forms. Those verbs that have participles in *me—e* have Series III forms in *me—e*, while those in *lə—(e)* have Series III forms with the same circumfix. The person–number conjugation is indicated by means of the auxiliary *xwi, xi, li,* and so forth 'be', the participial portion of the form being invariant. The Old Georgian facts are parallel.

A similar relationship between past passive participles and Series III forms of Class 2 verbs must have existed also in Zan, though it is being eroded. Asatiani (1970) lists numerous Mingrelian textual examples, from which the following are drawn.

(49) *ḳoči si ˀoperekə*
man/NOM you/NOM you/be/III
'Why, you must be a man!' (Kipshidze 1914:15, 3)

(50) *iripeli arto dočvere*
everything/NOM one/as it/burn/III
'Everything has burned up as one.' (Kipshidze 1914:14, 4)

Each of these Class 2 verbs has Series III forms composed of an optional preverb, *do-* in (50), verb root, *ˀop*, *č̣v,* the participial formant *-er/el,* and a screeve marker *-e*. In (49), the second person singular subject suffix *-k(ə)* also occurs; the third person singular subject suffix *-n* deletes in (50) as always when it is word-final in Mingrelian (see §16.1.5). Asatiani (1970:145) observes that while these forms are frequent in texts recorded earlier in the century (Kipshidze 1914; Xubua 1937), in 1956 in the village of J̌vari, she found them only infrequently in the speech of the old people. These are being replaced by forms like those in the examples below (elicited in the Xobi dialect in 1981).

(51) *ḳoč doγure*
man/NOM he/die/III
'Apparently the man died.'

(52) *nodari doškvid(el)e*
Nodar/NOM he/drown/III
'Apparently Nodar drowned.'

These forms consist of a preverb (*do-*), the verb root (*γur, škvid*), and the formant *-e*. For (52) the consultant pro·ided parallel forms with and without *-el* (cf. *škvid-el-i* past passive participle, Nadareishvili 1962:181). Thus, in Mingrelian the participial formant *-er/el* is being dropped from the forms, which otherwise retain their morphology, syntax, and function.

While the *-er/el* suffix, participial in origin, is now used in a New Series III with verbs of all classes in Laz (Kartozia 1976), it must originally have occurred just in the forms of Class 2 verbs, as do the participial formants in Svan, Georgian, and Mingrelian.

There is evidence from all four languages for the use of a past passive participle in the formation of Series III forms of Class 2 verbs. Old Georgian and Svan provide clear evidence of the use of a copula auxiliary with this, constituting a periphrastic evidential. While the Class 2 evidentials in Svan appear to retain their periphrastic nature (see Table 13.7), those in Georgian have been reanalyzed morphologically, so that the one-time auxiliaries now function as person markers (see Baramidze 1964). The auxiliary is less obvious in Laz and Mingrelian, but it is believed that the formant *-e,* which follows *-er,* is from *ore,* the copula in Zan (Asatiani 1970:147ff., attributed to Kipshidze). Hence, we may conclude that in CK the Series III forms of Class 2 verbs were formed periphrastically from the past passive participle and the copula and that in Georgian, Laz, and Mingrelian these were reanalyzed as organic formations.

13.2.5. Conclusions

In this section I have shown that sources for all of the morphology of Series III pre-existed the development of that series as an independent paradigm. In §3.1 it was shown that there was likewise a CK model for the syntax of Series III in the form of the inversion construction. These considerations lead to the conclusion that Series III is an internal development, though the development of the concept of the evidential may have been influenced by neighboring languages.[13]

In this section I set out in broad outline a hypothesis of how Series III developed. In the sections that follow, I deal with some specific questions that arise in connection with this series. Section 13.3 considers the question of the relation of Series III to the verb system as a whole, both synchronically and diachronically. Section 13.4 deals with the question of whether or not Series III has been reanalyzed in a way comparable to Series I. In §13.5 I discuss what can be determined about relative chronology.

13.3. THE PLACE OF THE EVIDENTIAL IN THE VERBAL SYSTEM

In this section I address the problem of the relationship of the evidential to the non-evidential. There are two aspects to this problem: one is morphological and the other pragmatic. In §13.3.1 I consider the pragmatic relationship of the unseen to the seen from a synchronic point of view in each language and in a few dialects of Modern Georgian. In §13.3.2 I show what the morphological relationships of the evidential screeves are to the other screeves. Section 13.3.3 presents a diachronic hypothesis that attempts to account for the apparently contradictory facts presented in §13.3.1 and §13.3.2. In this way we can see more precisely where Series III came from.

It should be observed first that syntax provides no evidence concerning the synchronic relationship of the evidential to the nonevidential (except in Mingrelian, §13.5) or concerning the ultimate source of the evidential. Class 1 and 3 verbs govern a particular syntactic construction—inversion—in Series III. Yet this construction can be derived from either Series I or II. This has been shown in Harris (1981b, Chap. 8); it can easily be seen by applying the case assignment patterns stated in Chapter 3 to the analysis of inversion proposed in §13.1. This is not an artifact of the analysis. Inversion exists for some verbs in each series; therefore, any adequate analysis would have to account for the fact that inversion is productively derivable in each series. For this reason, the syntax associated with Series III gives us no clue as to whether that set of screeves derives from Series I or II. We therefore turn to evidence from pragmatics and morphology.

13.3.1. Pragmatic Relationships

Thus far, our discussion has been limited to three series, but Mingrelian has a fourth. Like the other three, it is an independent set of verbal paradigms with their own morphology. Unlike the others, it does not involve a distinct syntactic feature. The functional (not morphological or syntactic) relationships among the series in Mingrelian are summarized in Table 13.8.[14] This table indicates that Series III expresses the unseen corresponding to Series II seen, and Series IV holds the parallel pragmatic relationship to Series I. The individual screeves of Series IV correspond to those of Series I, as in Table 13.9. In Svan and in some of the western dialects of Georgian, a system comparable to that in Table 13.9 is found, though the correspondences are less complete (Rogava 1953:27–29). That

Table 13.8

System of Series in Mingrelian[a]

Seen	Unseen
Series I	Series IV
Series II	Series III

[a]After Rogava (1953).

Table 13.9

Screeve Correspondences in Mingrelian

Series I	Series IV
Present	Third evidential
Imperfect	Fourth evidential
Subjunctive I	Subjunctive IV
Conditional I	Conditional IV
Future	

is, both Svan and some western dialects of Georgian have additional evidential screeves, constituting a Series IV, that correspond to some, but not all, screeves of Series I. In Mingrelian, Svan, and the western Georgian dialects, case marking is just as in Series I; surface subjects are in the nominative, surface objects in the dative (Rogava 1953:27–29; Topuria 1967:130–136). Agreement is also the same, and the syntax of Series IV in these dialects requires no special treatment.

Laz, too, has a Series IV corresponding to Series I. Laz has made the further innovation of introducing a New Series III (see Asatiani 1970; Kartozia 1976; Rogava 1953:26–27). The New and Old Series III function in parallel, as seen in Table 13.10, but the Old is being replaced by the New. In Laz, the Old Series III is characterized by inversion, governed by Class 1 and 3 verbs; this is not true of other series. In earlier chapters it is shown that Laz has extended active case marking to Series I. It is therefore not surprising that case marking in Series IV, as well as in the New Series III, is all of the active type. That is, with the inclusion of a rule of inversion of the kind proposed in §13.1, only one set of case assignment rules is required in Laz, unlike its sister languages. Parallel examples of the Old (a) and New (b) Series III from the Xopian dialect are given in (53); the first involves inversion, the second does not.

Table 13.10

System of Series in Laz

Seen	Unseen
Series I	Series IV
Series II	Old Series III New Series III

(53) a. *ḳoči-s* *uqvilun* *γeǯi*
man-DAT he/kill/it/INV/OLDIII pig/NOM
'Apparently the man killed a pig.'
b. *ḳoči-k* *doqvileren* *γeǯi*
man-NAR he/kill/it/NEWIII pig/NOM
'Apparently the man killed a pig.'

The evidential of Series IV has the same syntax as that of the New Series III, as seen in (54).

(54) *hemu-k* *zimupṭeren* *ia*
he-NAR he/measure/it/IV it
'Apparently he was measuring it.' (Chikobava 1936:141)

Thus, in Laz only the Old Series III requires any special treatment with regard to syntax.

At least some of the eastern dialects of Georgian also have a means of expressing the unseen that corresponds to Series I. Because it is formed periphrastically using a Series I form plus a particle, it is not considered to constitute a 'series', which is a label not traditionally used for collocations involving a particle. In keeping with the traditional use of the word, I have not labeled these 'Series IV' in Table 13.11, though they fill a parallel function. In Standard Modern Georgian, the particle *turme* indicates unseen and compensates for the lack of this category for certain forms (Kavtaradze 1956:179). The present, future, and imperfect are screeves of Series I; the aorist is a Series II screeve. The subjunctive, conditional, and imperative are not generally used with *turme* (Kavtaradze 1956:182). The particle *turme* may also be used with Series III forms.

Parts of the Ingilo dialect (spoken in the Azerbaijan SSR, and not contiguous with other Georgian dialects) use the particle *q̣opila* in a similar way (Imnaishvili 1955); while Xevsurian makes use of *q̣opilam,* which,

Table 13.11

System of Series in Georgian since the Twelfth Century

Seen	Unseen
Series I	Present + *turme* Future + *turme* Imperfect + *turme*
Series II	Aorist + *turme* Series III

with an indicative form, expresses the unseen (Arabuli 1980b). In each of these dialects, the syntax and case marking are the same as those governed by whichever indicative form is used with the particle. That is, when the particle is used with a Series I screeve, Series I case assignment is in effect; when the particle occurs with a Series II form, we find Series II case marking.

Kaxadze (1979) describes yet another system in a subdialect (in the village of Okroq̣ana) of Kartlian. As seen in Table 13.12, the Series III first evidential functions as the unseen of the present (Series I), while the other Series III forms function as the unseen of Series II screeves.[15] This contrasts with the situation in the literary dialect (Table 13.11), where all of Series III corresponds to Series II. Kaxadze illustrates the differing usage of the first evidential by the following examples. Waiting at a bus stop for a bus that did not appear, a resident of Okroq̣ana addressed to him the sentence in (55a); its Standard Georgian equivalent is (55b).

(55) a. *čven avṭobuz ar umušavnia, ai*
our bus/DAT NEG it/work/INV/1.EVID
(Kaxadze 1979:182)
b. *čveni avṭobusi ar mušaobs turme, ai*
our bus/NOM NEG it/work/PRES apparently
'Apparently our bus isn't working, you see.'
(after Kaxadze 1979:182)

This pattern can also be used in the affirmative, as in (56a) from Okroq̣ana and (56b) from Standard Georgian, and numerous other examples cited by Kaxadze.

(56) a. *umušavnia, ai*
it/work/INV/1.EVID (Kaxadze 1979:182)
b. *mušaobs turme, ai*
it/work/PRES apparently
'Apparently it is working, you see.' (Kaxadze 1979:182)

Table 13.12
System of Series in Okroq̣ana[a]

Seen	Unseen
Series I	First evidential
Series II	Second evidential

[a]After Kaxadze (1979).

Although the same first evidential form, *umušavnia,* exists in the literary dialect, it would not be used for the present tense but rather to mean 'apparently it worked' or 'it has worked', and so forth. The use of the first evidential in Okroqana is the same as that of Series IV in Laz, Mingrelian, Svan, and the western Georgian dialects (Kaxadze 1979). The first evidential in Okroqana governs Inversion, just as this FORM does in the other dialects; but its PRAGMATIC equivalent does not govern Inversion in the other dialects.

13.3.2. Morphological Relationships

In this section, I show briefly that morphological affinities favor the view that the first evidential (of Series III) developed out of Series I, while the remaining screeves of Series III developed out of Series II. Then I propose a hypothesis to account for the inconsistency, from a synchronic point of view, between the functional and morphological affinities.

13.3.2.1. First Evidential

The morphological properties of the first evidential connect it with Series I and distinguish it, though not unambiguously, from Series II. The Old Georgian facts are stated briefly below.

1. Class 1 forms of ablauting verbs have underlying forms with *e*-grade in Series I and *i*-grade in Series II (see Chap. 8). In the first evidential, these verbs have *e*-grade (e.g., *moudrekies* 'he has bent it'). This could be due to use of the Series I stem form or to the fact that the Series III Inversion forms were surface intransitives, transitivity having at one time governed the *e*/*i* alternation. The use of *i*-grade by other Series III screeves, also in the inversion construction, favors the former explanation.
2. A series marker occurs in all Series I forms, though for some lexical items this has a ∅ realization; series markers are not used in Series II. Generally, series markers occur in forms of the first evidential: *mouḳla**vs*** 'he has killed him', *migiγ**eb**ies* 'you have taken/received it', *ušen**eb**ies* 'he has built it'. On the other hand, some lexical items do not use a series marker in the first evidential even though they do in Series I. For example, while the present (Series I) form *iç̣qebs* 'he begins it' contains the series marker *-eb,* neither the aorist (Series II) *iç̣qo* 'he began it' nor the first evidential *uç̣qies* 'he has begun it' contains a series marker. Thus, while most Class 1 verbs use the Series I stem in the formation of the first evidential, some use the Series II stem.
3. The suffixes added to form all persons of the first evidential of Class 1 and 3 are found in the conjugation of inversion forms in the present

tense only; compare present *hgonies* 'he hears/believes it' and first evidential *miuγebies* 'apparently he took/received it'.

4. The auxiliary used in the formation of Class 2 first evidentials is the present tense form; compare *ars* 'he is' with *damalul ars* 'apparently he hid'.

5. Although there are relics of the use of *En*-Agreement in Series I in Old Georgian, Laz, and Mingrelian, the rule was no longer productive in this series in Old Georgian times but was still used in Series II. *En* is not used in the first evidential, either in transitive or intransitive forms; compare *dauçerian* 'apparently he wrote them', *mouḳlvan* 'apparently he killed them', and *damalul arian* 'they have hidden.' The fact that other screeves of Series III do have *En*-Agreement (see §13.3.2.2) confirms an affiliation between the first evidential and Series I.[16]

Laz and Mingrelian preserve some of the same Series I characteristics in the first evidential.

1. First evidential forms of Class 1 and 3 verbs in Laz and Mingrelian have *-u* (§13.1.2.2) with or without an additional full -VC series marker. When they have full series markers, these are typically different in form from the series markers used by the same forms in the present. Some examples are listed in Table 13.13, where the full series markers are in boldface. As shown in the table, the form of the series marker in the evidential is not related in an obvious way to that of the series marker in the present. In the Xopian dialect, from which the Laz examples were elicited, the expected form of series markers is -V*p*, while -V*m* is found

Table 13.13

Occurrence of Series Markers in Present and First Evidential

Present	First evidential		Class
Laz			
*qvil-**up**-s*	*u-qvil-u-n*	'kill'	1
*oškvid-**ap**-s*	*u-škvid-u-n*	'drown'	1
*qu-**ap**-s*	*u-qur-u-n*	'yell'	3
*γaγal-**ap**-s*	*u-γaγal-u-n*	'talk'	3
*gontx-**ip**-s*	*guntx-**im**-u-n*	'spread'	1
ister-s	*u-stir-**am**-u-n*	'play'	3
Mingrelian			
*ˀvil-**un**-s*	*duˀvil-u*	'kill'	1
*oškvid-**uan**-s*	*duškvid-**uap**-u*	'drown'	1
*ragad-**an**-s*	*u-ragad-u*	'talk'	3
*laˀap-**en**-s*	*u-laˀap-**in**-u*	'play'	3
*čxup-**en**-s*	*u-čxup-**eb**-u*	'fight'	3

in other Laz dialects and -V*n* in Mingrelian (see Table 9.2). The series marker *-eb* in the last example is found in Georgian but is not supposed to occur in Mingrelian; here and in other lexical items, it seems to occur in words borrowed from Georgian, though the Georgian does not necessarily have *-eb* (e.g., Georgian *čxub-ob-s* 'he is fighting', *u-čxub-n-i-a* 'apparently he fought').[17] Perhaps it would be most accurate to say that first evidential forms of Class 1 and 3 verbs in Laz and Mingrelian show TRACES of series markers.

2. The suffixal formant *-u* (see §13.1.2.2) occurs in the derivation of mediopassives in Series I and inversion constructions in the first evidential, but not in Series II. For example *-u* occurs in Laz *γur-**u**-nan* 'they are dying' and in *u-q̇vil-**u**-n* 'apparently he killed him'; but not in *do-γur-es* 'they died' in Series II.

3. In both Laz and Mingrelian, the present has characteristic third person agreement markers, which are carried over to the first evidential but which do not occur in Series II. For example, some verbs (see Chap. 15) take the third person singular subject marker *-n,* while in all other screeves the third person singular subject is marked by either *-s* or *-u*. The marker *-n* can be seen in the Laz present *γur-u-**n*** 'he is dying' and in the first evidential *u-bir-u-**n*** 'apparently he sang'.[18]

In Svan, the first evidential is derived with the invariant formant *-a,* which identifies it with the present (see §13.2.2). Most Svan verbs have ∅ series marker in Series I. Of those that have a non-null marker, most do not have it in first evidential forms, though some do. For example the present form *igem* 'he builds it' has the series marker *-em*; the first evidential in Lenṭex is *xogema* 'apparently he built it', which retains *-em,* but in other dialects the form is *xoga,* which lacks *-em* (Topuria 1967:171). In this respect, the first evidential more closely resembles Series II (which lacks series markers). Topuria (1967:170) observes, too, that verbs with stems suppletive for series use the Series II stem in the first evidential.

13.3.2.2. Other Series III Screeves

In Old Georgian and in Svan, the other screeves of Series III have a number of features in common with Series II and distinct from Series I.

1. In Old Georgian the second evidential of Class 1 forms of ablauting verbs has *i*-grade stems, as set out in Table 13.14.

2. As in Series II, series markers do not occur in the second evidential: *mo-e-ḳl-a* 'he had killed him', *aγ-e-šeyn-a* 'he had built it'. In this respect, the other Series III forms contrast with the first evidential and with Series I generally; see forms in §13.3.2.1.

3. Second evidential and other Series III forms of Class 2 verbs in Old Georgian are formed with a Series II form of the copula plus the past

Table 13.14

Distribution of Ablaut Grades in Old Georgian Transitives

Series I *e*-grade	First evidential *e*-grade
Series II *i*-grade	Second evidential *i*-grade

passive participle; compare *iqo* 'it was (Series II)' and *daçeril iqo* 'it had been written', *iqos* 'it will be' and *daçeril iqos* 'it will have been written'.[19]

4. While *En*-Agreement does not apply in the first evidential, it does apply in the other Series III screeves as in Series II. Second evidential examples of Class 1 verbs include *daeçernes* 'he had written them', *moeḳlnes* 'he had killed them', and subjunctive III *daeçernen* and *moeḳlnen.* These forms are entirely in accord with the generalization stated in Chapter 10 that plural direct objects, including initial direct objects in inversion, condition the occurrence of the suffix *-en/n.* In Series III forms of Class 2 verbs, *En*-Agreement, like all other agreement, shows up in the auxiliary, rather than in the participial element; for example, *daçeril iqvnes* 'they had been written" and *daçeril iqvnen* 'they will have been written'. These forms may be compared with those cited in §13.3.2.1, which show the lack of *-en/n* in the first evidential.[20]

In Svan, too, the second evidential and subjunctive III have morphological characteristics of Series II.

1. The stem used for Class 1 verbs is the same as the stem used for the same verbs in the first evidential, that is, it predominantly lacks a series marker and thus, is affiliated with Series II (Topuria 1967:173; see above).

2. The suffix *-än/an/ǟn,* otherwise used only in certain aorist forms, occurs in the second evidential; for example, Lenṭex *x-o-xaṭaw-an* 'he had painted him' (Topuria 1967:173). The suffix *-en/ēn,* otherwise used in the subjunctive II, occurs also in the corresponding forms of the subjunctive III; for example, Lenṭex *at-a-kač-en-s* 'he would have cut it' (Topuria 1967:177).

While Georgian and Svan show a clear relationship between Series II and the second evidential, subjunctive III, and habitual III, in Zan the affiliation of these Series III screeves seems to be closer to Series I.

1. Class 1 forms of the second evidential and subjunctive III have the series marker *-u,* otherwise limited to Class 2 forms in Series I; for ex-

ample, Mingrelian *do-u-ç̣ḳir-**u**-d-u* 'he had cut it' and *do-u-ç̣ḳir-**u**-d-a-s* 'he would have cut it' (forms from Rogava 1953:20, 18).

2. Similarly, the second evidential and subjunctive III have the formant *-d/ṭ*, some form of which is used in every Kartvelian language in the formation of Series I screeves; for example, *douç̣kirudu* and *douç̣kirudas*.

13.3.2.3. Summary

The morphological affiliations of Series III forms, from a synchronic point of view, are not the same in the various languages. The first evidential shows overwhelmingly Series I traits in Old Georgian, Laz, and Mingrelian; to a lesser extent, it has Series II traits in Svan. The remaining Series III screeves show a strong affiliation with Series II in Old Georgian and Svan; in Zan they are predominantly affiliated with Series I.

These data raise two questions. Why is there contradiction between the various languages concerning apparent morphological affiliations of particular screeves? Why do the morphological relationships described in this section not parallel the pragmatic ones set out in §13.3.1?

13.3.3. A Diachronic Account

In this section, I propose answers to the questions posed above, suggesting a diachronic explanation for these apparent anomalies.

I suggest that the second evidential, subjunctive III, and habitual III originally corresponded to Series II, not only in morphology but also in function.[21] The first evidential, on the other hand, must have developed as the morphological and functional parallel of Series I. Table 13.15 represents the reconstructed pragmatic and morphological relationships, shared by the Kartvelian languages and dialects, from which later systems must have developed. Note that the system set out in Table 13.15 is essentially the same as that preserved functionally in the village dialect of

Table 13.15

Reconstructed Pragmatic and Morphological Relationships among Screeves in Kartvelian

Seen	Unseen
Series I	First evidential
Series II	Second evidential Subjunctive III Habitual III

Okroqana (Table 13.12; Kaxadze 1979) and morphologically in Old Georgian. There is contradictory evidence concerning the question of the relative chronology of the developments that affected the system in Table 13.15 and concerning whether these developments took place sequentially or all at once. The problems are complex and need not be addressed at this time.

We may assume that something happened to upset the balance of the system outlined in Table 13.15. This event could have been the reinterpretation of Series I. For whatever reason, the first evidential must have come to be more tightly allied with the rest of Series III than with Series I. We thus have a shifting of functional affiliation from Series I toward Series II. Old Georgian seems to exemplify this transitional stage in the history of the first evidential. In some Old Georgian examples, the first evidential has a close pragmatic affiliation with the present—an affiliation notably lacking from the meaning of the first evidential in Standard Modern Georgian (Kavtaradze 1956:184–185). In other Old Georgian examples, the first evidential alternates with the aorist (Kavtaradze 1956:185–186). An ambivalence of this kind would seem to be consistent with the hypothesis that Old Georgian reflects a change of the type proposed.

When the first evidential became more closely associated with Series II, it destroyed the nearly perfect correspondence between the screeves of Series II and those of Series III (see Table 13.3). Perhaps as a result of that, we find that the screeves of Series II do not correspond individually to those of Series III in Standard Modern Georgian.

Clearly this change would leave a vacuum in the expression of the unseen that is parallel to Series I. Svan, Laz, Mingrelian, and some of the western Georgian dialects seem to have filled this void by developing Series IV. Series IV is affiliated with Series I, not only pragmatically, but also morphologically and syntactically (see Rogava 1953), and need not concern us further.

The eastern dialects must also have felt a need to fill the void created by this change. Some of them did so by creating new forms consisting of an old screeve and a particle. In Old Georgian, the use of the particle *ture, turme* to express the unseen with an appropriate indicative (seen) screeve seems to have developed in the literary dialect by the twelfth century (Kavtaradze 1956:183). In the Xevsurian dialect, *qopilam* is used in a similar way, and in Ingilo, *qopila*. In each of these dialects, the syntax of the construction with the particle is the same as that of the screeve employed.

The reaffiliation of the first evidential left the languages with a Series III containing screeves with inconsistent morphological properties. That is, the first evidential had morphological relations with Series I, and the remaining Series III screeves, with Series II. We may assume that in Svan this inconsistency was rectified by restructuring the first evidential in accordance with the second evidential and subjunctive III. Relics of its original morphology are the series markers that persist with some verbs in some dialects (see above). This change is consistent with the functional relationship of Series III to Series II.

In Mingrelian, the converse change was made. The second evidential, subjunctive III (and the additional screeve, the conditional III) were restructured in accordance with the first evidential. At first glance it seems most odd that this approach should be taken, given the pragmatic affiliations. That is, Series III functions as the expression of the unseen of Series II; yet we hypothesize that it was restructured morphologically to correspond to Series I. A syntactic motivation for this apparently anomalous change is suggested in §13.5.

I have hypothesized that Series III was in origin a disparate development, the first evidential coming from Series I and the other screeves from Series II. Neither of the other logically possible hypotheses would account in a reasonable way for subsequent developments in one or another of the daughter languages. Thus, if we hypothesize instead that Series III developed uniformly from Series II, we are unable to explain the strong morphological similarity between Series III and Series I in Mingrelian. On the other hand, if we propose that Series III developed uniformly from Series I, we are unable to explain the pragmatic and morphological affiliation between Series III and II in Svan or that between some Series III screeves and Series II in Georgian.

13.4. INVERSION AND THE HISTORY OF NUMBER AGREEMENT

In the Kartvelian languages we find a variety of systems for the assignment of markers of number agreement and a comparable diversity in the markers themselves. Diversity suggests change, and in this section I describe various systems synchronically (§13.4.1) and propose ways of relating some of them diachronically. With respect to number agreement, the first and second persons often differ from the third. I concentrate here on the third person; unless otherwise specified, statements made here pertain to the third person but not necessarily to the first or second.

13.4.1. Old Georgian

The rule of *En*-Agreement in Old Georgian is described in Chapter 10. Operating in conjunction with it was a rule that assigned plural marking to surface subjects. In the third person, subject marking was inflectional. The singular subject markers varied by screeve and included *-s, -a, -o, -n*. Plural subject markers likewise varied: *-en, -an, -n, -es, -ed*. For example, *imalebi-s* 'he hides' beside *imalebi-an* 'they hide'. These markers were conditioned strictly by the number of the final subject. Thus, in inversion it was the initial direct object that controlled the number of the final subject markers. For example in the hypothetical (57), the surface subjects *igi* 'it' versus *igini* 'them' controls *-s* versus *-an,* while number of the initial subject (= final indirect object) has no effect on the verb form.

(57) a. *upq̣ries* *mas* */mat* *igi*
he/hold/it/INV/I he/DAT they/DAT it/NOM
'He has it.' 'They have it.'
b. ***upq̣rian*** *mas* */mat* ***igini***
he/hold/them/INV/I he/DAT they/DAT them/NOM
'He has them.' 'They have them.'

Thus, the verb varies for the number of the surface subject. For the third person, we can state the generalization in (58).

(58) The plural markers *-en* (*-an,-n*), *-es, -ed* are controlled by final subjects.

When the surface subject is also the initial direct object, both plural subject marking and *En*-Agreement apply in screeves that permit the latter. This occurs in inversion and other constructions (see Chap. 10). For example, corresponding to the examples above, we find *epq̣r-a* 'he had it' 'they had it'; *epq̣r-n-es* 'he had them' 'they had them', where both *-n* (< **en*) and *-es* are conditioned by the plurality of the nominative-nominal.

In Old Georgian, plurality of the indirect object does not condition agreement. For example *utkuams* 'he says it to him' is invariant for a plural indirect object: *utkuams mat* 'he says it to them', where the number of the indirect object is indicated only by the plural pronoun *mat* (see Imnaishvili 1971:239). The examples below show that this is so.

(59) a. *da hrkua* *peṭres*
and he/say/it/to.him/II Peter/DAT
'and he said to Peter' (Mt 26:40)
b. *da hrkua mat*
them/DAT
'and he said to them' (Mt 26:45)

Although the number of the indirect objects in (59a) and (59b) varies, the forms are the same. This shows clearly that indirect objects do not trigger number agreement.

13.4.2. Laz and Mingrelian

In the Zan languages, third person subjects control number agreement, while third person objects do not. This is shown for each language below. For brevity, examples are given from one series only; Series I and II are the same in this respect.

(60) Laz

a. *baba-k* *cxeni* *meču* *skiri-s*
father-NAR horse/NOM he/give/it/to.him/II child-Dat
'The father gave a horse to (his) son.'

b. ***baba-nana-k*** *cxeni* ***mečes*** *skiris*
father-mother-NAR horse/NOM they/give/it/to.him/II child/DAT
'The parents gave a horse to (their) son.'

c. *babak* *cxen-epe* *meču* *skiris*
father/NAR horse-PL/NOM he/give/it/to.him/II child/DAT
'The father gave horses to (his) son.'

d. *babak* *cxeni* *meču* *skir-epe-s*
father/NAR horse/NOM he/give/it/to.him/II child-PL-DAT
'The father gave a horse to (his) sons.'

In (60a) each nominal is singular; in the examples that follow, the subject, direct object, and indirect object are pluralized in turn. Comparison of the verb form in (60a) with those in the other examples shows that only the plural subject in (60b) conditions verb agreement. Parallel examples from Mingrelian show that it has the same system of number agreement:

(61) Mingrelian

a. *muma-k* *cxen-i* *kimeču* *skua-s*
father-NAR horse-NOM he/give/it/to.him/II child-DAT
'The father gave a horse to (his) son.'

b. ***mšoblem-k*** *cxeni* ***kimečes*** *skuas*
parent/PL-NAR horse/NOM they/give/it/to.him/II child/DAT
'The parents gave a horse to (their) son.'

c. *mumak* *cxen-ep(i)* *kimeču* *skuas*
father/NAR horse-PL/NOM he/give/it/to.him/II child/DAT
'The father gave horses to (his) son.'

d. *mumak* *cxeni* *kimeču* *skual-em-s*
father/NAR horse/NOM he/give/it/to.him/II child-PL-DAT
'The father gave a horse to (his) sons.'

Subjects control number agreement in Laz and Mingrelian; direct and indirect objects do not.

In inversion, the dative-nominal (initial subject) controls number agreement, as the (b) examples show. The nominative-nominal (= final subject) does not trigger plural agreement, as the (c) examples show.

(62) Laz
a. *baba-s* *cxeni* *nučamun* *skiri-ša*
father-DAT horse/NOM he/give/it/INV/III child-ALL
'The father has given a horse to (his) son.'
b. ***nana-baba-s*** *cxeni* *nučamun**an*** *skiriša*
mother-father-DAT horse/NOM they/give/it/INV/III child/ALL
'The parents have given a horse to (their) son.'
c. *babas* *cxen-epe* *nučamun* *skiriša*
father/DAT horse-PL/NOM he/give/it/INV/III child/ALL
'The father has given horses to (his) son.'

(63) Mingrelian
a. *ḳos* *duˀvilu* *γeǰ-i*
man/DAT he/kill/it/INV/III pig-NOM
'The man has killed a pig.'
b. ***ḳoč-em-s*** ***duˀviluna*** *γeǰi*
man-PL-DAT they/kill/it/INV/III pig/NOM
'The men have killed a pig.'
c. *ḳos* *duˀvilu* *γeǰ-ep-i*
man/DAT he/kill/it/INV/III pig-PL-NOM
'The man has killed (some) pigs.'

On the other hand, in noninversion clauses in Series III, that is, those containing Class 2 verbs, it is the nominative-nominal (final subject) that controls number agreement, as shown by the examples below.

(64) Laz
a. *bere* *oxoris* *doskideren*
child/NOM house/DAT he/stay/III
'The child has stayed at home.'
b. ***bere-pe*** *oxoris* *doskideren**an***
child-PL/NOM house/DAT they/stay/III
'The children have stayed at home.'

(65) Mingrelian
a. *baγana* *ˀudes* *kudoskilade*
child/NOM house/DAT he/stay/III
'The child has stayed at home.'

b. ***baγan-ep*** *ʔudes* *kudoskiladena*
child-PL/NOM house/DAT they/stay/III
'The children have stayed at home.'

We can make the following generalization concerning the conditioning of number agreement by third person nominals in Laz and Mingrelian:

(66) Number agreement is controlled by the first subject that is a final term.

Given the analyses proposed above, rule (66) states that in inversion, number agreement will be controlled by initial subjects of Class 1 and 3 verbs (which are final indirect objects) and by final subjects of Class 2 verbs. In other constructions (including passives, unaccusatives, causatives, etc.), number agreement is conditioned by final subjects, as stated in (66).

13.4.3. The Modern Georgian Literary Norm

Number agreement in Standard Modern Georgian has been described many times, and the facts will not all be repeated here (see Chikobava 1968b; Harris 1978; 1981b:211–217; Tschenkéli 1958:463, 510–511). The system of number agreement control stated in (66) is characteristic of this dialect of Georgian, with one difference. In Laz and Mingrelian, a suffix *-nan* (Mingrelian *n*→∅/____#) may be triggered by final subjects, as in (64b) and (65b), or final indirect objects, as in (62b) and (63b), as long as they satisfy the condition stated in (66). In Georgian, the same nominals trigger plural markers; (67) is parallel to (62b) and (63b), and (68) is parallel to (64b) and (65b).

(67) ***mšobl-eb-s*** *miuciat* *cxen-i* *švilistvis*
parent-PL-DAT they/give/it/INV/III horse-NOM child-for
'The parents have given a horse to (their) child.'

(68) ***bavšv-eb-i*** *saxlši* *darčenilan*
child-PL-NOM house/in they/stay/III
'The children have stayed at home.'

The suffix *-an* in (68) is used elsewhere in Georgian to mark plural third person subjects, just as *-nan* is in Laz and *-na(n)* in Mingrelian. However, the *-t* that occurs in (67) is never used to mark plurality of third person subjects except in inversion and is, in the third person, to be considered a marker of object plurality (see also §13.4.6). This fact provides additional support for the final indirect-objecthood of the dative-nominal in inversion.

13.4.4. Svan

In Svan, the third person plural subject triggers the marker *-x,* suffixed to the singular form; for example, *annaqe* versus *annaqe-x* in the sentences below from the village of Leǯera (Upper Bal dialect).

(69) a. *dīna-d* *annaqe* *ḳubd-är*
girl-NAR she/bake/it/II pastry-PL/NOM
'The girl baked Svan meat pastries.'
b. ***dīn-äl-d*** ***annaqex*** *ḳubdär*
girl-PL-NAR they/bake/it/II pastry/PL/NOM
'The girls baked Svan meat pastries.'

For some subdialects of Upper Bal, plural direct objects condition the suffix *-ar* or its variants (*-al, -är, -āl,* etc.); see Topuria (1967:233–234) and Sharadzenidze (1954). This is illustrated in (70b).

(70) a. *māre-d* *anərde* *čäž* (Mesṭia)
man-NAR he/raise/it/II horse/NOM
'The man raised a horse.'
b. *māred* ***anərdāle*** ***čaž-är*** (Mesṭia)
man/NAR he/raise/them/II horse-PL/NOM
'The man raised some horses.'

The plural direct object in (70b) triggers *-āl* in the verb. Occurrence of this suffix in finite verb forms is optional for the speakers interviewed.[22] For these speakers, plural *-ar* is conditioned only by final direct objects, not by initial direct objects that are the final subjects of unaccusatives.

(71) ***šed-är*** ***ädḳušurānx*** (Mesṭia)
dish-PL/NOM they/break/II
'The dishes broke.'

In (71) and similar examples, the plural nominative-nominal conditions the plural marker *-x,* but not *-ar* or its variants. This is noteworthy since in participles, *-ar* is conditioned by nominals syntactically parallel to *šedär* 'dishes' in (71) (Sharadzenidze 1954). The distribution of *-ar* in finite forms may well have once been the same as the systems in participles described by Sharadzenidze. As described in §9.4, this suffix may also indicate iterative or repeated action.

Ordinary indirect objects do not control number agreement in Svan (Topuria 1967:22).

Turning to inversion, we find that either the dative-nominal or the nominative-nominal may condition the plural subject marker, *-x,* as shown in (72) from Mesṭia.

(72) a. *bepšw-s* *čuätkarwän* *xäm* (Mesṭia)
child-DAT he/lose/it/INV/II pig/NOM
'The child lost a pig.'
b. ***bopš-är-s*** *čuätkarwän**x*** *xäm* (Mesṭia)
child-PL-DAT he/lose/it/INV/II pig/NOM
'The children lost a pig.'
c. *bepšw-s* *čuätkarwän**x*** ***xam-är*** (Mesṭia)
child/DAT he/lose/it/INV/II pig-PL/NOM
'The child lost pigs.'

Topuria (1967:21) states that while the occurrence of *-x* with plural initial subjects, as in (72b), is obligatory, its occurrence with plural final subjects, as in (72c), is optional. The failure of *-x* to occur in the latter circumstance is illustrated by (21b). The plural initial direct object in inversion, as in (72c), does not trigger *-ar* and its variants, just as that in (71) does not.

In those Series III forms that do not involve Inversion (i.e., Class 2 verbs), *-x* is triggered by the final subject: Lower Bal *xäṗžəna* 'he has hidden from him' versus *xäṗžəna**x*** 'they have hidden from him'.

Thus, with respect to finite verb forms, *Ar*-Agreement is conditioned by final direct objects in some dialects, while in other dialects the rule does not exist (see example 69). With respect to the assignment of the plural marker *-x,* we can tentatively make the following generalization:

(73) a. The marker *-x* is controlled by the first subject that is a final term.
b. Other final subjects trigger *-x* optionally.

13.4.5. *Q̣e*-Agreement

In some dialects of Georgian an enclitic particle, *-q̣e,* marks agreement with objects. Chikobava (1923:34) lists the following dialects as having *-q̣e* or its phonetic variants: Račian, Lečxumian, Imerian, Kiziqian, Ingilo, Ḳaxian, Mtiul, Moqevian, and Fereidan. The examples below are from Upper Imerian and are representative, also, of other western dialects (see for example, Kiziria 1974); examples (74)–(75) are from Dzotsenidze (1973:239, 195, 70).

(74) a. *utxari**q̣e*** ***imat***
you/say/it/to.them/II them/DAT
'You said it to them.' 'Say it to them!'
b. *davzarde**q̣e*** ***švilebi***
I/raise/them/II child/PL/DAT
'I raised children.'

Example (74a) shows that *qe* marks agreement with indirect objects, and (74b), with direct objects. These examples are from Series II, and the same system is used in Series I. In inversion, *qe* indicates plurality of the surface indirect object. This is true both in Series III inversion, (75a), and with inversion verbs in other Series, (75b).

(75) a. ***kolmeurneeps*** *gouḳetebiaq̣e* *nalia*
farmer/PL/DAT they/make/it/INV/III granary/NOM
'The collective-farmers have built a corn granary.'

b. *venaxi* *ke* *kondaq̣e*
vineyard/NOM indeed they/have/it/INV/I
'Indeed they have a vineyard.'

In these western dialects, *Qe*-Agreement is controlled by final objects.[23]

In some of the eastern dialects in which *qe* is used, it occurs regularly in examples like (74a) and (75), but only rarely in the indication of plural direct objects in the nominative case, that is, in Series II (on Ingilo, see Imnaishvili 1959; on Ḳaxian, see Martirosovi and Imnaishvili 1956:128). Martirosovi and Imnaishvili suggest that this use of *qe* comes from Series I and that this suffix formerly marked agreement only with dative-nominals.

13.4.6. *T*-Agreement in Eastern Dialects of Georgian

Some eastern dialects have a noteworthy variation on the assignment of *-t,* described in §13.4.3. In Standard Modern Georgian, indirect objects, apart from those in Inversion, do not control agreement. Chikobava (1968b:275) cites the following as exemplifying the literary norm:

(76) a. *utxra* *mas*
he/say/it/to.him/II him/DAT
'He said it to him.'

b. *utxra mat*
them/DAT
'He said it to them.'

While the standard does not permit number agreement with indirect objects other than those in inversion, in some dialects the agreement rules have been simplified (see also *Normebi* 1970:182–183; Tschenkéli 1958:484–490).

(77) *eḳitxebodat:* *"ra* *moxda?"*
he/ask/it/to.them/I what/NOM it/happen/II
'He asked them, "What happened?" ' (Chikobava 1968b:276)

In this dialect, verbs may agree with ordinary indirect objects. Chikobava (1968b:276) makes the following observation:

> In the language of some writers who come from eastern Georgia, one finds verb [number] agreement with the *third person* dative-nominal *even* when this *dative indicates the real object*, that is, when the verb is not in inversion. . . . *As a process*, however, we must have a new factor in the formation of the third person: *a dialectal norm*.

In the passage quoted, Chikobava goes on to develop the hypothesis that this new possibility in some dialects is the result of the influence of *Q̣e*-Agreement. He suggests that *-t* is replacing *-q̣e* in this function, and that *-q̣e* itself is falling into disuse in some dialects (p. 277). As an alternative hypothesis, we might suppose that the use of *-t* for indirect objects in examples like (77) is a natural extension of its use in connection with final indirect objects in Inversion, as in (67). However, Chikobava's hypothesis receives support from facts in Ḳaxian. As reported by Martirosovi and Imnaishvili (1956:128), in this eastern dialect, *-t* is not only used for noninversion indirect objects but also occasionally for direct objects just as *-q̣e* is.[24] They illustrate the control of *-t* by a direct object with the example in (78).

(78) *c̣aiγot* ***oriveni*** *maγla haerši*
he/take/them/II both/PL/NOM high air/in
'He took them both high in the air.'

Thus, while the control of *-t* is limited to final indirect objects in inversion in Standard Modern Georgian, in some nonstandard dialects it may be conditioned by all final indirect objects, and in Ḳaxian by all final objects.[25]

13.4.7. A Historical View

From comparative evidence it appears that there has been a great flux in plural agreement in the Kartvelian dialects. Leaving aside the first and second persons and the problem of the shapes of the morphemes, we can list some of the changes that have taken place:

1. In Old Georgian, *-en, -es,* and so forth were conditioned by plural final subjects; in Standard Modern Georgian these suffixes are not triggered by the final subjects in inversion (which, however, trigger the Subject Agreement markers in Table 13.2).
2. In Old Georgian, *-t* was not conditioned by third person nominals; in Standard Modern Georgian it is triggered by those that are initial subjects and final indirect objects.[26]

3. In some eastern dialects, all final indirect objects may condition *-t*.
4. In Ḳaxian all final objects may condition *-t*.
5. From the evidence presented in §10.2, we may conclude that *En*-Agreement once applied in Series I and was later lost in that environment.
6. In historical times; *En*-Agreement was lost in Georgian in all other environments.
7. The third person plural subject marker *-nan* of Laz must have originated, as did Old Georgian *-n-es,* from the juxtaposition of two plural markers (see §10.1.2). This means that *-n-an* must originally have been triggered only by direct objects advanced to subject as *-n-es* was in Georgian. Its functions, however, have been reanalyzed and extended, so that today its use is determined by both class and screeve.
8. Mingrelian also underwent the changes described in 7. A productive rule in Mingrelian drops word-final *n,* so that in some screeves, third person singular subjects are realized with a $\emptyset$ ($<$ *n*), and third person plural subjects are marked with *-na* ($<$ *nan*). That *-n* is present in underlying forms is shown by the fact that it shows up whenever an enclitic particle is used; for example, compare *renan-o*? 'are they?' with *rena* from *renan* 'they are' (Chikobava 1936:97).
9. It is probable that *-qe* was formerly conditioned by final indirect objects, including initial direct objects; with the reanalysis of Series I, it was controlled by dative-nominals and later was extended to include all final objects.
10. In some dialects, *-qe* was extended also to marking iterative or habitual action (see Chikobava 1923:43; Deeters 1930: §107.)
11. From the fact that *-ar, -al,* and so forth mark plurality of direct objects and at least some intransitive subjects in participles in Upper Bal (Sharadzenidze 1954), it would appear that in the speech of Mesṭia, this morpheme has been restricted in finite forms to final direct objects, while for the nearby Lex̌era sub-dialect it has been entirely lost from finite forms.

This list is by no means exhaustive. The Svan marker *-ar, -al* in particular seems to have undergone a variety of extensions, but in most cases the direction of change is not at present recoverable. The list above is suggestive of the kinds and extent of changes that can occur.

13.5. REANALYSIS OF SERIES III

In Part III of this book it is shown that Series I originated as an aspect (durative) that governed a syntactic rule, Object Demotion. Series I later underwent reanalysis. The initial direct object, which had become a final indirect object through the application of Object Demotion, was reanalyzed as final direct object. In the sections above, I have shown that Series III originated as a status (unseen) that governed a syntactic rule, Inversion. Although Inversion is quite different from Object Demotion, the origins of these series are in some ways parallel. It is, therefore, only reasonable to ask whether Series III, like Series I, has undergone reanalysis, or whether the rule of Inversion applies productively. The answer, of course, may be different in the various languages.

As proposed in §13.1, the initial and final levels of derivation in inversion may be characterized as in Table 13.16. It might be proposed that the dative-nominal of inversion was reanalyzed as the final subject, the rule of Inversion itself being lost. In Georgian, there are insuperable difficulties that would prevent our making such an analysis. In §13.1 it is shown that, if Inversion is a productive rule, no special rule is needed to account for reflexivization, assignment of case, verb agreement, and a wide variety of other phenomena. The inclusion of Inversion as a productive rule in the grammar does make it necessary to complicate the rule that determines which nominal triggers number agreement (see §13.4 above; Harris 1981b: Chap. 15).

If, on the other hand, we propose that inversion has been reanalyzed, we require many more complications of the grammar:

1. The grammar required by the reanalysis hypothesis would include a third set of case marking rules in addition to those already necessary for Series I and for Series II.
2. In addition to the set of rules assigning the subject markers of Table 13.2 to subjects in Series I and II, that grammar would require another set of rules relating subject markers to direct objects just in case the verb

Table 13.16

Grammatical Relations in Inversion

	Dative	Nominative	Oblique
Initial	Subject	Direct object	Indirect object
Final	Indirect object	Subject	Retired indirect object

form was a Class 1 or 3 verb in Series III or was another verb that formerly governed inversion.

3. The grammar required by the reanalysis hypothesis would similarly require additional rules to assign indirect object markers to subjects just in those environments where Inversion had formerly applied.

4. That grammar would further require an exception feature on the rule assigning direct object agreement markers that would state that they are not assigned when the verb form is one that formerly governed Inversion.

5. While this grammar would be able to simplify the rule that determines which nominal triggers number agreement in examples like (67), it would have to introduce a complication into the rule that assigns the agreement marker. If the dative nominal had been reanalyzed as a simple subject, it should trigger a marker of subject plurality (see Table 13.2). Instead, it is marked by *-t,* a plural marker indeed, but one never otherwise used in the marking of a third person subject.

6. In the many dialects with *Q̣e*-Agreement, the reanalysis hypothesis would require a rule that *-q̣e* is conditioned by objects in Series I and II, while in Series III it is not conditioned by objects but is conditioned by subjects.

7. The reanalysis hypothesis would likewise require a complication of the rule of Object Camouflage (Harris 1981b:123–124), not discussed here.

8. In inversion in Series III, initial indirect objects become retired indirect objects (Chap. 11; Harris 1981b: Chap. 8). In Old Georgian, retired indirect objects, in this and other constructions, were marked with the dative case or with the allative case (§11.2.4). If Series III had undergone reanalysis comparable to that of Series I, the initial indirect object would be marked either in the way it was before reanalysis (dative or allative) or the way indirect objects are marked in other series (dative). It is not. The marking assigned to retired indirect objects has changed (Harris 1979); and in Standard Modern Georgian all nominals in this relation, including retired indirect objects in inversion, are marked with the postposition *-tvis* (Harris 1981b:171–173). The fact that the marking of this nominal in Series III has changed along with the other retired indirect objects in recent times establishes that this nominal is still perceived as bearing this relation. It has not undergone reanalysis.

A grammar of Georgian based on the reanalysis hypothesis would fail to relate the facts of the grammar to one another in a meaningful way. It would treat as a coincidence the fact that one nominal is case marked as an indirect object and triggers indirect object agreement, for it would call that nominal the subject. It would fail to relate all of that to a similar displacement of subject characteristics, referring to that surface subject as a direct object. While requiring a rule that assigns the appropriate case or postposition (see Chap. 11) to a retired indirect object, it would add a rule that assigned that same case or postposition to unretired indirect objects in Series III. It is clear that speakers could not fail to notice these relationships. So, the syntactic reanalysis hypothesis must be rejected for Georgian.[27]

When we turn to Mingrelian, we find a different situation. Although surface case patterns and agreement in Series III are similar to those in Georgian, there are differences that support the hypothesis that in Mingrelian, Series III has been reanalyzed. First, plural dative-nominals in inversion condition the marker *-na(n)* (see 63b), which marks third person plural subjects in some other screeves (e.g., *skidu-na* 'they remain', *γuru-na* 'they die'). This contrasts sharply with point 5 above concerning the literary dialect of Georgian. Second, since Series III is functionally related to Series II (Rogava 1953), we would expect the former to derive from the latter if Inversion were still productive. However, in Mingrelian, Series II case marking has changed and Series III is no longer derivable from it.[28] This is exactly the sort of positive evidence of reanalysis that is conspicuously absent from Standard Modern Georgian. Thus, it may be that in Mingrelian Series III has been reanalyzed; yet there remain problems with this hypothesis.

There is an alternative hypothesis. Series III case marking, verb agreement, and so forth could be derived productively from Series I. In §13.3.2 I show that Series III is morphologically derived from Series I and is no longer related morphologically to Series II. This is so in spite of the fact that originally part of Series III developed from Series II morphologically and in spite of the fact that they remain functionally related. If Series III derives syntactically from Series I as a productive process, this would explain why its morphology has been reanalyzed to accord with that of Series I. Thus, it may be that a detailed investigation of Mingrelian syntax would show that Inversion is productive in Series III, that Series I is unmarked, and that Series II exists apart as a special expression.[29]

It can be seen that a related change is underway in Laz. However, it is not that Series III is being reanalyzed, but rather that the original forms and syntax are being replaced by a newer parallel construction. Both are exemplified in (53), and are further discussed in Chapter 15, on extensions. The Lower Ač̣arian dialect of Georgian is losing or has lost inversion in Series III. This, too, has been effected by extension, rather than reanalysis, and is treated in Chapter 15. Other dialects cannot be individually considered here; some may have reanalyzed Series III.

In the course of developing an argument regarding universals of syntactic change, Cole *et al.* (1980) assume that the change in number agreement from Old Georgian to Standard Modern Georgian is part of the "acquisition of subject properties" on the part of the dative-nominal (1980:735–741). Leaving aside other aspects of that discussion, it involves the assumption that Series III (and inversion in other series) is undergoing reinterpretation. While I show above that Georgian has not already undergone such a reinterpretation, the question of whether such a change is presently underway is a distinct issue.

Although direct object properties are not mentioned in the discussion in Cole *et al.* (1980), we may assume that if the dative-nominal is being reinterpreted as final subject, the nominative-nominal must be in the throes of reanalysis as final direct object.[30] The authors interpret the fact that third person dative-nominals begin to determine number agreement (marking with *-t*) as evidence that they are becoming more like subjects. Yet they overlook the fact that the nominative-nominals at about the same time cease to determine *En*-Agreement, thus relinquishing a direct object property (see Chap. 10). Thus, when we view the whole clause, rather than the initial subject alone, we see that while the language gained a rule that refers to initial grammatical relations (marking with *-t*), it lost a different rule that referred also to initial grammatical relations (*En*-Agreement). If we consider the whole clause, there has been no clear overall change in orientation of the grammar toward initial versus final grammatical relations. The construction remains, as it has long been, one in which both initial and final grammatical relations must be taken into account.

Other factors, too, suggest that the change in number agreement in inversion may not be indicative of reinterpretation of that construction. First, as observed above, for centuries there has been a general flux in number agreement rules in the Kartvelian languages; some of the changes have had no effect on the inversion construction. Since most of the other changes could not possibly have been part of a reanalysis of a construction, to attribute this to one of many changes is an over-interpretation of the data. Second, the morpheme *-t,* which marks the plurality of the dative-nominal in inversion, is not otherwise used to mark plurality of a third person subject. While the control of plural marking is associated with other grammatical subjects, the form the marker takes is associated with grammatical objects. Thus, there are a number of additional factors that must be taken into account in determining whether a change is underway; it would appear that the inversion clause as a whole is not more oriented toward initial grammatical relations than it was in Old Georgian.

There is an alternative explanation for the change in number agreement that took place between Old and Modern Georgian. In §13.2 and 13.3 it was emphasized that the first evidential in Old Georgian was formally identical to certain relative intransitives in the present tense, while the second evidential and subjunctive III were identical to the aorist and subjunctive II of relative intransitives. In Old Georgian the rules of number agreement left this identity intact; in Modern Georgian they provide a partial distinction between Series III and the screeves on which it was originally modeled.[31] Compare the partial paradigms in Table 13.17. It is not possible to provide adequate glosses in English. The relative intransitives mean roughly 'the written message is in his possession'; it does not imply that the dative-nominal 'he' necessarily did the writing. In the evidential, on the other hand, the act of writing is ascribed to the dative-nominal, though with the proviso inherent in the unseen meaning. Number agreement is not the only means by which these screeves are distinguished; other features have been secondarily added to one or another, making them diverge. For example, the Series III forms in Modern Georgian are most often accompanied by a preverb. And, of course, number agreement would not differentiate the two meanings where both terms were singular; nevertheless, it does serve to distinguish partially between these screeves. Similarly, the standard dialect distinguishes the aorist of relative intransitives from the second evidential of transitive verbs in part by number agreement; for example, *mat eḳarga* 'he is lost to them' versus *eḳargat* 'they have lost him'. The number agreement markers emphasize the structural difference between the inversion forms and the formally related screeves—the fact that the dative-nominal is an initial subject in inversion, but not in the relative intransitive. Because the rule refers to the initial subject relation, it emphasizes the difference between these historically related screeves and thus constitutes one of the features that differentiates them in Modern Georgian.

Table 13.17

Differences in Number Agreement (Modern Georgian)

Present of relative intransitive verb (Series I)	
mas uc̣eria is	'he has it written'
mat uc̣eria is	'they have it written'
*mas uc̣eri*___an isini___	'he has them written'
First evidential of transitive verb (Series III)	
mas uc̣eria is	'he has written it'
mat *uc̣eri*___at___ *is*	'they have written it'
mas uc̣eria isini	'he has written them'

If Series III has not been reinterpreted, as Series I was, why not? One possible answer to this lies in the relative degree of identification of the final grammatical relations. In Series I, only the initial direct object of transitive verbs bore a final grammatical relation different from that which it bore in Series II. The surface indirect-objecthood of this nominal was coded by case and by person agreement. Apart from case, the identification of the direct object as a final indirect object was clear only when there was no initial indirect object and the direct object was third person (see Chap. 11). Because a clear marking of the initial direct object's final grammatical relations was restricted in this way, it was relatively easy for the case marking to be reinterpreted. In inversion, on the other hand, the initial subject, direct object, and indirect object all bear final grammatical relations different from those they bear in Series II. Further, the surface indirect object and surface subject are clearly coded in all forms. The marking of the retired indirect object with the same case or postposition that is used for retired indirect objects in other constructions is a further indication of the surface grammatical relations. Thus, for Series III to undergo a reanalysis equivalent to that undergone by Series I would entail reinterpreting many more rules. The change in the grammar occasioned by the reanalysis of Inversion would be much greater than that which resulted from the reinterpretation of Object Demotion.

13.6. THE ORIGIN OF SERIES III AND OTHER CHANGES IN THE GRAMMAR

13.6.1. The Relative Chronology of the Origin of Series III

When we turn to the problems of the relative chronology of the origin of Series III and other changes discussed in this work, we find little evidence that can be interpreted with certainty. In facing this issue, we must keep in mind that the first evidential is formally and semantically apart from the other screeves in Series III, and they may have arisen at different times or at the same time.

The morphology of Series III cannot be taken as evidence in this issue, because the relationships between the various screeves that existed when Series III arose continued long after it was established as an independent set of forms. As evidence of this, at least the following two changes have taken place historically in Georgian, affecting relative intransitives in the present tense and the similar forms in the first evidential. (a) The formant *-ie* became *-i;* for example, Old Georgian *mgonies,* Modern Georgian *mgonia* 'I think, believe it' (see Natadze 1955:82ff.). (b) The first and second person surface subject began to be marked by secondary markers, forms of the copula in origin; for example, Old Georgian *mo(v)uḳlav,* Modern Georgian *mo(v)uḳlavar, mo(v)uḳvlivar* 'he has killed me' (see Baramidze 1964:113). Given that these changes were essentially limited to forms of this type, we cannot assume that other changes did not take place before historical times in the morphology of related screeves, keeping them parallel. For example, the use of *e*-grade of ablauting verbs in the first evidential and *i*-grade in the second evidential suggests, at first glance, that these screeves were formed *after* the *i/e* alternation had been reinterpreted for Class 1 forms as markers of Series II versus Series I instead of transitive versus intransitive, which had been an earlier use. However, we cannot rule out the possibility that the Series III forms were reshaped and their ablaut grades changed in order to keep them parallel to the Series I and II screeves to which they corresponded.

Georgian scholars have long assumed that Series III is a more recent formation than Series I or II on the grounds that Series III derives from both of the latter by means of Inversion (Chikobava 1948:5). This assumes, however, that all screeves of Series III were formed at once. There is no reason to exclude the possibility that the second evidential, subjunctive III, and habitual III were formed from the corresponding Series II screeves before the creation of Series I and the first evidential.

A different reason for supposing Series III to be new is that examples of it in Old Georgian are not very frequent, and some particular forms are either unknown or very scarce in the oldest manuscripts. Kavtaradze (1956:184) has argued that the second evidential is newer than the first evidential on the grounds that the latter occurs more frequently than the former. Sarjveladze (1972:149) has similarly argued that the habitual III originated in the literary language only in the tenth century A.D. Natadze (1955:98) and Baramidze (1964:105–107) have argued that the absence of Series III forms of relative intransitives in manuscripts before the tenth century and their infrequency for some time thereafter shows that these are new forms. Sometimes this is interpreted as evidence that Series III as a whole is relatively recent. Imnaishvili (1971:358) has questioned the basis of this argument. The fact that these forms are infrequent, he argues, does not necessarily indicate that they are not old.

The diverse morphology used in the formation of Series III screeves in the various languages may also suggest late creation. I show above how the various Series III forms of Class 1 and 3 verbs may have been analogically reshaped in some languages and have proposed reasons for this. The Series III forms of Class 2 verbs, however, appear to be even more diverse. To draw any conclusions about the date of origin of those forms would require assumptions about the nature of linguistic change that I am not prepared to make.

It is not improbable that Series III is a recent formation or that, at least, part of it is. Nevertheless, the evidence traditionally adduced to support this claim has been based on assumptions that need to be reevaluated.

13.6.2. Series III and Other Changes in the Grammar

Series III and Inversion, while they produce a new surface pattern of case marking, fall outside the question of the origin of case assignment systems. If it could be positively established that Series III had undergone reanalysis, there would indeed be a different pattern. In fact, however, there is no clear evidence that this has happened, though it must be considered a candidate for such a change. If Series III underwent simple reanalysis (in any of the Kartvelian languages) the resulting system would be of the active type,[32] since the subjects of transitive and of active intransitive verbs are marked with one case (dative) while the final subjects of inactive intransitives are marked with another (nominative), as in the Mingrelian examples below.

(79) a. Transitive (Class 1)
zaza-s *duškviduapu* *nodar-i*
Zaza-DAT he/drown/him/INV/III Nodar-NOM
'Zaza has drowned Nodar.'
b. Active Intransitive (Class 3)
ʒγabi-s *teli* *dγas* *umušebu*
girl-DAT whole day she/work/INV/III
'The girl has worked all day.'
c. Inactive Intransitive (Class 2)
nodar-i *doškvidele*
Nodar-NOM he/drown/III
'Nodar has drowned.'

If Series III underwent simple reanalysis, retaining the surface pattern of case distribution (as occurred in the reinterpretation of Series I), it would be as a case system of active alignment. By the same token, the productive rule of Inversion may be said to be a rule of active alignment, applying as it does to the subjects of transitive and of active intransitives and not to the subjects of inactive intransitives. That this is so may be seen by examining the examples in (79). The subjects of the (a) and (b) examples have been made indirect objects, while the subjects of inactive intransitives do not undergo the rule (see Harris 1981b:247–249).

The pattern noted above for Mingrelian is found in all of the Kartvelian languages. It is even found in the Naḳra-Laxamula subdialect of Svan, where we might expect to find instead an ergative pattern (see §6.4.1). The examples below are typical of Series III in that subdialect.

(80) a. Transitive (Class 1)
dina-s *oxmara* *ḳubdär*
girl-DAT she/prepare/it/INV/III pastry/PL/NOM
'The girl has prepared Svan meat pastries.'
b. Active Intransitive (Class 3)
mara *xočamd* *otγirala*
man/DAT well he/sing/INV/III
'The man has sung well.'
c. Inactive Intransitive (Class 2)
bepšw *xäpžəna* [33]
child/NOM he/hide/to.him/III
'The child has hidden from him.'

The government of Inversion in Series III, like case marking in Series II, is a partly lexical phenomenon in all of the Kartvelian languages. A verb that is an exception to one will almost surely be an exception to the other. However, in Old Georgian, those Class 3 verbs that govern nominative case marking as a relic in Series II (see §6.2.2) nevertheless govern Inversion in Series III. Compare (81) with example (7) of Chapter 6.

(81) *eq̇ivnos* *katam-sa*
it/crow/INV/III chicken-DAT
'[when] the cock has [not even] crowed.' i.e., '[before] the cock has crowed' (Mt 26:75AB; J 13:38AB)

It appears that only inversion forms of this verb are found in Series III (also L 22:34; J 13:38Ad), and it would seem, therefore, that Inversion was obligatory. Given the strongly lexical nature of syntactic rule government in Kartvelian (see above; Harris 1981b:268ff.) and the fact that this verb exceptionally governs nominative case subjects in Series II, we would expect this verb to be an exception in Series III if any were.

In Laz, the Class 3 verbs that exceptionally take nominative subjects as an option, govern Inversion in Old Series III. We find, for example, *bere-s ustiramun* 'child-DAT has played/III' and *bere-s uγaγalun* 'child-DAT has talked/III' (see §6.3.2).

Thus, even those Class 3 verbs that are exceptions in taking nominative case subjects in the active case system (§6.2.2, 6.3.2, 6.4) are regular in governing Inversion in Series III in Old Georgian, in Naḳra-Laxamula, and in Laz. In the sense that Inversion applies to all and only initial subjects (i.e., subjects of Class 1 and 3 verbs), it is a rule of active alignment. Given the consistency of evidence, Inversion must be reconstructed as a rule of active alignment in Common Kartvelian as well.

Finally, we may note that the presence of a rule of Inversion in the grammar of a language is entirely unrelated to the alignment of its case marking and agreement rules. Inversion appears as a productive rule in languages with ergative case marking and agreement, such as Avar (Chikobava and Cercvadze 1962), in languages with active agreement, such as Choctaw (Davies 1981: Chap. 7), and in languages with accusative case marking and agreement, such as Kannada (Sridhar 1976). The analysis of Series III is thus independent of analysis of case marking in other series.

NOTES

[1]In glosses of verb forms in this chapter, inversion forms are glossed with "INV"; this practice is not followed in other chapters. The subject and object glosses represent the initial structure, rather than agreement.

[2]Here *mananas* is apparently a surface indirect object.

[3]This generalization does not include emphatics, such as in (82), though they have forms similar to reflexives.

(82)	*rametu*	*araray*	*[me]*	*tavsa*	*čemsa*	*šemicnobies*
	for	nothing/NOM	I/DAT	self	my	I/know/it/INV/III

'For I myself know nothing.' (1 Cor 4:4)

[4]The possessive pronoun *miča* in (13), (14b), and (15) was probably given only because the examples were elicited by translation from Georgian, where the possessive reflexive *tavisi* is used with the full pronoun; see (11)–(12). In textual examples, such as (16)–(17), *miča* is absent.

[5]This verb governs Lexical Object Demotion, which accounts for the case of the object; see analysis and examples (39)–(40) in Chapter 6.

[6]In Harris 1981b, I did distinguish Class 4, inversion verbs, from Class 2. For present purposes this additional distinction is unnecessary.

[7]The exact forms of these suffixes vary with the person and number of the final subject and with the dialect (see Topuria 1967:194, 179, and 173–175).

[8]There are exceptions; for example, the initial direct object bears the dative case in 1 Cor 16:17AB and a postposition in 1 Cor 16:17CD. This is comparable to certain Modern Georgian impersonal constructions (Harris 1981b:144–145).

[9]The meanings of the Series III screeves are points of some contention; see Shanidze (1973: §281–283), Kavtaradze (1956), and Chikobava (1962) on this problem in Old Georgian.

[10]I am following Natadze (1955) and others, rather than Topuria (1967), in use of the labels 'first evidential', and 'second evidential'.

[11]Except for the regular verb 'write', the intransitives listed are absolute, not relative, as some lack relative forms. It is the intransitive STEM only that is at issue.

[12]This discussion is limited to absolute intransitives; on the sources of the morphology of relative intransitives in Series III, see Imnaishvili (1971:348–358).

[13]The possibility of Azerbaijani influence in the development of a periphrastic evidential in Ingilo and Xevsurian is discussed in Imnaishvili (1955) and Arabuli (1980b).

[14]This section relies to a great extent on Rogava (1953) and follows his schema and much of his terminology.

[15]This seems to be the general pattern, but Kaxadze reports that some first evidential forms express the unseen of the imperfect or aorist.

[16]Additional affinities include the fact that *-n* (singular) and *-ed* (plural) occur as third person subject markers for indicative screeves only in Series I and in the first evidential. It is true, however, that they are found in the Series II imperative.

[17]The morphology of Series III in Mingrelian and of Old Series III in Laz is only incompletely described in the works available to me. For Mingrelian first evidentials of Class 1 verbs, the few examples I find in the literature lack full series markers; for example, *u-č̣ḳir-u* 'apparently he cut it' (Rogava 1953:19), *u-č̣ar-u* 'apparently he wrote it'. Both verbs, however, take series markers in Series I. Parallel forms with and without the series marker have been recorded in Laz: *u-ʒir-u-n, u-ʒir-am-u-n* 'apparently he saw it' (Rogava 1953:27; see Baramidze 1964:137). However, for the one speaker with whom I worked on this, a series marker occurred in a majority of forms. I lack suffficient data to form a generalization. The use of a different series marker in the first evidential may be compared with the use, in some of the mountain Georgian dialects, of one series marker (*-av*) in the first evidential of all verbs, regardless of which series marker the verbs govern in Series I (Baramidze 1977).

[18]A further connection between the present and first evidential in Zan is that the latter preserves the ablaut grade reconstructible for Series I in CK, **e*-grade, CK *e having the regular reflex *a* in Zan; the original **e*-grade has been lost in Series I (Gamkrelidze and Machavariani 1965:188).

[19]While these are the Series III forms corresponding to Series II forms such as *daiçera* 'it was written', (Imnaishvili 1971:239–240; Shanidze 1976:110–114), in Old Georgian they still functioned also as analytic passives in the meanings 'it was written' and 'it will be written', respectively. Each underwent later, separate changes.

[20]Series III forms of relative intransitives, on the other hand, have predominantly Series I morphological characteristics. They have been omitted from this discussion because their existence has not yet been confirmed earlier than the tenth century (Imnaishvili 1971:358).

[21]I am purposely avoiding the question of the original function of Series III. Shanidze (1973: §281–283) emphasizes the unseen, but observes, in his own way, the perfect function as well. Natadze (1955:86–88) suggests that the first evidential originally expressed the perfect, drawing a parallel with the German perfect. Kavtaradze (1956:191) suggests that the unseen use appeared later in what had developed as a perfect.

[22]One consultant in Mesṭia, given verb forms with and without *-ar* and asked to make up sentences, consistently gave plural objects corresponding to the *-ar* forms

and singular corresponding to those lacking *-ar*. The same consultant, asked to translate sentences with plural objects from Georgian into Svan, sometimes gave *-ar* forms and sometimes did not. On another day he was given his own sentences, but with *-ar* added for the plural object, and judged these grammatical, correcting for the form of the suffix. For other speakers this suffix may have a wider distribution.

[23]Dzotsenidze (1973:239) observes that in one subdialect the control of *-q̣e* (here *-ḳen*) has spread to certain subjects (see also Kiziria 1974).

[24]Martirosovi and Imnaishvili (1956:128) have observed at least one instance of a final subject in inversion conditioning *-t*.

[25]The suffix *-t* is also conditioned by indirect objects other than inversion nominals in Kartlian (Imnaishivili 1974:236) and in Ingilo (G. Imnaishvili 1966:138).

[26]This shift may be attributed to the fact that the initial subject is the topic of the inversion clause; on topics in agreement, see Givón (1976:154ff).

[27]This does not rule out the possiblity of systematic change in the semantics associated with Series III, which indeed seems to have occurred.

[28]If the Series III patterns were productively derived by Inversion of Series II, we would find in Mingrelian the following system: initial subjects of Class 1 and 3 verbs in the dative and initial direct objects of Class 1 and of Class 2 verbs in the narrative. This is in fact attested by one example from an old man, resident in J̌vari (Asatiani 1970:147). However, this is not the regular pattern, exemplified in this chapter (see especially example 79).

[29]The verbs 'come, go', 'sit', 'stand', and 'lie' govern Inversion (optionally?) in Series III in Mingrelian (Uridia 1960:170) and Laz (e.g., *emixtimun* 'I (IO) have gone up' Dumézil 1937:101, 12). In Chapter 6 it is shown that these verbs have only partially regularized the inherited constructions, governing either nominative or narrative subjects under certain circumstances in Laz and some Georgian dialects. The government of Inversion by these verbs in Series III is another part of the regularization of their syntax in both Mingrelain and Laz. Note that this phenomenon is not reanalysis, but regularization of the existing system.

[30]This reflects the assumption that only one nominal can bear a particular grammatical relation at a particular level of derivation (the Stratal Uniqueness Law).

[31]While this distinction is required by the literary norm (see *Normebi* 1970:182–183; Tschenkéli 1958:406–407, 463, 484–490, 511; Kiziria 1954:146–148), it has been eroded in some dialects (see §13.4.6 and sources cited there, Tschenkéli 1958:486).

[32]Reanalysis combined with another change could produce a different system.

[33]Although this is formally a relative intransitive and is glossed as such here, this form and others like it were elicited with Georgian absolute forms from the three consultants tested on this matter. It may be that the Svan relative forms are used for relative and absolutive alike (see also Topuria 1967:203).

14

Ergative to Active: The Mechanism of Change in Georgian

In Part II, a system of ergative case marking was reconstructed to CK on the basis of comparative data, primarily from Svan, Laz, and Georgian. Among Kartvelologists there has generally been agreement that the change involved an enlargement of the functions of the narrative case (see Deeters 1927:21; Shanidze 1973:483–484). Although it is widely accepted that the nominative case once marked the subjects of all intransitives, there is little agreement concerning the mechanism by which the narrative became the subject case governed by Class 3 intransitives. It is the problem of this mechanism that is addressed in this chapter on the basis of data from Georgian.

Concerning the mechanism of this change, the following points are made: (a) Rather than making a single leap from the generalized ergative system reconstructed in Chapter 6 to the active found in Old Georgian the language probably passed through an intermediate stage of restricted ergative marking (§14.1 and 14.2). (b) It is likely that the change from generalized to restricted ergative proceeded by means of reanalysis of contructions that were underlying transitives and surface intransitives, together with reinterpretation of other structures which were grammatically transitive, but which functioned as intransitives (§14.1). (c) The change from restricted ergative to active involved the generalization of the narrative case subject to a natural class of predicates, many of which were intransitive at all levels and therefore, did not participate in the shift described above (§14.2). (d) The two changes were actualized gradually. Although the rule changes were made before attested Old Georgian, relics of the ancient system still exist in Modern Georgian (§14.3). (e) As one of the concomitants of the change to an active case system, a new morphological class was established in Georgian and a new morphology was developed to set it apart from Classes 1 and 2 (§14.3.2).

In §14.4, four previous proposals concerning the mechanism of this change are examined, and compared with the one outlined above.

The changes described in this chapter must have taken place after the introduction of Series I, since a generalized ergative system was crucial to that development. The new case system, like the Inversion rule of Series III, identifies the subjects of Class 3 verbs with those of Class 1 verbs, contrasting both with the final subjects of Class 2. Although a relative chronology cannot be established with certainty, it seems probable that the introduction of Inversion in Series III led to a closer unity of Classes 1 and 3, in the sense described above, and eventually brought about the changes described in the present chapter, which culminated in active case marking.

14.1. THE TRANSITION FROM GENERALIZED TO RESTRICTED ERGATIVE

Two distinct sorts of ergative case marking were defined in §6.6.1[1]. The generalized ergative type appears to be much more common among languages of the world; in this type, derived intransitives have absolutive case subjects. For example, (1b) is an incorporated object construction in Tongan, corresponding to the transitive, (1a). Cases are marked by particles preceding a noun.

(1) a. *Naʔe haka ʔe he sianá ʔa e ika*
PAST cook ERG the man ABSL the fish
'The man cooked a fish.' (Chung 1978:152)
b. *Naʔe haka-ika ʔa e sianá*
PAST cook-fish ABSL the man
'The man cooked fish.' (Chung 1978:152)

Restricted ergative case rules, on the other hand, mark subjects of derived intransitives with the ergative case. For example, (2) is an incorporated object construction in Dargwa.

(2) *nuni jaħ-barra*
I/ERG patience-do
'I endured.' (Abdullaev 1971:82)

Although (2) is finally intransitive, its subject is in the ergative case; in this respect Dargwa differs significantly from Tongan.

In languages with a rule of active alignment, there is no change of subject case in transitive–intransitive pairs of this sort. Example (3b) is an incorporated object construction in Onondaga and corresponds to the canonical transtive, (3a).

(3) a. *waʔhahnínúʔ neʔ oyv́ʔkwaʔ*
TNS/he:it/buy/ASP PARTICLE it/tobacco/SF
'He bought the tobacco.' (Woodbury 1975:14–15)
b. *waʔhayvʔkwahní:nuʔ*
TNS/he:it/tobacco/buy/ASP
'He bought tobacco.'
(Woodbury 1975:14–15: ASP aspect; TNS, tense/mode; SF, noun suffix)

In Onondaga it is agreement rather than case that has active alignment. The agreement marker, *-ha-*, is the same in the canonical transitive and in the incorporated object construction. In this respect, an active system is like a restricted ergative; this fact seems to be one key to the development of the active from the restricted ergative in Georgian.

In §6.7 and 6.8 it is shown on the basis of comparative data that CK must have had generalized ergative marking, structurally like that illustrated in (1). It is suggested here that the introduction of incorporated-object constructions is one of the ways in which marking shifted to the restricted type. Structurally, marking in incorporated-object constructions in Old Georgian is like that in Dargwa. Since in both the restricted ergative and in the active there is no contrast between subject case in canonical transitives and object incorporation, this construction became an intermediate step in the development of active alignment (§14.1.1).

The change from generalized to restricted ergative likewise involved reanalysis of certain transitives as intransitive; this is described in §14.1.2.

14.1.1. Reanalysis via Incorporation

Incorporation was widely used in Old Georgian as a way of forming expressions such as 'baptize', 'receive baptism', 'worship', and 'honor'. Both direct objects and predicate adjectives could be incorporated, and incorporated forms could occur in both Series I and Series II.

In addition, there are some Class 3 verbs that have synthetic forms in Series I but have only incorporated forms in Series II (see Baramidze 1964:95; Kavtaradze 1954:19; Kavtaradze 1964b:162; Osidze 1960:269; Shanidze 1976:128). Some of these active intransitives are listed in Table 14.1.

I suggest that incorporated forms in Table 14.1 arose because the literal meaning of such compounds is compatible with the punctual aspect of Series II, while the meaning of the synthetic forms is not. Holisky (1979, 1981a:137ff.) has shown that Class 3 verbs in Georgian are atelic. She describes atelic verbs as denoting "activities which do not have to wait for a goal for their realization; they are realized as soon as they begin." They contrast with telic verbs that "describe action which is directed towards a goal or end point," where the goal may or not be attained (Holisky 1981a:138–139). Thus, telic verbs may be punctual–perfective or they may be durative–imperfective. Atelic verbs, on the other hand, are generally durative and cannot be perfectivized. This explains the often-observed fact that Class 3 verbs seldom occur in Series II in Old Georgian (Boeder 1979:465 and references cited there; also Kavtaradze 1954:23; Shanidze 1973:483ff.). For example, 'he cried out' was generally expressed as durative aspect, Series I, *γaγadebda*. While the punctual aspect was not generally used with this verb, a punctual periphrastic construction could occur, with the structure:

(4) (*man*) *γaγad* *q̣o*
he/ERG cry/ABSL he/make/it/II
Lit., 'he made a cry'

Later, the aorist became the general, unmarked past tense, and structures like (4) were used more frequently.

Table 14.1

Incorporated Forms of Class 3 Verbs in Series II in Old Georgian

Series I	Series II
sc̣qalobda 'he felt pity for him'	*c̣qaloba-qo* 'he took pity on him'[a]
qṁobda 'he called, was calling out'	*q̇ma-qo* 'he made a call'
γaγadebda 'he cried, was crying'	*γaγaḋ-qo* 'he made noise, made a cry'
hbrʒoda 'he fought, was fighting them (IO)'	*brʒola-u̇q̣o* 'he took up the fight against them (IO)'
qvioda 'it neighed, was neighing'	*qviv-q̣o* 'it gave a neigh'

[a]Not to be confused with the inverted form, which occurs in both series: *ec̣qalis* 'he pities him', *šeec̣qala* 'he pitied him' (see Kavtaradze 1954:107–108).

I suggest that the forms in the right-hand column of Table 14.1 arose as a reinterpretation of structure (4), where (4) is a simple transitive periphrastic clause. In §14.1.1.1, I argue that the forms in the right-hand column of Table 14.1 are originally and underlyingly transitive, where the incorporated noun is the underlying direct object. In §14.1.1.2, I argue that the same forms were reinterpreted as surface intransitives, and I show the role these structures played in the transition from generalized to restricted ergative marking.

14.1.1.1. Underlying Transitivity

As evidence that the forms in the right-hand column of Table 14.1 are underlying transitive, consider that the verb *qopa* 'make' is transitive and always takes a direct object.[2] Further, if the nominal portion occurs unincorporated, it has the case marking appropriate for a direct object, as in (5a) and (6a), beside the incorporated (b) versions.

(5) a. *romel-man q̣o ç̣q̣aloba-y mis tana*
who/REL-NAR he/make/it/II pity-NOM him with
'who took pity on him' (L 10:37Ad)

b. *da gamovida, ixila er-i mravali da*
and he/come/II he/see/it/II people-NOM many and
ç̣q̣aloba-q̣o mat zeda
pity-he/make/it/II them on
'He came out, saw the multitude, and took pity on them.' (Mk 6:34Ad)

(6) a. *da q̣u siṭq̣ua mat tana*[3]
and he/make/it/II talk/NOM them with
'And he reckoned with them.' (Mt 25:19Ad)

b. *da siṭq̣ua-hq̣o mat monata tana*
and talk/NOM-he/make/it/II DET slave/PL/GEN with
'And he reckoned with the slaves.' (Mt 25:19A)

These examples make it clear that the incorporable nominal is the direct object in (5a) and (6a), and we may assume on this basis that it is the underlying direct object in (5b) and (6b).

A third argument for the underlying direct-objecthood of incorporated nominals is the fact that they may trigger *En*-Agreement in Series II. In Chapter 10 it is shown that this rule is triggered by initial direct objects. Example (7) shows that plural incorporated nouns are also *-en* triggers. (See Chap. 10, example 10, where there is also no overt marker of plurality in the noun.)

(7) ***c̣am-uq̣vna*** *mas* *simon-peṭre*[4]
(eye)lash-he/make/them/to.him/II him/DAT Simon-Peter
'Simon-Peter beckoned to him.' (J 13:24B)

The verb in (7) is *q̣o* as in previous examples; in (7) the root, *q̣v*, is preceded by the version marker *u-* (< *i* / *x* + ____ +, with deletion of *x*) and followed by the plural marker *-n* (< *en*) and the third person singular subject marker for the aorist, *-a*.

These three facts show that the incorporated noun was historically and underlyingly the direct object of the verb, most frequently, *q̣opa* 'make'. Having a direct object as well as a subject, the clauses were underlyingly transitive.

14.1.1.2. Surface Intransitivity

While the forms in the right-hand column of Table 14.1 were originally transitive and derived from a structure like (4), they were eventually reinterpreted as surface intransitives.

The first argument that the incorporated noun is not a final direct object is based on case marking. In Series II, direct objects occur in nominative case forms, *-i*, *-y*, or Ø (see Chaps. 3 and 4); in Series I they are in the dative case. If the incorporated nominal were the surface direct object, it would bear the nominative or dative case, as determined by the series of the governing verb form. In fact, however, the incorporated nominal is in stem form or the dative case WITHOUT REGARD TO THE SERIES of the verb form. For example, with a Series II form, the incorporated noun is in the stem form in (8a) and the dative in (8b). With Series I forms, we find the stem form in (9a) and the dative in (9b).

(8) a. *ambur-uq̣o*
kiss-I/make/it/to.him/II (Mt 26:48B)
b. *ambors-uq̣o*
kiss/DAT-I/make/it/to.him/II
'I will kiss him.' (Mt 26:48AdA)

(9) a. *natel-iγebdes*
light-they/receive/it/I (Mt 3:6AdA)
b. *natels-iγebdes*
light/DAT-they/receive/it/I
'They were baptized.' (Mt 3:6B)

Since surface direct objects can never be in the dative in Series II or in the stem form in Series I, I conclude that these are not final direct objects.[5]

The use of the stem form for incorporated nominals may be due to the fact that these nouns were originally surface direct objects at a time when the stem was the regular form of the nominative case (see Chap. 4). On the other hand, the stem form may represent absence of any case connection, that is, an unmarked form. The use of the dative is probably due to the fact that this case was a marker of retired direct objects in Old Georgian (Harris 1979). This is further support for the proposal that the incorporated nominal is not a final direct object.

An additional argument that the incorporated noun loses its direct-objecthood is based on causatives. In Georgian, organic causatives may be formed from complex initial structures consisting of a matrix clause with an abstract predicate (CAUS), a subject, and a sentential direct object. In the final structure, the matrix subject remains subject. The final grammatical relations of the remaining nominals depend on the transitivity of the embedded clause. If the embedded clause is intransitive, its subject becomes the final direct object and its indirect object the final indirect object. The former is illustrated in (10).

(10)	*upal-man*	*γmert-man . . .*	*gananatl**nes***	***igini***
	lord/NAR	god/NAR	he/CAUS/light/them/II	them/NOM

'The Lord God will light them.' (Rev 22:5)

The fact that 'them' is marked with the nominative case in Series II and triggers *En*-Agreement (in boldface type) shows that it is a direct object. If, on the other hand, the embedded clause is transitive, its subject becomes the final indirect object, while its direct object is the final direct object of the causative, as in (11).

(11)	*ʒma-ta*	*sač̣mel-i*	*moaγebiis*	*tavisa*	*c̣ina*
	brother-PL/DAT	food-NOM	he/CAUS/bring/it/II	self	before

'He makes the brothers bring food before him.'
(Javaxishvili 1946:**70** [5])

In (11) the dative case marking and the fact that it does not trigger any number agreement show that *ʒmata* 'brothers' is the final indirect object. The contrast between the final grammatical relation assigned to the initial embedded subject in (10) and that in (11) gives us a test for transitivity and thus, for the presence of a direct object in the embedded clause (see Harris 1981:182–184). The causative test can be applied to an incorporated simplex structure, comparable to (12).

(12)	*da*	*mat*	*taq̇uanis-hsces*	*mas*
	and	they/NAR	worship-they/give/it/to.him/II	him/DAT

'And they worshiped him.' (L 24:52Ad)

In (12), *mat* 'they/NAR' is the subject, *taq̇uanis* 'worship' the direct object (at least initially), and *mas* 'him/DAT' the indirect object.[6] If this were a surface transitive, we would expect the subject of the embedded clause in the corresponding causative to be in the dative, as is *ʒma-ta* 'brothers-DAT' in (11). This is not what we find. The examples in (13) show that the subject of the initial embedded clause bears the nominative case of a direct object.

(13) a. *taq̇uanis-vacemie* *igi* *paṭiosan-sa*
worship-I/CAUS/give/him/to.it/II him/NOM venerable-DAT
ǰuar-sa
cross-DAT
'I made him worship the venerable cross.'[7]
(Abuladze 1960:51, 5)

b. *taq̇uanis-aceminnes* *cecxl-sa*
worship-they/CAUS/give/**them**/to.it/II fire-DAT
'They made them worship fire.' (Abuladze 1963:244, 12)

c. *q̇ovelni ḳac-ni* *taq̇uanis-aceminnes*
all man-PL/NOM worship-they/CAUS/give/**them**/to.it/II
ḳerp-ta
idol-PL/DAT
'They made all men worship idols.' (Abuladze 1963:244, 7)

In these examples, the initial direct object of the matrix clause, *taq̇uanis-* 'worship', is a final nonterm. The initial indirect objects of the matrix clause, *paṭiosansa ǰuarsa* 'venerable cross', *cecxlsa* 'fire', and *ḳerpta* 'idols', are final indirect objects. The initial subjects of the embedded clauses, *igi* 'he/him' and *q̇ovelni ḳacni* 'all men', are final direct objects. Final direct-objecthood is shown by the case of the nominal—nominative, since these clauses are in Series II. The plural initial subjects in (13b, c) condition *En*-Agreement, which provides additional proof of their status as final direct objects. If the embedded clause, structurally comparable to (12), were perceived as a transitive, in constructions like (13), its initial subject would be in the dative, as in (11). The fact that the initial subjects are final direct objects in causatives is additional evidence that the incorporated object constructions are derivatively intransitive.

Because the incorporating verb is formally transitive, because incorporable nouns in parallel construction bear direct object cases (see examples 5 and 6), and because incorporated nouns may trigger *En*-Agreement, we must conclude that these nominals are initial direct objects and that the clauses in which they occur are thus initially transitive. On the basis of the cases of the incorporated nominal and the grammatical relation of the initial subject of an incorporating verb when embedded in a causative construction (see example 13), we must conclude that incorporated objects are not final direct objects and that the clauses in which they occur are derivatively intransitive.[8]

When the rule of Object Incorporation began to apply to structures like (4) and they were reinterpreted as surface intransitives, the subject remained in the narrative case. Such constructions are examples of clauses in which the narrative case was assigned on the basis of underlying, rather than surface, transitivity. If we assume that case marking still had ergative alignment at the time Object Incorporation was introduced, this construction could have been the first stage in a transition from generalized to restricted ergative marking, setting a precedent for assigning case on the basis of INITIAL transitivity.

14.1.2. Reanalysis via Unemphatic Pronoun Drop

The transition to restricted ergative case marking also involved a reinterpretation of clauses in which the direct object had been dropped.

14.1.2.1. Class 3 Transitives

Many verbs that are Class 3 intransitives in Modern Georgian were optionally grammatically transitive in Old Georgian. These fall into several subclasses, which are not mutually exclusive. That is, a single verb form may belong to more than one of the types enumerated below.

One group of verbs had a direct object optionally, as illustrated in (14).

(14) a. *ċarmart-ni-ca* *iglovdes* *codva-ta-tvis*
gentile-PL/NOM-too they/mourn/I sin-PL/GEN-for
'The gentiles, too, mourned for the sin.'
(Shanidze 1959:235, 38)

b. *iglova* *igi* *q̇ovel-man* *er-man*
he/mourn/him/II him/NOM all-NAR people/SG-NAR
hrom-isa-man
Rome-GEN-NAR
'All the people of Rome mourned him.'
(Kekelidze 1918:132, 18)

Example (14a) is intransitive; the thing mourned over is an oblique nominal marked with the postposition *-tvis*, which governs the genitive case. Example (14b) is transitive, as shown by the fact that the one mourned over is in the direct object case, nominative. Other verbs which, like *glov*, could take an optional direct object are *ṭiris* 'he cries' and *mγeris* 'he sings' (see Nozadze 1974:28).

A second group of Class 3 verbs could optionally take a cognate object.

(15) a. *da imarxvides moçape-ni iovanesni*
and they/fast/I disciple-PL/NOM of John
'And the disciples of John fasted.' (Mk 2:18Ad)

b. *nu uḳue(y) marxva-y imarxet čem tvis*
whether fasting-NOM you/fast/II me for
'whether you fasted (a fast) for me' (Zak 7:5)

Additional examples of this type include *iloca locvay* 'he prayed a prayer' (cf. Modern Georgian *iloca* 'he prayed'), *dγesascauli idγesascaula* 'he celebrated a celebration' (cf. Modern Georgian *idγesascaula* 'he celebrated'), and *qumilvida qumilvasa* 'he was watching a watch' (not continued in Modern Georgian) (Nozadze 1974:49). Examples with cognate objects may occur in both series, but it is characteristic for the cognate object to be present in Series II and absent in Series I.

A third type of grammatical transitive has as its direct object the body part that performs the action. An example is given in (16).

(16) *aγixilna* ***tual-ni*** *zecad*
he/look/them/II eyes-PL/NOM heaven/ADV
'He looked up toward Heaven.' (L 9:16)

Another expression of this type is *iγrč̣enda ḳbilta* 'he gnashed (with) his teeth' (see Vogt 1947a:60). In some examples the direct object does not appear on the surface but must be in the underlying form, as shown by the *En*-Agreement it triggers (see Chap. 10); an example of this sort is given in (17).

(17) *ganicin**n**a sara gul-sa tvis-sa*
she/laugh/**them**/II Sarah heart-DAT self's-DAT
'Sarah laughed in her heart.' (Gen 18:12)

(Additional examples are cited in Imnaishvili 1971:344–345.) The *n* in the above examples is not part of the verb root and does not occur in Series I forms. It must refer to a grammatical direct object, just as that in (16) does.

A fourth type of grammatical transitive consists of reflexive intransitives. As a framework for the discussion of these, we may set out the Series II patterns (18).

(18) a. NAR verb NOM
b. NAR verb self-NOM
c. NOM verb
d. NAR verb

Pattern (18a) represents a canonical transitive, and (18b) a transitive with coreference between subject and direct object; both are Class 1 forms. Pattern (18c) expresses the reflexive as a Class 2 intransitive with nominative subject; as shown in Chapter 6, this is an ancient construction. Pattern (18d) is a newer construction, which signifies the reflexive as a Class 1 transitive with an unexpressed direct object. For most verbs, verbal morphology would distinguish among the several constructions, though there are differences from one verb to another, as discussed below.

The root *mzad* 'prepare' preserves the ancient pattern, having (a), (b), and (c) constructions.

(19) a. *ganmzadenit* *gza-ni* *uplisani*
you.PL/prepare/them/II path-PL/NOM lord/GEN/PL/NOM
'Prepare the paths of the Lord.' (L 3:4A)

b. [*mat*] *ganimzadnes* *tav-ni* *matni brʒolad*
they/NAR they/prepare/them/II self-PL/NOM their to.fight
'They prepared themselves to fight.' (Shanidze 1959:277, 31)

c. [*igini*] *ganemzadnes* *brʒolad*
they/NOM they/prepare/MP/II to.fight
'They prepared to fight.' (Shanidze 1959:273, 2)

Example (19a) is a realization of (18a), (19b) of (18b), and (19c) of (18c). These constructions are continued in Modern Georgian.

The root *ban* 'bathe' continues (18a, b, and d) instead of (18c). The examples in (20) are from Modern Georgian.

(20) a. *deda-m* *švili-i* *dabana*
mother-NAR child-NOM she/bathe/him/II
'The mother bathed her child.'

b. *deda-m* *ṭan-i* *daibana*
mother-NAR body-NOM she/bathe/it/to.her/II
'The mother bathed her body.'

d. *deda-m* *daibana*
mother-NAR she/bathe/II
'The mother bathed [herself].'

Example (20d) is derived from the corresponding (b) construction. However, unlike in ordinary Unemphatic Pronoun Drop, it is not necessary to establish in context the referent of the direct object. In this sense, the (d) examples function independently as intransitives.

The root *kec* 'return' preserves both (c) and (d) variants, as well as a canonical transitive.

(21) a. *da* [*man*] *miakcia . . . igi vecxl-i*
and he/NAR he/return/it/II DET silver-NOM
mγdelt-moʒγuar-ta
priest-elder-PL/DAT
'And he returned the silver to the priests and elders.'
(Mt 27:3AB)

c. *moikcen igini šenda*
they/return/MP/II they/NOM you/ALL
'May they return to you.' (Jer 15:19IO)

d. *moakcion mat šenda*
they/return/II they/NAR you/ALL
'May they return to you.'
(Jer 15:19W, cited in Danelia 1965:77)

While the (d) construction is rare with this verb in Old Georgian, it occurs also in a *xanmeṭi* fragment in Jeremiah 18:8 (Blake 1932:240). In both instances the (d) clause may be interpreted as transitive, as the verb has the prefix *a-*, which is characteristic of transitives. It is the (c) construction that is continued in Modern Georgian, though the meaning has changed somewhat, for example, *is gaikca* 'he fled'. Notice that this means that although the older (c) construction alternated with the newer (d) in Old Georgian, it is the older that continues, rather than the newer as one would ordinarily expect. A similar instance of a lexical item that begins to undergo a change, only to return to its former state is English *seem*.[9]

Another Old Georgian verb that has attested examples of both (c) and (d) constructions is *suen*.

(22) c. [*ganis*]*uennet*
you/rest/MP/II
'Rest [yourselves]. (Mt 26:45, Birdsall 1971:65)

d. *ganisuenos mis zeda sul-man γmrtisaman*
it/rest/II him on spirit-NAR god
'The spirit of God rested on him.' (Isaiah 11:2)

Other manuscripts have in Mt 26:45, *ganisuenet*, which lacks the morphology of a Class 2 form.[10] The Class 1, (d), construction is continued in Modern Georgian; (c) is not.

As a productive type, the ancient Class 2 reflexive intransitive (18c) construction has been replaced by (18d).

14.1.2.2. Unemphatic Pronoun Drop

In all of the Kartvelian languages, Unemphatic Pronoun Drop is very common and applies to objects as well as subjects. Example (23) illustrates the application of Unemphatic Pronoun Drop in Svan, (24) in Laz, and (25) in Mingrelian; see examples in §14.1.2.1 for the same rule in Georgian.

(23) Svan

a. *sosruq̣w-d* *laxṭix* *šīra*
Sosrukw-NAR he/return/it/to.him/II millstone/NOM
nart-äl-s
Nart-PL-DAT
'Sosrukw returned the millstone to the Narts.'
(Shanidze and Topuria 1939:394, 8–9)

b. *atxe sosruq̣w-d* *laxṭix* *i* *ečxāwxwäy*
now Sosrukw-NAR he/return/it/to.him/II and there many
adgär
he/kill/him/II
'Now Sosrukw returned it to them (again) and he killed many there.' (Shanidze and Topuria 1939:394, 11–12)

(24) Laz
ška-s *kogudu* *toḳi. . . .* *oxorǰa-k* *kaniçḳu,*
waist-DAT he/put/it/II rope/NOM woman-NAR she/untie/it/II
ḳapi-s *kogyudu*
stump/DAT she/put/it/II
'He put a rope on her waist. . . . The woman untied it (and) put it on a stump.' (Asatiani 1974:**51** [7] and [9])

(25) Mingrelian
arti čxom-i *opç̌ʔopi,* *mara . . .* *ḳoni guṭev-a*
one fish-NOM I/catch/it/II but back I/leave/it/II-QUOT
' "I caught a fish, but . . . I put it back," he said.'
(Kluge 1916:80, 2–3)

Unemphatic Pronoun Drop does not detransitivize a clause. In the Svan example, (23), it is clear that the clause is a surface transitive (i.e., there is a surface direct object) because the transitive form of the root is used; for this verb, surface intransitives have the stem form *ṭex* (see Chap. 8). In Modern Georgian, interaction with Causative Clause Union and Retired Term Marking show that verbs that take an obligatory direct object are not detransitivized by Unemphatic Pronoun Drop (Harris 1981b: Chap. 12).

The change that took place in Kartvelian was that some of the grammatically transitive clauses that had undergone Unemphatic Pronoun Drop of the direct object were reinterpreted as surface intransitives. The examples in (26) are constructed to illustrate the way in which Unemphatic Pronoun Drop could have facilitated the transition to restricted ergative marking. The letters assignd to the examples correspond to those used above in (18)–(22).

(26) a. *man* *igi* *iglova*
he/NAR him/NOM he/mourn/him/II
'He mourned him.'

c. *igi* *(i)glova*
he/NOM he/mourn/II
'He mourned.'

d. *man iglova*
'He mourned (him).'

The verb morphology is not at issue here but is discussed in §14.3.2. Example (26c) is unattested for this verb and is reconstructed on the basis of examples like (7) and (9) in Chapter 6 and (19c) and (21c) in §14.1.2.1. Example (26c) represents the original intransitive construction. With this particular verb, the intransitive could optionally include an oblique phrase of the sort illustrated in (14a). For the verbs discussed in §14.1.2.1, there was a corresponding transitive, represented as (26a).

Transitive clauses with cognate direct objects, such as (15), clauses with body-part direct objects that are constant for a given verb, such as (16) and (17), and clauses with reflexive unexpressed direct objects, such as (19c), (20d), and (21c, d), functioned as intransitives in the following sense: Their direct objects were entirely predictable; and the referents did not have to be established in context, as required for ordinary Unemphatic Pronoun Drop.[11] In this way, these clauses functioned as intransitives, though they were grammatically transitive.

I suggest that structures like (26d) first occurred as variants of the (a) construction, where the referent of the direct object pronoun was dropped by Unemphatic Pronoun Drop. In this way, clauses like (26d), originally transitive, were reinterpreted as final intransitives. This reinterpretation was possible in part because the narrative case occurred with transitives that were made intransitive by Object Incorporation, as described above, and in part because transitives like (18d) functioned as intransitives in the sense stated above. Similar reanalyses were made with other grammatically transitive verbs described above.

14.2. THE TRANSITION FROM ERGATIVE TO ACTIVE

Consider again the difference between ergative and active case marking. As the table of alignment types (Table 1.1, repeated here as Table 14.2)

Table 14.2

Alignment Types[a]

	Direct object	*Subject of intransitive*		*Subject of transitive*
		Inactive	*Active*	
Ergative	A	A		B
Active	A	A	B	B
Accusative	A	B		B

[a]After Sapir (1917).

shows, they differ only in the case assigned to the subject of active intransitive verbs, and it is in the change of this case marking that we find the shift from ergative to active in Georgian.

It is suggested above that Georgian first allowed the ergative case to be assigned on the basis of underlying transitivity in constructions like (4) and (5b)–(6b); then it applied the same principle to clause types discussed in §14.1.2, reanalyzing them as surface intransitives. The transition from that stage to the active involves the further reanalysis of (26d) and other Class 3 transitives as simple intransitives, that is, as clauses that are intransitive initially and finally, replacing the original intransitive construction, (26c).

Reanalysis of (26d) as a simple intransitive, replacing (26c), was possible because of the infrequent occurrence of either construction in Series II at this stage of the language, as observed above and as noted by other linguists (see p. 49). When active intransitives do occur in Series II in Old Georgian, they very rarely have an expressed subject. As pointed out above, their near-failure to occur in Series II is due to their atelic nature and the punctual aspect of Series II forms.[12]

The reanalysis of underlyingly transitive clauses as simple intransitives with narrative case subjects would have been further facilitated by the fact that the constructions in Table 14.1 took narrative case subjects, yet corresponded to the simple intransitives in the left-hand column of that table.

By no means all of the active intransitives in Old Georgian occurred in one of the grammatically transitive constructions discussed in §14.1.1 and 14.1.2. Nor did the verbs that became Class 3 in Modern Georgian constitute a clear morphological class in Old Georgian. Class 3 was not distinguished as a whole from Class 1 by any morphological characteristic (see Chap. 3). How, then, could the narrative case have been analogically extended to verbs such as *qiva* 'it crew' or *mepa* 'he reigned' (see examples in Chap. 6), which were never transitive at any level of derivation? Why was this case not systematically extended to the final subjects of inactive expressions like *is daixrčo* 'he drowned', is *gaçitlda* 'he blushed', *is daiγala* 'he got tired', or *is gaizarda* 'he grew (up)'? This can only be explained within a theory of universal grammar that recognizes a class of active intransitive predicates. Within such a theory, these predicates constitute a natural class, and it is not surprising that the grammar of a language would generalize case marking or some other morphological or syntactic process over this natural class.

I conclude then that the marking assigned to the subjects of the clauses discussed in §14.1.2 was generalized to the natural class of active intransitives and that in this way the language shifted from ergative- to active-type marking. Because the aorist eventually became the unmarked past tense, examples of this type began to occur more frequently in Series II. The narrative case was assigned to the subjects of active intransitives, regardless of whether or not they belonged to one of the transitive types described in §14.1.

14.3. THE ACTUALIZATION OF CHANGE

As observed in Chapter 2, it is necessary to distinguish between REANALYSIS, which is a change in the rules of grammar, and the ACTUALIZATION of change, which is the gradual fulfillment of the rules of the grammar (see Timberlake 1977). By the period of attested Georgian the reanlaysis from ergative to active case marking in Series II had already taken place, and the actualization of that change was in progress in Old Georgian and is today in Modern Georgian. If the change in case marking types had not already occurred, there would be no examples like (27), where a clause that is intransitive at all derivational levels has a subject in the narrative case, since without reanalysis there would be no basis on which the narrative case could be assigned to a purely intransitive subject.

(27) *da isiʒva man-ca*
and she/fornicate/II she/NAR-too
'And she, too, fornicated.' (Jer 3:8)

The occurrence of examples such as (27) could not have preceded reanalysis of the case system, as there would then be no explanation for the fact that narrative case subjects occurred only with those intransitives that were semantically active.

In §14.3.1 the gradual actualization of the change from ergative to active is examined in several verb types. In §14.3.2 I describe the morphology of the change. Throughout this section it must be borne in mind that, with a few irregular exceptions, there is in Georgian a strict correlation between the morphological class to which a verb form belongs and the syntax of the clause it governs, including the case of the subject. It must also be kept in mind that a given verb root may have forms in only one morphological class or in several (see Harris 1981b:259–261).

14.3.1. Gradual Actualization

The shift from ergative to active case marking has been actualized most completely among those active intransitives that do not correspond to a noncausative transitive. As described in Holisky (1981a), such "basic" intransitives fall into several clear semantic categories, including verbs that express the noises made by animals or humans (e.g., *drṭvinavs* 'murmur, grumble', *q̣ivis* 'screech'), verbs that evaluate actions (e.g., *celkobs* 'he behaves in a naughty manner'), verbs that express that the subject partook of something (e.g., *sadilobs* 'he partook of the noon meal'), verbs that express motion in place (e.g., *ḳanḳalebs* 'he trembles'), and verbs that express displacement motion (e.g., *goravs* 'he rolls') (see Holisky 1981a, especially 85ff., 43ff., 63ff., 98ff., 109ff.). Although the glosses may be misleading, these verbs are intransitive and agentive (active, controllable) (Harris 1981b:235ff.; Holisky 1981a:161ff.). These verb categories are large and productive and morphologically regular (Holisky 1981a; Nozadze 1974); they regularly govern narrative case subjects in Series II.[13]

Some Old Georgian verbs were transitive grammatically but were functionally intransitive. This includes verbs with cognate objects, such as *iloca locvay* 'he prayed a prayer', and some of the verbs with incorporated objects, such as *γaγad-q̣o* 'he cried out' and the other verbs in Table 14.1. Both types developed regular Series II forms and now regularly govern narrative case subjects. For example, Modern Georgian has *man iloca* 'he/NAR prayed' and *man iγaγada* 'he/NAR cried out'. For verbs of these two types, the actualization of the reanalysis has been complete.

With respect to verbs illustrated in (16)–(17), the actualization appears at first to be complete. We find an active case subject in Series II:

(28)	*vano-m*	*dascina*	*andro-s*
	Vano-NAR	he/laughed/to.him/II	Andro-DAT
	'Vano laughed at Andro.'		

Case marking and person agreement show that in (28) *vano* is the subject and *andro* the indirect object. The verb *dascina* is irregular in retaining its obligatory initial direct object, which, however, never shows up on the surface. There are two syntactic tests for transitivity in Modern Georgian. Retired transitive subjects are marked with the postposition *mier*, while retired intransitive subjects are marked with the genitive case. Subjects of transitives become final indirect objects in the corresponding causative constructions, while subjects of intransitives become final direct objects. These tests show that most Class 1 verbs are transitive, while Class 3 verbs have a direct object optionally or not at all (Harris 1981b, Chap. 12). A few Class 3 verbs, however, retain the obligatory initial direct object that they had historically. These tests show that the verbs in (16)–(17) retain their obligatory underlying direct object, although they cannot take an overt direct object.

(29) *nino-m* *daacinvina* *vano-s* *andros-tvis*
Nino-NAR she/CAUS/laugh/him/II Vano-DAT Andro-for
'Nino made Vano laugh at Andro.'

Example (29) is a causative corresponding to (28). The subject of the embedded clause, *vano*, is treated here as the subject of a transitive is, being made final indirect object; the subject of an embedded intransitive would be the final direct object (§14.1.1.2; Harris 1981b: Chap. 5). In addition, the indirect object of the embedded clause, *andro*, is treated as the indirect object of a transitive, being marked with the postposition *-tvis*; the indirect object of an embedded intransitive would be a final indirect object, marked with the dative case (Harris 1981b: Chap. 5). Thus, although the direct object can no longer occur on the surface, the verb *cineba* 'laugh' retains the syntactic peculiarity it showed in Old Georgian, (17). A complete actualization of the changes would involve loss of the underlying direct object.

Perhaps the least amount of change has occurred with verbs that take an optional direct object. Many of the verbs of this type in Old Georgian continue the same range of constructions in Modern Georgian. For example, *ṭirili* 'weep, mourn' was such a verb in Old Georgian and continues to occur as an intransitive or transitive. Like other verbs of this type in Class 3, it has the properties of a transitive just when it has an overt direct object (cf. *tamaši* 'play (it)', Harris 1981b:181–187). One verb of this category, *iʒaxa* 'he called (it) to him (Old Georgian *ʒaxeba*/*zaxeba*) takes an optional direct object, as in *iʒaxa saxeli* 'he called out the name to him'. If it lacks an overt direct object, it has a covert one as *dascina* has.[14] Both are unlike most Class 3 verbs in this respect and have not fully conformed to the regular patterns of the language.

It has already been shown that among the reflexive intransitives, some preserve the ancient construction, (18c), (e.g., *ganemzadnes* in 19c), while others have replaced this with the new construction, (18d), (e.g., *diabana* in 20d). Still others represent parital actualization of the ergative-to-active shift. For example, the verb *ḳrič* (< *ḳreč*) 'shave' has a transitive, *ḳričavs*, which takes the direct object 'beard' or 'face'. It has the (18d) construction, *ikričavs*, which is grammatically transitive but which fulfills the function of an active intransitive, meaning 'he shaves (himself)'. Beside this we find the ancient intransitive, construction (18c) with Class 2 syntax and morphology, *ikričeba*. The ancient intransitive, *ikričeba*, is restricted to a special meaning, 'his head is shaved for him to become a priest'. For this root, the newer construction has replaced the older in the general meaning, but the ancient construction is retained in a specialized sense; in this way the shift in case system has been partially actualized for this verb.

As described in §6.2.1, the change has been more fully actualized in some regional dialects of Georgian than in the literary standard.

14.3.2. Morphological Class

The shift in the syntax of active intransitive verbs cannot be entirely divorced from the changes in morphology and the development of morphological classes. In Old Georgian, active intransitives did not constitute a distinct morphological class, but all verbal types soon changed. In Old Georgian, Series II forms were not specially marked; but eventually Classes 1 and 2 began to use a preverb, together with the old screeve markers, to indicate Series II forms. Class 3, on the other hand, developed the use of the prefix *i-* with screeve markers for this purpose.[15]

The use of *i-* to form Series II of Class 3 intransitives coincided approximately with the use of the narrative case for the subjects of these verbs, and the two developments are undoubtedly related. For example, we find *igi mepa* 'he/NOM reigned' replaced by *man imepa* 'he/NAR reigned' (see §6.2.2) and (30a) replaced by (30b).

(30) a. *katam-i* *qiva*
chicken-NOM it/crow/II
'The cock crowed.' (Mt 26:74; L 22:60; J 18:27)

b. *mamal-ma iqivla*
cock-NAR it/crow/II
'The cock crowed.' (Shanidze 1973:484)

On the basis of these data, we may consider the hypothesis that the use of the narrative case is crucially dependent upon this change in the morphology. With respect to this hypothesis, the following points are made below: (a) The prefix *i-* is associated also with other classes. (b) In spite of the circumstantial evidence offered by the replacement of (30a) by (30b), the correlation between the occurrence of the narrative case and *i-* is not absolute in Old Georgian. (c) Comparison with sister languages does not support a correlation of *i-* with narrative and its absence with nominative. We must therefore conclude that the occurrence of *i-* is not crucial to the use of the narrative case.

The prefix *i-* is not particular to Class 3. It occurs productively in Series I and II as a formant of Class 2 intransitives such as ***i**-ç̣ereba* 'it is written/ I', ***i**-ç̣era* 'it was written/II' (see Appendix to Chap. 3). The prefix *i-* likewise occurs with Class 1 in Series I and II as a productive marker of benefactive–possessive version or as a prefix required with certain meanings; for example, *aγ**i**γebs* 'he takes it up/I', *aγ**i**γo* 'he took it up/II'. With some Class 3 verbs, too, *i-* may occur in both series, as shown below. In every Kartvelian language, *i-* occurs with some verbs from each class.

In Old Georgian a few Class 3 verbs occurred with narrative case subject and without the prefix *i-*; examples are *ç̣inaç̣armeṭq̇uela* 'he prophesied' and *kadaga* 'he preached', both of the *iglova*-type syntactically. Since a large number of Class 2 intransitives are formed with *i-* and govern nominative case subjects in Series II, it is clear that the occurrence of this prefix in a form is neither necessary nor sufficient for the use of a narrative case subject.

Although verbs of each class may have the *i-*, it is only with verbs of Class 3 that this prefix can mark a form as Series II. In Old Gerogian, some Class 3 verbs already had an opposition of Series I with Ø to Series II with *i-*; for example, *ṭirs, iṭira* 'he cries/I', 'he cried/II'. Others had *i-* in both series; for example *icinis, ganicinna* 'he smiles/I', 'he smiled/II'. Some verbs that belonged to this latter conjugation in Old Georgian later developed an opposition of Ø in Series I to *i-* in Series II; for example, *imarxavs* 'he fasts/I' is replaced by *marxulobs*, beside *imarxa* 'he fasted/ II'. It is this that has become the productive conjugational type in Modern Georgian, where *i-* in Series II (and secondarily in the future subseries of I) opposes Ø in the present subseries of I. In the conjugation of *mepobs, mepa* 'he reigns/I', 'he reigned/II', the prefix is absent from both series; in Modern Georgian this is replaced by *mepobs, imepa* in the same meanings. Some verbs belonged to more than one conjugational type in Old Georgian, for example, *glovs, iglovs* 'he mourns/I', *iglova* 'he mourned/II' (Nozadze 1974:33–36).

In the other Kartvelian languages, *i-* also plays a part in the morphology of Class 3. In Svan this prefix occurs in Series I and II forms of verbs that have the *-al* suffix characteristic of Class 3; for example, Naḳra ***i**šwep̣inäl* 'he whistles/I', ***i**šwep̣inal* 'he was whistling/I', *äd**i**šwep̣inal* (<*ad-**i**-*) 'he whistled/II'. Among Class 3 verbs lacking this suffix, one paradigm likewise has *i-* in both series (e.g., Naḳra *isḳora* 'he was thinking/I', *ädsḳore* (< *ad-i-*) 'he thought/II', Upper Bal *iqešda* 'it was barking/I', *läiqešde* 'it barked/II'). A second conjugational type of Class 3 verbs has *i-* in Series II but not in Series I; for example, Upper Bal *šwep̣da* 'he was whistling/

I', *läišwep* 'he whistled/II' (see Nozadze 1974:39).[16] In addition, some Class 3 verbs lack *i-* in both series, for example, Upper Bal *ačk̦uārda* 'he was thinking/I' (with the variant *ičk̦uārda*), *adčk̦ūre* 'he thought/II'.

In Laz, *i-* likewise occurs in both Series I and II of one conjugation of Class 3 verbs; for example, *ibirs* 'he sings/I', *isters* 'he plays/I', *ibiru* 'he sang/II', *isteru* 'he played/II'. Another conjugation of Class 3 verbs in Laz has *i-* in Series II but not in Series I (e.g., *xoronaps, ixoronu* 'he dances/I', 'he danced/II'), while a third has *i-* in neither (e.g., *peṭelaps, peṭelu* 'it bleats/I', 'it bleated/II') (Nozadze 1974:42). Mingrelian is the same in this respect (Nozadze 1974:42–44).

Thus, Old Georgian, Svan, Laz, and Mingrelian all have conjugational types in which (a) *i-* occurs in both series, (b) *i-* occurs in Series II but not in the original screeves of Series I (see n. 16, this chapter), and (c) *i-* occurs in neither series. On this basis, all three conjugational types must be reconstructed to CK. In the course of the history of Georgian, conjugational type (a) was replaced by (b) for some verbs, and (c) was replaced by (b) for the few verbs for which it is attested (at least *mepa* 'he reigned', *q̣iva* 'it crew', *kadaga* 'he preached', *c̣inac̣armeṭquela* 'he prophesied'). Conjugational type (b) has become the most widespread and productive type in Georgian.[17] Since type (c), illustrated in (30a), occurs in all four languages, we must reconstruct it for CK. It was replaced in Georgian by type (b), illustrated in (30b), as part of a widespread regularization of the conjugation of Class 3, which remains incomplete.

If the shift from nominative case subjects to narrative in examples like (30) were dependent upon the change in verbal morphology, we would expect to find that the (c) type in Laz and Svan governs nominative case subjects. Since Series II has undergone reanalysis in Mingrelian, we would not expect to find that situation there. To the extent that this can be investigated on the basis of published materials, verbs of conjugational type (c) in Laz take narrative case subjects, including the following examples: *mčxuri-k peṭelaps* 'sheep-NAR bleats' (Chikobava 1938:306), *cxeni-k xixinaps* 'horse-NAR neighs' (Chikobava 1938:428), *mončva-k k̦oxams* 'hen-NAR clucks' (Chikobava 1936, II:76, 19), *k̦ulani-k xoronaps* 'girl-NAR dances' (fieldwork). The only example of this conjugational type in my Svan data is *adčk̦ūre* 'he thought', which takes a narrative case subject in all dialects investigated; for example, Lašx *ejnēm adčk̦ore* 'he/NAR thought', Upper Bal *deded adčk̦ūre* 'the mother/NAR thought'. Thus, in the data available we find no support for the hypothesis advanced above.[18]

Since there is no causative relation between the occurrence of the *i-* prefix and the use of the narrative case, how do we account for the replacement of (30a) by (30b)?

On the basis of the facts discussed in Part II and in this chapter, I suggest the following development. At the earliest stages, the two sorts of intransitive were not distinguished grammatically and governed the same subject case, nominative. Some verbs of each class had *i-* and others lacked it; the original function of the prefix is obscure (but see Shanidze 1973:§418). The prefix *i-* is shared among all the languages because it was in CK. The ergative-to-active shift provided the impetus for the development of morphology to set Class 3 apart from the other classes; but this change followed the case shift, taking place after the separation of Georgian from Zan. Morphology from a variety of sources was developed in language-specific ways to set apart Class 3; this is one of the concomitants of the ergative-to-active shift and is explored further in Chapter 16. In Georgian, conjugational type (b) was generalized at the expense of types (a) and (c) as a defining characteristic of Class 3.

Thus, the *i-* prefix is very old with some verbs that have reflexes in Class 3, having occurred with them in CK, as shown by comparative evidence. The spread of conjugational type (b) in Georgian is one of the concomitants of the ergative-to-active shift, as is the development of other morphology that sets apart Class 3. The replacement of (30a) by (30b) is part of the actualization of the ergative-to-active shift and part of the generalization of conjugational type (b) in Georgian. Narrative subjects occurred with a few Class 3 verbs like *ċinaċarmeṭquela* because the development of Class 3 morphology, including the (b)-type conjugational use of *i-*, followed the ergative-to-active shift.

14.4. ALTERNATIVE ACCOUNTS

In this section I briefly consider hypotheses that have been advanced by other linguists to explain the use of the narrative case with intransitive verbs. All theories described here involve the transitivity of Class 3 verbs in some sense, but there remain important differences among them.

Shanidze (1973:472ff., and earlier works) suggests that the syntax and morphology of Class 3 verbs are "borrowed" from the corresponding active [Class 1] forms. For example, it is suggested that *iḳivla kal-ma* 'cried out/II woman-NAR' derives from the "subjective version" of the Class 1 form, *aḳivlebs* 'he causes someone to cry out' (Shanidze 1973:473–474). Thus, Shanidze accounts for the spread of the narrative case to the subjects of Class 3 by relating this class to transitives; he accounts for the prefix *i-* that occurs on many Class 3 forms by relating it likewise to Class 1 forms, which may have such a prefix.

So-called subjective version occurs only with transitive verbs and expresses that the subject possesses the direct object or that the action benefits the subject. For example, the transitive verb *garecxa* 'he washed it' has the subjective version form *gairecxa* 'he washed it for himself' or 'he washed something of his own'. Although Shanidze's hypothesis provides an account of the source of *i*-, it is impossible to reconcile the syntax of Class 3 verbs with that of actual subjective version. The causative of 'cry out' and other Class 3 intransitives cannot express that the subject possesses the direct object or that the action benefits the subject. Without an explanation of the fact that Class 3 verbs lack the notions of causation and possession-benefaction essential to the Class 1 forms proposed as a source, this hypothesis provides an incomplete account of the change.

Although we have seen that some Class 3 verbs occurred in various transitive constructions, illustrated in §14.1, many never occurred as transitives, such as *qivis* 'crows', *qeps* 'barks', and so forth. Without a linguistic theory that recognizes active intransitives as a natural class, there is no principled basis on which to explain how the narrative case was extended to those Class 3 verbs that have no corresponding transitives.

Finally, as shown in §14.3.2, there is only circumstantial evidence that the use of the narrative case is crucially related to the occurrence of the *i*- prefix. Comparative data shows that the narrative may occur also with Class 3 verbs that lack *i*-.

Additional arguments against such a borrowing proposal are made by Nozadze (1974:31–32), who advances his own hypothesis concerning the origin of the use of the narrative with Class 3. Nozadze (1974:47ff.) proposes that Class 3 verbs are all transitive and that their direct objects form the stems of the verbs. That is, he distinguishes verbs with "external" direct objects, such as *ḳlavs* 'kills', from verbs with "internal" direct objects, such as *mepobs* 'reigns' (related to *mepe* 'monarch'). There are several problems with such an account. First, although some Class 3 verbs are clearly related to nominals, there is no basis for claiming that the nominals to which they are related are in any sense their direct objects. Holisky argues that they are related, instead, by a lexical rule (1981a:43–51, 70–71) and suggests that in some instances nominals are formed lexically from Class 3 verbs, rather than the other way around (1981a:108–109). Second, one productive type of Class 3 verb is derived from other verbs (Holisky 1981a:73–81), while other productive classes are not related to nouns or verbs (Holisky 1981a:83ff.). Third, this theory entails that Class 3 verbs have always been "transitive" and have always had narrative case subjects (Nozadze 1974:48). It is therefore unable to explain the occurrence of examples like (30a) and sentences discussed in Chapter 6, where the subject is in the nominative case. Finally, if the direct object forms the stem of a verb of this class, then we have no explanation for the occurrence of another direct object optionally with some verbs of this class; for example, *itamaša nardi* 'he played backgammon', *imγera nanina* 'he sang a lullaby'.

Nebieridze (in press), citing examples similar to (5b) and (6b) and (15)–(17), proposes that all Class 3 verbs have a deep structure direct object. If the direct object and the verb have "the same referential meaning", as do *iloca locvay* 'he prayed a prayer', the direct object is deleted in Modern Georgian. On this basis he proposes deep structure transitives corresponding to surface structure intransitives. However, data from Old Georgian cannot necessarily be assumed to represent underlying structures in Modern Georgian.

If all Class 3 verbs were underlyingly transitive, there would be no way to account for the difference between causatives like (32b), on the one hand, and (32a) and (31) on the other.

(31) a. *vano-s* *davaçerine* *çeril-i*
Vano-DAT I/CAUS/write/it/to.him/II letter-NOM
'I got Vano to write a letter.'
b. *vanos* *davaçerine*
Vano-DAT I/CAUS/write/it/to.him/II
'I got Vano to write it.'

(32) a. *vano-s* *vatamaše* *nard-i*
Vano-DAT I/CAUS/play/him/II backgammon-NOM
'I got Vano to play backgammon.'
b. *vano* *vatamaše*
Vano/NOM I/CAUS/play/him/II
'I got Vano to play.' (Harris 1981b:182–183)

'Write' is a Class 1 verb; even when its direct object is not overt, it remains transitive. The initial subject of 'write' is a final indirect object in the corresponding causative (31), whether or not the initial direct object is expressed (see above; Harris 1981b: Chap. 5). 'Play', on the other hand, is a Class 3 verb. If it always had a deep structure direct object, as hypothesized by Nebieridze, then we could not explain the fact that the initial subject of 'play' in (32b) is the final direct object, as for other INtransitive verbs. His hypothesis is also unable to account for alternations in the marking of retired subjects of Class 3 verbs (Harris 1981b:184–186). Finally, if cognate direct objects are posited for all Class 3 verbs (**imepa mepoba* 'he reigned a reigning'), we still need a principled linguistic explanation for the lack of cognate direct objects with Class 2 verbs, such as **darča darčeba* 'he remained a remaining'.

Without reference to any particular language, Dixon has speculated that a change of the sort described here might take place by reanalysis of transitives:

> We might speculatively posit an original ergative system, and then suggest that some transitive verbs underwent a semantic shift that led to the elimination of previously obligatory object NP's: they would be reanalysed as intransitive verbs with the S NP marked by ergative case. (1979:100)

By "S NP," Dixon means the intransitive subject. Although Dixon did not apparently have Georgian in mind, his description is partially applicable to it. Some of the transitive verbs described in §14.1.2 do seem to have undergone a semantic shift.For example, *imarxa* in (15) originally meant 'keep' and later 'fast' (Deeters 1927:21). Nevertheless, there is no evidence that all of the verbs that took optional cognate objects changed semantically. The verbs illustrated in (16)–(17) could be considered to have changed semantically. Many Class 3 verbs never occurred in any one of the transitive patterns illustrated in §14.1, yet developed the use of the narrative case. Among these, several are listed in §6.1 and 6.5 as CK or CGZ roots, and these seem not to have changed semantically in any significant way. The occurrence of the ancient type (30a) gives us every reason to believe that the prototype of the Class 3 verb took subjects in the nominative case.

All of the hypotheses discussed here are based on transitives being reinterpreted as intransitives, and all have something in common with the account proposed in this chapter. All of them differ from my hypothesis in that they attribute transitivity at some level, or in some period, to all Class 3 verbs, even though there is every indication that many of them were always intransitive. If active intransitives like *qiva* 'it crew' were originally transitive, there would be no explanation for the occurrence of the nominative case subject with this ancient type. Those initial transitives that were reinterpreted as final intransitives never occurred with nominative case subjects; see examples (14b)–(17). The distinction between initial intransitive subjects and direct objects provides a principled basis by which to account for the development of active case marking without attributing transitivity to every active intransitive. The fact that certain active intransitives occurred in one or another transitive construction and could be reinterpreted as final intransitives made possible the reanalysis of the case marking system, as described in §14.1 and 14.2.

14.5. CONCLUSION

Unlike most of the changes described in this work, the ergative-to-active shift seems to have taken place by means of the reinterpretation of several surface constructions. It is likely that the ergative-to-active shift itself was preceded by a change from generalized to restricted ergative marking.

As a summary of this chapter, we state, in (33), the rules for case marking in Series II that applied after the ergative-to-active shift. These may be compared with those of CK, stated as (54) of Chapter 6 (see p. 142).

(33) a. The final subject of a transitive or active intransitive is marked with the narrative case.
b. The final subject of an inactive intransitive is marked with the nominative case.
c. A final direct object is marked with the nominative case.
d. A final indirect object is marked with the dative case.

While these are accurate generalizations, there are exceptions.

The changes in the case system were actualized gradually and have some residue in Svan, Laz, and Georgian, described in Chapter 6 and in this chapter. As one concomitant of the case shift, each language developed morphology that sets Class 3 apart from other classes (§14.3.2 and Chapter 16). Other changes that may be construed as results of the ergative-to-active shift are described in Chapter 15.

APPENDIX. OVERGENERALIZATION: THE CASE OF EXPRESSIVES

EXPRESSIVES is the name given here to onomatopoetic or "echo" verbs, which use sound symbolism or special phonological patterns to describe certain types of activities, as explained in greater detail below.

Cross-Linguistic Characterization

Emeneau has done important research on expressives (see especially Emeneau 1980b); it is clear from work by him and by a number of other linguists that expressives are likely to stand outside of the regular system of a language in several respects. (a) Expressives are not accorded full status in a language, either by speakers or by linguists (Emeneau 1980a:9). (b) Expressives may have a structure or rules that are not viable in the rest of the language (Emeneau 1980c:264). (c) They may constitute an exception to an otherwise-valid language universal (Campbell 1980:22–23). (d) It has been suggested that expressives are capable of being created or of diffusing rapidly to form a complete system in a short time (Hoffman 1952).[19] (e) Expressives seem to be a semantically coherent subsystem, both from a language-internal and from a cross-linguistic point of view. Although points (b) and (c) have been studied primarily from the point of view of phonology, Diffloth (1972) suggests that expressives are likewise likely to be exceptional from a syntactic perspective, and the data from Georgian confirms this.

The Subsystem of Georgian Expressives

The phonology of expressive verbs in Georgian has been studied by Asatiani (1975), and their morphology, syntax, and semantics has been studied by Holisky (1981a). It is from Holisky's work that the lists of verbs in Tables 14.3–14.6 are drawn.

Many expressive verbs in Georgian are reduplicating, as illustrated by those in Table 14.3. Among expressives formed with reduplication, some seem to be formed from simple (nonreduplicated) stems with a similar meaning, as in Table 14.4.

Apart from those formed by reduplication, many expressives fall into the pattern *Cial-ebs* or *Ca/uCun-ebs/obs*, as illustrated in Tables 14.5 and 14.6, respectively.

Table 14.3

Expressives with Reduplication in Georgian[a]

bubun-ebs	'it roars, bellows'
buqbuq-ebs	'it murmurs, gurles, rumbles'
gużguż-ebs	'it crackles'
zanzar-ebs	'it rattles (of panes of glass)'
ḳivḳiv-ebs	'it gobbles'
gizgiz-ebs	'it flickers (of hearth fire)'
varvar-ebs	'it glows, flames'
ḳamḳam-ebs	'it gleams, shines'
ḳašḳaš-ebs	'it shines, beams'
laplap̣-ebs	'it gleams, shines (of clean dishes, etc.).'
baban-ebs	'it trembles, shakes'
bibin-ebs	'it waves (of grass in a field)'
zanzar-ebs	'it rattles, shakes (of loose panes)'
tamtam-ebs	'it shakes (of loose flesh)'
taxtax-ebs	'it trembles, quakes'

[a]Adapted from Holisky (1981a:84–100).

Table 14.4

Simple and Reduplicated Expressives[a]

si-v-is	'hiss, whizz'	*si-si-n-ebs*	'hiss'
živ-is	'twitter'	*živ-živ-ebs*	'twitter'
zu-is	'buzz'	*zu-zu-n-ebs*	'buzz'
q̣iv-is	'screech'	*q̣iv-q̣iv-ebs*	'screech'

[a]Adapted from Holisky (1981a) and Tschenkéli (1960–1974).

Table 14.5

Cial-ebs Pattern[a]

bzrial-ebs	'it hums, buzzes'
zrial-ebs	'it rattles, clinks'
žrial-ebs	'it clinks, clatters'
bdγvrial-ebs	'it flashes, sparkles'
brial-ebs	'it blazes, flares'
brč̣qvial-ebs	'it glitters, twinkles'
ḳrial-ebs	'it gleams, shines'

[a]Adapted from Holisky (1981a:84–97).

Table 14.6

Ca/uCun-ebs/obs Pattern[a]

bzuḳun-ebs	'it buzzes'
gruxun-ebs	'it thunders'
ḳruxun-ebs	'it cackles'
žγarun-ebs	'it rings, chimes'
sluḳun-ebs	'it sobs'

[a]Adapted from Holisky 1981a:(84–97).

Additional patterns can be seen in the data cited by Holisky. Semantically, they fall into two macrogroups: active expressives, such as *bγavis* 'it bleats', *bγuis* 'it moos', and inactive expressives, such as most of those illustrated in Tables 14.3–14.6. Most of the active expressives express controllable noises made by animals or humans. Among inactive expressives are verbs of noncontrollable noise, light, and motion. Holisky (1981a:102–105) observes that a single verb may express two or more of these notions.

As noted in the preceding section, it has been suggested that a fully developed subsystem of expressives can be quickly formed by a language, and there are indications that this is true of inactive expressives in Georgian. The roots of some Georgian expressives can be identified as inheritances from CK, and others from CGZ. Among these, some seem to have developed the productive patterns relatively recently. For example, the CK root *ḳr is preserved in the Georgian inactive expressive *ḳrialeba* 'gleam, shine' and in Svan *liḳre*, which has the same meaning (Klimov 1964:114), but the Svan form apparently lacks the formant *-ial-eb* (see Table 14.5), which must have been added in Georgian. The view that the subsystem has developed (or redeveloped) relatively recently is supported by the regularity of word formation found among inactive expressives, including the fact that the inactive expressives are almost exclusively formed with the two most productive and most recent of the series markers, *-eb* and *-ob* (see Chap. 9).

While many examples of active expressives may be found in Old Georgian, few inactive ones occur. Among the inactive expressives that do occur, few, if indeed any, fall into the regular patterns described and illustrated above. For example, Holisky's category of verbs of light (*gizgizebs* class) contains 23 verbs that fall into one of the productive phonological patterns described above and illustrated in Table 14.3 and 14.5, and 5 verbs that do not fit one of these patterns. Not one of the 23 regular verbs is listed by Abuladze (1973), while 4 out of the 5 others are listed by him: *elvareba* 'sparkle, flash', *bzinva* 'flash, sparkle', *brç̣qinva* 'gleam, glitter', and *(gamo)ḳrtoma* 'sparkle'. While these data are only suggestive, the fact that those that fall outside the regular patterns are attested supports the view that the patterns illustrated in Tables 14.3, 14.5, and 14.6 are a recent development, while those expressives that fall outside these patterns are older.

On the basis of the facts discussed above, it appears that the regular, productive patterns for the formation of inactive expressives—and to this extent the subsystem of inactive expressives found in Modern Georgian—has recently developed, while those few inactive expressives that fall outside of the patterns described reflect an older set of inactive expressives.

Inactive Expressives in the Larger System

In previous chapters it is established that verb forms in Kartvelian fall into one of three classes, as summarized in Table 3.1, repeated here as Table 14.7. The observation that Class 3 verbs are atelic and Classes 1 and 2 telic (or stative) comes from Holisky (1981a). The case named in the second column of Table 14.7 refers to the case governed by verbs of the various classes for their subjects in Series II.

While active expressives, such as *zmuis* 'it moos', clearly fit into Class 3, inactive expressives, such as *katkatebs* 'it shimmers', do not, precisely

Table 14.7

Morphological–Syntactic–Semantic Correlations

Morphological	Syntactic	Semantic
Class 1	transitive narrative case	active (or inactive) telic
Class 2	intransitive initial direct object nominative case	inactive telic or stative
Class 3	intransitive initial subject narrative case	active atelic

because they are inactive, rather than active. On the other hand, inactive expressives differ from other inactive intransitives (Class 2) in being atelic. Thus, they fall outside the set of correspondences listed in Table 14.7.

To account for the relative newness of the subsystem of inactive expressives in Georgian, I propose the following hypothesis. In CK, as reconstructed in Part II, there was no grammatical distinction made among intransitive verbs. Later, with the introduction of Series III and the shift from the use of the nominative to the narrative case for the subjects of Class 3 verbs in Series II, a grammatical distinction based on the opposition of initial intransitive subjects (active) to initial intransitive objects (inactive) was introduced. At first, inactive expressives were identified with Class 2 on the basis of their syntax; this would have entailed no morphological change regarding this subclass. At this stage some inactive expressives are attested in Series II, as in (34).

(34) *cvima-y arγara dasc̣ueta kueq̣anasa zeda*
rain-NOM NEG it/drip/II earth on
'The rain no longer dripped down on the earth.' (Ex 9:33)

Note that these have the Class 2 property of governing a nominative case subject in Series II. Later, the emphasis shifted from the syntactic opposition to a semantic contrast of atelic to telic. Inactive expressives were grouped with active expressives, rather than with other inactives, with which they conflicted on the telic versus atelic criterion. In this way, inactive expressives became members of Class 3, and on the basis of that membership they govern narrative case subjects in Series II in Modern Georgian. For example, in Modern Georgian, the verb in (34) may take a subject in the nominative or narrative, but the latter is preferred (Harris 1981b:246).

Implications

The inclusion of inactive expressives in Class 3 in Modern Georgian makes it impossible to type all verbs in the language according to a single semantic criterion. For most verbs in the language the active versus inactive distinction divides Classes 1 and 3 from Class 2, while transitivity generally distinguishes Class 1 from Class 3. This statement applies also to active expressives but not to inactive expressives. In several ways inactive expressives fall outside the regular patterns of Georgian syntax (Holisky 1981a:160–168), and their deviant status in other languages, as discussed in the first section of this appendix, reinforces the conclusion that they are best considered exceptions in Georgian, both synchronically and diachronically.

NOTES

[1]It is not intended that these types be interpreted as an absolute dichotomy; it is entirely possible that in some language, case is assigned on the basis of final transitivity in one construction and on the basis of initial transitivity in another.

[2]In some incorporated forms it is not the initial direct object, but an adjective or adverb, that is incorporated, for example, *c̦rpel-qo* 'he made it straight', and *šeuracx-qo* 'he scorned him'. This type is transitive at all levels of derivation and is not discussed further here.

[3]The form *qo* is usual, not *qu* (see Blake 1976:140 in the *apparatus criticus*). The form *qo* comes from *qv* plus *a*, where *qv* is the root 'make' and *-a* is the third person singular subject marker for the aorist; see example (7).

[4]The subjects in (7), (17), and some other examples are proper names, which occur in stem form for both narrative and nominative case. Other examples show that these verbs govern narrative case subjects.

[5]The dative case marking in Series II cannot be an indicator of surface indirect-objecthood in this instance, since these dative plurals can trigger *En*-Agreement, as shown in (35); see also example (7).

(35) ***tualt*-*uqvnes*** *niḳodimoz-s*
eye/PL/DAT-they/make/them/to.him/II Nikodemos-DAT
'They beckoned to Nikodemos.'
(Anan. Ebr. 427, cited in Abuladze 1973:183b)

Yet the examples in (22) of Chapter 10 show that initial direct objects that are final indirect objects do not trigger *En*-Agreement.

[6]Imnaishvili (1957:188–189) has argued convincingly that *taquanis* or *tavqanis* is itself composed of *tav*, which in Old Georgian could mean 'honor, obeisance', and *qan-is*, genitive of 'field,' here 'low(ly)'. Thus, unlike other items incorporated with finite verbs forms, *taquanis* bears a genitive ending as the indication of the relation between *tav* and *qana*.

[7]Old Georgian causative constructions differ from those in Modern Georgian in that the retired indirect object of the embedded clause may be marked with the dative case, rather than with the postposition *-tvis* as in Modern Georgian (Harris 1981:81–85). For this reason, in Old Georgian the case marking of the initial embedded indirect object in a transitive is not distinct from that of one in an intransitive. Therefore, the case of *ǰuarsa* in (13a) does not form the basis for an additional argument for intransitivity as it would in Modern Georgian.

[8]A similar conclusion, in more traditional terms, is reached by Shanidze (1976:125). Shanidze (1942) argues for initial direct-objecthood on the basis of the parallel unincorporated examples; he argues that these are not final direct objects on the basis of the case of the incorporated nominal and because in some instances person markers may precede the incorporated nominal; for example, *v-γaγad-q̣av*, where *v-* is the first person subject marker, *γaγad* is the incorporated element, and *q̣av* is the verb root.

[9]For example, in (36), the experiencer is in the nominative case, rather than in the dative, which is required by both the old and the modern constructions for this verb.

(36) *Do as ye seems best.* (c. 1430 Generydes, 6007)
(Example cited in Butler 1977:166.)

In (37), on the other hand, the case marking is regular, but the verb fails to agree with its surface subject; the expected form is *seemeth*.

(37) *Me-seem my head doth swim.* (1571 Damon and Pithias, 79)
(Example cited in Visser 1963:31.)

[10]Another example that appears, on the basis of case, to be of type (c) is (38).

(38) *c̣mida-y peṭre-y ganisuena*
holy/NOM Peter/NOM he/rest/II
'Saint Peter rested (i.e., died).' (Marr 1974:723, 19)

[11]The occurrence of direct objects with these forms adds no lexical information but contributes to the expression of punctual–perfective aspect. It is probably for this reason that in Series II, which expressed punctual–perfective aspect, the transitives listed above were relatively plentiful while their intransitive counterparts are rare.

[12]Some linguists have interpreted the infrequency of Class 3 verbs in Series II in Old Georgian as an indication that at an earlier period, all active intransitives were restricted to Series I (e.g., Kavtaradze 1954:23). A lack of Series II forms is not a prerequisite to the changes described in §14.1. The hypothesis that active intransitives never occurred in Series II is not consistent with the occurrence of ancient verb morphology and ancient marking patterns in this series, as in examples (27) and (30a).

[13]Most Kartvelologists have overlooked the systematic nature of the use of narrative case for subjects of Class 3 verbs and have described this as an irregularity in an ergative system (for example, Boeder 1979:443ff., Fähnrich 1967; Klimov

1973, 1976.) This approach is critiqued in greater detail in Harris (1981b:Chapter 16).

[14]It appears that this verb has become a regular transitive Class 1 verb in some dialects (Dzidziguri 1941:250; G. Imnaishvili 1966:139; Martirosovi and Imnaishvili 1956:131), but another interpretation has also been proposed (G. Imnaishivli 1966:139).

[15]Aorists in *a——d* have sometimes been incorrectly identified as forms of Class 3 verbs; for example, *ṭiris* versus *aṭirda*. The *a——d* verbs are actually inceptives (members of Class 2), formed on the same root (see Harris 1981b:251–252; Holisky 1981a, 1983b; Nozadze 1974).

[16]More precisely, while *i-* is not found in the present, imperfect, and other original Series I screeves with verbs of this conjugational type, it does occur in secondarily formed Series I screeves, such as the future imperfect (Nozadze 1974:39).

[17]On the basis of the same data, Nozadze (1974:36) concludes instead that other (all?) Class 3 verbs in Georgian originally had *i-* in the present but had lost it before the manuscripts that are considered were written. This is methodologically unsound, given that Laz and Mingrelian have abundant examples of conjugational types in which *i-* is absent from Series I only (type b) and from both series (type c). If all daughter languages exhibit each of the conjugational types, all must be reconstructed for the proto-language (see §2.2.4).

[18]Chikobava (1938:298, 306) lists examples of two of these verbs with subjects in nominative case forms. These occur in the Maxo and Artašen dialects where the case system differs from that of Standard Laz (see §15.3.3 and §15.5, respectively). Since use of the nominative is regular for these dialects, the examples are irrelevant to the question at hand.

[19]Emeneau (1980c:264) does not entirely accept this.

15

Case Changes Resulting from the Ergative-to-Active Shift

In this chapter I describe a number of changes involving cases, which seem to have arisen because of the ergative-to-active shift discussed in the preceding chapter. In §15.1 I describe the reanalysis of Series I and show why it is probable that it resulted from the ergative-to-active shift. Section 15.2 deals with a change in the form of the narrative marker. Extensions of the functions of cases in Mingrelian, two Laz dialects, and one Georgian dialect are described in §15.3 and are discussed in more general terms in §15.4. Section 15.5 contains a description of a shift in alignment that resulted in part from phonological erosion.

15.1. REANALYSIS OF SERIES I

In Chapter 11 I show that the surface case patterns used in Series I in Georgian, Mingrelian, and Svan, and reconstructed for this series in Middle and Late Common Kartvelian, are derivable by application of the general case rules reconstructed for Early Common Kartvelian, together with the rule of Object Demotion. We see in Chapter 14, however, that these general case rules underwent an ergative-to-active shift, involving a change from nominative to narrative for the marking of subjects of active intransitives. Although this change is described on the basis of Georgian data alone, it probably took place in Common Georgian-Zan (See §6.7, argument 2). The first three rules from CK are repeated as (1), and their counterparts from CGZ as (2). The full sets of rules are stated in Chapters 11 and 14.

(1) a. The final subject of a transitive is marked with the narrative case.
b. The final subject of an intransitive is marked with the nominative case.
c. A final direct object is marked with the nominative case.

(2) a. The final subject of a transitive or active intransitive is marked with the narrative case.
b. The final subject of an inactive intransitive is marked with the nominative case.
c. A final direct object is marked with the nominative case.

While the CK case rules, stated as (1), account for the surface patterns found in Series I, the CGZ rules, (2), do not. In Series I, the rule of Object Demotion makes direct objects into indirect objects, leaving all clauses surface intransitives. Rule (1b) correctly states that surface subjects in Series I, all being the subjects of intransitives, are marked with the nominative case. By the corresponding new rules, (2), some subjects in Series I would not be assigned the nominative case. When a transitive clause, such as 'he is reading the book' is made into an intransitive comparable to 'he is reading in the book', the verb remains active, controllable, volitional. The underlyingly transitive clauses that were made intransitive by Object Demotion in Series I were mostly active. If the new rules, (2), had been applied to them, (2a) would have marked the subject with the narrative. This, however, did not happen. Instead, the original surface patterns were retained, and a new set of principles was introduced to account for them. The rules in (2) never applied in Series I; they are applicable to Series II. The new rules in (3) account for case assignment in Series I.

(3) a. A final subject is marked with the nominative case.
b. A final object is marked with the dative case.

Although the surface case distribution found in Series I had long existed as the result of Object Demotion and the CK case rules (1), it was only with the reanalysis of Series I that the addition of the new set of rules, (3), was effected. The probable cause for the reanalysis of Series I was the change in Series II case marking.

The reanalysis of Series I entails the loss of Object Demotion as a productive rule; it is retained as a rule that is lexically governed by a handful of verbs, as discussed in Chapter 1. The change also entailed the reinterpretation of some, but not all, surface structures in Series I. Only initial transitives were affected by Object Demotion, and only they were reinterpreted. As an illustration, consider a hypothetical example, (4), using Modern Georgian lexical items and morphology.

(4) *vano* *ceril-s* *scers* *deda-s*
Vano/NOM letter-DAT he/write/it/to.her/I mother-DAT
'Vano is writing a letter to his mother.'

Referring to this as though it were a sentence of CK and CGZ, Table 15.1 represents the reconstructed two-level structure for such clauses in CK and the reinterpretation of them as single-level structures in CGZ. In CK, the initial direct object, *cerils* 'letter' in (4), was made a grammatical indirect object by Object Demotion (see Chap. 7). In reinterpreting the surface structure, speakers analyzed *cerils* as the direct object. This would have been consistent with the grammatical relation of the same nominal in a Series II equivalent of (4). Thus, the reanalysis suggested is consistent with other parts of the language (Series II) and with the semantic structure of the clause, related to the initial structure in CK.

It appears that there is a natural correlation between the object demotion construction and imperfective–durative aspect, as a number of other languages also oppose these to a perfective or punctual that does not involve Object Demotion (see Chap. 7). When Series I was reanalyzed, it no longer functioned as the object demotion counterpart of Series II; and the aspectual opposition between the two series was later likewise eroded. In all of the modern languages there are some screeves in Series I that represent perfective or punctual aspect, generally indicated by the

Table 15.1

Schematic Representation of Structure of Example (4) in CK and in CGZ

	vano	*ceril-s*	*deda-s*
Common Kartvelian			
Initial structure	subject	direct object	indirect object
Final structure	subject	indirect object	retired indirect object
Common Georgian-Zan	subject	direct object	indirect object

presence of a preverb. In Old Georgian the aspectual opposition of Series I to Series II as imperfective–durative versus perfective–puntual was still intact. As Series I had already been reanalyzed by Old Georgian times, the concomitant change in the aspect system must have taken place after the reanalysis, rather than being part of it.

It was shown in Chapter 9 that the series markers were introduced to the verb system as indicators of durative aspect, having originated as collective suffixes in the noun. The restructuring of the aspect system must have been accompanied or preceded by a reinterpretation of the series markers. Series markers now occur in perfective–punctual screeves as well as in imperfective–durative ones, and they no longer retain their original value. In Modern Georgian, for example, they occur in the (imperfective) present (e.g., *xaṭ-av* 'you paint it') and in the (perfective) future (e.g., *da-xaṭ-av* 'you will paint it'), but not in the (perfective) aorist (*da-xaṭ-e* 'you painted it'). Laz and Mingrelian are similar to Georgian in this respect (see Chikobava 1936, esp. 118–119; Machavariani 1974). Series markers are used by few verbs in Svan and play a slight role in the verb system (see Topuria 1967).

When Object Demotion operated as a productive rule, every clause in Series I was a surface intransitive, either because of an initial intransitive structure or because of application of this rule. At this time, ∅- or *e*-grade stems were used in all Series I forms, since the *i* versus *e* alternation had been interpreted as an indicator of transitive versus intransitive. This had produced the distribution represented in Table 15.2, reconstructed for CK in Chapter 8, where *e*-grade stands also for the ∅-grade derived from it. The 'transitive' and 'intransitive' of Table 15.2 refer to CK *initial* structure, but *e*- versus *i*-grade was assigned on the basis of *final* structure. When Series I was reanalyzed and Object Demotion dropped, the initially transitive clauses in Series I were no longer final intransitives, but rather final transitives. Thus, the distribution of ablaut grades summarized in Table 15.2 was no longer motivated by the syntax. It was reinterpreted and restructured in different ways in the various languages. For most verbs in Georgian, *e* versus *i* was restructured as one marker of series alternation,

Table 15.2

Summary Distribution of Ablaut Grades, Reconstructed to CK

	Transitive	Intransitive
Series I	*e*-grade	*e*-grade
Series II	*i*-grade	*e*-grade

but only within transitive forms (see Tables 8.26 and 8.27).[1] On the other hand, for most ablauting verbs in Svan, *e* versus *i* was reinterpreted as a marker of intransitive versus transitive and was extended throughout Series I, II, and III. This is illustrated in Table 15.3. In Laz and Mingrelian, ablaut functions mostly as an indicator of transitivity, *i*-grade appearing in transitives and the regular reflexes of *e*- and Ø-grade in intransitives (see Gamkrelidze and Machavariani 1965:187–194, 214–225). The restructuring of ablaut is discussed in greater detail in Chapter 8.

When clauses that were formerly surface intransitives were reinterpreted as in Table 15.1, there was a need to reinforce their transitivity. One means for doing so was causative morphology, used now in a transitive, rather than truly causative, function (Gamkrelidze and Machavariani 1965:195, 206, 214; Vogt 1947a, esp. §30, 31, 49, etc.). For example, in Laz, the intransitive *do-ṭib-u* 'it heated up' corresponds to a transitive with the causative suffix *-in, do-ṭub-**in**-es* 'they heated it up'. (Forms, cited in Chikobava 1938:326, vary because they are from different dialects—root *i* versus *u*—and because of the number of the subject—*u* versus *es*.)

The rule of *En*-Agreement is reconstructed for Series I and II at least as far back as CGZ (see Chap. 10, especially §10.2). If it originally applied in both series according to the same principles retained productively in Series II for Old Georgian, then it would have been triggered in Series I only by plural subjects of Class 2 verbs (see §10.2.1). When Series I was reinterpreted in such a way that its structure did not differ from that of Series II, the surface pattern of distribution of *en* in Series I was incon-

Table 15.3

Ablaut in Svan[a]

	Transitive	Intransitive
Present (I)	*ṭix-e* 'you return it'	*ṭex-n-i* 'you return'
Aorist (II)	*a-ṭəx* < **a-ṭix-e* 'you returned it' *a-ṭix* 'he returned it'	*a-ṭex* 'you returned'
First evidential (III)	*x-o-ṭīx-a* 'he has returned it'	*la-x-ṭex-a*[b] 'he has returned to him'

[a]Forms are from Topuria (1967).

[b]The relative form is cited here because it is formed directly from the stem. The absolute form, *ämṭexēli* (Topuria 1967:204) also has *e*-grade, but it is formed from the past participle (Lenṭex *me-ṭex-e*), which independently requires the *e*-grade stem (Topuria 1967:221).

sistent with that in Series II. There having been no final direct objects in Series I prior to its reanalysis, they had not conditioned *En*-Agreement, while final direct objects had in Series II. This inconsistency was resolved in various ways. If *En*-Agreement ever existed in Svan, it disappeared, apparently without a trace. In Zan, too, it disappeared, but left as a relic the reduced form, *n*, in the present tense third person plural subject marker (see §10.2.3). In Georgian, on the other hand, *En*-Agreement as a productive rule was restricted to Series II, leaving some relics in the third person plural subject forms of a few Class 2 verbs (see §10.2.2).[2] Around the twelfth century, *En*-Agreement was lost also from Series II of most Georgian dialects, leaving relics in the form of an aorist third person plural subject marker, *-nen* from **-en-en,* restricted to Class 2 verbs.[3] The rule of *En*-Agreement is retained in a few dialects.

As shown in Chapter 12, we must reconstruct a stage at which the third person object marker, **x,* was conditioned by surface indirect objects alone, including those in Series I that were initial direct objects, as well as those in Series III that were initial subjects. It may be that this does not represent the ORIGINAL distribution of that morpheme (Gamkrelidze 1979:47), but it must have characterized **x* at some point. The reanalysis left the occurrence of this marker in some Series I forms unmotivated since initial direct objects no longer fitted the criterion of being final indirect objects. Reanalysis of the marker was effected in various ways. In Svan and literary Georgian, reflexes of **x* were restricted once again to surface indirect objects; after the reinterpretation of Series I, this category excluded Series I initial direct objects. This morpheme and Georgian *u* (< *i*/*x* + ___+, with deletion of *x*) are still used for those initial indirect objects that are final indirect objects, for initial subjects made indirect objects by Inversion, and for oblique objects advanced to indirect object by so-called Version rules (see handbooks). In Zan **x* was lost, but left as a relic the prefixal form *u-*, derived from **x + i,* as seen in the partial paradigm in Table 15.4. Because Inversion makes the initial subject a final indirect object in the screeve illustrated in Table 15.4, this nominal

Table 15.4

Some First Evidential Forms in Zan

Laz	Mingrelian	
m-i-qvilun	*do-m-ˀvilu* (< **do-m-i-*)	'I have killed it'
g-i-q̇vilun	*do-y-ˀvilu* (< **do-g-i-*)	'you have killed it'
u-q̇vilun	*d-u-ˀvilu* (< **do-x-i-*)	'he has killed it'

is marked by the object markers *m-*, *g-*, and **x*. A number of Georgian dialects have lost **x* except in the form *u-*, in a way parallel to Zan.

In many dialects of Georgian, the assignment of a reflex of **x* is a variable rule. In the north, south, and central subdialects of Kartlian, for example, we find the following hierarchy:

(5) final indirect objects >
final direct objects in Series I >
final direct objects in Series II.

The first entry, final indirect objects, nearly always trigger a reflex of **x*, for example, *ʒmeps misc̣era* 'to.brothers he/wrote/it/to.him', where *s* is the reflex of **x* before *c̣*. In Series I, where direct objects bear the same case as indirect objects, they frequently trigger a reflex of **x;* for example, *p̣urs šč̣amda* 'he was eating bread', with *š* as the reflex of **x* before *č̣*. In Series II, where direct objects bear a case different from that assigned to indirect objects, a reflex of **x* is infrequently triggered by the direct object; for example, *mohḳla* 'he killed him', with *h* before *ḳ*, beside the more usual *moḳla* in the same meaning. (Analysis and examples of Kartlian are based on Imnaishvili 1974:216–219; see also Shanidze 1957c: §65.)

The enclitic particle, *-q̣e,* which marks object plurality was mentioned in §13.4.5. It is used in a number of dialects; and in some of these it occurs, like **x*, according to the hierarchy in (5). In Ingilo and Ḳaxian, *-q̣e* regularly indicates plurality of indirect objects and of direct objects in Series I (i.e., in the dative case) and is used only occasionally for direct objects in Series II (i.e., in the nominative case) (Imnaishvili 1959:183; Martirosovi and Imnaishvili 1956:127–128).[4]

The variable assignments of **x* reflexes and of *-q̣e* seem to be relics of an earlier stage when these markers were conditioned by final indirect objects, including initial direct objects that were final indirect objects in Series I before reanalysis.

When Series I was reanalyzed and Object Demotion was lost as a productive rule, many morphological features were left unmotivated from a synchronic point of view, occasioning changes in the criteria upon which they were assigned. Some remained markers of a distinction between Series I and II, but their original values changed. This is particularly true of series markers in Georgian and Zan, but to some extent case marking, *En*-Agreement, ablaut, and the reflexes of **x* serve this purpose in some dialects. Because reinterpretation of Series I involved a reanalysis of the transitivity of some forms, some morphemes were restructured as markers of a transitive versus intransitive distinction. The clearest example of this is ablaut in Svan and to some extent in Zan and Georgian. Rules that no longer made sense could be dropped, as was *En*-Agreement in Zan; they could be restricted, as the same rule was in Georgian; or they could enlarge their functions on the basis of reanalyzed grammatical relations, as *q̣e* probably did.

15.2. A CHANGE IN CASE MORPHOLOGY

The marker of the narrative case in CK has been reconstructed as **n,* **d,* where the original distribution of the allomorphs is not clear (Chap. 4; see also Machavariani 1970). Georgian replaced this with the suffix *-man,* which itself retains narrative *-n;* relics of *-n* remain in a few words. Laz and Mingrelian replaced the original suffix with *-k* (see Chap. 4 on sources for both).[5] Below I present two hypotheses for the causes of these changes.

Zhghenti (1953) has suggested that there was a general process that weakened, then dropped, word-final *n.* If the narrative case had the form **n* in CGZ, then phonological erosion of the original desinence could have been the motivation for the replacements. In Mingrelian, loss of word-final *n* is still a productive rule (see §16.1.5). In Laz, word-final *n* has been lost in some words in some dialects. In most Laz dialects, *n* has been lost from the pronouns *man* 'I, me', *sin* 'you/SG', *čkun/čkin* 'we, us', and *tkvan* 'you/PL' (Chikobava 1936:72). Some dialects have the screeve formants *-dore* and *-ḳo,* while others have *-doren* and *-ḳon* (Zhghenti 1953:135). In Georgian, there have been a few losses of *n* word-finally. Most dialects have *me* (< *men*) 'I, me'. In the Xevsur and Pšavian dialects, *n* is lost from the postposition *-ḳen* 'toward' (Zhghenti 1953:136).

There are two problems with this hypothesis. First, although Laz and Georgian, as well as Mingrelian, replaced the inherited narrative desinence, both retain many instances of word-final *n* that are reconstructible to CGZ. For example, both languages retain the third person singular subject marker *-n* in the present and the third person plural subject marker *-en/an* (see Table 5.2, §16.1.5). Most dialects retain the final *n* in *-ḳen,* as well as in other postpositions, such as *-gan* 'from', *-dan* 'from', *-tan* 'with, at'. Most Georgian dialects retain the final *n* in the pronouns *šen* 'you/SG', *čuen* 'we, us', and *tkuen* 'you/PL'; one Laz dialect retains *n* in these pronouns. Thus, loss of *n* in word-final position is highly restricted in Georgian and not general in Laz.

A second problem with this proposal is that, while Zan replaced **n* with *-k,* Georgian replaced it with *-man.* The final *n* was indeed lost in historical times, occurring in Modern Georgian as *-ma.* Nevertheless, the hypothesis that it was phonological erosion that triggered replacement of the narrative case marker entails that the segment being eroded was retained for some time in the new marker adopted in Georgian.

An alternative view is that *n, *d was replaced because it had been an ERGATIVE case ending (i.e., was assigned only to subjects of transitives), and a new marker was needed to avoid confusion between the old and new functions. If this is correct, Georgian used its own ERGATIVE case pronoun (*man* 'he') as the new marker of the ACTIVE case.

There is insufficient evidence at present to determine which of these views is the more accurate. It is also possible that both a phonological erosion of word-final *n* and the syntactic change contributed to the morphological replacement of *n, *d.

15.3. EXTENSIONS

For Late CGZ, after the ergative-to-active shift and the reanalysis of Series I, the reconstructed two-part case system is as represented in Table 15.5. In the remainder of this chapter, grammatical relations in tables and text refer to the final level of derivation; Class 2 in the tables includes inversion constructions.

Table 15.5

Reconstructed Distribution of Cases in Late CGZ

	Subject of Class 1	Subject of Class 3	Subject of Class 2	Direct object	Indirect object
Series I	NOM	NOM	NOM	DAT	DAT
Series II	NAR	NAR	NOM	NOM	DAT

15.3.1. Mingrelian

Apparently no further changes in case marking were made after the separation of Zan from Georgian until Mingrelian and Laz had separated from one another. Then, Mingrelian extended the functions of the narrative case as stated in Table 15.6 (examples in support of this in Chap. 3). In Mingrelian there are two distinct systems, both having accusative alignment. The system represented in Table 15.6 must be derived from that of CGZ, represented in Table 15.5, by extending the narrative case from the subjects of Class 1 and 3 verbs to include those of Class 2.[6]

Table 15.6

Distribution of Cases in Mingrelian

	Subject of Class 1	Subject of Class 3	Subject of Class 2	Direct object	Indirect object
Series I	NOM	NOM	NOM	DAT	DAT
Series II	NAR	NAR	NAR	NOM	DAT

It is well known that among the languages of the world the unmarked case is the one assigned to subjects of inactive intransitives and to predicate nominals. In the opposition ergative versus absolutive, ergative is the marked member, as is accusative in nominative versus accusative. That is, it is the marked member of the opposition that is assigned only to subjects of transitives in the first type and to direct objects of transitives in the second. However, in Mingrelian, these generalizations do not hold. The *-k* case is marked with respect to the case in *-i,* both diachronically and synchronically. Diachronically, the *-i* case originally had a ∅ suffix (Chap. 4). Synchronically, it is the only case in Mingrelian to have ∅ allomorphs, occurring in the declension of vowel-final stems, such as *ḳoṭo-∅* 'pot' (Chikobava 1936:47; see Table 4.7). Even with consonant-final stems, where *-i* is part of the declension, it is dropped in conversation (see Chap. 4, n. 3). Further, the case in *-i* or ∅ is the sole citation form, for example, *ḳoči* 'man'. The forms in *-k* are never used in citation; and *-k* is not dropped but is often augmented to *-kə*. These criteria establish that the *-k* case is the marked member of the opposition. Yet in Series II in Mingrelian, this marked case includes among its functions the marking of subjects of inactive intransitives. It likewise marks predicate nominals, as the examples below show.

(6) *tik* *iʔū* *xaceci-k*
she/NAR she/become/II bride-NAR
'She became a bride.' (Xubua 1937: 220, 18)

(7) *tina-k* *oḳo* *iʔuas* *tiši komonǰ-k*
he-NAR MOD he/be/II her husband-NAR
'He must be her husband.' (Xubua 1937: 35, 2–3)

The unmarked case likewise defies our expectations in that in Series II it is assigned only to direct objects of transitives, as illustrated in (8).

(8) *ndii-kə mideʔunu ate vitožiri ǰimal-ep-i muši*
ogre-NAR he/lead/him/II this twelve brother-PL-NOM his
ʔudeša
house/ALL
'The ogre led these twelve brothers to his house.'
(Bleichsteiner 1919:**VII** [11])

Thus, in Mingrelian, the generalizations based on many languages of the world fail to be met. It is clear that the reason for this is historical. It is shown above that the unmarked case originally did indicate subjects of inactive intransitives, while the marked case was assigned only to subjects of transitives. In the ergative-to-active shift and in the Mingrelian-particular extension described above, the functions of the marked case were gradually expanded and those of the unmarked case contracted. Mingrelian thus represents a diachronic exception to an otherwise-valid universal (see Campbell 1980; Chung and Seiter 1980).

15.3.2. Standard Laz

The descriptions of Laz syntax presented above, especially the case marking facts of Chapter 3, are largely drawn from the Xopian dialect, but they are also representative of other parts of the Laz-speaking area, with the exception of Maxo and Artašen, discussed in §15.3.3 and 15.5. The Laz spoken outside the Maxo and Artašen areas is here termed 'Standard Laz' for ease of reference. Case marking is summarized in Table 15.7 from Chapter 3.

The facts in Table 15.7 can be summarized by saying that Standard Laz has one case system for Series I and II and that this case system is active in alignment. The Standard Laz case system must have been derived by applying the Series II rules in Series I, that is, by extending the Series II rules.

Table 15.7

Distribution of Cases in Standard Laz

	Subject of Class 1	Subject of Class 3	Subject of Class 2	Direct object	Indirect object
Series I	NAR	NAR	NOM	NOM	DAT
Series II	NAR	NAR	NOM	NOM	DAT

A further change that might be considered an extension is underway in Laz. As shown in Chapter 13, Series III originated as a system in which Class 1 and 3 verbs governed inversion obligatorily. The reflex of this development is the Laz Old Series III, which retains this characteristic syntax, as well as some of the original morphology. Beside it has developed a New Series III, without inversion, and with a different morphology. Parallel examples in the Old (a) and New (b) Series III are given in (9).

(9) a. *ḳoči-s uq̇urun*
man-DAT he/cry/OLDIII
b. *ḳoči-k q̇ureleren*
man-NAR he/cry/NEWIII
'The man apparently cried out.'

Similar examples of a Class 1 verb appear as (53) in Chapter 13. The Old Series III forms are rare in texts, and seem to be disappearing. The original construction is not being reanalyzed but is being REPLACED by forms with a new morphology. Since the case system of active alignment applies in the New Series III, this might be considered an extension. In the same sense, the case systems found in Series IV of both Laz (active) and Mingrelian (accusative) might be considered extensions of the Series I system in each language. It must be borne in mind, however, that these extensions differ from others considered here in that the target construction itself is new, and the morphology and case marking probably developed together.

15.3.3. Maxo

Case marking in the Maxo subdialect differs from that in Standard Laz in one respect: In Series I, subjects of Class 1 and 3 verbs may be either in the narrative case, as in Standard Laz, or in the nominative case, as in reconstructed CGZ.[7] The case pattern in the latter instance, however, is not fully comparable to that in CGZ, as the direct object is marked with the nominative, rather than with the dative.

(10) a. *usta-k oxori ḳodums*
carpenter-NAR house/NOM he/build/it/I
b. *usta oxori ḳodums*
carpenter/NOM
'A carpenter builds the house.'

(11) a. *ʔavǰi-k ʔilums mtuti*
hunter-NAR he/kill/it/I bear/NOM
b. *ʔavǰi ʔilums mtuti*
hunter/NOM
'The hunter kills a bear.'

(12) a. *kyatibi-k nč̣arums karṭali*
writer-NAR he/write/it/I paper/NOM
b. *kyatibi nč̣arums karṭali*
writer/NOM
'The writer writes a paper.'

Consultants rejected examples with a dative direct object; for example, **nč̣arums karṭalis*. The (a) variants of (10)–(12) are preferred (Chikobava 1936:181 and Part II: 2, n.1). Subjects of Class 3 verbs may also be marked with the nominative case in Series I in this dialect, as shown in the examples below.

(13) *monč̣a ḳroxams*
hen/NOM she/cluck/I
'A hen clucks.'

(14) *mamuli ḳiams*
rooster/NOM he/crow/I
'A rooster crows.'

In Series II, only the narrative subject may be used in these clause types.

(15) *usta-k oxori doḳodu*
carpenter-NAR house/NOM he/build/it/II
'The carpenter built a house.'

(16) *kyatibi-k donč̣aru karṭali*
writer-NAR he/write/it/II paper/NOM
'The writer wrote a paper.'

Examples (10)–(16) are from Chikobava (1936, II:2,1-21); all examples in this section are from one speaker.

These data are summarized in Table 15.8.

Table 15.8

Distribution of Cases in Maxo

	Subject of Class 1	Subject of Class 3	Subject of Class 2	Direct object	Indirect object
Series I	NOM NAR	NOM NAR	NOM	NOM	DAT
Series II	NAR	NAR	NOM	NOM	DAT

15.3.4. Lower Ačarian

In the Ačarian dialect of Georgian, we find some variations on case marking that further shed light on the way in which extensions are made. Some other Georgian dialects have made some of the changes found in Ačarian, or they have made other changes. However, Lower Ačarian was selected as an example because it is a dialect in which the changes have been rather extensive.

Ačara is in the southwest of Georgia and was under Turkish influence for some three hundred years, though it never lost contact with Georgian (Nizharadze 1975:5–9; Mikeladze 1980:90). The variety of Ačarian discussed here is spoken in the Čorox Valley; Kiziria (1974:78) names the villages of Ḳirnat, Maradid, Čarnal, Txilnar, and Ḳobalaur. The discussion below is based on examples and generalizations in Jajanidze (1970:259–261), Kiziria (1974:78–79), and Nizharadze (1975:156–157).

In Lower Ačarian, case marking differs from that in other Kartvelian dialects. In Series I, the subject may be in the narrative case, and the object may be in the dative or nominative.

(17) *sakatme* *ver* *gaaḳeteps* *ḳac-ma*
chicken/house/NOM NEG he/make/it/I man-NAR
'The man will not be able to make a chicken house.'
(Kiziria 1974:78)

(18) *turk-eb-ma* *paṭronoben* *sopeli*
Turk-PL-NAR they/rule/it/I village/NOM
'The Turks rule the village.' (Jajanidze 1970:259)

(19) *lobio-s* *ḳurdγel-ma* *čams*
bean-DAT rabbit-NAR he/eat/it/I
'The rabbit is eating beans.' (Kiziria 1974:78)

(20) *glex-eb-ma* *xmarobs* *miça-s*
peasant-PL-NAR he/use/it/I earth-DAT
'The peasants use the earth.' (Jajanidze 1970:259)

Examples (17)–(20) contain transitive verbs; (17)–(18) have direct objects in the nominative, and (19)–(20) have them in the dative. Active intransitives may also take narrative case subjects in Series I, as in (21) and (22).

(21) *baγn-eb-ma tamašoben*
child-PL-NAR they/play/I
'The children are playing.' (Kiziria 1974:79)

(22) *baγn-eb-ma ṭiroden*
they/cry/I
'The children were crying.' (Jajanidze 1970:260)

The patterns illustrated above coexist with those of literary Georgian, illustrated elsewhere. Thus, for transitive verbs we find the three patterns summarized in Table 15.9. Apparently the choice among the three patterns is free. From discussions in the sources cited above, it appears that direct objects in the nominative case are not combined with subjects in the nominative case.

In Series II, we find variation as well. As in literary Georgian, the narrative case is used for the subjects of Class 1 and 3 verbs. Class 2 verbs may have narrative or nominative case subjects, as exemplified below.

(23) *cxen-ma deiγala*
horse-NAR he/tire/II
'The horse got tired.'

(24) *ḳac-ma avat gaxta*
man-NAR ill he/become/II
'The man became ill.'

(25) *dat-ma çiskvilši darča*
bear(?)-NAR mill/in he/remain/II
'The bear(?) remained in the mill.'

(26) *ḳaṭa-m moxucda*
cat-NAR he/age/II
'The cat aged/became old.' (Jajanidze 1970:260)

Table 15.9

Case Patterns in Series I, Lower Ač̣arian

Subject	Direct object	
NOM	DAT	(= Series I pattern in Standard Modern Georgian)
NAR	DAT	(= innovative mixed pattern)
NAR	NOM	(= Series II pattern in all Georgian dialects)

(27) *tavǰdumare . . . čevda*
chairman/NOM he/go.down/II
'The chairman went down.' (Nizharadze 1975:156)

(28) *cxvar-eb-i darčen šyer-eb-i*
sheep-PL-NOM they/remain/II hungry-PL-NOM
'The sheep remained hungry.' (Kiziria 1974:79)

In Standard Georgian, all of the verbs in (23)–(28) govern nominative case subjects in Series II, as well as in I. According to Nizharadze (1975:156), the use of the nominative case for subjects of intransitive verbs in Series II, as in (27)–(28), is infrequent in comparison with the use of narrative case subjects. Nevertheless, both are possible (Jajanidze 1970:259; Kiziria 1974:79).

Jajanidze (1970:259), Kiziria (1974:79), and Nizharadze (1975:157) also describe clauses in which the third person singular pronoun *man* occurs as the direct object. In the literary dialect, *man* is the narrative case form. This phenomenon is illustrated below.

(29) *γmert-ma ar čameiq̣vana . . . man*
God-NAR NEG he/bring/him/II him
'God did not bring him here.' (Nizharadze 1975:157)

This is probably best viewed as nascent case syncretism, rather than as an additional function of the narrative case.[8] This analysis is supported by the following facts: (a) In the literature describing constructions like those in (29), it is stated that this is possible only with this pronoun. Nouns in the narrative case cannot function as direct objects. (b) The same form occurs in other uses of the nominative case, where the narrative is not found. Nizharadze (1975:156) cites examples from Upper Ač̣arian, which has noun case marking in Series I like that of Standard Georgian yet which permits the use of *man* for subjects in this series. If this were an additional function of the narrative case, as such, it would not be limited to the third person singular pronoun. Thus, on the basis of data available at this time, it appears that *man* is best viewed as a syncretic form, representing both the nominative and narrative cases, just as *me* represents both cases of the first person singular pronoun, and *šen* both cases of the second person singular. Nevertheless, the standard nominative is still in use (Nizharadze 1975:124). The case syncretism, if this analysis is correct, has not become complete.

Aside from this use of *man,* direct objects in Series II are illustrated only in the nominative case in the sources consulted, as in (30).

(30) *kal-ma* *beuri sakme* *gaaḳeta* *čvenši*
woman-NAR many deed/NOM she/do/it/II us/in

'The woman did many deeds among us.' (Jajanidze 1970:260)

While the types illustrated in (17)–(28) and (30) are amply exemplified in the literature cited, I do not have examples of clauses of all types in both Series I and II, and therefore, cannot display a summary table comparable to those given above. It appears, though, that Lower Ač̣arian is approaching an accusative case system in both series, where the narrative will mark subjects, the nominative will mark direct objects, and the dative indirect objects.[9]

The extensions of cases in Lower Ač̣arian differ from those described in subsections above, in that this dialect of Georgian was probably influenced by its neighbors, Laz and Mingrelian, while the changes in those languages must have been internally motivated. In particular, the changes in Series II are usually ascribed to Mingrelian influence, those in Series I to Laz. (Nizharadze 1975:156, 157, attributes this hypothesis originally to Chikobava.) While these languages may well have influenced Lower Ač̣arian, the Georgian dialect did not simply take over the Laz and Mingrelian sentence patterns. Lower Ač̣arian does not adopt the narrative case marker from Zan, *-k*, but uses the inherited *-m/ma*. It uses at least one pattern of distribution not widely found in either Zan language, namely that exemplified in (19)–(20).[10] Further, the Laz and Mingrelian systems are very different from one another, yet Lower Ač̣arian has managed to mesh elements of each according to definite, but variable, rules. For these reasons it seems justified to consider Lower Ač̣arian an instance of case extension under the influence of Laz and Mingrelian, rather than an outright borrowing of Laz or Mingrelian case assignment rules. It is therefore included in the general discussion of extension that follows.

Lower Ač̣arian has made an additional extension. In this subdialect, Inversion has been lost with at least some of those lexical items that govern this rule in Standard Modern Georgian, as shown in (31).

(31) *gamḳetebel-ma* *ar* *esmis* *ra-ina*
doer-NAR NEG he/understand/it/I what-MOD
gaaḳetos *da* *seit* *c̣adis*
he/do/it/II and whither he/go/II
'The doer (one doing a thing) doesn't understand what he should do and where he goes.' (Jajanidze 1970:259)

In the literary dialect, *esmis* 'he understands it' governs Inversion; and thus its initial subject is a final indirect object and bears the dative case. In (31), on the other hand, it is marked with the narrative case, as the subjects of other transitive verbs are in (17)–(20). In Lower Ač̣arian, Inversion has also been lost or has become optional in Series III, as the following examples illustrate.

(32) *am moadgile-m pasuxi ver guucia*
this assistant-NAR answer/NOM NEG he/give/it/III
'This assistant could not give an answer.' (Jajanidze 1970:261)

(33) *kaǰ-eb-ma sačečl-it deečxliṭ**en** saçqal kal-i*
fiend-PL-NAR comb-INST **they**/stick/her/III poor woman-NOM
'The fiends stuck the poor woman repeatedly with a carding comb.' (Jajanidze 1970:261)

Examples (32) and (33) differ from their equivalents in the literary dialect in two significant respects. First, the case of the subject would be dative rather than narrative in Standard Georgian. Second, in Lower Aç̣arian the pluralizer *-en* is a marker of third person subject plurality in a wide variety of screeves. In Series III, the literary dialect would use instead *-t*, which in the third person marks plurality of surface objects only, never of surface subjects. Both features suggest that inversion constructions in Series III, as in (31), have been reanalyzed, retaining the initial subject as surface subject. It is now case marked as a surface subject, and triggers number agreement markers used by surface subjects.[11] In both these respects it differs from literary Georgian.

Neither Laz nor Mingrelian has made this particular change. In Laz, the Old Series III forms still exist but are being replaced by a new set of forms, which do not govern Inversion and which have the case marking found in Series I and II (§15.3.2). Where the Old Series III forms are used, Inversion is maintained intact; where Inversion does not apply, new forms are used. The interpretation of the Mingrelian situation is not straight-forward on the basis of data available, as discussed in §13.5. In Mingrelian, the narrative case is not extended to initial subjects, as it is in the Lower Aç̣arian examples (32)–(33). In the literature, one example has been cited showing the extension of Mingrelian Series II case marking into Series III (Chap. 13, n. 28), but this is not the regular Mingrelian pattern. Lower Aç̣arian differs from both Laz and Mingrelian in that (a) it retains the original verb forms, apart from agreement, (b) it has lost Inversion or made it optional, and (c) it has extended Series II case marking into Series III.

15.4. EXTENSION AS A MECHANISM IN THE CHANGE OF CASE ALIGNMENT

In the discussion of earlier changes in case systems, explicit mechanisms of change were identified. The initial split between Series I and II originated as a productive syntactic construction, which was later reanalyzed, giving rise to a new set of case rules. The ergative-to-active shift was made possible by the discrepancies between underlying and surface transitivity and eventually was generalized to other verbs of the same class. In contrast, in the preceding discussion of rule extensions in Standard Laz, Maxo, Mingrelian, and Lower Aç̣arian, the mechanism of change is not made explicit. This section develops a hypothesis of how extensions occur.

It is impossible to suppose that there are not universal constraints governing extensions of a case to new functions. In the absence of constraints, a subject case might be extended to mark an object, with the object case in the same clause marking the subject. It would then be impossible, unless other conventions were established, for the sentence encoded with complementary extensions of this kind to be accurately decoded. Communication could not be maintained. It appears from the data presented above, as well as from evidence from other languages (esp. Payne 1979, 1980), that extensions are made in an orderly, constrained fashion, in part determined by the grammar of the language.

The functional role of a contrast between two cases in distinguishing the subject of a clause from its object has been emphasized in the discussion of case alignment (e.g., Anderson 1976:19; Comrie 1978:380ff.) It is clear that this functional role of case contrast is important in limiting the variety of alignment types. We may hypothesize, therefore, that extensions in the use of a case are functionally constrained by the need to keep the subject distinct from the object. This principle is invoked by Fähnrich (1967:41–42) as an explanation for the use of the narrative case in certain situations in Georgian. A principle of this kind would account for the fact that the narrative case, limited to the marking of certain subjects in CGZ (Table 15.5), was extended to additional subjects in Mingrelian (Table 15.6), Standard Laz (Table 15.7), Maxo (Table 15.8), and Lower Aç̣arian (§15.3.4). The nominative case is unmarked relative to other cases in the sense that it is the citation form, has a Ø realization in some phonological environments in Georgian and Mingrelian, and has been reanalyzed as Ø in Laz (see Chap. 4); for these reasons we might suppose that it would have been extended. The functional principle would explain why it was not. Because it was used in CGZ to mark both subjects and objects, in an extension of its use, it would be unclear whether it represented subject or object.

On the other hand, the need to maintain a distinction between subject and object cannot explain the occurrence of examples (10)–(12b) in Maxo. In (11b) the failure of the cases to distinguish subject from object is particularly remarkable, since either nominal could logically fill either role. Further, the functional principle provides no basis to exclude the possibility of extending the use of the narrative case from the CGZ base to subjects of Class 2 verbs just in Series I. Such an extension is highly unlikely, perhaps impossible, since in the reconstructed system Class 2 verbs never governed narrative case subjects. Yet the functional principle would make this change seem as likely as the ones that actually took place.

An approach with greater explanatory value is based on the notion that an extension is the removal of a condition from a rule. The source for the extensions discussed above is the reconstructed case system of CGZ, repeated here for ease of reference.

(34) If the verb is in Series I:
a. A final subject is marked with the nominative case.
b. A final object is marked with the dative case.

(35) If the verb is in Series II:
a. The final subject of a transitive or active intransitive is marked with the narrative case.
b. The final subject of an inactive intransitive is marked with the nominative case.
c. A final direct object is marked with the nominative case.
d. A final indirect object is marked with the dative case.

Rule (35) is not stated in the most compact way; this is done in order that the parts may be easily referred to. Reference to the series and to the type of the governing verb are conditions on the rule. ("If the verb is in Series II, and if the verb is an inactive intransitive, its subject is marked with the nominative case.") The core of the rule, that part that excludes conditions, includes the final grammatical relation and the case itself.[12] This view of extensions recognizes explicitly that they are a kind of analogy and that they result in greater efficiency.

Examining the changes described in the sections above from this point of view, we can provide a natural account of the process of extension. In Mingrelian, the condition on rule (35a), "of a transitive or active intransitive" was relaxed, making it possible to mark the subjects of inactive intransitives with the narrative case and producing the distribution summarized in Table 15.6. While I know of no direct evidence in Mingrelian that this change took place gradually, on the basis of Series II in Lower Aç̣arian (examples 23–28), it seems likely that for some time there was variability in the application of rules (35a) and (35b), the condition being maintained only some of the time. To account for the variability of case marking in Series II of Aç̣arian, and probably in a transitional stage of Mingrelian, I assume that rules (35a) and (35b) are part of the grammar, together with a statement that the condition on (35a) may be ignored. In Mingrelian, (35b) was eventually lost altogether.

Changes in Series I are more complex, as they involve the marking of more nominals. The examples from Series I of the Lower Ač̣arian and Maxo dialects show that the condition, "If the verb is in Series II," may be relaxed from the rules of (35). Lower Ač̣arian examples (17)–(18) show that, in a clause, this condition may be ignored on (35a) and (35c) together. Both subject and object have cases appropriate to Series II. Examples (19)–(20) show that in a clause, the condition on (35a) alone may be relaxed, still marking the direct object according to the Series I system. The (b) examples in (10)–(12) from Maxo show that it is possible to relax the condition on (35c) alone. Thus, in extension, the conditions on the individual rules of (35) operate independently. Apparently Lower Ač̣arian has a language-particular constraint against applying (35c) in a clause unless (35a) is applied in the same clause. (Without language consultants one cannot be sure of this.) Notice that if the series condition on rules (35b) and (35d) is relaxed, no change in case marking results.

According to the data cited by Chikobava (1936:181, and Part II, p. 2), dative direct objects are not found in Maxo. Rule (34b) must have been dropped from its grammar, so that rules (35c) and (35d) apply now in both series. In Standard Laz (Table 15.7), rule (34a) has likewise dropped, with (35a) and (35b) taking its place.

It is not clear from data available whether or not it is possible at present in Lower Ač̣arian to remove both of the conditions on rule (35a) at the same time. There are clear examples of the application of (35a) to the subjects of inactive intransitives in Series II, (23)–(26), and of marking by this rule the subjects of transitives and active intransitives in Series I, (17)–(22). But I have been unable to find a clear example of this rule applying to the subject of an inactive intransitive in Series I.[13] While it is most likely that this is no more than an accidental gap in the data available, it is not impossible that there exists a constraint, perhaps temporary, against the relaxing of more than one condition at a time.

Exceptions to rules are another type of condition on them, and the relaxing of these conditions is another kind of extension. Certain verbs, discussed in §6.2 and in Chapter 14, are lexical exceptions to the assignment of subject cases in Series II in Georgian. For example, in the literary dialect the verb 'come, go', though usually semantically active (volitional), is exceptionally a Class 2 verb and has most of the grammatical characteristics of that class, including subject case marking. However, in a great many of the nonstandard dialects, this exception condition has been relaxed, and the verb 'come, go' may have either a nominative subject (by the exception condition on the old rule) or a narrative subject, by extension of rule (35a) (see §6.2.1). In Standard Laz, the verb 'play' was left as a lexical exception to the ergative-to-active shift and to the extension of Series II case marking (see examples in §6.3.2). This lexical exception condition to the case rules may be optionally observed or relaxed.

The extensions that have taken place have involved Series II rules applying in Series I, or the narrative case marking nominals not previously marked by it in Series II. There are no examples in Kartvelian of the complementary types of extensions, and this is probably no accident.

From the data cited above, we can make certain generalizations about how extensions proceed in language. First, an extension may take place gradually, in the sense that a given nominal may be variably marked according to the old, receding rule or according to the new, expanding rule; these two possibilities may coexist for some time. In Lower Ačarian the patterns of Table 15.9 all coexist, as do the patterns exemplified by (23)–(26), on the one hand, and by (27)–(28), on the other. In the Maxo dialect of Laz, the (a) and (b) patterns of (10)–(12) coexist. Even in Standard Laz, there remains some variability, but only on items that are exceptions (see above). In Mingrelian, we see a stable system, fully regularized within both series; it seems probable, however, that this change also involved variability in its initial phases.

A second insight derived from the data discussed above is that cases are not necessarily extended in whole-clause patterns; that is, the marking of one nominal may change independently of the marking of another in the same clause, as in examples (19)–(20) and in the (b) examples in (10)–(12). This fact is somewhat surprising, since in Standard Georgian, even for verbs that govern irregular case marking, the options are limited to one of the two patterns used productively (see Harris 1981:187–190, 268–274).

Finally, one cannot predict that new marking will be extended to the subject before the direct object, or vice versa. In the Lower Ačarian examples, (19)–(20), the subject, but not the direct object, has the new marking. In the Maxo examples, (b) of (10)–(12), on the other hand, the direct object, but not the subject, has new case marking.

The proposed view of extensions considers them a type of analogy. As a step toward formalizing this approach and at the same time constraining an otherwise too-powerful mechanism, (36)–(38) are suggested:

(36) Extension proceeds by relaxing conditions on rules.

(37) The relaxation of conditions is at first optional, producing variation in the application of the rules.

(38) Later, old rules may be lost.

This is an explicit statement of the insights from the study made above, together with an observation of what kinds of changes occur by extension.

Points (36)–(38) make specific statements about the types of change that occur by extension. In a language with coexistent systems, such as the coexistent case systems (Series I and II) in Kartvelian, there will be more conditions on the rules involved in this split. Point (36) explicitly acknowledges that extension is more likely in coexistent systems or in other systems with many conditions on rules. The same principle contains the observation that where there is variation, one variant will represent the original rule or set of rules. For example, in the instance of 'come, go', discussed above, one variant is the Georgian norm; in the Maxo dialect, one variant is the CGZ norm. At the same time, (36) predicts that the second variant will not be arbitrary. For example, it rules out the possibility that the dative case would be extended to subjects in Series I or II. It does not rule out the possibility of subjects becoming marked by the dative via some other mechanism, only via extension. The Australian examples discussed as extensions by Dixon (1977b) and the Iranian examples treated by Payne (1980) conform to (36)–(38), and I suggest that it stand as a definition of extension.

15.5. ARTAŠEN

Artašen is a subdialect of Laz known from texts published by Chikobava (1936, Part II: 109–138) and by Dumézil and Esenç (1972). In this subdialect, subjects, direct objects, and indirect objects are in stem form in Series I and II. As observed in Chapter 4, Laz has reanalyzed the various case markers and stems such that all inherited and borrowed consonant-final roots (e.g., CK *$ḳac_1$ 'man') have a singular stem ending in *-i* (e.g., Standard Laz *ḳoči*). Although this *-i* at one time functioned as the desinence of the nominative case and continues to do so in the related languages, it cannot be considered a case marker synchronically in Laz, since it occurs in all singular forms (see paradigms in Chap. 4). Inherited and borrowed vowel-final roots have no suffix in the singular stem. It is the singular stem (e.g., *ḳoč-i*) or plural stem (e.g., *ḳoč-epe*) that occurs as subject and object in Artašen, as the following examples show. Here, ∅ indicates stem form.

(39) *avǰi . . . mtuti doilu*
hunter/∅ bear/∅ he/kill/it/II
'The hunter killed a bear.' (Chikobava 1936, II:111, 27)

(40) *xoǰa nusrettini a ndγa hem ezani ioxay*
hodja/∅ Nusrettin/∅ one day DET *ezan*/∅ he/call/it/I
'One day *Hodja* Nusrettin called out the *ezan* (call to prayers).'
(Dumézil and Esenç 1972:**3** [1])

(41) *lač̣i laloy*
dog/∅ he/bark/I
'A dog barks.' (Chikobava 1936, II:114, 29)

(42) *bere ǰur ç̣aneri diʔu*
child/∅ two year/∅ he/became/II
'The child became two years old.' (Chikobava 1936, II:121,24)

(43) *ar-co xoǰa uç̣u či . . .*
one-? *hodja*/∅ he/say/it/II that
'One of them said to the *hodja* that . . . .'
(Dumézil and Esenç 1972:**3** [4])

(44) *ǰur tane. . . ar didi mtuti konagey*
two shepherd/∅ one big bear/∅ they/encounter/it/II
'Two shepherds encountered a big bear.'
(Dumézil and Esenç 1972:**4** [1])

These examples illustrate the use of the stem form for the subject of transitive verbs, (39) and (40), for the subject of inactive intransitives, (42), for the subject of active intransitives, (41), for the direct object, (39) and (40), and for the indirect object (43). The phrase *ar didi mtuti* 'a big bear' may also be a final indirect object and is in the dative in some other dialects (see Dumézil and Esenç 1972).

The dative case desinence in Laz is *-s*, e.g., *ḳoči-s* 'man-DAT'. In the Artašen subdialect, there is a general weakening of word-final *s*. In this position, *s* or the consonant cluster of which it is a part is reduced to *y* (Chikobava 1936:28–30). This is formalized in (45) and (46).

(45) $s \rightarrow y / V \_\_\_ \#$

(46) $Cs \rightarrow y / \_\_\_ \#$

The application of these rules is shown in some forms in the sentences above; for example, *ioxay* from *ioxams* in (40), compared with Arkab *iǰoxums* (Dumézil and Esenç 1972:36); *laloy* from *laloms* in (41); *konagey* in (44), compared with Arkab *konages* (Dumézil and Esenç 1972:37).

If applied to the dative case form of a noun, this rule would leave only a slight contrast between the nominative and the surface form of the dative; for example, *ḳočis* 'man/DAT' becomes **ḳočiy*, beside *ḳoči* 'man/NOM'. Applied to appropriate forms of the third person pronoun, the rule would produce the form **himuy* (cf. Atinian *himus* 'he/DAT'). It seems likely that forms like **ḳočiy* and **himuy* functioned as the dative of these substantives at some time.

In some instances a variant of rule (45) reduces *s* to ∅, rather than *y*, following a vowel, as in (47).[14]

(47) *oxor-iša komoxte, dinǰirey*
house-ALL they/come/II they/sleep/II
'They came into the house (and) slept.'
(Chikobava 1936, II:123, 20)

Both verbs in (47) have the third person plural subject marker of the aorist, *-es*; in *komo-xt-e*, *-es* is reduced to *-e* and in *dinǰir-ey* to *-ey*. It is in no way surprising, then, that the *-s* of the dative is reduced to ∅ rather than *y*. The productive application of *s* → ∅ to a base form with word-final *s* is attested through the occurrence of forms like *himu* 'he/DAT' in another dialect (cf. Atinian *himus*), as in (48).

(48) *himu ǰuma kuonun*
he/DAT brother/NOM he/have/him/I
'He has a brother.' (Chikobava 1936:30, 5)

The sister dialects and languages have a dative in this function, as 'have' is a verb that governs Inversion. In the texts recorded by Dumézil and Esenç, on the other hand, *himu* is replaced by *him*, formerly the nominative form.

(49) *him č̣itxitu*
him/∅ you/ask/it/to.him/II
'Ask him!' (Dumézil and Esenç 1972:**1** [10])

(50) *ḳočepe him uçvey . . .*
man/PL/∅ him/∅ they/say/it/to.him/II
'The men said to him . . .' (Dumézil and Esenç 1972:**1** [1])

The Artašen examples, (49) and (50), may be compared with the Arkab equivalent, *hemus ḳitxit, hemus uçves* (Dumézil and Esenç 1972:33). The use of what was formerly the nominative suggests that a reanalysis has taken place, rather than that the surface form is derived by (45); (45), or its ∅ variant, and (46) apply productively only in verb forms.

The narrative desinence, *-k*, has also fallen away, leaving the stem forms; for example, *ḳoči-k* became *ḳoči*. This may also be related to a more general phenomenon, but there are a few items with word-final *-k*, since there are apparently no other derivational or inflectional suffixes making use of this segment. Two related lexical items do derive from forms in word-final *k*, namely *hay* 'here' and *hi* 'there'; forms in other Zan dialects are *hako, hak, ak* 'here' and *heko, hek, hik, ek* 'there' (Chikobava 1938:225). Both occur in (51).

(51) *huy ma hay bor, huy si hi or*
now I/∅ here I/be/I now you/∅ there you/be/I
'Now I am here, now you are there.'(Chikobava 1936, II:110, 3)

The loss of *k* in word-final position is apparently not part of a more general loss. This, together with the fact that there are so few lexical items that meet the structural description for the rule, suggests that the loss of *-k* originated as the loss of the narrative marker and was generalized to the few other occurrences of word-final *k*. For this reason it seems most likely that the loss of the narrative case desinence was occasioned by the loss of the dative suffix, which in turn resulted from a general weakening of *s* in word-final position.

The loss of the dative marker *-s* is attested in a number of Georgian dialects as well, not only in those that are geographically close to Laz, such as Ač̣arian (Nizharadze 1975:109–110) and Mesxian (Dzidziguri 1941:250), but also in some dialects that are quite far removed from the Black Sea, such as Kartlian (Imnaishvili 1974:194–195), Ḳaxian (Martirosovi and Imnaishvili 1956:69), and Ingilo (G. Imnaishvili 1966:85). While the Artašen subdialect of Laz shares with these Georgian dialects the general loss of the dative *-s*, this process in the Georgian dialects does not have the morpho–syntactic consequences it has in Artašen. In Georgian, the stem is the bare root, while the form with the suffix *-i* is the nominative case form. The difference can be seen in the comparative partial paradigm in Table 15.10.[15] When *-s* is lost from the dative with a consonant-final stem, in Ḳaxian the resulting form contrasts with the nominative and every other case. If *-s* were lost completely from dative forms of vowel-final stems, the resulting form would be the same as the nominative since the nominative *-i* is deleted after a vowel, for example, *ʒma* 'brother/NOM'. In order to maintain the distinction between the nominative and dative forms of vowel-final stems, *s* becomes *y*, rather than ∅, for example, Ḳaxian *ʒma-y* 'brother-DAT' (Martirosovi and Imnaishvili 1956:69). In Artašen, on the other hand, complete loss of *-s* produced a form identical to the nominative.

Table 15.10

Partial Paradigm of Comparative Case Forms (CK* *ḳac*$_1$ 'man')

	Standard Georgian	Ḳaxian	Standard Laz	Artašen
NOM	*ḳac-i*	*ḳac-i*	*ḳoč-i*	*ḳoč-i*
NAR	*ḳac-ma*	*ḳac-ma*	*ḳoč-i-k*	*ḳoč-i*
DAT	*ḳac-s*	*ḳac*	*ḳoč-i-s*	*ḳoč-i*

Taking the facts described above into consideration, the following seems the most likely account of the change in Artašen. As part of a general phenomenon found from east to west in southern Kartvelian dialects, in Artašen, word-final *s* underwent reduction to *y* or Ø. The contrast between a nominative terminating in *-i* and a dative in *-iy* may have been maintained for a time but was not significant enough to bear the functional load. The dative *-s* was lost as a distinct underlying form. This stimulated drop of the narrative desinence *-k* and generalized deletion of word-final *k*. The narrative form was also lost entirely, leaving a single syntactic case, which contrasts only with the several concrete cases. Thus, every syntactic function is filled by the stem form, producing a case distribution known in the linguistic literature as 'neutral' alignment. In the Artašen dialect we have a further instance of a change in case alignment, this time resulting from a phonological deletion rule and the resulting loss of case endings.

15.6. CONCLUSION

In this chapter I have described several changes that seem to be repercussions of the ergative-to-active shift. Although Series I surface patterns originated in Middle CK, it was only after the reanalysis of that series that a change in its case alignment was effected. The reanlaysis of Series I probably resulted from the ergative-to-active shift, and this reanalysis itself had numerous repercussions in the grammar. The extensions discussed in §15.3 and 15.4 probably resulted from the same shift, in the sense that they represent various ways of simplifying the system that it produced. The change in the desinence of the narrative case (§15.2) may result from its changed in function from ergative to active. The Artašen system is included here, in part for comparison with the other dialects discussed. In addition, the loss of *-s* and especially of *-k* may have been influenced by the general complexity of the case system.

NOTES

[1]This function of the *e* versus *i* alternation has been secondarily extended to a few Class 3 verbs, such as Modern Georgian *sṭvens* 'he whistles/I' versus *isṭvina* 'he whistled/II'.

[2]This discussion is based entirely on the third person, for although *En*-Agreement was controlled also by first and second persons in Series II in Old Georgian, it has left traces in Series I only in the third person. It may originally have been

limited to the third person, spreading to the first and second in Old Georgian. Alternatively, it may have applied originally in all persons, having left relic forms only in the restricted environment of the third.

[3]This new morpheme has been generalized to those Class 2 verbs that formerly did not have *En*-Agreement (see §10.1.4). However, in the aorist it is even now restricted to subjects of Class 2 verbs (see §16.1.3).

[4]There are also instances of **x* reflexes and *q̣e* being triggered by nominals not on the hierarchy, (5), whether as an innovation or an archaism (see Dzotsenidze 1973:239; Imnaishvili 1974:219).

[5]Schmidt (1978:254) has pointed out that this replacement of the narrative **d*, **n* (which he reconstructs as **ad*, **d*) constitutes loss only of its primary function, and that its original secondary function is preserved in the marking of the adverbial case in Georgian and Zan. In Svan, both the primary and secondary functions are retained.

[6]This change in Mingrelian is also described in Anderson (1977) and Schmidt (1973:115).

[7]This description is based on data in Chikobava (1936:181, and part II, p. 1ff). The property described was attested from Maxo, a village in the Viç̣ area. Not knowing the geographical extent of this type of case marking, I have taken the conservative course of assuming that it is restricted to Maxo. It may be more widespread, but it is not found in Xopian. See also Deeters (1930:98).

[8]In Laz, a similar change has taken place for one of the third person pronouns. The pronoun *muk*, originally the narrative case form, is now syncretic for narrative and nominative (Chikobava 1936:77).

[9]In Ač̣arian, the object prefix *h-* and its phonetic variants often mark agreement with a direct object in both Series I and II under circumstances that have not been fully delineated from a syntactic point of view (Lomtatidze 1937:135; Nizharadze 1957:42–44; Nizharadze 1961:86–89). While this may be related to the innovative case patterns described here, this distribution of *h-* is part of a more widespread agreement phenomenon, attested also in Gurian (Lomtatidze 1937) and Kartlian (see hierarchy in example 5).

[10]That is, in Laz and Mingrelian, a dative direct object may occur with a narrative subject in the object demotion construction, governed lexically by a few verbs (see Chap. 1, examples 7–8, and Chap. 6, example 38). The difference is that in Lower Ač̣arian this pattern is generalized.

[11]In Ač̣arian, *-en* also marks the plurality of an initial subject that HAS undergone Inversion, just as *-t* does in the litarary dialect (Nizharadze 1975:158).

[12]This approach is formally justifiable on the grounds that the grammar of each language explicitly recognizes, for example, 'final subject' as a notion relevant to all verb types through various rules, such as Subject Agreement (see Table 13.2).

[13]Some of the examples cited in the literature have the subject *man*, the problems of which are discussed above. Some contain verbs that, in other dialects, govern Inversion; in Lower Ač̣arian they have lost Inversion and are transitive. Some contain active intransitives which in literary Georgian are irregular members of Class 2 (e.g., *svla* 'come, go'). For these and other reasons, there is no satisfactory

example of an inactive intransitive with a narrative case in Series I in the available sources.

[14]From this subdialect there are also forms recorded in which the rules under discussion did not apply at all, for example, *gǰoxons* (Chikobava 1936, II: 111, 35) for the expected **gǰoxoy*, *hek* (Chikobava 1936, II:112, 2) for **he*.

[15]The dialect forms listed in Table 15.10 are not actually included in the works cited, but they follow the principles stated there and exemplified by a variety of other lexical items.

V

Kartvelian and Language Universals

16

Concomitants of Change

In each of the modern Kartvelian languages there are differences in agreement markers that distinguish among the classes of verbs. None of these can be reconstructed in its present distribution to CK. Several represent complications of the grammar: introductions of bifurcations where none existed before. We have a set of language-particular innovations, each of which serves, among other things, to distinguish among the verb classes.

The agreement features themselves are discussed in §16.1, and some possible interpretations of them in §16.2, together with some additional verb morphology.

16.1. CORRELATES

Some of these features have been discussed in other contexts in this work. Reference is made to the earlier discussion to avoid repetition.

16.1.1. Svan *-e* versus Ø

In Svan, with the partial exception of the Naḳra-Laxamula subdialect, the occurrence of the marker *-e* in the aorist identifies Class 1 and 3 verbs, contrasting with Class 2 verbs, which have Ø. This *-e* derives from the aorist screeve marker **i*, which occurred with Class 1, followed by the third person singular subject marker *a, which was common to verbs of all types (see §6.7, argument 1; Kaldani 1978). The suffix -*e* thus has its origins in ancient morphemes, but its present distribution is not the same as that of either of its components.

In the Nakra-Laxamula subdialect today this marker must occur if the subject is in the narrative case, and it is not permissible if the subject is in the nominative case (see Chap. 6, examples 18–26). In this subdialect, the subject of Class 3 verbs may be in either case, and the presence versus absence of -*e* correlates with the case. Thus, the Nakra-Laxamula dialect seems to represent a transitional stage between the distribution original to this marker and that found in other dialects today.

The strong correlation between the case of the surface subject and the presence versus absence of -*e* is the basis for the inference that the change in the distribution of -*e* is related to the change in the distribution of cases in Series II.[1] On this basis, I conclude that the distribution of -*e* is not its original one, and that the change is related to the change in case marking.

16.1.2. Georgian -*s* versus -*a*

Several features that have developed since Old Georgian distinguish among the verb classes. In Old Georgian, the third person singular form of every verb bore the agreement marker -*s* in the present screeve.[2] In Modern Georgian, Class 1 and 3 verbs continue to use this marker, while Class 2 verbs have the marker -*a* instead. The comparison of Old and Modern Georgian forms in Table 16.1 illustrates this. (As the examples show, -*ie* in statives became -*i*.) The same -*s* or -*a* suffix is used to mark third person singular subjects in the future, a screeve that did not exist in Old Georgian; for example, *daçer-s* 'he will write it', *iṭireb-s* 'he will cry', and *gatbeb-a* 'it will warm up'. There are exceptions to the generalization concerning -*s* versus -*a* with Class 2 verbs with irregular conjugations, for example, Modern Georgian *ari-s* 'he is'. A number of inversion verbs fall into this category, for example, Modern Georgian *akv-s* 'he has it' and *uqvar-s* 'he loves him'. However, most of those that are irregular in this respect in the present are regular in taking -*a* in the new future screeve; for example, *ikneb-a* 'he will be', *ekneb-a* 'he will have it', *eqvareb-a* 'he will love him', corresponding to the irregular present forms above. The use of -*a* as the marker of the third person singular subject in the present and future screeves is a characteristic that unites all of the types of Class 2 verbs, including markerless intransitives (*tbeba*), *i*- and *e*-intransitives (*imaleba, emaleba*), intransitives with the formant -*d* or -*d* from *n* (*ganmartldeba, šecuxḍeba*), stative passives (*sçeria*), and inversion verbs (*hgonia*); in this respect Class 2 opposes Classes 1 and 3.

Table 16.1

Comparison of Old and Modern Georgian Third Person Singular Subject Markers in the Present: *-s* and *-a*

Old Georgian	Modern Georgian	
Class 1		
c̣er-s	*c̣er-s*	'he writes it'
drek̥-s	*drek̥-s*	'he bends it'
k̥lav-s	*k̥lav-s*	'he kills it'
suam-s	*svam-s*	'he drinks it'
aṭpob-s	*atbob-s*	'he warms it up'
ašeyneb-s	*ašeneb-s*	'he builds it'
Class 3		
ṭir-s	*ṭiri-s*	'he cries, weeps'
qivi-s	*qivi-s*	'he cries out'
galob-s	*galob-s*	'he sings'
mepob-s	*mepob-s*	'he reigns'
Class 2		
ṭpebi-s	*tbeb-a*	'it warms up'
imalebi-s	*imaleb-a*	'he hides'
emalebi-s	*emaleb-a*	'he hides from him'
šec̣uxneb-s	*šec̣uxdeb-a*	'he grieves, worries, is grieved, worried'
ganmartldebi-s	*ganmartldeb-a*	'he becomes pure, just, etc.'
sc̣erie-s	*sc̣eri-a*	'it is written, stands written'
hgonie-s	*(h)goni-a*	'he hears, believes, thinks it'
up̣q̣rie-s	*up̣q̣ri-a*	'he has, holds it'

The suffix *-a* can be reconstructed as the third person singular subject marker for the aorist in Early CK (see Chap. 5). It occurs in this function with verbs of all types in Old and Modern Georgian and can be reconstructed on internal evidence in Svan (Kaldani 1979). Both Laz and Mingrelian have *u* in this function; likewise reconstructed as **a*.[3] The aorist - *a*, like other features of the aorist, was transferred to the imperfect with the creation of Series I (see Chap. 5), but this suffix was not originally used with the present, as shown by its absence from this screeve in Old Georgian, Svan, Laz, and Mingrelian. Its transfer to the present and future is a Georgian-particular innovation.

16.1.3. Georgian *-es* versus *-nen*

In Old Georgian, third person plural subjects were marked with *-es* in the aorist, for example, *c̣er-es* 'they wrote it'. If the direct object was plural, triggering *-en* (> *-n*), both suffixes appeared, for example, *c̣er-n-es* 'they wrote them'. Surface subjects of Class 2 verbs are underlying direct objects (see Appendix to Chapter 3). In their role as subject they triggered *-es* in the aorist, and as underlying objects they conditioned *-en*; for example, *ic̣er-n-es* 'they were written, got written' (see Chap. 10). In Old Georgian, *-en* (or its phonological variants *-n* or *-an*) was used in some screeves as a marker of third person plural SUBJECTS (see Table 5.2). When Old Georgian *En*-Agreement was dropped as a productive rule, the sequence *-n-es* was replaced by *-nen*, now reanalyzed as a single morpheme; for example, Modern Georgian *da-ic̣er-nen* 'they were written'. Further, it was extended to those Class 2 verbs that previously were exceptions to *En*-Agreement (see §10.1.4); for example, Old Georgian *(gan-)ṭp-es* replaced by *ga-tb-nen* 'they warmed up' and Old Georgian *(aγ-)šeyn-d-es* replaced by *a-šen-d-nen* 'they were built'. Thus, where no difference existed between the markers used by the different classes in Old Georgian, a distinction grew up in historical times, such that Class 1 and 3 use the ancient marker *-es* in the aorist, while Class 2 verbs use *-nen* in this function.

16.1.4. Laz Ø versus *-r* and Mingrelian *-k*

The suffix *-r* is conditioned by first and second person singular subjects, as illustrated by the paradigm in Table 16.2. It is believed that this originated in the present and later spread to other Series I screeves; for some speakers it occurs also in the plural forms of the first and second person (Lomtatidze 1946:133; Marr 1910:58, 65–67). The suffix *-r* occurs only with Class 2 verbs; with verbs of Classes 1 and 3 it does not occur, as illustrated in the paradigms of Tables 16.3 and 16.4.

In Mingrelian, a suffix *-k* is conditioned by first and second persons singular, just in the present tense. It occurs in verbs of all classes, as illustrated in Tables 16.5, 16.6, and 16.7.[4] While *-k* occurs in the singular of the first and second persons, it is replaced by *-t*, a general plural marker

Table 16.2

Conjugation of Class 2 Verb in Present Screeve in Laz (√ *skid* 'remain')

	Singular	Plural
1st person	*do-p-skid-u-r*	*do-p-skid-u-t*
2nd person	*do- skid-u-r*	*do- skid-u-t*
3rd person	*do- skid-u-n*	*do- skid-u-n-an*

Table 16.3

Conjugation of Class 1 Verb in Present Screeve in Laz
(√ *q̣uil* 'kill')

	Singular	Plural
1st person	*p-il-up* (< **v-q̣vil-up*)	*p -il-up-t*
2nd person	*q̣vil-up*	*q̇vil-up-t*
3rd person	*q̣vil-up-s*	*q̣vil-up-an*

Table 16.4

Conjugation of Class 3 Verb in Present Screeve in Laz
(√ *γa(r)γal* 'talk')

	Singular	Plural
1st person	*b-γaγal-ap*	*b-γaγal-ap-t*
2nd person	*γaγal-ap*	*γaγal-ap-t*
3rd person	*γaγal-ap-s*	*γaγal-ap-an*

Table 16.5

Conjugation of Class 1 Verbs in Singular of Present Screeve in Mingrelian

	√ *ˀvil* 'kill'	√ *arʒ* 'give'
1st person	*p-il-un-k* (**v-ˀvilunk*)	*v-arʒ-en-k*
2nd person	*ˀvil-un-k*	*arʒ-en-k*
3rd person	*ˀvil-un-s*	*arʒ-en-s*

Table 16.6

Conjugation of Class 3 Verbs in Singular of Present Screeve in Mingrelian

	√ *laˀap* 'play'	√ *ingar* 'cry'
1st person	*b-laˀap-en-k*	*imgar-k*
2nd person	*laˀap-en-k*	*ingar-k*
3rd person	*laˀap-en-s*	*ingar-s*

for these persons; for example, *pskidu-k* 'I remain' versus *pskidu-t* 'we remain' and *skidu-t* 'you(PL) remain'. Mingrelian *-k* is believed to be related to Laz *-r* (Asatiani 1973; Lomtatidze 1946).[5]

Table 16.7

Conjugation of Class 2 Verbs in Singular of Present Screeve in Mingrelian

	√ *skid* 'remain'	√ *γur* 'die'
1st person	*p-skid-u-k*	*b-γur-u-k*
2nd person	*skid-u-k*	*γur-u-k*
3rd person	*skid-u-n*	*γur-u-n*

Table 16.8

Forms of the Copula in the Singular of the Present Screeve[a]

	Laz	Old Georgian	Svan (Upper Svan and Lent̩ex)
1st person	*v-ore*	*v-ar*	*xv-äri*
2nd person	*ore*	*x-ar*	*x-äri*
3rd person	*ore-n*	*ar-s*	*äri*

[a]Laz example is from Chikobava (1936:171); Svan is from Gagua (1976:22).

Lomtatidize (1946) has shown that Laz *-r* comes from the copula. This is consistent with the fact that this auxiliary occurs enclitic to a few verbs in Georgian in the present tense, as well as in some dialects of Svan (see Baramidze 1964, esp. 142 on the development of person markers from auxiliary verbs). The verb 'be' can be reconstructed to CK on the basis of the forms listed in Table 16.8. Variants have been omitted from this table. Svan *i* regularly causes umlaut in a preceding vowel; *äri* comes from **ari*. The Great Zan Vowel Shift made CK **a* into Zan *o*. Thus, the Laz forms are the regular correspondents of CK **ar-*, as are the Svan forms. The Mingrelian forms are essentially like those of Laz with the addition of *-k*: *v-ore-k*, (*o*)*re-k*, (*o*)*re-*(*n*). On the basis of these facts, we reconstruct CK **ar-* as the present stem of the verb 'be'. Therefore, Laz *-r* must have come from a form of the copula with a vowel preceding *r*, either **a* or the *o* found today. This being the case, there can be no phonological explanation for the failure of *-r* to occur in the appropriate forms listed in Tables 16.3 and 16.4. That is, even if **q̣vil-up-r* were blocked by phonological rules, **q̣vil-up-or* would be possible from a phonotactic point of view. Thus, the explanation for the restriction of *-r* to Class 2 must be other than phonological. Diachronically, *-r* must have cliticized just to inactive intransitive verb forms. Synchronically, on the other hand, the situation is slightly different. In general, Class 2 verbs have the properties listed in

Table 16.9. The last two morphological characteristics listed for each class are discussed in subsections below. In general, Class 2 verbs have vowel-final present stems and take *-r*. There are, however, a few exceptional verbs that are apparently inactive and take nominative case subjects yet have the morphological characteristics listed for Class 1 and 3 verbs, for example, *melams* 'it falls' and *pacxalaps* 'it flutters'. Thus, the correlation between vowel-final stems and the occurrence of *-r* is closer than that between *-r* and the syntax of inactive verbs.[6] Those few verbs that are exceptions with respect to Series I stem form are also characteristically exceptions with respect to the other morphological properties listed in Table 16.9. While the synchronic correlation is phonologically based, this cannot have been the original situation. The fact that a vowel preceding *r* in the root of the copula is clearly reconstructible to CK requires us to explain the development of *-r* in terms of a relationship to Class 2. Later it was redistributed on the basis of vowel-final present stems.

Table 16.9

Morphological–Syntactic–Semantic Correlations: Laz

Morphological	Syntactic	Semantic
Class 1		
consonant-final Series I stem	transitive	active (or inactive)
does not take *-r*		telic
takes *-s*	narrative case	
takes *-an*	*inversion in Old Series III*	
Class 2		
vowel-final Series I stem	intransitive	inactive
takes *-r*	initial direct object	telic or stative
takes *-n*	nominative case	
takes *-nan*	no inversion in Old Series III	
Class 3		
consonant-final Series I stem	intransitive	active
does not take *-r*	initial subject	atelic
takes *-s*	narrative case	
takes *-an*	inversion in Old Series III	

16.1.5. Zan *-s* versus *-n*

As the paradigms above illustrate, in both Laz and Mingrelian, the third person subject marker in the present screeve is *-s* for Class 1 and 3 verbs

(Tables 16.3, 16.4, 16.5, and 16.6) and *-n* for Class 2 verbs (Tables 16.2 and 16.7). Forms with *-n* listed for Mingrelian in Table 16.7 are the underlying forms. In word-final position, *n* deletes in Mingrelian, and the surface forms corresponding to those in the table are *skidu* 'he remains' and *γuru* 'he dies'. That *-n* is present in underlying forms in Mingrelian is shown by its surface occurrence when followed by the enclitic question particle, *-o*; for example, *xe* 'he sits' (< *xe-n*), *xe-n-o* 'does he sit?' (Chikobava 1936:97). The marker is optionally retained in *ren* (or *re*) 'he/it is'.

The suffix *-s* as a third person singular subject marker certainly dates to CK, as it is found in subjunctive screeves in all four languages. While it is not found in the present in Svan, *-s* in this screeve must date at least to CGZ, and probably to CK.

In Old Georgian a third person singular subject marker *-n* also occurred, and forms with *-n* usually express habitual or generic present; for example, *c̣er-n* 'he writes (it)' beside *c̣er-s* 'he is writing it', though the distinction between these is not always maintained.[7] While *-n* in Georgian may occur with dynamic verbs, such as *c̣er-* 'write', it is most common with stative verbs; for example, *ar-n* 'he is', *dga-n* 'he stands' and *aku-n* 'he has it'. Stative verbs are regularly in Class 2, though this class also includes dynamic verbs. It is natural that stative verbs would appear frequently in the habitual present, rather than the 'actual' present; compare this with English *he is tall* versus **he is being tall* and *he has a dog* versus **he is having a dog*. Whether the expression of the habitual is a primary or secondary function of *-n*, it seems likely that in CGZ it connected either with stativity or with habitual aspect and that in Zan it was reanalyzed as a property of Class 2 verbs.[8]

Still later, Zan reanalyzed the distribution of *-n* as conditioned by vowel-final present stems, in opposition to *-s* with consonant-final present stems. Thus, synchronically it is phonetically conditioned, like the alternation of ∅ and *-r* in Laz and *-an* and *-nan* in both Laz and Mingrelian. It should be added that synchronically there is no *s* versus *n* alternation in Zan apart from these morphemes, either of the form $n \rightarrow s$ / C ____ # or of the form $s \rightarrow n$ / V ____ #. This, together with the fact that both *-s* and *-n* probably date to CK as third person subject markers, shows that the current phonetically based distribution must be the result of reanalysis.

16.1.6. Zan *-an* versus *-n-an*

In both Laz and Mingrelian, Class 1 and 3 verbs have the third person plural subject marker *-an*, while Class 2 verbs have the corresponding form *-nan*.[9] In Mingrelian, the deletion of word-final *n* reduces the opposition to the surface forms *-a* and *-na*, as illustrated in Table 16.10. The suffixes

Table 16.10

Third Person Plural Subject Forms in Mingrelian

Class 1 and 3 examples		Class 2 examples	
ˀvilun-a	'they kill it'	*skidu-na*	'they remain'
arʒen-a	'they give it'	*γuru-na*	'they die'
laˀapen-a	'they play'	*iškvidu-na*	'they drown'
ibir-a	'they sing'		
ingar-a	'they cry'[a]		

[a]Chikobava (1938:259) lists the forms *mgar* and *bgar* for the root of this verb in Laz and *gar* in Mingrelian. In both languages it takes the third person plural suffix *-a(n)*: Laz *ibgaran, imgaran* and Mingrelian *ingara* 'they sing'. However, in Laz, *r* may assimilate to the following *n*, giving *imganan*. Dumézil (1937:125, 7) has recorded *ibgarnan*. Although both forms appear to have the suffix *-nan*, both are due to the assimilation of *r* from underlying *imgaran, ibgaran* (see Zhghenti 1965:68).

-en, *-un*, and *-u* in the examples of the first three lines are series markers and occur in all persons and numbers, as can be seen by comparison with the forms in Tables 16.5, and 16.6, and 16.7. The deletion exemplified in Table 16.10 is a synchronic rule; see above.

In both languages, the distribution of *-a(n)* versus *-na(n)* is synchronically governed by whether the present stem is consonant- or vowel-final. Historically, on the other hand, *-nan* was two morphemes, *-n-an* from **-en-an*, where *-n-* is a relic of *En*-Agreement (§10.2.3). The original distribution of *En*-Agreement put it in Series I only with verbs of Class 2 (§10.2.1), and it remains with that class still.[10]

16.1.7. Summary

I have described six alternations in agreement markers in the four languages. Each represents an opposition of Classes 1 and 3 to Class 2. With the exception of Svan *-e* versus ∅, which seems to have developed out of a Class 1 versus Classes 2 and 3 (i.e., transitive versus intransitive) opposition, each of these represents a complication of the grammar. Each is a recent development. The three Zan rules discussed are governed synchronically by phonetic environment, and this in turn has a close correlation with the type of verb, as shown in Table 16.9. For each of these three pairs, it is shown that the alternation developed on some other basis and was only later reinterpreted as dependent on the phonetics of the verb stem. The three rules in Georgian and Svan are stated on the basis of class; they cannot be correlated with a phonetic environment.

16.2. INTERPRETATION

We cannot escape the observation that the development of these oppositions is new; there are no comparable oppositions that can be reconstructed to CK. Are they then related to some aspect of the modern languages that was not present in the parent language?

16.2.1. The Typological Consistency Hypothesis

In the diachronic study of word order change, it has been suggested that languages develop toward typological consistency. Universally, there is a high degree of correlation between the following orders: object–verb; genitive attribute–head noun; postpositions; main verb–auxiliary; and standard of comparison–comparative adjective. Complementary to this, we find the following: verb–object; head noun–genitive attribute; prepositions; auxiliary–main verb; comparative adjective–standard of comparison.[11] In explanation of this, Vennemann has suggested the Principle of Natural Serialization: "Languages tend to serialize operator–operand hierarchies unidirectionally" (1975:288). The notion of typological consistency has also been developed in Lehmann (1973) and elsewhere and has been used as a basis for word order reconstruction (Lehmann 1974).

The term 'ergative language', which permeates the literature on rule alignment, suggests that a language, rather than a rule, may be ergative. It is, of course, well known that ergative rules may coexist in a language with accusative rules. In spite of this, 'ergative language' suggests whole-language typology, the notion that other characteristics of a language are correlated with the alignment of a rule. The alignment of one rule is thought by some to be affected particularly by the alignment of another.

It is consistent with these two trends in linguistics to formulate the hypothesis that in the course of time, languages universally tend toward typological consistency with respect to rule alignment. I refer to this as the TYPOLOGICAL CONSISTENCY HYPOTHESIS.

In support of this hypothesis, we may note particularly that it appears that all four Kartvelian languages have introduced or realigned agreement rules to be consistent with the active case system, which is likewise new in all of them. The Svan *-e* versus ∅ alternation is particularly striking, since the original distribution of this marker seems to have correlated, instead, with the reconstructed ergative case system of Series II. That is, in reconstructed proto-Svan, the subjects of transitive verbs bore the narrative case, and their verbs had the suffixes *-*i*-*a* (> -*e*) in the third person, while intransitive verbs governed nominative case subjects and were marked *-*a* (> ∅) in the third person. While this situation is partially retained in Naḳra-Laxamula, in other dialects the narrative case and -*e* are associated with subjects of transitive and active intransitives only.

A second striking example would seem to be the difference between Laz -*r* and Mingrelian -*k*, if we assume with Asatiani (1973), Lomtatidze (1946), and others that these two are related. Laz has nominative case subjects for inactive intransitives only, and these verbs also have -*r* in appropriate screeves. In Mingrelian, on the other hand, the nominative is used for all subjects in the series where -*k* is used, and this suffix likewise occurs in all verbs.

Other examples are found in Ačarian. As shown in §15.3.4, the lower subdialect, in particular, is tending toward accusative case marking, that is, the use of one case for surface subjects of all verb types. At the same time it is losing the constrast between -*s* and -*a* in the present and that between -*es* and -*en* (-*nen* in other dialects) (Mikeladze 1980:101; Nizharadze 1975: 142–143). These three trends could be viewed as parallel developments of case and agreement rules.

In spite of this apparent support for the typological consistency hypothesis, a closer look reveals that is not upheld by the data. First, except for Svan -*e* versus ∅, no agreement rule in the modern languages actually has active alignment. While each of the rules discussed distinguishes subjects of inactive intransitives from those of transitive and active intransitive verbs, there is more to active alignment than this, as shown by the table of alignment types, Table 16.11. If, for example, the Laz -*s* versus -*n* rule had active alignment, -*n* would be triggered not only by the subjects of inactive intransitives, but also by direct objects of transitives, as is A in

Table 16.11

Some Alignment Types

	Direct Object	Subject Intransitive		Subject Transitive
		Inactive	Active	
Ergative	A	A		B
Active	A	A	B	B
Accusative	A	B		B
Active-tripartite	A	B	C	C

Table 16.11. The case marking rule, on the other hand, is one of active alignment, such that both subjects of inactive intransitives and direct objects are assigned the nominative case. The actual distribution of each of these agreement rules is that set out as 'active-tripartite' in Table 16.11. In the Laz *-s* versus *-n* alternation, for example, A has the value Ø, B the value *-n*, and C the value *-s*. Put differently, it is not nominative-nominals that trigger *-n* in the appropriate screeves in Laz: it is only a proper subset of these, nominative case subjects. The same is true of the other rules described in §16.1, except *-e* versus Ø in Svan, which does have active alignment in most dialects.

A second argument against the typological consistency hypothesis is that the Georgian *-s* versus *-a* rule and the Mingrelian *-s* versus *-n* and *-a(n)* versus *-na(n)* rules have developed in an inappropriate series. All three rules apply in Series I, which has accusative case marking in both languages, as well as in CGZ. The development of a secondary bifurcation in these markers cannot be viewed as a contribution to consistency of alignment, as it is not consistent with other rules in that series.

It is noteworthy, too, that where there exists any flexibility, there is apparently no attempt to correlate various characteristics of a class in a clause. In §6.3.1 I show that the verbs 'come, go' in Laz are irregular in that they may take either narrative case subjects (as Class 3 verbs) or nominative case subjects (as Class 2), the latter being archaic. In the examples below from texts, the subject cases selected do not correlate by class with the agreement markers. (See also examples in Chapter 6.)

(1) *beepe* *komul**an***
child/PL/NOM they/come/I
'The children will come.' (Asatiani 1974: **15** [8])

(2) *mamuni-k . . . **ulun***
midwife-NAR she/come/I
'The midwife comes.' (Asatiani 1974: **18** [4])

In (1), the subject is in the nominative, as with Class 2 verbs; yet the third person plural subject marker is *-an*, as for a Class 3 verb. With this subject we might expect, instead, *kom-ul-u-nan*. On the other hand, in (2) the same verb has a narrative case subject, as do Class 3 verbs, and uses the third person singular subject marker *-n*, as do Class 2 verbs. This verb is certainly irregular. Yet if the language tended toward consistency of rule alignment, we might also expect to find consistent adherence to characteristics of one class in a clause.

We may note further that *En*-Agreement in Old Georgian is one Kartvelian agreement rule that does have active alignment, if we discount the exceptions to it discussed in §10.1.4.[12] It was triggered both by subjects of inactive intransitives and by direct objects, and it applied in the series where case marking was of the active type. It would seem to be inconsistent with the spirit of the typological consistency hypothesis that the language lost this agreement rule, which had the same alignment as the case assignment rule in its series, while retaining person agreement rules, which have accusative alignment.

We must conclude that the typological consistency hypothesis in the form stated above is not supported by the changes that have taken place in agreement morphology.[13]

16.2.2. Reinforcement

Although the typological consistency hypothesis is not upheld by the data discussed in §16.1, it is clear that we would be missing a significant generalization concerning the diachronic development of syntax in Kartvelian if we failed to make any connection between the changes described above.

We can summarize the facts this way. In the Kartvelian languages, at least two rules were introduced—case marking in Series II and Inversion in Series III—which made reference to an opposition between transitive and active intransitive verb forms, on the one hand, and inactive intransitive forms, on the other. Previous grammatical rules had opposed transitive to intransitive, such as the original case marking system, or made no opposition, referring to primary surface grammatical relations. Each of the Kartvelian languages made innovations that REINFORCED the new opposition, making the differences between the two verb groups greater. The innovative differences were not limited to the two series where the active case marking and Inversion apply but occur throughout the verb conjugation. While only one of the innovations described in §16.1 has true active alignment, each reinforces the distinction between Classes 1 and 3 versus Class 2.

While inflectional bifurcations consistently differentiate Class 2 from Classes 1 and 3, derivational innovations distinguish each class from the others. Unlike the agreement markers discussed in §16.1, the derivational distinctions described below are in several instances limited to a subclass of a larger class. They nevertheless serve to identify unambiguously the class to which the verb form belongs.

In Svan, the derivational suffix *-al,* or one of its phonological variants, characterizes many Class 3 verbs and distinguishes them from verbs of other classes. This morpheme appears to be related to several others in Svan. (a) The most common noun pluralizer is *-ar, -al,* or phonological variants of these (see §9.3). (b) In parts of the Upper Bal dialect, there are remnants of *-al, -ar* as a marker of object plurality in finite and non-finite verb forms (see §9.4 and 13.4.4). (c) A morpheme of the same form may indicate interative action. These are discussed in Sharadzenidze (1954) and Topuria (1967:231–234).

There is no evidence that a morpheme cognate to *-al* serves as a formant of Class 3 verbs in any of the other languages. That is, the use of this morpheme as a marker of Class 3 must be a Svan development. The morpheme *-al* may derive from an ancient pluralizer (see §9.3) and from that function developed into a marker of object plurality and iterative action, which are related functions that often co-occur in a language. It is probable that its use in marking the interative led to its characterizing Class 3. Verbs of this class express ongoing activity (see Holisky 1981a and examples in Chapter 3, this volume), which is semantically close to repeated action.

Class 2 Svan verbs, with the exception of a few irregular members, differ from verbs of other classes in one or another conjugational feature. Non-ablauting Class 2 verbs are distinguished by a form of the suffix *-an* in the aorist, while ablauting Class 2 verbs are characterized by *e*-grade and by a form of the suffix *-en* in the present. The origins of the suffixes *-an* and *-en* and their variants are not known. Topuria (1979b:33ff and 1967:241–242) has suggested that Svan *-en* is equivalent to Georgian *-eb;* on *-eb-i* in Class 2, see below.

Even in Old Georgian there were features that distinguished Class 2 verbs from Classes 1 and 3. In the present screeve most Class 2 verbs used either a series marker plus *i* (e.g., *ṭp-**eb-i**-s* 'it warms up', *imal-**eb-i**-s 'he hides', šeçuxn-**eb-i**-s* 'he grieves, worries' and *ganmartld-**eb-i**-s* 'he becomes pure, just, straight') or *-ie* (e.g., *hgon-**ie**-s* 'he hears, believes, thinks it' and *hpqr-**ie**-s* 'he has, holds it').

In Modern Georgian, Class 3 is set apart by conjugational use of the prefix *i*. On the origin of this marker and its adaptation as a characteristic of Class 3 in Georgian, see §14.3.2. A second characteristic of Class 3, not found productively in the other classes, is the use of the formant *-n* in Series III forms (see examples (30)–(31) of Chap. 10); for example, *umušav-n-ia* 'he has worked' and *utamaš-n-ia* 'he has played'. This is a Georgian development not found in the sister languages (but see Chap. 9, n. 5).

In Zan, Class 1 and 3 Series I stems end in consonants, while those of Class 2 are vowel-final. This opposition has no single source. Class 1 verbs typically have Series I stems formed with a series marker having the form -VC; for example, *qvil-up* 'kill', *meč-ap* 'give', and *čar-um* 'write'. A number of Class 3 verbs have the same structure; for example, *qu-ap* (< **qur-*

ap) 'cry out', *xoron-ap* 'dance', and *γaγal-ap* 'talk'. Verb roots in Kartvelian are characteristically consonant-final (Gamkrelidze and Machavariani 1965:303–306), and many Class 3 verbs have Series I stems consisting of an optional prefix and the root with no suffix; for example, *ister-* 'play', *ibir-* 'sing', and *imgar-* 'cry'. These two facts account for consonant-final stems for Classes 1 and 3. In Laz and Mingrelian, Class 2 verbs typically have Series I stems formed with the series marker *-u* or with *-e* (Chikobava 1936:112–115; Danelia 1976).[14] There is no parallel contrast in Svan or Georgian that would lead us to reconstruct to CK the distribution found today in Zan.

In this section I have surveyed a number of morphemes that identify a verb form as belonging to a particular class, even though some do not occur with every verb in that class. The morphemes described in this section cannot be viewed in terms of alignment at all. They are properties of verbs and are not conditioned or governed by nominals. Most of the affixes discussed here have more than one function, among which is identifying the class of the verb form.

16.3. CONCLUSIONS

In Chapter 15 it is shown that several of the Kartvelian languages and dialects have simplified or unified case marking by entending an extant rule into new domains. In §16.2.1 it was shown that on the contrary, there has been no overwhelming tendency to simplify the grammar as a whole by aligning rules of different types in a single way. In particular, with the exception of *En*-Agreement, which eventually died out, and Svan *-e* versus *∅* (§16.1.1), there has been no agreement rule introduced or realigned with true active alignment. As applied to the alignment of rules, the typological consistency hypothesis is not supported by Kartvelian data. The implications of this observation are important for diachronic syntax: The alignment of one rule in a language cannot be used as a basis for reconstructing the alignment of another.

On the other hand, it cannot be an accident that case marking in Series II, Inversion in Series III, *-e* versus *∅* aorist agreement in Svan, and the Old Georgian *En*-Agreement all have active alignment. In addition, the agreement markers described in §16.1.2–16.1.6 are innovative bifurcations that exclusively reinforce a distinction between Class 2 and Classes 1 and 3. These have a distribution related to, but not the same as, active alignment, as set out in Table 16.11. Some other verb morphology cannot be described in terms of alignment at all, yet distinguishes one class from the others. Thus, a number of recent independent changes in the several daughter languages serve either to separate Class 2 from Classes 1 and 3 or to separate each class from the others. It has been suggested that all of these serve in part to REINFORCE class distinctions.

In considering whether or not the changes that reinforce class distinctions have anything to do with the changes in case marking systems, it is useful to recall that (a) in the Naḳra-Laxamula dialect, there is a close correlation between the choice of case and the distribution of the suffix *-e* (see Chap. 6), and (b) in Georgian there developed a correlation between the case of the subject and the morphology of the verb, as discussed in §14.3.2. On the other hand, the Maxo subdialect of Laz also permits an alternation in subject case (see §15.3.3), and there we find no correlation between the choice of case and the third person singular and plural marker alternants. The morphology of a particular verb is invariant, as shown by examples (10)–(12) of Chapter 15. In Xopian, too, irregular verbs do not maintain a correlation as (1)–(2) of the present chapter show.

We cannot arrive at an understanding of the relationship between the changes discussed in this chapter and the changes in case marking described above until these facts are compared with facts in other language groups that have undergone comparable change. Payne (1980, esp. 161, 165, 168, 173, 178, 181, 184–185) has shown that the loss of ergative case marking is, in some of the Pamir (Iranian) languages, accompanied by a weakening of conjugational distinctions between transitive and intransitive. While these facts are suggestive, their importance for diachronic syntax can be assessed only through a detailed comparison of the data in additional language groups.

At this stage in our understanding of linguistic universals and the principles of diachronic syntax, it would be mere speculation to suggest that all of the changes described in this chapter are related in a systematic way to the changes in case systems discussed in earlier chapters. I do not support the view that the changes in case alignment bear a causal relation to all of the changes described here. The changes that occurred at about the same time as or subsequent to the various case changes are recorded here in the hope that future research will, through comparison with other language families, discover what relationship exists between the changes in case systems and the verb morphology described above: whether it is a necessary correlate, a relative correlate, an accident, or something else. It is in this spirit that these facts are included here.

NOTES

[1]The change in distribution discussed here is that associated with the class of the verb. In fact, this marker was also generalized from third person singular to

all plural subject persons in the screeves and classes where it occurs; for this reason, it is often not considered a marker of agreement. Kaldani (1978:154, note 12) has observed that in Upper Bal, not only *-e* has been redistributed, but also the umlauted vowel that characterizes the last syllable of first and second person subject forms in the aorist. In Lower Bal the latter change has not occurred.

[2]For the sake of simplicity, I have assumed here the system schematized in Table 5.1. Another view, equally valid, is described in note 7 of the present chapter, but is irrelevant to the *-s* versus *-a* alternation.

[3]See Gamkrelidze and Machavariani (1965:358–359). The regular reflex of CK **a* is *o* in Zan, and Zan *o* generally became *u* in word-final position (Machavariani 1969).

[4]This is the distribution stated by Chikobava (1936:96, 115) and by Lomtatidze (1946:131). Kluge (1916:27, 29) records *-k* in the future for certain verbs; he also shows the conjugation of some verbs as lacking *-k* and the *n* of the series marker, -V*n*.

[5]Asatiani (1973) records that she discovered the suffix *-r*, rather than *-k* or Ø, used by Mingrelian speakers over the age of 83 in 1956 in the village of J̌vari, as well as in material recorded by Kipshidze in 1914. In the Mingrelian examples, *-r* is limited also to what appear to be Class 2 verbs, though the distribution of this suffix in Mingrelian is not identical to that of *-r* in Laz. On the basis of individual lexical items, she argues that *-k* is new, replacing *-r* in this function.

[6]The morphological properties listed for Classes 1 and 3 in Table 16.9 were originally believed to characterize transitive verbs (Class 1) only, and those listed for Class 2 to characterize intransitives. Oniani (1978:72–73, attributed to lectures by Gudava) points out that the choice between *-s* and *-n* in Mingrelian is most closely related to consonant- versus vowel-final Series I stems. (According to the forms listed in Chikobava 1938:273, the verb 'go' is an exception: *ma meuli* 'I go' and *tina meurs* 'he goes', not *meuli(n)* or *meuri(n)*.) The consonant- versus vowel-final stem is, in turn, dependent upon class (see Oniani 1978:170), and is related to the semantic, syntactic, and other morphological features included in Table 16.9.

[7]According to one analysis, *-s* functioned as the third person singular subject marker in the present screeve, while *-n* filled the same function in the present habitual screeve, which happens to be defective for person (Imnaishvili 1971; Kiknadze 1961:231; Shanidze 1957c, 1976). According to a second analysis, there is not distinct present habitual screeve, and *-n* and *-s* are simply alternants (Arabuli 1980a; Chikobava 1940, 1948:77–80, 1968:136, 163). Both sides in this debate agree that forms with *-n* usually had a habitual meaning (see esp. Chikobava 1940:21). The form *-d* also exists in this function.

[8]Topuria (1967:2–8) observes that five Svan verbs preserve a third person (singular and plural) subject prefix *l-* and suggests that it is related to CGZ **-n*. Kaldani (1959b) presents Svan data showing that *n-* and *y-* also occur in this function in "nearly all" verbs after the preverb *la-* in certain dialects. In Kaldani (1979) he argues that *l-* is the basic form and that the others developed from it. The variation seems to be determined in part by phonetic environment and in part by dialect. Topuria (1967:3) cites data that show that *l-* co-occurs with the third person singular subject marker *-s*, which is limited to subjunctives; for example,

Lower Bal *lä-l-em-e-s* 'may he eat it'. Kaldani (1979:209) provides examples of the occurrence of the allomorph *y-* with verbs of each class; for example, *la-y-te* (Class 1) 'he mowed it', *lä-y-γiral* (Class 3) 'he sang for a little while', and *lä-y-çərnan* (Class 2) 'he/it became red'. If it is correct to associate Svan *l/n/y-* with CGZ *-n*, there is no evidence in the published data on Svan to suggest that the distribution of this morpheme in CK was related to class, to habitual versus actual present, or (in alternation with *s*) to the phonetic environment. It seems probable, on the contrary, that the distribution proposed here for CGZ was the result of reanalysis of some previous situation.

[9]From textual examples, it appears that the Artašen subdialect of Laz, which has lost both narrative and the dative cases (see §15.5), has maintained all three of the Laz bifurcated agreement markers discussed here. A contrast between Ø and *-r* can be seen in the forms *ioxam* 'you call it' (transitive) (Dumézil and Esenç 1972:**3** [5]) and *bγuru-r* 'I am dying' (inactive intransitive) (Chikobava 1936, II:122, 6). As discussed in Chapter 15, in Artašen a word-final complex composed of a consonant plus *s* is regularly reduced to *y*. The contrast between underlying *-s* and *-n* is maintained in this form: for example, *šu-y* (< **šums*) 'he drinks it' (Class 1) (Chikobava 1936, II: 109, 24) and *ore-n*, *o-n* 'it is' (Class 2) (Chikobava 1936, II: 109, 27). In the following examples the parallel differentiation of *-an* and *-nan* can be seen: *šum-an* 'they drink it' (Class 1) (Chikobava 1936, II: 109, 24) and *goišaše-nan* 'they were astonished' (Class 2) (Dumézil and Esenç 1972: **3** [2]).

[10]The morphemes used in the present were carried over to Series III forms; the function of *-nan* there has been reanalyzed in a way consistent with the syntax of that series.

[11]The correlations stated here, made by Lehmann, Venemann, and others, are based on Greenberg (1963).

[12]The Svan suffix *-ar*, *-al* in Mesṭia is conditioned today in finite forms only by final direct objects, but its distribution in participles suggests that it may have occurred in a broader set of environments (see Sharadzenidze 1954; §13.4.4 this volume). Neither its alignment in participles nor its original alignment can be definitely determined from data available, but it appears to have been either ergative or active.

[13]Outside the realm of agreement, there is additional evidence against the typological consistency hypothesis in alignment. In the course of the history of Georgian, Retired Term Marking has changed from a rule for which no clear alignment type may be specified (Harris 1979) to a rule of ergative alignment (Harris 1981b). According to the typological consistency hypothesis, it would have been expected to develop either active marking, consistent with cases in Series II, or accusative, consistent with Series I.

[14]The origin of *-u* from **av* is discussed in Chapter 9 and Danelia (1976:169). In other instances CGZ **av* has the reflex *-up*, *-um*, *-un* in Zan. I hypothesize that in Zan the different reflexes are conditioned by class, reflecting the incipient need to distinguish among classes.

17

Case Alignment: Diachrony and Synchrony

This chapter summarizes the contributions of the study of Kartvelian case alignment changes to an understanding of diachronic syntax. Although agreement has been discussed in this work in several different contexts, the conclusions reached here are based on case alignment changes only, as those are at present better understood. In this chapter the following diachronic aspects of case marking are discussed: the mechanisms by which changes in case alignment occur (§17.1), possible directions of change (§17.2), and the nature and explanation of these shifts (§17.3). Comparison of grammars of the different languages also contributes to an understanding of some synchronic aspects of case alignment. Some aspects of the nature of active alignment are discussed in §17.4, and the nature of alignment splits in §17.5.

17.1. MECHANISMS

It has been known for some time that the surface structure of passives can be reinterpreted. The subject of the passive, which is an underlying direct object, bears the same marking as the subject of intransitives, which do not undergo Passivization. While these two are marked in one way, the agent of the passive, which is equivalent to the subject of a transitive, is marked a second way, thus leading to an ergative alignment. In this way, passives have been reanalyzed as part of an ergative system in various Indo-Aryan and Iranian languages[1] (Allen 1950; Anderson 1977; Bynon 1980; Matthews 1952; Payne 1979, 1980; Pirejko 1979, etc.), Australian (Hale 1970), and Polynesian (Chung 1977, 1978; Chung and Seiter 1980: §7; Hohepa 1969).

In Part III it is shown that Series I originated in Common Kartvelian as a set of forms denoting durative aspect. In this aspect, the productive rule of Object Demotion applied, making initial direct objects final indirect objects. Much later, a reinterpretation of the surface forms led to accusative case marking. A productive construction of the sort reconstructed for Series I in Kartvelian is attested in many languages of the world, for example, Dyirbal (Dixon 1972:66; 1977b:369) and Kalkatunga (Blake 1976), Greenlandic Eskimo (Woodbury 1977:323), and Tongan and Samoan (Chung 1978:54, 56). Like the passive-to-ergative reanalysis in other language families, the object demotion-to-accusative reanalysis in Kartvelian was a reinterpretation of the surface patterns of a once-productive syntactic construction and resulted in a realignment of case marking.

A second productive syntactic construction, inversion, was found in Series III in Common Kartvelian. The inherited construction is being replaced by new forms not involving Inversion in Laz (§15.3.2). In the Lower Ačarian dialect of Georgian, the forms of the verb are partially preserved, but inversion is being lost. On the basis of available data, no dialect can be positively identified as having reanalyzed Series III surface structures in a way comparable to the two reanalyses discussed above. It appears, however, that this is being prevented only by the fact that the surface grammatical relations in this construction are coded by so many devices in Kartvelian. Were this not so, it seems likely that inversion would have been reinterpreted in some dialects in a way comparable to passive in other languages and object demotion in Kartvelian.

Two other constructions, of more limited scope, were shown to play a role in the ergative-to-active shift. The initial direct object of some transitives was incorporated into the verb, making the clause finally intransitive; e.g., *γaγad-qo* 'noise-he/made/it'. This construction, though lexically limited, was liable to reanalysis as a simple intransitive; the form was replaced by *iγaγada,* with the same meaning. Verbs that took grammatical direct objects that were semantically redundant were likewise subject to reanalysis as intransitives through the dropping of unemphatic pronominal direct objects (see Chap. 14). Unlike the changes in alignment discussed above, the ergative-to-active shift is not entirely explained by these two mechanisms, as it included lexical items not occurring in either construction.

Thus, it seems likely that a wide variety of syntactic rules produce surface structures that can be reanalyzed, resulting in a realignment of case marking or of some other coding rule. Reinterpretation of surface patterns, which may result from more than one kind of rule, is an important mechanism for change in the alignment of coding rules.

It has been suggested that phonological processes can change the alignment of case marking or another coding rule (see Anderson 1977; Dixon 1977b). As is well known, the erosion of case markers in some Germanic languages played a part in the loss of cases, resulting in the case marking type known as 'neutral', that is, a system in which all subjects and direct objects bear the same marking (see Eliasson 1980; Jespersen 1927:208). A similar result was effected in Artašen by the loss of narrative *-k* and dative *-s*. At least the loss of *-s* was part of a widespread loss and weakening of this segment in word-final position.

A third mechanism that has been discussed in the literature is the extension of a case to a new function. Dixon (1977b) suggests that this occurred in the Dyirbal pronominal system, while Anderson (1977:353) proposes it as a mechanism for the change in Mingrelian described in Chapter 15. Additional instances of extension have been described in Chapter 15 in Standard Laz, the Artašen and Maxo dialects of Laz, and in the Lower Ač̣arian dialect of Georgian.

One change has elements of several of the mechanisms named above; the ergative-to-active shift apparently did not take place by a single process. There is evidence in Georgian that it involved (a) reinterpretation of surface structures resulting from Object Incorporation, and (b) reinterpretation of clauses in which Unemphatic Pronoun Drop had obscured the direct objects of verbs that were grammatically transitive but filled the roles of intransitives (see Chap. 14). To explain the spread of the use of the narrative case to the subjects of active intransitives not occurring in these constructions, we must assume rule generalization. Ontomatopoeia also played a role in this shift, as shown in the Appendix to Chapter 14.

Diffusion is not identified as the major factor in any of the alignment changes dealt with here. As discussed in Chapter 7, borrowing has been proposed as the mechanism by which accusative case marking was introduced in Series I in CK. That hypothesis must be rejected, as it does not account for the full range of facts. Contact may, however, have influenced the reanalysis of Series I. It is clear that Series I originated as the expression of durative aspect and involved object demotion. After Series II case marking shifted to active, the surface pattern of Series I could no longer be related to Series II by productive rules. At that point many alternatives existed, including the complete loss of Series I, restructuring it to be compatible with Series II, as well as the reanalysis that was actually made. The selection of reanalysis from among the possibilities may have been due in part to the influence of neighboring languages.

In the other alignment changes, it is unlikely that extrafamilial contact played a significant role. It must be assumed that the ergative-to-active shift was an internal development, since there is no known source from which it might have been borrowed. The languages with which Kartvelian was in contact—Greek, Armenian, Persian, Ossetian, Turkish, Azerbaijani, and those of the North East Caucasian and North West Caucasian families—have either accusative or ergative case marking, if they use case at all. The only known exception to this is (in part) Batsbi, or Tsova-Tush, (see Holisky 1983a), a member of the Nakh branch of North East Caucasian, spoken in one village in the Republic of Georgia. To the extent that Batsbi has active case marking, it must be due to the influence of Georgian upon this tiny nationality, rather than vice versa. The Laz extension of active case assignment, too, must have been an entirely internally motivated change.

In the Mingrelian and Lower Ačarian extensions of accusative case marking, contact with non-Kartvelian languages may have played some role. There were, however, extant analogues for accusative alignment—person agreement and Series I case marking—internal to the dialects, as well as the internal need for simplification. The role of external influence cannot be determined in these instances.

The existence of perfects and evidentials in neighboring languages may have influenced the development of this status of the verb in Kartvelian. Internal sources of both the syntax and morphology of the construction are clear (see Chap. 13).

While extrafamilial contact cannot definitely be shown to be responsible for the origin of any of the syntactic constructions discussed here, intrafamilial diffusion is the probable mechanism of spread of several phenomena. First, it has been shown that active case marking in Series II of Svan is probably due to contact with Georgian (see §6.7, argument 2). If it is correct to view the reanalysis of Series I as a result of the ergative-to-active shift (see §15.1), then the former change in Svan may also be the result of diffusion, though it is clear that the INTRODUCTION of Series I was a CK innovation.

It is probable, too, that diffusion is responsible for the spread of Series IV, an evidential that corresponds functionally to Series I and has the syntax of that series (see §13.3.1). While the morphology of this construction may have diffused to some extent (e.g., Mingrelian and certain western dialects of Georgian share a prefixed *no/na-* and use of the auxiliary 'be'), the category itself is more widespread (e.g., Series IV in Svan seems to be morphologically unrelated to that noted above; see Rogava 1953).

Further examples—mostly morphological—of diffusion in Kartvelian are listed in §2.2.5.

17.2. DIRECTIONS

Several distinct realignments of case marking have been considered in this work, and their directions are summarized in Table 17.1. The verb 'spawn' refers here to one type giving rise to a second type, which then coexists with the first, rather than replacing it. At least one change has been omitted from Table 17.1. While Lower Ac̣arian has lost Inversion and restructured Series III, there is not enough data on it available to determine the alignment of case marking there. The same is true of Series I in the same dialect, but in that instance it appears that the new system is accusative (see §15.3.4). If this is correct, then it represents one accusative case system replacing another by altering the system of which case marks which grammatical relations.

The ergative-to-active shift in CGZ, together with the active-to-accusative shift in Mingrelian, may be viewed as a continuous development, a gradual ergative-to-accusative change in Series II. On this view, Georgian and Laz would be seen as representing, in Series II, an intermediate stage. However, it would be false to assume on this basis that the active systems in Georgian and Laz are unstable or about to change. Georgian has maintained active case marking at least since its earliest attestation, about a millenium and a half ago (see Chap. 3). A system with that degree of stability cannot be viewed as merely transitional.

When the changes studied here are combined with the relatively abundant instances of accusative-to-ergative change, it appears that alignment change may proceed without constraint in any direction. While it is im-

Table 17.1

Directions of Change in Kartvelian

Changes	Examples
Ergative spawned accusative	Series I in CK
Ergative replaced by active	Series II in CGZ or CK
Accusative replaced by active	Series I in Laz
Active replaced by accusative	Series II in Mingrelian and Lower Ac̣arian
Active replaced by neutral	in Artašen

probable that any a priori limits on change exist, there are some structural limits on the direction of any particular mechanism.

As noted above, there are several examples of accusative case marking being replaced by ergative via reanalysis of passives. However, if the original system had active alignment, rather than accusative, the results would be different. Table 17.2 represents surface patterns in a language with accusative case marking. In this and other tables, *'by'* is an abbreviation for the various postpositions, prepositions, particles, and oblique cases used to mark the initial subject of a passive. In a language with active case marking, the surface pattern would be as in Table 17.3. In Table 17.2 the surface pattern of markers is ergative: One marker is assigned to the initial subjects of transitives, while another marker is assigned to the subjects of intransitives and to initial direct objects of transitives. In a language with active case alignment, on the other hand, three different markers are used; this marking is attested in Modern Georgian (see Harris 1981b). If such a system were reanalyzed, it would lead to an active-tripartite alignment (see Chap. 16), unless some further change took place. Thus, alignment

Table 17.2

Case Patterns with Passivization in a Language with Accusative Case Marking

	Transitive			Intransitive	
	Subject	+	Direct object	Subject of active intransitive	Subject of inactive intransitive
Results of passivization	oblique		subject	—	—
Accusative case assignment	*by*		NOM	NOM	NOM

Table 17.3

Case Patterns with Passivization in a Language with Active Case Alignment

	Transitive			Intransitive	
	Subject	+	Direct object	Subject of active intransitive	Subject of inactive intransitive
Results of passivization	oblique		subject	—	—
Accusative case assignment	*by*		INACT	ACT	INACT

of the output is determined both by the syntactic rule (here, Passivization) and by the alignment of the input system.

In a similar way it can be shown that the surface patterns of Object Demotion are determined by the alignment of the case rules of the original system. If case marking is ergative, as it was in Common Kartvelian, the output has an accusative distribution. If the original case marking were accusative, reanalysis of the surface patterns would lead to disuse of the original accusative case marker, but it would not result in a realignment of the rule. If the protolanguage had active case marking, the result would be another active-tripartite alignment.

Other things being equal, any one of these surface patterns could be reinterpreted in a way parallel to the reanalyses that have taken place in the Indic, Iranian, Polynesian, and Kartvelian languages. Perhaps things are not equal. As several of the logically possible types are not (yet) known to have occurred, it may be that languages avoid the active-tripartite pattern as unnatural. The fact that Kartvelian languages have introduced several different agreement rules with precisely this distribution would seem to undercut this hypothesis to some extent. Of course, the Kartvelian languages introduced these rules only in the special circumstance of having an active case system. In spite of the Kartvelian rules, the lack of other attestation suggests that active-tripartite alignment is unnatural in most situations. It may be that any reanalysis that would result in alignment of this type is either avoided or immediately followed by an additional change, in this way conforming to one of the better-represented types.

Thus, there are inherent structural limitations on what changes can be effected by which mechanism. Reanalysis of surface patterns produced by a productive rule can, in all probability, lead to accusative (via Object Demotion), active (via Inversion), or ergative (via Passive) rules. The potentially reanalyzable surface patterns are limited both by the syntactic rule that applies and by the alignment of the original rules. In addition, it is likely that reinterpretation is either avoided altogether or is followed by further change if such reanalysis would lead to certain alignment types, among them the active-tripartite.

It seems likely, too, that some universal constraints exist on the extensions that can be made at any one time. In §15.4 it is shown that a functional constraint, based on the need to distinguish subject from object in a transitive clause, is alone not sufficient to account for the variety of change found. It is suggested there that extension is structurally constrained in that it proceeds by the removal of conditions from one or more rules. Each language determines which rule(s) and which condition(s) will be simplified. This constraint recognizes that a greater variety of extensions are logically possible in a language that has coexistent rule systems, such as the coexistent case marking systems in some Kartvelian, Iranian, and Indic languages. Whether or not further research in other language families confirms this particular hypothesis, it seems likely that structural constraints on extension exist.

17.3. THE NATURE AND EXPLANATION OF CHANGE

The emphasis of this study is on how changes in case alignment took place, what repercussions case changes may have had on other parts of the grammar, and, to some extent, the cause of the changes. All of these are approached from the point of view of Kartvelian in order to understand the changes in the context of the whole system within which they occurred. The study of particular changes alone cannot reveal universal properties of change. The generalizations made below are rather recognitions that these are viable possibilities, though not necessarily the only ways in which change proceeds.

17.3.1. The Origin of Series I

The development of an independent case marking system in Series I occurred in two stages. First, the patterns were created, including the verbal morphology and the surface distribution of case marking. Much later, this was reinterpreted; this involved the addition of new rules to assign the cases in the same surface patterns used before reinterpretation of the syntactic structure.

It is clear that the new patterns originated for the purpose of expressing an aspectual opposition, having developed out of a system that was apparently relatively impoverished in tense and aspect distinctions.

The reanalysis itself was necessitated by another change in the grammar, the ergative-to-active shift (see §15.1). Because Series I could no longer be synchronically derived from Series II, it was imperative that some change be made. The fact that Series I was retained may be due to a language-internal need to maintain the durative versus punctual (later imperfective versus perfective) opposition. Why was Series I reanalyzed on the basis of its surface patterns, rather than being restructured, with the new case marking rules of Series II applying in the other series as well? The fact that Object Demotion exists as a rule governed by a few lexical items in Georgian (Chap. 1; Harris 1981b:188–189) suggests that there is nothing inconsistent about its occurring with active case assignment. If Series I had been restructured with active case marking, the Series I versus Series II opposition would not be realized as a contrast of accusative versus active case marking, but only as an opposition of dative versus nominative as the case assigned to logical direct objects. The choice of reanalysis over restructuring could be due to the influence of languages with which Kartvelian was in contact, or it could result from some structural limitation on the extent to which a shift like the ergative-to-active can apply in derived syntactic constructions (see Chung 1977).

It is instructive to compare the events that occurred in Kartvelian with a set of changes in some of the Pama Nyungan languages. Many of the languages of this family have or had an object demotion construction structurally parallel to that reconstructed for Common Kartvelian (Klokeid 1976, 1978). Many, including Nyamal and Yukulta, retain this as a productive construction. In Lardil, the object demotion construction has been reanalyzed in a way comparable to that of Kartvelian, the case that now marks direct objects being historically the dative (indirect object) case (Klokeid 1976; 1978). Thus, both language groups had a productive rule of Object Demotion, and in Lardil and Kartvelian, it was reinterpreted as an accusative system.

In Lardil the accusative marking system replaced the inherited ergative rules, rather than coexisting with them, as in Kartvelian. Klokeid attributes the reanalysis of the object demotion construction in Lardil in part to the fact that a phonological rule deleted or reduced the ergative marker, making it desirable to adopt a new system for the marking of grammatical relations (Klokeid 1978:599, 607–608). A similar situation may have obtained in Kartvelian. Zhghenti (1953) suggests that word-final *n* was eroded in Kartvelian. I propose this as one explanation for the replacement of the inherited narrative desinence (probably **n* in CGZ) in Georgian and in Zan (see §15.2). Why did Lardil, in this situation, completely lose the ergative case system, replacing it with the accusative, while Kartvelian replaced the old narrative case markers, permitting the two systems to coexist? The answer may lie simply in the availability of markers. As shown in Chapter 4, Georgian drew on post-nominal articles as a source for renewing case markers. The source of the new narrative marker in Laz–Mingrelian has not been definitely identified, but some possibilities are discussed in Chapter 4.

It is possible, as an alternative view, that the loss of the inherited narrative case marker was not due to phonological processes and that it was replaced as part of the ergative-to-active shift. On this hypothesis, the new form was added to distinguish the new function from the old (see §15.2). If this view is the more accurate one, then it would seem that Kartvelian retained two systems because both were renewed and revitalized and because the aspectual opposition was vital.

Unlike some of the other changes discussed in this work, the reanalysis of Series I must have taken place all at once. Although the development of an independent accusative case system occurred in two stages, it was not gradual, either in the sense the extensions were (§17.3.3) or in the sense the ergative-to-active shift was (§17.3.4). The reanalysis of Series I applied to all affected parts of the language at one time, leaving only two lexical relics (see §5.3). The actualization of the reanalysis, with respect to rules that originally interacted with Object Demotion, was gradual, for at least some rules. The original aspectual opposition of Series I to Series II was still intact in Old Georgian, and it changed gradually thereafter. The original alternation of ablaut had been lost by Old Georgian times and it continued to change gradually. By Old Georgian, *En*-Agreement had been dropped from Series I, leaving only a few relics; this process continued until the rule dropped from the language altogether. Third person indirect object agreement (*x*/*h*/*x*) with direct objects continued sporadically, then was lost (see §15.1). Thus, while the reanalysis took place all at once, the actualization of the change has been gradual (see Chung 1977; Timberlake 1977). The characteristics of the reanalysis of Series I, in contrast to the other changes discussed here, are summarized in (1).

(1) a. The surface patterns developed for the expression of a grammatical opposition: aspect.
  b. Reanalysis of the surface patterns had an external impetus, the ergative-to-active shift having made object demotion not synchronically derivable from Series II.
  c. The reanalysis occurred all at once, applying to all affected parts of the language. Actualization was gradual.

It seems probable that some of these characteristics, in their general form, are universal properties of change that occurs by means of reanalysis of surface patterns.

17.3.2. The Loss of Case in Artašen

Although it is suggested above that the loss of case markers in Artašen is due in part to phonological change, this is not enough to explain the entire change that occurred. The erosion of word-final *s*, which functions as the dative case desinence in other dialects, is a general process both in Artašen and in other Kartvelian dialects (see §15.5). However, in many instances, *s* is reduced to *y* instead of deleting altogether. If *s* → *y* had applied in the dative suffix, too, there still would be a contrast between the dative (e.g., *ḳoči-y* 'man-DAT') and nominative (*ḳoči*). Further, although there seem to be other examples of the loss of word-final *-k*, which functions as the narrative desinence in other dialects, the process is so restricted that it requires some other explanation. That is, there are few instances of word-final *k*, and there is apparently no general process of deletion of word-final velars or of word-final voiceless aspirates. The changes in Artašen were probably triggered by the weakening of *-s*. Other languages, such as some in the Germanic family, have also lost case marking in response to phonological erosion of desinence. Yet loss of case marking is only one of the responses possible in such a situation. Both Lardil and CGZ made different adaptations under similar circumstances (§17.3.1).

17.3.3. Extensions

The purpose of the extensions described here is to attain simplicity and efficiency of the language viewed as a whole. In the instances studied here, the grammatical oppositions were retained intact. That is, in Laz, Mingrelian, and Lower Ač̣arian, Series I verb forms are still distinct from those of Series II. It appears that it is proliferation or complication of rules that leads to simplification by extension of cases to new functions.

The extensions studied here occurred gradually in two senses. First, in the course of the change there is variation between the inherited rules and the innovative rules. This occurs both in the Maxo examples (§15.3.3) and in Lower Ač̣arian (§15.3.4). The extension may also be gradual in the sense that the marking of only one nominal is changed at a time. In the extension of Series II active case marking to Series I in Maxo, the marking of direct objects was changed first, while the shift in the case of subjects is still in progress. Series I examples from Lower Ač̣arian, on the other hand, show a change in the marking of subjects applying before any change in direct objects.

Payne (1980) has described a number of changes in Pamir languages that are comparable to those made in Laz, Mingrelian, and the Lower Ač̣arian dialect of Georgian. In this group of Iranian languages, a passive (or possessive) construction was reanalyzed as ergative, resulting in coexistant systems similar to those in Kartvelian. In the Pamir languages, the present tense governed accusative case marking and the past governed ergative. The various extensions that have occurred in the several languages, like those in Kartvelian, have taken place gradually in both senses. Variation in case assignment in the system undergoing extensions is permitted (Payne 1980:161, 162–163, 169, 172). In some dialects, only the marking of one nominal has yet been changed; for example, in Rošani (Payne 1980:153–161) and Maxo; in others, the marking of all nominals has been changed, for example, in Iškašmi (Payne 1980:176–178) and Standard Laz. The parallels between concomitants of these changes in Pamir languages and those in the Kartvelian languages were discussed in Chapter 16.

Payne notes that several of the Pamir languages have initiated the use of a preposition or of a suffix to mark direct objects in the present tense, but no realignment of case marking has occurred in that system. In contrast, a variety of changes have occurred in the past tense system of those languages. In the Iranian languages, the syntax of the present tense is the direct reflex of the inherited system, while that of the past tense is due to reanalysis of a once-productive construction. In this respect it is more or less complementary to Kartvelian. In the Kartvelian languages, extensions have affected both the original system, Series II (Mingrelian, Lower Ač̣arian), and the innovative system, Series I (Laz, Lower Ač̣arian). This may be due to the fact that Series II was realigned at about the same time that Series I was reanalyzed.

The characteristics of the extensions studied here are summarized in (2).

(2) a. Extensions are motivated by a need to simplify.
  b. Extensions are effected gradually.
    1. Variation is tolerated in transitional stages.
    2. The change may affect the marking of first one nominal, then another.

17.3.4. The Ergative-to-Active Shift

As observed in §17.1, the ergative-to-active shift differs in terms of mechanism from those changes labeled 'extension'. Like extensions, the shift occurred gradually, but in a rather different sense. The reanalysis of surface structures involved in this change may have taken place sequentially. Because some verbs governed one kind of initially transitive structure, and some another, the change, applying first to one of these structures then to others, affected first one group of lexical items then another and another. Later, through lexical diffusion, the narrative case assignment rule was generalized to active intransitives that had not occurred in a transitive structure. Thus, the ergative-to-active shift was a lexically governed change, and in this respect it occurred gradually.[2] It is probable that during the period of transition, variation in the marking of nominals was likewise tolerated. Beyond this, it appears that those intransitives that are related to transitives are slower to undergo this change than are basic intransitives (see §6.6 and 14.1).

It has been observed that members of the Tibeto-Burman family are moving away from ergativity in case marking as well as agreement (Bauman 1975). Although it is not clear that the end point of these changes will be either accusative or active case marking (Bauman 1979:430–431), they seem to be comparable in some respects to the changes that brought about the ergative-to-active shift in Kartvelian. In particular, Givón (1980:50–52) has suggested that an ongoing shift away from ergative case marking in Sherpa is proceeding in part through object-incorporation that maintains an ergative-marked subject, in a way similar to that described for Georgian in §14.1.1. A further similarity is the fact, noted by Givón (1980:54–55), that the gradual change is in part verb-governed. There are suggestive parallels between the situations in the two language families, but caution is called for in the interpretation of these facts.

The ergative-to-active shift in Kartvelian may have been an indirect result of the introduction of Series III, where Inversion applies to the subjects of Class 1 and 3 verbs and not to those of Class 2 verbs. The then-ergative case rules of Series II would have grouped the subjects of Class 3 verbs with those of Class 2 verbs, opposing both to Class 1. The ergative-to-active shift would have altered case marking in Series II just enough to have coordinated its alignment with that of the Inversion rule in the new Series III. The change in case marking in Series II thus REINFORCED the distinction between Classes 1 and 3 and Class 2 in the sense defined in Chapter 16.

Characteristics of the ergative-to-active shift are summarized in (3).

(3) a. The ergative-to-active shift may have occurred as a REINFORCEMENT of an existing distinction.
  b. The shift was effected gradually.
    1. It is lexically governed.
    2. Variation may have been tolerated in transitional phases.
  c. The change leaves lexical residue.
  d. The change is affected by external factors, especially onomatopoeia.

17.3.5. Varieties of Alignment Types

It has been suggested that linguistic universals cannot be violated diachronically (Weinreich, Labov, and Herzog 1968:100). Yet studies have documented instances of the diachronic violation of otherwise-valid universal laws (Campbell 1980; Chung and Seiter 1980; §15.3.1).

Sapir (1917) lists five types of case marking, and more recent investigations from the point of view of universals of alignment have not expanded this inventory (Anderson 1976; Dixon 1979; Fillmore 1968), except that Comrie (1978) adds the double-oblique type, attested in some Pamir languages (Payne 1980). In Chapter 16 I show that five distinct rules in Georgian, Laz, and Mingrelian have a distribution that I refer to as active-tripartite, distinct from any of the other types. These are agreement rules, rather than case marking. However, it is believed that agreement rules exist in the same alignment types as case marking, and the active-tripartite is therefore included in summary Table 17.4.

Payne (1980) and the present study both describe some infrequently found phenomena. Both the upper dialect of Waxi (Pamir) and Mingrelian have coexistent accusative case marking systems, distinguished from one another by the cases used in some functions, rather than by a difference in alignment. In Waxi, this does not occur outside first and second person pronouns; in Mingrelian, it occurs only with substantives other than first and second person pronouns. The acceptability of variation in case marking (without semantic significance) likewise occurs among both language groups.[3] In the present study, synchronic variation has been described in the Naḳra-Laxamula dialect of Svan, the Lower Ač̣arian dialect of Georgian, and the Maxo dialect of Laz.

The types listed in Table 17.4 do not all have the same status. It is necessary both to recognize that the double-oblique type and the active-tripartite type exist and to observe that they have been attested only in languages where there has been recent change in the coding rules of the relevant type. Perhaps the scarcely attested tripartite type occurs only under similar circumstances. It appears that while ergative, active, accusative, and neutral alignments occur naturally in coding rules in languages of many families, other types may occur, but only under certain circum-

Table 17.4
Alignment Types

<table>
<tr><th rowspan="2"></th><th rowspan="2">Direct Object</th><th colspan="2">Subject of Intransitive</th><th rowspan="2">Subject of Transitive</th></tr>
<tr><th>Inactive</th><th>Active</th></tr>
<tr><td>Ergative</td><td>A</td><td colspan="2">A</td><td>B</td></tr>
<tr><td>Active</td><td>A</td><td>A</td><td>B</td><td>B</td></tr>
<tr><td>Active-tripartite</td><td>A</td><td>B</td><td>C</td><td>C</td></tr>
<tr><td>Accusative</td><td>A</td><td colspan="2">B</td><td>B</td></tr>
<tr><td>Tripartite</td><td>A</td><td colspan="2">B</td><td>C</td></tr>
<tr><td>Double-oblique</td><td>A</td><td colspan="2">B</td><td>A</td></tr>
<tr><td>Neutral</td><td>A</td><td colspan="2">A</td><td>A</td></tr>
</table>

stances, including change in alignment. Coexistent systems of the same alignment and acceptable variation in the assignment of cases may also be limited to transitional stages.

17.4. THE NATURE OF ACTIVE ALIGNMENT IN KARTVELIAN

Throughout this work it has been emphasized that in the Kartvelian languages, verb forms fall into one of three classes, each of which is a combination of semantic, syntactic, and morphological properties. These groups of verbs are strict, in the sense that verb forms do not slide in and out of a class (exceptions to this generalization are discussed in §6.3 and in Harris 1981b:268–274). A given lexical item may occur in different classes, with appropriate changes in morphology.

The correlations that have been established here are listed in Table 17.5. The case listed under syntax refers to that governed for subjects in the active systems: Series II for Svan and Georgian, Series I and II (as well as the New Series III and IV) for Laz. It does not apply to Mingrelian, where this property is not found. The terms 'inversion' and 'no inversion' refer to whether or not these verbs condition Inversion in Series III (in Old Series III, for Laz). The morphological properties referred to by class differ for each language and are discussed in Chapters 3 and 16. For Class 1 verbs, 'active (or inactive)' indicates that the majority of verbs of this class are active, though it is entirely regular for those transitives that are inactive to be members of this class; an example is Georgian *miiγo* 'he received it'.

Table 17.5

Morphological–Syntactic–Semantic Correlations

Morphological	Syntactic	Semantic
Class 1	transitive narrative case inversion	active (or inactive) telic
Class 2	intransitive initial direct object nominative case no inversion	inactive telic or stative
Class 3	intransitive initial subject narrative case inversion	active atelic

Although the generalizations summarized in Table 17.5 are valid throughout the Kartvelian family, there are some exceptions. Individual exceptions to the correlations in Old Georgian, Laz, and Svan are discussed in §6.2, 6.3, 6.4, and 6.6. Individual exceptions in Modern Georgian are described in Harris 1981b:187–190, 268–274; a group of verbs that are inactive and atelic are discussed above in the Appendix to Chapter 14.

In none of the Kartvelian languages is case determined semantically by context, such that a given verb form has a subject in one case when it is controllable and in another case when it is not controllable. In all of the Kartvelian languages, case is strictly determined by the verb form, whether by its syntactic or morphological features. One form governs just one case (exceptions in §6.2–6.3; Harris 1981b:268–274).

17.5. THE NATURE OF ALIGNMENT SPLITS

Linguistic literature contains a number of discussions of so-called split ergativity (e.g., DeLancey 1981; Dixon 1979; Hopper and Thompson 1980; Tasaku 1981). One type of 'split' refers to the coexistence of different alignments for a single rule type. It has been said that such splits are made on the basis of tense or aspect, such that ergative case marking occurs in the past tense or perfective aspect, opposing accusative case marking in nonpast tenses or imperfective aspect.

In this work it has been shown that this relationship between case marking types and aspect obtained in Common Kartvelian: Series I expressed durative aspect and had accusative case marking while Series II expressed predominantly punctual aspect and had ergative case marking. A study of changes in the Kartvelian languages makes it possible for us to learn more about the nature of such splits in general.

First, we may observe that it is possible for a split to exist on the basis of other categories of the verb. In Kartvelian, Series III and, where it exists, Series IV oppose Series II and I in terms of status (seen vs. unseen, see Chap. 13). As discussed in §13.5, it is probable that it is only agreement phenomena in Series III that have prevented its being reanlayzed as an additional coexistant case system. It seems probable that status (in the sense of Aronson 1977:13; Friedman 1979) could become the basis for a split.

A further basis for such a split is finite versus nonfinite. While many languages mark the terms of a nonfinite verb form in the same way as those of a finite form, many other languages use different cases and a different alignment. In Modern Georgian, for example, case marking in

Series I has accusative alignment, in Series II active alignment, and with most nonfinite forms ergative alignment (Harris 1981b). Thus, case marking splits can exist on the basis of finiteness.

It is important to observe that although the split in Kartvelian originated on the basis of an aspectual distinction, it exists today neither on that basis nor on the basis of past versus nonpast nor on the basis of any other single semantic feature. There are both perfective and imperfective forms in Series I and in Series II in all Kartvelian languages (Holisky 1981b; Machavariani 1974; Schmidt 1963). This may be illustrated in Table 17.6 with forms from Mingrelian (examples from Machavariani 1974:133). Since the case marking split is according to Series I versus II, aspect is irrelevant to it. And it is not continued today on the basis of nonpast versus past as these examples might suggest. Series I also contains a past tense; compare *zimundu* 'he was measuring it' (Series I, imperfective) with *zimu* 'he measured it' (Series II, imperfective) (Chikobava 1936:138, 137). Modern Georgian has essentially the same characteristics as Mingrelian in this respect, and examples can be found in the handbooks. In Svan, too, both perfective and imperfective forms exist in Series I: for example, Upper Bal *asqēne* 'he builds it, is building it' (imperfective) versus *ansqēne* 'he will build it' (perfective) (examples from Topuria 1967, analysis in Machavariani 1974:136). Svan, however, is conservative in having essentially only perfective forms in Series II; in this way, it retains part of the original structure of the aspectual contrast between the series.[4] Like Mingrelian, Svan has past tenses in both series and, thus, with both case marking systems: Upper Bal *amāra* 'he was preparing it' (Series I) and *anmāre* 'he prepared it' (Series II) (Topuria 1967:73, 136). Thus, although Mingrelian, Georgian, and Svan all preserve a case marking split, it is not maintained on the basis of an aspectual opposition, a tense opposition, (i.e., past versus nonpast), or the basis of any other single criterion. While the split originated on the basis of an aspectual opposition, that category has been reanalyzed in all of the daughter languages. The split in Kartvelian is historically motivated but synchronically arbitrary. It must be

Table 17.6

Aspectual Oppositions in Mingrelian

Series I	
imperfective	*vc̣arunk* 'I write it, I am writing it'
perfective	*dovc̣arunk* 'I will write it'
Series II	
imperfective	*vc̣ari* 'I wrote it'
perfective	*dovc̣ari* 'I wrote it'

recognized in general linguistics that it is possible for a split to be maintained on an arbitrary basis.

A second fact that is established here about splits of this sort is that synchronically they need not be restricted to ergative versus accusative. Again, the Kartvelian split originated as this much-discussed distribution but does not continue it precisely in any of the daughters, except the Naḳra-Laxamula dialect. In Georgian and most of the Svan dialects, one system is accusative, the other active. In Mingrelian, both systems in the split are accusative; the split is instantiated by using DIFFERENT cases, albeit in the same alignment.

Consideration of these facts thus provides a more complete view of case splits conditioned by verbal categories. It is likewise important that historically, Kartvelian confirms the narrower view represented in the literature, namely that splits involve accusative versus ergative case marking and are based on an aspectual (or tense) opposition.

17.6. CONCLUSION

In the Introduction to *Mechanisms of Syntactic Change*, Li poses two questions, "(1) how does an accusative language become ergative? (2) how does an ergagtive language become accusative?" He goes on to remark that "while the passive-to-ergative reanalysis appears to be an important mechanism for the development of ergative languages and thus constitutes an answer to question (1), we have not yet come to grips with question (2)" (1977:xiv–xv). Klokeid (1976, 1978) has since discussed the development of an ergative-to-accusative change in Lardil through the mechanism of reanalysis of an object demotion construction. With the addition of Kartvelian, the importance of this mechanism in the development of accusative case marking, one outcome of this work, is established.

A second result of this work is to establish as a viable method in syntactic reconstruction the comparison of the syntax of morphologically cognate expressions. By comparing Series II verb forms with Series I, it is shown that the former are older than the latter, thus leading to the hypothesis that the case marking used with them might likewise be older (Chap. 5). Comparison of the case marking used in Series I in the various languages reveals that it had accusative alignment (Chap. 5). Change in case alignment, like phonological change, may leave relics; and it is with the aid of these that ergative alignment can be reconstructed for case marking in Series II (Chap. 6). This reconstruction is confirmed many times over by the account in Part III of the development and reanalysis of Series I from the base of Series II. Similar techniques are applied to the reconstruction of the marking of retired indirect objects (Chap. 11), the alignment of *En*-Agreement (Chap. 10), the alignment of several rules of agreement (Chap. 12 and §13.4) as well as to many morphological problems (Chaps. 4, 5, 8, 9, etc.).

A third result is a study of the repercussions of these changes on other parts of the grammer (Chaps. 15 and 16). Many of these facts cannot be fully evaluated on the basis of Kartvelian alone, but await comparison with data from other language groups.

NOTES

[1]Anderson (1977:341) distinguishes the passive from a "possessive," that is, an analytic perfect (see Benveniste 1952). While these are distinct, they are similar and may be conflated for present purposes.

[2]The extensions that took place in Laz, Mingrelian, and Lower Ač̣arian could not be studied in sufficient detail to determine whether or not they involve lexical diffusion. The data discussed in §6.3 suggest that the extension that occurred in Laz was lexically governed, but these are limited to a few lexical items.

[3]This variation is not the same as the optional occurrence of the ergative case marker reported for some languages of Australia and New Guinea (e.g., in Dixon 1979:72–73). In each of the Kartvelian dialects, it is the nominative form, not the stem form, that alternates with the narrative. Further, in Kartvelian the alternations in case are constrained by series and verb class.

[4]"In constrast to other Kartvelian languages, in Svan imperfective forms (without preverb) of the aorist are very seldom encountered" (Machavariani 1974:137). Holisky (1981b) gives examples of both aspects in Series I in Georgian, where the aspectual opposition is expressed through means other than a preverb.

References

Abbreviations

BK	*Bedi Kartlisa*
BLS	*Proceedings of the nth Annual Meeting of the Berkeley Linguistics Society*
CLS	*Papers from the nth Regional Meeting of the Chicago Linguistic Society*
Enimḳis Moambe	*Enis, Isṭoriisa da Maṭerialuri Ḳulṭuris Insṭiṭuṭis Moambe*
IF	*Indogermanische Forschungen*
IJAL	*International Journal of American Linguistics*
IḲE	*Iberiul-Ḳavḳasiuri Enatmecniereba*
IRSL	*International Review of Slavic Linguistics*
KESS	*Kartvelur Enata Sṭrukṭuris Saḳitxebi*
KZ	*Zeitschrift für Vergleichende Sprachforschung*
Macne	*Sakartvelos SSR Mecnierebata Aḳademiis Macne, Enisa da Liṭeraṭuris Seria*
NELS	*Papers from the nth Annual Meeting, North Eastern Linguistic Society*
NTS (NJL)	*Norsk Tidsskrift for Sprogvidenskap (Norwegian Journal of Linguistics)*
TUM	*Ṭpilisis (Tbilisis) Universiṭeṭis Moambe*
TUŠ	*Tbilisis Saxelmc̣ipo Universiṭeṭis Šromebi*
SMOMPK	*Sbornik Materialov Dlja Opisanija Mestnostej i Plemen Kavkaza*
SMAM	*Sakartvelos SSR Mecnierebata Aḳademiis Moambe*
V Ja	*Voprosy Jazykoznanija*

LINGUISTIC LITERATURE

Kartvelian texts consulted are listed in a separate section following this list.

Abdullaev, Z.G. (1971). *Očerki po sintaksisu darginskogo jazyka.* Moskva: Nauka.

Abuladze, I. (1973). *ʒveli Kartuli enis leksiḳoni.* [Dictionary of the Old Georgian language] Tbilisi: Mecniereba.

Allen, B.J., and Frantz, D.G. (1978). Verb agreement in Southern Tiwa. *BLS,* **4,** 11–17.

Allen, W.S. (1950). A study in the analysis of Hindi sentence structure. *Acta Linguistica,* **6,** 68–86.

Anderson, S.R. (1976). On the notion of subject in ergative languages. In *Subject and topic,* ed. by C.N. Li, 1–23. New York: Academic Press.

Anderson, S.R. (1977). On mechanisms by which languages become ergative. In *Mechanisms of syntactic change,* ed. by C.N. Li, 317–363. Austin: University of Texas Press.

Arabuli, A. (1980a). Sporadulad gamovlenil III piris *-n/-d, -en/-ed* supiksta punkciisatvis ʒvel Kartulši. [On the function of sporadically occurring third person *-n/-d, -en/-ed* suffixes in Old Georgian]. In *Narḳvevebi Iberiul-Ḳavḳasiur enata morpologiidan,* ed. by G. Bedoshvili and B. Jorbenadze, 31–40. Tbilisi: Mecniereba.

Arabuli, A. (1980b). Turmeobitis analizuri c̣armoebis tavisebureba Kartvelur enata zog dialekṭši. [A peculiarity in the analytic formation of the evidential in some dialects of Kartvelian languages]. *Macne,* **1,** 149–154.

Aronson, H.I. (1977). Interrelationships between aspect and mood in Bulgarian. *Folia Slavica,* **1,** 9–32.

Aronson, H.I. (1979). Towards a typology of transitivity: The strange case of the Georgian subject. *The elements,* CLS parasession volume, 297–306.

Asatiani, I. (1970). *-Ere* supiksiani turmeobiti Megrulši. [The evidential with the suffix *-ere* in Mingrelian] *IḲE,* **17,** 144–151.

Asatiani, I. (1973). *-R* supiksis ḳvali Megrul zmnaši. [Traces of the suffix *-r* in the Mingrelian verb] *IḲE,* **18,** 273–283.

Asatiani, R. (1975). Poneṭiḳuri simbolizmis zogierti saḳitxi. [Some questions of phonetic symbolism]. Unpublished manuscript. Oriental Institute of the Georgian Academy of Sciences.

Austin, P. (1982). Transitivity and cognate objects in Australian languages. In *Studies in transitivity (Syntax and semantics, Vol. 15),* ed. by P.J. Hopper and S.A. Thompson, 37–47. New York: Academic Press.

Bach, E. (1971). Questions. *Linguistic Inquiry,* **2,** 153–166.

Baramidze, L. (1964). Zogierti ṭipis mešvel-zmnian pormata časaxva da ganvitareba Kartulši. [On the origin and development of certain types of auxiliary verb constructions in Georgian]. *ʒveli Kartuli Enis Ḳatedris Šromebi,* **9,** 95–150. Tbilisi: Universiṭeṭi.

Baramidze, L. (1976). Vnebiti gvaris zmnata ac̣mq̣os daboloebisatvis ʒvel Kartulši. [On the ending of the present of passive voice verbs in Old Georgian]. *ʒveli Kartuli Enis Ḳatedris Šromebi,* **19,** 79–95. Tbilisi: Universiṭeṭi.

Baramidze, L. (1977). P̣irveli turmeobitis c̣armoebis zogi tavisebureba Kartuli enis mtis ḳiloebši. [Some peculiarities of the formation of the first evidential in the mountain Georgian dialects]. *ʒveli Kartuli Enis Ḳatedris Šromebi,* **20,** 37–51. Tbilisi: Universiṭeṭi.

Bauman, J.J. (1975). *Pronouns and pronominal morphology in Tibeto-Burman.* Unpublished doctoral dissertation, University of California, Berkeley.

Bauman, J.J. (1979). An historical perspective on ergativity in Tibeto-Burman. In *Ergativity,* ed. by F. Plank, 419–433. New York: Academic Press.

Benveniste, É. (1952). La construction passive du parfait. *Bullétin de la Societé de Linguistique de Paris,* **48,** 52–62.
Birdsall, J.N. (1980). The Georgian version of the book of Revelation. *Studia Biblica 1978, III. (Journal for the Study of the New Testament.* Supplement Series, **3.**)
Birdsall, J.N. (1981). Evangelienbezüge im georgischen Martyrium der hl. Schuschaniki. *Georgica,* **4,** 20–23.
Blair, R.W. (1964). *Yucatec Maya noun and verb morpho-syntax.* Unpublished doctoral dissertation, Indiana University.
Blake, B.J. (1976). On ergativity and the notion of subject: Some Australian cases. *Lingua,* **39,** 281–300.
Blake, R.P. (1932). Khanmeti palimpsest fragments of the Old Georgian version of Jeremiah. *Harvard Theological Review,* **25,** 225–272.
Boeder, W. (1979). Ergative syntax and morphology in language change: The South Caucasian languages. In *Ergativity,* ed. by F. Plank, 435–480. New York: Academic Press.
Braithwaite, K. (1973). *Case shift and verb concord in Georgian.* Unpublished doctoral dissertation, University of Texas at Austin.
Butler, M.C. (1977). Reanalysis of object as subject in Middle English impersonal constructions. *Glossa,* **11,** 155–170.
Bynon, T. (1980). From passive to active in Kurdish via the ergative construction. In *Papers from the 4th International Conference on Historical Linguistics,* ed. by E.C. Traugott, R. Labrum, and S. Shepherd, 152–163. Amsterdam: John Benjamins.
Campbell, L. (1980). Explaining universals and their exceptions. In *Papers from the 4th International Conference on Historical Linguistics,* ed. by E.C. Traugott, R. Labrum, and S. Shepherd, 17–26. Amsterdam: John Benjamins.
Campbell, L., and Mithun, M. (1980). The priorities and pitfalls of syntactic reconstruction. *Folia Linguistica Historica,* **1,** 19–40.
Catford, J.C. (1976). Ergativity in Caucasian languages. *NELS,* **6,** 37–48.
Chafe, W. (1970). *Meaning and the structure of language.* Chicago: University of Chicago Press.
Chantladze, I. (1979). Orpuʒianobis saḳitxisatvis Kvemosvanurši. [On the question of two-base declension in Lower Svan]. *IḲE,* **21,** 115–128.
Chikobava, B. (A.) (1923). *Q̣e* naçilaḳi Pereydnulši da misi mnišvneloba gramaṭiḳa-loγiḳis urtiertobis tvalsazrisit. [The particle *qe* in Fereidan and its meaning from the point of view of the relationship between grammar and logic]. *Çeliçdeuli,* **1–2,** 32–68.
Chikobava, A. (1927). Pereidnulis mtavari taviseburebani. [The main characteristics of Fereidan]. *TUM,* **7,** 196–221.
Chikobava, A. (1929b). Rit aris çarmodgenili mravlobitis saxelobitši dasmuli morpologiuri obieḳṭi ʒvel Kartulši? [By what means is the morphological object in the nominative plural represented in Old Georgian?]. *TUM,* **9,** 107–119.
Chikobava, A. (1936). *Çanuris gramaṭiḳuli analizi.* [A grammatical analysis of Laz]. Tbilisi: Aḳademia.
Chikobava, A. (1938). *Çanur–Megrul-Kartuli šedarebiti leksiḳoni.* [Laz–Mingrelian–Georgian comparative dictionary]. Tbilisi: Aḳademia.
Chikobava, A. (1939). Motxrobiti brunvis genezisisatvis Kartvelur enebši. [On the origin of the narrative case in the Kartvelian languages]. *TUŠ,* **10,** 2829–2838.
Chikobava, A. (1940). Mesame p̣iris subieḳṭis uʒvelesi nišani Kartvelur enebši. [The ancient marker of the third person subject in the Kartvelian languages]. *Enimḳis Moambe,* **5–6,** 13–42.
Chikobava, A. (1942). Ergaṭiuli ḳonsṭrukciis problemisatvis Ḳavḳasiur enebši: Am ḳonsṭrukciis sṭabiluri da labiluri varianṭebi. [On the problem of the ergative construction in

Caucasian languages: Stable and labile variants of this construction]. *Enimḳis Moambe,* **12,** 221–239.

Chikobava, A. (1943). P̣ermansivis ('xolmeobitis') isṭoriuli adgilisatvis Kartuli zmnis uγvlilebis sisṭemaši. [The historical position of the permansive (habitual) in the conjugational system of the Georgian verb]. SMAM, **4,** 91–6.

Chikobava, A. (1948). *Ergaṭiuli ḳonsṭrukciis problema Iberiul–Ḳavḳasiur enebši, I.* [The problem of the ergative construction in the Ibero–Caucasian languages, I]. Tbilisi: Aḳademia.

Chikobava, A., (ed.). (1950–1964). *Kartuli enis ganmarṭebiti leksiḳoni.* [An explanatory dictionary of the Georgian language]. Tbilisi: Aḳademia.

Chikobava, A. (1954). Mravlobitobis supiksta genezisisatvis Kartulši. [On the origin of the suffixes of plurality in Georgian]. *IḲE,* **6,** 67–76.

Chikobava, A. (1956a). Isṭoriulad gansxvavebuli ori morpologiuri ṭipisatvis Kartul brunvata šoris. [On two historically distinct morphological types among Georgian cases]. In *Saxelis brunebis isṭoriisatvis Kartvelur enebši,* ed. by V. Topuria, 265–268. Tbilisi: Universiṭeṭi. (first published, 1942)

Chikobava, A. (1956b). Mimartulebiti (gardakceviti) brunvis mnišvnelobisa, c̣armoebisa da isṭoriisatvis. [On the meaning, formation, and history of the directional (transformative) case]. In *Saxelis brunebis isṭoriisatvis Kartvelur enebši,* ed. by V. Topuria, 10–29. Tbilisi: Universiṭeṭi. (first published, 1936).

Chikobava, A. (1961). *Ergaṭiuli ḳonsṭrukciis problema Iberiul–Ḳavḳasiur enebši, II.* [The problem of the ergative construction in the Ibero–Caucasian languages, II]. Tbilisi: Aḳademia.

Chikobava, A. (1962). Kartuli zmnis naḳvteulta daǰgupebis p̣rincip̣isatvis. [On a principle of grouping of Georgian verb forms]. *IḲE,* **13,** 93–107.

Chikobava, A. (1964). Ac̣mqos puʒis c̣armokmnis isṭoriisatvis: 1. *-av, -am,* da *-ev, -em* supiksis isṭoriuli urtiertoba. [On the history of the formation of the present stem: 1. The historical relation between the *-av, -am,* and *-ev, -em* suffixes]. *IḲE,* **14,** 127–134.

Chikobava, A. (1968a). *Marṭivi c̣inadadebis problema Kartulši, I.* [The problem of the simple sentence in Georgian, I]. Tbilisi: Mecniereba.

Chikobava, A. (1968b). Marṭivi c̣inadadebis evoluciis ʒiritadi ṭendenciebi Kartulši. [Basic tendencies of the evolution of the simple sentence in Georgian]. *Marṭivi c̣inadadebis problema Kartulši, I,* 269–280. Tbilisi: Mecniereba. (first published, 1941).

Chikobava, A. and Cercvadze, I. (1962). *Xunʒuri ena.* [The Avar language]. Tbilisi: Universiṭeṭi.

Chincharauli, A. (1960). *Xevsurulis taviseburebani.* [Characteristics of Xevsurian]. Tbilisi: Aḳademia.

Chomsky, N. (1982). *Lectures on government and binding.* Dordrecht: Foris Publications. (first published, 1981).

Chung, S. (1977). On the gradual nature of syntactic change. In *Mechanisms of syntactic change,* ed. by C.N. Li. Austin: University of Texas Press.

Chung, S. (1978). *Case marking and grammatical relations in Polynesian.* Austin: University of Texas Press.

Chung, S., and Seiter, W.J. (1980). The history of raising and relativization in Polynesian. *Language,* **56,** 622–638.

Chxubianishvili, D. (1972). *Inpiniṭivis saḳitxisatvis ʒvel Kartulši.* [On the question of the infinitive in Old Georgian]. Tbilisi: Mecniereba.

Cole, P., Harbert, W., Hermon, G., and Sridhar, S.N. (1980). The acquisition of subjecthood. *Language,* **56,** 719–743.

Comrie, B. (1973). The ergative: Variations on a theme. *Lingua,* **32,** 239–253.

Comrie, B. (1976a). 'Definite' direct objects and referent identifiability. Unpublished manuscript, University of Southern California.

Comrie, B. (1976b). Review of *Očerk obščej teorii èrgativnosti,* by G.A. Klimov, 1973. *Lingua,* **39,** 252–260.

Comrie, B. (1978). Ergativity. In *Syntactic typology: Studies in the phenomenology of language,* ed. by W.P. Lehmann, 329–394. Austin: University of Texas Press.

Danelia, K. (1965). Ieremias ç̣inasç̣armeṭqvelebis ʒveli Kartuli versiebis zogierti sinṭaksuri tavisebureba. [Some syntactic characteristics of the Old Georgian versions of the prophecy of Jeremiah]. *TUŠ,* **105,** 75–81.

Danelia, K. (1975). Ucxo enata gavlenis ḳvali ʒveli Kartuli ç̣erilobiti ʒeglebis enaši. [Vestiges of the influence of foreign languages in the language of Old Georgian written monuments]. *Macne,* **4,** 79–90.

Danelia, K. (1976). Vnebiti gvaris ç̣armoebisatvis Ḳolxurši. [On the formation of the passive voice in Kolxur]. *ʒveli Kartuli Enis Ḳatedris Šromebi,* **19,** 165–174. Tbilisi: Universiṭeṭi.

Davies, W.D. (1980). Inversion in Choctaw. Unpublished manuscript. University of California, San Diego.

Davies, W.D. (1981). *Choctaw clause structure.* Unpublished doctoral dissertation, University of California, San Diego.

Deeters, G. (1927). Armenisch und Südkaukasisch, II. *Caucasica,* **4,** 1–64.

Deeters, G. (1930). *Das kharthwelische Verbum.* Leipzig: Kommissionsverlag von Markert & Petters.

Deeters, G. (1954). 'Haben' im Georgischen. *Sprachgeschichte und Wortbedeutung: Festschrift Albert Debrunner,* 109–119. Bern: Francke Verlag.

Deeters, G. (1963). Die kaukasischen Sprachen. *Handbuch der Orientalistik,* I Abt., VII Band, 1–79. Leiden: E. J. Brill.

DeLancey, S. (1981). An interpretation of split ergativity and related patterns. *Language,* **57,** 626–657.

Derbyshire, D.C. (1982). Ergativity and transitivity in Paumarí. Unpublished manuscript. Summer Institute of Linguistics.

Diffloth, G. (1972). Notes on expressive meaning. *CLS,* **8.** 440–447.

Dik, S.C. (1978). *Functional grammar.* Amsterdam: North-Holland.

Dixon, R.M.W. (1972). *The Dyirbal language of North Queensland.* Cambridge: Cambridge University Press.

Dixon, R.M.W. (1977a). *A grammar of Yidiɲ.* Cambridge: Cambridge University Press.

Dixon, R.M.W. (1977b). The syntactic development of Australian languages. In *Mechanisms of syntactic change,* ed. by C.N. Li, 365–415. Austin: University of Texas Press.

Dixon, R.M.W. (1979). Ergativity. *Language,* **55,** 59–138.

Dixon, R.M.W. (1981). Grammatical reanalysis: An example of linguistic change. *Australian Journal of Linguistics,* **1,** 91–112.

Donaldson, T. (1976). Wangaybuwan. In *Grammatical categories in Australian languages,* ed. by R.M.W. Dixon. Canberra: Australian Institute of Aboriginal Studies.

Dondua, K.D. (1956a). K voprosu o roditel' nom èmfatičeskom v drevneliteraturnom gruzinskom jazyke. In *Saxelis brunebis isṭoriisatvis Kartvelur enebši,* ed. by V. Topuria, 204–217. Tbilisi: Universiṭeṭi. (first published, 1930).

Dondua, K.D. (1956b). O dvux suffiksax množestvennosti v gruzinskom. In *Saxelis brunebis isṭoriisatvis Kartvelur enebši,* ed. by V. Topuria, 290–312. Tbilisi: Universiṭeṭi. (first published, 1932).

Dressler, W. (1971). Über die Rekonstruktion der indogermanischen Syntax. *KZ,* **85,** 5–22.

Dryer, M.S. (1983). Indirect objects in Kinyarwanda revisited. In *Studies in Relational Grammar, 1,* ed. by D.M. Perlmutter, 129–140. Chicago: University of Chicago Press.

Dzidziguri, S. (1941). Mesxuri dialekṭis aγçeriti analizi sxva ḳiloebtan mimartebis tvalsazrisit. [A descriptive analysis of the Mesxian dialect from the point of view of its relation to other dialects]. *Enimḳis Moambe,* **10,** 237–253. (reprinted in *3iebani Kartuli dialekṭologiidan,* 131–146, 1954).
Dzidziguri, S. (1971). *Gruzinskie varianty nartskogo èposa.* Tbilisi: Merani.
Dzidzishvili, M. (1956). Nanatesaobitari vitarebiti 3vel Kartulši (VII–X ss. ʒeglebis enis mixedvit). [The degenitive adverbial in Old Georgian (according to the language of monuments of the 7th–10th centuries)]. In *Saxelis brunebis isṭoriisatvis Kartvelur enebši,* ed. by V. Topuria, 33. Tbilisi: Universiṭeṭi.
Dzidzishvili, M. (1958). Gramaṭiḳuli movlenata ṭendenciebi Gurulši. [Tendencies of grammatical phenomena in Gurian]. *IḲE,* **9–10,** 193–200.
Dzotsenidze, K. (1973). *Zemoimeruli ḳiloḳavi.* [The Upper Imerian dialect]. Tbilisi: Universiṭeṭi.
Eliasson, S. (1980). Case, word order and coding in a historical linguistic perspective. In *Historical morphology,* ed. by J. Fisiak, 127–139. The Hague: Mouton.
Emeneau, M.B. (1980a). Linguistic area: Introduction and continuation. *Language and linguistic area,* 1–18. Stanford: Stanford University Press.
Emeneau, M.B. (1980b). Bilingualism and structural borrowing. *Language and linguistic area,* 38–65. Stanford: Stanford University Press.
Emeneau, M.B. (1980c). Onomatopoetics in the Indian linguistic area. *Language and linguistic area,* 250–293. Stanford: Stanford University Press.
Fähnrich, H. (1967). Georgischer Ergativ im intransitiven Satz. *Beiträge zur Linguistik und Informationsverarbeitung,* **10,** 34–42.
Faltz, L.M. (1978). On indirect objects in universal syntax. *CLS,* **14,** 76–87.
Fillmore, C.J. (1968). The case for case. In *Universals in linguistic theory,* ed. by E. Bach and R.T. Harms, 1–88. New York: Holt, Rinehart, and Winston.
Friedman, V.A. (1979). Toward a typology of status: Georgian and other non-Slavic languages of the Soviet Union. *The elements,* CLS parasession volume, 339–350.
Gagua, K. (1976). *Dronaḳli zmnebi Svanurši.* [Tense-defective verbs in Svan]. Tbilisi: Mecniereba.
Gamkrelidze, T.V. (1959). *Sibilanṭta šesaṭqvisobani da Kartvelur enata uʒvelesi sṭruḳṭuris zogi saḳitxi.* [Sibilant correspondences and some questions of the oldest structure of the Kartvelian languages]. Tbilisi: Aḳademia.
Gamkrelidze, T.V. (1966). A typology of Common Kartvelian. *Language,* **42,** 69–83.
Gamkrelidze, T.V. (1967). Kartvelian and Indo-European: A typological comparison of reconstructed linguistic systems. In *To honor Roman Jakobson, 707–717.* The Hague: Mouton.
Gamkrelidze, T.V. (1979). Zmnis 'pirianoba' da 'valenṭoba'. ['Personalism' and 'valence' of the verb]. In *Saenatmecniero ḳrebuli,* ed. by S. Dzidziguri, 33–50. Tbilisi: Mecniereba.
Gamkrelidze, T.V., and Machavariani, G.I., (1965). *Sonanṭta sisṭema da ablauṭi Kartvelur enebši.* [The system of sonants and ablaut in the Kartvelian languages]. Tbilisi: Mecniereba.
Gamkrelidze, T.V., and Mačavariani, G.I. (1982). *Sonantensystem und Ablaut in den Kartwelsprachen.* Tübingen: Gunter Narr Verlag. (Gamkrelidze and Machavariani 1965, translated from the Russian with a Supplement by W. Boeder)
Getsadze, D. (1957). Sampiriani zmnata III seriis pormebis šesaxeb 3vel Kartulši. [On Series III forms of three-person verbs in Old Georgian]. *Kutaisis Sax. P̣edagogiuri Insṭiṭuṭis Šromebi,* **17,** 465–471.
Gigineishvili, B. and Sarjveladze, Z. (1978). Nanatesaobitari mimartulebitisa da nanatesaobitari danišnulebitis adgili 3veli Kartulisa da Kartveluri enebis brunvata sisṭemaši. [The place of the degenitive directional and of the degenitive designative in the system of cases of Old Georgian and the Kartvelian languages]. *Mravaltavi,* **6.** 123–136.

Givón, T. (1976). Topic, pronoun, and grammatical agreement. In *Subject and topic,* ed. by C.N. Li, 149–188. New York: Academic Press.
Givón, T. (1980). The drift away from ergativity: Diachronic potentials in Sherpa. *Folia Linguistica historica,* **1,** 41–60.
Greenberg, J.H. (1957). The problem of linguistic sub-groupings. *Essays in linguistics,* 46–55. Chicago: The University of Chicago Press.
Greenberg, J.H. (1963). Some universals of grammar with particular reference to the order of meaningful elements. In *Universals of language,* ed. by J.H. Greenberg, 73–113. Cambridge: MIT Press.
Greenberg, J.H. (1978). How does a language acquire gender markers? In *Universals of human language,* ed. by J.H. Greenberg, C.A. Ferguson, and E.A. Moravcsik, 47–82. Stanford: Stanford University Press.
Gudava, T. (1974). Puʒedreḳadi zmnebi Megrulši. [Verbs with stem vowel alternation in Mingrelian]. *Macne,* **4,** 132–138.
Gudava, T. (1979). Bagismieri tanxmovnebi čkamierta c̣in Megrulši. [Labial consonants before obstruents in Mingrelian]. In *Saenatmecniero ḳrebuli,* ed. by S. Dzidziguri, 81–88. Tbilisi: Mecniereba.
Hale, K. (1970). The passive and ergative in language change: The Australian case. In *Pacific linguistic studies in honour of Arthur Capell* (*Pacific Linguistics,* Series C, No. 13), ed. by S.A. Wurm and D.C. Laycock, 757–781. Canberra: The Australian National University.
Hale, K. (1973). Person marking in Walbiri. In *A Festschrift for Morris Halle,* ed. by S.R. Anderson and P. Kiparsky, 308–344. New York: Holt, Rinehart, and Winston.
Hale, K. (1976). Dja:bugay. In *Grammatical categories in Australian languages,* ed. by R.M.W. Dixon, 321–326. Canberra: Australian Institute of Aboriginal Studies.
Harris, A.C. (1978). Number agreement in Modern Georgian. In *The classification of grammatical categories,* ed. by Bernard Comrie, 75–98. Edmonton, Alberta: Linguistic Research.
Harris, A.C. (1979). Retired term marking in Old Georgian. *The elements,* CLS parasession volume, 377–389.
(Harris) Harisi, A. (1981a). Vnebiti Kartulši. [The passive in Georgian]. *Macne,* **3.** 109–116.
Harris, A.C. (1981b). *Georgian syntax: A study in relational grammar.* Cambridge: Cambridge University Press.
Harris, A.C. (1981c). On antipassives in Udi. Unpublished manuscript. Vanderbilt University.
Harris, A.C. (1982). Georgian and the Unaccusative Hypothesis. *Language,* **58,** 290–306.
Harris, A.C. (1984). Case marking, verb agreement, and Inversion in Udi. In *Studies in relational grammar, 2,* ed. by D.M. Perlmutter and C. Rosen, 243–258. Chicago: University of Chicago Press.
Hetzron, R. (1976). Two principles of genetic reconstruction. *Lingua,* **38,** 89–108.
Hoffmann, K. (1952). 'Wiederholende' Onomatopoetika im Altindischen. *IF,* **60:** 254–264.
Hohepa, P.W. (1969). The accusative-to-ergative drift in Polynesian languages. *Journal of the Polynesian Society,* **78,** 295–329.
Holisky, D.A. (1978). Stative verbs in Georgian and elsewhere. *The classification of grammatical categories,* ed. by Bernard Comrie, 139–162. Edmonton, Alberta: Linguistic Research.
Holisky, D.A. (1979). On lexical aspect and verb classes in Georgian. *The elements,* CLS parasession volume, 390–401.
Holisky, D.A. (1981a). *Aspect and Georgian medial verbs.* Delmar, NY: Caravan Press.

Holisky, D.A. (1981b). Aspect theory and Georgian aspect. In *Tense and aspect (Syntax and semantics, Vol. 14),* ed. by P.J. Tedeschi and A. Zaenen, 127–144. New York: Academic Press.

Holisky, D.A. (1983a). The case of the intransitive subject in Tsova–Tush (Bats). Unpublished manuscript. George Mason University.

Holisky, D.A. (1983b). On derived inceptives in Georgian. *Studies in the languages of the USSR* (*Papers in Linguistics,* 16), ed. by Bernard Comrie; 147–170. Edmonton, Alberta: Linguistic Research.

Hopper, P.J., and Thompson, S.A. (1980). Transitivity in grammar and discourse. *Language,* **56,** 251–299.

Imnaishvili, G. (1955). P̣irveli turmeobitisa da sṭaṭiḳur zmnata çarmoeba Ingilourši. [The formation of the first evidential and of stative verbs in Ingilo]. *IḲE,* **7,** 119–123.

Imnaishvili, G. (1959). Ingilouris mtavari sinṭaksuri taviseburebani. [The major syntactic idiosyncracies of Ingilo]. *IḲE,* **11,** 179–190.

Imnaishvili, G. (1966). *Kartuli enis Ingilouri dialekṭis taviseburebani.* [Idiosyncracies of the Ingilo dialect of the Georgian language]. Tbilisi: Mecniereba.

Imnaishvili, G. (1974). *Kartluri dialekṭi, I.* [The Kartlian dialect, I]. Tbilisi: Mecniereba.

Imnaishvili, I. (1956). Çrpelobiti brunvis saḳitxi saḳutar saxelebši. [The question of the absolutive case in personal names]. In *Saxelis brunebis isṭoriisatvis Kartvelur enebši,* ed. by V. Topuria, 59–75. Tbilisi: Universiṭeṭi. (first published, 1943).

Imnaishvili, I. (1957). *Saxelta bruneba da brunvata punkciebi 3vel Kartulši.* [The declension of nouns and the functions of cases in Old Georgian]. *(3veli Kartuli Enis Ḳatedris Šromebi,* **4**). Tbilisi: Universiṭeṭi.

Imnaishvili, I. (1971). *Kartuli enis isṭoriuli kresṭomatia, I, 2.* [A historical chrestomathy of the Georgian language, I, 2]. *(3veli Kartuli Enis Ḳatedris Šromebi,* **14***.)* Third edition. Tbilisi: Ganatleba.

Imnaishvili, I. (1975). *Sinuri Mravaltavi: Gamoḳvleva da leksiḳoni.* [The Sinai Mravaltavi: Analysis and lexicon]. *(3veli Kartuli Enis Ḳatedris Šromebi,* **17***.)* Tbilisi: Universiṭeṭi.

Imnaishvili, V. (1977). Ḳvlav šereuli kavširebitis šesaxeb 3vel Kartulši. [Once more on the mixed subjunctive in Old Georgian]. *TUŠ,* **187,** 13–24.

Jacobsen, W. (1969). The analog of the passive transformation in ergative-type languages. Unpublished manuscript. University of Nevada.

Jajanidze, P. (1970). Sinṭaksuri movlenebi Gurulši. [Syntactic phenomena in Gurian]. *Kutaisis Saxelmçipo P̣edagogiuri Insṭiṭuṭis Šromebi,* **33,** 249–262.

Jakobson, R. (1958). Typological studies and their contribution to historical comparative linguistics. In *Proceedings of the VIII International Congress of Linguists,* ed. by E. Silversten, 17–25. Oslo: Oslo University Press.

Jeffers, R.J. (1976). Review of *Proto–Indo-European syntax,* by Winfred P. Lehmann, 1974. *Language,* **52,** 982–988.

Jensen, H. (1959). *Altarmenische Grammatik.* Heidelberg: Carl Winter–Universitätsverlag.

Jespersen, O. (1927). *A Modern English grammar on historical principles,* Vol. III. Copenhagen: Ejnar Munksgaard.

Johnson, D.E. (1977). On Keenan's definition of 'subject of'. *Linguistic Inquiry,* **8,** 673–691.

Jorbenadze, B.A. (1975). *Zmnis gvaris pormata çarmoebisa da punkciis saḳitxebi Kartulši.* [Questions of the formation and function of voice forms of verbs in Georgian]. Tbilisi: Universiṭeṭi.

Kaldani, M. (1955). Svanuri enis Laxamuluri ḳiloḳavis poneṭiḳuri taviseburebani. [Phonetic characteristics of the Laxamula subdialect of the Svan language]. *IḲE,* **7,** 138–192.

Kaldani, M. (1956). Svanuri enis Laxamuluri ḳiloḳavis gramaṭiḳuli taviseburebani. [Grammatical characteristics of the Laxamula subdialect of the Svan language]. *IḲE,* **8,** 161–176.

Kaldani, M. (1959a). Svanuri enis Čubexeuri meṭqvelebis taviseburebani. [Characteristics of the Čubexe subdialect of the Svan language]. *IḲE,* **11,** 213–233.

Kaldani, M. (1959b). *Y*-s genezisisatvis Svanurši. [On the origin of *y* in Svan]. *KESS,* **1,** 91–99.

Kaldani, M. (1961). Svanuri enis Lenṭexuri ḳilos zogierti poneṭiḳuri taviseburebani. [Some phonetic characteristics of the Lenṭex dialect of the Svan language]. *KESS,* **2,** 167–182.

Kaldani, M. (1962). Svanuri enis Bečouri ḳiloḳavis poneṭiḳuri taviseburebani. [Phonetic characteristics of the Bečo subdialect of the Svan language]. *IḲE,* **13,** 191–206.

Kaldani, M. (1964). Ḳitxviti, gansazγvrebiti da gaʒlierebiti naçilaḳebi Svanurši. [Question, definite, and emphatic particles in Svan]. *IḲE,* **14,** 227–234.

Kaldani, M. (1968). *E/a* xmovantmonacvleobis zogi saḳitxisatvis Svanur zmnaši. [On some questions of *e/a* vowel alternation in the Svan verb]. *IḲE,* **16,** 132–143.

Kaldani, M. (1969). *Svanuri enis poneṭiḳa, I: Umlauṭis sisṭema Svanurši.* [The phonetics of the Svan language, I: The system of umlaut in Svan]. Tbilisi: Mecniereba.

Kaldani, M. (1974). Saxelobiti brunvisa da mravlobiti ricxvis maçarmoebel supiksta saḳitxisatvis Svanurši. [On the question of the formant suffixes of the nominative case and of plural number in Svan]. *KESS,* **4,** 148–164.

Kaldani, M. (1978). Aorisṭis çarmoeba Svanurši. [The formation of the aorist in Svan]. *IḲE,* **20,** 150–161.

Kaldani, M. (1979). Mesame subiekṭuri piris nišnis saḳitxisatvis Svanurši. [On the question of the marker of the third person subject in Svan]. In *Saenatmecniero ḳrebuli,* ed. by S. Dzidziguri, 208–222. Tbilisi: Mecniereba.

Kartozia, G. (1976). Arainversiul turmeobitta çarmoebisatvis Lazurši. [On the formation of non-inverted evidentials in Laz]. *Macne,* **3,** 121–129.

Kavtaradze, I. (1954). *Zmnis ʒiritadi ḳaṭegoriebis isṭoriisatvis Ʒvel Kartulši.* [On the history of basic verbal categories in Old Georgian] Tbilisi: Aḳademia.

Kavtaradze, I. (1956). Unaxaobis ḳaṭegoriis isṭoriisatvis Kartulši. [On the history of the category of unseen in Georgian]. *IḲE,* **8,** 179–192.

Kavtaradze, I. (1960). Mqopadis erti saxeobis isṭoriisatvis Kartulši. [On the history of one type of future in Georgian]. *IḲE,* **12,** 199–208.

Kavtaradze, I. (1961). Xolmeobitis ḳaṭegoriis isṭoriidan Kartulši. [From the history of the habitual category in Georgian]. *KESS,* **2,** 1–26.

Kavtaradze, I. (1964a). *Kartuli enis isṭoriisatvis: XII–XVIII ss, I.* [On the history of the Georgian language: 12th–18th centuries, I]. Tbilisi: Universiṭeṭi.

Kavtaradze, I. (1964b). Zmnis aγçeriti pormebis organulit šecvlis isṭoriidan Kartulši. [From the history of the replacement of periphrastic verb forms by organic ones in Georgian]. *IḲE,* **14,** 161–174.

Kaxadze, O. (1979). Açmqos turmeobitis šesaxeb Kartulši. [About the present evidential in Georgian]. In *Arnold Čikobavas,* ed. by S. Dzidziguri, 180–185. Tbilisi: Mecniereba.

Keenan, E.L. (1976). Towards a universal definition of 'subject'. In *Subject and topic,* ed. by C.N. Li, 303–333. New York: Academic Press.

Kekelidze, K. (1960). *Kartuli liṭeraṭuris isṭoria, I.* Tbilisi: Sabčota Sakartvelo.

Kiknadze, L. (1947). P̣irveli seriis mçḳrivta çarmoebastan daḳavširebuli saḳitxebi. [Questions related to the formation of the screeves of Series I]. *TUŠ,* **30,** 317–343.

Kiknadze, L. (1961). Uçqveṭlis xolmeobitis mçḳrivi Ʒvel Kartulši. [The imperfect habitual screeve in Old Georgian]. *Ʒveli Kartuli Enis Ḳatedris Šromebi,* **7,** 229–279. Tbilisi: Universiṭeṭi.

Kiknadze, L. (1967). Šereuli xolmeobitis mçķrivi ʒvel Kartulši. [The mixed habitual screeve in Old Georgian]. In *Orioni: Aķaķi Šaniʒes,* ed. by I. Imnaishvili and A. Urushadze, 184–199. Tbilisi: Universiṭeṭi.

Kiparsky, P. (1974). Remarks on analogical change. In *Historical linguistics, II,* ed. by J.M. Anderson and C. Jones, 257–275. Amsterdam: North-Holland.

Kiziria, A. (1954). *Saero mçerlobis ʒeglta enis sinṭaksis zogierti saķitxi (XII–XVIII ss).* [Some questions about the syntax of the language of the monuments of national writers (12th–18th centuries)]. *IĶE,* **6,** 137–155.

Kiziria, A. (1955). *-Eb* nišniani mravlobiti ricxvis sinṭaksuri ʒalisatvis ʒvel Kartulši. [On the syntactic strength of plurals in *-eb* in Old Georgian]. *IĶE,* **7,** 35–40.

Kiziria, A. (1959). Micemitši dasmuli pirmiumartavi damaṭeba ʒvel Kartulši. [The dative complement not triggering agreement in Old Georgian]. *IĶE,* **11,** 169–177.

Kiziria, A. (1963). *Marṭivi çinadadebis šedgeniloba ʒvel Kartulši.* [The structure of the simple sentence in Old Georgian]. Tbilisi: Aķademia.

Kiziria, A. (1974). Kvemdebare-šemasmenlis urtiertoba Kartuli enis dasavluri dialekṭebis mixedvit. [The subject–predicate relation in western dialects of the Georgian language]. *KESS,* **4,** 75–91.

Klimov, G.A. (1962). *Sklonenie v kartvel'skix jazykax v sravnitel'no-istoričeskom aspekte.* Moskva: Akademija.

Klimov, G.A. (1964). *Ètimologičeskij slovar' kartvel'skix jazykov.* Moskva: Akademija.

Klimov, G.A. (1972). K xarakteristike jazykov aktivnogo stroja. *V Ja,* **4,** 3–12.

Klimov, G.A. (1973). *Očerk obščej teorii èrgativnosti.* Moskva: Nauka.

Klimov, G.A. (1976). Anomalii èrgativnosti v lazskom (čanskom) jazyke. *Aγmosavluri Pilologia,* **4,** 150–159.

Klimov, G.A. (1977). *Tipologija jazykov aktivnogo stroja.* Moskva: Nauka.

Klokeid, T.J. (1976). Revaluations and case assignment in Pama Nyungan. Unpublished manuscript.

Klokeid, T.J. (1978). Nominal inflection in Pamanyungan: A case study in relational grammar. In *Valence, semantic case, and grammatical relations,* ed. by W. Abraham, 577–615. Amsterdam: John Benjamins.

Kluge, T. (1916). *Beiträge zur mingrelischen Grammatik.* Berlin: Verlag von W. Kohlhammer.

Kuryłowicz, J. (1964). On the methods of internal reconstruction. In *Proceedings of the Ninth International Congress of Linguists,* ed. by H. Lunt, 9–29. The Hague: Mouton.

Lake, K., Blake, R.P., and New, S. (1928). The Caesarean text of the Gospel of Mark. *Harvard Theological Review,* **21,** 207–404.

Lawler, J.M. (1977). *A* agrees with *B* in Achenese: A problem for relational grammar. In *Grammatical relations. (Syntax and semantics, Vol. 8),* ed. by P. Cole and J.M. Sadock, 219–248. New York: Academic Press.

Lehmann, W.P. (1968). Review of *Sonanṭta sisṭema da ablauṭi Kartvelur enebši,* by T. Gamkrelidze and G. Machavariani, 1965. *Language,* **44,** 404–407.

Lehmann, W.P. (1973). A structural principle of language and its implications. *Language,* **49,** 47–66.

Lehmann, W.P. (1974). *Proto-Indo-European syntax.* Austin: University of Texas Press.

Li, C.N. (1977). Introduction. *Mechanisms of syntactic change,* ed. by C.N. Li, xi–xix. Austin: University of Texas Press.

Lightfoot, D.W. (1979). *Principles of diachronic syntax.* Cambridge: Cambridge University Press.

Lomtatidze, K. (1937). Naštebi mesame piris obiekṭuri prepiksisa Gurulsa da Ačarulši. [Remains of the third person object prefix in Gurian and Ačarian]. *TUŠ,* **6,** 123–138.

Lomtatidze, K. (1946). *-K* supiksisatvis Megrul zmnebši. [On the suffix *-k* in Mingrelian verbs]. *IĶE,* **1,** 131–140.

Lomtatidze, K. (1952). *Tbeba* ṭipis zmnata isṭoriisatvis Kartulši. [On the history of *tbeba*-type verbs in Georgian]. IḲĖ, **4,** 75–81.
Machavariani, G.I. (1955). Maxvilis saḳitxisatvis Kartvelur enebši. Unpublished manuscript; summary published in *Mimomxilveli,* **6–9,** 506–509. 1972.
Machavariani, G.I. (1959). 'Unišno vnebiti' Kartvelur enebši. [The 'markerless passive' in the Kartvelian languages]. *KESS,* **1,** 101–129.
Machavariani, G.I. (1960). Brunebis erti ṭipis genezisisatvis svanurši. [On the origin of one type of declension in Svan]. TUŠ, **93,** 93–104.
Machavariani, G.I. (1963). O trex rjadax sibiljantnyx spirantov i affrikat v kartvel'skix jazykax. *Trudy XXV Meždunarodnogo kongressa vostokovedov, III,* 532–535. Moskva: Bostočnoj Literatury.
Machavariani, G.I. (1966). K tipologičeskoj xarakteristike obščekartvel'skogo jazyka-osnovy. *V Ja,* **1,** 3–9.
Machavariani, G.I. (1969). Kartvelur enata diakroniuli ponologiis zogierti saḳitxi. [Some questions of the diachronic phonology of the Kartvelian languages]. In *Giorgi Axvledians,* ed. by S. Dzidziguri, 156–165. Tbilisi: Universiṭeṭi.
Machavariani, G.I. (1970). The system of ancient Kartvelian nominal flection as compared to those of the Mountain Caucasian and Indo-European languages. In *Theoretical problems of typology and the northern Eurasian languages,* ed. by L. Dezsö and P. Hajdu, 165–169. Amsterdam: B.R. Grüner.
Machavariani, G.I. (1974). Aspeḳṭis ḳaṭegoria Kartvelur enebši. [The category of aspect in the Kartvelian languages]. *KESS,* **4,** 118–141.
Machavariani, G.I. (1980). Namqo usruli Svanurši da misi adgili Kartvelur enata uγvlilebis sisṭemaši. [The imperfective past in Svan and its place in the conjugational system of the Kartvelian languages]. *IḲE,* **22,** 207–217.
Malkiel, Y. (1981). Drift, slope, and slant. *Language,* **57,** 535–570.
Marr, N. (1910). *Grammatika čanskago (lazskogo) jazyka. (Materialy po jafetičeskomu jazykoznaniju, II).* S. Peterburg: Akademija.
Martirosovi, A. (1955). Masdaruli ḳonsṭrukciis genezisisatvis Ʒvel Kartulši. [On the origin of the masdar construction in Old Georgian]. *IḲE,* **7,** 43–59.
Martirosovi, A. (1958). Absṭrakṭul saxelta çarmoeba da saçarmoebel apiksta šedgeniloba Ʒvel Kartulši. [The derivation of abstract nouns and the formation of derivational affixes in Old Georgian]. *IḲE,* **9–10,** 121–129.
Martirosovi, A. (1959). *Čemda, šenda . . .* ṭipis nacvalsaxelta çarmoeba da punkciebi Kartvelur enebši. [The formation and functions of *čemda-, šenda*-type pronouns in the Kartvelian languages]. *IḲE.* **11,** 107–128.
Martirosovi, A. (1964). *Nacvalsaxeli Kartvelur enebši.* [The pronoun in the Kartvelian languages]. Tbilisi: Aḳademia.
Martirosovi, A. (1979). Saxelis gansazγvruloba–ganusazγvrelobis ḳaṭegoria Ʒvel Kartulši. [The definite–indefinite category in substantives in Old Georgian]. In *Arnold Čikobavas,* ed. by S. Dzidziguri, 125–138. Tbilisi: Mecniereba.
Martirosovi, A., and Imnaishvili, G. (1956). *Kartuli enis Ḳaxuri dialekṭi.* [The Kaxian dialect of the Georgian language]. Tbilisi: Aḳademia.
Matthews, W.K. (1952). The ergative construction in Indo–Aryan. *Lingua,* **3,** 391–406.
McKay, G.R. (1976). Rembarnga. In *Grammatical categories in Australian languages,* ed. by R.M.W. Dixon, 494–505. Canberra: Australian Institute of Aboriginal Studies.
McLendon, S. (1978). Ergativity, case, and transitivity in Eastern Pomo. *IJAL,* **44,** 1–9.
Meillet, A. (1954). *La méthode comparative en linguistique historque.* Paris: Librairie Ancienne Honoré Champion.
Meillet, A. (1964). *Introduction á l'étude comparative des langues indo-européennes.* University, Alabama: University of Alabama Press.

Melikishvili, D. (1977). Inḳluziv–eksḳluzivis ḳaṭegoriis gamoxaṭvis isṭoriisatvis Kartul zmnaši. [On the history of the expression of the category of inclusive–exclusive in the Georgian verb]. *Macne,* **4,** 159–165.
Mikeladze, N. (1980). Morpologiuri taviseburebani Ačaraši moγvaçe mçeralta txzulebebši. [Morphological peculiarities in the compositions of writers working in Ačara]. *Macne,* **4,** 90–107.
Nadareishvili, L. (1962). Mimγeoba Zanurši. [The participle in Zan]. *IḲE,* **13,** 177–190.
Nadareishvili, L. (1970). Masdaris çarmoebis šesaxeb Čanurši. [On the derivation of the masdar in Laz]. *IḲE,* **17,** 136–143.
Natadze, N. (1955). Mesame seriis dro-ḳilota çarmoebisatvis Kartulši. [On the formation of the tense-aspects of Series III in Georgian]. *IḲE,* **7,** 81–98.
Natadze, N. (1959). Temis nišnebi Kartvelur enebši. [Thematic markers in the Kartvelian languages]. *IḲE,* **11,** 129–149.
Natadze, N. (1961). Mqopadisatvis Kartvelur enebši. [On the future in the Kartvelian languages]. *KESS,* **2,** 29–51.
Nebieridze, G.S. (In press). Problema ergativnoj konstrukcii v kartvel'skix jazykax. In *G. Axvledianisadmi miʒγvnili ḳrebuli.* Tbilisi.
Nizharadze, S. (1957). *Zemoačarulis taviseburebani.* [Characteristics of Upper Ačarian]. Batumi: Ačaris ASSR Saxelmçipo Gamomcemloba.
Nizharadze, S. (1961). *Kartuli enis Zemoačaruli dialekṭi.* [The Upper Ačarian dialect of the Georgian language]. Batumi: Saxelmçipo Gamomcemloba.
Nizharadze, S. (1975). *Ačaruli dialekṭi.* [The Ačarian dialect]. Batumi: Sabčota Ačara.
(Normebi) (1970). *Tanamedrove Kartuli Saliṭeraṭuro enis normebi.* [The norms of the Modern Literary Georgian language]. Tbilisi: Mecniereba.
Nozadze, L. (1958). In-eniani vnebitis urtiertobis saḳitxisatvis Kartulši. [On the question of the relation between the *i-* and *e*-passives in Georgian]. *IḲE,* **9–10,** 129–135.
Nozadze, L. (1974). Medioakṭiv zmnata çarmoebis zogi saḳitxi Kartulši. [Some questions of the formation of medioactive verbs in Georgian]. *IḲE,* **19,** 25–51.
Oniani, A. (1978). *Kartvelur enata isṭoriuli morpologiis saḳitxebi* [Questions of the historical morphology of the Kartvelian languages]. Tbilisi: Ganatleba.
Osidze, E. (1960). *γaγad-qo* ṭipis zmnebi ʒvel Kartulši. [*γaγad-qo*-type verbs in Old Georgian]. IḲE, **12,** 267–273.
Osidze, E. (1963). Erti ṭipis zmnata açmqos puʒis agebulebisatvis Kartulši. [On the construction of the present stem of one type of verb in Georgian]. *KESS,* **3,** 11–18.
Osthoff, H., and Brugman, K. (1878). Vorwort to *Morphologische Untersuchungen auf dem Gebiete der indogermanischen Sprachen.* Leipzig: Verlag von S. Hirzel.
Palmaiti, L. (1978). 'Empaṭiḳuri *-a*' saxelta morpologiis ʒiritad saḳitxebtan daḳavširebit. ['Emphatic *-a*' in relation to fundamental questions of the morphology of nouns]. *Macne,* **1,** 113–124.
Palmaiti, L. (1979). Šenišvnebi Svanuri brunebis šesaxeb. [Remarks on Svan declension]. *Macne,* **3,** 113–124.
Panchvidze, V. (1960). Nazmnari saxelis mier saxelis martva brunvaši Udur enaši. [Government of the case of a nominal by deverbal nouns in the Udi language]. *IḲE,* **12,** 404–409.
Panchvidze, V. (1974). *Uduris gramaṭiḳuli analizi.* [A grammatical analysis of Udi]. Tbilisi: Mecniereba.
Pätsch, G. (1952). Die georgische Aoristkonstruktion. *Wissenschaftliche Zeitschrift der Humboldt-Universität Berlin (Gesellschafts- und sprachwissenschaftliche Reihe),* **1,** 5–13.
Pätsch, G. (1967). Das georgische präsens—Indoeuropäischer Einfluss oder eigengesetzliche Entwicklung? *BK,* **23–24,** 143–152.

Payne, J. (1979). Transitivity and intransitivity in the Iranian languages of the USSR. *The elements,* CLS parasession volume, 436–447.
Payne, J. (1980). The decay of ergativity in Pamir languages. *Lingua,* **51**, 147–186.
Peeters, P. (1935). Sainte Sousanik, Martyre en Arméno–Georgie. *Analecta Bollandiana,* **53**, 5–48.
Perlmutter, D.M. (1978a). Evidence for Inversion in Russian, Japanese and Kannada. Unpublished manuscript. University of California, San Diego.
Perlmutter, D.M. (1978b). Impersonal passives and the Unaccusative Hypothesis. *BLS,* **4**, 157–189.
Perlmutter, D.M. (1982). Syntactic representation, syntactic levels, and the notion of subject. In *The nature of syntactic representation,* ed. by P. Jacobson and G.K. Pullum, 283–340. Dordrecht: D. Reidel.
Perlmutter, D.M., and Postal, P.M. (1983a). Toward a universal characterization of passivization. In *Studies in relational grammar, 1,* ed. by D.M. Perlmutter, 3–29. Chicago: University of Chicago Press.
Perlmutter, D.M., and Postal, P.M. (1983b). Some proposed laws of basic clause structure. In *Studies in relational grammar, 1,* ed. by D.M. Perlmutter, 81–128. Chicago: University of Chicago Press.
Perlmutter, D.M., and Postal, P.M. (1984). The 1-Advancement Exclusiveness Law. *Studies in relational grammar, 2,* ed. by D.M. Perlmutter and C. Rosen, 81–125. Chicago: University of Chicago Press.
Pirejko, L.A. (1979). On the genesis of the ergative construction in Indo-Iranian. In *Ergativity,* ed. by F. Plank, 481–488. New York: Academic Press.
Plank, F. (Ed.). (1979). *Ergativity: Towards a theory of grammatical relations.* New York: Academic Press.
Pochxua, B. (1961). Mravlobitis *n*ariani maçarmoeblebi ʒvel Kartulši. [*N*-indicators of the plural in Old Georgian]. *KESS,* **2,** 53–62.
Postal, P.M. (1970). The method of universal grammar. In *Method and theory in linguistics,* ed. by P.L. Garvin, 113–131. The Hague: Mouton.
Reed, I., Miyaoka, O., and Jacobson, S. (1977). *Yup'ik Eskimo grammar.* Fairbanks: Alaska Native Language Center, University of Alaska.
Rogava, G. (1953). Dro-ḳilota meotxe ǯgupis naḳvetebi Kartvelur enebši. [Forms of the fourth tense-mood Series in the Kartvelian languages]. *IḲE,* **5,** 17–31.
Rogava, G. (1954). Namqo-usrulis *-od* supiksis šedgenilobisatvis Kartulši. [On the structure of the suffix *-od* of the imperfective past in Georgian]. *IḲE,* **6,** 79–84.
Rogava, G. (1968). Mravlobiti ricxvis mesame subieḳṭuri piris *-an* supiksisatvis Kartulši. [On the *-an* suffix of the third-person plural subject in Georgian]. *IḲE,* **16,** 74–77.
Rogava, G. (1975). Nominaṭiuri ḳonsṭrukciis mkone gardamavali zmnis genezisisatvis Kartvelur enebši. [On the genesis of transitive verbs that have the nominative construction in the Kartvelian languages]. *Çeliçdeuli,* **2,** 273–279.
Sapir, E. (1917). Review of *Het passieve karakter van het verbum transitivum of van het verbum actionis in talen van Noord-Amerika,* by C.C. Uhlenbeck, 1916. *IJAL,* **1,** 82–86.
Sarjveladze, Z. (1972). Axali masalebi mesame xolmeobitis šesaxeb. [New materials on the third habitual]. *Macne,* **3,** 147–149.
Schmidt, K.H. (1962). *Studien zur Rekonstruktion des Lautstandes der südkaukasischen Grundsprache. (Abhandlungen für die Kunde des Morgenlandes, XXXIV, 3).* Wiesbaden: Kommissionsverlag Franz Steiner GMBH.
Schmidt, K.H. (1963). Zu den Aspekten im Georgischen und in indogermanischen Sprachen. *BK,* **15–16,** 107–115.

Schmidt, K.H. (1966). Tempora im Georgischen und in indogermanischen Sprachen. *Studia Caucasica,* **2,** 48–57.
Schmidt, K.H. (1968). Review of *Sonanṭta sisṭema da ablauṭi Kartvelur enebši,* by T. Gamkrelidze and G. Machavariani, 1965. *IF,* **73,** 395–397.
Schmidt, K.H. (1971). Sprachstruktur und Sprachbund. *BK,* **28,** 262–268.
Schmidt, K.H. (1973). Transitive und Intransitive. In *Indogermanische und allgemeine Sprachwissenschaft,* ed. by G. Redard, 9–24. Wiesbaden: Reichert.
Schmidt, K.H. (1976). Kasus, Präverb, und Postposition in den Kaukasischen Sprachen. *Aγmosavluri Pilologia,* **4,** 144–149.
Schmidt, K.H. (1978). On the reconstruction of Proto-Kartvelian. *BK,* **36,** 246–265.
Schmidt, K.H. (1980). Casus indefinitus bei Eigennamen. *BK,* **38,** 233–238.
Shanidze, A. (1926). Kartuli zmnis sakcevi. [Version in the Georgian verb]. *TUM,* **6,** 312–338.
Shanidze, A. (1942). Zmnata gardamavlobis saḳitxisatvis Kartvelur enebši, II. [On the question of transitivity of verbs in the Kartvelian languages, II.] *SMAM,* **3,** 289–293.
Shanidze, A. (1945). Mc̣ḳrivta moʒγvrebisatvis, I: Sami mc̣ḳrivis c̣armoebis taviseburebani ʒvel Kartulši. [On the doctrine of screeves, I: Characteristics of the formation of three screeves in Old Georgian]. *SMAM,* **6,** 835–844.
Shanidze, A. (1956). C̣odebitis pormis adgilisatvis gramaṭiḳaši. [On the place of the form of the vocative in the grammar]. In *Saxelis brunebis isṭoriisatvis Kartvelur enebši,* ed. by V. Topuria, 48–55. Tbilisi: Universiṭeṭi. (first published, 1942).
Shanidze, A. (1957a). Kartuli ḳiloebi mtaši. [Georgian dialects in the mountains]. *Kartuli enis sṭrukṭurisa da isṭoriis saḳitxebi, I,* 9–19. Tbilisi: Universiṭeṭi. (first published, 1915).
Shanidze, A. (1957b). Nasaxelari zmnebi Kartulši. [Denominal verbs in Georgian]. *Kartuli enis sṭrukṭurisa da isṭoriis saḳitxebi, I,* 35–44. Tbilisi: Universiṭeṭi. (first published, 1919).
Shandize, A. (1957c). Subiekṭuri prepiksi meore pirisa da obiekṭuri prepiksi mesame pirisa Kartul zmnebši. [The subject prefix of the second person and the object prefix of the third person in the Georgian verb]. *Kartuli enis sṭrukṭurisa da isṭoriis saḳitxebi, I,* 111–263. Tbilisi: Universiṭeṭi. (first published, 1920).
Shandize, A. (1957d). Umlauṭi Svanurši. [Umlaut in Svan]. *Kartuli enis sṭrukṭurisa da isṭoriis saḳitxebi, I,* 323–372. Tbilisi: Universiṭeṭi. (first published, 1925).
Shandize, A. (1973). *Kartuli enis gramaṭiḳis sapuʒvlebi, I.* [Fundamentals of the grammar of the Georgian language, I]. Second edition. *(ʒveli Kartuli Enis Ḳatedris Šromebi, 15.)* Tbilisi: Universiṭeṭi. (first published, 1953).
Shandize, A. (1976). *ʒveli Kartuli enis gramaṭiḳa.* [A grammar of the Old Georgian language]. *(ʒveli Kartuli Enis Ḳatedris Šromebi, 18.)* Tbilisi: Universiṭeṭi.
Sharadzenidze, T. (1954). Saxelta mravlobiti ricxvis c̣armoeba Svanurši Balszemouri ḳilos mixedvit. [The formation of the plural of substantives in Svan, according to the Upper Bal dialect]. *IḲE,* **6,** 189–203.
Sharadzenidze, T. (1955). Brunebata ḳlasipiḳaciisatvis Svanurši. [On the classification of declensions in Svan]. *IḲE,* **7,** 125–133.
Sharadzenidze, T. (1956). *-Ta* supiksiani mravlobiti mokmedebitsa da vitarebits brunvebši. [The plural with the suffix *-ta* in instrumental and adverbial cases]. In *Saxelis brunebis isṭoriisatvis Kartvelur enebši,* ed. by V. Topuria, 271–285. Tbilisi: Universiṭeṭi. (first published, 1942).
Sharadzenidze, T. (1961). Orpuʒianobis erti ṭipis šesaxeb Svanur saxelta brunebaši. [On one type of two-base declension in Svan]. *KĖSS,* **2,** 221–231.
Sherozia, R. (1980). P̣oṭencialisis ḳaṭegoria da mastan daḳavširebuli zogi saḳitxi Kartvelur enebši. [The category of potential and some questions related to it in the Kartvelian

languages]. In *Narḳvevebi Iberiul-Ḳavḳasiur enata morpologiidan,* ed. by G. Bedoshvili and B. Jorbenadze, 119–126. Tbilisi: Mecniereba.

Silverstein, M. (1976). Hierarchy of features and ergativity. In *Grammatical categories in Australian languages,* ed. by R.M.W. Dixon, 112–171. Canberra: Australian Institute of Aboriginal Studies.

Sridhar, S.N. (1976). Dative subjects. *CLS,* **12,** 582–593.

Suxishvili, M. (1976). *Sṭaṭiḳuri zmnebi Kartulši.* [Stative verbs in Georgian]. Tbilisi: Mecniereba.

Takaishvili, A. (1974). Ḳauzaṭivis ҫarmoebis zogi saḳitxi Kartulši. [Some questions of the formation of the causative in Georgian]. *KESS,* **4,** 5–34.

Tasaku, T. (1981). Split case-marking patterns in verb-types and tense–aspect–mood. *Linguistics,* **19,** 389–438.

Timberlake, A. (1977). Reanalysis and actualization in syntactic change. In *Mechanisms of syntactic change,* ed. by C.N. Li, 141–177. Austin: University of Texas Press.

Topuria, G. (1977). Mokmedebiti brunvis isṭoriisatvis Svanurši. [On the history of the instrumental case in Svan]. *Macne,* **3,** 111–114.

Topuria, V. (1923). Sinṭaksuri analogiis erti šemtxveva Kartulši dialekṭebis mixedvit. [One instance of syntactic analogy in Georgian dialects]. *Čveni mecniereba,* **1,** 113–121.

Topuria, V. (1927). Saxelta daboloebis isṭoriisatvis Svanurši. [On the history of the ending of nouns in Svan]. *TUM,* **7,** 285–315.

Topuria, V. (1937). Zogierti brunvis genezisisatvis Megrul– Ҫanurši. [On the origin of certain cases in Mingrelo–Laz]. *Enimḳis moambe,* **1,** 179–182.

Topuria, V. (1942a). Mesame ṭipis vnebitis ҫarmoeba Kartulši. [The formation of type three passives in Georgian]. *SMAM,* **3,** 965–972.

Topuria, V. (1942b). Zmnis uʒvelesi supiksaciisatvis Kartulši. [On ancient verbal suffixation in Georgian]. SMAM, **3,** 489–496.

Topuria, V. (1944). Brunebis sisṭemisatvis Svanurši sxva Kartvelur enata brunebastan šedarebit. [On the system of declension in Svan in comparison with declension in the other Kartvelian languages]. SMAM, **5,** 339–347.

Topuria, V. (1953). Enis ganvitarebis šinagan ḳanonta erti nimuši Kartulši. [One example in Georgian of internal laws of the evolution of language]. *IKE,* **5,** 519–528.

Topuria, V. (1954). Gramaṭiḳul movlenata ertgvarovani procesi Kartvelur enebši. [A uniform process of grammatical phenomena in the Kartvelian languages]. *IḲE,* **6,** 445–455. (reprinted in *Šromebi, III,* 173–183. Tbilisi: Mecniereba. 1979).

Topuria, V. (Ed.). (1956a) *Saxelis brunebis istoriisatvis Kartvelur enebši.* [On the history of noun declension in the Kartvelian languages]. Tbilisi: Universiṭeṭi.

Topuria, V. (1956b). Ҫodebiti brunvisatvis. [On the vocative case]. In *Saxelis brunebis isṭoriisatvis Kartvelur enebši,* ed. by V. Topuria, 36–47. Tbilisi: Universiṭeṭi. (first published, 1935).

Topuria, V. (1956c). Vitarebiti brunvis daboloebis saḳitxisatvis Kartulši. [On the question of the ending of the adverbial case in Georgian]. In *Saxelis brunebis isṭoriisatvis Kartvelur enebši,* ed. by V. Topuria, 32. Tbilisi: Universiṭeṭi.

Topuria, V. (1963). Kartvelur enata dialekṭebis šesҫavlis mdgomareoba da amocanebi. [The status and problems of the study of dialects of the Kartvelian languages]. *KESS,* **3,** 161–188.

Topuria, V. (1967). *Svanuri ena, I: Zmna.* [The Svan Language, I: The verb]. *(Šromebi, I)* Tbilisi: Mecniereba. (first published, 1931).

Topuria, V. (1979a). Poneṭiḳuri daḳvirvebani Kartvelur enebši, I. [Observations on the phonetics of the Kartvelian languages, I]. *Šromebi, III,* 5–26. Tbilisi: Mecniereba. (first published, 1926).

Topuria, V. (1979b). Poneṭiḳuri daḳvirvebani Kartvelur enebši, II. [Observations on the phonetics of the Kartvelian languages, II]. *Šromebi, III*, 27–39. Tbilisi: Mecniereba. (first published, 1930).

Topuria, V. (1979c). Redukciisatvis Kartvelur enebši. [On reduction in the Kartvelian languages]. *Šromebi, III*, 145–171. Tbilisi: Mecniereba. (first published, 1946).

Tschenkéli, K. (1958). *Einführung in die georgische Sprache, I.* Zürich: Amirani.

Tschenkéli, K. (1960–1974). *Georgisch–Deutsches Wörterbuch.* Zürich: Amirani.

Tsereteli, G.V. (1966). La théorie des sonantes et des ablauts dans les langues Kartvéliennes. *BK*, **21–22**, 30–51.

Uridia, O. (1960). Megrulis sinṭaksuri taviseburebani Kartultan mimartebit. [The syntactic peculiarities of Mingrelian in relation to Georgian]. *TUŠ*, **93**, 167–178.

Vennemann, T. (1975). An explanation of drift. In *Word order and word order change*, ed. by C.N. Li, 269–305. Austin: University of Texas Press.

Visser, F.T. (1963). *An historical syntax of the English language, I.* Leiden: E.J. Brill.

Voegelin, C.F., Ramanujan, R.A., Voegelin, F.M. (1960). Typology of density ranges I: Introduction. *IJAL*, **26**, 198–205.

Vogt, H. (1936). *Esquisse d'une grammaire du géorgienne moderne.* Oslo: A.W. Brøggers. (also published in 1938 in *NTS*, **9**, 5–114 and **10**, 5–188).

Vogt, H. (1938). Arménien et caucasique du sud. *NTS*, **9**, 321–338.

Vogt, H. (1939). Alternances vocaliques en géorgien. *NTS*, **11**, 118–135.

Vogt, H. (1947a). Suffixes verbaux en géorgien ancien. *NTS*, **14**, 38–82.

Vogt, H. (1947b). Le system des cas en géorgien ancien. *NTS*, **14**, 98–140.

Vogt, H. (1971). *Grammaire de la langue géorgienne.* Oslo: Universitetsforlaget.

Watkins, C. (1963). Preliminaries to a historical and comparative analysis of the syntax of the Old Irish verb. *Celtica*, **6**, 1–49.

Watkins, C. (1964). Preliminaries to the reconstruction of Indo-European sentence structure. In *Proceedings of the Ninth International Congress of Linguists*, ed. by H. Lunt, 1035–1042. The Hague: Mouton.

Watkins, C. (1976). Towards Proto–Indo–European syntax: Problems and pseudo-problems. *Diachronic syntax*, CLS parasession volume, 305–326.

Weinreich, U., Labov, W., and Herzog, M.I. (1968). Empirical foundations for a theory of language change. In *Directions for historical linguistics*, ed. by W.P. Lehmann and Y. Malkiel, 95–195. Austin: University of Texas Press.

Wixman, R. (1980). *Language aspects of ethnic patterns and processes in the North Caucasus.* Chicago: University of Chicago, Dept. of Geography, Res. Paper No. 191.

Woodbury, A.C. (1977). Greenlandic Eskimo, ergativity, and relational grammar. In *Grammatical relations. (Syntax and semantics, Vol. 8)*, ed. by P. Cole and J.M. Sadock, 307–336. New York: Academic Press.

Woodbury, H. (1975). *Noun incorporation in Onondaga.* Unpublished doctoral disseration, Yale University. New Haven, CN.

Zhghenti, S. (1949). *Svanuri enis poneṭiḳis ʒiritadi saḳitxebi.* [Principal questions of the phonetics of the Svan language]. Tbilisi: Aḳademia.

Zhghenti, S. (1953). Kartvelur enata dialekṭebis šesçavlis zogierti saḳitxi. [Some questions of the study of the dialects of the Kartvelian languages]. *TUŠ*, **49**, 129–142.

Zhghenti, S. (1965). *R* ponema Megrul–Čanurši. [The phoneme *r* in Mingrelo–Laz]. *Kartvelur enata poneṭiḳis saḳitxebi*, 54–60. Tbillisi: Ganatleba. (first published, 1949).

Zorrell, F. (1930). *Grammatik zur altgeorgischen Bibelübersetzung.* Rome: Pontificium Institutum Biblicum.

EDITED KARTVELIAN TEXTS

Georgian

Abuladze, I. (1955). *Mamata sc̣avlani.* (Ʒveli Kartuli Enis Ʒeglebi, **8**.) Tbilisi: Ạkademia.

Abuladze, I. (1957). *Balavarianis Kartuli redakciebi. (Ʒveli Kartuli Enis Ʒeglebi,* **10.**) Tbilisi: Ạkademia. [Manuscript A (J 140), quoted here, the "Complete Balavariani," was written in the second half of the eleventh century, on the basis of ninth–tenth century sources (p. 8).]

Abuladze, I. (1960). *Ioane Mosxi, "Limonari." Tbilisi: Ạkademia.*

Abuladze, I. (1963). *Ʒveli Kartuli agiograpiuli liṭeraṭuris ʒeglebi,* I. Tbilisi: Ạkademia.

Birdsall, J.N. (1971). Khanmeti fragments of the Synoptic Gospels from Ms. Vind. Georg. 2. *Oriens Christianus,* **55,** 62–89.

Birdsall, J.N. (1972). Palimpsest fragments of a khanmeti Georgian version of I Esdras. *Le Muséon,* **85,** 97–105.

Blake, R.P. (1974). *The Old Georgian version of the Gospel of Mark. Patrologia Orientalis,* **20,** fasc. 3. (first edition, 1928).

Blake, R.P. (1976). *The Old Georgian version of the Gospel of Matthew. Patrologia Orientalis,* **24,** fasc. 1. (first edition, 1933).

Blake, R.P., and Briére, M. (1950). *The Old Georgian version of the Gospel of John. Patrologia Orientalis,* **26,** fasc. 4.

Blake, R.P., and Briére, M. (1961). *The Old Georgian version of the Prophets. Patrologia Orientalis,* **29,** fasc. 2–5.

Blake, R.P., and Briére, M. (1963). *The Old Georgian version of the Prophets: Apparatus criticus. Patrologia Orientalis,* **30,** fasc. 3.

Briére, M. (1955). *La version géorgienne ancienne de L'évangile de Luc. Patrologia Orientalis,* **27,** fasc. 3.

Dzotsenidze, K., and Danelia, K. (1974). *P̣avles Episṭoleta Kartuli versiebi. (Ʒveli Kartuli Enis Ḳatedris Šromebi,* **16.**) Tbilisi: Universiṭeṭi.

Garitte, G. (1955). *L'ancienne version géorgienne des Actes des Apôtres.* Louvain: Publications Universitaires.

Imnaishvili, I. (1961). Iovanes gamocxadeba da misi targmaneba. *Ʒveli Kartuli Enis Ḳatedris Šromebi,* **7,** 1–205. Tbilisi: Universiṭeṭi.

Imnaishvili, I. (1966). *Saḳitxavi c̣igni Ʒvel Kartul enaši, II. (Ʒveli Kartuli Enis Ḳatedris Šromebi,* **10.**) Tbilisi: Universiṭeṭi.

Imnaishvili, I. (1970a). C̣amebay C̣midisa Šušaniḳisi Dedoplisay. In *Kartuli enis isṭoriuli kresṭomatia, I, 1. (Ʒveli Kartuli Enis Ḳartedris Šromebi,* **13.**), 133–143. Tbilisi: Universiṭeṭi (first published, 1949). [This is considered by some to date from A.D. 476–483 (Kekelidze 1960: 117ff.), placing it among the oldest attested Georgian writings; others place it later (Birdsall 1981; Peeters 1935).]

Imnaishvili, I. (1970b). Cxorebay da mokalakobay γmert-šemosilisa neṭarisa mamisa čuenisa Serapionisi. In *Kartuli enis isṭoriuli kresṭomatia, I, 1.* (*Ʒveli Ḳartuli Enis Katedris Šromebi,* **13.**) 189–202. Tbilisi: Universiṭeṭi.

Imnaishvili, I. (1970c). Mqectatvis saxisa siṭquay. In *Kartuli enis isṭoriuli krestomatia, I, 1.* (*Ʒveli Kartuli Enis Ḳatedris Šromebi,* **13.**) 235–241. Tbilisi: Universiṭeṭi.

Imnaishvili, I. (1970d). Šromay da moγuac̣ebay γirsad cxorebisay c̣midisa da neṭarisa mamisa čuenisa Grigolisi. In, *Kartuli enis isṭoriuli kresṭomatia, I. 1. (Ʒveli Kartuli Enis Ḳatedris Šromebi,* **13.**) 203–226. Tbilisi: Universiṭeṭi.

Ingorokva, P. (1913). *Ʒvel-Kartuli sasuliero poezia, I. Ṭpilisi: Saeḳlesio Muzeumi.*

Javaxishvili, I. (1946). *Giorgi Mtac̣mideli, "Cxorebay Iovanesi da Eptvimesi." (Ʒveli Kartuli Enis Ʒeglebi,* **3.**) Tbilisi: Ạkademia.

Kauxchishvili, S. (1973). *Kartlis cxovreba, IV: Baṭonišvili Vaxusṭi, "Aγçera sameposa Sakartvelosa."* Tbilisi: Sabčota Sakartvelo.
Kekelidze, K. (1918). *Kartuli hagiograpiuli ʒeglebi. Naçili pirveli. Ḳimeni. I.* Ṭpilisi: Sakart. Rḳ. Gz. Sammartvelos Ṭipo-liṭograpia.
Kekelidze, K. (1946). *Kartuli agiograpiuli ʒeglebi. Naçili pirveli. Ḳimeni. II.* Tbilisi: Aḳademia.
Marr, N. (1911). *Georgij Merčul, "Žitie sv. Grigorija Xandztijskago."* S. Peterburg: Aḳademija.
Marr, N. (1974). *Le synaxaire géorgienne. Patrologia Orientalis,* **29,** fasc. 5. (first edition, 1926).
Shanidze, A. (1935). *Ʒveli Kartulis kresṭomatia leksiḳoniturt, 1: Kresṭomatia. (Caucasus Polyglottus,* I). Ṭpilisi: Universiṭeṭi.
Shanidze, A. (1947). *Çignni ʒuelisa aγtkumisani, I. 1. (Ʒveli Kartuli Enis Ʒeglebi,* **4**.) Tbilisi: Aḳademia.
Shanidze, A. (1948). *Çignni ʒuelisa aγtkumisani, I. 2. (Ʒveli Kartuli Enis Ʒeglebi,* **4**.) Tbilisi: Aḳademia.
Shanidze, A. (1959). *Sinuri mravaltavi 864 çlisa. (Ʒveli Kartuli Enis Ḳatedris Šromebi,* **5**.) Tbilisi: Universiṭeṭi.
Shanidze, M. (1960). *Psalmunis Ʒveli Kartuli redakciebi, 1, (Ʒveli Kartuli Enis Ʒeglebi,* **11**.) Tbilisi: Aḳademia.

Svan

Davitiani, A. (1973). *Svanuri andazebi.* [Svan proverbs]. Tbilisi: Aḳademia. [Translations and glosses are based on Davitiani's translations into Georgian.]
Davitiani, A., Topuria, V., and Kaldani, M. (1957). *Svanuri prozauli ṭeksṭebi, II: Balskvemouri ḳilo.* [Svan prose texts, II: The Lower Bal dialect]. Tbilisi: Aḳademia. [Translations are based on Dzidziguri 1971, which provides Georgian translations of several of the Svan versions of the Nart sagas.]
Gabliani, E. (1925). Ʒveli da axali Sakartvelo. [Old and new Georgia]. Tbilisi. [Contains some poetry and some proverbs. Transations are based on Georgian translations provided by Gabliani. The pieces reflect the Upper Bal dialect.]
Shanidze, A., and Kaldani, M. (1978). *Svanuri enis kresṭomatia. (Ʒveli Kartuli Enis Ḳatedris Šromebi,* **21**.) [Chrestomathy of the Svan language]. Tbilisi: Universiṭeṭi.
Shanidze, A., and Topuria, V. (1939). *Svanuri prozauli ṭeksṭebi, I: Balszemouri ḳilo.* [Svan prose texts, I: Upper Bal dialect]. Tbilisi: Aḳademia. [Translations are based on Dzidziguri 1971, which provides Georgian translations of several of the Svan versions of the Nart sagas.]
Shanidze, A., Topuria, A., and Gujejiani, M. (1939). *Svanuri poezia, I.* [Svan poetry, I]. Tbilisi: Aḳademia. [Translations are based on Georgian translations provided by the editors.]

Laz

Asatiani, I. (1974). *Çanuri (Lazuri) ṭeksṭebi.* [Laz texts]. Tbilisi: Mecniereba. [Translations are based on Georgian translations provided by Asatiani.]
Chikobava, A. (1929a). *Çanuri ṭeksṭebi (Xopuri ḳiloḳavi).* [Laz texts: The Xopian dialect]. Tbilisi: Universiṭeṭi.

Chikobava, A. (1936). *Çanuris gramaṭiḳuli analizi.* [A grammatical analysis of Laz]. Part II: Texts. Tbilisi: Aḳademia.
Dumézil, G. (1937). *Contes lazes.* Paris: Institut d'ethnologie. [Translations of examples based on Dumézil's French translations. The transcription has been altered to be consistent with the system used here.]
Dumézil, G., and Ensenç, T. (1972). Textes en laze d'Ardeşen. *BK,* **29–30**, 32–41. [Translations are based upon French translations provided by Dumézil and Esenç. Transcriptions have been altered to be consistent with the system used here.]

Mingrelian

Bleichsteiner, R. (1919). *Kaukasische Forschungen: Georgische und mingrelische Texte.* Wien. [Translations are based on Bleichsteiner's German translations. Transcriptions have been altered to be consistent with the system used here.]
Kipshidze, I. (1914). *Grammatika mingrelskogo (iverskogo) jazyka s xrestomatieju i slovarem. (Materially po jafetičeskomu jazykoznaniju, VIII).* S. Peterburg: Akademija.
Kluge, T. (1916). *Beiträge zur mingrelischen Grammatik,* 79–89. Berlin: Verlag von W. Kohlhammer. [Translations are based on the German provided by Kluge. Transcriptions have been altered to be consistent with the system used here.]
Samushia, K. (1979). *Kartuli xalxuri poeziis saḳitxebi: Megruli nimušebi.* [Questions of Georgian folk poetry: Mingrelian illustrations]. Tbilisi: Mecniereba. [Translations are based on the Georgian provided by Samushia.]
Xubua, M. (1937). *Megruli ṭeksṭebi.* [Mingrelian texts]. Ṭpilisi: Aḳademia.

INDEX

A

*a/*e*, 191, 194, 223
Ablaut, 167–186
  distinguishing Series I from II, 99, 152–153, 265-266
  in bimorphemic stems in Series I and II, 172–176
  in monomorphemic stems in Series I and II, 167–170, 186–187
  in Series III, 300, 302–303, 322
  relation to origin of Series I, 170–172
  restructuring the paradigms, 184–185, 366–367
  support for proposed account, 176–184
Ablauting intransitive, 59
Absolute intransitive, *see* Relative intransitive, versus absolute
Absolutive form of nominative case, 86–87, *see also* Stem form
Ač̣arian, Lower, dialect, 318, 375–380, 383, 384, 405, 423
Accent, *see* Stress
Accusative alignment
  definition, 3, 4
  of case
    in Common Kartvelian, 93–94
    in Georgian, 51, 379, 405
    in Mingrelian, 57–58, 371
    in Svan, 46
    origin, 144, 151–164, 414
  of person agreement, 261, 405
Active alignment, 14, 409
  and incorporation, 331
  definition, 4, 12 (n. 3)
  of agreement, 218, 405, 406–407
  of case
    in Common Kartvelian, 94
    in Georgian, 51, 218
    in Kartvelian languages, 427–428
    in Laz, 55, 373
    in Svan, 46
    origin, 329–359
  of inversion, 323–324
Active case, 371
Active intransitive, *see* Class 3 verb
Active-tripartite alignment, 405–406, 419, 426–427
Active versus inactive verbs, 41, 111, 218, 223–224, 344, 356
Actualization of change
  ergative-to-active shift, 330, 344–350
  reanalysis of Series I, 364–370, 422
  theory, 25
Adverbial case
  marker, 74–75, 247
  use in marking retired indirect object, 237–238

Q

R

Z

SYNTAX and SEMANTICS

Volume 1
edited by *John P. Kimball*

Volume 2
edited by *John P. Kimball*

Volume 3, Speech Acts
edited by *Peter Cole* and *Jerry L. Morgan*

Volume 4
edited by *John P. Kimball*

Volume 5, Japanese Generative Grammar
edited by *Masayoshi Shibatani*

Volume 6, The Grammar of Causative Constructions
edited by *Masayoshi Shibatani*

Volume 7, Notes from the Linguistic Underground
edited by *James D. McCawley*

Volume 8, Grammatical Relations
edited by *Peter Cole* and *Jerrold M. Sadock*

Volume 9, Pragmatics
edited by *Peter Cole*

Volume 10, Selections from the Third Gronigen Round Table
edited by *Frank Heny* and *Helmut S. Schnelle*

Volume 11, Presupposition
edited by *Choon-Kyu Oh* and *David S. Dinneen*

Volume 12, Discourse and Syntax
edited by *Talmy Givón*

Volume 13, Current Approaches to Syntax
edited by *Edith A. Moravcsik* and *Jessica R. Wirth*

Volume 14, Tense and Aspect
edited by *Philip J. Tedeschi* and *Annie Zaenen*

Volume 15, Studies in Transitivity
edited by *Paul J. Hopper* and *Sandra A. Thompson*

Volume 16, The Syntax of Native American Languages
edited by *Eung-Do Cook* and *Donna B. Gerdts*

Volume 17, Composite Predicates in English
Ray Cattell

Volume 18, Diachronic Syntax: The Kartvelian Case
Alice C. Harris